MERGERS, ACQUISITIONS, AND OTHER RESTRUCTURING ACTIVITIES

MERGERS, ACQUISITIONS, AND OTHER RESTRUCTURING ACTIVITIES

An Integrated Approach to Process, Tools, Cases, and Solutions

Second Edition

DONALD M. DEPAMPHILIS, PH.D.

College of Business Administration
Loyola Marymount University
Los Angeles, California

ACADEMIC PRESS

An Imprint of Elsevier

Amsterdam   Boston   London   New York   Oxford   Paris
San Diego   San Francisco   Singapore   Sydney   Tokyo

Academic Press
An Imprint of Elsevier
525 B Street, Suite 1900, San Diego, California 92101-4495, USA
http://www.academicpress.com

Academic Press
84 Theobald's Road, London WC1X 8RR, UK
http://www.academicpress.com

Library of Congress Control Number: 2002111286

International Standard Book Number: 0-12-209552-9

PRINTED IN THE UNITED STATES OF AMERICA
04   05   06   9   8   7   6   5   4   3   2

*I extend my heartfelt gratitude to my wife, Cheryl,
and my daughter, Cara, without whose patience and understanding
this book could not have been completed, and to
my brother, Mel, without whose encouragement this book
would never have been undertaken.*

AUTHOR BIOGRAPHY

Donald M. DePamphilis has a Ph.D. in economics from Harvard University and has managed more than 30 acquisitions, divestitures, joint ventures, and minority investments, as well as licensing and supply agreements. He is currently Clinical Professor of Finance at the College of Business Administration at Loyola Marymount University in Los Angeles. He has also taught mergers and acquisitions and corporate restructuring at the Graduate School of Management at the University of California, Irvine, and Chapman University to undergraduates, MBA, and Executive MBA students. He has published a number of articles on economic forecasting, business planning, and marketing. As Vice President of Electronic Commerce at Experian, Dr. DePamphilis managed the development of an award winning web site. He was also Vice President of Business Development at TRW Information Systems and Services, Director of Planning at TRW, and Chief Economist at National Steel Corporation.

PRAISE for the FIRST EDITION:

"This is one of the finest books I have seen on the subject, and surely the most comprehensive. It's a primer on all corporate finance activities, and anyone seeking an education on the mergers and acquisition process and all of its ramifications should read this. As an active mergers and acquisitions practitioner myself, I want my dealmakers and colleagues to read this, too.

The book covers not only the basics, but also the detailed, specific knowledge needed by those individuals involved in almost every aspect of the mergers and acquisitions process. This includes buyers, sellers, bankers, lawyers, and accountants. It happily addresses not only the large public corporate transactions, but also the private middle market companies where the vast majority of mergers and acquisitions deals take place.

While it certainly is a comprehensive textbook, I found it truly 'easy reading' and especially enjoyed the many case studies—some with the drama of the 'Barbarians at the Gate.' Good stuff!"

—Marvin Kaulkin, CEO, Kaulkin Ginsberg Company

"Professor DePamphilis draws upon his years in academia and considerable industry experience to produce a book that should be valuable reading for both the student and practitioner of 'deal making.' I found it insightful and interesting."

—D. Van Skilling, Retired Chairman and CEO, Experian Corporation

CONTENTS

PREFACE TO THE SECOND EDITION   XVII

PART I

THE MERGERS AND ACQUISITIONS ENVIRONMENT

1

INTRODUCTION TO MERGERS AND ACQUISITIONS

Overview   4
Building a Common Vocabulary   5
Participants in the Mergers and Acquisitions Process   13
Common Motivations for Mergers and Acquisitions   19
Historical Merger and Acquisition Waves   29
Do Mergers and Acquisitions Pay Off for Shareholders?   32
Why Do Mergers and Acquisitions Often Fail to Meet Expectations?   38
Do Mergers and Acquisitions Pay Off for Society?   40
Things to Remember   41
Chapter Discussion Questions   43
Chapter Business Case: America Online Acquires Time Warner—The
    Emergence of a Vertically Integrated Internet and Media Giant*   44

Chapter Business Case: Vodafone AirTouch Acquires Mannesmann in a
     Record-Setting Deal   51
References   58

2

REGULATORY CONSIDERATIONS

Overview   66
Federal Securities Laws   68
Insider Trading Laws   71
Antitrust Laws   72
State Regulations Affecting Mergers and Acquisitions   96
Regulated Industries   97
Environmental Laws   101
Labor and Benefit Laws   101
Cross-Border Transactions   102
Things to Remember   103
Chapter Discussion Questions   104
Chapter Business Case: Exxon and Mobil Merger—The Market Share
     Conundrum*   105
Chapter Business Case: GE's Aborted Attempt to Merge with
     Honeywell   106
References   111

3

COMMON TAKEOVER TACTICS AND DEFENSES

Overview   113
Alternative Takeover Tactics   114
The Takeover Decision Tree   130
Alternative Takeover Defenses: Prebid and Postbid   132
Things to Remember   151
Chapter Discussion Questions   152
Chapter Business Case: Tyco Rescues AMP from AlliedSignal*   153
Chapter Business Case: Pfizer Acquires Warner-Lambert in a Hostile
     Takeover   157
References   162

PART II

THE MERGERS AND ACQUISITIONS PROCESS: PHASES 1–10

4

PLANNING: DEVELOPING BUSINESS AND ACQUISITION PLANS—PHASES 1 AND 2 OF THE ACQUISITION PROCESS

Overview   168
A Planning-Based Approach to Mergers and Acquisitions   169
Phase 1: Building the Business Plan   172
The Business Plan as a Communication Document   197
Phase 2: Building the Merger/Acquisition Implementation Plan   199
Things to Remember   205
Chapter Discussion Questions   207
Chapter Business Case: Consolidation in the Global Pharmaceutical
    Industry Continues: The Glaxo Wellcome and SmithKline Beecham
    Example*   207
Chapter Business Case: Pepsi Buys Quaker Oats in a Highly Publicized
    Food Fight   210
Appendix A: Common Sources of Economic, Industry, and
    Market Data   215
References   216

5

IMPLEMENTATION: SEARCH THROUGH CLOSING—PHASES 3–10

Overview   218
Phase 3: The Search Process   219
Phase 4: The Screening Process   222
Phase 5: First Contact   224
Phase 6: Negotiation   227
Phase 7: Developing the Integration Plan   243
Phase 8: Closing   245

Phase 9: Implementing Postclosing Integration 250
Phase 10: Conducting a Postclosing Evaluation 252
Things to Remember 253
Chapter Discussion Questions 255
Chapter Business Case: When Companies Overpay—Mattel Acquires the
    Learning Company* 255
Chapter Business Case: First Union Buys Wachovia Bank: A Merger of
    Equals? 262
Appendix A: Legal Due Diligence Preliminary Information Request 265
References 275

6

INTEGRATION: MERGERS, ACQUISITIONS, AND BUSINESS ALLIANCES

Overview 278
The Role of Integration in Successful Mergers and Acquisitions 278
Viewing Integration as a Process 282
Integrating Business Alliances 316
Things to Remember 318
Chapter Discussion Questions 319
Chapter Business Case: Daimler Acquires Chrysler—Anatomy of
    a Cross-Border Transaction* 320
Chapter Business Case: The Travelers and Citicorp Integration
    Experience 323
References 326

PART III

MERGER AND ACQUISITION TOOLS AND CONCEPTS

7

A PRIMER ON MERGER AND ACQUISITION VALUATION

Overview 332
Required Returns 332

Analyzing Risk   335
Calculating Free Cash Flows   337
Time Value of Money   342
Alternative Approaches to Valuation   345
Applying Income or Discounted Cash-Flow Methods   348
Estimating the Market Value of the Firm's Debt   357
Applying Market-Based (Relative Value) Methods   360
Applying Asset-Oriented Methods   365
Valuing the Firm Using the Weighted Average Method   367
Valuing Nonoperating Assets   369
Adjusting the Target Firm's Equity Value for Nonoperating Assets and
    Liabilities   376
Things to Remember   378
Chapter Discussion Questions   380
Chapter Practice Problems and Answers   380
Chapter Business Case: The Hunt for Elusive Synergy—@Home
    Acquires Excite*   387
References   388

8

APPLYING FINANCIAL MODELING TECHNIQUES TO VALUE AND STRUCTURE MERGERS AND ACQUISITIONS

Overview   392
The Limitations of Financial Data   393
The Model-Building Process   398
Factors Affecting Postmerger Share Price   411
Key M&A Model Formulas   415
Business Case: Determining the Initial Offer Price: The Gee Whiz Media
    and Go Go Technology Saga   418
Maintaining Shareholder Value in a Stock-for-Stock Exchange   438
Things to Remember   441
Chapter Discussion Questions   442
Chapter Practice Problems   442
Chapter Business Case: Tribune Company Acquires the Times Mirror
    Corporation in a Tale of Corporate Intrigue*   444
Chapter Business Case: Ford Acquires Volvo's Passenger
    Car Operations   451
Appendix A: Commonly Used Financial Ratios   457
References   459

9

ANALYSIS AND VALUATION OF PRIVATELY HELD COMPANIES

Overview   462
Challenges of Valuing Privately Held Companies   463
Adjusting the Income Statement   467
Applying Valuation Methodologies to Private Companies   473
Reverse Mergers   484
Calculating Ownership Share: The Venture Capital Method   487
Using Leveraged Employee Stock Ownership Plans to Buy Private
    Companies   488
Analyzing Private Shareholder Returns   489
Things to Remember   489
Chapter Discussion Questions   491
Chapter Business Case: Valuing a Privately Held Company*   492
Chapter Business Case: Pacific Wardrobe Acquires Surferdude Apparel by
    a Skillful Structuring of the Transaction   492
References   496

10

STRUCTURING THE DEAL: PAYMENT, LEGAL, TAX, AND ACCOUNTING CONSIDERATIONS

Overview   500
The Deal-Structuring Process   501
Form of Acquisition Vehicle   505
Postclosing Organization   507
Legal Form of Selling Entity   508
Form of Payment or Total Consideration   509
Form of Acquisition   513
Tax Structures and Strategies   521
Financial Reporting of Business Combinations   531
Things to Remember   538
Chapter Discussion Questions   539
Chapter Business Case: Consolidation in the Wireless Communications
    Industry: Vodafone Acquires AirTouch*   540
Chapter Business Case: JDS Uniphase-SDL Merger Results in
    Huge Write-Off   547
References   553

PART IV

ALTERNATIVE STRATEGIES AND STRUCTURES

11

LEVERAGED BUYOUT STRUCTURES AND VALUATION

Overview   558
The Origins of Leveraged Transactions   559
Alternative Financing Options   561
Common Forms of Leveraged Buyout Structures   570
Critical Success Factors   572
Impact on Shareholder Returns of Leveraged Buyouts   574
Analyzing Leveraged Buyouts   578
Case Study: Pacific Investors Acquires California Kool in a Leveraged
       Buyout   584
Things to Remember   589
Chapter Discussion Questions   589
Chapter Business Case: Evaluating a Leveraged Buyout Opportunity*   590
Chapter Business Case: RJR Nabisco Goes Private—Key Shareholder and
       Public Policy Issues   591
References   594

12

SHARED GROWTH AND SHARED CONTROL STRATEGIES: JOINT VENTURES, PARTNERSHIPS, STRATEGIC ALLIANCES, AND LICENSING

Overview   598
Motivations for Business Alliances   601
Critical Success Factors for Business Alliances   611
Alternative Legal Forms of Business Alliances   613
Strategic and Operational Plans   619
Business Alliance Deal Structuring   620
Empirical Findings   633
Things to Remember   634
Chapter Discussion Questions   635

Chapter Business Case: Bell Atlantic and Vodafone Form Wireless
     Operation to Expand Geographic Coverage*   636
Chapter Business Case: Coca-Cola and Procter & Gamble's Aborted Effort
     to Create a Global Joint Venture Company   638
References   640

13

ALTERNATIVE EXIT AND RESTRUCTURING STRATEGIES: DIVESTITURES, SPIN-OFFS, CARVE-OUTS, SPLIT-UPS, BANKRUPTCY, AND LIQUIDATION

Overview   644
Motives for Exiting Businesses   645
Divestitures   652
Spin-Offs and Split-Ups   656
Equity Carve-Outs and Split-Off Initial Public Offerings   658
Tracking, Targeted, and Letter Stocks   661
Voluntary Liquidations (Bust-Ups)   664
Comparing Alternative Exit Restructuring Strategies   664
Choosing Among Divestiture, Carve-Out, and Spin-Off
     Restructuring Strategies   665
Returns to Shareholders   667
Business Failure   671
Things to Remember   689
Chapter Discussion Questions   690
Chapter Business Case: Allegheny Teledyne Restructures*   691
Chapter Business Case: AT&T—A Poster Child for Restructuring
     Gone Awry   692
References   698

PART V

PUTTING IT ALL TOGETHER

14

THE ACQUISITION PROCESS:
THE GEE WHIZ MEDIA CASE

Part I: Planning   703
Part II: Implementation   711
Gee Whiz Media Case Study Discussion Questions   729

APPENDIX
Solutions to Selected Chapter Business Case Study Discussion
        Questions   733

INDEX   759

*A solution for this business case is provided in the appendix at the back of this book.

PREFACE
TO THE SECOND EDITION

THE FUTURE OF DEAL-MAKING

Following the carnage wrought on the dotcoms, the recession, and the approximate 20% drop in the major stock indices during the early years of the new millenium, it is easy to be negative about the outlook for M&A. During the heyday of deal making in the late 1990s, the likes of Bernie Ebbers of Worldcom and Dennis Kozlowski of Tyco exemplified a breed of dealmakers that emphasized growth through acquisition. This generation of dealmakers viewed acquisitions as the primary means of achieving and sustaining a high growth rate. Keeping their firms' stock prices at lofty levels was critical to maintaining this strategy, because it gave them the wherewithal to continue this highly aggressive strategy.

By 2002, conditions had changed dramatically. Highly acquisitive firms, such as Conseco, WorldCom, and Tyco, were clearly out of favor, their stocks having fallen to only a fraction of their previous peaks. High-profile bankruptcies such as Enron, Global Crossing, and Kmart seriously eroded investor confidence in the veracity of publicly available financial information, as investors wondered aloud if these firms simply represented the "tip of the iceberg." The nation's financial markets were indeed in the throes of a crisis of investor confidence.

Is this period really any different from what we have seen in the past? While it is clear that the volume of transactions worldwide dropped precipitously from the heady days of the late 1990s, it is unclear if this is simply a normal cyclical downturn in transactions or the start of a long-term "bear market" for M&A. History can be very instructive in providing insights in this matter.

M&A activity has historically fallen and surged with the ebb and flow of the stock market and the economy. This was readily apparent in the wake of the 1973–1975 recession and the recession of the early 1980s and the subsequent recovery. More recently, the collapse of many highly leveraged firms in the wake of the 1980s M&A feeding frenzy followed by a recession in the early 1990s dampened M&A activity through 1994. What deals were consummated were largely done with cash and very little debt. However, this preceded the longest economic recovery and the largest bull market in stocks in history. This in turn triggered record levels, both in terms of the number and dollar volume, of M&As during the second half of the 1990s.

A cleansing period, in which many companies focus on what they do best, is inevitable. Divestitures and spin-offs will become increasingly commonplace as companies focus on markets in which they have a clearly defined leadership position. High-tech companies like Cisco Systems, JDS Uniphase, and Ariba will not be able to grow rapidly by using their lofty stock prices as a means to acquire revenue streams. Acquisitions for a time will be financed with more cash and less debt and stock. But history shows that these developments are temporary. Consequently, there is little reason to believe that the current recovery in the economy and the stock market will not reignite another long-term boom in M&A activity.

BUSINESS COMBINATIONS ARE A CRITICAL PART OF THE FABRIC OF DOING BUSINESS

The explosive growth in the number, size, and complexity of mergers, acquisitions, and alliances during the 1990s demonstrates how ingrained business combinations have become in the global business community. Despite these developments, studies show that a disproportionately large number of such combinations fail to satisfy their participants' expectations, suggesting a need to think and act differently in conceiving and implementing corporate restructuring activities. The increasing complexity of transactions demands that managers and analysts alike continuously update their skills to reflect the inevitable changes in their operating environments. Central to the process is the need to clearly understand how the various activities contributing to successful business combinations fit together in an integrated framework. Because business combinations often entail a common set of activities, the manager or analyst is able to view mergers, acquisitions, or business alliances in the context of a process or logical sequence of activities. A properly articulated process disciplines the manager or analyst to consider all relevant activities in an orderly manner, to understand how the various activities interact, to review the range of reasonable options, and to select the option that best satisfies the primary needs of all parties involved. This book is intended to help the reader think of all the activities that contribute to the success or failure of M&As in an integrated way.

THE UNIQUENESS OF THIS BOOK

This book is unique in its ability to integrate the subject matter in a coherent way. Most books on mergers, acquisitions, and other forms of corporate restructuring focus on a very narrow slice of the subject matter, such as the challenges of planning, valuation, or integration. Authors of such texts often argue that their focus represents the most important part of the acquisition process, and they downplay other M&A activities as being secondary to the success of the transaction. In contrast, this book addresses subjects often overlooked or treated only superficially in corporate restructuring texts. These include negotiation, premerger planning, postmerger integration; business alliances as alternatives to M&As; the application of sophisticated financial modeling techniques to analyzing and structuring M&A deals; and assumptions-driven valuation. To ignore these areas is to ignore the importance of approaching M&A in an integrated way.

Integration is addressed in this book in three important ways: (1) as a process, (2) in the context in which M&A activities actually occur, and (3) in a highly realistic and comprehensive business case. This case study (Chapter 14) enables the reader to understand how normal business challenges are resolved through a transaction described from conception through completion.

The process outlined in this book consists of 10 interrelated phases and is sufficiently flexible to be applicable to businesses of various sizes and in different industries. The first two phases make up the planning stage and comprise the development of a business plan, defining where and how a firm chooses to compete, and an acquisition plan—if management believes that an acquisition is the most desirable option for implementing the business plan. The remaining eight phases make up the implementation stage, comprising such activities as search, screen, first contact, negotiation, integration planning, and closing, as well as postmerger integration and evaluation. The negotiation phase is highlighted as the most dynamic aspect of the M&A process, consisting of a continuous refinement of the preliminary valuation, deal structure, and financing plan based on information obtained through due diligence. This iteration continues until a decision is made either to proceed to closing or to "walk away." In this crucial negotiation phase, all elements of the purchase price are actually determined.

The tools and concepts required to solve common problems faced in the M&A process are discussed in contexts in which they normally occur. For example, deal structuring is most often treated as a series of largely independent events most often handled by lawyers. In practice, deal structuring is a highly interactive process supported by numerous analysts possessing different types of expertise. Deal structuring is conceptualized as a process consisting of six interdependent components discussed in Chapter 10. These include the acquisition vehicle, the postclosing organization, the form of payment, the legal form of the seller, the form of acquisition, and the tax structure. Another example of contextual integration involves the discussion of takeover tactics and defenses in Chapter 3, which emphasizes that the takeover tactics employed often reflect the defenses in place at the target company. Similarly, the defenses initiated following the initial bid for the target often depend on the type of takeover tactics employed by the suitor.

Although largely fictional, the Gee Whiz Media case study (Chapter 14) reflects the author's extensive experience as both a practitioner and teacher of the subject matter. The case illustrates the application of the planning-based approach to M&As presented in this book. Although the case takes place in a rapidly changing high-technology environment, the approach transfers across industries, and the challenges described are common to most transactions. The case illustrates the importance of "up-front planning," techniques for searching for and screening potential acquisition candidates, and initiating contact. In addition, the case explores the concurrent phases of the negotiation process, methods for identifying sources and destroyers of value, events common to the closing activity, and the hazards of postclosing integration.

WHO MIGHT BE INTERESTED IN THIS BOOK

The text is intended for students of M&As, corporate restructuring, business strategy, industrial organization, and entrepreneurship courses at both the undergraduate and the master in business administration level. Moreover, the material has worked effectively in Executive MBA, development, and training programs. The book should also interest those actively pursuing careers as financial analysts, chief financial officers, corporate treasurers, operating managers, investment bankers, business brokers, portfolio managers, or investors, as well as corporate development and strategic planning managers. Others who may have an interest include bank lending officers, venture capitalists, business appraisers, actuaries, government regulators and policy makers, and entrepreneurs. Hence, from the classroom to the boardroom, this text offers something for anyone with an interest in M&As, business alliances, and other forms of corporate restructuring.

TO THE INSTRUCTOR

This book equips the instructor with the information and tools needed to communicate effectively with students from diverse backgrounds and with differing levels of preparation. The generous use of examples and contemporary business cases makes the text suitable for distance learning and self-study programs as well as large, lecture-focused courses. Prerequisites for this text include familiarity with basic accounting, finance, economics, and general management concepts.

MANY PRACTICAL, TIMELY, AND DIVERSE EXAMPLES AS WELL AS CURRENT BUSINESS CASES WITH SOLUTIONS

Each chapter begins with a vignette based on the author's own experience, intended to illustrate a key point or points that will be described in more detail as the chapter unfolds. Hundreds of examples, business cases, tables, and figures illustrate the application of key concepts and tools. Many exhibits and diagrams summarize otherwise diffuse information and the results of numerous empirical studies substantiating key points made in each chapter. Each chapter concludes with a series of ten discussion questions and two integrative Chapter Business Cases intended to stimulate critical thinking and test the reader's understanding of the material. Solutions to selected Chapter Business Cases are found in the back of the book. Solutions to all Chapter Business Cases and discussion questions are provided in the Instructor's Manual that accompanies this book.

COMPREHENSIVE YET FLEXIBLE ORGANIZATION

Although the text is sequential, each chapter was developed as a self-contained unit to enable adaptation of the text to various types of students and teaching strategies. The flexibility of the organization also makes the material suitable for courses of various lengths, from one quarter to two full semesters. The amount of time required depends on the students' level of sophistication and the desired focus of the instructor. Undergraduates have consistently demonstrated the ability to master at least 8 or 9 chapters of the book during a typical semester, while graduate-level students are able to cover effectively 12 to 13 chapters during the same period.

EXCITING NEW CONTENT IN THE SECOND EDITION

- *Up-to-date information*: Each chapter, including business cases, has been updated to reflect current developments and the latest academic and empirical research. Documentation is extensive.
- *Practical financial modeling techniques*: Chapter 8's discussion of financial modeling has been substantially expanded and includes a step-by-step explanation of how to perform sophisticated financial modeling techniques to analyze, value, and structure deals. The chapter includes a detailed example of how to create and apply financial models for these purposes.
- *Deal structuring and valuation model*: Based on Microsoft Excel, the model embodies realism, sophistication, relative ease of use, and flexibility. Although it uses real data to illustrate the financial modeling techniques discussed in Chapter 8 of this book, the reader may use it to value and structure deals by simply inserting their own data and modifying the model to reflect the unique aspects of their situation.
- *Eighteen new business cases*: All 70 case studies, whether contained within or at the end of the chapter, include discussion questions, many of which have solutions in the back of the book. See the Business Case listing at the end of the preface for the titles of all business cases included in this book.
- *Practice problems and solutions*: Numerous practice problems and answers are found at the end of both Chapters 7 and 10.

- *Techniques for choosing restructuring strategies*: Chapter 13's discussion of common restructuring strategies provides a framework for selecting the appropriate restructuring strategy ranging from spin-offs to carve-outs to divestitures.
- *Expanded usage of "key idea" section headings*: These headings enable the student to understand more easily the key point in each section of each chapter.
- *Transaction-tested due diligence question list*: Chapter 5 provides a detailed listing of questions commonly used to evaluate target firms doing due diligence.
- *Primer on using financial ratios*: Chapter 8 has been extended to include a convenient summary of commonly used financial ratios and suggestions as to how they may be used to evaluate target companies.
- *Detailed sources of publicly available data*: Chapters 4 and 5 include lengthy lists of both online and "hard copy" sources of information including economic, industry, market, and financial data.
- *Strategy selection guidelines*: Chapter 4 has been expanded to provide tools for assisting in the selection of corporate and business unit level strategies.
- *Instructor's Manual*: The manual contains suggested learning objectives, chapter presentations for creating lectures or providing students with study guides, more than 750 test questions and answers (including true/false, multiple-choice, essay questions, and practice problems), and solutions to all chapter business case studies in the book. The manual also contains detailed course syllabi that have been used extensively for both undergraduate and graduate classes and suggested ways for teaching the materials.

ACKNOWLEDGMENTS

I would like to express my sincere appreciation for the many helpful suggestions received from numerous anonymous reviewers and the many resources of Academic Press. Finally, I would like to thank John Mellen, Jim Healy, and Chris Manning for their many constructive comments and J. Scott Bentley, Executive Editor, and Mara Conner, Marketing Director, at Academic Press, for their ongoing support.

BUSINESS CASE STUDIES

1-1.   The Man Behind the Legend at Berkshire Hathaway
1-2.   America Online Acquires Time Warner—The Emergence of a Vertically Integrated Internet and Media Giant
1-3.   Vodafone AirTouch Acquires Mannesmann in a Record-Setting Deal

2-1.   BP Amoco and Arco Vow to Contest the FTC's Ruling
2-2.   Justice Department Requires AlliedSignal and Honeywell to Divest Overlapping Businesses

2-3. FTC Prevents Staples from Acquiring Office Depot
2-4. Justice Department Blocks Microsoft's Acquisition of Intuit
2-5. JDS Uniphase Acquires SDL—What a Difference Seven Months Makes!
2-6. MCI WorldCom Blocked from Acquiring Sprint
2-7. How the Microsoft Case Could Define Antitrust Law in the "New Economy"
2-8. FCC Uses Its Power to Stimulate Competition in the Telecommunications Market
2-9. Exxon and Mobil Merger: The Market Share Conundrum
2-10. GE's Aborted Attempt to Merge with Honeywell

3-1. Alcoa Easily Overwhelms Reynolds' Takeover Defenses
3-2. Hewlett Packard Family Members Oppose Proposal to Acquire Compaq
3-3. Tyco Rescues AMP from AlliedSignal
3-4. Pfizer Acquires Warner Lambert in a Hostile Takeover

4-1. Dell Computer's Drive to Eliminate the Middleman
4-2. Is Sustainable Competitive Advantage Possible?
4-3. Consolidation in the Global Pharmaceutical Industry Continues—The Glaxco Wellcome and SmithKline Beecham Example
4-4. Pepsi Buys Quaker Oats in a Highly Publicized Food Fight

5-1. The Cash Impact of Product Warranties
5-2. McKesson HBOC Restates Revenue
5-3. When "Reps and Warranties" Don't Provide Adequate Protection
5-4. Vodafone Finances the Acquisition of AirTouch
5-5. The Downside of Earnouts
5-6. Sleepless in Philadelphia: A Dramatic Closing
5-7. When Companies Overpay—Mattel Acquires the Learning Company
5-8. First Union Buys Wachovia Bank—A Merger of Equals?

6-1. M&A Gets Out of Hand at Cisco
6-2. Case Corporation Loses Sight of Customer Needs in Integrating New Holland Corporation
6-3. Exxon Mobil—A Study in Cost Cutting
6-4. Albertson's Acquires American Stores—Underestimating the Costs of Integration
6-5. Overcoming Culture Clash—Allianz AG Buys Pimco Advisors LP
6-6. Avoiding the Merger Blues—American Airlines Integrates TWA
6-7. Daimler Acquires Chrysler—Anatomy of a Cross Border Transaction
6-8. The Travelers and Citicorp Integration Experience

7-1. The Hunt for Elusive Synergy: @Home Acquires Excite

8-1. Determining the Initial Offer Price: The Gee Whiz Media and Go Go Technology Saga
8-2. Northrop Grumman Makes a Bid for TRW: How Collar Arrangements Affect Shareholder Value
8-3. Tribune Company Acquires the Times Mirror Corporation in a Tale of Corporate Intrigue
8-4. Ford Acquires Volvo's Passenger Operations

9-1. Due Diligence Uncovers Misstated Revenue
9-2. Loss of Key Employee Causes Carpet Manufacturer's Profits to Go Flat
9-3. GHS Helps Itself by Avoiding an IPO
9-4. The Corporate Shell Game
9-5. Valuing a Privately Held Company
9-6. Pacific Wardrobe Acquires Surferdude Apparel by Skillfully Structuring the Transaction

10-1. Consolidation in the Wireless Communications Industry: Vodafone Acquires AirTouch
10-2. JDS Uniphase-SDL Merger Results in Huge Write-Off

11-1. Pacific Investors Acquires California Kool in a Leveraged Buyout
11-2. Evaluating a Leveraged Buyout Opportunity
11-3. RJR Nabisco Goes Private: Key Shareholder and Public Policy Issues

12-1. Getting Wired: Walmart-America Online and Other Internet Marketing Alliances
12-2. General Motors Buys 20% of Subaru
12-3. Automotive Manufacturers Join Forces in an Online Purchasing Consortium
12-4. Bridgestone Acquires Firestone's Tire Assets
12-5. Johnson & Johnson Sues Amgen
12-6. Bell Atlantic and Vodafone Form Wireless Operation to Expand Geographic Coverage
12-7. Coca-Cola and Proctor & Gamble's Aborted Effort to Create a Global Joint Venture Company

13-1. Hughes Corporation Moves from the Defense Business Into the Entertainment Industry
13-2. Gillette Announces Divestiture Plans
13-3. Baxter to Spin-Off Heart Care Unit

13-4.   United Parcel Services Goes Public in an Equity Split-Off IPO

13-5.   Hewlett Packard Spins Out Its Agilent Unit in a Staged Transaction

13-6.   USX Bows to Shareholder Pressure to Split Up the Company

13-7.   The Enron Shuffle—A Scandal to Remember

13-8.   PG&E Seeks Bankruptcy Protection

13-9.   Allegheny Teledyne Restructures

13-10. AT&T—A Poster Child for Restructuring Gone Awry

THE MERGERS AND ACQUISITIONS ENVIRONMENT

1

INTRODUCTION TO MERGERS AND ACQUISITIONS

Murphy's Law: "If anything can go wrong, it will."

O'Toole's Commentary on Murphy's Law: "Murphy was an optimist."

Watch the evening news or read the business section of any major city newspaper and it's not hard to be swept up in merger mania. Chief executive officers (CEOs) confidently communicate their visions for the combined businesses to assure shareholders that the transaction is in their best interests. The infectious camaraderie of the CEOs of the companies involved in the transaction radiates from the podium as they, sometimes almost giddily, announce the emergence of the latest behemoth. The CEOs seem to revel in the limelight, as they are asked how it feels to be running the largest firm in the industry. Egos and flamboyant personalities often dominate the stage. The CEOs are courting the support of their shareholders, Wall Street analysts, employees, and customers. They promise that projected synergies will be realized, customers will benefit from higher product quality and an expanded product offering, jobs in the long run will be more secure, and investors will prosper.

The press loves the big story. It gives them an opportunity to once again give mainstream America a glimpse of the arcane world of high finance. Wall Street, never inclined to ignore an oncoming gravy train, nods approvingly. The surrealistic surroundings often seem more appropriate for a Hollywood movie set than for the trappings of a major business transaction. The emphasis is clearly on appearance.

Amidst the euphoria surrounding the event, there are few willing to question the recordbreaking purchase price. After all, everyone seems to want to enjoy the moment. For those at the top, it is often their "15 minutes of fame." But reality soon sets in as the studio lights are dimmed and the attention of investors turns to the next big merger announcement. Away from the glare of the cameras, the CEOs and their subordinates hunker down to meet the challenge of making it all work. Their stress level rises. The promised synergies must be realized. Customers, employees, and investors cannot be disappointed. The CEOs are well aware that their jobs are at stake.

OVERVIEW

In terms of the intensity of merger and acquisition (M&A) activity, the decade of the 1990s was unlike any other in U.S. history. Following a drop in both the number of transactions and the total dollar volume during the 1990 recession, M&A activity rebounded sharply in 1992. By 1995, the number and dollar volume exceeded their previous record levels set in the mid-1980s, when many transactions were largely financially motivated. The five largest transactions completed during the 1990s averaged $77 billion—about five times the average of the five largest deals completed during the previous decade. The average purchase price continued to set new records year after year. During the 1990s, the dollar value of cumulative M&A transactions totaled $6.5 trillion in the United States, with more than one-half of the transactions during this period taking place during the last 2 years of the decade.

Deals during the 1990s tended to be more strategic in nature and used a lot less debt than in the 1980s. M&A activity was motivated by intensifying global competition, rapid industry consolidation, deregulation, and increasingly complex and rapidly changing technologies. The overall antitrust regulatory environment was generally supportive, as exemplified by the rapid consolidation in the cable, telephone, defense, and radio industries. In evaluating the competitive effects of mergers, regulators increasingly looked beyond simply the size of the transaction and more toward their potential for improving operating efficiency. The financial environment was also highly favorable, with soaring stock market multiples and relatively low interest rates.

The bursting of the "dotcom" speculative bubble and the slump in global equity markets in 2000, followed by the onset of the 2001 recession in the United States, resulted in a huge drop off in M&A activity both in terms of dollar volume and in the number of transactions. Despite more favorable economic conditions in 2002, continued weakness in the equity markets, disappointment with many of the mega-mergers of the 1990s, and concerns about the reliability of corporate financial data hampered the recovery in M&A activity.

The intent of this chapter is to provide the reader with the information necessary to understand the underlying dynamics of the M&A process. This includes a working knowledge of the relevant vocabulary, the role of the various participants in the M&A process, and the wide range of factors influencing M&A activity historically. The dynamics of the five major merger waves that have taken place since the close of the nineteenth century are also described. Moreover, the chapter addresses the question of whether mergers pay off for target and acquiring company shareholders as well as for society. The most frequently cited reasons for many M&A's failure to meet expectations also are discussed. The chapter concludes with several stimulating case studies. These include America Online's acquisition of Time Warner—an interesting combination of the "old" and "new" economies and the largest transaction in U.S. history—and the Vodafone and Mannesmann merger—the largest cross-border transaction on record.

BUILDING A COMMON VOCABULARY

Any field of endeavor tends to have its own jargon. The study of buying and selling entire businesses or parts of businesses is no exception. Understanding the field requires a familiarity with the vocabulary. This section defines terms that will be used frequently throughout the book.

CORPORATE RESTRUCTURING

Actions taken to expand or contract a firm's basic operations or fundamentally change its asset or financial structure are referred to as *corporate restructuring* activities. Corporate restructuring is a catchall term that refers to a broad array of activities from mergers, acquisitions, and business alliances to divestitures and spin-offs. In the literature, corporate restructuring activities often are broken into two specific categories: operational and financial restructuring. *Operational restructuring* usually refers to the outright or partial sale of companies or product lines or to downsizing by closing unprofitable or nonstrategic facilities. *Financial restructuring* describes actions by the firm to change its total debt and equity structure. An example of financial restructuring would be to add debt to either lower the corporation's overall cost of capital or as part of an antitakeover defense (see Chapter 3).

ACQUISITIONS, DIVESTITURES, AND BUYOUTS

Generally speaking, an *acquisition* occurs when one company takes a controlling ownership interest in another firm, a legal subsidiary of another firm, or selected assets of another firm such as a manufacturing facility. An acquisition may involve the purchase of another firm's assets or stock, with the acquired firm continuing to exist as a legally owned subsidiary of the acquirer. In contrast, a *divestiture* is the sale of all or substantially all of a company or product line to another party for cash or securities. A *leveraged buyout* (LBO) or *highly leveraged transaction* involves the purchase of a company financed primarily by debt. The term often is applied to a firm borrowing funds to buy back its stock to convert from a publicly owned to a privately owned company (see Chapter 11). A *management buyout* is a leveraged buyout in which managers of the firm to be taken private are also equity investors. A firm that attempts to acquire or merge with another company is called an *acquiring company* or *acquirer*. The *target company* or the *target* is the firm that is being solicited by the acquiring company. *Takeovers* or *buyouts* are generic terms referring to a change in the controlling ownership interest of a corporation.

MERGERS AND CONSOLIDATIONS

Mergers can be described from a legal or structural perspective and an economic perspective. Certain types of mergers must satisfy the specific legal requirements as prescribed by the state or states in which the parties to the merger are chartered. From an economic perspective, mergers may be grouped by the relatedness of the firms or by whether they are a customer or supplier to the potential merger partner. This distinction is relevant to later discussions in this book concerning deal structuring, regulatory issues, and strategic planning.

A Legal or Structural Perspective

A structural perspective refers to the legal structure used to consummate the transaction. Such structures may take on many forms depending on the nature of the transaction. From a structural standpoint, a *merger* is a combination of two firms in which only one firm's identity survives. In a typical merger, shareholders of the target firm exchange their shares for those of the acquiring firm. A *statutory merger* is one in which the acquiring company assumes the assets and liabilities of the target in accordance with the statutes of the state in which it is incorporated. A *subsidiary merger* of two companies occurs when the target becomes a subsidiary of the parent (e.g., General Motors and Electronic Data Systems [EDS]). Note that following an acquisition of a target firm, the parent firm may choose to operate the target firm as a legal subsidiary and, at a later date, decide to merge the subsidiary into the parent. Because the parent firm is the primary shareholder in the subsidiary, the merger does not require approval of the parent's shareholders in some states. Such a merger is called a *short form merger*. However, many states do not permit this type of a merger.

Although the terms *mergers* and *consolidations* often are used interchangeably, a *statutory consolidation*, which involves two or more companies joining to form a new company, is technically not a merger. All legal entities that are consolidated are dissolved during the formation of the new company. In a merger, either the acquirer or the target survives. The 1999 combination of Daimler-Benz and Chrysler to form DaimlerChrysler is a recent example of a consolidation. The new corporate entity created as a result of consolidation or the surviving entity following a merger usually assumes ownership of the assets and liabilities of the merged or consolidated organizations. Stockholders in merged companies typically exchange their shares for shares in the new company.

A *merger of equals* is a merger framework usually applied whenever the merger participants are comparable in size, competitive position, profitability, and market capitalization. Under such circumstances, it is unclear if either party is ceding control to the other and which party is providing the greatest synergy. Consequently, target firm shareholders rarely receive any significant premium for their shares. It is common for the new firm to be managed by the former CEOs of the merged firms who will be co-equal and for the composition of the new firm's board to have equal representation from the boards of the merged firms. The 1998 formation of Citigroup from Citibank and Travelers is an example of a merger of equals.

An Economic Perspective

Business combinations also may be classified as horizontal, vertical, and conglomerate mergers. How a merger is classified depends on whether the merging firms are in the same or different industries and on their positions in the corporate value chain (Porter, 1985).

Horizontal and Conglomerate Mergers

Horizontal and conglomerate mergers are best understood in the context of whether the merging firms are in the same or different industries. A *horizontal merger* occurs between two firms within the same industry. Examples of horizontal acquisitions include Exxon and Mobil (1999), SBC Communications and Ameritech (1998), and NationsBank and BankAmerica (1998). *Conglomerate mergers* are those in which the acquiring company purchases firms in largely unrelated industries. An example would be U.S. Steel's acquisition of Marathon Oil to form USX in the mid-1980s.

Vertical Mergers

Vertical mergers are best understood operationally in the context of the corporate value chain (see Figure 1-1). Vertical mergers are those in which the two firms participate at different stages of the production or value chain. A simple value chain in the basic steel industry may distinguish between raw materials, such as coal or iron ore; steel making, such as "hot metal" and rolling operations; and metals distribution. Similarly, a value chain in the oil and gas industry would separate exploration activities from production, refining, and marketing. An Internet value chain might distinguish between infrastructure providers, such as Cisco and MCI WorldCom; content providers, such as Bloomberg and Dow Jones; and portals,

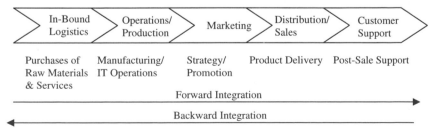

FIGURE 1-1.   Corporate value chain.

such as Yahoo. Companies that do not own operations in each major segment of the value chain may choose to backward integrate by acquiring a supplier or to forward integrate by acquiring a distributor. An example of forward integration is the 1993 merger between Merck, then the world's largest pharmaceutical company, and Medco, the nation's largest seller of discount drugs. An example of backward integration in the natural resources industry is Chevron Oil's 1984 purchase of Gulf Oil to augment its reserves. A more recent example of backward integration in the technology industry is America Online's purchase of media and content provider Time Warner in 2000.

FRIENDLY VERSUS HOSTILE TAKEOVERS

In a *friendly* takeover of control, the target's management is receptive to the idea and recommends shareholder approval. To gain control, the acquiring company generally must offer a premium to the current price of the stock. The excess of the offer price over the target's current share price is called a *control premium*. If the stockholders approve, the transaction is consummated through a purchase of the target company's shares for cash, stock, debt, or some combination of all three. In contrast, an *unfriendly* or *hostile takeover* occurs when the initial approach was unsolicited, the target was not seeking a merger at the time of the approach, the approach was contested by the target's management, and control changed hands (i.e., more than half of the target's common stock was acquired). The acquirer may attempt to circumvent management by going directly to the target's shareholders and by buying shares in the marketplace. This is accomplished by a *tender offer*, which is an offer to buy the shares of a company for cash, securities, or both with the intent to take control of the corporation.

Bidders usually find friendly takeovers preferable to hostile transactions because they often can be consummated at a lower purchase price. A hostile takeover attempt may put the target "into play" and attract new bidders. In the ensuing auction environment, the final purchase price may be bid up to a point well above the initial offer price. In addition, acquirers prefer friendly takeovers because the postmerger integration process usually can be accomplished more expeditiously and effectively when both parties are cooperating fully. Although the number of bids classified as hostile and unsolicited has been rising, most deals of this type are ultimately unsuccessful and subsequently withdrawn. According to Thomson Financial Securities Data Corporation, only about 17% of such M&A transactions in the United States during the 1990s were successful. However, almost 40% of the targeted firms ultimately were sold to another bidder and 6% were sold to *white knights*, firms perceived as friendly by the target firm. The remaining target firms remained independent.

G. William Schwert (2000) argues that the distinction between hostile and friendly takeovers is largely perceptual and often cannot be substantiated based on accounting and stock price data. The perceived differences between the two may depend on how information is released to the public. Transactions in which negotiations are not made public until an agreement is reached often are viewed as friendly. In contrast, transactions may be viewed as hostile when negotiations are made public before all issues are resolved. To put pressure on the target's management, such information may be leaked to the public by the bidder.

THE ROLE OF HOLDING COMPANIES IN
MERGERS AND ACQUISITIONS

A *holding company* is a legal entity having a controlling interest in one or more companies. The primary function of a holding company is to own stock in other corporations. In general, it has no wholly owned operating units of its own. The segments owned by the holding company are separate legal entities, which in practice are controlled by the holding company. This differs from firms having multiple divisions or profit centers reporting to a single corporate headquarters.

The Holding Company as an Investment Vehicle

The primary advantage of the holding company structure is the potential leverage that can be achieved by gaining effective control of other companies' assets at a lower overall cost than would be required if the firm were to acquire 100% of the target's outstanding shares. Effective control sometimes can be achieved by owning as little as 20% of the voting stock of another company. This is possible when the target company's ownership is highly fragmented, with few shareholders owning large blocks of stock. Consequently, the holding company frequently is able to cast the deciding votes by voting its shares as a block on important issues of corporate strategy and governance. In this manner, investors through a holding company are able to gain effective control of substantially more assets than they could through a merger.

Effective control largely determines how a subsidiary's financial performance will be treated for accounting purposes. Gaining effective control of assets with relatively little equity investment can magnify fluctuations in the holding company's earnings because the firm's consolidated statements, for financial reporting purposes, reflect 100% of a subsidiary's earnings but less than 100% of the subsidiary's assets. The amount of the subsidiary's assets included on the parent's consolidated statements generally will be equal to the holding company's percentage share of the subsidiary's equity. Effective control generally is achieved by acquiring less than 100% but usually more than 50% of another firm's equity. One firm is said to have *effective control* over another when control has been achieved through the purchase of voting stock, it is not likely to be temporary, there are no legal restrictions on control such as from a bankruptcy court, and there are no powerful minority shareholders.

Companies controlled by the holding company generally are referred to as wholly or partially owned subsidiaries, depending on the percentage of voting shares held by the holding company. As explained in Chapter 10, the percentage of ownership has significant implications for accounting and tax purposes.

Disadvantages of Holding Companies

Despite the potential for gaining control of another company at a lower cost than through an acquisition, the holding company structure can create significant management challenges. Because the holding company can gain effective control with less than 100% ownership, the holding company is left with a significant number of minority shareholders, who may not always agree with the strategic direction of the company. Consequently, implementing holding company strategies may become very contentious. Furthermore, in highly diversified holding companies, managers also may have difficulty making optimal investment decisions because of their limited understanding of the different competitive dynamics of each business. The holding company structure also can create significant tax problems for shareholders of the holding company. Subsidiaries of holding companies pay taxes on their operating profits. The holding company then pays taxes on dividends they receive from their subsidiaries. Finally, holding company shareholders pay taxes on dividends they receive from the holding company. This amounts to triple taxation of subsidiary operating earnings.

THE ROLE OF EMPLOYEE STOCK OWNERSHIP PLANS IN MERGERS AND ACQUISITIONS

An employee stock ownership plan (ESOP) is a trust that invests in the securities of the firm sponsoring the plan. Such plans are defined contribution employee benefit pension plans that invest at least 50% of the plan's assets in the common shares of the firm sponsoring the ESOP. The plans may receive stock or cash, which is used to buy the sponsor's stock. The sponsoring corporation can make tax-deductible contributions of cash, stock, or other assets into the trust. The plan's trustee holds title to the assets for the benefit of the employees (i.e., beneficiaries). The trustee is charged with investing the trust assets productively; and, unless specifically limited, the trustee can sell, mortgage, or lease the assets. The assets are allocated to employees and are not taxed until withdrawn by employees. Both interest and principal payments on ESOP loans are tax deductible by the firm sponsoring the ESOP. Dividends paid on stock contributed to ESOPs are also deductible if they are used to repay ESOP debt. The sponsoring firm could use tax credits equal to .5% of payroll if contributions in that amount were made to the ESOP.

There are also tax advantages to lenders making loans to ESOPs owning more than 50% of the sponsoring firm's stock. Only one-half of the interest earned on such loans is taxable to the lender.

In 2000 there were about 11,500 ESOPs covering almost 9 million employees (www.csopassociation.org). Of these, 9% were in publicly traded companies. About three-fourths were leveraged using borrowed funds to purchase the sponsoring firm's stock. ESOPs owned about $500 billion in stock in the sponsoring firms. Approximately 2500 of the firms with ESOP were majority owned by the ESOP; about 1500 were 100% owned. Early studies (U.S. General Accounting Office, 1987) were not able to establish a direct link between gains in worker productivity

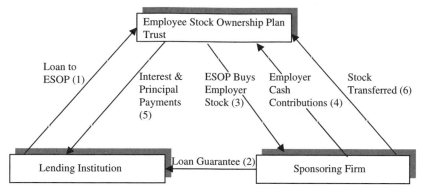

FIGURE 1-2. Leveraged employee stock ownership plan.

and the profitability of the sponsoring firms. However, a later study found that the financial returns of public companies with ESOPs were significantly higher than comparable firms without ESOPs (Conte, Biasi, Kruse, and Jampani, 1996).

Establishing an ESOP

Figure 1-2 illustrates the steps involved in establishing an ESOP. The ESOP borrows from financial institutions (step 1), and the employer sponsoring the ESOP guarantees the loan (step 2). The ESOP uses the borrowed funds to purchase stock from the sponsoring employer, and the stock is used to provide collateral for the loan (step 3). The employer then makes periodic cash contributions to the ESOP (step 4). The interest and principal on the loan are repaid by cash contributions to the ESOP from the sponsoring firm (step 5). Because it has a contingent liability (loan guarantee), the sponsoring firm transfers ownership of the stock to the ESOP only as portions of the loan principal are repaid (step 6).

ESOPs as an Alternative to Divestiture

If a subsidiary cannot be sold at what the parent firm believes to be a reasonable price, and liquidating the subsidiary would be disruptive to customers, the parent may initiate a sale directly to employees through a shell corporation. A *shell corporation* is one that is incorporated but has no significant assets or operations. The shell sets up the ESOP, which borrows the money to buy the subsidiary. The parent guarantees the loan. The shell operates the subsidiary, whereas the ESOP holds the stock. As income is generated from the subsidiary, tax-deductible contributions are made by the shell to the ESOP to service the debt. As the loan is paid off, the shares are allocated to employees who eventually own the firm.

ESOPs and Management Buyouts

ESOPs commonly are used by employees in leveraged or management buyouts to purchase the shares of owners of privately held firms. This is particularly common where the owners have most of their net worth tied up in their firms. The mechanism is similar to a sale initiated by the owner to employees.

ESOPs as an Antitakeover Defense

A firm concerned about the potential for a hostile takeover creates an ESOP. The ESOP borrows with the aid of the sponsoring firm's guarantee and uses the loan proceeds to buy stock issued by the sponsoring firm. While the loan is outstanding, the ESOP's trustees retain voting rights on the stock. Once the loan is repaid, it generally is assumed that employees will tend to vote against bidders who they perceive as jeopardizing their jobs.

BUSINESS ALLIANCES

In addition to mergers and acquisitions, businesses also may combine through joint ventures (JVs), strategic alliances, minority investments, franchises, and licenses. These alternative forms of combining businesses are addressed in more detail in Chapter 12. The term *business alliance* will be used to refer to all forms of business combinations other than mergers and acquisitions.

Alternative Structures

Joint Ventures

JVs are cooperative business relationships formed by two or more separate parties to achieve common strategic objectives. The JV is usually an independent legal entity in the form of a corporation or partnership. JV corporations have their own management reporting to a board of directors consisting of representatives of those companies participating in the JV. The JV generally is established for a limited time. Each of the JV partners continues to exist as separate entities.

Strategic Alliances

Strategic alliances generally fall short of creating a separate legal entity. They can be an agreement to sell each firm's products to the other's customers or to codevelop a technology, product, or process. Such agreements often are cancelable without significant penalties. The terms of such an agreement may be legally binding or largely informal, with the primary motivation of both participants being the desire to achieve shared objectives.

Minority Investments

Passive minority investments require little commitment of management time and may be highly liquid if the investment is in a publicly traded company. Investing companies may choose to assist small or start-up companies in the development of products or technologies useful to the investing company. The investing company often receives representation on the board of the firm in whom the investor has made the investment.

Franchises

From a legal perspective, a franchise is a privilege given to a dealer by a manufacturer or franchise service organization to sell the franchiser's products or services in a given area, with or without exclusivity. Such arrangements sometimes are formalized with franchise agreements. Under the agreement, the franchiser may offer the franchisee consultation, promotional assistance, financing, and other benefits in exchange for a share of the franchise's revenue. Franchises represent a low-cost way to expand because the capital usually is provided by the franchisee; however, the success of franchising has been limited largely to such industries as fast food services and retailing.

License Agreements

Licenses require no initial capital and represent a convenient way for a company to extend its brand to new products and new markets by licensing their brand name to others. Alternatively, a company may gain access to a proprietary technology through the licensing process. A franchise is a specialized form of a license agreement.

Advantages and Disadvantages of Alternative Business Alliance Structures

The major attraction of these alternatives to outright acquisition is the opportunity for each partner to gain access to the other's skills, products, and markets at a lower commitment of management time and financial resources. The JV also allows for the sharing of ongoing operating expenses. Major disadvantages include limited control and, in the case of JVs, independent management that may have divided loyalties between the various owners of the JV, the requirement that each party share the profits, and the potential for loss of trade secrets and skills. The latter exposure is greatest in license arrangements, in which controls tend to be very limited.

PARTICIPANTS IN THE MERGERS AND ACQUISITIONS PROCESS

Even the best ideas founder if they are not executed properly. Moving from the concept stage to a completed transaction requires an array of highly skilled advisors. Each advisor specializes in a specific aspect of the M&A process. Understanding the roles of the various players is helpful in sorting out what types of resources will be required for a specific transaction. Good advice is worth its weight in gold; bad advice can be disastrous. Like all professions, the quality of advisors can vary widely. Although major financial institutions may provide "one-stop" M&A advisory services, they are unlikely to have highly competent people to support all aspects of a transaction. Although investment bankers and lawyers frequently get the greatest press in the largest transactions, there are many other professionals who play an essential role in the successful completion of the deal.

INVESTMENT BANKERS

Investment bankers are often at the forefront of the acquisition process. They offer strategic and tactical advice and acquisition opportunities; screen potential buyers and sellers; make initial contact with a seller or buyer; and provide negotiation support, valuation, and deal structuring. Investment bankers help to identify the firm's strategic objectives and assist in evaluating alternative strategies for achieving these objectives. The major investment banking firms usually have groups within corporate finance departments that offer advice on M&A strategies. According to Mergerstat, the top five investment banks in terms of their share of the dollar value of 2001 M&A transactions were Goldman Sachs, Merrill Lynch, Morgan Stanley Dean Witter, Credit Suisse First Boston, and Citigroup/Salomon Smith Barney (Mergerstat, 2002).

Fairness Opinion

A *fairness opinion letter* is a written and signed third-party assertion certifying the appropriateness of the price of a proposed deal involving a tender offer, merger, asset sale, or leveraged buyout. It discusses the price and terms of the deal in the context of comparable transactions. The focus in the opinion is on strategic considerations that might make a particular deal worth more or less than others. A typical fairness opinion provides a range of fair prices, with the presumption that the actual deal price should fall within that range. Often the range is wide.

Although such opinions are intended to inform investors, they actually are developed as legal protection for members of the boards of directors against possible shareholders' challenges of their decisions. They tend to bolster the position of the corporate board approving the deal. They are not a substitute for due diligence because the investment bankers preparing such deals may have an inherent bias in favor of ratifying such transactions. Public accounting firms and consultants often also prepare fairness opinions. They compete with investment bankers on the basis of greater independence and expertise as well as lower fees. Under any circumstance, the investor should consider the motives of whatever organization prepares the fairness opinion.

The size of an investment banking advisory fee is often contingent on the completion of the deal and may run about 1–2% of the value of the transaction. Such fees generally vary with the size of the transaction. The size of the fee paid may exceed 1–2% if the advisors achieve certain incentive goals. Fairness opinion fees often amount to about one-fourth of the total advisory fee paid on a transaction (Sweeney, 1999). Although the size of the fee may vary with the size of the transaction, the fairness opinion fee usually is paid whether or not the deal is consummated.

Large Versus Small Investment Banks

The size of the transaction often will determine the size of the investment bank that can be used as an advisor. The largest investment banks are unlikely to consider any transaction valued at less than $100 million. Large investment banks do not necessarily provide the best advice. So-called investment boutiques can be very helpful in providing specialized industry knowledge. However, the larger firms are likely to offer easier entree at higher levels in potential corporate buyers and sellers. Investment banks often provide large databases of recent transactions, which are critical in valuing potential target companies. For highly specialized transactions, the investment boutiques are apt to have more relevant data. Finally, the large investment banks are more likely to be able to assist in funding large transactions because of their current relationships with institutional lenders and broker distribution networks.

Financing Services

In large transactions, a group of investment banks, also referred to as a *syndicate*, agrees to purchase a new issue of securities (e.g., debt, preferred, or common stock) from the acquiring company for sale to the investing public. Within the syndicate, the banks underwriting or purchasing the issue are often different from the group selling the issue. The selling group often consists of those firms with the best broker distribution networks.

Following registration with the Securities and Exchange Commission (SEC), such securities may be offered to the investing public as an *initial public offering* (IPO) at a price agreed on by the issuer and the investment banking group or they may be *privately placed* with institutional investors, such as pension funds and insurance companies. Unlike a public offering, a private placement does not have to be registered with the SEC if the securities are purchased for investment rather than for resale.

LAWYERS

The legal framework surrounding a typical transaction has become so complex that no one individual can have sufficient expertise to address all the issues. On large, complicated transactions, legal teams can consist of more than a dozen attorneys, each of whom represents a specialized aspect of the law. Areas of expertise include the following: M&As, corporate, tax, employee benefits, real estate, antitrust, securities, and intellectual property. In a hostile transaction, the team may grow to include litigation experts. According to Mergerstat, the leading law firms in terms of their share of the dollar value of transactions in 2001 include Wachtell Lipton Rosen & Katz, Simpson Thatcher & Bartlett, Skadden Arps Slate Meagher & Flom, Sullivan & Cromwell, and Davis Polk & Wardwell (Mergerstat, 2002).

ACCOUNTANTS

Services provided by accountants include advice on the optimal tax structure, on financial structuring, and on performing financial due diligence. Tax accountants or tax attorneys are vital in determining the appropriate tax structure. A transaction can be structured in many different ways, with each having different tax implications for the parties involved (see Chapter 10). In conducting due diligence for a friendly takeover, accountants perform the role of auditors by reviewing the target's financial statements and operations through a series of onsite visits and interviews with senior and middle-level managers.

PROXY SOLICITORS

Proxy battles are attempts to change management control of a company by gaining the right to cast votes on behalf of other shareholders. In contests for the control of the board of directors of a target company, it is often difficult to compile mailing lists of stockholders' addresses because many addresses are held by brokerage houses. Proxy solicitation companies often are hired by an acquiring company or dissident shareholder for this purpose. Proxy solicitors can represent both dissident shareholders and management.

Contests for control, particularly unsolicited tender offers, are a critical test of a company's leadership. For corporations defending themselves against takeover bids or making tender offers, success depends on the ability to quickly identify shareholders and to communicate effectively with these shareholders. Whether a hostile bid or an unsolicited tender offer, the proxy solicitation company designs strategies to educate shareholders and communicate why shareholders should follow the Board's recommendations. The major companies in this business are Georgeson & Company and D. F. King & Company. Georgeson & Company (2000) claims to have won 77% of the proxy contests representing management (66 of 86) and 65% representing dissident shareholders (57 of 88).

PUBLIC RELATIONS

Communicating a consistent position during a takeover attempt is vital. Inconsistent messages reduce the credibility of the parties involved. From the viewpoint of the acquiring company in a hostile takeover attempt, the message to the shareholders must be that their plans for the company will increase shareholder value more than the plans of incumbent management. The target company's management frequently will hire private investigators, such as Kroll Associates (acquired by O'Gara in 1997), to look into the backgrounds and motives of those managing the takeover attempt. Private investigators may be hired to develop detailed financial data on the company and to do background checks on key personnel. Such information may be used by the target firm to discredit publicly the management of the acquiring firm. Major public relations firms with significant experience in the

M&A arena include Kekst & Company, Hill & Knowlton, and Robinson Lerer & Montgomery.

INSTITUTIONAL INVESTORS

Institutional investors include public and private pension funds, insurance companies, investment companies, bank trust departments, and mutual funds. Although a single institution generally cannot influence a company's actions, a collection of institutions can. Before 1992, for an institutional investor to submit a slate of candidates for the board of directors and to get support for its candidates it had to file a proxy statement with the SEC and mail copies to all other shareholders of the company. Today, however, federal regulations require only institutional shareholders who are seeking actual proxies or who hold a large percentage of a company's stock to file a proxy statement with the SEC. Shareholders may announce how they intend to vote on a matter and advertise their position to seek support. Consequently, institutional shareholders now have more influence than ever before.

ARBITRAGEURS

When a bid is made for a target company, the target company's stock price often trades at a small discount to the actual bid. This reflects the risk that the offer may not be accepted. *Merger arbitrage* refers to an investment strategy that attempts to profit from this spread. If the merger is successful, the arbitrageur captures the arbitrage spread. However, if the merger fails, the arbitrageur incurs a loss, usually much greater than the profits obtained if the deal succeeds.

Arbitrageurs ("arbs") buy the stock and make a profit on the difference between the bid price and the current stock price if the deal is consummated. Arbs may accumulate a substantial percentage of the stock held outside of institutions to be in a position to influence the outcome of the takeover attempt. For example, if other offers appear, arbs promote their positions directly to managers and institutional investors with phone calls and through leaks to the financial press. Arbs also provide market liquidity during transactions. Arbs make it possible for institutional investors, who are willing to accept less rather than risk losing their entire profit if the transaction is not completed, to sell their holdings of the target company shares before completion of the transaction.

With the number of merger arbitrageurs increasing, arbs are becoming more proactive in trying to anticipate takeover situations (i.e., firms that appear to be undervalued). Arbs monitor rumors and stock price movements to determine if investors are accumulating a particular stock. Their objective is to identify the target before the potential acquirer is required by law to announce its intentions. Empirical studies show that the price of a target company's stock often starts to rise in advance of the announcement of a takeover attempt. Also, if one firm in an industry is acquired, it is commonplace for the share prices of other firms in the same industry to also increase because they are viewed as potential targets.

Merger arbitrage has the potential to be highly profitable. A number of studies find that such arbitrage generates financial returns ranging from 4.5% to more than 100% in excess of what would be considered normal in a highly competitive market (Dukes, Frohlich, and Ma, 1992; Jindra and Walkling, 1999; Karolyi and Shannon, 1998; Mitchell and Pulvino, 2001). Exhibit 1-1 illustrates the implementation of a typical merger arbitrage strategy.

EXHIBIT 1-1. MERGER ARBITRAGE IN PRACTICE

Normally, following an announced merger the price of the target's stock rises but not to the offering price because of the uncertainty associated with completing the transaction. A transaction may not be consummated because it does not receive regulatory or shareholder approval or the acquirer cannot arrange financing. The difference between the target's trading price and the offer price is called the discount. The amount of the discount increases with the expected length of time until closing and the likelihood that the deal will not close. The arb seeks to lock in this spread. To do this when the offer is a cash offer, the arbitrageur merely has to buy the stock of the target. However, when the offer is an exchange of securities, the investor also must hedge against the possibility of the acquirer's stock falling. This can be accomplished by selling the acquirer's stock short.[1]

Assume an acquirer offers to exchange one share of its stock for each share of the target's stock; the acquirer's and target's stocks currently are trading at $90 and $70 per share, respectively; and an arb buys the target's stock at $85. This is the price the target's share reached immediately after the announcement. The arb hedges his or her position by selling the acquirer's stock short at $90. As the merger date approaches, this $5 spread between the arb's purchase price for the target's stock and the acquirer's share price (i.e., the offer price) will diminish as the prices of the target's and acquirer's stock converge.

Once the merger is consummated and the target's stock is converted to the acquirer's stock, the arb locks in the $5 gain regardless of the current price of the acquirer's stock. The arb covers the short sale with the acquirer's stock valued at $90. If during the interim the market has declined, sending the acquirer's stock down to $70, the investor makes $20 on the short sale of the acquirer's stock at $90, less the loss of $15 on the target's shares for which the investor paid $85.

Arbitrage Strategy: Buy 1 share of target at $85/sell short 1 share of acquirer stock at $90.

Scenarios After Merger	Gain (Loss) on Long Position of $85	Gain (Loss) on Short Position of $90	Total Gain (Loss)
Rise in Acquirer's Stock to $110:	$25	($20)	$5
Fall in Acquirer's Stock to $70:	($15)	20	$5

If the merger takes 6 months to complete from the announcement date, the 5% profit realized in this example equates to a compound annualized gain of 10.25%, [i.e., $(1.05) \times (1.05)$]. If the arb had borrowed half of the total investment in the arbitrage transaction, the annualized return would double.

The risk is that the merger will not be completed. The target's stock price should return to its original price of $70. The result would be a loss of $15 on the purchase of the target's stock at $85. Similarly, even if the acquirer's share price had fallen after the merger announcement, the acquirer's share price should return to its previous price of $90 after the transaction is called off. This occurs as short sellers cover their positions buying the acquirer's stock. Any investor who sold the acquirer's stock short at less than $90 would incur a loss on their short position in addition to the loss incurred on the target's shares.

[1] A short sale is the sale of a security not owned by the seller. This technique is used to take advantage of an anticipated decline in the security's price or to protect a profit in securities currently held by the seller. To implement this strategy, an investor borrows stock certificates for delivery at the time of the short sale. If the buyer can buy that stock later at a lower price, a profit is realized; if the price increases, a loss is incurred.

COMMON MOTIVATIONS FOR MERGERS AND ACQUISITIONS

There are numerous theories of why mergers and acquisitions take place. In reality, most M&As are a result of a number of different motivations. Table 1-1 lists some of the more prominent theories about why mergers happen. Each of these theories is discussed in greater detail in the remainder of this section.

SYNERGY

Synergy is a widely used, albeit often misused, justification for making acquisitions. Synergy is the rather simplistic notion that the combination of two businesses can create greater shareholder value than if they are operated separately. There are two basic types of synergy: operating and financial.

Operating Synergy (Economies of Scale and Scope)

Operating synergy consists of both economies of scale and economies of scope. Gains in efficiency can come from either factor and from improved managerial

TABLE 1-1   Common Theories of What Causes Mergers and Acquisitions

Theory	Motivation
Synergy	$1 + 1 = 3$
Operating Synergy Economies of Scale Economies of Scope	Improve operating efficiency through economies of scale or scope by acquiring a customer, supplier, or competitor
Financial Synergy	Lower cost of capital by smoothing cash flow, realizing financial economies of scale, and better matching of investment opportunities with internal cash flows
Diversification New Products/Current Markets New Products/New Markets Current Products/New Markets	Position the firm in higher growth products or markets
Market Power	Increase market share to improve ability to set and maintain prices above competitive levels
Strategic Realignment Technological Change Regulatory and Political Change	Acquire needed capabilities to adapt more rapidly to environmental changes than could be achieved if they were developed internally
Hubris (Managerial Pride)	Acquirers believe that their valuations of targets are more accurate than the market's, causing them to overpay by overestimating the gains from synergy
Buying Undervalued Assets (q-Ratio)	Acquire assets more cheaply when the stock of existing companies is less than the cost of buying or building the assets
Mismanagement (Agency Problems)	Replace marginally competent managers or managers who are not acting in the best interests of the owners
Managerialism	Increase the size of a company to increase the power and pay of managers
Tax Considerations	Obtain unused net operating losses and tax credits, asset write-ups, and substitute capital gains for ordinary income

practices. Both economies of scale and scope assume a level of management talent in place to realize the benefits of operating synergy.

Economies of Scale (Fixed Per Unit Costs Decline as Output Increases)

Economies of scale refer to the spreading of fixed costs over increasing production levels. Scale is defined by such fixed costs as depreciation of equipment and amortization of capitalized software; normal maintenance spending; obligations such as interest expense, lease payments, and union, customer, and vendor contracts; and taxes. Such costs are fixed in the sense that they cannot be altered in the short run. Consequently, for a given scale or amount of fixed expenses, the dollar value of fixed expenses per dollar of revenue decreases as output and sales increase.

Economies of scale most frequently are seen in manufacturing operations, although they can be important in any business having substantial fixed overhead expenses. Declining per-unit expenses reflect improving labor productivity as workers and managers learn how to improve workflow. Per-unit costs continue to fall until the firm begins to experience inefficiencies associated with managing very large organizations. Economies of scale are most evident in very high fixed-cost industries such as utilities; steelmaking; and pharmaceutical, chemical, and aircraft manufacturing.

There is only marginal empirical support for using mergers to achieve economies of scale. Some research suggests a correlation between changes in ownership and improvements in efficiency (Lictenberg and Siegel, 1987). However, simple correlation does not demonstrate a causal link between corporate takeovers and lower operating costs resulting from economies of scale. There is some evidence that operating efficiencies in vertical integration may be significant. By combining firms at different stages of production, better communication and coordination as well as less customer–vendor bargaining may result in improved product planning and implementation (Klein, Crawford, and Alchian, 1978). By acquiring a supplier, a firm may avoid potential disruptions in supply that might occur when independent supplier agreements expire (Carlton and Perloff, 1994).

The importance of consolidation to achieve economies of scale is evident in the semiconductor and pharmaceutical industries. In 2002, a typical semiconductor fabrication plant cost between $2 billion and $3 billion compared with $1 billion just 5 years ago. By the late 1990s, it cost pharmaceutical firms more than $800 million to develop and get approval of a new drug, six times the cost 20 years earlier (Dreazen, Ip, and Kulish, 2002). The rapid recovery of these huge initial capital outlays requires that semiconductor and pharmaceutical manufacturers achieve and maintain high utilization rates of their manufacturing facilities.

Economies of Scope (Producing Multiple Products with the Same Resources)

Economies of scope refer to using a specific set of skills or an asset currently employed in producing a specific product or service to produce related products or services. For example, Proctor and Gamble, the consumer products giant, uses its highly regarded consumer marketing skills to market a full range of personal care as well as pharmaceutical products. Honda utilizes its skills in enhancing internal combustion engines to develop motorcycles, lawn mowers, and snow blowers, as well as automobiles. Sequent Technology lets customers run applications on UNIX and NT operating systems on a single computer system. Citigroup uses the same computer center to process loan applications, deposits, trust services, and mutual fund accounts for its bank's customers. Small banks, which do not have sufficient revenue to provide trust services and investment advice, may be able to afford to provide such services if they merge (Mester, 1987).

Financial Synergy (Lowering the Cost of Capital)

Financial synergy refers to the impact of mergers and acquisitions on the cost of capital of the acquiring firm or the newly formed firm resulting from the merger or acquisition. Theoretically, the cost of capital could be reduced if the merged firms have uncorrelated cash flows, realize financial economies of scale, or result in a better matching of investment opportunities with internally generated funds.

Financial Economies of Scale (Reducing Transactions Costs)

Another example of financial synergy is the reduction in the cost of capital resulting from lower securities and transactions costs (Levy and Sarnat, 1970). Larger firms should be able to issue debt at a lower average interest rate and also lower average cost to issue the debt because SEC registration fees, legal fees, and printing costs are spread over the firm's larger bond issue. Similar logic applies to issuing common equity.

Better Matching of Opportunities with Internally Generated Funds

Combining a firm with excess cash flows with one whose internally generated cash flow is insufficient to fund its investment opportunities may result in a lower cost of borrowing (Nielsen and Melicher, 1973). A firm in a mature industry whose growth is slowing may produce cash flows well in excess of available investment opportunities. Another firm in a high-growth industry may have more investment opportunities than the cash to fund them. Reflecting their different growth rates and risk levels, the firm in the mature industry may have a lower cost of capital than the one in the high-growth industry. Combining the two firms might result in a lower cost of capital for the merged firms. This result may be achieved because investors perceive a lower level of risk associated with the combined firms, savings in flotation and transactions costs, and because of a more efficient allocation of capital as the higher growth opportunities are funded by cash generated by the more mature business.

DIVERSIFICATION

Diversification refers to a strategy of buying firms outside of a company's current primary lines of business. There are two commonly used justifications for diversification.

Firms often justify diversification on the basis of reducing shareholder risk by stabilizing overall revenue through shifting a portion of the firm's assets from a cyclical industry to what is perceived to be a more stable industry. If the two firms have cash flows that are uncorrelated, their combined cash flow may be less volatile than their cash flows viewed separately. Consequently, investors may believe that the combined firms are less likely to default on their obligations than the firms viewed separately and require a lower rate of return to invest in the combined firm's securities. This also is referred to as "co-insurance." This was the announced

TABLE 1-2 Product–Market Matrix

	Markets	
Products	Current	New
Current	Lower Growth/Lower Risk	Higher Growth/Higher Risk
New	Higher Growth/Higher Risk	Highest Growth/Highest Risk

motivation for U.S. Steel's mid-1980s acquisition of Marathon Oil to form USX. At the time, oil and gas revenues appeared to be considerably more predictable than steel industry revenues. This justification for diversification by firms always has been on shaky theoretical grounds (Levy and Sarnat, 1970). Shareholders can more efficiently spread their investments and risk among industries, thus obviating the need for companies to diversify on behalf of their shareholders.

The second common argument for diversification is for firms to shift from their core product lines or markets into product lines or markets that have higher growth prospects. The product–market matrix illustrated in Table 1-2 illustrates this strategy. If a firm is facing slower growth in its current markets, it may be able to accelerate growth by selling its current products in new markets that are somewhat unfamiliar and, therefore, more risky. Similarly, the firm may attempt to achieve higher growth rates by developing new products, untested in the marketplace, and selling them into familiar and less risky current markets. In each instance, the firm is assuming additional risk.

Benefits of Unrelated Diversification Questionable

The performance of diversified companies has changed dramatically over time. In a study of the highly diversified conglomerates of the 1960s, Schipper and Thompson (1983) found that the share prices of such firms responded positively to announcements of new acquisitions before 1967. After 1967, legislation such as the Williams Act of 1968 and the Tax Reform Act of 1969 created new challenges to the types of M&A activity that took place during the 1960s (see Chapters 2 and 10).

With the passage of time, the perceived value of diversification diminished significantly. In a comparison of the stock performance of 13 conglomerates with the Standard and Poor's (S&P) 500, Ravenscraft and Scherer (1988) showed that investments in conglomerates made before 1968 dramatically outperformed the overall market through 1983. However, investments made in 1968, the peak in conglomerate share prices, underperformed the S&P 500 through 1983. These findings were contradicted in a study of 337 mergers between 1957 and 1975 in which the share prices of conglomerate mergers outperformed nonconglomerate mergers in the sample (Elgers and Clark, 1980).

More recent studies have supported the conclusion that investors do not benefit from unrelated diversification. Investors perceive companies diversified in unrelated areas as riskier because they are difficult for management to understand and management often fails to fully fund the most attractive investment opportunities (Morck, Shleifer, and Vishny, 1990). Empirical studies also show that unrelated acquisitions are four times more likely to be divested than those related to the acquirer's core business (Kaplan and Weisbach, 1992). Berger and Ofek (1995) reported that between 1986 and 1991, for a sample of 100 large firms, the market value of the average diversified firm was about 13–15% less than the value of the sum of its divisions if valued independently. Lins and Servaes (1999) find *a conglomerate discount* of a similar magnitude for firms in the United Kingdom and Japan.

Although more recent studies also conclude that diversified firms often destroy value, they attribute some portion of the magnitude of the discount to the fact that diversifying firms are often poor performers before becoming conglomerates. Consequently, the entire magnitude of the discount is not necessarily a result of the simple act of diversification (Campa and Simi, 1999; Hyland, 2001). Graham, Lemmon, and Wolf (2002) argue that the size of the discount may be overstated because the firms used to value the conglomerate's divisions are not truly comparable.

Focused Firms Tend to Outperform Diversified Companies

In a study of corporate performance during the 1980s, Comment and Jarrell (1993) found that stock returns tended to increase as firms increased their focus. They concluded that greater corporate focus is consistent with shareholder wealth maximization. This conclusion was supported in a study of corporate spin-offs, a process in which a parent would dividend the stock in a wholly owned subsidiary to its shareholders (see Chapter 13). The increase in market value of firms spinning off businesses in unrelated industries was substantially greater than for firms getting rid of businesses operating in the same industry as the parent firm's core business (Daley, Mehrotra, and Sivakumar, 1996). Berger and Ofek (1996) found that asset sales lead to an improvement in operating performance in the year following the sale; the improvement occurs mainly in firms that increase their focus.

Although the empirical evidence suggests that corporate performance is likely to be greatest for firms that tend to pursue a more focused corporate strategy, there are always exceptions. Among the most famous are Berkshire Hathaway (see Case Study 1-1) and General Electric (see Case Study 2-10, Chapter 2 of this book).

CASE STUDY 1-1: THE MAN BEHIND THE LEGEND AT BERKSHIRE HATHAWAY

Although not exactly a household name, Berkshire Hathaway ("Berkshire") has long been a high flier on Wall Street. The firm's share price has outperformed the total return on the Standard and Poor's 500 stock index in 32 of the 36 years that Warren Buffet has managed the firm. Berkshire Hathaway's share price rose from $12 per share to $71,000 at the end of 2000, an annual rate of growth of 27%. With revenue in excess of $30 billion, Berkshire is among the top 50 of the Fortune 500 companies.

What makes the company unusual is that it is one of the few highly diversified companies to consistently outperform the S&P 500 over many years. As a conglomerate, Berkshire acquires or makes investments in a broad cross-section of companies. It owns operations in such diverse areas as insurance, furniture, flight services, vacuum cleaners, retailing, carpet manufacturing, paint, insulation and roofing products, newspapers, candy, shoes, steel warehousing, uniforms, and an electric utility. The firm also has "passive" investments in such major companies as Coca-Cola, American Express, Gillette, and the *Washington Post*.

Warren Buffet's investing philosophy is relatively simple. It consists of buying businesses that generate an attractive sustainable growth in earnings and leaving them alone. Synergy among his holdings never seems to play an important role. He has shown a propensity to invest in relatively mundane businesses that have a preeminent position in their markets; he has assiduously avoided businesses he felt he did not understand such as those in high technology industries. He also has shown a tendency to acquire businesses that were "out of favor" on Wall Street.

He has built a cash-generating machine, principally through his insurance operations that produce "float" (i.e., premium revenues that insurers invest in advance of paying claims). In 2000, Berkshire acquired eight firms. Usually flush with cash, Buffet has developed a reputation for being nimble. This most recently was demonstrated in his acquisition of Johns Manville in late 2000. Manville generated $2 billion in revenue from insulation and roofing products and more than $200 million in after-tax profits. Manville's controlling stockholder was a trust that had been set up to assume the firm's asbestos liabilities when Manville had emerged from bankruptcy in the late 1980s. After a buyout group that had offered to buy the company for $2.8 billion backed out of the transaction on December 8, 2000, Berkshire contacted the trust and acquired Manville for $2.2 billion in cash. By December 20, Manville and Berkshire reached an agreement.

STRATEGIC REALIGNMENT

The strategic realignment theory suggests that firms use M&As as ways of rapidly adjusting to changes in their external environments. Although change can come from many different sources, only changes in the regulatory environment and technological innovation are considered. During the 1990s these two factors have been major forces in creating new opportunities for growth or threats to a firm's primary line of business.

Regulatory Change

M&A activity in recent years has centered in industries that have been subject to significant deregulation. These industries include financial services, health care, utilities, media, telecommunications, and defense. There is significant empirical evidence that takeover activity is higher in deregulated industries than in regulated ones (Jensen, 1993; Mitchell and Mulherin, 1996; Mulherin and Boone, 2000).

The advent of deregulation broke down artificial barriers in these industries and stimulated competition. In some states, utilities now are required to sell power to competitors, which can resell the power in the utility's own marketplace. Some utilities are responding to this increased competition by attempting to achieve greater operating efficiency through mergers and acquisitions. In financial services, commercial banks are moving well beyond their historical role of accepting deposits and granting loans and into investment banking, insurance, and mutual funds. The Financial Services Modernization Act of 1999 repealed depression-era legislation that prevented banks, securities firms, and insurance companies from merging. The legislation accelerated the trend toward huge financial services companies typified by the 1998 Citicorp-Travelers merger.

Historically, local and long-distance phone companies were not allowed to compete against each other. Cable companies were essentially monopolies. Following the Telecommunications Reform Act of 1996, local and long-distance companies are actively encouraged to compete in each other's markets. Cable companies are moving to offer Internet access and local telephone service. During the first half of the 1990s, the U.S. Department of Defense actively encouraged consolidation of the nation's major defense contractors to improve their overall operating efficiency. Radio and television broadcasters now are permitted to own far more stations.

The trend in deregulation continued into the new millennium in some industries. In early 2002, a Federal Appeals Court rejected a Federal Communications Commission regulation that prohibited a company from owning a cable television system and a TV station in the same city. Moreover, it also overturned a rule that barred a company from owning TV stations that reach more than 35% of U.S. households. These rulings may trigger combinations among the largest media companies or purchases of smaller broadcasters.

Technological Change

Technology has disrupted the status quo throughout history. Certain technological advances have created new competitors, products, markets, and industries at a blinding pace. The advent of the railroad opened up the western United States, allowing a more rapid and less expensive flow of products between the eastern and western states. The development of the airplane provided faster, easier access to more distant geographic areas and created new industries, such as the passenger airline, avionics, and satellite industries. The vacuum tube, transistor, and microchip provided the basis for the television, radio, and personal computer. The telephone ultimately evolved into wireless communication.

The emergence of satellite delivery of cable network to local systems ignited explosive growth in the cable industry. Today, with the expansion of broadband technology, we are witnessing the convergence of voice, data, and video technologies on the Internet.

As the pace of technological change accelerates, M&A often is viewed as a way of rapidly exploiting new products and markets made possible by the emergence of new technologies. Large, more bureaucratic firms often are unable to exhibit the creativity and speed smaller, more nimble, niche players display. With engineering talent often in short supply and product life cycles shortening, firms often do not have the luxury of time or the resources to innovate. Consequently large companies often look to mergers and acquisitions as a fast and sometimes less expensive way to acquire new technologies and proprietary know-how to fill gaps in their current product offering or to enter entirely new businesses. Acquiring technologies also can be used as a defensive weapon to keep important new technologies out of the hands of competitors.

HUBRIS AND THE "WINNER'S CURSE"

The hubris hypothesis is an explanation of why mergers may happen even if the current market value of the target firm reflects its true economic value. As a result of hubris, managers believe that their own valuation of a target firm is superior to the market's valuation. Thus, the acquiring company tends to overpay for the target because of overoptimism in evaluating potential synergies. Even in the presence of significant synergies, competition among bidders is likely to result in the winner overpaying because of hubris, even if significant synergies are present (Roll, 1986). Senior managers tend to be very competitive and sometimes self-important. The desire not to lose can result in a bidding war that can drive the purchase price of an acquisition well in excess of the actual economic value of that company. Hubris or ego-driven decision making is a factor contributing to the so-called "winner's curse." In an auction environment where there are many bidders, there is likely to be a wide range of bids for a target company. The winning bid is often substantially in excess of the expected value of the target company, given the difficulty all participants have in estimating the actual value of the target and the competitive nature of the process. The winner is cursed in the sense that he paid more than the company is worth (Capen, Clapp, and Campbell, 1971).

BUYING UNDERVALUED ASSETS (THE q-RATIO)

The q-ratio is the ratio of the market value of the acquiring firm's stock to the replacement cost of its assets. Firms interested in expansion have a choice of investing in new plant and equipment or obtaining the assets by acquiring a company whose market value is less than the replacement cost of its assets (i.e., q-ratio <1). This theory was very useful in explaining M&A activity during the

1970s when high inflation and interest rates depressed stock prices well below the book value of many firms. High inflation also caused the replacement cost of assets to be much higher than the book value of assets. In the late 1970s and early 1980s, T. Boone Pickens, the then-CEO of Mesa Petroleum, found it less expensive to purchase companies with proven reserves than to explore for oil. In this instance, the stock price of these target firms did not reflect fully the market value of their reserves.

MISMANAGEMENT (AGENCY PROBLEMS)

Agency problems arise when there is a difference between the interest of incumbent managers and the firm's shareholders. This happens when management owns a small fraction of the outstanding shares of the firm. These managers are more inclined to focus on maintaining job security and a lavish lifestyle than maximizing shareholder value. When the shares of a company are widely held, the cost of mismanagement is spread across a large number of shareholders. Each shareholder bears only a small portion of the cost. This allows for such mismanagement to be tolerated for long periods. According to this theory, mergers take place to correct situations where there is a separation between what the managers may want and what the owners want. Low stock prices put pressure on managers to take actions to raise the share price or become the target of acquirers, who perceive the stock to be undervalued (Fama and Jensen, 1983).

TAX CONSIDERATIONS

There are two important issues in discussing the role of taxes as a motive for M&As. The first involves the tax benefits associated with the target's unused net operating losses and tax credits as well as the revaluation or write-up of acquired assets. The second concerns the tax-free status of the deal. These issues are discussed in greater detail in Chapter 10.

Tax benefits, such as loss carry forward and investment tax credits, can be used to offset the combined firms' taxable income. Additional tax shelter is created if the acquisition is recorded under the purchase method of accounting, which requires the book value of the acquired assets to be revalued to their current market value. The resulting depreciation of these generally higher asset values also shelters future income generated by the combined companies (see Chapter 10).

The taxable nature of the transaction frequently will play a more important role in determining if the merger takes place than any tax benefits that accrue to the acquiring company. The tax-free status of the transaction may be viewed by the seller as a prerequisite for the deal to take place. A properly structured transaction can allow the target shareholders to defer any capital gain resulting from the transaction. If the transaction is not tax-free, the seller normally will want a higher purchase price to compensate for the tax liability resulting from the transaction.

MARKET POWER

This theory suggests that firms merge to improve their monopoly power to set product prices at levels not sustainable in a more competitive market. Early empirical studies failed to support this theory. In one study of 11 mergers challenged by antitrust authorities, only 2 of the 11 mergers examined displayed statistically significant (i.e., results not due to chance) abnormal positive financial returns (Stillman, 1983). Another study hypothesized that if the market power theory is correct, mergers that are likely to be challenged as anticompetitive should show abnormal negative financial returns when they are first announced. In a sample of 126 horizontal and vertical mergers, the study found statistically significant positive abnormal returns when the merger was first announced but no negative returns when investigations were undertaken by the regulatory authorities (Eckbo, 1981). These results suggest that investors apparently did not believe that the regulatory authorities would find these business combinations anticompetitive. Presumably, the motivation for these mergers was something other than a desire to gain market power. However, more recent studies do show that market power may be a motive in some instances. According to one study, mergers in the airline industry in the late 1980s did result in higher ticket prices (Kim and Singal, 1993).

MANAGERIALISM

Self-serving managers are presumed to make poorly planned acquisitions to increase the size of the acquiring firm and their own compensation. This theory assumes that compensation received by senior management is determined by the size of their firm (D. C. Mueller, 1969). However, this basic premise may be incorrect because there is empirical evidence that management compensation is determined more by profitability than size (Lewellen and Huntsman, 1970).

HISTORICAL MERGER AND ACQUISITION WAVES

M&A activity in the United States came in five multiyear waves in the last century, each of which was characterized by an easily identifiable underlying trend (see Figure 1-3). Two preceded and three followed World War II (Gaughan, 1996; Golbe and White, 1988). Each merger movement occurred when the economy experienced sustained high rates of growth and coincided with specific developments in the economy. Each merger wave corresponded to the emergence of some key economic factor such as a rising stock market and low interest rates or technological development. Whereas important economic factors affecting the overall economy provide a favorable environment for M&A activity, developments in specific industries largely determine where such activity will be concentrated (Mitchell and Mulherin, 1996).

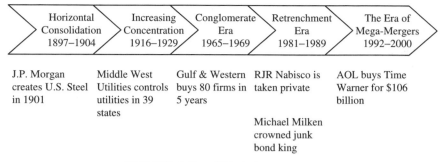

Horizontal Consolidation 1897–1904	Increasing Concentration 1916–1929	Conglomerate Era 1965–1969	Retrenchment Era 1981–1989	The Era of Mega-Mergers 1992–2000
J.P. Morgan creates U.S. Steel in 1901	Middle West Utilities controls utilities in 39 states	Gulf & Western buys 80 firms in 5 years	RJR Nabisco is taken private Michael Milken crowned junk bond king	AOL buys Time Warner for $106 billion

FIGURE 1-3.   Historical merger waves.

THE FIRST WAVE:
HORIZONTAL CONSOLIDATION, 1897–1904

M&A activity was spurred by a drive for efficiency, lax enforcement of the Sherman Anti-Trust Act, westward migration, and technological change. Mergers during this period were largely horizontal and resulted in increased concentration in primary metals, transportation, and mining. Fraudulent financing and the 1904 stock market crash ended this boom. During this period, large companies absorbed small ones. In 1901, J. P. Morgan created America's first billion-dollar corporation, U.S. Steel. U.S. Steel was formed by the combination of 785 separate companies, the largest of which was Carnegie Steel. Other giants that were formed during this era included Standard Oil, Eastman Kodak, American Tobacco, and General Electric.

THE SECOND WAVE:
INCREASING CONCENTRATION, 1916–1929

Activity during this period was a result of the entry of the United States into World War I and the postwar economic boom. Mergers also tended to be horizontal and further increased industry concentration. For example, Samuel Insull built his utilities empire, consisting of operations in 39 states. This era came to a close as a consequence of the stock market crash of 1929 and the passage of the Clayton Act, which further defined what constituted monopolistic practices. See Chapter 2 of this book for a more detailed discussion of antitrust regulation.

THE THIRD WAVE: THE CONGLOMERATE ERA, 1965–1969

This period of M&A activity was characterized by the emergence of financial engineering and conglomeration. A rising stock market and the longest period of uninterrupted growth in the nation's history up to that time resulted in record price-to-earnings (P/E) ratios. Companies given high P/E ratios by investors learned how to grow earnings per share (EPS) through acquisition rather than through reinvestment. Companies with high P/E ratios often would acquire firms with lower P/E ratios and increase the EPS of the combined companies. The increase in EPS boosted the share price of the combined companies, as long as the P/E applied to the stock price of the combined companies did not fall below the P/E of the acquiring company before the transaction. However, for this pyramiding effect to continue, target companies had to have earnings growth rates sufficiently attractive to convince investors to apply the higher multiple of the acquiring company to the combined companies. In time, the number of high-growth, relatively low P/E companies declined as conglomerates bid their P/Es up. The higher prices paid for the targets, coupled with the increasing leverage of the conglomerates, caused the "pyramids" to collapse.

THE FOURTH WAVE:
THE RETRENCHMENT ERA, 1981–1989

The 1980s saw the rise of the corporate raider and the emergence of the hostile takeover. Before this period, there were relatively few hostile takeovers. The decade of the 1980s was characterized by a breakup of many of the major conglomerates and a proliferation of financial buyers using the hostile takeover and the LBO as their primary acquisition strategies. Management buyouts and takeovers of U.S. companies by foreign acquirers became more common. Conglomerates began to divest unrelated acquisitions made in the 1960s and early 1970s. Of the acquisitions made outside of the acquirer's main line of business between 1970 and 1982, 60% were sold by 1989 (Wasserstein, 1998). In 1988, the mega-railroad Burlington Northern spun off Burlington Resources, its energy properties, for $4.2 billion. The same year Mobil Oil sold retailer Montgomery Ward for $3.8 billion. In 1989, Paramount, formerly Gulf and Western Industries, sold its finance company, Associates First Capital, for $3.4 billion.

For the first time, takeovers of U.S. companies by foreign firms in the 1980s exceeded in number and dollars the acquisitions by U.S. firms of companies in Europe, Canada, and the Pacific Rim, excluding Japan. The motivation for foreign purchases of U.S. companies stemmed from the size of the market, limited restrictions on takeovers, the sophistication of U.S. firm's technology, and the weakness of the dollar against major foreign currencies. Foreign companies also tended to pay substantial premiums for U.S. companies because the strength of their currencies lowered the effective cost of acquisitions. Moreover, favorable accounting practices allowed foreign buyers to write off goodwill in the year in which it occurred, unlike U.S. firms that had to charge goodwill expense against earnings for many years. The largest cross-border deals of the 1980s included the Beecham Group PLC (UK) purchase of the SmithKline Beckman Corporation for $16.1 billion in 1989. In 1987, British Petroleum Corporation acquired the remaining 45% of Standard Oil Corporation for $7.8 billion. Campeau Corporation of Canada purchased Federated Department Stores for $6.5 billion in 1988.

The fortunes of LBOs waned during the second half of the decade. RJR Nabisco exemplified the challenges faced by LBOs during this period.

Kohlberg, Kravis & Roberts (KKR) paid $24.5 billion for the company in 1988, a record purchase price at the time. Despite going public in 1991, RJR Nabisco struggled under the burden of its massive debt until the mid-1990s, when improving cash flow enabled the firm to pay off a significant portion of its debt. (For a more detailed discussion of the RJR Nabisco LBO, see Case Study 11-3 in Chapter 11 of this book.) Other LBO transactions also fell on hard times. Toward the end of the decade, the level of merger activity tapered off in line with a slowing economy and widely publicized LBO bankruptcies. Moreover, the junk bond market dried up as a major source of financing with the demise of Drexel Burnham, the leading underwriter and "market-maker" for high-yield securities.

THE FIFTH WAVE:
THE AGE OF THE STRATEGIC MEGA-MERGER, 1992–2000

After the 1980s, many believed that the M&As during this decade largely were overpriced and overleveraged. Moreover, junk bond or high-yield financing was thought unlikely to recover from its pummeling during the late 1980s. Consequently, many assumed that takeovers would not return to their levels of this period. Although M&A activity did taper off during the 1990 recession, the number of transactions and the dollar volume rebounded sharply beginning in 1992. The combination of the information technology revolution, continued deregulation, reductions in trade barriers, and the global trend toward privatization powered the longest economic expansion and stock market boom in U.S. history.

According to Thompson Financial Services, the announced dollar volume of global M&A activity in 2000 set a new record of $3.48 trillion, 5.4% higher than 1999's $3.31 trillion. In the United States, the year 2000's announced dollar volume rose by a more robust 16.6% over its 1999 level of $1.57 trillion to $1.83 trillion. Reflecting a slowdown in business investment and a weak stock market, worldwide volume tumbled in 2001 by 49% from 2000 to about $1.7 trillion. In the United States, $796 billion of mergers and acquisitions were announced in 2001, down 57% from the prior year.

Reflecting the huge run-up in purchase prices during the 1990s, the average purchase price of the top five transactions during the 1990s was about 4 times the average during the 1980s but 400 times the average during the 1950s (DePamphilis, 2001). Average purchase prices slumped between 2000 and 2001 in line with the global economic slowdown and decline in equity prices.

DO MERGERS AND ACQUISITIONS
PAY OFF FOR SHAREHOLDERS?

Unfortunately, the answer to the question "Do mergers and acquisitions pay off for shareholders?" is ambiguous. The answer seems to depend on for whom and over what period of time. Around the announcement date of the transaction, average returns to target firm shareholders, including both friendly and hostile takeovers, are about 30%. In contrast, the shareholders of acquiring firms generally show returns that range from slightly negative to modestly positive around the announcement date. Over longer periods, many M&As either underperform their industry peers or destroy shareholder value. Two approaches have been used to measure the impact of takeovers on shareholder value. The first approach, premerger returns, involves the examination of abnormal stock returns to the shareholders of both bidders and targets around the announcement of an offer and includes both successful and unsuccessful takeovers. Such analyses are referred to as "event" studies, with the event being the takeover announcement. The second approach, postmerger returns, measures the impact on shareholder value after the merger has been completed.

PREMERGER RETURNS TO SHAREHOLDERS

Positive abnormal returns represent gains for shareholders, which could be explained by such factors as improved efficiency, pricing power, or tax benefits. They are abnormal in the sense that they exceed what an investor would expect to earn for accepting a certain level of risk. The average results of numerous studies of returns to shareholders of both bidding and target firms are summarized in Table 1-3. These returns are computed over a preacquisition period starting immediately before the announcement and ending on or before the effective date of the tender offer for both mergers and tender offers. Despite the difficulty in distinguishing between the two different types of takeovers (Schwert, 2000), these studies often associate tender offers and mergers with hostile and friendly takeovers, respectively. An acquisition often is classified as a tender offer in empirical studies if the bidder purchases the majority of the target's stock through a tender offer (i.e., an unwanted or hostile bid). Moreover, these studies usually assume that share prices fully adjust to anticipated synergies that could materialize as a result of the acquisition; therefore, they reflect both the short- and long-term effects of the acquisition.

Target Shareholders Realize Exceptional Returns in Both Successful and Unsuccessful Bids

These studies suggest that average excess or abnormal returns to target company shareholders for successful tender offers have risen from 22% during the 1960s, to 35% during the 1970s and 1980s, and in some studies to more than 50% in the early 1990s. These substantial returns reflect the frequent bidder strategy of offering a substantial premium to preempt other potential bidders and the potential for revising the initial offer because of competing bids. Other contributing factors include the increasing sophistication of takeover defenses, as well as federal and state laws requiring bidders to notify target shareholders of their intentions before completing the transaction (see Chapters 2 and 3 for more details). Moreover, the abnormal gains tend to be higher for shareholders of target firms, whose financial

TABLE 1-3　Empirical Evidence on Returns to U.S. Bidders and U.S. Targets Around Announcement Dates

Outcome of takeover attempt	Impact on shareholder value	
	Target	Bidder
Average Return on Mergers		
1960s[1]	20%	0%
1970s[1,3]	20%	0.5%
1980s[3,9]	20%	1%
1990s[10,11]	20%	0.7%
Average Return on Tender Offers		
1960s[1,2,4,5]	22%	4%
1970s[1,4,5,6]	35%	2.4%
1980s[4,5,6,7]	38%	(1.3)%
1990s (1989–1992)[8]	52%	N/A
Jensen and Ruback (1983)[1]	30% (Tender offers only)	4% (Tender offers only)
(Review of 13 studies during 1960s and 1970s)	20% (Mergers only)	0% (Mergers only)
Asquith (1983)[2]	20% (1962–1976)	2% (1962–1976)
(Sample = 211 successful tender offers)		
You, Caves, Smith, and Henry (1986)[3]	20% (1975–1984)	1% (1975–1984)
(Sample = 133 mergers)		
Jarrell, Brickley, and Netter (1988)[4]	19% (1962–1965)	4% (1962–1965)
(Sample = 663 successful tender offers)	30% (1970–1979)	2% (1970–1979)
	35% (1980–1985)	1% (1980–1985)
Bradley, Desai, and Kim (1988)[5]	19% (1963–1969)	4% (1963–1969)
(Sample = 236 successful tender offers)	35% (1968–1980)	1.3% (1968–1980)
	35% (1981–1984)	3% (1981–1984)
Bhagat and Hirshleifer (1996)[6]	45% (1958–1984)	1.3% (1958–1984)
(Sample = 290 successful tender offers)		
Schwert (1996)[7]	35% (1975–1991)	0% (1975–1991)
(Sample size = 1814 tender offers)		
Cotter, Shivdasani, and Zenner (1997)[8]	62% (1989–1992) Highly	Not applicable
(Sample = 169 successful tender offers)	independent board	
	41% (1989–1992)	
	Less independent board	
Ghosh and Lee (2000)[9]	20.3% (1981–1990)	Not applicable
(Sample = 1587 mergers)	28% (1981–1990)	
	Underperforming firms	
Mulherin and Boone (2000)[10]	21.2% (1990–1999)	0.7 (1990–1999)
(Sample = 376 mergers)		
Akhigbe, Borde, and Whyte (2000)[11]	18.4% (1987–1996)	Not applicable
(Sample = 135 mergers)		

performance is expected to deteriorate over the long term (Ghosh and Lee, 2000). This may suggest that the bidding firms see the highest potential for gain among those target firms whose management is viewed as ineffective.

These returns compare to about 20% for presumed friendly mergers since the 1960s. The magnitude of such returns has been remarkably stable over time. Leeth and Borg (2000) found evidence that abnormal returns to target shareholders in friendly transactions typically exceeded 15% as far back as the 1920s. Returns from tender offers typically exceed those from friendly mergers, which are characterized by less contentious negotiated settlements between the boards and management of the bidder and the target firm. Moreover, mergers often do not receive competing bids.

Unsuccessful takeovers also may result in significant returns for target company shareholders around the announcement date, but much of the gain dissipates if another bidder does not appear. Studies show that the immediate gain in target share prices following a merger announcement disappears within 1 year if the takeover attempt fails (Akhigbe, Borde, and Whyte, 2000; Asquith, 1983; Bradley, Desai, and Kim, 1988; Sullivan, Jensen, and Hudson, 1994). Consequently, target firm shareholders, in an unsuccessful bid, must sell their shares shortly after the announcement of a failed takeover attempt to realize abnormal returns.

Bidder's Shareholders Often Disappointed in Both Successful and Unsuccessful Offers

For successful takeovers, returns are modest to slightly negative for both tender offers and mergers. Bidder returns generally have declined slightly over time, as the premiums paid for targets have increased.

In a perfectly competitive market, bidding firms should not receive returns in excess of what is normal for the amount of risk being assumed. Therefore, the empirical studies suggest that the market for "corporate control" is highly competitive. For unsuccessful takeovers, bidder shareholders have experienced negative returns in the 5% to 8% range (Bradley, Desai, and Kim, 1988).

Cross Border Returns Comparable to U.S. Empirical Results

Event studies involving U.S. buyers of foreign firms or foreign firms' acquisitions of U.S. firms give results that are remarkably similar to those involving completely domestic transactions. Target company shareholders experience large, abnormal positive returns, whereas buyer shareholders experience little or no abnormal returns (Doukas and Travlos, 1988; Eun, Kolodny, and Scheraga, 1996; Harris and Ravenscraft, 1991; Seth, Song, and Petit, 2000).

POSTMERGER RETURNS TO SHAREHOLDERS

The second approach to measuring the performance of M&As has been to examine accounting or other performance measures, such as cash flow and operating profit, during the 3- to 5-year period following completed transactions.

TABLE 1-4   Postmerger Performance Studies: Returns to Merged Companies Versus Industry Average Returns (3–5 Years Following Announcement Date)

Underperform Industry Average	Approximate Industry Average	Overperform Industry Average
McKinsey & Company (1990)	Mueller (1985)	Healy, Palepu, and Ruback (1992)
Mangenheim and Mueller (1988)	Ravenscraft and Sherer (1987–1991)	Kaplan and Weisbach (1992)
Franks, Harris, and Titman (1991)	Bradley and Jarrell (1988)	Rau and Vermaelen (1998)[2]
Agrawal, Jaffe, and Mandelker (1992)		
Sirower (1997)		
Gregory (1997)		
Loughran and Vijh (1997)		
Rau and Vermaelen (1998)[1]		
Agrawal and Jaffe (1999)[1]		
Black, Carnes, and Jandik (2000)		
Deogun and Lipin (2000)		
Sanford Bernstein & Company (2000)		

[1]Pertains to business combinations involving mergers.
[2]Pertains to business combinations involving tender offers.

Unfortunately, these studies, as shown in Table 1-4, provide conflicting evidence about the long-term impact of M&A activity. Although some find a better than average chance that M&As create shareholder value, others have found that as many as 50–80% underperform their industry peers or fail to earn their cost of capital. The diversity of conclusions about postmerger returns may be the result of sample and time period selections, methodology employed in the studies, or factors unrelated to the merger such as a slowing economy (Barber and Lyon, 1997; Fama, 1998; Lyon, Barber, and Tsai, 1999). Presumably, the longer the postmerger time period analyzed the greater the likelihood that other factors, wholly unrelated to the merger, will affect financial returns. Thus, the results of postmerger studies should be viewed with considerable caution.

Long-Term M&A Performance Similar to Alternative Growth Strategies

Even if a substantial percentage of M&As underperform their peers or fail to earn appropriate financial returns, it is important to note that there is no compelling evidence that business growth strategies that are undertaken as an alternative to

M&As fare any better. Such alternatives include reinvestment of excess cash flows in the firm, business alliances including joint ventures, licensing, franchising, and minority investments. See Chapters 4 and 12 of this book for a more detailed discussion of these issues.

Key Findings

Acquirers Tend to Overpay for Growth Firms

In an exhaustive study of 22 different papers examining long-run postmerger returns, Agrawal and Jaffe (1999) separate financial performance following mergers (i.e., those presumed to be friendly) from tender offers (i.e., unsolicited or hostile bids). Although the authors review a number of arguments purporting to explain postmerger performance, the argument that acquirers tend to overpay for so-called high-growth glamour companies based on their past performance is believed to be the most convincing. Consequently, the postmerger share price should underperform broader industry averages as their future growth slows to more normal levels.

Shareholders Profit by Selling Around Merger Announcement Dates

Loughran and Vijh (1997) found that in the case of stock mergers, the gains experienced around the announcement date tend to dissipate within 5 years even if the acquisition succeeds. These findings imply that shareholders, selling around the announcement dates, may realize the largest gains from either tender offers or mergers. Those who hold onto the acquirer's stock received in payment for their shares may see their gains diminish over time.

M&As May Be More Likely to Succeed Today Than in the Past

In a 1997 study of 215 acquisitions, each valued at more than $500 million, Mercer Management Consulting (MMC) found that 52% of the mergers completed during the 1990s achieved above-industry-average shareholder returns during the 3 years following closing, as compared with only 37% completed during the 1980s. MMC attributes this favorable trend to improved postmerger integration.

Acquirer Experience Improves Long-Term Performance of Combined Companies

Not surprisingly, cumulative experience increases the likelihood that M&As will create shareholder value. The importance of experience was documented in a 1995 joint study by MMC and *Business Week* of 248 acquirers, which purchased 1045 companies from January 1990 through July 1995. Experienced acquirers tended to substantially outperform less experienced acquirers in terms of returns to shareholders during the 3 years following the transaction when they were compared with their industry peers (Lajoux, 1998). Experienced acquirers were defined as those that had completed six or more transactions annually; less experienced buyers were those that completed less than five transactions per year. Experienced buyers constituted 24% of the entire sample. Of the firms in this group, 72%

generated returns in excess of their industry average. In contrast, only 55% of those firms in the less experienced group earned financial returns above their industry average.

In a study of 21 highly diversified corporate acquirers and financial buyers, Anslinger and Copeland (1996) found that 80% of the 839 acquisitions made by these companies earned their cost of capital over the 10-year period ending in 1994. During this period, the corporate buyers exhibited average annual rates of returns to shareholders of at least 18%, whereas the financial buyers studied averaged more than 35% per year during the same period. The cumulative experience of this sample was substantial, with each firm averaging 40 acquisitions during this period.

The role of experience in dealmaking has been particularly noticeable for high-tech firms. For the 10-year period ending in 2000, high-tech companies averaging 39% annual growth in total return to shareholders undertook as many as twice as many acquisitions and as many as 10 times as many alliances as less profitable firms. Although experience seems to be a factor contributing to long-term prof-itability, the size of the average transaction also may play an important role. Deals for these high-tech acquirers tended to be small, with an average transaction value of less than $400 million, about 1% of the market value of the acquiring firms (Frick and Torres, 2002).

Method of Payment May Affect Longer-Term Returns

Bidding firms using cash to purchase the target seem to exhibit a higher long-term performance than do those using stock (Linn and Switzer, 2001; Loughran and Vijh, 1997; Sanford Bernstein & Company, 2000; Sirower, 1997). The use of stock to acquire a firm seems to negatively impact the return to the bidders' shareholders during the 3–5 years following the transaction. Stock is more likely to be used to finance larger transactions than smaller ones. Acquirers may not be able to borrow enough to finance the major portion of the purchase price of large transactions with cash. To induce the target to accept its stock, the bidder may have to offer a higher price than would have been necessary using some other form of payment. This results in more frequent overpayment for target firms. In particular, the Sanford Bernstein & Company study found that large stock-for-stock transactions tended to underperform the S&P 500 the most because the degree of overpayment tends to be the greatest.

WHY DO MERGERS AND ACQUISITIONS OFTEN FAIL TO MEET EXPECTATIONS?

OVERPAYING, SLOW INTEGRATION, AND POOR BUSINESS STRATEGIES

There are many reasons given for the failure of takeovers to meet expectations. Table 1-5 identifies 10 of the most commonly cited reasons ranked by the number

TABLE 1-5 Commonly Cited Reasons for M&A Failure[1]

Overestimating synergy/overpaying[2]	Bekier, Bogardus, and Oldham (2001)
	Chapman, Dempsey, Ramsdell, & Bell (1998)
	Agrawal and Jaffe (1999)
	Rau and Vermaelen (1998)
	Sirower (1997)
	Mercer Management Consulting (1998)
	Hillyer and Smolowitz (1996)
	Bradley, Desai, and Kim (1988)
	McKinsey & Company (1990)
Slow pace of integration	Coopers & Lybrand (1996)
	Anslinger and Copeland (1996)
	Mitchell (1998)
	Business Week (1995)
	McKinsey & Company (1990)
Poor strategy	Mercer Management Consulting (1998)
	Bogler (1996)
	McKinsey & Company (1990)
	Salter & Weinhold (1979)
Form of payment[3]	Sanford Bernstein & Company (2000)
	Loughran & Vijh (1997)
	Sirower (1997)
	Gregory (1997)
Poor postmerger communication	Mitchell (1998)
	Chakrabarti (1990)
Conflicting corporate cultures	Mercer Management Consulting (1998)
	Hillyer and Smolowitz (1996)
Weak core business	McKinsey & Company (1990)
	Anslinger and Copeland (1996)
Large size of target company	McKinsey & Company (1990)
Inadequate due diligence	Mercer Management Consulting (1998)
Poor assessment of technology	Bryoksten (1965)

[1] Factors are ranked by the number of times they have been mentioned in studies.

[2] Some studies conclude that postmerger underperformance is a result of overpayment. However, it is difficult to determine if overpayment is a cause of merger failure or a result of other factors such as overestimating synergy, the slow pace of integration, a poor strategy, or simply the bidder overextrapolating past performance.

[3] These studies find that firms that pay for an acquisition using stock generally are overvalued and their performance subsequent to the merger is simply a reversion to their industry's average performance.

of studies in which they are mentioned. The top three include overestimation of synergy or overpaying, the slow pace of postmerger integration, and a flawed strategy. Conversely, acquiring firms that tend not to overpay, focusing on rapid integration of the target firm, and having a well-thought-out strategy tend to meet or exceed expectations.

THE LEGACY OF OVERPAYING

As a result of the extent to which acquirers tended to overpay in the late 1990s, an estimated $1.3 trillion in goodwill is expected to be written off during 2002 and 2003 because of a change in accounting standards (Baer, 2002). Goodwill is the difference between the purchase price paid for a target firm and the actual fair market value (see Chapter 10). Historically, such goodwill could be deducted against future earnings for many years. However, the Financial Accounting Standards Board, the rulemaking body for the accounting industry, changed the regulations in 2001 such that companies now must assess goodwill annually to determine if it is impaired (i.e., no longer reflective of the true economic value of the acquisition). If the goodwill is found to be impaired, the firm must take a one-time write-down of the asset.

Although many firms had begun this process in 2001 in anticipation of the rule change, others were forced to do so in 2002. As a result of the decline in the stock market in 2000 and 2001, many firms' share prices were trading at levels significantly less than book value. In a recordsetting quarterly write-off, AOL admitted in effect that it had overpaid for Time Warner by more than one-half when it announced in the first quarter of 2002 that it would reduce the value of the goodwill associated with the transaction by $60 billion. This exceeded the previous recordsetting write-off by the former telecom high flier JDS Uniphase of $41.8 billion announced during the first quarter of 2001. Battered by the dramatic drop in the share prices of telecommunications companies, WorldCom and Qwest Communications announced that they would write down goodwill by $20 and $30 billion, respectively. See Chapter 10 for a more detailed discussion of this subject.

DO MERGERS AND ACQUISITIONS
PAY OFF FOR SOCIETY?

Although postmerger performance study results are ambiguous, event studies show generally consistent results. Such studies suggest that M&A activity tends to improve aggregate shareholder value (i.e., the sum of the shareholder value of both the target and acquiring firms). If financial markets are indeed efficient, the large increase in the combined shareholder values of the two firms will reflect future efficiencies that are expected to result from the merger. However, the bulk of this increase in combined shareholder value often is captured by the target firm's shareholders.

Moreover, there is no evidence that M&A activity results in increasing industry concentration. Mergers and acquisitions have continued to increase in number and average size during the last 30 years. Despite this trend, M&A activity has not increased industry concentration in terms of the share of output or value produced by the largest firms in the industry, either in manufacturing or in the overall economy, since 1970 (Carlton and Perloff, 1999).

Finally, recent research suggests that gains in aggregate shareholder value are attributable more to the improved operating efficiency of the combined firms than to increased market power (Akhigbe, Borde, and Whyte, 2000; Benerjee and Eckard, 1998; Song and Walking, 2000). In an exhaustive study of 10,079 transactions between 1974 and 1992, Maksimovic and Phillips (2001) conclude that corporate transactions result in an overall improvement in efficiency by transferring assets from those who are not using them effectively to those who can.

THINGS TO REMEMBER

Deals in the 1990s tended to be more strategically focused and used substantially less debt than the financially driven takeovers of the 1980s. Deals were motivated by corporations wanting to realign strategies to exploit new opportunities created by changing government regulation or accelerating technological innovation. Intensifying global competition contributed to rapid industry consolidation to achieve cost savings through economies of scale and scope. Government antitrust regulatory authorities seemed less concerned about the size of a transaction and more interested in its implications for improving the overall efficiency of the combined businesses. Finally, soaring stock prices and relatively low interest rates throughout most of the 1990s contributed greatly to the stratospheric prices paid in the megadeals of the decade. The slowing economy and the stock market collapse between 2000 and 2002 contributed to a greater than 50% decline in the dollar volume of M&A transactions. However, the drop in transactions was largely cyclical and temporary. Transaction volume will continue to be governed over the long term by such powerful forces as ongoing globalization, industry consolidation, deregulation, and technological innovation.

There are myriad theories of why M&As take place. Operating and financial synergies are commonly used rationales for takeovers. *Operating synergy* consists of both economies of scale—the spreading of fixed costs over increasing production levels—and economies of scope—the use of a specific set of skills or an asset currently used to produce a specific product to produce related products. *Financial synergy* is the reduction in the cost of capital as a result of more stable cash flows, financial economies of scale, or a better matching of investment opportunities with available funds. **Diversification** is a strategy of buying firms outside of the company's primary line of business. There is little evidence that shareholders benefit from a company's efforts to diversify on their behalf because investors can more efficiently spread their investments and risk among industries on their own. Recent studies suggest that corporate strategies emphasizing focus deliver more benefit to shareholders.

Strategic realignment suggests that firms use takeovers as a means of rapidly adjusting to changes in their external environment such as deregulation and technological innovation. **Hubris** is an explanation for takeovers that attributes a tendency to overpay to excessive optimism about the value of a deal's potential synergy or excessive confidence in management's ability to manage the acquisition. The **undervaluation of assets** theory states that takeovers occur when the market value of a target is less than the replacement value of its assets. The **mismanagement** or **agency theory** postulates that mergers take place when there are differences between what managers and shareholders want. Low share prices of such firms pressure managers to take action to either raise the share price or become the target of an acquirer.

Tax considerations are generally not the driving factor behind acquisitions. The value of tax benefits may represent a significant but relatively small percentage of the target's total value. A more important factor is the tax status of the deal. The seller may make a tax-free transaction a prerequisite for the deal to take place. The **market power** hypothesis suggests that firms merge to gain greater control over pricing, but the empirical support for this notion is limited. According to the **managerialism** theory, managers acquire companies to increase the acquirer's size and their own remuneration. In practice, management compensation seems to be more determined by profitability than size.

Most acquisitions require a broad array of different skills to complete a corporate takeover. Few firms have all of the needed skills in-house. Investment bankers offer strategic and tactical advice, acquisition opportunities, screening of potential buyers and sellers, making contact with a buyer or seller, negotiation support, valuation, and deal structuring. Legal expertise often is required in such specialized areas as mergers and acquisitions, corporate, tax, employee benefits, real estate, antitrust, securities, and intellectual property law. Accountants provide advice on financial structuring, on tax issues, and on performing due diligence. Proxy solicitation companies often are hired to compile lists of stockholder mailing addresses. Public relations advisors ensure that both the target and acquiring companies present a compelling and consistent message to their respective constituencies.

Although there is substantial evidence that mergers pay off for target company shareholders around the time the takeover is announced, shareholder wealth creation in the 3–5 years following closing is problematic. Abnormal returns to target shareholders around takeover tender offer announcement dates have risen from an average of 22% in the 1960s to 35% in the 1970s and 1980s. Recent studies suggest that such returns in the early 1990s could have averaged more than 50%.

Returns to shareholders around the date of merger announcements have remained remarkably stable at 20% since the 1960s. In contrast, excess or abnormal returns to acquirer shareholders have declined from slightly positive to slightly negative levels.

Studies suggest as many as 50% to almost 80% of M&As fail to outperform their peers or to earn their cost of capital. Not surprisingly, the performance for more experienced acquirers is much better. The most commonly cited reasons for failure is the overestimation of synergies and subsequent overpayment, the slow pace of postmerger integration, and the lack of a coherent business strategy. Empirical studies also suggest that M&As tend to pay off for society because on average the summation of bidder and target shareholder value tends to increase. More often than not, this increase seems to be related to improved operating efficiency of the combined firms rather than an increase in market power.

Despite the somewhat disappointing success rate for many mergers and acquisitions, it is important to note that the experience for M&As is very similar to alternative growth strategies that may be undertaken. Such strategies may include reinvesting excess cash flow in the firm, business alliances, licensing, franchising, and minority investments. Corporations, holding companies, ESOPs, and JVs represent alternative vehicles for engaging in various types of business combinations intended to enhance shareholder value.

CHAPTER DISCUSSION QUESTIONS

1-1. Discuss why mergers and acquisitions occur.

1-2. What are the advantages and disadvantages of a holding company structure in making acquisitions?

1-3. How might a leveraged ESOP be used as an alternative to a divestiture, to make a company private, or as a defense against an unwanted takeover?

1-4. What is the role of the investment banker in the M&A process?

1-5. Describe how arbitrage typically takes place in a takeover of a publicly traded company.

1-6. In your judgment, why is potential synergy often overestimated by acquirers in evaluating a target company?

1-7. What are the major differences between the merger waves of the 1980s and 1990s?

1-8. In your opinion, what are the motivations for two mergers or acquisitions currently in the news?

1-9. What are the arguments for and against corporate diversification through acquisition? Which do you support and why?

1-10. What are the primary differences between operating and financial synergy? Give examples to illustrate your statements.

CHAPTER BUSINESS CASE

CASE STUDY 1-2: AMERICA ONLINE ACQUIRES TIME WARNER—THE EMERGENCE OF A VERTICALLY INTEGRATED INTERNET AND MEDIA GIANT

Time Warner, itself the product of the world's largest media merger in a $14.1 billion deal a decade ago, celebrated its 10th birthday by announcing on January 10, 2000, that it had agreed to be taken over by America Online (AOL). AOL had proposed the acquisition in October 1999. In less than 3 months, the deal, valued at $160 billion as of the announcement date ($178 billion including Time Warner debt assumed by AOL), became the largest on record up to that time. To some it looked as if the minnow had swallowed the whale. AOL had less than one-fifth of the revenue and workforce of Time Warner, but AOL had almost twice the market value. As if to confirm the move to the new electronic revolution in media and entertainment, the ticker symbol of the new company is AOL.

Time Warner

Time Warner is the world's largest media and entertainment company, and it views its primary business as the creation and distribution of branded content throughout the world. Its major business segments include cable networks, magazine publishing, book publishing and direct marketing, recorded music and music publishing, and filmed entertainment consisting of TV production and broadcasting as well as interests in other film companies. Its major brands include, among others, *Time*, Cable News Network (CNN), Warner Brothers, *Sports Illustrated*, *People*, Home Box Office (HBO), Turner Broadcasting System (TBS), and Turner Network Television (TNT). Time Warner owns the nation's largest collection of cable companies. Subscribers also are able to receive broadband technology. Such technology divides a frequency range into multiple independent channels, allowing voice, video, and data signals to be transmitted at the same time. Broadband technology is 10–80 times faster than standard telephone dialup services. Many believe that the proliferation of this technology will promote electronic commerce, interactive TV, and Internet phone service.

The 1990 merger between *Time* and Warner Communications was supposed to create a seamless marriage of magazine publishing and film production, but the company never was able to put that vision into place. Time Warner's stock underperformed the market through much of the 1990s until the company bought TBS in 1996.

America Online

Founded in 1985, AOL views itself as the world leader in providing interactive services, Web brands, Internet technologies, and electronic commerce services. AOL operates two subscription-based Internet services and, at the time of the announcement, had 20 million subscribers plus another 2 million through

CompuServe. Other leading brands include ICQ (Internet telephony service), AOL Instant Messenger (an online email alert service), Digital City, Netscape, AOL.com, AOL MovieFone (the nation's largest movie listing guide and ticketing service), and Spinner and Nullsoft (leaders in providing music on the Internet). Through a strategic alliance with Sun Microsystems, AOL provides hardware and systems support for companies doing business on the Internet. AOL believes that its cumulative investment in its information infrastructure and network enables it to design, develop, and operate Web sites very efficiently. AOL claims that this investment enables it to design, implement, and operate Web sites at about one-fifth the cost of major competitors such as Yahoo.

Before the announcement, AOL had been pushing the regulatory authorities to require all cable TV operators to open their systems to Internet service provider (ISP) subscribers. At that time, cable companies usually had exclusive relationships with ISPs (e.g., AT&T cable subscribers had to use Excite@Home as their ISP). To gain access to alternative broadband technologies, AOL also was developing alliances with local phone companies to enable AOL subscribers to access the Internet using the digital subscriber line (DSL) capabilities of these companies and had a minority interest in DirecTV's satellite business.

AOL's growth has benefited greatly from the relatively benign government policies to protect Internet user privacy and the decision to impose a moratorium on taxing e-commerce transactions. Moreover, the Federal Communications Commission decision not to subject ISPs to the same local telephone company access fees that are paid by long-distance carriers has promoted e-commerce activity. However, pending privacy legislation could severely restrict how personal information is used for marketing and promotional purposes, and state and local government pressure is mounting to tax the growing volume of transactions on the Internet. Differences in European Union (EU) and U.S. privacy policies may make it impossible to share consumer information to engage in cross-border promotion activities.

Strategic Fit (From a 1999 Perspective)

On the surface, the two companies look quite different. Time Warner is a media and entertainment content company dealing in movies, music, and magazines, whereas AOL is largely an ISP offering access to content and commerce. There is very little overlap between the two businesses. AOL says it is buying access to rich and varied branded content, to a huge potential subscriber base, and to broadband technology to create the world's largest vertically integrated media and entertainment company. Time Warner cable systems serve 20% of the country, giving AOL a more direct path into broadband transmission than it has with its ongoing efforts to gain access to DSL technology and satellite TV. The cable connection will facilitate the introduction of AOL TV, a service introduced in 2000 and designed to deliver access to the Internet through TV transmission.

The Time Warner deal seemed to solve AOL's need to gain access to broadband technology. AOL had been lobbying for open access, under which cable-system operators would open their systems and their large subscriber bases to ISPs for a negotiated fee. Time Warner's Roadrunner gives AOL access to one of the nation's largest cable modem ISPs. With all this bandwidth, AOL Time Warner would be able to deliver a broad array of content directly to consumers. Together, the two companies have relationships with almost 100 million consumers. At the time of the announcement, AOL had 23 million subscribers and Time Warner had 28 million magazine subscribers, 13 million cable subscribers, and 35 million HBO subscribers. The combined companies expect to profit from its huge customer database to assist in the cross promotion of each other's products.

At the time of the announcement, AOL Time Warner projected that the combined businesses would have $40 billion in revenue and earnings before interest, taxes, depreciation, and amortization of $10 billion during the first full year of operation. (This broader measure of earnings, often called EBITDA, is often used as a proxy for operating cash flow.) The companies were expected to realize cost savings by combining sales forces and back-end functions such as sales and customer service call centers. The new company expected to generate at least $1 billion in operating cash flow from realizing these synergies. AOL Time Warner projected annual growth in EBITDA in the 8–12% range.

Terms of the Transaction

To secure the deal, AOL paid a 71% premium over the value of Time Warner's stock price before the announcement. However, at the time of closing, the deterioration in AOL's share price caused the premium to virtually evaporate. AOL shareholders received one share in the new company for each of their shares, and Time Warner shareholders received 1.5 shares for each of their Time Warner shares. As such, AOL shareholders would own 55% and Time Warner shareholders would own 45% of the combined companies on the closing date. AOL agreed to assume $18 billion in debt on the balance sheet of Time Warner.

Market Confusion Following the Announcement

AOL's stock was immediately hammered following the announcement, losing about 19% of its market value in 2 days. Despite a greater than 20% jump in Time Warner's stock during the same period, the market value of the combined companies was actually $10 billion lower 2 days after the announcement than it had been immediately before making the deal public. Investors appeared to be confused about how to value the new company. The two companies' shareholders represented investors with different motivations, risk tolerances, and expectations. AOL shareholders bought their company as a pure play in the Internet, whereas investors in Time Warner were interested in a media company. Before the announcement, AOL's shares traded at 55 times earnings before interest, taxes, depreciation, and amortization have been deducted. Reflecting its much lower growth rate, Time Warner traded at 14 times the same measure of its earnings. Could the new company achieve growth rates comparable to the 70% annual growth that AOL had achieved before the announcement? In contrast, Time Warner had been growing at less than one-third of this rate. The final multiple placed on the combined companies depends on whether investors see the new company as more like America Online or Time Warner.

Wall Street investors continued to wrestle with how to value the behemoth during the balance of 2000: Is it an Internet company, a media company, or some hybrid? But the Internet is not as exciting a place as it once was, especially in the consumer markets. Many of the entertainment companies on the Internet such as NBCi and MTVi announced large layoffs in late 2000 and in early 2001. Talk of companies, such as Yahoo!, becoming major media companies has dwindled as potential buyers such as Disney currently are reducing their investment in such Internet-related investments as Go.com. Although few expect e-commerce activity to shrink, current projected growth rates tend to be much lower than previously believed.

Shareholder Protection

The decline in AOL shares could have been less stinging to the Time Warner shareholders if a "collar" had been in place. Simply stated, a "collar" is a safety measure written into the sales agreement to automatically readjust terms if the two companies' stocks trade outside a designated range before the deal closes. It appears that Time Warner did not insist on such an arrangement because of the inherent volatility in AOL stock. AOL stock historically had traded as a premier technology stock. Moreover, the two parties have stated publicly that the use of a collar would have suggested a lack of commitment to getting the deal done. Besides the breakup fees (i.e., the cost of walking away from the deal) were substantial, with AOL required by contract to pay $5.4 billion to Time Warner and Time Warner to pay AOL $4 billion. (*Business Week*, November 6, 2000).

Regulatory Approval

After the announcement, it became clear that the proposal would face substantial scrutiny from regulatory authorities—the Federal Trade Commission (FTC) and the Federal Communication Commission (FCC)—in the United States and their European counterparts. The proposed merger received approval from the EU in mid-November but only after AOL agreed to sever all of its alliances with Bertelsmann AG, Europe's largest media company. In addition, Time Warner agreed to suspend any further efforts to create a joint venture with EMI, owner of the EMI and Virgin record labels. The EU regulators were concerned that the merger between Time Warner and AOL would have given too much control over the online distribution of music to a single company.

More than 11 months after the announcement of the merger, antitrust regulators in the United States gave approval on December 15, 2000, with safeguards to ensure that Americans will have broad choices as the Internet evolves. U.S. FTC officials feared that the deal could stymie the development of Internet technology that has been characterized by openness, diversity, and easy access. The leading concern seemed to involve maintaining consumer choice for Internet providers.

Under the terms of the 5-year "consent decree" with the FTC, AOL and Time Warner agreed to offer subscribers at least three Internet providers, in addition to AOL, within 3 months of offering services to the public as a combined company. This concession is intended to ensure that consumers could select from a variety of Internet providers in offering a range of dial-up and broadband services. The FTC settlement also contains key provisions that bar the companies from discriminating against Internet companies, besides AOL, that want to carry Time Warner's popular content. Moreover, AOL Time Warner cannot discriminate against content from other sources that it uses on its Internet systems or interactive television service. As such, AOL has agreed not to withhold its popular service from other companies that offer high-speed Internet access over competing mediums such as phone lines or satellite systems.

Typically the FCC waits for a ruling by the FTC before announcing its decision. On January 12, 2001, 2 days after the 1-year anniversary of the merger's announcement, the FCC gave its approval. William Kennard, the then-FCC chairman, said, "the marriage of old and new media presented the agency with unusual challenges. The Commission sought to safeguard consumer choice for new Internet services; but, at the same time, it did not want to regulate too heavily the emerging technologies." (Srinivasan, January 12, 2001). As part of AOL Time Warner's agreement with the FCC, AOL agreed to make its next generation of instant messaging services offered over Time Warner's cable lines work with competing systems such as Microsoft, Excite@Home, and AT&T. (Note that since this FCC consent decree was signed, Excite@Home declared bankruptcy in late 2001.)

Integration Challenges

Integrating two vastly different organizations is a daunting task. Internet company AOL tended to make decisions quickly and without a lot of bureaucracy. Media and entertainment giant Time Warner is a collection of separate fiefdoms, from magazine publishing to cable systems, each with its own subculture. During the 1990s, Time Warner executives did not demonstrate a sterling record in achieving their vision of leveraging the complementary elements of their vast empire of media properties. The diverse set of businesses never seemed to reach agreement on how to handle online strategies among the various businesses.

Top management of the combined companies included icons of the digital world such as Steve Case and Robert Pittman of the digital world and Gerald Levin and Ted Turner of the media and entertainment industry. Steve Case, former chair and CEO of AOL, was appointed chair of the new company, and Gerald Levin, former chair and CEO of Time Warner, remained as chair. Under the terms of the agreement, Levin could not be removed until at least 2003, unless at least three-quarters of the new board consisting of eight directors from each company agree. Ted Turner was appointed as vice chair. The presidents of the two companies, Bob Pittman of AOL and Richard Parsons of Time Warner, were named co-chief operating officers (COOs) of the new company.

AOL Time Warner Identifies Postclosing Challenges

Immediately after receipt of FCC approval, the AOL and Time Warner merger finally closed in January 2001. Although one of the largest deals in history in terms of price paid, the passage of more than a year had taken its toll on the value of the AOL shares received by Time Warner shareholders. On the closing date, the transaction was valued at $106 billion, down from $165 billion on the announcement date 1 year earlier. This decline in value erased almost two-thirds of the premium AOL had originally offered Time Warner shareholders. AOL Time Warner immediately following closing identified a series of major challenges that had to be overcome; after 1 year, however, the firm's progress seems to be mixed (*Business Week*: January 15, 2001). The publicly stated challenges included making good on commitments to grow revenue and profits at 12–15% annually and a 30% increase in cash flow in 2001 alone, getting Time Warner operating on the Internet, breaking down barriers between businesses, and stimulating advertising revenues.

The Disparity Between Projected and Actual Performance Becomes Apparent

Despite all the hype about the triumph of a "new media" company (AOL) over an "old media" firm (Time Warner) and the pending culture clash between AOL techies and the Time Warner's showbiz crew, several facts have emerged since the closing. First, in May 2002, Richard Parsons, formerly CEO of Time Warner, replaced Jerry Levin as CEO of AOL Time Warner, when Levin surprisingly announced his retirement. Second, Robert Pittman became the COO of the Company. Third, because of the relative maturity of these businesses, achieving the growth rates that AOL Time Warner has proclaimed publicly falls squarely on AOL.

Despite all the hype about the emergence of a vertically integrated new media company, AOL seems to be more like a traditional media company, similar to Bertelsmann in Germany, Vivendi in France, and Australia's News Corp. A key part of the AOL Time Warner strategy was to position AOL as the preeminent provider of high-speed access in the world, just as it is in the current online dial-up world. High-speed connections have become a strategic imperative for AOL because the more traditional dial-up or "narrowband" market is fast approaching saturation. Because most Americans who want to get online are already online (the rest are simply uninterested, low income, or elderly), AOL's greatest growth opportunities lie overseas. Even in such developed foreign markets as Germany, Britain, France, Brazil, and Japan, people have been slower to sign up for Internet access than in the United States. With service offerings in 8 languages in 16 countries, AOL is the only company that sells Internet access globally.

Despite pronouncements to the contrary, AOL Time Warner seems to be backing away from its attempt to become the premier provider of broadband services.

The firm has had considerable difficulty in convincing other cable companies, who compete directly with Time Warner Communications, to open up their networks to AOL. Cable companies are concerned that AOL could deliver video over the Internet and steal their core television customers. Moreover, cable companies are gearing up to compete head-on with AOL's dial-up and high-speed services by offering a tiered pricing system giving subscribers more options than AOL. Even if AOL is able to expand its geographic coverage through alliances with other cable firms, it is likely to find such broadband relationships to be only modestly profitable business because of the need to share revenue. In early April 2002, Bob Pittman, AOL Time Warner's COO, was given the responsibility for also managing AOL because of the significant shortfall in AOL's advertising revenues and deceleration in the growth of its subscriber base.

At $23 billion at the end of 2001, concerns mounted about AOL's leverage. Under a contract signed in March 2000, AOL gave German media giant Bertelsmann, an owner of one-half of AOL Europe, a put option to sell its half of AOL Europe to AOL for $6.75 billion. In early 2002, Bertelsmann gave notice of its intent to exercise the option. AOL will have to borrow heavily to meet its obligation, and it will be stuck with all of AOL Europe's losses, which totaled $600 million in 2001. The firm's problems are likely to be compounded by AT&T's effort to sell back to AOL its 25.5% stake in Time Warner Communications, which is believed to be worth as much as $10 billion (Shook, 2002).

In late April 2002, AOL Time Warner rocked Wall Street with a first quarter loss of $54 billion, including a $60 billion write-down of goodwill. Although investors had been expecting bad news, the reported loss simply reinforced anxieties about the firm's ability to even come close to its growth targets set immediately following closing. Rather than growing at a projected double-digit pace, EBITDA actually declined by more than 6% from the first quarter of 2001. Most of the sub-par performance stemmed from the Internet side of the business (Peers, 2002).

At about $20 per share, AOL Time Warner stock stood at less than one-third of its value on the day the deal was announced. Analysts were increasingly vocal about the wisdom of the deal, and others were calling for the spin-off of AOL. One study concluded that virtually all the value of the combined companies was concentrated in Time Warner. What had been billed as the greatest media company of the twenty-first century appeared to be on the verge of a meltdown. The irony is that many of these critics were among the biggest boosters of the merger when it was first announced early in 2000.

Case Study Discussion Questions

1. What were the primary motives for this transaction? How would you categorize them in terms of the historical motives for mergers and acquisitions discussed in this chapter?
2. Although the AOL–Time Warner deal is referred to as an acquisition in the case, why is it technically more correct to refer to it as a consolidation? Explain your answer.

3. Would you classify this business combination as a horizontal, vertical, or conglomerate transaction? Explain your answer.
4. What are some of the reasons AOL Time Warner may fail to satisfy investor expectations?
5. What would be an appropriate arbitrage strategy for this all-stock transaction?

Solutions to these questions are found in the Appendix at the back of the book.

CHAPTER BUSINESS CASE

CASE STUDY 1-3: VODAFONE AIRTOUCH ACQUIRES MANNESMANN IN A RECORD-SETTING DEAL

On February 4, 2000, Vodafone AirTouch Plc, the world's largest wireless communications company, agreed to buy Mannesmann AG in a $180.0 billion stock swap, subject to shareholder and regulatory approval. The deal is the largest transaction in M&A history. The value of this transaction exceeded the value of the AOL Time Warner merger at closing by an eye-popping $74 billion. Including $17.8 billion in assumed debt, the total value of the transaction soared to $198 billion. After a protracted and heated contest with Mannesmann's management as well as German labor unions and politicians, the deal finally closed on March 30, 2000 (Vodafone AirTouch, 2000). In this battle of titans, Klaus Esser, CEO of Mannesmann, the German cellular phone giant, managed to squeeze nearly twice as much money as first proposed out of Vodafone, the British cellular phone powerhouse. This transaction illustrates the intricacies of international transactions in countries in which hostile takeovers are viewed negatively and antitakeover laws generally favor target companies. (See Chapter 3 for a more detailed discussion of antitakeover laws.)

Transaction Timeline

Vodafone AirTouch and Mannesmann had worked together for years in the mobile-phone business in Germany, France, and Italy. Mannesmann's acquisition of Orange, the U.K.'s third-largest mobile phone company, in 1999 made it Europe's top wireless company and sparked Vodafone AirTouch's takeover attempt. Its initial "friendly" offer, valued at $107 billion plus assumed debt, to management on November 14, 1999, was quickly rebuffed by Klaus Esser, Mannesmann's CEO, as not in the best interests of Mannesmann's shareholders. In less than a week, Vodafone AirTouch sweetened the offer to about $131 billion; 1 week later, Mannesmann rejected the improved bid.

Frustrated by Esser's continued resistance, Gent decided to circumvent the Mannesmann board and go directly to the firm's shareholders through a tender offer. His objective was to raise the pressure on Esser and the Mannesmann board

TABLE 1-6   Vodafone AirTouch/Mannesmann Transaction Timeline

Date	Event
October 21, 1999	Mannesmann pays $36 billion for Orange, Britain's third-largest mobile phone operator.
November 12, 1999	Vodafone AirTouch indicates a wish to deepen its ties with Mannesmann.
November 14, 1999	Vodafone AirTouch proposes a friendly merger with Mannesmann, based on 43.7 of its own shares for each Mannesmann share.
November 14, 1999	Vodafone's AirTouch merger proposal is rejected by Mannesmann.
November 19, 1999	Vodafone raises the offer to 53.7 shares.
November 28, 1999	Mannesmann rejects improved proposal.
December 23, 1999	Vodafone AirTouch launches formal bid to shareholders, offering 53.7 shares.
January 14, 2000	Mannesmann rejects formal offer and publicly values itself at more than $200 billion.
January 18, 1999	Mannesmann, seeking a "white knight," starts talks with Vivendi.
January 25, 2000	Mannesmann-Vivendi talks end.
January 31, 2000	Vodafone AirTouch and Vivendi agree to Internet pact.
February 3, 2000	Mannesmann accepts improved Vodafone offer of 53.96 shares.
February 7, 2000	Mannesmann shareholders approve Vodafone Airtouch's offer.

Source: CNNfn, "Vodafone Seals Deal," February 7, 2000,
http://cnnfn.com/2000/02/04/europe/vodafone.

to accept the offer. Two days before Christmas, Mannesmann released a document to its shareholders in which it claimed to be worth at least $200 billion, about 53% higher than Vodafone AirTouch's latest bid. Simultaneously, Mannesmann sought another buyer, a so-called "white knight," in Vivendi, which they thought would be more likely to retain Mannesmann's current management and allow them to continue to pursue their current strategy. However, talks with Vivendi collapsed and Vodafone AirTouch raised the bid to the heretofore unheard of figure of $180 billion. Esser and the board relented to investor pressure and agreed to support the offer. See Table 1-6.

Vodafone AirTouch Corporate Profile

Business Strategy: Become Global Leader in Wireless Communication

Vodafone AirTouch, itself the product of a $60 billion acquisition of U.S.-based AirTouch Communications in early 1999, is focused on becoming the global leader in wireless communication. Although it believes the growth opportunities are much greater in wireless than in wired communication systems, Vodafone AirTouch has pursued a strategy in which customers in certain market segments are offered a package of integrated wireless and wired services. Vodafone has grown historically through third-party commercial agreements, such as with Cable & Wireless and

Energis in the United Kingdom or through the acquisition of assets where market and regulatory conditions make this attractive.

Technological and Product Innovator

Vodafone AirTouch is widely recognized for its technological innovation and for pioneering creative new products and services. Vodafone AirTouch has been a leader in the development of new technologies, including the design of the radio link protocol. In the United Kingdom, Vodafone AirTouch has developed a wide range of data applications and is one of the leaders in short messaging services. Europolitan, a Vodafone AirTouch-controlled firm, is recognized as a world leader in data services for the corporate market.

Extensive Geographic Coverage

Vodafone introduced cellular service on the analogue network into the United Kingdom on January 1, 1985. Vodafone has been a leader since 1986 in terms of the number of customers, with more than 7.5 million at the end of 2000. It was the first network operator to introduce a network based on the global system modem (GSM) standard and is one of the world's first operators to introduce international roaming, with agreements covering more than 100 countries. Vodafone also introduced a highly popular Pay-As-You-Talk prepaid service. This enormously popular service represented more than one-half of Vodafone AirTouch's U.K. customer base by the end of 2000.

Vodafone AirTouch's operations cover the vast majority of the European continent, as well as potentially high-growth areas such as Eastern Europe, Africa, and the Middle East. At the end of 2000, Vodafone AirTouch had more than 12 million customers. Vodafone AirTouch's geographic coverage received an enormous boost in the United States by entering into the joint venture with Bell Atlantic. Vodafone AirTouch has a 45% interest in the joint venture. The JV has 23 million customers (including 3.5 million paging customers). Covering about 80% of the U.S. population, the joint venture offers cellular service in 49 of the top 50 U.S. markets and is the largest wireless operator in the United States. (See Chapter 12 for a more detailed discussion of this JV.)

Mannesmann's Corporate Profile

Business Strategy: Become a Global Leader in Cellular Communications

Mannesmann is an international, German-headquartered corporation focused on the telecommunications, engineering, and automotive markets. Mannesmann transformed itself during the 1990s from a manufacturer of steel pipes, auto components, and materials-handling equipment into Europe's biggest mobile-phone operator. Rapid growth in its telecom activities has accounted for much of the growth in the value of the company in recent years. In 1998, Mannesmann announced plans to spin off the manufacturing business, allowing it the freedom to grow its telecommunications operations.

Mannesmann Telecommunications: Excellent European Geographic Coverage

With telecommunications operations in Germany, Italy, France, and Austria, Mannesmann is one of Europe's largest telecommunications providers. Mannesmann is the largest player in mobile communications in Germany, with more than 8 million network subscribers. In Italy the company is the second largest mobile operator, with more than 9 million subscribers. Mannesmann has grown internationally through acquisitions, minority investments, and applications for new licenses.

Other Mannesmann Operations

The engineering segment of the company is a leading global supplier of hydraulics, material-handling equipment, flow controls, and process and laser technology. The automotive segment is a systems developer, with two main divisions: Mannesmann VDO (information systems, cockpit systems, and audio and navigation systems) and Mannesmann Sachs (components and systems primarily for chassis and power trains). Finally, Mannesmann Tube is one of the world's largest producers of steel tubes.

Strategic Rationale for the Merger

Although Vodafone AirTouch is the world's largest mobile telecommunications in terms of subscribers, the company doesn't dominate Europe, trailing Telecom Italia SpA. Although it has stakes in markets from Sweden to Greece, most are minority positions, and it doesn't control Germany and Italy, the European markets with the most cellular-phone subscribers. With Mannesmann, Vodafone AirTouch would get control of Germany's biggest cellular company, Mannesmann Mobilfunk, and the second-biggest in Italy, Omnitel Pronto Italia SpA.

With Mannesmann, Vodafone AirTouch intends to consolidate its position in Europe and then to undertake a global brand strategy. In Europe, Vodafone and Mannesmann will have controlling stakes in 10 European markets, giving the new company the most extensive European coverage of any wireless carrier. Vodafone AirTouch will benefit from the additional coverage provided by Mannesmann in Europe, whereas Mannesmann's operations would benefit from Vodafone AirTouch's excellent U.S. geographic coverage. The merger will create a superior platform for the development of mobile data and Internet services, which are poised to become significant drivers of growth. Vodafone AirTouch's Asian presence gives it the opportunity to benefit from growth in this region, as well as providing a window on some of the leading mobile Internet applications currently available. Vodafone AirTouch's global reach also facilitates the spread of best practices and technology for the benefit of its customers.

The combined firm's major concentration of customers is in Europe, with 29 million in 11 countries. The combined companies will have 42 million customers worldwide, with the potential to serve as many as 510 million. The new company is seeking to establish a single standard format enabling mobile customers to use the same phone wherever they travel. This is in marked contrast to current mobile phone systems around the world, which are largely incompatible with one another.

The sheer size of the combined companies together with the global brand could make it the partner of choice for suppliers and other providers as well as the operator of choice for multinational companies and consumers. Significant synergies are expected to arise from the ability to leverage best practices and purchasing economies, as well as the creation of a global brand and the introduction of new Internet and data applications. The combined firms' were expected to generate after-tax cash flow from synergies of at least $750 million in 2003 and $900 million in 2004.

Mannesmann's "Just Say No" Strategy

What supposedly started on friendly terms soon turned into a bitter battle, involving a personal duel between Chris Gent and Klaus Esser. In November 1999, Vodafone AirTouch had announced for the first time its intention to make a takeover bid for Mannesmann. Mannesmann's board rebuked the overture by stating, "The offer by Vodafone AirTouch is not attractive to Mannesmann shareholders since Mannesmann has a more favorable strategic position than Vodafone AirTouch" (CNNfn, November 26, 1999). Mannesmann argued that Mannesmann's strategy of combining traditional and cellular services would provide greater value for the company's shareholders than Vodafone AirTouch's narrower focus on mobile services.

Vodafone AirTouch Approaches Mannesmann Shareholders

After the Mannesmann management had refused a second, more attractive bid, Vodafone AirTouch went directly to the Mannesmann shareholders with its offer. A central theme in Vodafone AirTouch's appeal to Mannesmann shareholders was what it described as the extravagant cost of Mannesmann's independent strategy. "Developing further in Europe will be very expensive ... dilution of (shareholder) interests would seem the inevitable consequence if Mannesmann remains independent" (CNNfn, December 23, 1999). Both companies' managers had appealed to Mannesmann's major shareholders for support in tours across Europe and the United States. Relations between Chris Gent and Klaus Esser turned highly contentious.

Vodafone AirTouch's board decided to approach the shareholders of Mannesmann with a highly attractive and "final" tender offer, so that they can decide on the merits of the combination for themselves. The terms of the transaction communicated to the Mannesmann shareholders included 53.7 Vodafone AirTouch shares for each Mannesmann share based on Mannesmann's closing price on November 18, 1999. This offer constituted a 54% premium over the Mannesmann closing price on October 18, 1999, the last business day before speculation regarding a possible transaction between Mannesmann and Orange. It also constituted a premium of 67% over the Mannesmann closing price on October 21, 1999, the day following the announcement of Mannesmann's formal offer for Orange.

The decision to undertake a hostile takeover (i.e., one not supported by the management of the target firm) was highly risky. Numerous obstacles stood in the way of foreign acquirers of German companies.

Culture Clash

Hostile takeovers of German firms by foreign firms are rare. It is even more rare when it turns out to be one of the nation's largest corporations. Vodafone AirTouch's initial offer immediately was decried as a job killer. The German tabloids painted a picture of a pending bloodbath for Mannesmann and its 130,000 employees if the merger took place. Vodafone AirTouch had said that it was only interested in Mannesmann's successful telecommunications operations and that it was intending to sell off the companies' engineering and automotive businesses, which employ about 80% of Mannesmann's total workforce. Mannesmann had announced that it was considering doing the same thing just 1 month before it received the takeover proposal from Vodafone AirTouch. The prospect of what was perceived to be a less caring foreign firm doing the same thing led to appeals from numerous political factions for government protection against the takeover.

German law also stood as a barrier to an unfriendly takeover. German corporate law requires that 75% of outstanding shares be tendered before control is transferred. In addition, the law allows individual shareholders to block deals with court challenges that can drag on for years. In a country where hostile takeovers are rare, public opinion was squarely behind management. Even Chancellor Gerhard Schroeder, a Social Democrat often attacked by his party's left wing for being too market friendly, came out strongly against the hostile takeover bids, urging the "utmost possible caution." "Hostile takeovers destroy corporate culture and harm the target but they also, over the medium term, harm the predator as well" (Stanley, 1999).

To defuse the opposition from German labor unions and the German government, Chris Gent, CEO of Vodafone AirTouch, said that the deal would not result in any job cuts and the rights of the employees and trade unions would be fully preserved. Moreover, Vodafone would accept fully the Mannesmann corporate culture including the principle of codetermination through employee representation on the Mannesmann supervisory board. As a consequence of these reassurances, the unions decided to support the merger.

Mannesmann Hits Some Roadblocks

Mannesmann suffered a series of setbacks. On November 19, 1999, a High Court judge in London upheld U.S. investment bank Goldman Sachs' authority to advise Vodafone in its pursuit of Mannesmann. Mannesmann had argued that, while advising Orange, Goldman Sachs had obtained confidential information that could help Vodafone make a hostile bid. Mannesmann's negotiating position also was weakened when potential white knight Vivendi, which had been seen as a possible Mannesmann ally, backed out of the talks.

The Offer Mannesmann Couldn't Refuse

When it became clear that Vodafone's attempt at a hostile takeover might succeed, the Mannesmann management changed its strategy and agreed to negotiate the terms for a friendly takeover. The final agreement is based on an improved offer for Mannesmann shareholders to exchange their shares in the ratio of 58.96 Vodafone AirTouch shares for one Mannesmann share, an improvement over the previous offer of 53.7 to 1. Furthermore, the agreement defined terms for the integration of the two companies and their further development. For example, Dusseldorf was retained as one of two European headquarters with responsibility for Mannesmann's existing continental European mobile and fixed-line telephone business. Moreover, with the exception of Esser, all of Mannesmann's top managers would remain in place.

Who Won?

Undoubtedly, the Mannesmann shareholders could celebrate their sweet victory. Mannesmann's CEO Klaus Esser managed to extract excellent value for his company, despite his expression of personal concerns about the deal. Throughout the hostile takeover battle, Vodafone AirTouch had said that it was reluctant to offer Mannesmann shareholders more than 50% of the new company; in sharp contrast, Mannesmann had said all along that it would not accept a takeover that gives its shareholders a minority of new company. Esser managed to get Mannesmann shareholders almost 50% ownership in the new firm, despite Mannesmann contributing only about 35% of the operating earnings of the new company. After 3 months of fending off Vodafone AirTouch's hostile offer, which would have left Mannesmann shareholders with 47.2% of the combined companies, the German company relented, giving its shareholders 49.5% of the new firm.

Only time will tell if Vodafone AirTouch's shareholders will benefit significantly from this transaction. However, Chris Gent was not willing to wait to see the long-term performance of the combined firms. He had his eyes focused on accelerating the growth of the new firm. Despite just closing the largest deal in history, the audacious Gent vowed "to keep his eyes open" for takeover opportunities in Asia and to further consolidate the firm's position in Spain by trying to secure a majority stake in Spanish telecom company Airtel (CNNfn, February 4, 2000). There is little rest for the ambitious.

The Vodafone AirTouch-Mannesmann struggle highlighted the failure of the rest of Europe to adopt a U.S.-style and British-style, takeover-friendly environment. The Mannesmann battle drew attention to the slow pace of corporate law overhaul in Germany, which has been trying to replace a voluntary takeover code and remove a host of antitakeover defenses open to target managers. Public and official reaction against the Mannesmann bid stood in stark contrast to the efforts of ". . . the German reformers striving to create a market for corporate control as vigorous as Britain's," and to ". . . the European Commission . . . trying to impose some British discipline on the rest of Europe" (*The Economist*, 1999).

Case Study Discussion Questions

1. Who do you think negotiated the best deal for their shareholders, Chris Gent or Klaus Esser? Explain your answer in terms of short- and long-term impacts.
2. Both firms were pursuing a similar strategy of expanding their geographic reach. Does this strategy make sense? Why or why not? What are the risks associated with this strategy?
3. Do you think the use of all stock, rather than cash or a combination of cash and stock, to acquire Mannesmann helped or hurt Vodafone AirTouch's shareholders? Explain your answer.
4. Do you think that Vodafone AirTouch conceded too much to the labor unions and Mannesmann's management to get the deal done? Explain your answer.
5. What problems do you think Vodafone AirTouch might experience if they attempt to introduce what they view as "best operating practices" to the Mannesmann culture? How might these challenges be overcome? Be specific.

REFERENCES

Agrawal, Anup and Jeffrey F. Jaffe, "The Post-Merger Performance Puzzle," Working Paper Series, Social Science Research Network, December 1999.

Agrawal, Anup, Jeffrey F. Jaffe, and Gershon N. Mandelker, "The Post-Merger Performance of Acquiring Firms: A Reexamination of an Anomaly," *Journal of Finance*, 47, September 1992, pp. 1605–1621.

Akhigbe, Aigbe, Stephen F. Borde, and Anne Marie Whyte, "The Source of Gains to Targets and Their Industry Rivals: Evidence Based on Terminated Merger Proposals," *Financial Management*, 29 (4) (Winter 2000), pp. 101–118.

Anslinger, P. and T. Copeland, "Growth Through Acquisitions: A Fresh Look," *Harvard Business Review*, January/February, 1996.

Asquith, Paul, "Merger Bids and Stock Returns," *Journal of Financial Economics*, 11 (1), 1983, pp. 51–83.

Baer, Justin, "Overvalued Acquisitions May Cost $1 Trillion in Write-Downs," *Bloomberg News* as reported in *the Orange County Register*, January 11, 2002, p. C3.

Barber, Brad M. and John D. Lyon, "Detecting Long-Run Abnormal Stock Returns: The Empirical Power and Specification of Test Statistics," *Journal of Financial Economics*, 43, 1997, pp. 341–372.

Bekier, Matthias M., Anna J. Bogardus, and Tim Oldham, "Why Mergers Fail," *McKinsey Quarterly*, 4, 2001, p. 3.

Benerjee, Ajeyo and E. Woodrow Eckard, "Are Mega-Mergers Anti-Competitive? Evidence from the First Great Merger Wave," *Rand Journal of Economics*, 29 (Winter 1998), pp. 803–827.

Berger, Phillip G. and Eli Ofek, "Bustup Takeovers of Value Destroying Diversified Firms," *Journal of Finance*, Vol. 51, September 1996, pp. 1175–1200.

Berger, Phillip G. and Eli Ofek, "Diversification's Effect on Firm Value," *Journal of Financial Economics*, 37 (1), January 1995, pp. 39–65.

Bhagat, Sanfai and David Hirshleifer, "Do Takeovers Create Value?: An Intervention Approach," University of Michigan Business School, Working Paper 9505-03-R, http://eres.bus.umich.edu/docs/workpap/wp9505-03-R.pdf, December 1996, p. 35.

Black, Ervin L., Thomas A. Carnes, and Tomas Jandik, "The Long-Term Success of Cross-Border Mergers and Acquisitions," Social Science Research Network Electronic Paper Collection, December 2000, http://papers.ssrn.com/5013/delivery.cfn/ssrn_id272782_010705100.pdf.

Bogler, Daniel, "Post-Takeover Stress Disorder," Summary of a PA Consulting Study in *Financial Times*, May 22, 1996, p. 11.

Bradley, Michael, Anand Desai, and E. Han Kim, "Synergistic Gains from Corporate Acquisitions and Their Division Between the Stockholders of Target and Acquiring Firms," *Journal of Financial Economics*, 21, 1988, p. 3.

Bradley, Michael and Gregg Jarrell, "Comment on Mergers and Acquisitions," Chapter 15 in John Coffee, Jr., Louis Lowenstein, and Susan Rose-Ackerman, eds., *Knights, Raiders, and Targets*, Oxford, England: Oxford University Press, 1988, pp. 253–259.

Bryoksten, Johan, "Merger Lemons," *Mergers & Acquisitions*, Fall 1965, pp. 36–41.

Business Week, "The Case Against Mergers," October 31, 1995, p. 122.

Business Week, "21st Century," January 15, 2001, pp. 37–47.

Business Week, "Gerald Levin Looks Ahead," Media Section, November 6, 2000, pp. 157–160.

Business Week, "Show Time for AOL Time Warner," January 15, 2001, pp. 57–64.

Campa, Jose and Kedia Simi, "Explaining the Diversification Discount," Working Paper, Harvard University, 1999.

Capen, E. C., R. V. Clapp, and W. M. Campbell, "Competitive Bidding in High Risk Situations," *Journal of Petroleum Technology*, 23, June 1971, pp. 641–653.

Carlton, Dennis and Jeffrey Perloff, *Modern Industrial Organization* (2nd ed.), New York: Harper Collins, 1994, p. 502.

Carlton, Dennis and Jeffrey Perloff, *Modern Industrial Organization* (3rd ed.), New York: Addison-Wesley Longman, 1999, p. 27.

Chakrabarti, Alok K., "Organizational Factors in Post-Acquisition Performance," *IEEE Transactions on Engineering Management*, 37 (4), November 1990, p. 135.

Chapman, Timothy L., Jack J. Dempsey, Glenn Ramsdell, and Trudy J. Bell, "Purchasing's Big Moment—After a Merger," *The McKinsey Quarterly*, 1, 1998, pp. 56–65.

Comment, Robert and Gregg A. Jarrell, "Corporate Focus and Stock Returns," *Journal of Financial Economics*, 37 (1), 1993, pp. 67–87.

CNNfn, "Vodafone Seals Deal," February 4, 2000, http://cnnfn.com/2000/02/04/europe/vodafone.

CNNfn, "Vodafone Raises Bid to $138 Billion," December 23, 1999, http://cgi.cnnfn.com/output/pfv/1999/12/23/europe/vodafone/.

CNNfn, "Board Rejects Vodafone Bid," November 26, 1999, http://cnnfn.com/1999/11/26/europe/vodafone.

Conte, Michael A., Joseph Biasi, Douglas Kruse, and Rama Jampani, "Financial Returns of Public ESOP Companies: Investor Effects vs. Manager Effects," *Financial Analysts Journal*, 52, July/August 1996, pp. 51–61.

Coopers & Lybrand, "Most Acquisitions Fail, C&L Study Says," *Mergers & Acquisitions*, Report 7 (47), November 1996, p. 2.

Cotter, James F., Anil Shivdasani, and Marc Zenner, "Do Independent Directors Enhance Target Shareholder Wealth during Tender Offers?," *Journal of Financial Economics*, 43 (2), February 1997, pp. 237–266.

Daley, Lane, Vikas Mehrotra, and Ranjini Sivakumar, "Corporate Focus and Value Creation: Evidence from Spin-Offs," *Journal of Financial Economics*, 45 (2), 1996, pp. 257–281.

Deogun, Nikhil and Steven Lipin, "Big Mergers in '90s Prove Disappointing to Shareholders," Salomon Smith Barney study quoted in *The Wall Street Journal*, October 30, 2000, p. C12.

DePamphilis, Donald M., *Mergers, Acquisitions, and Other Restructuring Activities: An Integrated Approach to Process, Tools, Cases, and Solutions*, Academic Press: San Diego, 2001, p. 34.

Doukas, Hohn and Nickolaso G. Travlos, "The Effect of Corporate Multinationalism on Shareholders' Wealth: Evidence from International Acquisitions," *Journal of Finance*, 43, December 1988, pp. 1161–1175.

Dreazen, Yochi J., Greg Ip, and Nicholas Kulish, "Why Oligopolies Are on the Rise," *The Wall Street Journal*, February 25, 2002, p. 7.

Dukes, William, Cheryl Frohlich, and Christopher Ma, "Risk Arbitrage in Tender Offers: Handsome Rewards—and Not for Insiders Only," *Journal of Portfolio Management*, 18 (4), 1992, pp. 47–55.

The Economist, "Barriers to Entry," December 18, 1999, pp. 122–123.

Elgers, Pieter T., and John J. Clark, "Merger Types and Shareholder Returns: Additional Evidence," *Financial Management*, Summer 1980, pp. 66–72.

Eun, C., R. Kolodny, and C. Scheraga, "Cross-Border Acquisitions and Shareholder Wealth: Tests of the Synergy and Internationalization Hypothesis," *Journal of Banking and Finance*, 20, 1996, pp. 1559–1582.

Fama, E. F., and M. C. Jensen. "Separation of Ownership and Control," *Journal of Law and Economics*, 26, 1983, pp. 301–325.

Fama, Eugene F., "Market Efficiency, Long-Term Returns, and Behavioral Finance," *Journal of Financial Economics*, 47, 1998, pp. 427–465.

Franks, Julian R., Robert S. Harris, and Sheridan Titman, "The Post-Merger Share-Price Performance of Acquiring Firms," *Journal of Financial Economics*, 29, 1991, pp. 81–96.

Frick, Kevin A. and Alberto Torres, "Learning from High Tech Deals," *McKinsey Quarterly*, 1, 2002, p. 2.

Gaughan, Patrick A., *Mergers, Acquisitions and Corporate Restructurings*, John Wiley & Sons, Inc., 1996, pp. 18–53.

Georgeson & Company, "Proxy Solicitation," www.georgeson.com/proxy/proxy.html, 2000.

Ghosh, Aloke and Chi-Wen Jevons Lee, "Abnormal Returns and Expected Managerial Performance of Target Firms," *Financial Management*, 29 (1), Spring 2000, pp. 40–52.

Golbe, Devra L. and Lawrence J. White, "A Time-Series Analysis of Mergers and Acquisitions in the U.S. Economy," Chapter 9 in Alan J. Auerbach, ed., *Corporate Takeovers: Causes and Consequences*, Chicago: The University of Chicago Press, 1988, pp. 265–309.

Graham, John R., Michael L. Lemmon, and Jack G. Wolf, "Does Corporate Diversification Destroy Value?," *Journal of Finance*, 57 (2), 2002, pp. 695–720.

Gregory, Alan, "An Examination of the Long-Run Performance of UK Acquiring Firms," *Journal of Business Finance and Accounting*, 24, 1997, pp. 971–1002.

Harris, Robert S. and David Ravenscraft, "The Role of Acquisitions in Foreign Direct Investment: Evidence from the U.S. Stock Market," *Journal of Finance*, 46, 1991, pp. 825–844.

Healy, Paul M., Krishna G. Palepu, and Richard S. Ruback, "Does Corporate Performance Improve After Mergers?," *Journal of Financial Economics*, 31, 1992, pp. 135–175.

Hillyer, Clayton and Ira Smolowitz, "Why Do Mergers Fail to Achieve Synergy?" *Director's Monthly*, January 1996, p. 13.

Hyland, David, "Why Firms Diversify: An Empirical Examination," Working Paper, University of Texas, Arlington, 2001.

Jarrell, Gregg A., James A. Brickley, and Jeffry M. Netter, "The Market for Corporate Control: The Empirical Evidence Since 1980," *Journal of Economic Perspectives*, 2, 1988, pp. 49–68.

Jensen, M. C., "The Modern Industrial Revolution: Exit, and the Failure of Internal Control Systems," *Journal of Finance*, 48, 1993, pp. 831–880.

Jensen, Michael C., and Robert S. Ruback, "The Market for Corporate Control: The Scientific Evidence," *Journal of Financial Economics*, 11, 1983, pp. 5–53.

Jindra, Jan and Ralph Walkling, "Arbitrage Spreads and the Market Pricing of Proposed Acquisitions," Working Paper, Ohio State University, 1999.

Kaplan, Steven N. and Michael N. Weisbach, "The Success of Acquisitions: Evidence from Divestitures," *Journal of Finance*, 47 (1), March 1992, pp. 107–138.

Karolyi, G. Andrew and John Shannon, "Where's the Risk in Risk Arbitrage?," Working Paper, Richard Ivey School of Business, The University of Western Ontario, 1998.

Kim, E. Han and Vijay Singal, "Mergers and Market Power: Evidence from the Airline Industry," *American Economic Review*, 83 (3), June 1993, pp. 549–569.

Klein, B. R. Crawford, and A. Alchian, "Vertical Integration, Appropriate Rents, and the Competitive Contracting Process," *Journal of Law and Economics*, 21, October 1978, pp. 207–326.

Lajoux, Alexandra Reed, *The Art of M&A Integration*, New York: McGraw-Hill, 1998, p. 8.

Leeth, John D. and J. Rody Borg, "The Impact of Takeovers on Shareholders' Wealth During the 1920's Merger Wave," *Journal of Financial and Quantitative Analysis*, 35 (2), June 2000.

Levy, Haim and Marshall Sarnat, "Diversification, Portfolio Analysis and the Uneasy Case for Conglomerate Mergers," *Journal of Finance*, 25, September 1970, pp. 795–802.

Lewellen, W. G. and B. Huntsman, "Managerial Pay and Corporate Performance," *American Economic Review*, 60, September 1970, pp. 710–720.

Lictenberg, Frank and Donald Siegel, "Productivity and Changes in Ownership of Manufacturing Plants," *Brookings Papers on Economic Activity*, 3, 1987, pp. 643–683.

Linn, Scott C. and Jeannette A. Switzer, "Are Cash Acquisitions Associated with Better Post Combination Operating Performance Than Stock Acquisitions," *Journal of Banking and Finance*, 25 (6), June 2001, pp. 1113–1138.

Lins, Karl and Henri Servaes, "International Evidence on the Value of Corporate Diversification," *Journal of Finance*, 54, 1999, pp. 2215–2239.

Loughran, Tim and Anand M. Vijh, "Do Long-Term Shareholders Benefit from Corporate Acquisitions?" *Journal of Finance*, 22, April 1997, pp. 321–340.

Lyon, John D., Brad M. Barber, and Chih-Ling Tsai, "Improved Methods for Tests of Long-Run Abnormal Stock Returns," *Journal of Finance*, 54, 1999, pp. 165–201.

Maksimovic, Vojislav and Gordon M. Phillips, "The Market for Corporate Assets: Who Engages in Mergers and Asset Sales and Are There Efficiency Gains," *Journal of Finance*, December 2001, pp. 332–355.

Mangenheim, Ellen B. and Dennis C. Mueller, "Are Acquiring Firm Shareholders Better Off After an Acquisition," Chapter 11 in John Coffee Jr., Louis Lowenstein, and Susan Rose-Ackerman, eds., *Knight, Raiders, and Targets*, Oxford, England: Oxford University Press, 1988, pp. 171–193.

McKinsey & Company, "Creating Shareholder Value through Merger and/or Acquisition: A McKinsey & Company Perspective," an internal 1987 memorandum cited in Tom Copeland, Tim Koller, and Jack Murrin, *Valuation: Measuring and Managing the Value of Companies*, New York: John Wiley & Sons, 1990, p. 321.

Melicher, Ronald W. and Edgar A. Norton, *Finance: Introduction to Institutions, Investments, and Management*, Cincinnati: Southwestern College Publishing, 1999, p. 320.

Mercer Management Consulting, 1995 and 1997 surveys cited in Alexandra Reed Lajoux, *The Art of Integration*, New York: McGraw-Hill, 1998, pp. 19–21.

Mergerstat LP, "Dealmakers Hope for Better Days Ahead in 2002," Press Release, January 2, 2002, www.mergerstat.com.

Mester, Loretta L. "Efficient Product of Financial Services: Scale and Scope Economies." *Review*, Federal Reserve Bank of Philadelphia, January/February 1987, pp. 15–25.

Mitchell, David, Survey conducted by Economist Intelligence Unit, cited in Alexandra Reed Lajoux, *The Art of M&A Integration*, New York: McGraw-Hill, 1998, p. 19.

Mitchell, M. L. and Mulherin, J. H., "The Impact of Industry Shocks on Takeover and Restructuring Activity, *Journal of Financial Economics*, 41, 1996, pp. 193–229.

Mitchell, Mark L. and Todd C. Pulvino, "Characteristics of Risk and Return in Arbitrage," *Journal of Finance*, December 2001, pp. 206–220.

Morck, Randall, Andrei Shleifer, and Robert W. Vishny, "Do Managerial Objectives Drive Bad Acquisitions?" *Journal of Finance*, 45 (1), March 1990, pp. 31–48.

Mueller, D. C., "A Theory of Conglomerate Mergers," *Quarterly Journal of Economics*, 83, 1969, pp. 643–659.

Mueller, Dennis, "Mergers and Market Share," *Review of Economics and Statistics*, 47, 1985, pp. 259–267.

Mulherin, J. Harold and Audra L. Boone, "Comparing Acquisitions and Divestitures," Working Paper Series, Social Sciences Research Network, April 19, 2000, p. 17.

Nerney, Chris, "CMGI's Long, Cold Winter," Internet.com, January 22, 2001, http://boston.internet.com/stocks/article.html.

Nielsen, J. F. and R. W. Melicher, "A Financial Analysis of Acquisitions and Merger Premiums," *Journal of Financial and Quantitative Analysis*, 8, March 1973, pp. 139–162.

Peers, Martin, "AOL Posts $54.24 Billion Net Loss," *The Wall Street Journal*, April 25, 2002, p. 11.

Porter, Michael, *Competitive Advantage*, New York, The Free Press, 1985.

Rau, P. Raghavendra and Theo Vermaelen, "Glamour, Value, and the Post-Acquisition Performance of Acquiring Firms," *Journal of Financial Economics*, 49 (2), August, 1998, pp. 223–253.

Ravenscraft, David and Frederic Scherer, *Mergers, Selloffs and Economic Efficiency*, Washington, DC: Brookings Institution, 1987a.

Ravenscraft, David and Frederick Scherer, "Life After Takeovers," *Journal of Industrial Economics*, 36, 1987b, pp. 147–156.

Ravenscraft, David and Frederick Scherer, "Mergers and Managerial Performance," in John Coffee, Louis Lowenstein, and Susan Rose Ackerman, eds., *Knights and Targets*, New York: Oxford University Press, 1988, pp. 194–210.

Roll, Richard, "The Hubris Hypothesis of Corporate Takeovers," *Journal of Business*, 59 (2), April 1986, pp. 197–216.

Salter, Malcolm S. and Wolf A. Weinhold, *Diversification Through Acquisition: Strategies for Creating Economic Value*, New York: The Free Press, 1979, pp. 30–31.

Sanford Bernstein & Company, "Net Equation," *Business Week*, January 31, 2000, pp. 39–41.

Schipper, Katherine and Rex Thompson, "Evidence on the Capitalized Value of Merger Activity for Merging Firms," *Journal of Financial Economics*, 11, 1983, pp. 85–119.

Schwert, G. William, "Hostility in Takeovers: In the Eyes of the Beholder," *Journal of Finance*, 55 (6), December 2000, pp. 2599–2640.

Schwert, William, "Markup Pricing in Mergers and Acquisitions," *Journal of Financial Economics*, 41, 1996, pp. 153–192.

Seth, Anju, Kean P. Song, and Richard Petit, "Synergy, Managerialism or Hubris: An Empirical Examination of Motives for Foreign Acquisitions of U.S. Firms," *Journal of International Business Studies*, 31, 2000, pp. 387–405.

Shook, David, "Will AOL and Yahoo Trade Places?," *BusinessWeek Online*, April 10, 2002.

Sirower, Mark, *The Synergy Trap*, New York: The Free Press, 1997.

Song, H.H. and R.A. Walking, "Abnormal Returns to Rivals of Acquisitions Targets: A Test of the Acquisition Probability Hypothesis," *Journal of Financial Economics*, 55 (2), 2000, pp. 439–457.

Srinivasan, Kalpana, "AOL-Time Warner Merger Approved," Associated Press, *Los Angeles Times*, Business, January 12, 2001, p. 2.

Stanley, Bruce, "Vodafone Ups Hostile Bid," Associated Press, November 19, 1999, http://abcnews.go.com/sections/business/dailynews/mannesmann_vodafone991119.html.

Sullivan, M.J., M.R.H. Jensen, and C.D. Hudson, "The Role of Medium of Exchange in Merger Offers: Examination of Terminated Merger Proposals," *Financial Management*, 23 (3), 1994, pp. 51–62.

Sweeney, Paul, "Who Says It's A Fair Deal?," *Journal of Accountancy*, 188 (2), August 6, 1999, p. 6.

Thompson Financial Services, various news releases, www.tfibcm.com.

United States General Accounting Office, "Employee Stock Ownership Plans: Little Evidence of Effects on Corporate Performance," Washington, DC, 1987.

Vodafone AirTouch Press Release, "Final Results of Offer for Mannesmann," March 30, 2000, http://www.vodafone.com/media/press_releases/8864.

Wasserstein, Bruce. *Big Deal: the Battle for Control of America's Leading Corporations*, Warner Books, New York, 1998, pp. 113 116.

You, Victor, Richard Caves, Michael Smith, and James Henry, "Mergers and Bidders' Wealth: Managerial and Strategic Factors," Chapter 9 in Lacy Glenn Thomas, III, ed., *The Economics of Strategic Planning*, Lexington, MA: Lexington Books, 1986, pp. 201–220.

2

REGULATORY
CONSIDERATIONS

Character is doing the right thing when no one is looking.
—J.C. Watts

As chief executive officer (CEO) of one of the nation's largest direct marketing companies, Maria was convinced that the proposed merger between her firm and the third largest competitor in the industry would result in substantial cost savings and expanded geographic coverage. Lower overall operating expenses for the combined companies would result from the elimination of overlapping administrative and support positions at the corporate level and the shutdown of one of the two data centers currently operated by the two companies. Moreover, the increased leverage of the combined companies would result in significant savings in purchasing mailing addresses and certain demographic information such as age or marital status from regional vendors specializing in the collection of such data. Finally, because the target company owned information on both consumers and small businesses in geographic areas not currently covered by Maria's firm, the combined companies would have a truly national database suitable for developing and selling mailing lists to retailers and financial service companies interested in conducting national marketing campaigns.

The merger would not come cheap. Maria knew that she would have to pay at least $4 billion, resulting in a premium of almost 50% over the target's current share price. "But it would be worth it," she reasoned, "if the anticipated synergy could be realized in a timely manner." Although Maria was confident that she could get shareholder approval for the proposed transaction, she was less sanguine about receiving regulatory approval without making significant concessions to the Federal Trade Commission (FTC). The FTC was concerned that the combined firms would own the most comprehensive database in the industry and effectively could exclude other direct marketing firms from gaining access to certain types of data highly valued by retailers and financial services companies. Maria worried that the FTC might make approval of the transaction conditional on her willingness to license such information to others. She knew that such a requirement could materially reduce the value of the data by creating competitors.

Maria was a veteran of a number of transactions. She knew that completing the deal would ultimately depend on receiving FTC approval under conditions that would be acceptable to all parties involved. She was prepared to walk away from the transaction if the requirements to receive regulatory approval threatened her ability to achieve the synergy necessary to justify the purchase price.

OVERVIEW

Regulations that affect merger and acquisition (M&A) activity exist at all levels of government. Regulatory considerations can be classified as either general or industry-specific. General considerations are those that affect all firms, whereas industry-specific considerations affect only certain types of transactions in specific industries. General considerations include federal security, antitrust, environmental, racketeering, and employee benefits laws. Examples of industries that are subject to substantial regulation include insurance, banking, broadcasting, telecommunications, defense contracting, transportation, and public utilities. M&A activities in these industries may require government approvals to transfer government-granted licenses, permits, and franchises. For example, the Federal Communications Commission (FCC) must grant approval to transfer a communications license.

In addition to federal regulations, numerous state statutes have to be considered in M&As. For example, state antitakeover statutes place limitations on how and when a hostile takeover may be implemented. Moreover, approval may have to be received to make deals in certain industries at both the state and federal levels. Cross-border transactions may be even more complicated because it may be necessary to get approval from regulatory authorities in all countries in which the acquirer and target companies do business.

This chapter will focus on the key elements of selected federal and state regulations and their implications for M&As. Considerable time is devoted to discussing the prenotification and disclosure requirements of current legislation and how decisions are made within the key securities law and antitrust enforcement agencies. This chapter provides only an overview of the labyrinth of environmental, labor, and benefit laws affecting M&As. Because a detailed discussion is well beyond the scope of this book, the intent of this overview is simply to make the reader aware of the challenges of complying with all of the applicable laws. See Table 2-1 for a summary of applicable legislation.

TABLE 2-1 Laws Affecting M&A

Law	Intent
Federal Securities Laws	
Securities Act (1933)	Prevents the public offering of securities without a registration statement; defines minimum data requirements and noncompliance penalties
Securities Exchange Act (1934)	Empowers Securities and Exchange Commission (SEC) to revoke registration of a security if issuer is in violation of any provision of the 1934 act
Section 13	Defines content and frequency of, as well as events triggering, SEC filings
Section 14	Defines disclosure requirements for proxy solicitation
Williams Act (1968)	Regulates tender offers
Section 13D	Defines disclosure requirements
Federal Antitrust Laws	
Sherman Act (1890)	Establishes criminal penalties for behaviors that unreasonably limit competition
Section 1	Makes mergers creating monopolies or "unreasonable" market control illegal
Section 2	Applies to firms already dominant in their served markets to prevent them from "unfairly" restraining trade
Clayton Act (1914)	Created the Federal Trade Commission (FTC) and established civil penalties for behaviors illegally restraining trade
Celler–Kefauver Act of 1950	Amended Clayton Act to cover asset as well as stock purchases
Hart–Scott–Rodino Antitrust Improvement Act (1976)	Requires waiting period before a transaction can be completed and regulatory data submission requirements
Title I	Defines what must be filed
Title II	Defines who must file and when
Title III	Enables state attorneys general to file triple damage suits on behalf of injured parties
State Antitakeover Laws	Define conditions under which a change in corporate ownership can take place; may differ by state
State Antitrust Laws	Similar to federal antitrust laws; states may sue to block mergers, even if the mergers are not challenged by federal regulators
Industry Specific Regulations	Banking, communications, railroads, defense, insurance, and public utilities
Environmental Laws (federal and state)	Define disclosure requirements
Labor and Benefit Laws (federal and state)	Define disclosure requirements
Applicable Foreign Laws	Cross-border transactions subject to jurisdictions of countries in which the bidder and target firms have operations

FEDERAL SECURITIES LAWS

Whenever either the acquiring or the target company is publicly traded, the firms are subject to the substantial reporting requirements of the current federal securities laws. Passed in the early 1930s, these laws were a direct result of the loss of confidence in the securities markets following the crash of the stock market in 1929. See the Securities and Exchange Commission Website (www.sec.gov), Loss and Seligman (1995), and Gilson and Black (1995) for a comprehensive discussion of federal securities laws.

SECURITIES ACT OF 1933

Originally administered by the FTC, the Securities Act of 1933 requires that all securities offered to the public must be registered with the government. Registration requires, but does not guarantee, that the facts represented in the registration statement and prospectus are accurate. However, the law makes providing inaccurate or misleading statements in the sale of securities to the public punishable with a fine, imprisonment, or both. The registration process requires the description of the company's properties and business, a description of the securities, information about management, and financial statements certified by public accountants. The legislation is intended to enable investors to have an opportunity to realistically evaluate the worth of securities they are being offered. Section 8 of the law permits the registration statement to automatically become effective 20 days after it is filed with the SEC. However, the SEC may delay or stop the process by requesting additional information.

SECURITIES EXCHANGE ACT OF 1934

The Securities Exchange Act of 1934 extends disclosure requirements stipulated under the Securities Act of 1933 covering new issues to include securities already trading on the national exchanges. In 1964 coverage was expanded to include securities traded on the Over-the-Counter (OTC) Market. Moreover, the act prohibits brokerage firms working with a company and others related to the securities transaction from engaging in fraudulent and unfair behavior such as insider trading. The act also covers proxy solicitations (i.e., mailings to shareholders soliciting their vote on a particular issue) by a company or shareholders. For a more detailed discussion of proxy statements, see Chapter 3.

Registration Requirements

Companies that are required to register are those with assets of more than $1 million and with more than 500 shareholders. Even if both parties are privately owned, an M&A transaction is subject to federal securities laws if a portion of the purchase price is going to be financed by an initial public offering of stock or a public offering of debt by the acquiring firm.

Frequency of Filings

After registration of securities, companies must file annual and other periodic reports to update data in the original filing. Section 13 of the Securities and Exchange Act covers periodic reporting requirements. These include the 10K or annual report, the Form 10Q or quarterly report, and the Form 8K. The 8K must be submitted within 15 days of the occurrence of certain specified events, such as the acquisition or divestiture of a significant amount of assets. Acquisitions and divestitures are deemed significant if the equity interest in the acquired assets or the amount paid or received exceeds 10% of the total book value of the assets of the registrant and its subsidiaries.

Section 13: Periodic Reports

The Form 10K or annual report summarizes and documents the firm's financial activities during the preceding year. The four key financial statements that must be included are the income statement, balance sheet, statement of retained earnings, and the statement of cash flows. The statements must be well documented with information on accounting policies and procedures, calculations, and transactions underlying the financial statements. The Form 10K also includes a relatively detailed description of the business, the markets served, major events and their impact on the business, key competitors, and competitive market conditions. The Form 10Q is a highly succinct quarterly update of such information.

In the event an acquisition or divestiture is deemed significant, the Form 8K must describe the assets acquired or disposed, the nature and amount of consideration (i.e., payment) given or received, and the identity of the person or persons for whom the assets were acquired. In the case of an acquisition, the Form 8K also must identify the source of funds used to finance the purchase and the financial statements of the acquired business.

Section 14: Proxy Solicitations

Where proxy contests for control of corporate management are involved, the Act requires the names and interests of all participants in the proxy contest. Proxy materials must be filed in advance of their distribution to ensure that they are in compliance with disclosure requirements. If the transaction involves the shareholder approval of either the acquirer or target firm, any materials distributed to shareholders must conform to the SEC's rules for proxy materials.

WILLIAMS ACT: REGULATION OF TENDER OFFERS

Until the late 1960s, most M&A activity involved negotiated settlements between the management of the acquirer and the target companies. During the era of conglomerate mergers in the late 1960s, mergers grew more hostile. Tender offers were becoming more commonplace. Regulatory officials became increasingly concerned about whether target shareholders had sufficient time to make informed decisions about such offers. See Chapter 3 for a more detailed discussion of tender offers.

Passed in 1968, the Williams Act consists of a series of amendments to the Securities Act of 1934. The Williams Act was intended to protect target firm shareholders from lightning-fast takeovers in which they would not have enough information or time to adequately assess the value of an acquirer's offer. This protection was achieved by requiring more disclosure by the bidding company, establishing a minimum period during which a tender offer must remain open, and authorizing targets to sue bidding firms. The disclosure requirements of the Williams Act apply to anyone, including the target, asking shareholders to accept or reject a takeover bid. The major sections of the Williams Act as they impact M&As are in Sections 13(d) and 14(d). Note that the procedures outlined in the Williams Act for prenotification must be followed diligently. Failure to deliver copies of the required documents to all parties stipulated in the law can result in a violation of U.S. securities laws.

Section 13(d)

Section 13(d) of the Williams Act is intended to regulate "substantial share" or large acquisitions and serves to provide an early warning for a target company's shareholders and management of a pending bid. Any person or firm acquiring 5% or more of the stock of a public corporation must file a Schedule 13D with the SEC within 10 days of reaching that percentage ownership threshold. The disclosure is necessary even if the accumulation of the stock is not followed by a tender offer.

Under Section 13(g), any stock accumulated by related parties such as affiliates, brokers, or investment bankers working on behalf of the person or firm are counted toward the 5% threshold. This prevents an acquirer from avoiding filing by accumulating more than 5% of the target's stock through a series of related parties. Institutional investors, such as registered brokers and dealers, banks, and insurance companies, can file a Schedule 13G, a shortened version of the Schedule 13D, if the securities were acquired in the normal course of business.

The information required by the Schedule 13D includes the identities of the acquirer, their occupation and associates, sources of financing, and the purpose of the acquisition. If the purpose of the acquisition of the stock is to take control of the target firm, the acquirer must reveal its business plan for the target firm. The plans could include the breakup of the firm, the suspension of dividends, a recapitalization of the firm, or the intention to merge it with another firm. Otherwise, the purchaser of the stock could indicate that the accumulation was for investment purposes only. Whenever a material change in the information on the Schedule 13D occurs, a new filing must be made with the SEC and the public securities exchanges. The Williams Act is vague when it comes to defining what constitutes a material change. It is generally acceptable to file within 10 days of the material change.

Section 14(d)

Although Section 14(d) applies to public tender offers only, it applies to acquisitions of any size. The 5% notification threshold also applies.

Obligations of the Acquirer

An acquiring firm must disclose its intentions, business plans, and any agreements between the acquirer and the target firm in a Schedule 14D-1. The schedule is called a *tender offer statement*. The commencement date of the tender offer is defined as the date on which the tender offer is published, advertised, or submitted to the target.

Schedule 14D-1 must contain the identity of the target company and the type of securities involved; the identity of the person, partnership, syndicate, or corporation that is filing; and any past contracts between the bidder and the target company. The schedule also must include the source of the funds used to finance the tender offer, its purpose, and any other information material to the transaction.

Obligations of the Target Firm

The management of the target company cannot advise its shareholders how to respond to a tender offer until it has filed a Schedule 14D-9 with the SEC within 10 days after the tender offer's commencement date. This schedule is called a *tender offer solicitation/recommendation statement*. Target management is limited to telling its shareholders to defer responding to the tender offer until it has completed its consideration of the offer. The target also must send copies of the Schedule 14D-9 to each of the public exchanges on which its stock is traded.

Shareholder Rights: 14(d) (4)–(7)

The tender offer must be left open for a minimum of 20 trading days. The acquiring firm must accept all shares that are tendered during this period. The firm making the tender offer may get an extension of the 20-day period if it believes that there is a better chance of getting the shares it needs. The firm must purchase the shares tendered at the offer price, at least on a pro rata basis, unless the firm does not receive the total number of shares it requested under the tender offer. The tender offer also may be contingent on attaining the approval of such regulatory agencies as the Department of Justice (DoJ) and the FTC. Shareholders have the right to withdraw shares that they may have tendered previously. They may withdraw their shares at any time during which the tender offer remains open. The law also requires that when a new bid for the target is made from another party, the target firm's shareholders must have an additional 10 days to consider the bid.

INSIDER TRADING LAWS

Insider trading involves individuals buying or selling securities based on knowledge not available to the general public. Historically, insider trading has been covered under the Securities and Exchange Act of 1934. Section 16(a) of the Act defines insiders as corporate officers, directors, and any person owning 10% or more of any class of securities of a company. This section also requires that insiders must report to the SEC all transactions involving their purchase or sale of the firm's stock on a monthly basis. Section 16(b) of the Act provides that the corporation or any of its security holders may file suit against an insider to force the return of alleged profits from illicit trading activities to the corporation with respect to transactions completed within the preceding 6 months.

The SEC is responsible for investigating insider trading. Regulation 10b-5 issued by the SEC under powers granted by the 1934 Securities and Exchange Act prohibits the commission of fraud in relation to securities transactions. In addition, regulation 14e-3 prohibits trading securities in connection to a tender offer based on information not available to the general public. According to the Insider Trading Sanctions Act of 1984, those convicted of engaging in insider trading are required to give back their illegal profits, and they also are required to pay a penalty three times the magnitude of such profits. A 1988 U.S. Supreme Court ruling gives investors the right to claim damages from a firm that falsely denied it was involved in negotiations that subsequently resulted in a merger. The Supreme Court argued that such denials are misleading and provide the basis for investors who sold stock during the period of negotiations to be compensated for profits they would have earned had they held the stock until the merger was announced to the public.

ANTITRUST LAWS

Federal antitrust laws exist to prevent individual corporations from assuming too much market power such that they can limit their output and raise prices without concern for any significant competitor reaction. The DoJ and the FTC have the primary responsibility for enforcing federal antitrust laws. The FTC was established in the Federal Trade Commission Act of 1914 with the specific purpose of enforcing antitrust laws such as the Sherman, Clayton, and Federal Trade Commission Acts.

The attitude of the government regulatory agencies has changed dramatically over the years. After a short period of relative activism in the early 1960s under Robert Kennedy's Department of Justice, the goals of government antitrust policy and business seemed to become increasingly aligned. Under Lyndon Johnson, the federal government adopted a conciliatory government policy, noting that a merger should not be attacked simply because the companies were large. During the administrations of Ronald Reagan (1981–1988) and George Bush (1989–1992), antitrust challenges to M&As were relatively infrequent, as regulators assumed a more pro-free-market stance. In short, during the 1980s and early 1990s, antitrust regulators tended not to intercede as long as a proposed combination tended to enhance efficiency and promote innovation (Champlin and Knoedler, 1999).

During the second half of the 1990s, the pendulum shifted once again to a somewhat more aggressive enforcement of antitrust laws. This shift is illustrated by the federal government's blocking of Microsoft's attempted acquisition of Intuit in 1995, Rite Aid's proposal to purchase Revco in 1996, the Office Depot and Staples merger in 1997, and MCI WorldCom's attempt to purchase Sprint in 2000.

Although it is true that some notable mergers were disallowed, more than $2 trillion in M&A activity was allowed to take place in 2000 alone. The election of George W. Bush in 2001 may resurrect the less activist antitrust policy reminiscent of the 1980s. As illustrated by the concerns expressed during their review of the AOL Time Warner merger in 2000, antitrust regulators during the Clinton years were acutely concerned about the potential for mergers to create future monopolies. Whereas Timothy Muris, the current FTC chair, has called for continuity in antitrust policy, the George W. Bush administration seems to view the "new economy" as posing unique competitive problems. This administration's actions, particularly its early termination of the Microsoft antitrust case, suggest that it will be more cautious in taking action because of the extreme difficulty in projecting future changes in competitive conditions (see Muris, 2001). For excellent discussions of antitrust law, see the DoJ (www.usdoj.gov) and FTC (www.ftc.gov) Websites, Gaughan (1999), and Ton and Lipsky (1992).

SHERMAN ACT

Passed in 1890, the Sherman Act makes illegal all contracts, combinations, and conspiracies that "unreasonably" restrain trade (U.S. Department of Justice, 1999). Examples include agreements to fix prices, rig bids, allocate customers among competitors, or monopolize any part of interstate commerce. Section I of the Sherman Act prohibits new business combinations that result in monopolies or in a significant concentration of pricing power in a single firm. Section II applies to firms that already are dominant in their targeted markets. The Sherman Act remains the most important source of antitrust law today. The Act defines broad conditions and remedies for such firms that are deemed to be in violation of current antitrust laws.

The Act applies to all transactions and businesses involved in interstate commerce or, if the activities are local, all transactions and business "affecting" interstate commerce. The latter phrase has been interpreted to allow broad application of the Sherman Act. Most states have comparable statutes prohibiting monopolistic conduct, price-fixing agreements, and other acts in restraint of trade having strictly local impact. The sheer breadth of the Act underscores Congress's intent to cover all types of anticompetitive activities. However, the breadth of the wording of the Act reduced its effectiveness because it stated that all contracts that restrained trade were illegal. This implies that virtually all contracts are illegal. Historically, courts have had substantial difficulty in enforcing this part of the law.

CLAYTON ACT

Passed in 1914 to strengthen the Sherman Act, the Clayton Act created the FTC to regulate the actions of businesses. Section 5 of the Act made price discrimination between customers illegal unless it could be justified by cost savings associated with bulk purchases. Tying of contracts—in which a firm refused to sell certain important products to a customer unless the customer agreed to buy other products from the firm—also was prohibited. Under Section 7 of the Act, it is illegal for one company to purchase the stock of another company if their combination results in reduced competition within the industry. Interlocking directorates also were made illegal when the directors were on the boards of competing firms.

Unlike the Sherman Act, which contains criminal penalties, the Clayton Act is a civil statute. The Clayton Act allows private parties injured by the antitrust violation to sue in federal court for three times their actual damages. State attorneys general also may bring civil suits. If the plaintiff wins, costs must be borne by the party violating prevailing antitrust law, in addition to the criminal penalties imposed under the Sherman Act.

Acquirers soon learned how to circumvent the original statutes of the Clayton Act of 1914, which applied to the purchase of stock. They simply would acquire the assets, rather than the stock, of a target firm. In the Celler–Kefauver Act of 1950, the Clayton Act was amended to give the FTC the power to prohibit asset as well as stock purchases. The FTC also may block mergers if it believes that the combination will result in increased market concentration (i.e., fewer firms having increased market shares) as measured by the sales of the largest firms.

HART–SCOTT–RODINO ANTITRUST
IMPROVEMENTS ACT OF 1976

Acquisitions involving companies of a certain size cannot be completed until certain information is supplied to the federal government and until a specified waiting period has elapsed. The premerger notification allows the FTC and the DoJ sufficient time to challenge acquisitions believed to be anticompetitive before they are completed. Once the merger has taken place, it is often exceedingly difficult to break it up. See Table 2-2 for a summary of prenotification filing requirements.

Before the Hart–Scott–Rodino Act (HSR), antitrust actions usually were taken after a merger was completed. In some cases, the combined firms had been operating for several years before a court ruling was made. This made it politically unpopular to "de-merge" the combined firms because of the potential deleterious impact on employees, communities, customers, suppliers, and shareholders. Thus, HSR strengthened the regulatory powers of the DoJ and FTC by requiring approval before a merger could take place.

TABLE 2-2 Summary of Regulatory Prenotification Filing Requirements

	Williams Act	Hart–Scott–Rodino (HSR) Act
Required filing	1. Schedule 13D within 10 days of acquiring 5% stock ownership in another firm 2. Ownership includes stock held by affiliates or agents of bidder 3. Schedule 14D-1 for tender offers 4. Disclosure required even if 5% accumulation not followed by a tender offer	HSR filing IS necessary when: 1. One firm has assets >$50 million or 2. A firm has assets of <$10 million but a purchase price of >$200 million
File with whom	**Schedule 13D** 1. 6 copies to SEC 2. 1 copy via registered mail to target's executive office 3. 1 copy via registered mail to each public exchange on which target stock traded **Schedule 14D-1** 1. 10 copies to SEC 2. 1 copy hand delivered to target's executive offices 3. 1 copy hand delivered to other bidders 4. 1 copy mailed to each public exchange on which target stock traded (each exchange also must be phoned)	1. Pre-Merger Notification Office of the Federal Trade Commission 2. Director of Operations of the DoJ Antitrust Division
Time period	1. Tender offers must stay open a minimum of 20 business days 2. Begins on date of publication, advertisement, or submission of materials to target	1. Review/waiting period: 30 days 2. Target must file within 15 days of bidder's filing 3. Period begins for all cash offer when bidder files; for cash/stock bids, period begins when both bidder and target have filed 4. Regulators can request 20-day extension

Title I: What Must Be Filed?

Title I of the Act gives the DoJ the power to request internal corporate records if it suspects potential antitrust violations. In some cases, the requests for information result in truckloads of information being delivered to the regulatory authorities because of the extensive nature of the prenotification form. The information requirements include background information on the "ultimate parent" of the acquiring and target parents, a description of the transaction, and all background studies relating to the transaction. The "ultimate parent" will be the corporation that is at the top of the chain of ownership if the actual buyer is a subsidiary. In addition, the reporting firm must supply detailed product line breakdowns, a listing of competitors, and an analysis of sales trends.

By receiving background studies relating to the proposed transaction, the government is gaining access to such information as internal memoranda describing the deal. In Microsoft's proposed acquisition of Intuit in 1994, the DoJ uncovered several communications, including one in which Intuit's CEO, Scott Wood, noted that the transaction would leave financial institutions "with one clear option" for financial software and would eliminate a "bloody (market) share war." In another communication, a Microsoft executive noted that "as a combination [Microsoft and Intuit] would be dominant" (Wasserstein, 1998, p. 758). Such information was used by the DoJ to eventually block the proposed acquisition on the grounds that the combined companies would have too much market power in the personal financial software market.

Title II: Who Must File and When?

Title II defines the length of the premerger notification period. On February 1, 2001, this section of HSR was amended by Congress to extend the amount of time regulators have to review submitted documents from 20 days to 30 days. The amendment also increased the minimum asset threshold that requires filing from $15 million to $50 million. The minimum threshold will be adjusted upward by the annual rate of increase in gross domestic product. If the target firm has assets of less than $10 million but a purchase price of greater than $200 million, the transaction must be reported.

Bidding firms must execute a HSR filing at the same time as they make an offer to a target firm. The target firm also is required to file within 15 days following the bidder's filing. Filings consist of information on the operations of the two companies and their financial statements. The required forms also request any information on internal documents, such as the estimated market share of the combined companies made before the offer being made. Consequently, any such analyses should be undertaken with the understanding that the information ultimately will be shared with the antitrust regulatory authorities.

If the regulatory authorities suspect anticompetitive effects, they will file a lawsuit to block completion of the proposed transaction. Although it is rare that either the bidder or the target contest the lawsuit because of the expense involved, it does happen (see Case Study 2-1). If fully litigated, a government lawsuit can result in substantial legal expenses as well as a significant use of management time and attention. Even if the FTC's lawsuit is ultimately overturned, the perceived benefits of the merger often have disappeared by the time the lawsuit has been decided. This is especially true in the fast-changing environment of high-technology businesses. Nevertheless, both the combining companies and the regulatory authorities may choose to file lawsuits as part of the negotiation process.

CASE STUDY 2-1: BP AMOCO AND ARCO
VOW TO CONTEST THE FTC'S RULING

Reflecting their concern about the effect on gasoline prices on the West Coast, the FTC commissioners rejected on February 3, 2000, the merger of BP Amoco and Atlantic Richfield Corporation (Arco) and directed its staff to file a court injunction to block the proposed $30 billion transaction. If it had been allowed, the combination would have resulted in the second largest non-government-owned oil company at the time, behind Exxon Mobil, whose merger had been approved by the FTC in November 1999.

The primary concern of the Commission is that the combined companies would have too much control over Alaskan oil production. BP Amoco and Arco together account for 70% of the oil on Alaska's North Slope. That accounts for 45% of the oil refined in California, Oregon, and Washington. The FTC's staff recommended against the proposed acquisition in December 1999, suggesting that the combination would lead to higher gasoline prices on the West Coast. This allegation had been strongly denied by BP Amoco and Arco. During negotiations with the FTC, BP Amoco sought to allay antitrust concerns by agreeing to reduce its North Slope production by 13% by selling interests in the oil fields. However, these concessions were not enough for the FTC, which noted that even with the sales, BP Amoco and Arco still would control 55% of Alaska's oil production. Despite FTC opposition, BP Amoco decided to proceed with the merger. Although a settlement was possible, the prognosis in early February was for a lengthy court battle.

The rejection of this highly visible merger seemed to represent the introduction of a more stringent application of current antitrust laws. Comments made by Robert Pitofsky, chair of the FTC at that time, suggested as much. On February 18, 2000, Pitofsky stated in a speech before international antitrust lawyers that the agency's reviews of mergers and acquisitions are going to be more rigorous than in the past. In particular, Pitofsky noted that, "We (the agency) have seen more frequent proposals that are so extensive and complex that it is impossible to predict with any confidence that competition will be restored and consumer welfare will be protected." The harsher stance was being taken for two reasons. First, deals are currently more strategic in nature and are capable of changing the competitive landscape. Second, regulators now believe that despite efforts to require companies to sell off operations to protect competition, it often does not work that way. Currently, the FTC reviews about 4% of all mergers and acquisitions and challenges about 2%.

By March 2000, the posturing by both sides seemed to have resulted in substantial progress toward receiving regulatory approval. Both sides assumed a more conciliatory position following further action taken by BP Amoco and Arco. The FTC voted to approve the proposed merger between

Arco and BP Amoco following the announcement of the pending sale of Arco's Alaskan operations to Phillips Petroleum. This would bring the amount of oil on the North Slope of Alaska controlled by the combined companies to less than 50%. However, the completion of the transaction was still dependent on BP Amoco reaching some accommodation with Exxon Mobil, which claimed to have a right of first refusal to purchase the Arco reserves in Alaska. By late April 2000, this issue was resolved and the transaction was completed.

Case Study Discussion Questions

1. Why were the antitrust authorities so focused on the market share of the combined businesses? What other factors should they have considered? Explain your answer.
2. Why did Pitofsky state that the business combinations today are becoming increasingly complex?
3. The FTC reviews and challenges only a small percentage of all mergers. Do you believe they can be effective in ensuring that markets remain competitive? Why or why not?

The waiting period begins when both the acquirer and target have filed. Either the FTC or the DoJ may request a 20-day extension of the waiting period for transactions involving securities and 10 days for cash tender offers. If the acquiring firm believes that there is little likelihood of anticompetitive effects, it can request early termination. However, the decision is entirely at the discretion of the regulatory agencies.

How Does HSR Affect State Antitrust Regulators?

Title III expands the powers of state attorneys general to initiate triple damage suits on behalf of individuals in their states injured by violations of the antitrust laws. This additional authority gives states the incentive to file such suits to increase state revenues.

PROCEDURAL RULES

When the DoJ files an antitrust suit, it is adjudicated in the federal court system. When the FTC initiates the action, it is heard before an administrative law judge at the FTC. The results of the hearing are subject to review by the commissioners of the FTC. Criminal actions are reserved for the DoJ, which may seek fines or imprisonment for violators. Individuals and companies also may file antitrust lawsuits. The FTC reviews complaints that have been recommended by its staff and approved by the Commission. Each complaint is reviewed by one of the FTC's hearing examiners. The Commission as a whole then votes whether to accept or reject the hearing examiner's findings. The decision of the Commission then can be appealed in the federal circuit courts.

Historically, once the FTC files a challenge, it has taken years to work through the Commission's review process from complaint to final commission ruling. In 1999 the FTC implemented new "fast-track" guidelines that commit the FTC to making a final decision on a complaint within 13 months. The 12-month resolution of the challenge of the $81 billion Exxon-Mobil merger suggests that the new guidelines may be working.

As an alternative to litigation, a company may seek to negotiate a voluntary settlement of its differences with the FTC. Such settlements usually are negotiated during the review process and are called ***consent decrees***. The FTC then files a complaint in the federal court along with the proposed consent decree. The federal court judge routinely approves the consent decree.

THE CONSENT DECREE

A typical consent decree requires the merging parties to divest overlapping businesses or to restrict anticompetitive practices. If a potential acquisition is likely to be challenged by the regulatory authorities, an acquirer may seek to negotiate a consent decree in advance of consummating the deal. In the absence of a consent decree, a buyer often requires that an agreement of purchase and sale includes a provision that allows the acquirer to back out of the transaction if it is challenged by the FTC or the DoJ on antitrust grounds.

In a report evaluating the results of 35 divestiture orders entered between 1990 and 1994, the FTC concluded that the use of consent decrees to limit market power resulting from a business combination has proven to be successful (Federal Trade Commission, 1999). Most divestitures have created viable competitors in the markets that the FTC felt were most likely to be affected. The study also found that the success of the divestiture is more likely with the divestiture of an ongoing business than with the divestiture of a single product line or proprietary technology. Moreover, the divestiture is also likely to be more successful if it is made to a firm in a related business rather than a new entrant into the business. (see Case Study 2-2.)

CASE STUDY 2-2: JUSTICE DEPARTMENT REQUIRES ALLIEDSIGNAL AND HONEYWELL TO DIVEST OVERLAPPING BUSINESSES

AlliedSignal Inc. and Honeywell Inc. were ordered to divest significant portions of their avionics—airplane electronics systems—businesses in 1999 to resolve the Justice Department's competitive concerns involving their proposed $16 billion merger. Both companies are major providers of avionics and other advanced technology products to a broad range of commercial, space, and U.S. defense customers. The DoJ concluded that the transaction as originally proposed would have been anticompetitive, resulting in higher prices and lower quality for these products.

The department's Antitrust Division filed a lawsuit and proposed a consent decree in U.S. District Court in Washington, DC. The consent decree, if approved by the Court, would resolve the issue. According to the complaint, the proposed merger would have substantially lessened competition in four product areas: traffic alert and collision avoidance systems, search and surveillance weather radar, reaction and momentum wheels, and inertial systems. In each of these product areas, the merger would leave at most two or three major competitors. Consequently, the DoJ alleged that these competitors would have been able to coordinate their pricing and more easily increase prices for customers.

Under the consent decree, AlliedSignal divested its search and surveillance weather radar business in Olathe, Kansas; its space and navigation business in Teterboro, New Jersey; its MRG business in Cheshire, Connecticut, and a related repair business in Newark, Ohio; and its MEMs business in Redmond, Washington, and related MEMs licenses. Also, Honeywell divested its traffic alert and collision avoidance systems business located in Glendale, Arizona.

Case Study Discussion Questions

1. Do you believe consent decrees involving the acquiring firm to dispose of certain target company assets is an abuse of government power? Why or why not?
2. What alternative actions could the government take to limit market power resulting from business combination?
3. Should the government be concerned about such factors as job loss and disruption to communities that may result from the merger if the merger is expected to result in improved overall efficiency for the combined firms? Why or why not?

ANTITRUST MERGER GUIDELINES
FOR HORIZONTAL MERGERS

Understanding an industry begins with understanding its market structure. Market structure may be defined in terms of the number of firms in an industry; their concentration, cost, demand, and technological conditions; and ease of entry and exit. The size of individual competitors does not tell one much about the competitive dynamics of an industry. Some industries give rise to larger firms than do other industries because of the importance of economies of scale or huge capital and research and development requirements. For example, although Boeing and Airbus dominate the commercial airframe industry, the nature of industry rivalry is intense.

Beginning in 1968, the DoJ issued guidelines indicating the types of M&As the government would oppose. Intended to clarify the provisions of the Sherman and Clayton Acts, the largely quantitative guidelines were presented in terms of specific market share percentages and concentration ratios. Concentration ratios were defined in terms of the market shares of the industry's top four or eight firms. Because of their initial rigidity, the guidelines have been revised over the years to reflect the role of both quantitative and qualitative data. Qualitative data include factors such as the enhanced efficiency that might result from a combination of firms, the financial viability of potential merger candidates, and the ability of U.S. firms to compete globally. In 1992, both the FTC and the DoJ announced a new set of guidelines indicating that they would challenge mergers creating or enhancing market power, even if there are measurable efficiency benefits. Market power is defined as a situation in which the combined firms will be able to profitably maintain prices above competitive levels for a significant period. M&As that do not increase market power are acceptable. The 1992 guidelines were revised in 1997 to reflect the regulatory authorities' willingness to recognize that improvements in efficiency over the long term could more than offset the effects of increases in market power. Consequently, a combination of firms, which enhances market power, would be acceptable to the regulatory authorities if it could be shown that the increase in efficiency resulting from the combination more than offsets the increase in market power.

In general, horizontal mergers, those between current or potential competitors, are most likely to be challenged by regulators. Vertical mergers or customer–supplier mergers are considered much less likely to result in anticompetitive effects, unless they deprive other market participants of access to an important resource. The antitrust regulators seldom contest conglomerate mergers involving the combination of dissimilar products into a single firm.

The 1992 guidelines describe the process the antitrust authorities go through to make their decisions. This process falls into five discrete steps.

Step 1: Market Definition, Measurement, and Concentration

Although a number of factors are examined to determine if a proposed transaction will result in a violation of law, calculating the respective market shares of the combining companies and the degree of industry concentration in terms of the number of competitors is the starting point for any investigation.

Defining the Market

Regulators generally define a market as a product or group of products offered in a specific geographic area. Market participants are those currently producing and selling these products in this geographic area as well as potential entrants. Regulators calculate market shares for all firms or plants identified as market participants based on total sales or capacity currently devoted to the relevant markets. In addition, the market share estimates include capacity that is likely to be diverted to this market in response to a small, but significant and sustainable, price increase.

In certain cases, the regulatory agencies have chosen to segment a market more narrowly by size or type of competitor. This is the approach adopted in the FTC's investigation of Staple's acquisition of Office Depot (Case Study 2-3).

CASE STUDY 2-3: FTC PREVENTS STAPLES FROM ACQUIRING OFFICE DEPOT

As the leading competitor in the office supplies superstore market, Staples' proposed $3.3 billion acquisition of Office Depot received close scrutiny from the FTC immediately after its announcement in September 1996. The acquisition would create a huge company with annual sales of $10.7 billion. Following the acquisition, only one competitor, OfficeMax with sales of $3.3 billion, would remain. The Commission requested documents to determine whether superstores lower prices in cities where they compete with other superstores.

Staples pointed out that the combined companies would comprise only about 5% of the total office supply market. However, the FTC considered the superstore market as a separate segment within the total office supply market. Using the narrow definition of "market," the FTC concluded that the combination of Staples and Office Depot would control more than three-quarters of the market and would substantially increase the pricing power of the combined firms. Despite Staples' willingness to divest 63 stores to Office Max in markets in which its concentration would be the greatest following the merger, the FTC could not be persuaded to approve the merger.

Staples continued its insistence that there would be no harmful competitive effects from the proposed merger because office supply prices would continue their long-term decline. Both Staples and Office Depot had a history of lowering prices for their customers because the efficiencies associated with their "superstores." The companies argued that the merger would result in more than $4 billion in cost savings over 5 years that would be passed on to their customers. However, the FTC argued and the federal court concurred that the product prices offered by the combined firms still would be higher, as a result of reduced competition, than they would have been had the merger not taken place. The FTC relied on a study showing that Staples tended to charge higher prices in markets in which it did not have another superstore as a competitor. In early 1997, Staples withdrew its offer for Office Depot.

Case Study Discussion Questions

1. How important is properly defining the market segment in which the acquirer and target companies compete to determining the potential increased market power if the two are permitted to combine? Explain your answer.

> 2. Why do you believe that the FTC would not approve the merger even though Staples agreed to divest 63 stores in which market concentration would be the greatest following the merger?

Determining Market Concentration

The number of firms in the market and their respective market shares determine market concentration (i.e., the extent to which a single or a few firms control a disproportionate share of the total market). Concentration ratios are an incomplete measure of industry concentration. Such ratios measure how much of the total output of an industry is produced by the "n" largest firms in the industry. The shortcomings of this approach include the frequent inability to define accurately what constitutes an industry, the failure to reflect ease of entry or exit, foreign competition, regional competition, and the distribution of firm size.

In an effort to account for the distribution of firm size in an industry, the FTC measures concentration by using the *Herfindahl-Hirschman Index* (HHI), which is calculated by summing the squares of the market shares for each firm competing in the market. For example, a market consisting of five firms with market shares of 30%, 25%, 20%, 15%, and 10% would have an HHI of 2250 ($30^2 + 25^2 + 20^2 + 15^2 + 10^2$). Note that an industry consisting of five competitors with market shares of 70%, 10%, 5%, 5%, and 5% will have a much higher HHI score of 5075 because the process of squaring the market shares gives the greatest weight to the firm with the largest market shares. The HHI measure takes into consideration all firms in the industry and is considered more complete than traditional concentration ratios.

Likely FTC Actions Based on the Herfindahl–Hirschman Index

The HHI ranges from 10,000 for an almost pure monopoly to approximately zero in the case of a highly competitive market. The index gives proportionately more weight to the market shares of larger firms to reflect their relatively greater market power. The FTC has developed a scoring system, described in Figure 2-1, which is used as one factor in determining whether the FTC will challenge a proposed merger or acquisition.

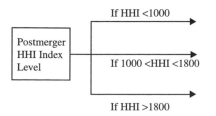

FIGURE 2-1.   Federal Trade Commission (FTC) actions at various market share concentration levels. HHI, Herfinahl-Hirschman Index. (From FTC Merger Guidelines, www.ftc.gov.)

Step 2: Potential Adverse Competitive Effects of Mergers

Market share and concentration data alone do not provide a complete picture of the ability of a single firm, or a small group of firms, to exercise market power. Market concentration and market share data are based on historical data. Consequently, changing market conditions may overstate the significance of market share. Suppose a new technology that is important to the long-term competitive viability of the firms within a market has been licensed to other firms within the market but not to the firm with the largest market share. Regulators may conclude that market share information overstates the potential for an increase in the market power of the firm with the largest market share. Therefore, before deciding to challenge a proposed transaction, regulators will consider factors other than simply market share and concentration to determine if a proposed merger will have "adverse competitive effects." These other factors include evidence of coordinated interaction, differentiated products, and similarity of substitute products.

Coordinated Interaction

Regulators consider the extent to which a small group of firms may exercise market power collectively by cooperating in restricting output or setting prices. Tacit collusion is not necessarily illegal unless competitors have the ability to detect and to punish firms deviating from agreed on competitive practices. Collusion may take the form of firms agreeing to follow simple guidelines such as maintaining common prices, fixed price differentials, stable market shares, or customer or territorial restrictions.

Where detection and punishment is likely to be easy, individual firms have few incentives to deviate from coordinated practices. Consequently, regulators are interested in understanding the extent to which key information, such as output levels, individual transactions, and selling prices for individual firms, is readily available to other competitors. If such information is not readily available, it may be difficult to detect deviations from collusive practices, allowing "cheating" to continue. Under this scenario, regulators are likely to be less concerned about the potential for collusion resulting from a merger or acquisition.

Differentiated Products

In some markets the products are differentiated in the eyes of the consumer. Consequently, products sold by different firms in the market are not good substitutes for one another. A merger between firms in a market for differentiated products may diminish competition by enabling the merged firms to profit by raising the price of one or both products above premerger levels.

Similarity of Substitutes

Market concentration may be increased if the merger of two firms whose products are viewed by customers as equally desirable merge. In this instance, market share may understate the anticompetitive impact of the merger if the products of the merging firms are more similar in their various attributes to one another than to other products in the relevant market. In contrast, market share may overstate the perceived undesirable competitive effects when the relevant products are less similar in their attributes to one another than to other products in the relevant market.

Step 3: Entry Analysis

The ease of entry into the market by new competitors is considered a very important factor in determining if a proposed business combination is anticompetitive. Ease of entry is defined as entry that would be timely, likely to occur, and sufficient to counter the competitive effects of a combination of firms that temporarily increases market concentration. Barriers to entry—such as proprietary technology or knowledge, patents, government regulations, exclusive ownership of natural resources, or huge investment requirements—can serve to limit the number of new competitors and the pace at which they enter a market. In such instances, a regulatory agency may rule that a proposed transaction will reduce competitiveness. In contrast, an acquisition may not be considered anticompetitive if new firms can enter relatively easily in response to higher product or service prices. Ease of entry appears to have been a factor in the DoJ's assessment of Microsoft's proposal to acquire Intuit (Case Study 2-4).

CASE STUDY 2-4:
JUSTICE DEPARTMENT BLOCKS
MICROSOFT'S ACQUISITION OF INTUIT

In 1994 Bill Gates saw dominance of the personal financial software market as a means of becoming a central player in the global financial system. Critics argued that, by dominating the point of access (the individual personal computer) to online banking, Microsoft believed that it may be possible to receive a small share of the value of each of the billions of future personal banking transactions once online banking became the norm (Radigan, 1994). With a similar goal in mind, Intuit was trying to have its widely used financial software package, Quicken, incorporated into the financial standards of the global banking system. In 1994 Intuit had acquired the National Payment Clearinghouse Inc., an electronic bill payments system integrator, to help the company develop a sophisticated payments system. By 1995 Intuit had sold more than 7 million copies of Quicken and had about 300,000 bank customers using Quicken to pay bills electronically.

Efforts by Microsoft to penetrate the personal financial software market with its own product, Money, were lagging badly. Intuit's product, Quicken, had a commanding market share of 70% compared to Microsoft's 30%. Intuit's success reflected both a product that was easier to use and a series of alliances with financial services firms.

In 1994 Microsoft made a $1.5 billion offer for Intuit. Eventually, it would increase its offer to $2 billion. To appease its critics, it offered to sell its Money product to Novell Corporation. Almost immediately, the Justice Department challenged the merger, citing its concern about the anticompetitive effects on the personal financial software market. Specifically, the Justice Department argued that, if consummated, the proposed transaction would add to the dominance of the number-one product Quicken, weaken the number two-product (Money), and substantially increase concentration and reduce competition in the personal finance/checkbook software market (Talmor, 1995). Moreover, the DoJ argued that there would be few new entrants because competition with the new Quicken would be even more difficult and expensive. The DoJ also noted that H&R Block had decided to exit the market because of the planned merger of Microsoft and Intuit by selling its finance software subsidiary, Meca Software, to Bank of America and NationsBank in May 1995.

Critics saw the sale of Microsoft's Money software to Novell as a ploy to distract the regulatory authorities. Further fueling the critics' ire were Microsoft's plans to introduce its new Microsoft Network (MSN). Critics believed that Microsoft's control over the personal computer desktop would be strengthened if Quicken were integrated into the Windows 95 software and the new online MSN service. This integration would provide consumers with a gateway to a host of financial and nonfinancial services (Bers, 1995).

Microsoft and its supporters argued that government interference would cripple Microsoft's ability to innovate and limit its role in promoting standards that advance the whole software industry. Only a Microsoft–Intuit merger could create the critical mass needed to advance home banking (Sraeel, 1995).

On May 20, 1995, Microsoft announced that it was discontinuing efforts to acquire Intuit. It said it wanted to avoid a protracted and expensive court battle with the Justice Department.

Case Study Discussion Questions

1. Explain how Microsoft's acquisition of Intuit might limit the entry of new competitors into the financial software market.
2. How might the proliferation of Internet usage in the twenty-first century change your answer to question 1?
3. Do you believe that the FTC might approve of Microsoft acquiring Intuit today? Why or why not?

Step 4: Efficiencies

Increases in efficiency that result from a merger or acquisition can enhance the combined firms' ability to compete and result in lower prices, improved quality, better service, or new products. However, efficiencies are difficult to measure and to verify because they will be realized only after the merger has taken place. Efficiencies are most likely to make a difference in the FTC's decision to challenge when the likely effects of market concentration are not considered significant. An example of verifiable efficiency improvements would be a reduction in the average fixed cost of production due to economies of scale.

Step 5: Alternative to Imminent Failure

Regulators also take into account the likelihood that a firm would fail and exit a market if it is not allowed to merge with another firm. The regulators must weigh the potential cost of the failing firm, such as a loss of jobs, against any potential increase in market power that might result from the merger of the two firms. The failing firm must be able to demonstrate that it is unable to meet its financial obligations, that it would be unable to successfully reorganize under the protection of the U.S. bankruptcy court, and that it has been unsuccessful in its good-faith efforts to find other potential merger partners.

ANTITRUST GUIDELINES FOR VERTICAL MERGERS

The guidelines described for horizontal mergers also apply to vertical mergers between customers and suppliers. Vertical mergers may become a concern if an acquisition by a supplier of a customer prevents the supplier's competitors from having access to the customer. Regulators are not likely to challenge this type of merger unless the relevant market has few customers and as such is highly concentrated (i.e., an HHI score in excess of 1800). Alternatively, the acquisition by a customer of a supplier could become a concern if it prevents the customer's competitors from having access to the supplier. The concern is greatest if the supplier's products or services are critical to the competitor's operations (Case Study 2-5).

CASE STUDY 2-5: JDS UNIPHASE ACQUIRES SDL—WHAT A DIFFERENCE 7 MONTHS MAKES!

What started out as the biggest technology merger in history saw its value plummet in line with the declining stock market, a weakening economy, and concerns about the cash-flow impact of actions the acquirer would have to take to gain regulatory approval. The $41 billion mega-merger, proposed on July 10, 2000, consisted of JDS Uniphase (JDSU) offering 3.8 shares of its stock for each share of SDL's outstanding stock (SDL Press Release, July 10, 2000). The challenge facing JDSU was to get Department of Justice approval of a merger that some feared would result in a supplier (i.e., JDS Uniphase/SDL) that could exercise enormous pricing power over the entire range of products from raw components to packaged products purchased by equipment manufacturers. The resulting regulatory review lengthened the period between the signing of the merger agreement by the two companies and the actual closing to 7 months.

The Participants: JDS Uniphase and SDL

Through an incredible series of 11 mergers and acquisitions totaling $18 billion since its formation in 1999, JDSU assembled the largest portfolio of optical components in the industry. In fact, JDSU is the product of a merger in mid-1999 between JDS FITEL and Uniphase Corporation. JDSU manufactures and distributes fiber-optic components and modules to telecommunication and cable systems providers worldwide. The company is the dominant supplier in its market for fiber-optic components. In 1999 the firm focused on making only certain subsystems needed in fiber-optic networks, but a flurry of acquisitions has enabled the company to offer complementary products. JDSU's strategy is to package entire systems into a single integrated unit, thereby reducing the number of vendors that fiber network firms must deal with when purchasing systems that produce the light that is transmitted over fiber (Hanks, November 2, 2000). SDL's products, including pump lasers, support the transmission of data, voice, video, and Internet information over fiber-optic networks by expanding their fiber-optic communications networks much more quickly and efficiently than would be possible using conventional electronic and optical technologies. Consequently, SDL fit the JDSU strategy perfectly.

As of July 10, 2000, JDSU had a market value of $74 billion. Annual 2000 revenues amounted to $1.43 billion. The firm had $800 million in cash and virtually no long-term debt. Including one-time merger-related charges, the firm recorded a loss of $905 million. With its price-to-earnings (excluding merger-related charges) ratio at a meteoric 440, the firm sought to use stock to acquire SDL, a strategy that it had used successfully since 1999.

Motivation for the Merger

The growth of the Internet has created an accelerating demand for bandwidth that is driving the construction of significantly more telecommunication network capacity. Telecommunication system providers are developing those network systems based on optical technologies that require advance components and modules with increasing levels of integration and complexity. JDSU believed that a merger with SDL would provide two major benefits. First, it would add a line of lasers to the JDSU product offering that strengthened signals beamed across fiber-optic networks. Second, it would bolster JDSU's capacity to package multiple components into a single product line.

Regulatory Concerns

Although few doubted the beneficial effects of the mergers on JDSU/SDL, regulators expressed concern that the combined entities could control the market for a specific type of laser (i.e., 980-nanometer wavelength pump lasers) used in a wide range of optical equipment. SDL is one of the largest suppliers of this type of laser, and JDS is one of the largest suppliers of the chips used to build them. Other manufacturers of pumped lasers, such as Nortel Networks, Lucent Technologies, and Corning, complained to regulators that they would have to buy some of the chips necessary to manufacture pump lasers from a supplier (i.e., JDSU), which in combination with SDL also would be a competitor. As required by the HSR Act of 1976, JDSU had filed with the U.S. DoJ seeking regulatory approval. On August 24, the firm received a request for additional information from the DoJ, which extended the HSR waiting period. Such a request was commonplace for mergers of this size involving new rapidly changing and important technologies.

JDS Uniphase Receives Regulatory Approval

On February 6, JDSU agreed as part of a consent decree to sell a Swiss subsidiary, which manufactures pump laser chips, to Nortel Networks Corporation, a JDSU customer, to satisfy DoJ concerns about the proposed merger. Canadian-based Nortel paid $2.5 billion in stock for the Swiss operation. Nortel agreed to pay another $500 million in Nortel common stock payable to the extent Nortel's future purchases from JDSU do not meet certain target levels (SDL Press Release, February 14, 2001). The divestiture of this operation set up an alternative supplier of such chips, thereby alleviating concerns expressed by other manufacturers of pump lasers that they would have to buy such components from a competitor. Following receipt of shareholder approval on February 12, 2001, the deal closed 2 days later. JDSU shares had fallen from their 12-month high of $153.42 to $53.19. SDL shares traded at $201.64. The deal that originally had been valued at $41 billion when first announced more than 7 months earlier had fallen to $13.5 billion on the day of closing, a staggering loss of more than two-thirds of its value.

Epilogue

Severe industry weakness from mid-2000 through late 2001 resulted in a dramatic erosion of JDSU's sales. Sales for the 3 months ending in June 31, 2001, were 35% below sales of $920 million for the quarter ended March 31, 2001, and 6% lower than sales for the quarter ended June 31, 2000. Despite aggressive cost-cutting efforts, the company reported a loss of $7.9 billion for the quarter ending June 31 and $50.6 billion for the 12 months ending June 31, 2001. The fiscal year loss included a reduction in the value of goodwill carried on the balance sheet of $38.7 billion to reflect the declining market value of assets purchased during a series of previous transactions. Most of this reduction was related to goodwill arising from the merger of JDS FITEL and Uniphase and the subsequent acquisitions of SDL, E-TEK, and OCLI (JDS Uniphase Press Release, July 27, 2001). (The reduction in goodwill resulting from the impairment of assets will be discussed further in Chapter 10.)

Case Study Discussion Questions

1. The JDS Uniphase/SDL merger proposal was somewhat unusual in that it represented a vertical rather than horizontal merger. Why does the FTC tend to focus primarily on horizontal rather than vertical mergers?
2. How can an extended regulatory approval process change the value of a proposed acquisition to the acquiring company?
3. Do you think that JDS Uniphase's competitors had legitimate concerns, or were they simply trying to use the antitrust regulatory process to prevent the firm from gaining a competitive advantage? Explain your answer.

ANTITRUST GUIDELINES FOR COLLABORATIVE EFFORTS

The formation of alliances or joint ventures (JVs) will generally not need approval of antitrust regulatory authorities in the United States if the combined strength of the partners does not infringe on a significant share of the global market for a specific product or service. Smaller companies not holding dominant shares will have little to be concerned about. Any efforts by alliance or JV partners to fix prices or geographically allocate customers or markets are likely to be considered illegal. Moreover, alliances cannot be used to deprive competitors of vital resources (Lynch, 1993).

The Role of Collaborative Arrangements in the U.S. Economy

The DoJ believes that alliances play a vital role in the growth of the U.S. economy. Consequently, the DoJ systematically has been removing regulatory obstacles. Such endeavors as collaborative research, even among major industry players, are being encouraged when the research is shared among all participants in the JV. The DoJ tends to favor project-oriented alliances. Even in very concentrated markets, the DoJ may be receptive to alliances if the partners in a horizontal alliance can show efficiency gains or that collaboration will result in new technologies. Purchaser–supplier alliances are treated in much the same way as vertical mergers and are generally not considered serious competitive threats.

Although the regulatory authorities often have viewed properly constructed alliances in a positive light during most of the 1980s and 1990s, they have been challenged a number of times as anticompetitive. These challenges occurred whenever alliances allegedly attempted to impose rules or standards in the marketplace that clearly tended to favor a single or a small number of competitors. In 1992 the

DoJ challenged Primestar, a JV consisting of cable companies intending to enter the direct broadcast satellite (DBS) industry. The JV included Time Warner, TCI, and other smaller cable companies. The DoJ claimed that the JV sought to delay the development of DBS by imposing rules on its members that discouraged them from providing programming to competing DBS companies. The case was settled with the elimination of the rules (*United States v. Primestar*, 1993). In the mid-1980s, similar concerns were raised when Visa and Mastercard created a single JV, known as Entree, to issue debit cards. A group of 13 state attorneys general challenged the formation of the JV, alleging that Visa and Mastercard intended to retard the development of an online debit payment system, which they believed would erode the profitability of credit cards. In 1990, Visa and Mastercard agreed to abandon the Entree JV. They have since created their own online debit card systems (*New York State v. Visa USA, Inc.*, 1990).

On October 1, 1999, the DoJ and the FTC circulated new guidelines to be applied to collaborative efforts among competitors such as JVs. JVs are unlikely to be challenged if they comprise less than 20% of the market in which they compete. Moreover, if the participants in the JV have incentives to compete against the JV, the JV will probably not be challenged.

The Limitations of Antitrust Laws

Efforts to measure market share or concentration inevitably must take into account the explosion of international trade during the last 20 years. Actions by a single domestic firm to restrict its output to raise its selling price may be thwarted by a surge in imports of similar products. Moreover, the pace of technological change is creating many new substitute products and services, which may make a firm's dominant position in a rapidly changing market indefensible almost overnight.

The Electronic Commerce Marketplace

The rapid growth of electronic commerce, as a marketplace without geographic boundaries, has tended to reduce the usefulness of conventional measures of market share and market concentration. What constitutes a market on the Internet is largely undefined. Marketers routinely refer to market segments on the Internet as "spaces" with largely undefined competitive boundaries. These ambiguities lead to challenges for regulators. Do anticompetitive practices arise when a single vendor such as Microsoft tends to dominate the PC desktop or when the preponderance of users enter the Internet through the same "portal" or access point such as America Online or Yahoo? When does control of electronic access to the home constitute a monopolistic practice?

Open-Access Issues

The FTC has expressed concern about the potential for anticompetitive practices on the Internet (Balto, 1999). Whereas medium-to-large-sized businesses have many ways to access the Internet, consumers are largely dependent on connecting to Internet service providers (ISPs). Because the technology is changing so rapidly, the FCC has chosen not to require owners of broadband systems to open access to everyone, preferring to let cable and telephone companies fight it out in the marketplace. The FCC has taken the position that high-speed cable access to the home does not constitute a monopoly because it competes with telephone companies' digital subscriber line (DSL) services as well as satellite delivery systems. On November 18, 1999, the FCC ruled that telephone companies must share their telephone lines into the home with DSL providers. This ruling should make DSL services more cost competitive with cable services. On December 7, 1999, AT&T, after months of resisting the notion of providing access to competing ISPs over its cable lines, took steps to make "open access" a part of its company policy. AT&T signed a deal with MindSpring to give its customers a choice between AT&T and MindSpring as their ISP.

ISPs are undergoing substantial consolidation. In the merger of MCI and World-Com, the DoJ, FCC, and the European Union (EU) alleged harm to competition. The consent decree settling the case required the divestiture of MCI's backbone infrastructure (WorldCom, 1998). The potential for increased concentration grew in late 1999 with MCI WorldCom's announcement of a merger with Sprint. In disallowing this merger in 2000, regulators at the FCC and DoJ were simply not convinced that the salutary effects of improved efficiency would lead to lower prices and more innovative products and offset the potentially anticompetitive effects of increasing concentration in the telecommunications industry (Case Study 2-6).

CASE STUDY 2-6: MCI WORLDCOM BLOCKED FROM ACQUIRING SPRINT

Background

On October 6, 1999, MCI WorldCom proposed to acquire Sprint in a stock-for-stock transaction valued at $115 billion, $129 billion including the assumption of debt. At this price, the merger would constitute the third largest transaction in history, behind Vodafone's acquisition of Mannesmann and AOL's takeover of Time Warner, and would provide Sprint's shareholders with a 50% premium over the market value of Sprint and its Sprint PCS business. Sprint's operations are divided into two separately traded stocks, one representing its long-distance network and the other its wireless operation. MCI increased the premium significantly from its first offer as a result of a series of competing bids for Sprint made by BellSouth.

The new company would have more than 40 million business and residential customers and 142,000 employees, as well as operations in

65 countries. The new company also would have revenue of $54 billion, compared with AT&T's $64 billion.

FCC Expresses Concern About Increasing Market Concentration

Within 1 day of the announcement, William Kennard, chair of the FCC, expressed concern that the proposed merger would not be good for consumers. He also said that the second and third largest long-distance telephone companies "would bear a heavy burden to show how consumers would be better off." The FCC was concerned particularly about the increased concentration in the long-distance market and in the Internet backbone (i.e., the telecommunications network access to the Internet).

With the loss of Sprint as a competitor, just two companies, AT&T and MCI WorldCom, would control 85% of the U.S. long-distance market. Qwest Communications, the third largest competitor, would control only 2% of the market. To approve the merger, the FCC considered requiring the companies to sell some portion of their Internet backbone capacity. Together, Sprint and MCI WorldCom currently control 43% of the access points to the Internet in the United States.

Increased Efficiencies Used to Justify the Proposed Merger

The companies argued that the economics of the combination are particularly compelling. Economies of scale and greater access to the capital markets could be expected to play a major role in reducing the combined firms' operating expenses. Operating synergies, primarily from consolidations, were expected to reach $9.7 billion. In addition, capital spending levels of the combined firms would be $5.2 billion less than if they remained separate. The combined companies would have the capital, marketing strength, and state-of-the-art networks to compete more effectively against both domestic and foreign carriers. The combined companies also would control about one-third of the U.S. long-distance market and offer wireless phone and paging services and access to the Internet.

The new company's strategy would be to provide customers, especially businesses, with the full range of telecommunication services including voice and data transmission, Internet access, and wireless and international calling. The new company would have access to more customers in more countries, and Sprint's wireless business would fill a hole in MCI WorldCom's strategy of offering its customers a full array of telecommunication services. Given its size, company officials believed that it would be able to effectively compete against AT&T, which controls about 45% of the long-distance market in the United States. Moreover, the new company would be in a better position to serve a larger market for its wireless and Internet products by bundling these services with its long-distance service.

Efficiency Loses Out to Market Share Concerns

After an intensive review, Attorney General Janet Reno announced that the Justice Department would block the proposed combination. Within days, WorldCom and Sprint's application for EU approval was rejected. U.S. regulators were concerned about increased concentration in the long-distance telephone market, whereas EU regulators concluded that the merger would sharply reduce competition for Internet connections.

The decision ultimately may have turned on how the regulators chose to define the market. U.S. regulators expressed alarm that the deal would put 80% of the long-distance market in the hands of two rivals, AT&T and WorldCom–Sprint. However, the decision was made just as the long-distance market was deteriorating. If the merger had been allowed, they indeed may have been able to cut costs in line with declining revenues. The decision by the regulators ignored the fact that AT&T's biggest competitive threat in the long-distance market no longer came from WorldCom and Sprint but rather from Verizon, SBC, and the wireless industry. Had these firms been included in the calculation of market share, WorldCom–Sprint would have had only 22% of the total U.S. telecommunications market. This example illustrates the importance of being able to properly define the market served by the firms that are seeking approval to combine.

Case Study Discussion Questions

1. How might economies of scale and increased access to capital markets have been used to justify the proposed merger of WorldCom and Sprint?
2. Should the emergence of alternative technologies such as satellite-based telecommunications systems have changed the FTC's position? Why or why not?
3. Comment on the ability of antitrust authorities to regulate effectively markets that are subject to rapidly changing competitive dynamics.

Promoting Innovation: The Microsoft Antitrust Case

The government's 1998 suit against Microsoft was based on its anticompetitive practices defined under the Sherman Antitrust Act of 1890. The suit was largely an effort to protect consumers by keeping prices down and promoting choice. In late 1999, Microsoft had been found guilty of anticompetitive practices. On April 28, 2000, the government submitted its proposed remedy to the federal courts. The proposal consisted of splitting the firm into operating systems and applications software companies in an effort to promote innovation as well as to encourage price competition and consumer choice.

The proposed remedy did not deal directly with Microsoft's dominance of the PC operating system market because the PC market does not represent the future of the computing industry. Rather, the proposed remedy reflected an effort to limit Microsoft's ability to dominate the server market, high-powered computers that run networks. At that time, Microsoft Exchange, the most popular e-mail program around, ran only on servers using Windows NT or its successors. Therefore, companies had to buy Windows server software if they wanted to deploy Exchange. Moreover, a number of features in the PC desktop version of Windows 2000 (e.g., automated back-ups) work only with servers operating on Windows NT. If Microsoft were split into two companies, it was assumed that the software applications business would have sufficient incentive to develop versions of Exchange and other Microsoft applications that would run on Linux, Sun Solaris, and IBM's Unix operating systems that directly compete with Windows NT.

But the proposal seemed to be based more on intuition than on empirical studies. According to the growth theories propounded by Paul Romer of Stanford University, a contributing author to the briefs supporting the government's case, innovation is the most important factor determining the well-being of consumers and the pace of innovation is highly responsive to incentives. Such incentives are much stronger in an economy characterized by competition than by monopoly. Small firms are more likely to innovate without fear of being overwhelmed by larger firms that choose to embrace and extend the smaller firms' new technological innovations. The presumed result is that consumers would receive new software more rapidly (*Business Week*, 2000). The implications of the increasing importance of innovation in antitrust enforcement are discussed in Case Study 2-7.

CASE STUDY 2-7: HOW THE MICROSOFT CASE COULD DEFINE ANTITRUST LAW IN THE "NEW ECONOMY"

Although the proposed remedy did not stand on appeal, the Microsoft case had precedent value because of the perceived importance of innovation in the information-based, technology-driven "new economy." The case illustrates how "trust busters" are increasingly viewing innovation as a central issue in enforcement policy. Regulators increasingly are seeking to determine whether proposed business combinations either promote or impede innovation.

Because of the accelerating pace of new technology, government is less likely to want to be involved in imposing remedies that seek to limit anticompetitive behaviors by requiring the government to monitor continuously a firm's performance to a consent decree. In fact, the government's frustration with the ineffectiveness of sanctions imposed on Microsoft in the early 1990s may have been a contributing factor in their proposal to divide the firm.

Antitrust watchdogs are likely to pay more attention in the future to the impact of proposed mergers or acquisitions on start-ups, which are viewed as major contributors to innovation. In some instances, business combinations among competitors may be disallowed if they are believed to be simply an effort to slow the rate of innovation. The challenge for regulators will be to recognize when cooperation or mergers among competitors may provide additional incentives for innovation through a sharing of risk and resources. However, until the effects on innovation of a firm's actions or a proposed merger can be more readily measured, decisions by regulators may appear to be more arbitrary than well reasoned.

The economics of innovation are at best ill-defined. Innovation cycles are difficult to determine and may run as long as several decades between the gestation of an idea and its actual implementation. Consequently, if it is to foster innovation, antitrust policy will have to attempt to anticipate technologies, markets, and competitors that do not currently exist to determine which proposed business combinations should be allowed and which firms with substantial market positions should be broken up.

Case Study Discussion Questions

1. Comment on whether antitrust policy can be used as an effective means of encouraging innovation.
2. Was Microsoft a good antitrust case in which to test the effectiveness of antitrust policy on promoting innovation? Why or why not?

STATE REGULATIONS AFFECTING MERGERS AND ACQUISITIONS

Numerous regulations affecting takeovers exist at the state level. The regulations often differ from one state to another, making compliance with all applicable regulations a challenge. State regulations often are a result of special interests that appeal to state legislators to establish a particular type of anti-takeover statute to make it more difficult to complete unfriendly takeover attempts. Such appeals usually are made in the context of an attempt to save jobs in the state.

STATE ANTITAKEOVER LAWS

States regulate corporate charters. **Corporate charters** define the powers of the firm and the rights and responsibilities of its shareholders, boards of directors, and managers. However, states are not allowed to pass any laws that impose restrictions on interstate commerce or that conflict in any way with federal laws regulating interstate commerce. State laws tend to apply only to corporations that are incorporated in the state or that conduct a substantial amount of their business within the state. These laws typically contain *fair price provisions* requiring that all target shareholders of a successful tender offer receive the same price as those tendering their shares. In a specific attempt to prevent highly leveraged transactions such as leveraged buyouts, some state laws include *business combination provisions*, which may specifically rule out the sale of the target's assets for a specific period. Because the sale of target assets is frequently a means of reducing indebtedness in highly leveraged transactions, these provisions effectively would preclude such transactions.

Other common characteristics of state antitakeover laws include cash-out and control share provisions. *Cash-out provisions* require a bidder, whose purchases exceed a stipulated amount, to buy the remainder of the target stock on the same terms granted to those shareholders whose stock was purchased at an earlier date. By forcing the acquiring firm to purchase 100% of the stock, potential bidders lacking substantial financial resources effectively are eliminated from bidding on the target. *Share control provisions* require that a bidder obtain prior approval from stockholders holding large blocks of target stock once the bidder's purchases of stock exceed some threshold level. The latter provision can be particularly troublesome to an acquiring company when the holders of the large blocks of stock tend to support target management.

Such state measures may be set aside if sufficient target firm votes can be obtained at a special meeting of shareholders called for that purpose. Ohio's share control law forced Northrop Grumman to increase its offer price from its original bid of $47 in March 2002 to $53 in mid-April 2002 to encourage those holding large blocks of TRW shares to tender their shares. Such shareholders had balked at the lower price, expressing favor for a counter proposal made by TRW to spin off its automotive business and divest certain other assets. TRW had valued its proposal at more than $60 per share. The Ohio law, among the toughest in the nation, prevented Northrop from acquiring more than 20% of TRW's stock.

STATE ANTITRUST LAWS

As part of the Hart–Scott–Rodino Act of 1976, the states were granted increased antitrust power. The state laws are often very similar to federal laws. Under federal law, states have the right to sue to block mergers they believe are anticompetitive, even if the DoJ or FTC does not challenge them.

REGULATED INDUSTRIES

In addition to the DoJ and the FTC, a variety of other agencies monitor activities in certain industries, such as commercial banking, railroads, defense, and cable TV. In each industry, the agency is typically responsible for both the approval of M&As and subsequent oversight. Mergers in these industries often take much longer to complete because of the additional filing requirements.

BANKING

According to the Bank Merger Act of 1966, any bank merger not challenged by the attorney general within 30 days of its approval by the pertinent regulatory agency could not be challenged under the Clayton Antitrust Act. Moreover, the Bank Merger Act stated that anticompetitive effects could be offset by a finding that the deal meets the "convenience and needs" of the communities served by the bank. Currently, three different agencies review banking mergers. Which agency has authority depends on the parties involved in the transaction. The comptroller of the currency has responsibility for transactions in which the acquirer is a national bank. The Federal Deposit Insurance Corporation oversees mergers where the acquiring or resulting bank will be a federally insured state-chartered bank that operates outside of the Federal Reserve System. The third agency is the Board of Governors of the Federal Reserve System. It has the authority to regulate mergers in which the acquirer or the resulting bank will be a state bank, which is also a member of the Federal Reserve System. Although all three agencies conduct their own review, they consider reviews undertaken by the DoJ. Using a modified version of the HHI, the DoJ generally will not challenge a bank merger unless its HHI score exceeds 1800 and increases the index by more than 200 points.

COMMUNICATIONS

The federal agency charged with oversight, the FCC, has deferred to the DoJ and the FTC for antitrust enforcement. The FCC is an independent U.S. government agency directly responsible to Congress. Established by the 1934 Communications Act, the FCC is charged with regulating interstate and international communication by radio, television, wire, satellite, and cable. Headed by five commissioners appointed by the president and approved by Congress, it has seven operating bureaus including Cable Services, Common Carrier, Consumer Information, Enforcement, International Mass Media, and Wireless. These bureaus are responsible for developing and implementing regulatory programs, processing applications for licenses, analyzing complaints, and conducting investigations. The FCC is responsible for the enforcement of such legislation as the Telecommunications Act of 1996. This act is intended to promote competition and reduce regulation while promoting lower prices and higher quality services. (See the Federal Communications Commission Website at www.fcc.gov.)

The FCC used an innovative solution to perceived competitive issues in the 1999 merger of Ameritech and SBC Communications (see Case Study 2-8). A tight timetable coupled with substantial fines, if certain conditions are not satisfied, was intended to accelerate the achievement of the objectives of the 1996 Telecommunications Act.

CASE STUDY 2-8: FCC USES ITS POWER TO STIMULATE COMPETITION IN THE TELECOMMUNICATIONS MARKET

Oh, So Many Hurdles

Having received approval from the Justice Department and the Federal Trade Commission, Ameritech and SBC Communications received permission from the Federal Communications Commission to combine to form the nation's largest local telephone company. The FCC gave its approval of the $74 billion transaction, subject to conditions requiring that the companies open their markets to rivals and enter new markets to compete with established local phone companies.

Satisfying the FCC's Concerns

SBC, which operates under Southwestern Bell, Pacific Bell, SNET, Nevada Bell, and Cellular One brands, has 52 million phone lines in its territory. It also has 8.3 million wireless customers across the United States. Ameritech, which serves Illinois, Indiana, Michigan, Ohio, and Wisconsin, has more than 12 million phone customers. It also provides wireless service to 3.2 million individuals and businesses.

The combined business would control 57 million, or one-third, of the nation's local phone lines in 13 states. The FCC adopted 30 conditions to ensure that the deal would serve the public interest. The new SBC must enter 30 new markets within 30 months to compete with established local phone companies. In the new markets, it would face fierce competition from Bell Atlantic, BellSouth, and U.S. West. The company is required to provide deep discounts on key pieces of their networks to rivals who want to lease them. The merged companies also must establish a separate subsidiary to provide advanced telecommunications services such as high-speed Internet access. At least 10% of its upgraded services would go toward low-income groups. Failure to satisfy these conditions would result in stiff fines. The companies could face up to $1.2 billion in penalties for failing to meet the new market deadline and could pay another $1.1 billion for not meeting performance standards related to opening up their markets.

A Costly Remedy for SBC

SBC has had considerable difficulty in complying with its agreement with the FCC. Between December 2000 and July 2001, SBC paid the U.S. government $38.5 million for failing to adequately provide rivals with access to its network. The government noted that SBC failed repeatedly to make available its network in a timely manner, to meet installation deadlines, and to notify competitors when their orders were filled.

Case Study Discussion Questions

1. Comment on the fairness and effectiveness of using the imposition of heavy fines to promote social policy.
2. Under what circumstances, if any, do you believe the government should relax the imposition of such fines in the SBC case?

RAILROADS

The Surface Transportation Board (STB), the successor to the Interstate Commerce Commission (ICC), governs mergers of railroads. Under the ICC Termination Act of 1995, the STB employs five criteria to determine if a merger should be approved. These criteria include the impact of the proposed transaction on the adequacy of public transportation, the impact on the areas currently served by the carriers involved in the proposed transaction, and the burden of the total fixed charges resulting from completing the transaction. In addition, the interest of railroad employees is considered, as well as whether the transaction would have an adverse impact on competition among rail carriers in regions affected by the merger.

DEFENSE

During the 1990s, the defense industry in the United States underwent substantial consolidation. The consolidation that has swept the defense industry is consistent with the Department of Defense's (DoD) philosophy that it is preferable to have three or four highly viable defense contractors that could more effectively compete than to have a dozen weaker contractors. Examples of transactions include the merger of Lockheed and Martin Marietta, Boeing's acquisition of Rockwell's defense and aerospace business, Raytheon's acquisition of the assets of defense-related product lines of Hughes Electronics, and Boeing's acquisition of Hughes space and communication business. However, regulators did prevent the proposed acquisition by Lockheed Martin of Northrop Grumman.

Although defense industry mergers are technically subject to current antitrust regulations, the DoJ and FTC have assumed a secondary role to the DoD. The DoD has a formal process of coordinating with the DoJ and the FTC. This involves the DoD making assessments of a proposed transaction on the country's defense industry and then making a recommendation to the DoJ and FTC based on their findings.

OTHER REGULATED INDUSTRIES

Insurance

The insurance industry is regulated largely at the state level. Acquiring an insurance company normally requires the approval of state government and is subject to substantial financial disclosure by the acquiring company.

Public Utilities

Public utilities are highly regulated at the state level. Like insurance companies, their acquisition requires state government approval.

Airlines

The acquisition of more than 10% of a domestic airline's shares outstanding is subject to approval of the Federal Aviation Administration.

ENVIRONMENTAL LAWS

Environmental laws create numerous reporting requirements for both acquirers and target firms. Failure to comply adequately with these laws can result in enormous potential liabilities to all parties involved in a transaction. These laws require full disclosure of the existence of hazardous materials and the extent to which they are being released into the environment. Such laws include the Clean Water Act (1974), the Toxic Substances Control Act (TSCA) of 1978, the Resource Conservation and Recovery Act (1976), and the Comprehensive Environmental Response, Compensation, and Liability Act (CERCLA or Super-fund) of 1980. These laws require the notification of government authorities in case of spills of hazardous materials and related emergencies. Moreover, the TSCA and related regulations require producers of chemicals to report on the existence and use of hazardous materials on their premises.

Additional reporting requirements were imposed in 1986 with the passage of the Emergency Planning and Community Right to Know Act (EPCRA). This act requires that businesses provide detailed information about the presence of extremely hazardous materials to facilitate state and local emergency response planning. The act also requires companies to contact local authorities immediately in the event such materials are released into the environment. Unlike other federal environmental laws, much of the information that is required by EPCRA is publicly available. In addition to EPCRA, several states also have passed "right-to-know" laws, such as California's Proposition 65. The importance of state reporting laws has diminished because EPCRA is largely implemented by the states.

LABOR AND BENEFIT LAWS

A diligent buyer also must ensure that the target is in compliance with the labyrinth of labor and benefit laws. These laws govern such areas as employment discrimination, immigration law, sexual harassment, age discrimination, drug testing, and wage and hour laws. Labor and benefit laws also include the Family Medical Leave Act, the Americans with Disabilities Act, and the Worker Adjustment and Retraining Notification Act (WARN). WARN governs notification before plant closings and requirements to retrain workers.

BENEFIT PLAN LIABILITIES

Employee benefit plans frequently represent one of the biggest areas of liability to a buyer. The greatest potential liabilities often are found in defined pension benefit plans, postretirement medical plans, life insurance benefits, and deferred compensation plans. Such liabilities arise when the reserve shown on the seller's balance sheet does not accurately indicate the true extent of the liability. The potential liability from improperly structured benefit plans grows with each new round of legislation starting with the passage of the Employee Retirement Income and Security Act of 1974. Laws affecting employee retirement and pensions were strengthened by additional legislation including the following: the Multi-Employer Pension Plan Amendments Act of 1980, the Retirement Equity Act of 1984, and the Single Employer Pension Plan Amendments Act of 1986; the Tax Reform Act of 1986; and the Omnibus Budget Reconciliation Acts of 1987, 1989, 1990, and 1993. Buyers and sellers also must be aware of the Unemployment Compensation Act of 1992; the Retirement Protection Act of 1994; and Statements 87, 88, and 106 of the Financial Accounting Standards Board (Sherman, 1998).

CROSS-BORDER TRANSACTIONS

Transactions involving firms in different countries are complicated by having to deal with multiple regulatory jurisdictions in specific countries or regions. Antitrust regulators tend to follow different standards and impose different fee structures from one country to another. The number of antitrust regulatory authorities has grown to 100 from 6 in the early 1990s (*The New York Times*, January 28, 2001).

Reflecting the effects of this mishmash of regulations and fee structures, Coca-Cola's 1999 acquisition of Cadbury Schweppes involved obtaining antitrust approval in 40 jurisdictions globally. Fees paid to regulators ranged from $77 in Austria to $2.5 million in Argentina. In contrast, the fee in the United States is limited to $280,000 for transactions whose value exceeds $500 million (Weston and Weaver, 2001). Following the failed merger attempt of Alcan Aluminum, Pechiney, and Alusuisse, Jacques Bougie, CEO of Alcan Aluminum, complained that his company had to file for antitrust approval in 16 countries and in eight languages. In addition, his firm had to submit more than 400 boxes of documents and send more than 1 million pages of email (Garten, 2000).

Several reports advocate the use of regional antitrust authorities created through multilateral rather than bilateral agreements to streamline the antitrust process and reduce administrative and financial burdens on businesses (Brookings Institute, November, 2000; U.S. Attorney General, February, 2000). However, recent developments suggest that even such agreements may not easily resolve fundamental philosophical differences.

The recent collapse of the General Electric and Honeywell transaction underscores how such philosophical differences can jeopardize major deals. Mario Monti, chief of the EU Competition Office, had taken a highly aggressive posture in this transaction. The GE-Honeywell deal was under attack almost from the day it was announced in October 2000. Rival aerospace companies including United Technologies, Rockwell, Lufthansa, Thales, and Rolls Royce considered it inimical to their ability to compete. Philosophically, U.S. antitrust regulators focus on the impact of a proposed deal on customers; in contrast, EU antitrust regulators are more concerned about the impact on rivals. Reflecting this disparate thinking, U.S. antitrust regulators approved the transaction rapidly, concluding that it would have a salutary impact on customers. However, EU regulators refused to approve the transaction without GE making major concessions, which it was unwilling to make. Jack Welch, CEO of GE, declared that such concessions would reduce substantially the value of the deal, and he walked away on July 4, 2001.

THINGS TO REMEMBER

The Securities Acts of 1933 and 1934 established the SEC and requires that all securities offered to the public must be registered with the government. The registration process requires the description of the company's properties and business, a description of the securities, information about management, and financial statements certified by public accountants.

Passed in 1968, the Williams Act consists of a series of amendments to the 1934 Securities Exchange Act, which were intended to provide target firm shareholders with sufficient information and time to adequately assess the value of an acquirer's offer. Any person or firm acquiring 5% or more of the stock of a public corporation must file a Schedule 13D with the SEC within 10 days of reaching that percentage ownership threshold. The disclosure is necessary even if the accumulation of the stock is not followed by a tender offer. Under Section 14(d) of the Williams Act, acquiring firms that initiate tender offers must disclose their intentions and business plans, as well as any agreements between the acquirer and the target firm, in a Schedule 14D-1.

Federal antitrust laws exist to prevent individual corporations from assuming too much market power such that they can raise prices without concern for any significant competitor reaction. Passed in 1890, the Sherman Act makes illegal such practices as agreements to fix prices and allocate customers among competitors, as well as attempts to monopolize any part of interstate commerce. In an attempt to strengthen the Sherman Act, the Clayton Act was passed in 1914 to make illegal the purchase of stock of another company if their combination results in reduced competition within the industry. Current antitrust law requires prenotification of mergers or acquisitions involving companies of a certain size to allow the FTC and the DoJ to have sufficient time to challenge business combinations believed to be anticompetitive before they are completed. Bidding firms must execute a HSR filing at the same time as it makes an offer to a target firm. The target firm also is required to file within 15 days following the bidder's filing. Before the takeover can be completed, a 30-day waiting period is required. Either the FTC or the DoJ may request a 20-day extension of the waiting period.

To determine which business combinations to challenge, antitrust regulators look at a variety of factors. These include the analysis of market concentration, the potential for anticompetitive practices such as price fixing, ease of new competitors entering the market, efficiencies that may result from the business combination, the likelihood that a firm will fail if it is not acquired, and the impact on innovation. A decision by the federal antitrust regulatory authorities may be appealed in the federal circuit courts. As an alternative to what is likely to be very expensive litigation, a company may seek to negotiate a voluntary settlement of its differences with the FTC. Such settlements usually are negotiated during the review process and are called consent decrees.

There are numerous state regulations affecting M&As such as state antitakeover and antitrust laws. A number of industries also are subject to regulatory approval at the federal and state level. Examples include banking, insurance, telecommunications, defense, public utilities, railroads, and airlines. Considerable effort also must be made to ensure that a transaction is in full compliance with applicable environmental and employee benefit laws. The resulting penalties for failure to do so can be litigation and fines that seriously could erode the profitability of the combined firms or result in bankruptcy.

CHAPTER DISCUSSION QUESTIONS

2-1. What was the motivation for the Federal Securities Acts of 1933 and 1934?

2-2. What was the rationale for the Williams Act?

2-3. What factors do U.S. antitrust regulators consider before challenging a merger or acquisition?

2-4. What are the obligations of the acquirer and target firms according to Section 14(d) of the Williams act?

2-5. Discuss the pros and cons of federal antitrust laws.

2-6. Why is premerger notification (HSR filing) required by U.S. antitrust regulatory authorities?

2-7. When is a person or firm required to submit a Schedule 13D to the SEC? What is the purpose of such a filing?

2-8. What is the rationale behind state antitakeover legislation?

2-9. Give examples of the types of actions that may be required by the parties to a proposed merger subject to a FTC consent decree?

2-10. How might the growth of electronic commerce affect the application of current antitrust laws?

CHAPTER BUSINESS CASE

CASE STUDY 2-9: EXXON AND MOBIL MERGER— THE MARKET SHARE CONUNDRUM

From the moment the proposed $81-billion merger was announced in December 1998, officials at the FTC promised a rigorous regulatory review. Following that review, they decided to challenge the Exxon–Mobil transaction on anticompetitive grounds. This paved the way for either a vigorous court challenge by the merger partners of the FTC's rulings, a negotiated settlement, or a withdrawal of merger plans. Before the merger, Exxon was the largest oil producer in the United States and Mobil was the next largest firm. The combined companies would create the world's biggest oil company in terms of revenues. Top executives from Exxon Corporation and Mobil Corporation argued that they needed to implement their proposed merger because of the increasingly competitive world oil market. Falling oil prices during much of the late 1990s put a squeeze on oil industry profits. Moreover, giant state-owned oil companies are posing a competitive threat because of their access to huge amounts of capital.

To offset these factors, Exxon and Mobil argued that they had to combine to achieve substantial cost savings. By combining their exploration and production activities, the two companies expected to save $2 billion annually in operating expenses. Analysts estimated that job cuts for the combined companies could reach 20,000, about 16% of the combined companies' workforce.

After a yearlong review, antitrust officials at the FTC approved the Exxon–Mobil merger after the companies agreed to the largest divestiture in the history of the FTC. The divestiture involved the sale of 15% of their service station network, amounting to 2400 stations. This included about 1220 Mobil stations from Virginia to New Jersey and about 300 in Texas. In addition, about 520 Exxon stations from New York to Maine and about 360 in California were divested. Exxon also agreed to the divestiture of an Exxon refinery in Benecia, California.

The FTC continuously had expressed its concern about the potentially anticompetitive effects of the deal. However, the FTC has noted that there is considerably greater competition worldwide. This is particularly true in the market for exploration of new reserves. The greatest threat to competition seems to be in the refining and distribution of gasoline.

Case Study Discussion Questions

1. How does the FTC define market share?
2. Why might it be important to distinguish between a global and a regional oil and gas market?
3. Why are the Exxon and Mobil executives emphasizing efficiencies as a justification for this merger?
4. Should the size of the combined companies be an important consideration in the regulators' analysis of the proposed merger?
5. How do the divestitures address perceived anticompetitive problems?

Solutions to these case study questions are found in the Appendix at the back of the book.

CHAPTER BUSINESS CASE

MARKET CASE STUDY 2-10: GE'S ABORTED ATTEMPT TO MERGE WITH HONEYWELL

It was billed by some as General Electric's CEO Jack Welch's last hurrah. The GE board even allowed him to postpone retirement for at least 8 months, although he would reach the firm's mandatory retirement age on April 1, 2001. The benefits of the proposed merger seemed palpable to GE and to many customers of both firms. Many observers anticipated significant regulatory review because of the size of transaction and the increase in concentration it would create in the markets served by the two firms. Nonetheless, most believed that after making some concessions to regulatory authorities, the transaction would be approved.

Although the pundits were indeed correct in noting that it would receive close scrutiny, they were completely caught off guard by divergent approaches taken by the U.S. and EU antitrust authorities. U.S. regulators ruled that the merger should be approved because of its potential overall benefits to customers. In marked contrast, EU regulators ruled against the transaction based on its perceived negative impact on competitors, with the potential positive impact on customers seeming to have only a secondary role in its decision-making process.

What happened? How could the two regulatory bodies looking at the same data come to such divergent conclusions? What are the implications of these fundamentally different rulings for future cross-border transactions? What can be done to reconcile differences between the two approaches to antitrust review?

Background

In an October 23, 2000, press conference, Jack Welch beamed as he announced GE's merger with aerospace and industrial products giant Honeywell International Inc. (Honeywell). Honeywell's merger agreement with GE came together quickly after Honeywell and United Technologies announced on October 19 that they were in merger talks. Welch spoke confidently of the potential value to be created by the deal, the dramatic benefits to customers, and the transaction's likely acceptance by the regulators. He even shrugged off the notion that he entered the transaction in an effort to stave off his retirement at 65 years of age.

Under the terms of the transaction, GE would pay 1.055 of its shares for each of Honeywell's 801 million outstanding shares. Based on GE's closing price of $52.13 on October 20, 2000, the deal valued Honeywell at $55.39 per share or about $42 billion. GE also agreed to assume Honeywell's outstanding debt. Honeywell's avionics and engines unit would add significant strength to GE's jet-engine business, an operation that would account for 13% of the combined companies' sales. The deal also would augment GE's product offerings in industrial controls and power generation businesses. The deal would add about 10 cents to GE's 2001 earnings and could eventually result in $1.5 billion in annual cost savings. The purchase also would enable GE to continue its shift away from manufacturing and into services, which already comprised 70% of its revenues in 2000 (*Business Week*, November 6, 2000).

The best fit is clearly in the combination of the two firms' aerospace businesses. Revenues from these two businesses alone would total $22 billion, combining Honeywell's strength in jet engines and cockpit avionics with GE's substantial business in larger jet engines. As the largest supplier in the aerospace industry, GE could offer airplane manufacturers "one-stop shopping" for everything from engines to complex software systems by cross-selling each other's products to their biggest customers. For example, GE builds the jet engines for the C-17 military tanker, and Honeywell supplies the avionics and pneumatic controls for the 717 commercial airliner, both of which are built at the same Boeing plant in Long Beach, California.

Although the potential benefits were clear, so were the risks. The combined firms would be enormously complex. With GE's annual revenues of $130 billion in 2000, the combined companies' revenues would total $176 billion in annual sales, and the combined companies would have 460,000 employees. Each firm had operations throughout the world. GE is in dozens of businesses, everything from aircraft engines to kitchen appliances to financial services to network television through its ownership of NBC. Honeywell is also highly diversified, with businesses in aerospace systems, power and transportation products, specialty chemicals, home security systems, and building controls (Ackman, October 23, 2000). Although GE had demonstrated an obvious ability to acquire and successfully integrate 134 acquisitions worth more than $17 billion in 1999 alone, Honeywell would be much larger than any it had ever done before. Honeywell, itself a product of the merger of the original Honeywell and Allied Signal Inc. 11 months earlier, had been burdened with a number of low-margin, low-growth businesses. GE would inherit the challenges Honeywell and AlliedSignal have been experiencing in attempting to construct a unified culture.

Honeywell had been on the block for a number of months before the deal was consummated with GE. Its merger with Allied Signal had not been going well, and it had contributed to deteriorating earnings and a much lower stock price. Honeywell's shares declined in price by more than 40% since its acquisition of Allied Signal. While the euphoria surrounding the deal in late 2000 lingered into the early months of 2001, rumblings from the European regulators began to create an uneasy feeling among GE's and Honeywell's management.

Regulatory Hurdles Slow the Process

Welch had hoped to close the transaction by early 2001. However, he had not anticipated the intensity of the regulatory scrutiny in Europe. Mario Monti, the European Competition Commissioner, leading an in-depth review of the transaction, noted that a decision would take at least until July 12, 2001. He expressed

concern about possible "conglomerate effects" or the total influence a combined
GE and Honeywell would wield in the aircraft industry. He was referring to GE's
perceived ability to expand its influence in aerospace industry through service
initiatives. GE's service offerings help differentiate it from others at a time when
prices of many industrial parts are being pressured by increased competition,
including low-cost manufacturers overseas. In a world in which manufactured
products are becoming increasingly commoditylike, the true winners are those
able to differentiate their product offering.

GE and Honeywell's European competitors complained to the EU regulatory
commission that GE would have a pernicious advantage. Critics alleged that its
extensive service offering would give it entrée into many more points of contact
among airplane manufacturers—from communications systems to the expanded
line of spare parts GE would be able to supply. This so-called "range effect" or
"portfolio power" is a relatively new legal doctrine that has not been tested in
transactions the size of this one (Murray, April 5, 2001).

U.S. Regulators Approve the Deal

On May 3, 2001, the U.S. Department of Justice approved the buyout after the
companies agreed to sell Honeywell's helicopter-engine unit and to take other steps
to protect competition. The U.S. regulatory authorities believed that the combined
companies could sell more products to more customers (especially in the aerospace
industry) and therefore could realize improved efficiencies, although it would not
hold a dominant market share in any particular market. Thus, customers would
benefit from GE's greater range of products and possibly lower prices, but they still
could shop elsewhere if they chose. The U.S. regulators expressed little concern
that bundling of products and services could hurt customers, particularly in the
aerospace industry, where sophisticated buyers choose among a relative handful
of suppliers.

Under the U.S. agreement, GE must sell the engine unit, which had $200
million in revenue in 2000, and outsource some of the maintenance and overhaul
of Honeywell aircraft engines and auxiliary-power units. Welch expressed pleasure
with the U.S. ruling and noted, "Now that the U.S. has completed its review of the
transaction, we can focus on continuing discussion with the European Commission
officials. . . . We remain positive about that process and hopeful that we can proceed
promptly to a just conclusion" (Wilke, May 3, 2001).

Understanding the European Union Position

To understand the European position it is necessary to understand the nature
of competition in the EU. France, Germany, and Spain have spent billions subsi-
dizing their aerospace industry over the years. The GE-Honeywell deal has been
heartily attacked by their European rivals from Rolls-Royce and Lufthansa to
French avionics manufacturer, Thales.

Although the EU imported much of its antitrust law from the United States,
the antitrust law doctrine has evolved in fundamentally different ways. In Europe,

the main goal of antitrust law is to guarantee that all companies should be able to compete on an equal playing field. The implication is that the EU is just as concerned about how a transaction affects rivals as it is consumers. This means that it is much easier for competitors to kill a deal in Europe than it is in the United States. This doctrine has resulted in a substantially different application of antitrust laws in Europe than in the United States. Complaints from competitors are taken more seriously in Europe, whereas in the United States it is the impact on consumers that constitutes the litmus test. Europeans have accepted the legal concept of "portfolio power," which argues that a firm may achieve an unfair advantage over its competitors by bundling goods and services. Also, in Europe, the European Commission's Merger Task Force can prevent a merger without taking a company to court. By removing this judicial remedy, the EU makes it possible for the regulators, who are political appointees, to be biased.

Lamenting the lack of a court review process, Jack Welch noted, "With the European Commission's rejection of the Honeywell acquisition, there was no review process. The bureaucrats can take the most extreme positions, and they do not have any incentive to compromise... Companies should have the right to a fair and public hearing in a reasonable time by an impartial tribunal" (Welch, 2001).

GE Walks Away from the Deal

The EU authorities continued to balk at approving the transaction without major concessions from the participants, concessions that GE believed would render the deal unattractive. On June 15, 2001, GE submitted its final offer to the EU regulators in a last-ditch attempt to breathe life into the moribund deal. GE knew that, if it walked away, it could continue as it had before the deal was struck, secure in the knowledge that its current portfolio of businesses offered substantial revenue growth or profit potential. Honeywell clearly would fuel such growth, but it made sense to GE's management and shareholders only if it would be allowed to realize potential synergies between the GE and Honeywell businesses.

GE said it was willing to divest Honeywell units with annual revenue of $2.2 billion, including regional jet engines, air-turbine starters, and other aerospace products. To GE, these were major concessions. Anything more would jeopardize the rationale for the deal. Specifically, GE was unwilling to agree not to bundle (i.e., sell a package of components and services at a single price) its products and services when selling to customers. Another stumbling block was GE Capital Aviation Services unit, the airplane-financing arm of GE Capital. The EU Antitrust Commission argued that this unit would use its clout as one of the world's largest purchasers of airplanes to pressure airplane manufacturers into using GE products. The Commission seemed to ignore that GE had only an 8% share of the global airplane leasing market and would therefore seemingly lack the market power the Commission believed it could exert.

Honeywell was in a far different position from GE. If the transaction was not consummated, it would have to find another buyer. While sitting in limbo since the announcement in October of 2000, the firm had seen its earnings plummet resulting from an economic slowdown and a rise in oil prices.

On July 4, 2001, the EU vetoed the GE purchase of Honeywell, marking the first time a proposed merger between two U.S. companies has been blocked solely by European regulators. Having received U.S. regulatory approval, GE could ignore the EU decision and proceed with the merger as long as it would be willing to forego sales in Europe. This clearly was an untenable option. GE decided not to appeal the decision to the EU Court of First Instance, knowing that it could take years to resolve the decision, and withdrew its offer to merge with Honeywell.

Within hours after the announcement, Honeywell's Chair and CEO Michael Bonsignore announced his resignation. He was replaced immediately by Larry Bossidy, the former chair and CEO of Allied Signal. He announced that Honeywell would move aggressively to improve its performance, further strengthen its management team, and rebuild the confidence of its shareholders, customers, and employees (Johnson, July 4, 2001).

The GE–Honeywell Legacy

The fallout from the EU's decision applies mainly to firms contemplating large cross-border mergers. Such transactions are likely to receive the closest scrutiny by the EU regulators. The EU's decision bodes ill for other companies planning big mergers involving companies with operations in Europe. Companies may be unwilling to go to the lengths GE did in subjecting its proposal to the intense review of the EU regulators. The issues raised in this deal could discourage big mergers by making their likelihood of receiving regulatory approval less predictable. To the extent that cross-border transactions contribute to improved efficiencies, the EU's decision could reduce efficiency not only in Europe but also around the world and especially in the United States, the world's largest airplane manufacturing market. It is more important than ever for government policymakers in different parts of the world to confer to resolve fundamental differences in antitrust policies if the full economic benefits of globalization are to be realized. If global antitrust policy is made consistent across countries, cross-border mergers could contribute to improved efficiency, lower prices, and higher living standards.

Case Study Discussion Questions

1. What are the important philosophical differences between U.S. and EU antitrust regulators? Explain the logic underlying these differences. To what extent are these differences influenced by political rather than economic considerations? Explain your answer.
2. This is the first time that a foreign regulatory body has prevented a deal involving U.S. firms only from occurring. What do you think are the long-term implications, if any, of this precedent?
3. What were the major stumbling blocks between GE and the EU regulators? Why do you think these were stumbling blocks? Do you think the EU regulators were justified in their position? Why or why not?

4. Do you think that competitors are using antitrust to their advantage? Explain your answer.
5. Do you think the EU regulators would have taken a different position if the deal had involved a less visible firm than General Electric? Explain your answer.

REFERENCES

Ackman, Dan, "Honeywell Hooks Up with GE," Forbes.com, October 23, 2000, http://www.forbes.com/2000/10/23/1023topnews.html.

Balto, David A., "Emerging Antitrust Issues in Electronic Commerce," Office of Policy and Evaluation, Bureau of Competition, Federal Trade Commission, November 2, 1999.

Bers, Joanna Smith, "Microsoft-DoJ suit exposes the pitfalls of electronic commerce," *Bank Systems & Technology*, 32 (6), June 1995, pp. 6–8.

Brookings Institute, "Antitrust Goes Global," November, 2000.

Business Week, "Antitrust for the Digital Age," May 15, 2000, pp. 46–48.

Business Week, "Jack's Risky Last Act," *Business Week*, November 6, 2000, pp. 40–45.

Champlin, Dell P. and Janet T. Knoedler, "Restructuring by Design: Government's Complicity in Corporate Restructuring," *Journal of Economic Issues*, 33 (1), March 1999, p. 41.

Federal Trade Commission, Bureau of Competition, "A Study of the Commission's Divestiture Process," 1999.

Federal Trade Commission, *Merger Guidelines*, 1999, www.ftc.com.

Gaughan, Patrick A., *Mergers, Acquisitions, and Corporate Restructurings* (2nd ed.), John Wiley & Sons, 1999, pp. 61–114.

Garten, Jeffery E., "As Business Goes Global, Antitrust Should Too," *Business Week*, November 13, 2000, p. 38.

Gilson, Ronald J. and Bernard S. Black, *The Law and Finance of Corporate Acquisitions* (2nd ed.), Westbury, NY: The Foundation Press, Inc., 1995.

Hanks, Vince, "Gigantic JDS Uniphase," The Motley Fool, Fool.com, November 2, 2000, www.fool.com/dripoport/2000/dripport001102.htm.

"JDS Uniphase and SDL agree to a $41 Billion Merger," SDL Press Release, July 10, 2000, www.sdli.com/about/release/pr_071000.html.

JDS Uniphase, JDS Uniphase Announces Fourth Quarter Results, Press Release, July 27, 2001.

Johnson, Linda, "Honeywell's CEO Quits After EU Move," *Associated Press and Orange County Register*, Business Section, July 4, 2001, p. 7.

Loss, Louis and Joel Seligman, *Fundamentals of Securities Regulation* (3rd ed.), Boston: Little, Brown, 1995.

Lynch, Robert Porter, *Business Alliances Guide, The Hidden Competitive Weapon*, John Wiley & Sons, Inc., 1993, pp. 257–258.

Motley Fool Lunchtime News, September 4, 1996. www.sur.be.fool.com/lunchnews/1996.

Muris, Timothy, "Current Changes at the FTC," Speech presented to the American Bar Association, Antitrust Section Annual Meeting, Chicago, August 7, 2001, p. 7.

Murray, Matthew, "GE's Honeywell Deal is More Than the Sum of Airplane Parts," *Wall Street Journal*, April 5, 2001, p. B6.

New York State v. Visa USA, Inc., 1990–1, Trade Case (CCH), 69016, SDNY, 1990.

New York Times, "The Spread of Antitrust Authorities," January 28, 2001, Section 3, p. 4.

Radigan, Joseph, "Look out home banking, here comes William the Conqueror," *United States Banker*, 104 (12), December 1994, pp. 22–26.

"Sale of Zurich Subsidiary to Nortel Networks Completed," SDL Press Release, February 14, 2001, www.sdli.com/about/release/pr_021301.html.

Sherman, Andrew J., *Mergers and Acquisitions from A to Z, Strategic and Practical Guidance for Small and Middle Market Buyers and Sellers*, AMACOM, 1998, pp. 78–94.

Sraeel, Holly, "Microsoft-DoJ appeal rejection of proposed antitrust settlement," *Bank Systems & Technology*, 32 (4), April 1995, pp. 6–8.

Talmor, Sharona, "Trials of the Game," *Banker*, 145 (832), June 1995, pp. 76–77.

Ton, Willard K. and Abbott B. Lipsky, Jr., *Antitrust Law Developments* (3rd ed.), Volume I, American Bar Association, 1992.

United States Department of Justice, Antitrust Division, www.usdoj.gov, 1999.

United States Attorney General, "Global Antitrust Regulation: Issues and Solutions," *Final Report of the International Competition Policy Advisory Committee*, February 2000.

United States v. Primestar, L.P., 58 Fed Reg, 33944, June 22, 1993 (Proposed Final Judgment and Competitive Impact Study).

Wasserstein, Bruce, *Big Deal: The Battle for Control of America's Leading Corporations*, New York: Warner Books, 1998.

Welch, Jack, *Jack*, New York: Warner Books, 2001, p. 375.

Weston, J. F. and Samuel C. Weaver, *Mergers and Acquisitions*, McGraw-Hill: New York, 2001, p. 34.

Wilke, Joseph, "Justice Department Backs GE-Honeywell Accord," *Wall Street Journal*, May 3, 2001, p. C2.

WorldCom, Inc., 13, FCC Ruling 18025, 1998.

3

COMMON TAKEOVER
TACTICS AND DEFENSES

There is no job so simple that it cannot be done wrong.
—Anonymous

As she is in the habit of doing eight or ten times a day, the chief executive officer (CEO) glances at a flickering monitor on a credenza behind her mahogany desk to review the price movement in her company's stock. Her eyes widen in amazement at the sharp jump in share price in the last hour. She knows that unexpectedly large movements are frequently a result of institutional trades of large blocks of stock to cover a short position or simply an overreaction to rumors on "the street." But this time something is different. The stock price has run up more than eight points in the last week, accompanied by an unusually large number of block trades for such a short period. In the last hour, the stock has surged upward by more than two points. Her heart pounds as she pushes away from her desk, unable to concentrate on the contents of her in-box, and zaps an e-mail to her chief financial officer, corporate attorney, and head of public affairs, setting up a meeting later in the morning. She can't get back to her daily routine until she knows what's going on. She has gone through this drill before in response to what appeared to be credible rumors. In all cases, they turned out to be all smoke and no fire. But maybe, just maybe, this time it's for real.

OVERVIEW

The corporate takeover has been dramatized in Hollywood as motivated by excessive greed, reviled in the press as a destroyer of jobs and of local communities, sanctified on Wall Street as a means of dislodging incompetent management, and often heralded by shareholders as a source of windfall gains. The reality is that corporate takeovers may be a little of all of these things. The purpose of this chapter is to discuss the commonly used tactics to acquire a company in a hostile takeover attempt and to evaluate the effectiveness of various takeover defenses. The chapter is divided into two major sections: alternative takeover tactics and alternative takeover defenses. Alternative takeover tactics are subdivided further into friendly and aggressive tactics. Aggressive tactics include the bear hug, proxy contests, open-market operations, and tender offers. Alternative takeover defenses are viewed in terms of two stages: prebid, those put in place before a bid is made; and postbid, those put in place in response to a bid. The impact on shareholder returns of the various types of takeover tactics and defenses also is discussed. Finally, the case at the end of the chapter, entitled "Tyco Saves AMP from AlliedSignal," provides an excellent illustration of how takeover tactics are used in a hostile takeover to penetrate a firm's defenses and common reactions by target firms to such tactics in a high stakes game of chess.

ALTERNATIVE TAKEOVER TACTICS

Takeovers may be classified as friendly or hostile. Friendly takeovers are negotiated settlements that often are characterized by bargaining, which remains undisclosed until the agreement of purchase and sale has been signed. An example of a friendly takeover is a company desirous of being acquired soliciting another firm to assess its interest in combining the two firms. A hostile takeover generally is considered an unsolicited offer made by a potential acquirer that is resisted by the target firm's management. Hostile transactions normally are disclosed in the press. Although it would seem easy to distinguish between friendly and hostile takeovers, the distinctions are sometimes more perceived than real.

An aggressive public rejection of an offer is often the first step in the process leading to a negotiated settlement. Public announcements are frequently part of a negotiating strategy. Sometimes firms engage in confidential negotiations before there is a public announcement of a bid or a completed transaction. In this instance, the transaction might be viewed as friendly. In other instances, the negotiations may start on a friendly basis but later become vitriolic. Bidders may choose to announce the negotiations publicly if they feel that this would put pressure on the board and management of the target firm to accede to their terms. Similarly, the target's management may reveal the existence of the negotiations to elicit alternative bidders.

Friendly takeovers may be viewed as ones in which a negotiated settlement is possible without the acquirer resorting to such aggressive tactics as the bear hug, proxy contest, or tender offer. A *bear hug* involves the mailing of a letter containing an acquisition proposal to the board of directors of a target company without prior warning and demanding a rapid decision. A *proxy contest* is an attempt by dissident shareholders to obtain representation on the board of directors or to change a firm's bylaws. A *tender offer* is a takeover tactic in which the acquirer bypasses the target's board and management and goes directly to the target's shareholders with an offer to purchase their shares. Unlike a merger in which the traditional legal doctrine holds that the minority must agree to the terms of the negotiated agreement, the tender specifically allows for the management and the board of the target firm to be bypassed. In some instances, the terms of the transaction may be *crammed down* or imposed on the minority. Alternatively, the acquirer may decide not to acquire 100% of the target's stock. In this case, the minority is subject to a *freeze-in*, in which the remaining shareholders are dependent on the decisions made by the majority shareholders.

Two theories have been proposed to explain the motives of target company management when approached by a potential acquirer. According to the *management entrenchment theory*, corporate managers take actions using various types of takeover defenses that are designed to ensure their longevity with the firm. Shareholders lose when the value of their shares declines in response to management's actions. In contrast, the *shareholder interests theory* argues that shareholders gain when management resists takeover attempts. Such resistance is viewed to be in the best interests of the shareholders if it is undertaken to hold out for a higher offer either from the initial bidder or from competing bidders. Although there is evidence to support both theories, there appears to be more empirical evidence that management resists takeover attempts to maximize shareholder value (Schwert, 2000).

THE FRIENDLY APPROACH: "SWEET-TALKING THE TARGET"

Friendly takeovers involve the initiation by the potential acquirer of an informal dialogue with the target's top management. In a friendly takeover, the acquirer and target reach agreement on key issues early in the process. These key issues usually include the combined businesses' long-term strategy, how the combined businesses will be operated in the short term, and who will be in key management positions. A *standstill agreement* often is negotiated, in which the acquirer agrees not to make any further investments in the target's stock for a stipulated period. This compels the acquirer to pursue the acquisition only on friendly terms, at least for the time period covered by the agreement. It also permits negotiations to proceed without the threat of more aggressive tactics, such as a tender offer or proxy contest. From the target's perspective, the standstill agreement is an indication of the acquirer's true intentions.

According to Thompson Financial Securities Data Corporation (2000), about four out of five transactions were classified as friendly during the 1990s. However, this was not always the case. The 1970s and early 1980s were characterized by blitzkrieg-style takeovers. The CEO of a target firm could wake up to a full-page ad in the *Wall Street Journal* announcing a cash offer for the business. The federal prenotification regulations have slowed the process dramatically (see Chapter 2). A number of states also require shareholder approval for certain types of offers.

Moreover, most large companies have antitakeover defenses in place, such as poison pills. Hostile takeovers are now more likely to last for months.

Although hostile takeovers today are certainly more challenging than in the past, they continue to have certain advantages over the friendly approach. In taking the friendly approach, the acquirer is surrendering the element of surprise. Even a warning of a few days gives the target's management time to take defensive action to impede the actions of the suitor. Negotiation also raises the likelihood of a leak and a spike in the price of the target's stock as arbitrageurs (arbs) seek to profit from the spread between the acquirer's and the target's stock prices. The speculative increase in the target's share price can add dramatically to the cost of the transaction because the initial offer by the bidder generally includes a premium over the target's current share price. Because a premium usually is expressed as a percentage of the target's share price, a speculative increase in the target firm's current share price will add to the overall purchase price paid by the acquiring firm. For these reasons, a potential bidder may opt for a more hostile approach.

THE AGGRESSIVE APPROACH

Successful hostile takeovers depend on the premium offered to the target's current share price, the composition of the board, the composition and sentiment of the target's current shareholders, the provisions of the target's bylaws, and the potential for the target to put in place additional takeover defenses.

Premium

The target's board will find it more difficult to reject offers exhibiting substantial premiums to the target's current stock price. Concern about their fiduciary responsibility and about stockholder lawsuits puts pressure on the target's board to accept the offer.

Board Composition

Despite the pressure of an attractive premium, the composition of the target's board greatly influences what the board does and the timing of its decisions. A board dominated by independent directors, nonemployees, or family members is more likely to resist offers in an effort to induce the bidder to raise the offer price or to gain time to solicit competing bids than to protect itself and current management. Shivdasani (1993), in an analysis of 169 tender offers from 1989 through 1992, concluded that the shareholder gain from the inception of the offer to its resolution is 62.3% for targets with an independent board, as compared with 40.9% for targets without an independent board.

Stock Ownership

The final outcome of a hostile takeover is also heavily dependent on the composition of the target's stock ownership and how stockholders feel about management's performance. To assess these factors, an acquirer must compile lists of stock ownership by category: management, officers, employee stock ownership plans (ESOPs), employees, and institutions such as pension and mutual funds. Sometimes the acquirer has to sue the company for shareholder lists. Once these categories are defined, an effort is made to determine the length of time that each group has held their stock. Such information can be used to estimate the target's "stock float." *Float* represents the amount of stock that can be most easily purchased by the acquirer. The float is likely to be largest for those companies that have been underperforming and where stockholders are disappointed with incumbent management. For this reason, tender offers often are made for the stock of firms whose performance has been lackluster.

Bylaws

The target's bylaws may provide numerous hurdles, which add to the cost of a takeover. Such provisions could include a staggered board, the inability to remove directors without cause, or super-majority voting requirements for approval of mergers. (These takeover defenses will be discussed in more detail later in this chapter.)

Potential Takeover Defenses

An astute bidder always will analyze the target's possible defenses, including golden parachutes for key employees, poison pills, or an authorization for a large number of shares that have not yet been issued. (These and other measures also will be discussed later in this chapter.)

THE BEAR HUG: LIMITING THE TARGET'S OPTIONS

If the friendly approach is considered inappropriate or is unsuccessful, the acquiring company may attempt to limit the options of the target's senior management by making a formal acquisition proposal, usually involving a public announcement, to the board of directors of the target. The intent is to move the board to a negotiated settlement. The board may be motivated to do so because of its fiduciary responsibility to the target's shareholders. Directors who vote against the proposal may be subject to lawsuits from target stockholders. This is especially true if the offer is at a substantial premium to the target's current stock price. Once the bid is made public, the company is effectively "put into play" (i.e., likely to attract additional bidders). Institutional investors and arbitrageurs add to the pressure by lobbying the board to accept the offer. Empirical data suggests significant abnormal returns associated with institutional activism (Bruner, 1999). Arbs are likely to acquire the target's stock and to sell the bidder's stock short (see Chapter 1). The accumulation of stock by arbs makes purchases of blocks of stock by the bidder easier. The public announcement also may attract other bidders for the target.

The target's board is unlikely to reject the bid without obtaining a "fairness" opinion from an investment banker stating that the offer is inadequate.

The fairness opinion may be used to defend the board if lawsuits are filed by target shareholders.

The acquisition of Reynolds Aluminum by Alcoa in 1999 is a classic case in which the combination of poor profitability, weak takeover defenses, and limited shareholder support enabled Alcoa to purchase the company at a very modest premium. This was accomplished simply by threatening more aggressive action unless Reynolds' management capitulated (Case Study 3-1).

CASE STUDY 3-1: ALCOA EASILY OVERWHELMS REYNOLDS' TAKEOVER DEFENSES

Alcoa reacted quickly to a three-way intercontinental combination of aluminum companies aimed at challenging its dominance of the Western World aluminum market by disclosing an unsolicited takeover bid for Reynolds Metals in early August 1999. The offer consisted of $4.3 billion, or $66.44 a share, plus the assumption of $1.5 billion in Reynolds' outstanding debt. Reynolds, a perennial marginally profitable competitor in the aluminum industry, appeared to be particularly vulnerable because other logical suitors or potential white knights, such as Canada's Alcan Aluminium, France's Pechiney SA, and Switzerland's Alusuisse Lonza Group AG, already were involved in a three-way merger.

Alcoa's bear hug letter from its chief executive indicated that it wanted to pursue a friendly deal but suggested that it may pursue a full-blown hostile bid if the two sides could not begin discussions within a week. Reynolds appeared to be highly vulnerable because of its poor financial performance amid falling aluminum prices worldwide and because of its weak takeover defenses. It appeared that a hostile bidder could initiate a mail-in solicitation for shareholder consent at any time. Moreover, major Reynolds' shareholders began to pressure the board. Its largest single shareholder, Highfields Capital Management, a holder of more than 4 million shares, demanded that the board create a special committee of independent directors with its own counsel and instruct Merrill Lynch to open an auction for Reynolds.

Despite pressure, the Reynolds' board rejected Alcoa's bid as inadequate. Alcoa's response was to say that it would initiate an all-cash tender offer for all of Reynolds' stock and simultaneously solicit shareholder support through a proxy contest for replacing the Reynolds' board and dismantling Reynolds' takeover defenses. Notwithstanding the public posturing by both sides, Reynolds capitulated on August 19, slightly more than 2 weeks from receipt of the initial solicitation, and agreed to be acquired by Alcoa. The agreement contained a 30-day window during which Reynolds could entertain other bids. However, if Reynolds should choose to go with another offer, it would have to pay Alcoa a $100 million breakup fee.

Under the agreement, which was approved by both boards, each share of Reynolds was exchanged for 1.06 shares of Alcoa stock. When announced, the transaction was worth $4.46 billion and valued each Reynolds share at $70.88, based on an Alcoa closing price of $66.875 on August 19, 1999. The $70.88 price per share of Reynolds suggested a puny 3.9% premium to Reynolds' closing price of $68.25 as of the close of August 19. The combined annual revenues of the two companies totaled $20.5 billion and accounted for about 21.5% of the Western World market for aluminum. To receive antitrust approval, the combined companies were required to divest selected operations.

Case Study Discussion Questions

1. Discuss the takeover strategy Alcoa used in its successful takeover of Reynolds.
2. In your judgment, why was Alcoa able to complete the transaction by offering such a small premium over Reynolds share price at the time the takeover was proposed?

PROXY CONTESTS IN SUPPORT OF A TAKEOVER

The two primary forms of proxy contests are those for seats on the board of directors and those concerning management proposals. Proxy fights sometimes are initiated if management opposes a takeover attempt. They may be used to replace specific board members or management with those more willing to vote for the merger. By replacing board members, proxy contests can be an effective means of gaining control without owning 51% of the voting stock, or they can be used to eliminate takeover defenses, such as poison pills, as a precursor of a tender offer. Alternatively, proxy contests can be initiated by dissident shareholders to stop management from initiating a takeover bid (Case Study 3-2).

CASE STUDY 3-2: HEWLETT-PACKARD FAMILY MEMBERS OPPOSE PROPOSAL TO ACQUIRE COMPAQ

Hewlett-Packard Attempts to Realign Its Strategy

On September 4, 2001, Hewlett-Packard (HP) announced its proposal to acquire Compaq Computer Corporation for $25 billion in stock. The proposed terms of the deal called for each Compaq share to be exchanged for one share of HP common stock, providing a premium of 18% over the price of Compaq common stock on the announcement date. The merger would produce a company with total annual revenue of $90 billion, comparable in size to IBM. The proposed transaction amounts to a renewed bet on the revival of the personal computer business and on a new operating system for computer servers developed by Intel and HP. The combined firms would dominate the personal computer and printer markets.

Both Compaq and HP shareholders suffered throughout 2001 as a result of the decline in technology stocks. Compaq's stock dropped 76% from its previous peak, and HP fell 66% from its previous high. HP's CEO, Carly Fiorina, believed that the combined firms could achieve annual cost savings of $2.5 billion within 2 years after closing. Both HP and Compaq had been hurt by price wars in the market for personal computers, where it has been difficult for manufacturers to differentiate themselves from their competitors. The combined firms would have a $15 billion consulting business, with 65,000 employees in consulting, support, and outsourcing. The HP strategy appears strikingly similar to IBM, which successfully moved into the services business as its hardware business became less profitable. HP would not only enjoy a dominant market share in printers, PCs, and storage devices, it would have the second-largest server business and the third-largest technical services organization. The combination also would double the sales force to 15,000, giving HP access to firms of all sizes. The combined firms would have two "cash cows" to fund future growth. These included the $9 billion ink cartridge business, which churned out $2 billion in profits annually, and a computer repair business generating annual profits of $1 billion.

Investors Are Unimpressed

Almost immediately, investors began to doubt the wisdom of the proposal. The new company would face the mind-numbing task of integrating overlapping product lines and 150,000 employees in 160 countries. The concern seems to have centered on the lack of a precedent of a merger in the technology industry of this size having been successful. Critics notes that many of Compaq's financial problems stemmed from its inability to effectively integrate its 1998 purchase of Digital Equipment. Historically, such mergers have created significant distractions during integration to cut costs to achieve greater efficiency than competitors such as Dell's, while not losing sight of product quality and customer service. Moreover, HP would have to pour money into research and development and consulting to take on IBM, EDS, and others in the services market. It was unclear to investors where this needed funding would come from because more than half of the new company's sales would come from low-margin PCs and printers. Reflecting these concerns, the value of the proposed merger had sunk to $16.9 million within 30 days following the announcement, in line with the decline in the value of HP's stock.

A Lack of Solidarity Among HP Shareholders Threatens the Merger

In November 2001, Walter Hewlett and David Packard, sons of the co-founders, and both the Hewlett and Packard family foundations, came out against the transaction. These individuals and entities controlled about 18% of HP's total shares outstanding. Both Carly Fiorina and Michael Capellas, Compaq's CEO, moved aggressively to counter this opposition by taking their case directly to the remaining HP shareholders. Their focus was on institutions that are major shareholders in both firms; an institutional advisory firm, Institutional Shareholder Services, whose advice could influence as much as 22% of total shares outstanding; and individual investors. Although individual investors rarely vote in proxy fights, they held 25% of HP's shares. HP management's efforts included a 49-page report written by HP's advisor Goldman Sachs to rebut one presented by Walter Hewlett's advisors. HP also began advertising in national newspapers and magazines, trying to convey the idea that this deal is not about PCs but about giving corporate customers everything from storage and services to printing and imaging.

The Proxy Battle Gets Personal

In a letter to their 900,000 shareholders dated January 18, 2002, the eight promerger members of the HP board of directors laid out their reasons why they believed the HP proposal to acquire Compaq was in the best interests of the shareholders. Although the letter did focus on the long process of deliberation that led to the deal, the letter also derided the experience of Walter Hewlett by referring to him as an "academic and musician ... who has never been involved in the direct management of the company." The letter trumpeted the merger as a means of "building a technology powerhouse with depth in high-end computing and services, and achieving profit improvement through cutting jobs and costs." The HP board urged shareholders not to return the proxy cards they had been sent by Hewlett, particularly in light of his not outlining any alternatives (*Reuters*, January 18, 2002).

These comments were intended to blunt Hewlett's earlier arguments to the shareholders that "the merger would bloat its (HP's) low-margin personal computer business and dilute the value of its (HP's) market leading position printer unit." In contrast, Hewlett argued that the merger would prove an enormous distraction to management, enabling competitors to grab customers. Moreover, HP's server business would suffer from ongoing aggressive price cutting by Dell. Hewlett also noted that despite the implementation of cost-cutting measures, Compaq's PC unit still lost $587 million in 2001. Hewlett countered that HP would do best on its own by making a series of smaller, strategic acquisitions. Focus should be on limiting PC and server operating losses by holding the line on price decreases rather than on chasing market share. A more focused HP could make its printer franchise more attractive by expanding its photo printer and "all-in-one" printer–copier–fax businesses.

HP Shareholders Narrowly Support the Merger

On March 23, 2002, HP declared victory in the proxy fight, as shareholders approved the takeover of Compaq by a vote of 838 million for (51.4% of the total vote) and 793 million against (48.6% of the total vote). This slender 2.8 percentage point margin of victory was among the smallest in history. The preliminary vote count was open to a review and challenge period before IVS Associates, a proxy counting firm, could certify a final count. Reminiscent of the 2000 U.S. presidential election, both sides could challenge anything from a blurry signature to the date on the proxy voting cards during this period. Knowing that it was very rare for a vote count to be overturned, Walter Hewlett decided to attack HP's management on a second front.

Hewlett Goes to Court

In a lawsuit filed on March 28, 2002, Hewlett claimed that HP had coerced and enticed Deutsche Bank, a major company shareholder, to change its votes to favor the merger after HP set up a multibillion-dollar credit facility that included the bank. He also accused HP of misleading shareholders about the status of its integration plans. The legal wrangling finally came to a close at the end of April when a Delaware Chancery Court judge dismissed the lawsuit.

The Legacy of the Hewlett/HP Proxy Battle

HP finally was able to purchase Compaq on May 7, 2002, for approximately $19 billion, after an 8-month proxy fight. In the short run, the delay in integrating the two firms probably resulted in the defection of some key employees, the loss of some customers and suppliers, the expenditure of millions of dollars of shareholder funds, and widespread angst among shareholders. In the long run, the outcome of the court battle helps to define what management can and cannot do in persuading shareholders to vote in their favor. To avoid a court fight, management must maintain an arms-length relationship in its dealings with those shareholders over which it may appear that they have undue influence. Moreover, management must be diligent in assuring the complete accuracy of statements communicated to shareholders. However, what may be more telling is the supposed independence of the various parts of Deutsche Bank. Although the judge exonerated HP executives, he expressed serious concern about the potential conflicts of interest at Deutsche Bank in how it decided to swing 17 million votes in HP's favor just before the vote. The judge also raised questions about the "ethical wall" that supposedly separates Deutsche Bank's asset management divisions from its commercial lending division.

Case Study Discussion Questions

1. Discuss the pros and cons of the proposed transaction. Which side would you support and why?
2. Explain why management rarely loses proxy contests. In your judgment, should the rules that govern proxy contests be changed? If so, how?

A proxy fight may be costly. Substantial fees must be paid to hire proxy solicitors, investment bankers, and attorneys. Other expenses include printing, mailing, and advertising. Litigation expenses also may be substantial. The cost of litigation easily can become the largest single expense item in highly contentious proxy contests. Nonetheless, a successful proxy fight represents a far less expensive means of gaining control over a target than a tender offer, which may require purchasing at a substantial premium a controlling interest in the target.

Implementing a Proxy Contest

When the bidder is also a shareholder in the target firm, the proxy process may begin with the bidder attempting to call a special stockholders' meeting. Alternatively, the bidder may put a proposal to replace the board or management at a regularly scheduled stockholders' meeting. Before the meeting, the bidder may undertake an aggressive public relations campaign consisting of direct solicitations sent to shareholders and full-page advertisements in the press in an attempt to convince shareholders to support their proposals. The target will undertake a similar campaign, but it will have a distinct advantage in being able to deal directly with its own shareholders. The bidder may have to sue the target corporation to get a list of its shareholders' names and addresses. Often such shares are held in the name of banks or brokerage houses under a "street name," and these depositories generally do not have the authority to vote such shares. Once the proxies are received by shareholders, they may then sign and send their proxies directly to a designated collection point such as a brokerage house or bank. The votes then are counted, often under the strict supervision of voting inspectors to ensure accuracy. Both the target firm and the bidder generally have their own proxy solicitors present during the tabulation process.

Legal Filings in Undertaking Proxy Contests

Securities Exchange Commission (SEC) regulations cover the solicitation of the target's shareholders for their proxy or right to vote their shares on an issue that is being contested. All materials distributed to shareholders must be submitted to the SEC for review 10 days before they are distributed. Proxy solicitations are regulated by Section 14(a) of the Securities Exchange Act of 1934. The party attempting to solicit proxies from the target's shareholders must file a ***proxy statement*** and Schedule 14A with the SEC and mail it to the target's shareholders.

Proxy statements include the date of the future shareholders' meeting at which approval of the transaction is to be solicited, details of the merger agreement, company backgrounds, reasons for the proposed merger, and opinions of legal and financial advisors. Proxy statements may be obtained from the companies involved, as well as on the Internet at the SEC site (www.sec.gov).

The Impact of Proxy Contests on Shareholder Value

Despite a low success rate, there is some empirical evidence that proxy fights result in abnormal returns to shareholders of the target company regardless of the outcome. The gain in share prices occurred despite only one-fifth to one-third of all proxy fights actually resulting in a change in board control. In studies covering proxy battles during the 1980s through the mid-1990s, abnormal returns ranged from 6% to 19%, even if the dissident shareholders were unsuccessful in the proxy contest (DeAngelo and DeAngelo, 1989; Dodd and Warner, 1983; Mulherin and Poulsen, 1998). Reasons for the gains of this magnitude may include the eventual change in management at most firms embroiled in proxy fights, the tendency for new management to restructure the firm, and investor expectations of a future change in control as a result of merger and acquisition activity. These conclusions were contradicted in a study by Ikenberry and Lakonishok (1993), who found that proxy contests appear to be a result of the poor performance of firms and that firms experienced predominately negative returns during periods associated with proxy contests.

PRE-TENDER OFFER TACTICS: PURCHASING TARGET STOCK IN THE OPEN MARKET

Potential bidders often purchase stock in a target before a formal bid to accumulate stock at a price lower than the eventual offer price. Such purchases are normally kept secret so as not to drive up the price and increase the average price paid for such shares. The primary advantage accruing to the bidder of accumulating target stock before an offer is the potential leverage achieved with the voting rights associated with the stock it has purchased. This voting power is important in a proxy contest to remove takeover defenses, to win shareholder approval under state antitakeover statutes, or for the election of members of the target's board. In addition, the target stock accumulated before the acquisition can be later sold, possibly at a gain, by the bidder in the event the bidder is unsuccessful in acquiring the target firm. This enables the losing bidder to recover some of the legal and investment banking expenses that it has incurred.

Street Sweep

Open-market purchases do not always lead to a tender offer. The bidder may conclude the stock is too closely held, that current shareholders are long-term investors, or that a tender offer is unlikely to garner as much stock as the bidder would like. In this circumstance, the bidder may choose to adopt a so-called street sweep strategy of purchasing as much stock as possible as quickly as possible to gain control. This involves seeking out owners of large blocks of target stock, such as arbs. Such purchases may be made clandestinely before prenotification ownership percentages are reached through the bidder's affiliates, partnerships, or investment bank.

Special Meetings

Once the bidder has established a toehold ownership position in the voting stock of the target through open-market purchases, the bidder may attempt to call a special stockholders' meeting. The purpose of such a meeting may be to call for a replacement of the board of directors or for the removal of takeover defenses. The conditions under which such a meeting can be called are determined by the firm's articles of incorporation governed by the laws of the state in which the firm is incorporated. Generally, such meetings can be called if a certain number of stockholders ask for the meeting.

Limitations to Open-Market Purchases

Federal and state antitrust and securities p\. ~otification laws make it extremely difficult for a bidder to acquire a controlling inte\. ' in a target without such actions becoming public knowledge (see Chapter 2). Und\. federal antitrust law, certain conditions require a Hart–Scott–Rodino filing with th\. Department of Justice and Federal Trade Commission. These conditions include t\. following: one of the firms involved in the deal has assets of more than $50 mi\. ~ or the target has assets of less than $10 million but a purchase price of more t\. ` $200 million. The transaction cannot be completed until a mandated 30-day wait\. ~ period has elapsed. Once a purchaser's intentions are made public, the target's s\.`ck price often will soar in anticipation of an offer for the company. This will dash a\.`hope the buyer may have of obtaining control at a lower average price than the even\.`al offer price. For this reason, the bidder may time the announcement of a tende\. offer to coincide with the first disclosure of its target stock holdings and intentions to achieve a controlling interest in the target.

TENDER OFFERS: CIRCUMVENTING THE TARGET'S BOARD

During the early 1980s, tender offers appeared to be virtually unstoppable. With the tender offer, the takeover battle is taken directly to the shareholders rather than to the target's board. Although the bidder may seek to work with the target's board and management, the tender offer is a deliberate effort to circumvent the target's board and management. Acquirers often resort to tender offers whenever a friendly negotiated settlement is not possible. The early successes of the tender offer generated new, more effective defenses, such as the poison pill, designed to raise the cost of a takeover to the potential acquirer. As a result of new defenses, discussed later in this chapter, tender offers rarely force a target to rapidly capitulate to the bidder. Takeover tactics had to adapt to the proliferation of more formidable takeover defenses. For example, during the 1990s, tender offers were used to go directly to shareholders in combination with proxy contests to overcome takeover defenses.

Implementing a Tender Offer

Tender offers can be for cash or for securities. Unlike mergers, tenders offers frequently use cash as the form of payment. Securities transactions involve a longer period for the takeover to be completed because new security issues must be registered with and approved by the SEC, as well as with states having security registration requirements. During the approval period, target firms are able to prepare defenses and to solicit other bids, resulting in a potentially higher purchase price for the target.

If t' ⸱ tender offer involves a share-for-share exchange, it is referred to as an **exch⸱ ⸱ge offer**. In either case, the proposal is made directly to the shareholders of tl target. The offer is extended for a specific period and may be unrestricted (an ⸱or-all offer) or restricted to a certain percentage or number of the target's sh ⸱e. Restricted tender offers may be oversubscribed. Because the Williams Act o 1968 requires that all shareholders tendering shares must be treated equally, ⸱ ⸱e bidder may either purchase all of the target stock that is tendered or purchase ⸱nly a portion of the tendered stock. For example, if the bidder has extended a tender offer for 70% of the target's outstanding shares and 90% of the target's stock actually is offered, the bidder may choose to prorate the purchase of stock by buying only 63% (63/90 = .70) of the tendered stock from each shareholder.

If the bidder chooses to revise the tender offer, the waiting period automatically is extended. If another bid is made to the target shareholders, the waiting period also must be extended by another 10 days to give them adequate time to consider the new bid. If securities are part of the tender offer, they must be registered with the SEC according to the Securities Act of 1933 as well as under the "Blue Sky Laws" of the states whose jurisdiction is applicable.

Once a tender offer is initiated, it is likely that the target eventually will be acquired, although not necessarily by the original bidder. Not surprisingly, uncontested tender offers result in the target being taken over more than 90% of the time. However, for contested tender offers, the target eventually is acquired about half of the time (Gaughan, 1999, p. 250).

The premium offered for the target's stock under a tender offer often is determined by attempting to forecast the stock price 6–12 months from the tender offer date. The bidder then offers some portion of the difference between the current market value and the forecasted market value to the target firm's shareholders in the form of a premium to the current value of the stock. The bidder is in effect saying to the target firm's shareholders that they can realize the future value of the shares today rather than wait for that value to be realized in the future.

Legal Filings in Undertaking Tender Offers

Federal securities laws impose a number of reporting, disclosure, and antifraud requirements on acquirers initiating tender offers. Once the tender offer has been made, the acquirer cannot purchase any target shares other than the number specified in the tender offer. Thus, what actions constitute a tender offer are of great interest to the potential acquirer.

Defining a Tender Offer for Regulatory Purposes: The Eight-Factor Test

The SEC has taken the position that the term "tender offer" applies to actions in addition to a public announcement and direct mailing of an offer to acquire stock held by the target company's shareholders. Privately negotiated and open-market purchases by the acquirer may be considered tender offers. The SEC has devised an eight-factor test to determine what constitutes a tender offer (Exhibit 3-1).

EXHIBIT 3-1. THE EIGHT-FACTOR TEST TO DETERMINE WHAT CONSTITUTES A TENDER OFFER[1]

Actions taken by a bidder may be considered a tender offer if they involve the following:

3-1. Active and widespread solicitation of public shareholders;

3-2. Solicitation of a substantial percentage of the issuer's stock;

3-3. The offer price provides a premium to the current market price;

3-4. The terms of the offer are firm rather than negotiated;

3-5. The offer is contingent on the tender of a fixed number of shares;

3-6. The offer is open for a limited time;

3-7. Shareholders are pressured to sell the stock; and

3-8. Public announcement of a plan to purchase shares precedes or accompanies rapid accumulation.

[1] The courts have ruled that not all of the factors must be present for an open-market purchase to be declared a tender offer.

Although there has been much litigation on what constitutes a tender offer, no court has ruled that open-market purchases by themselves constitute a tender offer. Even purchases of large blocks of the target's stock in the open market in a short time period, so-called "street sweeps," have not been classified by the courts as tender offers. The courts have ruled consistently that the purchase of stock from institutional investors is not subject to the Williams Act (*Kennecott Cooper Corp. v. Curtiss Wright Corp.*, 1978; *Stromfeld v. Great Atlantic & Pacific Tea Company*, 1980). The courts also have identified open-market purchases combined with privately negotiated purchases as tender offers. Such tactics generally were found to be tender offers whenever shareholders were under pressure to sell their stock. Shareholders were said to be subject to pressure created by a public announcement of the acquirer's intent to purchase the target's stock before a rapid purchase of stock by the acquirer (Wasserstein, 1998, pp. 622–623). Privately negotiated transactions generally have not been found to be tender offers by the courts. The key test seems to be the extent to which a privately negotiated transaction interferes with the stockholder's ability to consider the transaction in an unhurried manner.

Federal Securities Laws: Williams Act 14(d) Reporting Requirements

As noted in Chapter 2, Section 14(d) of the Williams Act covers tender offers. It requires that any individual or entity making a tender offer resulting in owning more than 5% of any class of equity must file a Schedule 14D-1 and all solicitation material with the SEC. In addition to the SEC, copies of the 14D-1 must be sent to the target's executive offices and to each of the public exchanges on which the target's stock is traded. The tender offer begins on the day when it is publicly announced, advertised, or submitted to the target firm. Once the tender offer begins, the bidder has 5 business days to disseminate all materials relating to the tender offer. The target must respond to the tender offer by filing a Schedule 14D-9 within 10 days of the tender offer's commencement date with the SEC and with each exchange on which its stock is traded. The target must indicate whether it recommends acceptance or rejection of the tender offer to its shareholders. The Williams Act also requires that a tender offer be held open for at least 20 days, that the bidder accept all shares that are tendered or at least on a pro rata basis, and that the bidder cannot buy any shares tendered until the end of the 20-day period. The bidder may extend the tender offer period if it believes that it can get the shares it is seeking by doing so, or the bidder may discontinue the tender offer if it does not receive the total number of shares requested under the terms of the tender offer.

Multi-Tiered Offers

A potential acquirer can make either a one-tier or a two-tiered offer for a target firm. The offer can consist of cash, stock, debt, or some combination. In a *one-tier offer*, the acquirer announces the same offer to all target shareholders. In a *two-tiered offer*, target shareholders typically receive two offers, which potentially have different values. In the two-tiered approach, the acquirer announces the price to be paid and the percentage of target shares sought in a first tier. The second-tier offer is referred to as a *back-end merger*. The merger is complete when the acquirer obtains the number of voting shares necessary to achieve control of the target firm. These shares include those acquired in the first tier plus those not owned by the acquirer but that are voted in favor of the merger. All target shares not owned by the acquirer are exchanged at the price or exchange rate announced when the two-tiered offer was initiated.

The purpose of the two-tiered approach is to exploit differences in target shareholders' valuations. The Williams Act of 1968 (see Chapter 2) requires that all

shares tendered to the potential acquirer in the first tier must be treated equally. By offering a higher price for shares tendered during the first tier than in the second tier, the potential acquirer is attempting to encourage target shareholders to tender their shares. If the first-tier offer is oversubscribed, the acquirer either must accept all shares tendered or prorate the difference between the shares tendered and the shares sought to the second tier to be in compliance with the Williams Act. For example, if the bidder is seeking 51% of the target's shares outstanding in the first tier but receives tenders for 80%, the bidder may purchase 40.8% $(.51 \times .80 = .408)$ of the shares tendered from each shareholder in the first tier and purchase any additional shares sought in the second tier. The advantage to the bidder is that the second-tier offer is usually lower than the first-tier offer.

Many states give target company shareholders *appraisal rights* such that target firm shareholders not tendering shares in the first or second tier may seek to have the state court determine a "fair value" for the shares. The appraised value for the shares may be more or less than the offer made by the bidding firm. A variation of the two-tier tender offer is the *toehold strategy*. This approach involves the buyer purchasing a minority position in the target firm through open-market purchases. The buyer subsequently initiates a tender offer to gain a controlling interest; finally after control has been achieved, the buyer offers a lower purchase price for any remaining shares. This lower price may be in the form of the buyer's shares or debt.

OTHER POTENTIAL TAKEOVER STRATEGIES

The process of acquiring another firm is often a very expensive proposition. Consequently, what actions a bidder is willing to take often depends on the perceived likelihood that the takeover attempt actually will succeed. To heighten the chance of success, the bidder will include a variety of provisions in a letter of intent designed to discourage the target firm from backing out of any preliminary agreements. The *letter of intent* (*LOI*) is a preliminary agreement between two companies intending to merge that stipulates major areas of agreement between the parties, as well as their rights and limitations.

The LOI may contain a number of features protecting the buyer. The *no-shop agreement* is among the most common. This agreement prohibits the takeover target from seeking other bids or making public information that is not currently readily available. Related agreements commit the target firm's management to use its best efforts to secure shareholder approval of the bidder's offer. Another means of ensuring that the deal will be completed is to include a *breakup or termination fee*, which would be paid to the initial bidder if the transaction is not completed. This fee reflects legal and advisory expenses, executive management time, and the costs associated with opportunities that may have been lost to the bidder who was involved in trying to close this deal. Another form of protection for the bidder is the *stock lockup*. This is an option granted to the bidder to buy the target firm's stock at the first bidder's initial offer that is triggered whenever a competing bid is accepted by the target firm. Because the target may choose to sell to a higher bidder, the stock lockup arrangement usually ensures that the initial bidder will make a profit on its purchase of the target's stock. The initial bidder also may require that the seller agree to a *crown jewels lockup*, in which the initial bidder has an option to buy important strategic assets of the seller if the seller chooses to sell to another party.

According to critics, target management grants lockup options to discourage competition to select the preferred buyer. The lack of competition is thought to lower purchase price premiums. However, Burch (2001) in a study of 2067 deals announced during 1988–1995 found that on average deals with lockup options have higher target and lower bidder abnormal returns around the date of the announcement. The data are consistent with the notion that target management uses lockup options to enhance their bargaining power in dealing with a bidding firm.

THE TAKEOVER DECISION TREE

The various tactics that may be used in the takeover process should not be viewed as discrete, independent events; they should be viewed as a reasonably structured series of decision points, with options usually well defined and understood before a takeover attempt is initiated. Careful planning should precede the selection of appropriate tactics. This planning involves a review of the target's current defenses, an assessment of the defenses that could be put in place by the target after an offer is made, and the size of the float associated with the target's stock. If minimizing the cost of the purchase and maximizing cooperation between the two parties is considered critical, the bidder may choose the "friendly" approach.

The friendly approach has the advantage of generally being less costly than more aggressive tactics and minimizes the loss of key personnel during the fight for control of the target. Friendly takeovers avoid an auction environment, which generally raises the target's purchase price. Moreover, as noted in Chapter 6, friendly acquisitions facilitate premerger integration planning and increase the likelihood that the combined businesses will be quickly and effectively integrated following closing. The primary risk of this approach is the loss of surprise. If the target is unwilling to reach a negotiated settlement, the acquirer is faced with the choice of abandoning the effort or resorting to more aggressive tactics. Such tactics are likely to be less effective because of the extra time afforded the target's management to put additional takeover defenses in place. In reality, the risk of loss of surprise may not be very great because of the prenotification requirements of the Williams and the Hart-Scott–Rodino Acts. As noted earlier, these requirements make it very difficult, if not impossible, to prevent the bidder's intentions from becoming public knowledge.

Reading Figure 3-1 from left to right, the bidder's options under the friendly approach are to either walk away or to adopt more aggressive tactics if the target's

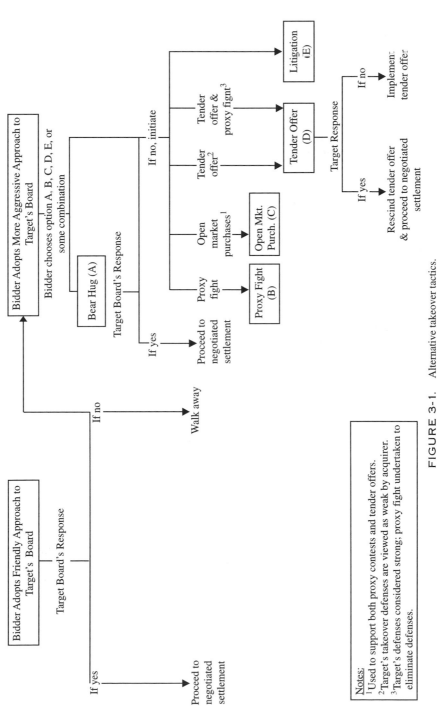

Bidder Adopts Friendly Approach to Target's Board

Target Board's Response

If yes → Proceed to negotiated settlement

If no →

Bidder Adopts More Aggressive Approach to Target's Board

Bidder chooses option A, B, C, D, E, or some combination

Walk away

Bear Hug (A)

Target Board's Response

If yes → Proceed to negotiated settlement

If no, initiate

Proxy fight → Proxy Fight (B)

Open market purchases[1] → Open Mkt. Purch. (C)

Tender offer[2] → Tender Offer (D)

Tender offer & proxy fight[3] → Tender Offer (D)

Litigation (E)

Target Response

If yes → Rescind tender offer & proceed to negotiated settlement

If no → Implement tender offer

Notes:
[1] Used to support both proxy contests and tender offers.
[2] Target's takeover defenses are viewed as weak by acquirer.
[3] Target's defenses considered strong; proxy fight undertaken to eliminate defenses.

FIGURE 3-1.   Alternative takeover tactics.

management and board spurn the bidder's initial offer. If the choice is to become more aggressive, the bidder may undertake a simple bear hug to nudge the target toward a negotiated settlement. The fiduciary responsibilities of the directors require that they consider all reasonable offers. The bear hug tactic presumes that large institutional shareholders and arbs will pressure the Board into agreement with the bidder.

If the bear hug fails to convince the target's management to negotiate, the bidder may choose to buy a sizable block of stock in the open market. This may enable the bidder to accumulate a sufficient number of voting rights to call a special stockholders' meeting if a proxy fight is deemed necessary to change management or board members or to dismember the target's defenses. If the target's defenses are viewed as relatively weak, the bidder may forego a proxy contest and initiate a tender offer for the target's stock. In contrast, if the target's defenses appear formidable, the bidder may implement concurrently a proxy contest and a tender offer.

Finally, litigation is a common tactic used to put additional pressure on the target board to relent to the bidder's takeover attempt or to remove defenses. Litigation may prove particularly effective if the firm's defenses appear to be especially onerous. The board may be accused of not giving the bidder's offer sufficient review or it may be told that the target's defenses are intended only to entrench senior management. As such, the acquirer will allege that the board is violating its fiduciary responsibility to the target firm's shareholders. Lawsuits may be used in support of or independently of other hostile takeover tactics.

ALTERNATIVE TAKEOVER DEFENSES: PREBID AND POSTBID

Alternative takeover defenses can be grouped into two categories: those put in place before receiving a bid and those implemented after receipt of a bid. Prebid defenses are used to prevent a sudden, unexpected hostile bid from gaining control of the company before management has time to assess their options properly. If the prebid defenses are sufficient to delay a change in control, the target firm has time to erect additional defenses after an unsolicited bid is received. Prebid defenses also may be referred to as preventive and postbid as active defenses. Table 3-1 identifies the most commonly used defenses. Public companies make use on average of about three of the various pre- and postbid defenses listed in this table (Field and Karpoff, 2000). These defenses are discussed in more detail later in this chapter.

PREDICTING THE LIKELIHOOD OF BEING ACQUIRED

Many attempts have been made to determine conditions under which firms would be more prone to being acquired. In numerous empirical studies of predictors

TABLE 3-1   Alternative Prebid and Postbid Takeover Defenses

Prebid (Preventive) Defenses	Postbid (Active) Defenses
Poison Pills	
First Generation (Preferred Stock Plans)	Greenmail (Bidder's investment purchased at a
Second Generation (Flip-Over Rights Plans)	premium to cost basis as inducement to refrain
Third Generation (Flip-In Rights Plans)	from any further activity)
Back-End Plans	
Poison Puts	
Shark Repellants (Implemented	
by Changing Bylaws or Charter)	
Strengthening the Board's Defenses	Standstill Agreements (Often used in conjunction
Staggered or Classified Board Elections	with an agreement to buy bidder's investment)
Cumulative Voting Rights	
"For Cause" Provisions	
Limiting Shareholder Actions	
Calling Special Meetings	
Consent Solicitations	
Advance Notice Provisions	
Super Majority Rules	
Antigreenmail Provisions (Discourages	
target's use of greenmail	
as a takeover tactic)	
Fair Price Provisions	
Super Voting Stock	
Reincorporation	
Golden and Silver Parachutes	Pac-Man Defense
	White Knights and White Squires
	Employee Stock Ownership Plans
	Recapitalization
	Share Repurchase Plans
	Corporate Restructuring
	Litigation
	"Just Say No" Defense

of hostile takeovers, only the size of the firm consistently proved to be a major deterrent to takeovers (Comment and Schwert, 1995; Worthington, 2001). Larger firms are simply less likely to be acquired than smaller ones. However, mega-mergers of recent years, such as Citicorp and Travelers and Exxon and Mobil Oil, clearly illustrate that no company is immune from takeover. Table 3-2 summarizes the results of six empirical studies.

THE ROLE OF PLANNING

Because there appears to be relatively few factors that suggest the likelihood of being taken over, the best defense against unwanted suitors may be advance planning and preparation. Large public companies routinely review their takeover defenses. Many companies have "stock watch" programs in place that

TABLE 3-2   Predictors of the Likelihood of Being Acquired

Study	Good Predictor	Poor Predictor
Worthington (2001)	Size	
Comment and Schwert (1995)	Size	
Shivadasani (1993)	Size, managerial holdings, and affiliate firm cross-holdings	Earnings growth and board composition (independent versus employee or family members)
Mikkelson and Partch (1989)	Size and affiliate firm cross-holdings	Leverage and managerial stockholdings
Morck, Shleifer, and Vishny (1988)	Size and market/book value (applies to both hostile and friendly takeovers)	
Palepu (1986)	Size, sales growth, and leverage	
Hasbrouck (1985)	Size and market/book value	Liquidity and leverage

are i. ¬nded to identify stock accumulations or stock price movements that reflect an impei. 'ing takeover attempt. Such a program tracks trading patterns in a company's stocк. Companies require their stock transfer agent to provide up-to-date and accurate stock transfer sheets and to report any unusual movements in stock transfer activity. For example, a large number of blocks of stock traded in the street name of brokerage houses may indicate that a potential suitor is accumulating stock. *Street name* refers to the name of the brokerage firm and not to the actual owner of the stock.

Stock watch programs routinely review SEC records for any Schedule 13D filings. Stock watch programs also may query specialists about large block trades in their stocks. Specialists are members of an exchange charged with maintaining an orderly market in a stock by buying and selling stock for its own account when there is an imbalance in the demand and supply of a stock. Market makers perform a similar function for the over-the-counter market.

Although a takeover attempt may be detectable before it is made public, the rapidity of subsequent events may make an effective defense impossible unless certain defenses are already in place. A preventive strategy involves building defenses that are adequate to the task of slowing down a bidder to give the target company's management and board time to assess the situation and to decide on an appropriate response to an offer. A company's strategy should never be to try to build insurmountable defenses. Courts will disallow defenses, which appear to be designed only to entrench the firm's management.

The "Casual Pass"

A takeover attempt often starts with a "casual pass" in the form of a call to a target board member or executive. Frequently, the individual contacted at the target firm is caught off guard and is ill prepared to respond. Ambiguous responses can be interpreted by the suitor as an expression of interest and invite an unwanted bid. The best response is a strong reaction intended to discourage any would-be suitor. Board members, the CEO, and other key members of management should be instructed to respond in this manner.

When Is Silence Appropriate?

Once a bid has been received, most companies choose never to comment on merger discussions until an agreement has been signed. Companies are understandably reluctant to disclose the receipt of an offer for fear of putting themselves in play. When such an event must be disclosed depends on how far along discussions are with the bidder. The U.S. Supreme Court has said that a company has an obligation to make accurate and nonmisleading statements once it has commented on a situation (see Wasserstein, 1998, p. 689). The Supreme Court also has said that a company's statement of "no comment" will be taken as silence and therefore will not be considered as misleading.

PREBID OR PREVENTIVE DEFENSES

Prebid or preventive defenses generally fall into three categories: poison pills, shark repellants, and golden parachutes. The prevalence and sophistication of such measures has increased dramatically since 1980 in lockstep with the proliferation and effectiveness of takeover tactics. The objective of these defensive measures is to slow the pace of the takeover attempt and to make it more costly for the bidder.

Poison Pills

Poison pills represent a new class of securities issued by a company to its shareholders. These securities have no value unless an investor acquires a specific percentage of the firm's voting stock. If this threshold percentage is exceeded, the poison pill securities are activated and typically allow the shareholder to purchase additional shares of the issuing firm's common stock. This has the effect of raising the cost of the acquisition to the acquirer. This occurs when target company shareholders exercise their rights to purchase more of the target's shares (often at a discount from their current market price) or convert existing preferred shares to common shares in the target company. Under either circumstance, this increases the buyer's total acquisition cost by increasing the number of target common shares to be purchased with cash or acquiring company shares in a share-for-share exchange. In the latter case, the increase in the number of acquirer shares reduces the portion of the combined firm's equity held by acquiring firm shareholders, thereby diluting their ownership share of the new company. Approximately 60% of publicly traded firms have poison pill plans in place (Field and Karpoff, 2002). Poison pills have evolved through three generations, as new versions were introduced to solve problems existing with earlier versions (Table 3-3).

TABLE 3-3 Advantages and Disadvantages of Prebid or Preventive Takeover Defenses—Poison Pills

Type of Poison Pill	Advantages for Target Firm	Disadvantages for Target Firm
First Generation (Preferred Stock Plans convertible into stock of the acquirer) Activated following completion of takeover	1. Dilutes ownership position of the acquirer and raises cost of acquisition 2. May result in positive abnormal returns to target shareholders if investors view that a takeover is imminent	1. Activated following completion of merger 2. Issuer may redeem only after an extended time period (sometimes 10 years); limits target's flexibility if it is later decided to pursue a merger 3. Increases leverage because preferred stock is often counted as debt by credit rating agencies
Second Generation (Flip-Over Rights to buy stock in the acquirer) Countdown to expiration begins whenever a specific event occurs such as a hostile tender for 40% of a firm's stock Exercisable after buyer purchases 100% of target's stock	1. No impact on leverage 2. Simpler to implement because does not require issuance of preferred stock with attendant SEC filing requirements 3. Rights redeemable by buying them back from shareholders at nominal price	1. Ineffective in preventing acquisition of less than 100% of target. Hostile bidders could buy controlling interest only and buy the remainder after rights expire 2. Subject to hostile tender contingent on target board's redemption of the pill 3. Makes issuer less attractive to White Knights
Third Generation (Flip-In Rights to buy stock in target) Activated by an event such as a less than 100% change in ownership	1. Effective in dealing with bidders buying less than 100% of target. Dilutes target stock regardless of amount of stock purchased by acquired 2. Flip in rights are discriminatory (i.e., not given to investor who activated the rights) 3. Rights are redeemable at any point before the triggering event	1. May not be permissible in certain states due to their discriminatory nature 2. No poison pill provides any protection against proxy contests
Back-End Plans	1. Back-end price set above market price, effectively setting a minimum price for a takeover. Deals effectively with two-tiered tender offer	1. Target's board put in position of effectively setting a sale price, while saying publicly that the company is not for sale
Poison Puts	1. Places large cash demands on the combined firms	1. Rendered ineffective if acquirer can convince put holders not to exercise their options. Particularly true if bond's coupon rate exceeds market rates of interest

First-Generation Poison Pills

The brainchild of Marty Lipton, the famous Wall Street attorney, the first-generation poison pill was developed in 1982 and involved issuing preferred stock in the form of a dividend to shareholders convertible into the common stock of the acquiring company following a takeover. If a target company were acquired and merged into the acquirer, target company shareholders owning the special preferred stock could convert the preferred stock into multiple shares of the acquirer's stock. This would dilute immediately the acquirer's ownership interest in the earnings of the combined companies. To implement this type of plan, companies customarily use *blank check preferred stock*, which is stock that has been authorized but not yet issued. The board normally has broad discretion to establish voting, dividend, conversion, and other rights for this stock.

Second-Generation Poison Pills

The second-generation poison pill included a rights plan or *flip-over pill*. The flip-over pill enables the holder of the security to purchase the acquirer's shares at a discount. By enabling target shareholders to buy shares at a discount in the surviving company, the pill has resulted in a dilution of the ownership position of the acquiring firm's shareholders. The target company's shareholders were said to flip over and become acquirer shareholders.

Third-Generation Poison Pills

The third-generation pill was referred to as the *flip-in* pill. Under this plan, shareholders receive a special dividend of one stock purchase right for each share they own. The rights are activated whenever an investor acquires a certain percentage of the stock of the company issuing the rights, without prior board approval. When the rights are activated, holders of the rights are allowed to buy stock in the issuing company (i.e., target firm) at a substantial discount. This increases the number of shares the acquirer must purchase, thereby raising the cost to the acquiring firm. More cash must be used to purchase the increased number of target shares or more acquirer shares must be issued in a share-for-share exchange. In the later case, the increased number of acquirer shares issued dilutes the ownership position of current acquirer shareholders. The flip-in plan is the type most commonly used today.

Back-End Plans and Poison Puts

Other types of poison pills include back-end plans and poison puts. With *back-end plans*, shareholders receive a dividend of rights, giving them the option of exchanging the rights for cash or senior debt securities at a specific price set by the target's board. The price usually is set above the current market price of the target company's shares. This effectively communicates to potential acquirers the asking price for the company as determined by the target's board. With *poison puts*, the target issues bonds containing put options exercisable if and only if an unfriendly takeover occurs. This enables holders of these puts to cash in their bonds, thereby placing substantial cash demands on the acquiring company.

Poison Pills Effectively Slow but Rarely Prevent Takeovers

Although the pill has proven to be an effective means of delaying a takeover and of increasing the overall expense to the acquiring company, pill defenses rarely prevent a firm from being acquired, although not necessarily by the initial bidder (Georgeson & Company, 1997a). Most pills are put in place with the caveat or *escape clause* that the board of the issuing company can redeem the pill through a nominal payment to the shareholders. This is necessary to avoid dilution of the bidder's ownership position in the event the acquiring company is considered friendly. In addition, the Delaware Supreme Court, in approving the poison pill as a defensive measure and as a means of enabling the target to secure higher bids, made its approval largely conditional on the existence of a redemption feature or escape clause. However, the existence of this redemption feature has made pill defenses vulnerable. For example, a tender offer may be made conditional on the board's redemption of the pill. The target's board will be under substantial pressure from institutions and arbs to redeem the pill if the bidder has offered a significant premium over the current price of the target's stock. Alternatively, such takeover defenses could be dismantled through a proxy fight. One strategy that has sometimes been used to mitigate this redemption feature is the *dead hand* poison pill. This security is issued with special characteristics, which prevent the board of directors from taking action to redeem or rescind the pill unless the directors were the same directors who adopted the pill.

SHARK REPELLANTS

Shark repellants are specific types of takeover defenses that can be adopted by amending either a corporate charter or its bylaws. The charter gives the corporation its legal existence. The *corporate charter* consists of the *articles of incorporation*, a document filed with a state government by the founders of a corporation, and a *certificate of incorporation*, a document received from the state once the articles have been approved. The charter contains the corporation's name, purpose, amount of authorized shares, and number and identity of directors. The corporation's powers thus derive from the laws of the state and from the provisions of the charter. Rules governing the internal management of the corporation are described in the *corporation's bylaws*, which are determined by the corporation's founders.

Shark repellants are put in place largely to reinforce the ability of a firm's board of directors to retain control. Although shark repellants predate poison pills, their success in slowing down and making takeovers more expensive has been mixed. These developments have given rise to more creative defenses such as the poison pill. Today, shark repellants are intended largely as supplements to the poison pill defenses. Their role is primarily to make gaining control of the board through a proxy fight at an annual or special meeting more difficult.

In conjunction with the firm's charter and bylaws, the laws of the state in which the firm is incorporated determine what may be enacted as a bylaw without shareholder approval. In practice, most shark repellants require amendments to the firm's charter, which necessitate a shareholder vote. Although there are many variations of shark repellants, the most typical include staggered board elections, restrictions on shareholder actions, anti-Greenmail provisions, super-voting, and debt-based defenses. Table 3-4 summarizes the primary advantages and disadvantages of each type of shark repellant defense.

Strengthening the Board's Defenses

Staggered or Classified Board Elections

Following an amendment to the firm's charter, the firm's directors are divided into a number of different classes. Only one class is up for reelection each year. For example, for a board consisting of 12 members, the directors may be divided into 4 classes with each director elected for a 4-year period. In the first year, the 3 directors designated as class 1 directors are up for reelection, in the second year class 2 directors are up for election, and so on. Consequently, an insurgent stockholder who may hold the majority of the stock still would have to wait for 3 elections to gain control of the board. Moreover, the size of the board is limited to preclude the insurgent stockholder from adding board seats to take control of the board. The target may have to accede to the majority stockholder's demands because of litigation initiated by dissident shareholder groups. The likelihood of litigation is highest and pressure on the board is greatest whenever the offer price for the target is substantially above the target firm's current share price. Approximately one-half of publicly traded firms have classified board defenses in place (Field and Karpoff, 2002).

Cumulative Voting Rights

Some firms have common stock carrying cumulative voting rights to maximize minority representation. Using the preceding example of a 12-member board, a shareholder, who has 100 shares of stock, has 300 votes for 3 open seats for class 1 directors. The shareholder may cumulate her votes and cast them for a specific candidate. An insurgent stockholder may choose this approach to obtain a single seat on the board to gain access to useful information that is not otherwise readily available. However, cumulative voting rights also may backfire against the dissident shareholder. Cumulative voting may be used to counter the ability of insurgents to gain control of the board by cumulating the votes of opposing shareholders and casting them for candidates who would vigorously represent the board's positions. Only about one-fifth of large companies have cumulative voting stock (see Bhagat and Brickley, 1984).

TABLE 3-4 Advantages and Disadvantages of Prebid or Preventive Takeover Defenses—Shark Repellents and Golden Parachutes

Type of Defense	Advantages for Target Firm	Disadvantages for Target Firm
Shark Repellents: Strengthening the Board's Defenses		
Staggered or Classified Boards	Delays assumption of control by a majority shareholder	May be circumvented by increasing size of board
Cumulative Voting	Delays assumption of control by a majority shareholder	Gives dissident shareholder a board seat and access to confidential information
Limitations on When Can Remove Directors	"For cause" provisions narrow range of reasons for removal	Can be circumvented unless supported by a super-majority requirement for repeal
Shark Repellents: Limiting Shareholder Actions		
Limitations on Calling Special Meetings	Limits ability to use special meetings to add board seats, remove or elect new members	States may require a special meeting if a certain percentage of shareholders request a meeting
Limiting Consent Solicitations	Limits ability of dissident shareholders to expedite a proxy contest process	May be subject to court challenge
Advance Notice Provisions	Gives board time to select its own slate of candidates and to decide an appropriate response	May be subject to court challenge
Super-Majority Provisions	May be applied selectively to events such as hostile takeovers	Can be circumvented unless a super-majority of shareholders are required to change the provision
Other Shark Repellents		
Antigreenmail Provision	Eliminates profit opportunity for raiders	Eliminates greenmail as a takeover defense
Fair Price Provisions	Increases the cost of a two-tiered tender offer	Raises the cost to a White Knight, unless waived by typically 95% of shareholders
Super Voting Stock	Gives "friendly" shareholders more voting power than others	Difficult to implement because requires shareholder approval; only useful when voting power can be given to promanagement shareholders; and only available to firms with such shares outstanding as of July 1988
Reincorporation	Takes advantage of most favorable state antitakeover statutes	Requires shareholder approval; time consuming to implement unless subsidiary established before takeover solicitation
Defenses Not Requiring Shareholder Approval		
Golden Parachutes	Emboldens target management to negotiate for a higher premium and raises the cost of a takeover to the hostile bidder	Negative public perception; makes termination of top management expensive

"For Cause" Provisions

Such provisions specify the conditions for removing a member of the board of directors. This narrows the range of reasons for removal and limits the flexibility of dissident shareholders in contesting board seats.

Limiting Shareholder Actions

Other means of reinforcing the board's ability to retain control include limiting the ability of shareholders to gain control of the firm by bypassing the board altogether. These include limiting their ability to call special meetings and to engage in consent solicitations and limiting the use of super-majority rules.

Calling Special Meetings

Many states require a firm to call a special meeting of the shareholders if it is requested by a certain percentage of its shareholders. If such a meeting is called by the shareholders, the board is confronted with several challenges. The first challenge arises when special meetings are used as a forum for insurgent shareholders to take control by replacing current directors with those who are likely to be more cooperative or by increasing the number of board seats. To limit this type of action, firms frequently include in their bylaws a provision that directors can be removed "for cause" defined in the charter or bylaws and a limitation on the number of board seats. The second major challenge occurs when shareholders engage in a nonbinding vote to remove certain types of defenses such as a poison pill. The board then must decide to ignore the will of the shareholders or to remove the defenses.

Consent Solicitations

In some states, shareholders may take action to add to the number of seats on the board, to remove specific board members, or to elect new members without a special meeting. All that is required is the written consent of shareholders. Although the consent solicitation must abide by the disclosure requirements applicable to proxy contests, dissident stockholders may use this process to expedite their efforts to seize control or to remove defenses. This process circumvents delays inherent in setting up a meeting to conduct a stockholder vote. Companies have attempted to limit shareholders' ability to use this procedure by amending charters or bylaws. Bylaw amendments may not require shareholder approval. However, the courts frequently have frowned upon actions restricting shareholder rights without shareholder approval.

Advance Notice Provisions

Some corporate bylaws require the announcement of shareholder proposals and board nominations well in advance of an actual vote. Some bylaws require advance notice of as long as 2 months. Such provisions buy significant time for the target's board to determine an appropriate response to an unsolicited offer.

Super-Majority Rules

These rules require that a higher level of approval is required for amending the charter or for certain types of transactions such as a merger or acquisition. Such rules are triggered if an "interested party" acquires a specific percentage of the ownership shares (e.g., 5–10%). Super-majority rules may require that as much as 80% of the shareholders must approve a proposed merger or a simple majority of all shareholders except the "interested party." Super-majority rules often include escape clauses, which allow the board to waive the requirement. For example, super-majority rules may not apply to mergers approved by the board.

Antigreenmail Provisions

During the 1980s, many raiders profited by taking an equity position in a target firm, threatening takeover, and subsequently selling their ownership position back to the target firm at a premium over what they paid for the target's shares. Many believed that the payment of greenmail only encouraged this type of behavior. Many corporations adopted charter amendments restricting the firm's ability to repurchase shares at a premium. By removing the incentive for greenmail, companies believed they were making themselves less attractive as potential takeover targets. As such, antigreenmail provisions may be viewed as an antitakeover tactic. About 10% of public companies have antigreenmail defenses in place (Field and Karpoff, 2002).

Fair-Price Provisions

A corporation may call for a shareholder vote to amend its charter to require that any acquirer pay minority shareholders at least a fair market price for their stock. The fair market price may be expressed as some historical multiple of the company's earnings or as a specific price equal to the maximum price paid when the buyer acquired shares in the company. Fair-price provisions are most effective when the target firm is subject to a two-tiered tender offer. The fair-price provision forces the bidder to pay target shareholders, who tender their stock in the second tier, the same terms offered to those tendering their stock in the first tier. Most such provisions do not apply if the proposed takeover is approved by the target firm's board of directors or if the bidder obtains a specified super-majority level of approval from the target's shareholders. About 40% of public companies make use of fair-price provisions (Field and Karpoff, 2000).

Super-Voting Stock

Companies may have more than one class of stock for many reasons, including the separating the performance of individual operating subsidiaries, compensating subsidiary operating management, and preventing hostile takeovers. As a takeover defense, a firm may issue several classes of stock having different voting rights. The objective is to concentrate stock with the greatest voting rights in the hands of those who are most likely to support management. One class of stock may have

10 to 100 times the voting rights of another class of stock. Such stock is said to have "super-voting" rights. This stock is issued to all shareholders along with the right to exchange it for ordinary stock. Most shareholders are likely to exchange it for ordinary stock because the stock with the multiple voting rights usually has a limited resale market and pays a lower dividend than other types of voting stock issued by the corporation. Management usually will retain the special stock. This effectively increases the voting control of the corporation in the hands of management. Today, the creation of a new class of stock with super-voting privileges is generally not allowed under the voting rights policies of the SEC, the New York Stock Exchange (NYSE), American Exchange, and the National Association of Securities Dealers. However, companies that issued such stock before July 1988, when such issues were allowed, are permitted to continue to issue such stock.

Reincorporation

A potential target firm may choose to change its state of incorporation to one in which the laws are more favorable for implementing takeover defenses. Several factors need to be considered in selecting a state for possible reincorporation. These include how the state's courts have ruled in lawsuits alleging breach of corporate director fiduciary responsibility in takeover situations and the state's statutes pertaining to the treatment of poison pills, staggered boards, and hostile tender offers. Reincorporation involves the creation of a subsidiary in the new state. The parent then is merged into the subsidiary at a later date. Shareholders normally must approve such a move because a merger of the parent is involved.

GOLDEN, SILVER, AND TIN PARACHUTES

Golden parachutes are employee severance arrangements, which are triggered whenever a change in control takes place. Such a plan usually covers only a few dozen employees and obligates the company to make a lump-sum payment to employees covered under the plan who are terminated following a change in control. A change in control usually is defined to occur whenever an investor accumulates more than a fixed percentage of the corporation's voting stock. Occasionally, changes in control as a result of friendly acquisitions may be exempted from triggering the plans. However, this obviates the stated purpose of the plans to retain key employees who may feel threatened by a pending change in control. *Silver parachutes* are severance agreements that cover far more employees and also are triggered in the same manner as golden parachutes. Although golden parachute payments may equal several years of an employee's pay, silver parachute payments are usually much less, consisting of 6 months to 1 year of severance. In some instances, *tin parachute* plans cover virtually all employees and consist of very modest severance payments. When triggered, payments under such parachute plans make the takeover much more expensive for the acquirer.

The board of directors generally can implement golden, silver, and tin parachutes without stockholder approval. Plans put in place before a specific takeover threat generally are protected by *the business judgment rule*, which states that management's actions are appropriate if they are implemented while management is acting in the stockholders' best interests (see *Buckhorn Inc. v. Ropak Corp.*, 1987). According to the courts, boards putting plans in place before a specific takeover threat must be able to demonstrate that the company conducted a reasonable, good-faith investigation of the perceived takeover threat and that the plan constituted a reasonable response (Wasserstein, 1998, p. 711). Public criticism of such plans has caused many corporations to create compensation committees consisting of outside directors to review all compensation and benefit plans before they are implemented. The 1986 Tax Act imposed stiff penalties on these types of plans if they create what is deemed an excessive payment. Excessive payments are those exceeding three times the employee's average pay over the last 5 years and are not tax deductible by the paying corporation. The employee receiving the parachute payment also must pay a 20% surcharge in addition to the normal tax due on the parachute payment.

DEFENSES UNDERTAKEN IN RESPONSE TO A BID (POSTBID OR ACTIVE DEFENSES)

Once an unwanted suitor has approached a firm there are a variety of additional defenses that can be introduced. These include greenmail to dissuade the bidder from continuing the pursuit; defenses designed to make the target less attractive, such as restructuring and recapitalization strategies; and efforts to place an increasing share of the company's ownership in friendly hands by establishing ESOPs and seeking white knights and squires. Table 3-5 summarizes the primary advantages and disadvantages of such postbid or active takeover defenses.

Greenmail

Greenmail is the practice of paying a potential acquirer to leave you alone. It usually consists of a payment to buy back shares at a premium price in exchange for the acquirer's agreement to not undertake a hostile takeover. In exchange for the payment, the potential acquirer is required to sign a standstill agreement, which typically specifies the amount of stock, if any, that the investor can own, the circumstances under which the raider can sell stock currently owned, and the term of the agreement. Despite their discriminatory nature, courts in certain states such as Delaware have found greenmail an appropriate response as long as it is made for valid business reasons. However, courts in other states, such as California, have favored shareholder lawsuits, based on the contention that greenmail constituted a breach of fiduciary responsibility (Wasserstein, 1998, pp. 719–720).

The importance of greenmail as a takeover defense has diminished since the late 1980s. Greenmail is arguably counterproductive because once such a payment becomes public others may feign a takeover attempt to receive

TABLE 3-5 Advantages and Disadvantages of Postbid (Active) Takeover Defenses

Type of Defense	Advantages for Target Firm	Disadvantages for Target Firm
Greenmail	Encourages raider to go away (usually accompanied by a standstill agreement)	Reduces risk to raider of losing money on a takeover attempt; unfairly discriminates against nonparticipating shareholders; often generates litigation; and triggers unfavorable tax consequences
Standstill Agreement	Prevents raider from returning for a specific time period	Increases amount of greenmail paid to get raider to sign standstill; provides only temporary reprieve
Pac-Man Defense	Sends message that target will defend itself at all costs	Requires that target can fund such a strategy and may emasculate both the target and the bidder
White Knights/White Squires	May be a preferable alternative to the hostile bidder	Necessarily involves loss of target's independence
ESOPs	Alternative to white knight and highly effective if used in conjunction with certain states' antitakeover laws	Employee support not guaranteed. ESOP cannot overpay for stock because transaction could be disallowed by federal employee benefit laws
Recapitalizations	Makes target less attractive to bidder and may increase target shareholder value if incumbent management motivated to improve performance	Increased leverage reduces target's debt capacity
Share Buy-Back Plans	Reduces number of target shares available for purchase by bidder, arbs, and others who may sell to bidder	Securities laws limit ability to self-tender without SEC filing once hostile tender under way. A reduction in the shares outstanding may facilitate bidder's gaining control
Corporate Restructuring	Going private may be attractive alternative to bidder's offer for target shareholders and for incumbent management	Going private, sale of attractive assets, making defensive acquisitions, or liquidation may reduce target's shareholder value vs. bidder's offer
Litigation	May buy time for target to build defenses and increases takeover cost to the bidder	May have negative impact on target shareholder returns
"Just Say No"	Buys time to build defenses	Must satisfy conditions established by the courts

similar payments. In addition, the federal tax code was changed in 1987 to impose a 50% tax on any gains associated with the payment of greenmail. To be subject to the tax, the payment must have been made to acquire stock from a shareholder making or threatening to make a tender offer for the paying company's stock and who has held the stock for less than 2 years. Finally, in response to public criticism, some firms have amended their charters with antigreenmail provisions requiring management to obtain approval of the majority or the super-majority of nonparticipating shareholders before repurchasing a specific investor's stock at a premium.

Pac-Man Defense

A rarely used, but highly aggressive, defense is for the target to make a hostile tender offer for the bidder. Such a defense is only effective if the target has the financial resources to make a legitimate bid for the bidder. Such a scenario may be mutually destructive because both companies may be left extremely highly leveraged in the wake of their attempts to implement hostile tenders for each other.

White Knights and White Squires

A target company seeking to avoid being taken over by a specific bidder may try to be acquired by another firm, a *white knight*, which is viewed as a more appropriate suitor. To complete such a transaction, the white knight must be willing to acquire 100% of the target on more favorable terms than those of the original bidder. The motivation for the white knight is generally more mercenary than chivalrous. Fearing that a bidding war might ensue, the white knight often demands some protection in the form of a *lock-up* in an agreement of purchase and sale eventually signed with the target. The lock-up may involve giving the white knight options to buy stock in the target that has not yet been issued at a fixed price or to acquire at a fair price target assets that are viewed as strategic by the white knight. Such lock-ups usually have the effect of making the target less attractive to the original bidder. In the event a bidding war ensues, the knight may exercise the stock options and sell the shares at a profit to the acquiring company.

White squires are firms that agree to purchase a large block of the target's stock. Such stock is often convertible preferred, which may have already been approved but has not yet been issued by the target company. If the target's stock trades on the NYSE, the target still will have to receive shareholder approval to sell such stock to a white squire. The NYSE requires shareholder approval if such shares are issued to officers or directors or if the number issued equals 20% of the target's shares outstanding. Warren Buffet is probably the most famous white squire following his investments in such companies as Gillette, Coca-Cola, U.S. Air, and Salomon Brothers. Blank check preferred stock may be issued to white knights and white squires.

Employee Stock Ownership Plans

ESOPs are trusts that hold a firm's stock as an investment for their employees' retirement program. ESOPs may be viewed as an alternative to a white knight or white squire defense. They can be established quickly, with the company either issuing shares directly to the ESOP or having an ESOP purchase shares on the open market. Any impact on earnings per share of issuing the stock to the ESOP can be offset by the firm repurchasing shares on the open market. The stock held by ESOPs is likely to be voted in support of management in the event of a hostile takeover attempt. However, this support is not guaranteed because according to federal benefits and tax laws, employees must be given the freedom to control how their ESOP stock is voted.

Recapitalization

To recapitalize a company may need shareholder approval, depending on the company's charter and the laws of the state in which it is incorporated. A company may recapitalize by assuming substantial amounts of new debt, which is used to either buy back stock or finance a dividend to shareholders. In doing so, the target becomes less attractive to a bidder because the additional debt reduces its borrowing capacity, which may have been used by the bidder to help finance the takeover of the target. Moreover, the payment of a dividend or a stock buyback may persuade shareholders to support the target's management in a proxy contest or hostile tender offer. The target firm is left in a highly leveraged position. Critics have viewed this strategy as equivalent to scorched earth policies. However, in practice, they may add significantly to shareholder value.

Whether the recapitalization actually weakens the target firm in the long term depends on its impact on the target firm's shareholder value. Shareholders will benefit from the receipt of a dividend or from capital gains resulting from a stock repurchase. Furthermore, the increased debt service requirements of the additional debt will shelter a substantial amount of the firm's taxable income and may encourage management to be more conscientious about improving the firm's performance. Thus, the combination of these factors may result in current shareholders benefiting more from this takeover defense than from a hostile takeover of the firm. As an alternative to taking on more debt, the target firm may issue additional shares to make it more difficult for a bidder to gain a controlling interest. The increase in the number of shares will dilute earnings per share and reduce the target's share price.

Share Repurchase or Buyback Plans

When used as an antitakeover tactic, share repurchase or buyback plans are intended to reduce the number of shares that could be purchased by the potential acquirer or by those such as arbitrageurs who will sell to the highest bidder. This tactic reflects the belief that when a firm initiates a tender offer (i.e., a self-tender) for a portion of its own shares the shareholders who offer their shares for sale are those most susceptible to a tender offer by hostile bidder. Therefore, for a hostile tender offer to succeed in purchasing the remaining shares, the premium offered would have to be higher. The resulting higher potential premium might discourage some prospective bidders (Bagwell, 1992). A share buyback may work well in combination with a white squire strategy in which the target can place stock in friendly hands.

The repurchase tactic may in fact be subject to the "law of unintended consequences." By reducing the number of shares on the open market, it may be easier for the buyer to gain control because fewer shares have to be purchased to achieve 51% of the target's outstanding voting shares. Moreover, self-tenders actually may attract potential bidders if they are seen as a harbinger of improving target company cash flows. Self-tenders are regulated by Section 13e of the Securities and Exchange Act of 1934. Federal securities law prohibits purchase by an issuer of its own shares during a tender offer for its shares. However, an exception is made if the firm files a statement with the SEC disclosing the identity of the purchaser, stock exchanges that will be used for the purchase, the intent of the purchase, and the intended disposition of the shares.

Restructuring

Restructuring may involve taking the company private, the sale of attractive assets, undertaking a major acquisition, or even liquidating the company. "Going private" typically involves the management team's purchase of the bulk of a firm's shares. This may create a win–win situation for shareholders who receive a premium for their stock and management who retain control. To avoid lawsuits, the price paid for the stock must represent a substantial premium to the current market price. Alternatively, the target may make itself less attractive by divesting assets the bidder wants. The cash proceeds of the sale could fund other defenses such as share buybacks or payment of a special stockholder dividend. A target company also may undertake a so-called *defensive acquisition* to draw down any excess cash balances and to exhaust its current borrowing capacity. Liquidation represents the most drastic alternative. A firm may choose to liquidate the company, pay off outstanding obligations to creditors, and distribute the remaining proceeds to shareholders as a liquidating dividend. This makes sense only if the liquidating dividend exceeds what the shareholders would have received from the bidder (see Chapter 13).

Litigation

Takeover litigation often includes antitrust concerns, alleged violations of federal securities laws, inadequate disclosure by the bidder as required by the Williams Act, and alleged fraudulent behavior. Targets often try to get a court injunction temporarily stopping the takeover attempt until the court has decided that the target's allegations are groundless. By preventing the potential acquirer from buying more stock, the target firm is buying time to erect additional takeover defenses. Litigation occurs in about one-third of takeover attempts (Jarrell, 1985).

"Just Say No" Defense

A target board may attempt to buy time when faced with a hostile takeover attempt by simply refusing to accede to the bidder's demands. However, the refusal cannot be arbitrary. The board cannot refuse to withdraw certain defenses or decline the bid without being able to satisfy two conditions (*Unocal v. Mesa*, 1985). The first condition is that the board must establish that it has well-founded grounds that the bid is inadequate and that it threatens existing corporate strategy. The second condition requires that actions taken to defend against a hostile takeover attempt be in proportion to the size of the threat. In other words, a target board cannot erect defenses that cannot be penetrated. Such scenarios are likely to invite shareholder litigation. In general, the "just say no" defense will crumble as a result of shareholder pressure if the offer price is attractive enough.

Impact on Shareholder Value of Takeover Defenses: Empirical Evidence

As noted in Chapter 1 of this book, average abnormal returns to target shareholders about the time of a tender offer announcement have increased dramatically since the 1960s to significantly more than 35%, whereas abnormal returns to acquirer shareholders have deteriorated from marginally positive to slightly negative. In contrast, the abnormal return to shareholders following merger announcements (i.e., those presumed to be "friendly") has remained remarkably stable at about 20%. The increase in target company shareholder returns may be attributable to potential improvements in efficiency, tax savings, or market power. However, if this were true, one would have expected abnormal returns for mergers to also show a correspondingly large increase over time. Consequently, other factors must be at work.

It is probably more than coincidental that the increase in abnormal returns began with the introduction of the 1967 Wallace Act notification period. This provided a respite for target firms to erect takeover defenses and to search for other potential bidders. Takeover defenses such as poison pills, although unlikely to prevent a takeover, could add significantly to the overall purchase price. The purchase price could be further boosted by any auction that might take place as the initial bidder lost precious time in trying to overcome myriad defenses the target may have in place. Thus, the increasing sophistication of takeover defenses since 1980 would seem to be a highly plausible factor explaining the sustained increase in abnormal returns to target shareholders following the announcement of a tender offer.

Unfortunately, it is difficult to substantiate this intuitive argument empirically. Although numerous empirical studies of the effects of takeover defenses have been undertaken during the last 20 years, it is difficult to reach any significant conclusions about their impact on shareholder returns. Most studies seem to have difficulty accounting for effects of takeover defenses announced shortly after a takeover attempt has been announced or rumored. Such tactics could be an attempt by management to negotiate a better price during negotiation. Investors could interpret this as a positive development. Moreover, an acquisition of one firm within an industry may initiate speculation that others in the industry will be acquired, thereby triggering a run-up in the share prices of all firms in the industry. This speculative run-up in share prices clearly could overwhelm any negative effects resulting from individual firm's takeover defenses.

Those studies showing a negative return to shareholders support the argument that incumbent management acts in its own self-interest—the management entrenchment hypothesis; studies showing a positive shareholder return support the argument that incumbent management acts in the best interests of shareholders—the shareholder interests hypothesis. For many takeover defenses, empirical results cannot be confirmed by multiple studies, the available evidence is largely contradictory, or the findings are statistically insignificant, perhaps because of chance. The empirical evidence seems to suggest that takeover defenses in general have virtually no statistically significant impact on shareholder returns or, as in the case of poison pills, have a positive impact. Thus, the empirical evidence taken together provides only weak support for the notion that managers tend to act in the best interests of shareholders.

In a comprehensive review of previous studies, Comment and Schwert (1995) found that most takeover defensives such as staggered boards, super-majority provisions, fair-price provisions, reincorporation, and dual capitalization resulted in a slightly negative decline in shareholder returns of about 0.5%. These studies included the following: Jarrell and Poulsen, 1987; Malatesta and Walkling, 1988; Ryngaert, 1988; Karpoff and Malatesta, 1989; and Romano, 1993. Other studies found no statistically significant negative results (DeAngelo and Rice, 1983; Linn and McConnell, 1983). A more recent study found that shareholder efforts to remove takeover defenses had no significant impact on shareholder returns, suggesting that such efforts were viewed by investors as largely inconsequential (Karpoff and Walkling, 1996). Field and Karpoff (2002) concluded in a study of 1019 initial public offerings between 1988 and 1992 that the presence of takeover defenses had no impact on the takeover premiums of those firms subsequently acquired.

The Comment and Schwert (1995) study also found that poison pills would have a positive impact on shareholder returns if they were viewed by investors as a signal that a takeover was imminent or that the firm's management would use such a defense to improve the purchase price during negotiation. The existence of poison pills often requires the bidder to raise its bid or to change the composition of its bid to an all-cash offer to put the target's board under pressure to dismantle its pill defenses. Timing also is important. For example, whenever a merger announcement or a rumor of an impending merger coincided with the announcement of a poison pill, abnormal returns to target shareholders increased by 3% to 4%. Moreover, according to a study by Georgeson & Company (1997a, 1997b), there is no evidence that the presence of poison pills increases the likelihood that a friendly takeover bid will be withdrawn or that a hostile bid will be defeated. The study also concludes that there is no indication that poison pills reduce the chance that a company will become a takeover target. In contrast, if investors viewed the introduction of the poison pill as deterring potential takeover attempts, the effect on shareholder returns would be negative.

THINGS TO REMEMBER

Takeovers often are divided into friendly and hostile categories. Friendly takeovers include those that reach a negotiated settlement without experiencing contentious proxy contests, tender offers, or litigation. A hostile takeover generally is considered an unsolicited offer made by a potential acquirer that is resisted by the target's management. The shareholder interests hypothesis suggests that target managers resist hostile offers to improve the terms of a takeover offer. The management entrenchment hypothesis suggests that target managers resist hostile offers to avoid being taken over. Although empirical evidence supports both hypotheses, the evidence seems to favor somewhat the belief that directors and managers resist hostile takeover bids to improve takeover premiums.

If the friendly approach is considered inappropriate or is unsuccessful, the acquiring company may attempt to limit the options of the target's senior management by making a formal acquisition proposal, usually involving a public announcement, to the board of directors of the target. This tactic is called a bear hug and is an attempt to pressure the target's board into making a rapid decision. Alternatively, the bidder may undertake a proxy contest. The two primary forms of proxy contests are those for seats on the board of directors and those concerning management proposals. By replacing board members, proxy contests can be an effective means of gaining control without owning 51% of the voting stock, or they can be used to eliminate takeover defenses, such as poison pills, as a precursor to a tender offer. In a tender offer, the bidding company goes directly to the target shareholders with an offer to buy their stock. The tender offer is a deliberate effort to circumvent the target's board and management.

Alternative takeover defenses can be grouped as prebid or preventive defenses and postbid or active defenses. The prevalence and sophistication of such measures has increased dramatically since 1980 in lockstep with the proliferation of new and more effective takeover tactics. Takeover defenses are designed to raise the overall cost of the takeover attempt and to provide the target firm with more time to install additional takeover defenses. Prebid or preventive defenses generally fall into three categories: poison pills, shark repellants, and golden parachutes.

Poison pills represent a new class of securities issued by a company to its shareholders, which have no value unless an investor acquires a specific percentage of the firm's voting stock. Takeover defenses that can be included in either a corporate charter or bylaws often are referred to as shark repellants or active defenses. These defenses are put in place largely to reinforce the ability of a firm's board of directors to retain control. Today, shark repellants are intended largely as supplements to the poison pill defenses. Golden parachutes are large severance packages granted senior management, which are activated if an individual or a single entity purchases a specific percentage of the target's outstanding voting stock.

Postbid or active defenses are those undertaken in response to a bid. One example is greenmail, which is the practice of paying a potential acquirer to leave you alone. A target company seeking to avoid being taken over by a specific bidder may try to be acquired by another firm, a white knight, which is viewed as a more appropriate suitor. Takeover litigation often is initiated under the guise of antitrust concerns, alleged violations of federal securities laws, inadequate disclosure by the bidder as required by the Williams Act, and alleged fraudulent behavior. Targets often try to get a court injunction temporarily stopping the takeover attempt until the court has decided that the target's allegations are groundless. Empirical evidence suggests that poison pills have the greatest positive impact on shareholder wealth, whereas most other defenses have either no measurable impact or a negative one.

CHAPTER DISCUSSION QUESTIONS

3-1. What are the management entrenchment and shareholder interests hypotheses? Which seems more realistic in your judgment?

3-2. What are the advantages and disadvantages of the friendly versus hostile approaches to a corporate takeover?

3-3. What are proxy contests and how are they used?

3-4. What is a tender offer? How do they differ from open-market purchases of stock?

3-5. How are target shareholders affected by a hostile takeover attempt?

3-6. How are the bidder's shareholders affected by a hostile takeover attempt?

3-7. What are the primary advantages and disadvantages of commonly used takeover defenses?

3-8. Of the most commonly used takeover defenses, which seem to have the most favorable impact on target shareholders?

3-9. How may golden parachutes for senior management help a target firm's shareholders? Are such severance packages justified in your judgment?

3-10. How might recapitalization as a takeover defense help or hurt a target firm's shareholders?

CHAPTER BUSINESS CASE

CASE STUDY 3-3: TYCO RESCUES AMP
FROM ALLIEDSIGNAL

Background

In late November 1998, Tyco International Ltd., a diversified manufacturing and service company, agreed to acquire AMP Inc. for $11.3 billion, thereby successfully fending off a protracted takeover attempt by AlliedSignal Inc. Tyco agreed to exchange 0.7839 shares of its stock for each AMP share outstanding, as long as Tyco's share price traded between $60 and $67 during the 10-day period before closing. The share exchange ratio was set to change if Tyco shares fluctuated outside the range, but the exchange would not exceed a value of $55.95 per AMP share. AMP shareholders could expect to receive a purchase price per share within a range of $47.03 ($60 × 0.7839) to $52.52 ($67 × 0.7839). However, if Tyco's stock rose above the range, AMP's shareholders could receive as much as $55.95 ($71.37 × 0.7839) at the time of closing. As part of the merger agreement with Tyco, AMP rescinded its $165 million share buyback offer and its plan to issue an additional 25 million shares to fund its defense efforts. Tyco, the world's largest electronics connector company, saw the combination with AMP as a means of becoming the lowest cost producer in the industry.

An electrical components supplier, AMP had been attempting to fend off an unwanted bid from AlliedSignal for 4 months until a court decision gave Allied-Signal permission to proceed with a $10 billion consent solicitation bid. As of February 1999, AlliedSignal owned 200 million AMP shares, or 9.1% of the total outstanding. It had purchased these shares before making its $10 billion bid. After the Third U.S. Circuit Court of Appeals reversed a ruling from a lower court, AlliedSignal was poised to vote on the Tyco proposal to buy the Pennsylvania-based AMP. The law said that purchasers of more than 20% of a company's stock cannot vote the stock without first getting the approval of the other shareholders. Although AlliedSignal had purchased less than 20%, the lower court ruled that the shares were "control shares" because they were purchased with the intent to acquire AMP. The appeals court ruled that the law requires the actual accumulation of at least 20% of the outstanding shares.

AlliedSignal Fires an Opening Salvo

Lawrence Bossidy, CEO of AlliedSignal, telephoned an AMP director in mid-1998 to inquire about AMP's interest in a possible combination of their two companies. The inquiry was referred to the finance committee of the AMP board for consideration. The committee concluded that such a combination did not offer any benefits to AMP's businesses and that there was no interest in merging with AlliedSignal. By early August, AlliedSignal announced its intention to initiate an unsolicited tender offer to acquire all of the outstanding shares of AMP common stock for $44.50 per share to be paid in cash. The following week AlliedSignal initiated such an offer and sent a letter to William J. Hudson, then CEO of AMP, requesting a meeting to discuss a possible business combination. Bossidy also advised AMP of AlliedSignal's intention to file materials shortly with the SEC as required by federal law to solicit consents from AMP's shareholders. The consent solicitation materials included proposals to increase the size of AMP's board from 11 to 28 members and to add 17 AlliedSignal nominees, all of whom were directors or executive officers of AlliedSignal. Within a few days, Hudson indicated in writing to Bossidy that it was premature for such a meeting because the board had not yet reviewed AlliedSignal's proposal.

AMP Rejects AlliedSignal's Offer

The AMP board decided to continue to aggressively pursue its current strategic initiatives because the AlliedSignal offer did not fully reflect the values inherent in AMP businesses. In addition, the AMP board also replaced Hudson with Robert Ripp as chair and CEO of AMP.

AMP Pressures Shareholders to Vote Against AlliedSignal's Proposals

The AMP board also authorized an amendment to the AMP rights agreement dated October 25, 1989. The amendment provided that the rights could not be redeemed if there were a change in the composition of the AMP board following the announcement of an unsolicited acquisition proposal such that the current directors no longer comprised a majority of the board. A transaction not approved by AMP's board and involving the acquisition by a person or entity of 20% or more of AMP's common stock was defined as an unsolicited acquisition proposal.

AlliedSignal Amends Its Offer

By early September, AlliedSignal amended its tender offer to reduce the number of shares of AMP common stock it was seeking to purchase to 40 million shares. AlliedSignal also stated that it would undertake another offer to acquire the remaining shares of AMP common stock at a price of $44.50 in cash following consummation of its offer to purchase up to 40 million shares. In concert with its tender offer, AlliedSignal also announced its intention to solicit consents for a proposal to amend AMP's bylaws. The proposed amendment would strip the AMP board of all authority over the AMP rights agreement and any similar agreements and to vest such authority in three individuals selected by AlliedSignal. In response, the AMP board unanimously determined that the amended offer from AlliedSignal was not in the best interests of AMP shareholders. The AMP board also approved another amendment to the AMP rights agreement, lowering the threshold that would make the rights nonredeemable from 20% to 10% of AMP's shares outstanding. AlliedSignal immediately modified its tender offer by reducing the number of shares it wanted to purchase from 40 million to 20 million shares at $44.50 per share to be paid in cash.

AMP Builds Additional Defenses

AMP announced a self-tender offer to purchase up to 30 million shares of AMP common stock at $55 per share. The AMP self-tender offer was intended to provide AMP shareholders with an opportunity to sell a portion of their shares of common stock at a price in excess of AlliedSignal's $44.50 per share offer. Also, on September 28, 1998, AMP stated its intention to create a new ESOP that would hold 25 million shares of AMP common stock to fund future AMP benefit and compensation requirements.

In early October, AlliedSignal announced that it had purchased 20 million shares of AMP common stock at a price of $44.50 per share. Following the commencement of the AMP self-tender offer, AlliedSignal indicated that if the AMP self-tender offer were consummated, it would reduce the consideration to be paid in any further offer undertaken by AlliedSignal to $42.64 per share. AlliedSignal indicated that the price could be even lower to take into account expenses incurred by AMP in connection with the AMP self-tender offer.

AMP Seeks a White Knight

Credit Suisse, AMP's investment banker, approached a number of firms, including Tyco, concerning their possible interest in acquiring AMP. In early November, Tyco stepped forward as a possible white knight. Based on limited information, L. Dennis Kozlowski, Tyco's CEO, set the preliminary valuation of AMP at $50.00 per share. This value assumed a transaction in which AMP shares would be exchanged for Tyco shares and was subject to the completion of appropriate due diligence.

AlliedSignal Blinks?

In mid-November, Ripp and Bossidy met at Bossidy's request. Bossidy indicated that AlliedSignal would be prepared to increase its proposed acquisition price for AMP by a modest amount and to include stock for a limited portion of the total purchase price. The revised offer also would include a minimum share exchange ratio for the equity portion of the purchase price along with an opportunity for AMP shareholders to participate in any increase in AlliedSignal's stock before the closing. The purpose of including equity as a portion of the purchase price was to address the needs of certain AMP shareholders, who had a low tax basis in the stock and who wanted a tax-free exchange. Ripp indicated that the AMP board expected a valuation of more than $50.00 per share. Bossidy indicated that AlliedSignal would not go that high. After conferring with his board, Ripp told Bossidy that the AlliedSignal offer was inadequate.

Tyco Ups Its Offer

Tyco indicated a willingness to increase its offer to at least $51.00 worth of Tyco common shares for each share of AMP common stock. The offer also would include protections similar to those offered in AlliedSignal's most recent proposal. On November 20, 1998, the AMP board voted unanimously to approve the merger agreement and to recommend approval of the merger to AMP's shareholders. They also voted to terminate the AMP self-tender offer, the ESOP, and AMP's share repurchase plan and to amend the AMP rights agreement so that it would not apply to the merger with Tyco.

AlliedSignal and Dissident AMP Shareholders Sue AMP

In early August, AlliedSignal filed a complaint against AMP in the United States District Court against the provisions of the AMP rights agreement. The complaint also questioned the constitutionality of certain antitakeover provisions of Pennsylvania state statutes. Concurrently, AMP shareholders filed four shareholder class-action lawsuits against AMP and its board of directors. The suits alleged that AMP and its directors improperly refused to consider the original AlliedSignal offer and wrongfully relied on the provisions of the AMP rights agreement and Pennsylvania law to block the original AlliedSignal offer.

AMP Countersues

In late August, AMP filed a complaint in the United States District court against AlliedSignal, seeking an injunction to prevent AlliedSignal from attempting to pack the AMP board of directors with AlliedSignal executive officers and directors. The complaint also alleged that the Schedule 14D-1 SEC filing by Allied-Signal was false and misleading. The complaint alleged that the filing failed to disclose that some of AlliedSignal's proposed directors had conflicts of interest and that the packing of the board would prevent current board members from executing their fiduciary responsibilities to AMP shareholders.

The Court Agrees with AMP

In early October, the court agreed with AMP and enjoined AlliedSignal's board-packing consent proposals until it stated unequivocally that its director nominees have a fiduciary duty solely to AMP under Pennsylvania law. The court also denied AlliedSignal's request to deactivate antitakeover provisions in the AMP rights agreement. The court further held that shareholders might not sue the board for rejecting the AlliedSignal proposal.

AlliedSignal Appeals the Lower Court Ruling

AlliedSignal immediately filed in the United States Court of Appeals for the Third Circuit. The court ordered that although AlliedSignal could proceed with the consent solicitation, its representatives could not assume positions on the AMP board until the court of appeals completed its deliberations. The district court ruled that the shares of AMP common stock acquired by AlliedSignal are "control shares" under Pennsylvania law. As a result, the court enjoined AlliedSignal from voting any of its AMP shares unless AlliedSignal's voting rights are restored under Pennsylvania law. AlliedSignal was able to overturn the lower court ruling on appeal.

Case Study Discussion Questions

1. What types of takeover tactics did AlliedSignal use?
2. What steps did AlliedSignal take to satisfy federal securities laws?
3. What antitakeover defenses were in place at AMP before AlliedSignal's offer?
4. How did the AMP board use the AMP rights agreement to encourage AMP shareholders to vote against AlliedSignal's proposals?
5. What options did AlliedSignal have to neutralize or circumvent AMP's use of the rights agreement?
6. After announcing it had purchased 20 million AMP shares at $44.50, why did AlliedSignal indicate that it would reduce the price paid in any further offers it might make?
7. What other takeover defenses did AMP use in its attempt to thwart AlliedSignal?
8. How did both AMP and AlliedSignal use litigation in this takeover battle?
9. Should state laws be used to protect companies from hostile takeovers?
10. Were AMP's board and management acting to protect their own positions (i.e., the management entrenchment hypothesis) or in the best interests of the shareholders (i.e., the shareholder interests hypothesis)?

Solutions to these questions are found in the Appendix at the back of this book.

CHAPTER BUSINESS CASE

CASE STUDY 3-4: PFIZER ACQUIRES WARNER-LAMBERT IN A HOSTILE TAKEOVER

Pfizer and Warner Lambert Develop a Strategic Relationship

In 1996 Pfizer and Warner Lambert (Warner) agreed to comarket worldwide the cholesterol-lowering drug Lipitor, which had been developed by Warner. The agreement gave Pfizer the exclusive right to promote the drug in certain foreign markets and in partnership with Warner in the United States for a one-time fee and other financial considerations. The combined marketing effort was extremely successful with combined 1999 sales reaching $3.5 billion, a 60% increase over 1998. Before entering into the marketing agreement, Pfizer had entered into a confidentiality agreement with Warner that contained a stand-still clause that, among other things, prohibited Pfizer from making a merger proposal unless invited to do so by Warner or until a third party made such a proposal.

Rumors About an Impending Warner Merger Circulate

In late 1998, Pfizer became aware of numerous rumors of a possible merger between Warner and some unknown entity. William C. Steere, chair and CEO of Pfizer, sent a letter on October 15, 1999, to Lodeijk de Vink, chair and CEO of Warner, inquiring about the potential for Pfizer to broaden its current strategic relationship to include a merger. More than 2 weeks passed before Steere received a written response in which de Vink expressed concern that Steere's letter violated the spirit of the standstill agreement by indicating interest in a merger. Speculation about an impending merger between Warner and American Home Products (AHP) came to a head on November 19, 1999, when an announcement appeared in the *Wall Street Journal* announcing an impending merger of equals between Warner and AHP. The merger with AHP was valued at $58.3 billion.

Pfizer Moves Aggressively with a Hostile Bid

The public announcement of the agreement to merge between Warner and AHP released Pfizer from the standstill agreement. Tinged with frustration and impatience at what Pfizer saw as stalling tactics, Steere fired off a letter stating his interest in a merger:

> I want to reiterate that I have repeatedly tried over the past few weeks to discuss with you the merits of a combination between Pfizer and Warner Lambert. Unfortunately, our efforts have been rejected—a response that is particularly disappointing given the substantial success represented by our partnership in developing and marketing Lipitor, which both our companies have publicly acknowledged. My letters dated November 3 and October 25—as well as our conversation on October 27—clearly demonstrated our desire to make the best possible proposal for your company and its shareholders within the "standstill" framework we had agreed to.
>
> Since the standstill agreement is no longer operative, we are now prepared to offer a tax-free merger in which your shareholders would receive 2 1/2 shares of Pfizer common stock for each outstanding share of common stock of Warner Lambert. Customary and appropriate provisions will be made for outstanding options and warrants. Based on yesterday's closing market price, this offer represents a $96.40 per share purchase price for each Warner Lambert share, a premium of 30% over the last month's average closing price of your shares. This $82.4 billion offer represents a very substantial premium over the proposed AHP transaction as well. In addition, our proposal envisions combining the Boards of both companies. Our offer is conditioned solely on the elimination of the egregious $2 billion "break-up fee" and the improper issuance of the stock option which would prevent us (but not AHP) from utilizing a pooling of interest[1] accounting for this transaction as well as entering into the appropriate documentation. (SEC S4 Filing: December 18, 1999)

---

[1] Pooling of interests is an accounting treatment used to account for transactions satisfying certain criteria for financial reporting purposes. Acquiring companies engaging in a share-for-share exchange often use this treatment to mitigate the unfavorable impact on earnings of alternative accounting treatments. Effective January 2002, this form of accounting for business combinations is no longer permitted. See Chapter 10 for additional detail on this subject.

Steere outlined in the letter the primary reasons why the proposed combination of the two companies made sense to Warner's shareholders. In addition to a substantial premium over Warner's current share price, Pfizer argued that combining the companies would result in a veritable global powerhouse in the pharmaceutical industry. Furthermore, the firm's product lines are highly complementary, including Warner's over-the-counter drug presence and substantial pipeline of new drugs and Pfizer's powerful global marketing and sales infrastructure. Steere also argued that the combined companies could generate annual cost savings of at least $1.2 billion annually within 1 year following the completion of the merger. These savings would come from centralizing computer systems and research and development (R&D) activities, consolidating more than 100 manufacturing facilities, and combining two headquarters and multiple sales and administrative offices in 30 countries. Pfizer also believed that the two companies' cultures were highly complementary.

Pfizer Takes Legal Action

In addition to the letter from Steerc to de Vink, on November 4, 1999, Pfizer announced that it had commenced a legal action in the Delaware Court of Chancery against Warner, Warner's directors, and AHP. The action sought to enjoin the approximately $2 billion termination fee and the stock option granted by Warner-Lambert to AHP to acquire 14.9% of Warner's common stock valued at $83.81 per share as part of their merger agreement. The lawsuit charges that the termination fee and stock options are excessively onerous and are not in the best interests of the Warner shareholders because they would discourage potential takeover attempts. Furthermore, Pfizer argued that Warner's directors breached their fiduciary duties to their stockholders by entering into the merger agreement with AHP without informing them of the Pfizer proposal. The legal action also alleges that AHP aided and abetted that breach of fiduciary duty. Pfizer's offer was contingent on the removal of these provisions.

"Not Interested"

On November 5, 1999, Warner explicitly rejected Pfizer's proposal in a press release and reaffirmed its commitment to its announced business combination with AHP. On November 9, 1999, de Vink sent a letter to the Pfizer board in which he expressed Warner's disappointment at what he perceived to be Pfizer's efforts to take over Warner as well as Pfizer's lawsuit against the firm. In the letter, he stated Warner-Lambert's belief that the litigation was not in the best interest of either company's stockholders, especially in light of their copromotion of Lipitor, and it was causing uncertainty in the financial markets. Not only did Warner reject the Pfizer bid, but it also threatened to cancel the companies' partnership to market Lipitor.

De Vink stated that Warner was very comfortable with the conduct of its directors and was prepared to respond to Pfizer in the courts. Further, the letter stated that Warner Lambert remained committed to the American Home transaction and wanted to resolve the legal issues quickly. He concluded by asking Pfizer to commit to moving the proceeding along as promptly as possible.

Pfizer Turns Up the Heat

Pfizer responded by exploiting a weakness in the Warner Lambert takeover defenses by utilizing a consent solicitation process that allows shareholders to change the board without waiting months for a shareholders' meeting. Pfizer also challenged in court two provisions in the contract with AHP on the grounds that they were not in the best interests of the Warner Lambert shareholders because they would discourage other bidders. Pfizer's offers for Warner Lambert were contingent on the removal of these provisions. On November 12, 1999, Steere sent a letter to de Vink and the Warner board indicating his deep disappointment as a result of their refusal to consider what Pfizer believes is a superior offer to Warner. He also reiterated his firm's resolve in completing a merger with Warner. Not hearing anything from Warner management, Pfizer decided to go straight to the Warner shareholders on November 15, 1999, in an attempt to change the composition of the board and to get the board to remove the poison pill and break-up fee.

In the mid-November proxy statement sent to Warner shareholders, Pfizer noted the following:

- The current Warner Lambert board has approved a merger agreement with American Home, which provides 30% less current value to the Warner-Lambert stockholders than the Pfizer merger proposal;
- Warner shareholders would benefit more in the long run in a merger with Pfizer because the resulting firm would be operationally and financially stronger than a merger created with AHP. Pfizer has a market capitalization that is 80% greater than American Home, and Pfizer's 3-year average revenue growth rate for continuing operations is 289% greater than American Home's;
- The Pfizer board also believes that American Home's recent proposed settlement of the class-action litigation caused by its diet drug known as "fen-phen," for which American Home took a pretax charge of $4.75 billion in the third quarter of 1999, may be a significant drain on American Home's financial resources;
- Pfizer has a better ability to raise capital than AHP because Pfizer's credit rating is one of the strongest in the industry and is superior to AHP's;
- Pfizer's international marketing strength is superior in the view of most industry analysts to that of American Home and will greatly enhance Warner-Lambert's foreign sales efforts; and
- The current Warner Lambert board is not acting in the best interests of its shareholders by refusing to even grant Pfizer permission to make a proposal. Pfizer also alleged that it is violating its fiduciary responsibilities by approving the merger agreement with American Home in which AHP

is entitled to a termination fee of approximately $2 billion and an option to buy almost 15% of Warner's stock. This option was designed to prevent an acquirer from using the pooling of interest treatment to account for a merger.[2]

Warner Relents Under Increasing Pressure

Pressure intensified from all quarters including such major shareholders as the California Public Employees Retirement System and the New York City Retirement Fund. After 3 stormy months, Warner Lambert agreed on February 8, 2000, to be acquired by Pfizer for $92.5 billion, forming the world's second largest pharmaceutical firm. Although they were able to have the Warner poison pill overturned in court as being an unreasonable defense, Pfizer was unsuccessful in eliminating the break-up fee and had to pay AHP the largest such fee in history (Bloomberg.com, 2000a).

The combined companies did indeed create a pharmaceutical juggernaut. The new company, also called Pfizer, had total annual sales of more than $29 billion, after-tax profits of $4.9 billion, and an R&D budget of $4.7 billion. Although the new company has slightly less than 7% of the world market for prescription drugs, it is expected to be able to more effectively develop new medicines and cut overhead expenses. Pfizer has been among the best performing drug companies during the 1990s, but its growth was expected to slow without the acquisition because of too few new "blockbuster" drugs in its R&D pipeline. Moreover, patents on a number of drugs that had been key to its growth were set to expire by 2005. Pfizer was anxious to acquire the rights to Lipitor, the best-selling cholesterol-reduction drug, and other drugs in development within Warner Lambert. On the surface, the merger seemed like the perfect medicine to sustain Pfizer's attractive growth rate.

The announced acquisition of Warner Lambert by Pfizer ended one of the most contentious corporate takeover battles in recent memory. The pending challenge for both companies is to put aside their nasty accusations and lawsuits and to integrate their respective research, sales, and manufacturing operations to make the combined companies successful. Pfizer's first step with Warner Lambert will be to achieve an estimated $2 billion in sustainable cost savings by 2002. The bulk of such savings are expected to come from layoffs. The track record for merged drug companies in recent years has been disappointing. Barrie G. James, president of Pharma Strategy Consulting, found that drug companies formed as a result of deals tended to lose market share in the years following the transaction when compared with those drug companies that had remained independent.

---

[2] To qualify for a pooling of interests treatment, an acquirer must be able to acquire "substantially all" of the target's outstanding voting shares. If exercised, this option would have prevented Pfizer from adopting this more favorable accounting treatment.

Case Study Discussion Questions

1. What takeover defenses did Warner use to ward off the Pfizer merger proposal? What tactics did Pfizer use to overcome these defenses? Comment on the effectiveness of these defenses.

2. What other defenses do you think Warner could or should have used? Comment on the effectiveness of each alternative defense you suggest Warner could have used.

3. What factors may have contributed to Warner Lambert's rejection of the Pfizer proposal?

4. What factors may make it difficult for this merger to meet or exceed industry average returns? What are the implications for the long-term financial performance of the new firm of only using Pfizer stock to purchase Warner Lambert shares?

5. What is a standstill agreement, and why might it have been included as a condition for the Pfizer-Warner Lambert Lipitor distribution arrangement? How did the standstill agreement affect Pfizer's effort to merge with Warner Lambert? Why would Warner Lambert want a standstill agreement?

REFERENCES

Bagwell, Laurie Simon, "Dutch Auction Repurchases: An Analysis of Shareholder Heterogeneity," *Journal of Finance*, 47, March 1992, pp. 71–105.

Bhagat, S. and J. A. Brickley, "Cumulative Voting: The Value of Minority Shareholders Rights," *Journal of Law and Economics*, 27, October 1984, pp. 339–366.

Bloomberg.com, "Pfizer's Stormy Courtship Ends," February 8, 2000a.

Bruner, Robert F., "An Analysis of Value Destruction and Recovery in the Alliance and Proposed Merger of Volvo and Renault," *Journal of Financial Economics*, 51 (1), January 1999, pp. 125–166.

Buckhorn Inc. v. Ropak Corp., 656 F, Supplement. 209 (S.D. Ohio) affected by summary order 815 F.2d 76 (6th Circuit, 1987).

Burch, Timothy R., "Locking Out Rival Bidders: The Use of Lockup Options in Corporate Mergers," *Journal of Financial Economics*, 60 (1), April 2001, pp. 103–141.

Comment, Robert and G. William Schwert, "Poison or Placebo: Evidence on the Deterrence and Wealth Effects of Modern Anti-Takeover Measures," *Journal of Financial Economics*, 39, 1995, pp. 3–43.

DeAngelo, Harry and Eugene Rice, "Anti-Takeover Charter Amendments and Stockholder Wealth," *Journal of Financial Economics*, 11, 1983, pp. 329–360.

DeAngelo, Harry and Linda DeAngelo, "Proxy Contests and the Governance of Publicly Held Corporations," *Journal of Financial Economics*, 23, 1989, pp. 29–60.

Dodd, Peter and Jerrold Warner, "On Corporate Government: A Study of Proxy Contests," *Journal of Financial Economics*, 11, 1–4, April 1983, pp. 401–438.

Field, Laura Casares and Jonathan M. Karpoff, "Takeover Defenses of IPO Firms," *Journal of Finance*, 57 (5), 2002, pp. 1629–1666.

Gaughan, Patrick A., *Mergers, Acquisitions, and Corporate Restructurings* (2nd ed.), New York: John Wiley & Sons, Inc., 1999, pp. 243–288.

Georgeson & Company, "Poison Pills and Shareholder Value: 1992–1996," 1997a, www.georgeson.com/pubs.

Georgeson & Company, "Institutional Voting on Poison Pill Rescission," 1997b, www.georgeson.com/pubs.

Hasbrouck, Joel, "The Characteristics of Takeover Targets," *Journal of Banking and Finance*, 9, 1985, pp. 351–362.

Ikenberry, David and Josef Lakonishok, "Corporate Governance Through the Proxy Contest: Evidence and Implications," *Journal of Business*, 66, July 1993, pp. 405–435.

Jarrell, Gregg, "Wealth Effects of Litigating by Targets: Do Interests Diverge in a Merger?" *Journal of Law and Economics*, 28, April 1985, pp. 151–177.

Jarrell, Gregg and Annette B. Poulsen, "Shark Repellents and Stock Prices: The Effects of Antitakeover Amendments Since 1980," *Journal of Financial Economics*, 19 (1), September 1987, pp. 127–168.

Karpoff, Jonathan M. and Paul H. Malatesta, "The Wealth Effects of Second Generation State Takeover Legislation," *Journal of Financial Economics*, 25, 1989, pp. 291–322.

Karpoff, Jonathan M. and Ralph A. Walkling, "Corporate Governance and Shareholder Initiatives: Empirical Evidence," *Journal of Financial Economics*, 42, 1996, pp. 365–395.

Kennecott Cooper Corp. v. Curtiss Wright Corp., 584 F. 2d 1195 (2nd Cir. 1978).

Linn, Scott C. and John J. McConnell, "An Empirical Investigation of the Impact of Anti-Takeover Amendments on Common Stock Prices," *Journal of Financial Economics*, 11 (1–4), April 1983, pp. 361–399.

Malatesta, Paul H. and Ralph A. Walkling, "Poison Pills Securities: Stockholder Wealth, Profitability and Ownership Structure," *Journal of Financial Economics*, 20, January/March 1988, pp. 347–376.

Mikkelson, Wayne H. and M. Megan Partch, "Managers' Voting Rights and Corporate Control, *Journal of Financial Economics*, 25, 1989, pp. 263–290.

Morck, Randall, Andrei Shleifer, and Robert W. Vishny, "Characteristics of Targets of Hostile and Friendly Takeovers," in Alan J. Auerbach, ed., *Corporate Takeovers: Causes and Consequences*, National Bureau of Economic Research: Chicago, 1988, pp. 101–129.

Mulherin, J. Harold and Annette B. Poulsen, "Proxy Contests and Corporate Change: Implications for Shareholder Wealth," *Journal of Financial Economics*, 47, 1998, pp. 279–313.

Palepu, Krishna G., "Predicting Takeover Targets: A Methodological and Empirical Analysis," *Journal of Accounting and Economics*, 8, 1986, pp. 3–35.

Reuters, "HP Board Belittles Merger Foe Hewlett," *Orange County Register*, Business Section, January 18, 2002, p. 7.

Romano, Roberta, "Competition for Corporate Charters and the Lesson of Takeover Statutes," *Fordham Law Review*, 61, 1993, pp. 843–864.

Ryngaert, Michael, "The Effects of Poison Pill Securities on Stockholder Wealth," *Journal of Financial Economics*, 20, January/March 1988, pp. 377–417.

Schwert, G. William, "Hostility in Takeovers: In the Eyes of the Bidder?" *Journal of Finance*, 55 (6), 2000, pp. 2599–2640.

Shivdasani, Anil, "Board Composition, Ownership Structure, and Hostile Takeovers," *Journal of Accounting and Economics*, 16, 1993, pp. 167–198.

Stromfeld v. Great Atlantic & Pacific Tea Company, 484F. Supplement, 1264 (S.D.N.Y. 1980), aff'd 6464 F. 2d 563 (2nd Circuit 1980).

Thompson Financial Securities Data Corporation, "The World is Not Enough . . . To Merge," Press release, January 5, 2000.

Unocal v. Mesa, 493 A.2d 949, (Del 1985).

Wasserstein, Bruce, *Big Deal: The Battle for Control of America's Leading Corporations*, New York: Warner Books, 1998, pp. 601–644.

Worthington, Andrew C., "Efficiency in Pre-Merger and Post-Merger Non-Bank Financial Institutions," *Managerial and Decision Economics*, 22 (8), December 2001, pp. 439–452.

THE MERGERS AND ACQUISITIONS PROCESS

PHASES 1–10

4

PLANNING

DEVELOPING BUSINESS AND ACQUISITION PLANS— PHASES 1 AND 2 OF THE ACQUISITION PROCESS

If you don't know where you are going, any road will get you there.

—Alice in Wonderland

Lee had a reputation throughout the industry and within his company as a "big picture" guy, a visionary who seemed to see things that others couldn't. His detractors often quipped that he made so many predictions that some would have to be true ... they just didn't know which ones or when. They were convinced that he did not know either.

He had come up through the ranks in his company during the 1990s when management agility and nimbleness in decision making often were viewed on Wall Street as signs of strong management. The virtues of "first mover advantage" often were used to justify deals that, had they been made in a less heady time, would have been viewed as reckless. Be first and fast. Build a brand name and market share to erect barriers to others who may choose to follow. After all, this was the age of accelerating change. This was the age of electronic commerce and the new economy. This was an age when it was cool to be brash.

Lee bought into this philosophy. After all, he was a visionary. Although his view of the future was understandably somewhat fuzzy, he reasoned that he did not have the time to consider his options. He had to act quickly or miss an opportunity. He had confidence in his instincts. He was a manager for the next millennium. Act first and ask for forgiveness later was his mantra. But he had forgotten what his driving instructor had told him when he was first learning to drive. "Sometimes," the instructor admonished, "speed kills."

OVERVIEW

A poorly designed or inappropriate business strategy is among the most frequently cited reasons for the failure of mergers and acquisitions (M&As) to satisfy expectations. Surprisingly, many textbooks on the subject of M&As fail to address adequately the overarching role that planning should take in conceptualizing and implementing business combinations. The purpose of this chapter is to introduce a planning-based approach to mergers and acquisitions, which discusses M&A activity in the context of an integrated process consisting of 10 interrelated phases. This chapter focuses on the first two phases of the process—building the business and acquisition plans—and on tools commonly used to evaluate, display, and communicate information to key constituencies both inside (e.g., board of directors and management) and outside (e.g., lenders and stockholders) of the corporation. Phases 3–10 are discussed in Chapter 5.

The literature on strategic planning that has emerged over the years runs the gamut from a focus on a more prescriptive and static approach involving the use of specific tools and checklists to more eclectic theories, which view planning as largely a dynamic and evolving process. Stryker (1986), Porter (1985), and Almaney (1992) make effective use of checklists to ensure that all key issues about a firm's internal and external operating environments are addressed. Other writers on the subject of strategic planning argue that planning is largely an iterative process in which the firm continuously must make "midcourse" corrections to its strategy as it adapts to changes in its operating environment. These writers view planning more as a way of thinking about the future (James, Mintzberg, and Quinn, 1988). However, such approaches, although conceptually appealing, are often difficult to apply in practice. Other approaches focus on the role of flexibility and nimbleness in implementing corporate strategies (Waterman, 1987). These approaches provide little guidance or discipline in their application. Still others advocate a rule-based approach to planning in which expert systems are developed to provide more disciplined guidance to the process (Chung and Davidson, 1987).

The planning tools described in this chapter are largely prescriptive in nature in that they recommend certain strategies based on the results generated by applying specific tools (e.g., experience curve) and answering checklists of relevant questions. Although these tools introduce some degree of rigor to strategic planning, their application should not be viewed as a completion of the planning process. Business plans must be updated frequently to account for changes in the firm's operating environment and its competitive position within that environment. Indeed, business planning is not an event—it is an evolving process.

There are few unambiguous answers. More often than not the planning process provides direction that is supported more by intuition than empirical evidence. This is particularly true in the current environment, which seems to be changing at an accelerating pace. In this volatile environment, planning is even more important. The ultimate value of a well-designed planning process is that it forces management to be introspective by asking the "tough" questions and answering them honestly. The planning process should compel management to specify clearly all key assumptions underlying their chosen strategies and to reassess these strategies as changes in the environment render important assumptions obsolete.

A PLANNING-BASED APPROACH TO MERGERS AND ACQUISITIONS

The acquisition process envisioned in this chapter can be separated into a planning and an implementation stage. The planning stage consists of the development of the business and the acquisition plans. The implementation stage includes the search, screening, contacting the target, negotiation, integration planning, closing, integration, and evaluation activities. To understand the role of planning in the M&A process, it is necessary to understand the purpose of the acquiring firm's mission and strategy.

KEY BUSINESS PLANNING CONCEPTS

A planning-based acquisition process consists of both a business plan and a merger/acquisition plan, which drive all subsequent phases of the acquisition process. The *business plan* articulates a mission or vision for the firm and a *business strategy* for realizing that mission for all of the firm's stakeholders. *Stakeholders* include such constituent groups as customers, shareholders, employees, suppliers, regulators, and communities. The business strategy is long-term oriented and usually cuts across organizational lines to affect many different functional areas. It is often broadly defined and provides relatively little detail.

With respect to business strategy, it is often appropriate to distinguish between corporate level strategy, where decisions are made by the management of a diversified or multiproduct firm, and business level strategy, where decisions are made by the management of the operating unit within the corporate organizational structure. *Corporate-level strategies* generally cut cross business unit organizational lines and entail such decisions as financing the growth of certain businesses, operating others to generate cash, divesting some units, or pursuing diversification. *Business-level strategies* pertain to a specific operating unit and may involve the business unit attempting to achieve a low-cost position in its served markets, differentiating its product offering, or narrowing its focus of the operation to a specific market niche.

The *implementation strategy* refers to the way in which the firm chooses to execute the business strategy. It is usually far more detailed than the business strategy. The *merger/acquisition plan* is a specific type of implementation strategy and describes in detail the motivation for the acquisition and how and when it will be achieved. *Functional strategies* describe in detail how each major function (e.g., manufacturing, marketing, and human resources) within the firm will support the business strategy. *Contingency plans* are actions that are taken as an alternative to the firm's current business strategy. The selection of which alternative action to pursue is often contingent on certain events occurring (e.g., failure to realize revenue targets or cost savings). Such events are called *trigger points*.

THE ACQUISITION PROCESS

It is sometimes convenient to think of an acquisition process as a series of largely independent events culminating in the transfer of ownership from the seller to the buyer. In theory, thinking of the process as discrete events facilitates the communication and understanding of the numerous activities that are required to complete the transaction. In practice, the steps involved in the process are frequently highly interrelated; do not necessarily follow a logical order; and involve, as new information becomes available, reiteration of steps in the process thought to have been completed.

Good Planning Expedites Sound Decision Making

Some individuals tend to shudder at the thought of following a structured process because of perceived delays in responding to both anticipated and unanticipated opportunities. Anticipated opportunities are those identified as a result of the business planning process. This process consists of understanding the firm's external operating environment, assessing internal resources, reviewing a range of reasonable options, and articulating a clear vision of the future of the business and a realistic strategy for achieving that vision (Hill and Jones, 2001). Unanticipated or unforeseen opportunities result from new information becoming available. Rather than delaying the pursuit of an opportunity, the presence of a well-designed business plan provides for a rapid yet substantive evaluation of the perceived opportunity based on work completed while having developed the business plan. Decisions made in the context of a business plan are made with the confidence that comes from already having asked and answered the difficult questions.

Mergers and Acquisitions Are a Process not an Event

Figure 4-1 illustrates the 10 phases of the acquisition process described in this chapter and in Chapter 5. These phases fall into two distinct sets of activities (i.e., pre- and postpurchase decision activities). The crucial phase of the acquisition process is the negotiation phase. Negotiation consists of four largely concurrent and interrelated activities. The decision to purchase or walk away is determined as a result of continuous iteration through the four activities comprising the negotiation phase. Assuming the transaction ultimately is completed, the price paid for the target is actually determined during the negotiation phase. The phases of the acquisition process are summarized as follows:

Phase 1.   Develop a strategic plan for the entire business (Business Plan).
Phase 2.   Develop the acquisition plan related to the strategic plan (Acquisition Plan).

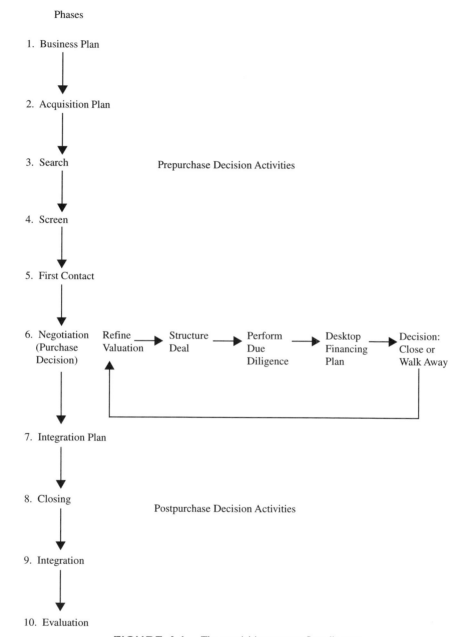

FIGURE 4-1.　The acquisition process flow diagram.

Phase 3.   Actively search for acquisition candidates (Search).
Phase 4.   Screen and prioritize potential candidates (Screen).
Phase 5.   Initiate contact with the target (First Contact).
Phase 6.   Refine valuation, structure deal, perform due diligence, and
           develop financing plan (Negotiation).
Phase 7.   Develop plan for integrating the acquired business (Integration
           Plan).
Phase 8.   Obtain all necessary approvals, resolve postclosing issues, and
           implement closing (Closing).
Phase 9.   Implement postclosing integration (Integration).
Phase 10. Conduct postclosing evaluation of acquisition (Evaluation).

PHASE 1: BUILDING THE BUSINESS PLAN

KEY ACTIVITIES

A well-designed business plan is a result of the following activities:

1. External analysis involves determining where to compete (i.e., the industry
   or market in which the firm has chosen to compete) and how to compete
   (i.e., conducting an external industry or market evaluation to determine
   how the firm can most effectively compete in its chosen market[s])
2. Internal analysis or self-assessment (i.e., conducting an internal analysis of
   the firm's strengths and weaknesses relative to its competition)
3. Defining a mission statement (i.e., summarizing where and how the firm has
   chosen to compete and the basic operating beliefs and values of management)
4. Setting objectives (i.e., developing quantitative measures of performance)
5. Business strategy selection (i.e., selecting the strategy most likely to
   achieve the objectives in an acceptable time period, subject to constraints
   identified in the self-assessment)
6. Implementation strategy selection (i.e., selecting the best means of
   implementing the business strategy from a range of reasonable options)
7. Functional strategy development (i.e., defines the roles, responsibilities,
   and resource requirements of each major functional area within the firm
   needed to implement the firm's business strategy)
8. Establishing strategic controls (i.e., monitoring actual performance to plan,
   implementing incentive systems, and taking corrective actions as necessary)

The first two activities, the external and internal analyses, often are referred
to in the planning literature as a *SWOT analysis* (i.e., the determination of a
business' strengths, weaknesses, opportunities, and threats). In practice, the
process of actually developing a business plan can be greatly facilitated by
addressing a number of detailed questions corresponding to each activity listed
previously. Extensive checklists can be found in Porter (1985) and Stryker (1986).

Answering these questions requires the accumulation of substantial amounts of economic, industry, and market information. See Appendix A for common sources of such data.

Figure 4-2 provides a convenient framework for understanding how the various activities involved in developing the business plan interact. This illustration is intended to underscore that planning is indeed an iterative process. Following an exhaustive and objective analysis of the external environment and introspective internal assessment of the firm, management has a clearer understanding of emerging opportunities and threats to the firm and of the firm's primary internal strengths and weaknesses. This information enables management to set an overall direction for the firm in terms of where and how the firm intends to compete, which is communicated to the firm's stakeholders in the form of a mission/vision statement and a set of quantifiable objectives.

Information gleaned from the external and internal analyses drives the development of business, implementation, and functional strategies. Each level of strategy involves an increased level of detail. The business strategy defines in general terms how the business intends to compete (i.e., through cost leadership, differentiation, or increased focus). The implementation strategy identifies how the business strategy will be realized (i.e., the firm acts on its own, partners with others, or acquires/merges with another firm). Finally, functional strategies define in considerable detail how each functional department (e.g., legal, finance, and human resources) in the firm will support the implementation strategy. Functional strategies often entail setting objectives and performance milestones for each employee supporting the implementation strategy.

Strategic controls are put in place to heighten the prospect that vision, objectives, and strategies will be realized on schedule. Such controls involve establishing bonus plans and other incentive mechanisms to motivate all employees to achieve their individual objectives on or ahead of schedule. Systems are also put in place to track the firm's actual performance to plan. Significant deviations from the plan may require modification of the implementation strategy by switching to contingency plans. If the deviations between actual performance and plan are large and sustained, the control mechanism might require a substantial change in the firm's business plan or vision.

The eight key activities involved in developing an appropriate business plan are discussed in more detail during the remainder of this chapter. Of the various implementation strategy alternatives, the merger/acquisition implementation plan is discussed in considerable detail. Shared growth/shared control or partnering strategies are discussed in detail in Chapter 12. Implementing solo ventures are beyond the scope of this book.

EXTERNAL ANALYSIS

This analysis involves the development of an in-depth understanding of the business's customers and their needs, underlying market dynamics or factors

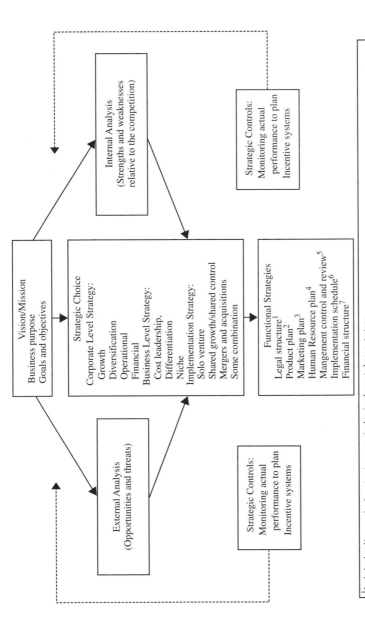

Vision/Mission
Business purpose
Goals and objectives

Internal Analysis
(Strengths and weaknesses relative to the competition)

External Analysis
(Opportunities and threats)

Strategic Choice
Corporate Level Strategy:
  Growth
  Diversification
  Operational
  Financial
Business Level Strategy:
  Cost leadership,
  Differentiation
  Niche
Implementation Strategy:
  Solo venture
  Shared growth/shared control
  Mergers and acquisitions
  Some combination

Functional Strategies
Legal structure[1]
Product plan[2]
Marketing plan[3]
Human Resource plan[4]
Mangement control and review[5]
Implementation schedule[6]
Financial structure[7]

Strategic Controls:
Monitoring actual performance to plan
Incentive systems

Strategic Controls:
Monitoring actual performance to plan
Incentive systems

[1] Includes legal/accounting/tax structures required to implement chosen strategy.
[2] Product plan includes management of supply chain from new product development, supplier/customer channel relationships, manufacturing & IT operations, customer service and postsale support.
[3] Includes product/brand positioning, promotion, and pricing.
[4] Includes organizational design and effectiveness, identifying staffing requirements, and plans for satisfying those requirements.
[5] Includes systems for monitoring performance to objectives, reward mechanisms, and contingency plans.
[6] Timeline for achieving business objectives, including milestones.
[7] Projected income, cash flow, and balance sheet statements, including how the chosen strategy will be financed.

FIGURE 4-2   Framework for developing the business plan.

determining profitability, and emerging trends that affect customer needs and market dynamics. This analysis starts with answering two basic questions, which involve determining where the firm should compete and how the firm should compete. The primary output of the external analysis is the identification of important growth opportunities and competitive threats.

DETERMINING WHERE TO COMPETE

Deciding where a firm should compete starts with identifying the firm's current and potential customers and their primary needs. This is the single most important activity in building a business plan and is based on the process of market segmentation.

Market Segmentation

Market segmentation involves identifying customers with common characteristics and needs. Collections of customers, whether individual consumers or other firms, comprise *markets*. A collection of markets is said to comprise an *industry*. In manufacturing, examples include the automotive industry, which could be defined to consist of the new and used car markets as well as the aftermarket for replacement parts. Markets may be further subdivided by examining cars by makes and model years. The automotive market also could be defined regionally (e.g., North America) or by country. Each subdivision, whether by product or geographic area, defines a new market within the automotive industry.

Identifying Market Segments

The process for identifying a target market involves a three-step procedure. The first step entails establishing evaluation criteria used to distinguish the market to be targeted by the firm from other potential target markets. This requires the management of the firm conducting the market segmentation to determine the factors likely to affect a firm's overall attractiveness. The evaluation criteria may include market size and growth rate, profitability, cyclicality, the price sensitivity of customers, amount of regulation, degree of unionization, and entry and exit barriers. Larger firms are more likely to establish minimum size requirements for selecting target markets. For example, in the mid-1980s, IBM announced that it would not pursue markets that could not generate at least $1 billion in total annual sales. Other firms may choose to avoid markets with extremely high growth rates because of the substantial investment levels required to sustain these high rates of growth.

The second step entails continuously subdividing industries and the markets within these industries and analyzing the overall attractiveness of these markets in terms of the evaluation criteria. For each market, the evaluation criteria are given a numerical weight reflecting the firm's perception of the relative importance of each criterion applied to that market to determine overall attractiveness. Higher numbers imply greater perceived significance. Note that some criteria may be given a zero weight. The evaluation criteria then are ranked from 1 to 5, with 5 indicating that the firm finds a market to be highly favorable in terms of a specific evaluation criterion.

In the third step, a weighted average score is calculated for each market and the markets are ranked according to their respective scores. The market with the highest score is considered to be the most attractive. How laborious the process becomes is largely dependent on management's willingness to narrow at the outset of the process the number of industries and markets to be analyzed. Some managers will require that a large number of industries be analyzed before selecting the target market. The intuitive appeal of this approach is that management is less likely to miss highly attractive markets. The practical risk to this approach is that it is likely to be much more time consuming and it tends to defer making the difficult decisions. The process of "thinking broadly" tends to contribute to "analysis paralysis." This three-step procedure is illustrated in Table 4-1. Such a matrix is constructed for each market evaluated.

Segmenting Markets When Available Data Are Limited

Although it is generally possible to collect a sufficient amount of data for established industries to develop selection criteria, reasonably accurate data are often not available for new or evolving industries. Despite the absence of good data, the market segmentation process still can be helpful in determining where the firm should compete.

For example, electronic commerce commonly is associated with the buying and selling of information, products, and services via computer networks. In broader terms, electronic commerce addresses the needs of organizations, merchants, and consumers to reduce costs while improving the speed at which transactions are consummated. Increasing interest in electronic commerce has spawned a headlong rush by both existing companies and start-ups to target products and services either for supporting the infrastructure requirements needed to support exploding usage (i.e., infrastructure providers) or for sale via the Internet (i.e., content providers). During the 1990s, companies that generated revenue by selling on the Internet or selling products and services that were used by companies during business on the Internet often were referred to simply as Internet companies. This lack of distinction among companies resulted in many companies exhibiting a high price-to-earnings ratio simply because their business was somehow related to the Internet.

Despite a lack of reliable data to measure the size and growth rate of segments, market segmentation techniques still can provide helpful insights by creating a simplistic framework for characterizing the industry. Market segmentation forces the analyst to group firms having common characteristics. Instead of labeling all firms with "dotcom" in their names as Internet companies, functionally similar firms are compared. Earthlink is clearly more closely related to other Internet service providers (ISPs) than with AOL Time Warner (AOL), although AOL Time Warner also provides Internet access. In other instances, the distinction may be

TABLE 4-1 Industry/Market Attractiveness Matrix

Industry or Market Evaluation Criteria[1]	Weight: (Relative Importance of Criteria)	Ranking: (5 = Highly Favorable; 1 = Highly Unfavorable)[2]	Weighted Score: (Weight × Ranking)
Market size: Is it large or small? Global, national, or regional?	.10	4	.40
Growth rate: Is it slowing, declining, or accelerating?	.20	5	1.00
Profitability: Is it currently profitable? Expected to remain so?	.20	4	.80
Cyclicality: Is profitability volatile?	.05	2	.10
Seasonality: Is profitability seasonal?	.00	3	.00
Customers: Are the number, average size, and needs changing?	.05	4	.20
Competitors: Is it currently highly competitive? Will competition intensify?	.10	4	.40
Suppliers: Are they reliable?	.00	3	.00
Culture: What are the emerging trends?	.00	4	.00
Regulation: Is the industry heavily regulated?	.06	4	.24
Politics: Is the political climate stable?	.05	3	.15
Labor unions: Is it heavily unionized? Are unions cooperative or militant?	.05	4	.20
Technology: What are the emerging technological trends?	.10	5	.50
Entry and exit barriers: Is it difficult to enter or leave?	.04	3	.12
Total	1.00		4.11

[1] Some of the criteria are viewed as insignificant when applied to this industry or market and are given a zero weight.

[2] The ranking is the extent to which each criterion is viewed as favorable by the firm.

less clear. Should Amazon.com be compared with other online booksellers or to other retailers offering a broader product offering?

Infrastructure activities consist of network, equipment, software, and systems integration expertise. Major telecommunications carriers manage the network backbone underlying the Internet. Access to the network is gained through regional carriers, which in turn sell access to consumers and small businesses through ISPs. Equipment suppliers provide modems, routers, and servers to support access, communication, and processing of information. All of these activities rely on sophisticated client and server software applications supplied by software vendors.

TABLE 4-2   Internet Focused Industries and Markets

Industry Segment	Market Segments (Representative Companies)				
Network providers	Internet backbone provider (MCI WorldCom)	Fiber optic network provider (QWEST)	Regional backbone access provider (PSINET)	Internet access providers (Earthlink)	Wireless technology (Vodafone AirTouch)
Equipment	Access (3 COM)	Backbone (Cisco)	Servers (Sun Microsystems)	Data networking (Lucent)	Transmission gear (Ascend)
Software	Client (Oracle)	Server (Sun)	Development tools (Oracle)	Security (Raptor)	Personalized transactions (Broadvision)
Expertise	Creative (Earthweb)	Systems integration (Andersen)	Reengineering (CSC)	Advertising services (Doubleclick)	Domain names (Network Solutions)
Enabling services	Directories and portals (Yahoo)	Security (Verisign)	Payment systems (First Data)	Rating services (I/Pro)	Website hosting (GTE)
Content	Entertainment (Sportsline)	Financial (Bloomberg)	Retailers (Amazon.com)	News feeds (Dow Jones)	Publishers (D&B)

System integrators must meld complex systems using disparate software and hardware vendors. Content providers are dependent on vendors providing such enabling services as payments processing, security, advertising, Web design, and search or directory services. Table 4-2 illustrates how this simple framework can be used to create discrete industry and market segments.

DETERMINING HOW TO COMPETE

Determining how to compete involves a clear understanding of the factors critical for successfully competing in the targeted market. This outward-looking analysis applies to the primary factors governing the environment external to the firm. Understanding market dynamics and knowing in what areas the firm must excel when compared with the competition is crucial if the firm is to compete effectively in its chosen market. This requires developing a snapshot or profile of the market expressed in terms of its key competitive characteristics.

Profiling the Targeted Markets

Market profiling entails collecting sufficient data to accurately assess and characterize a firm's competitive environment within its chosen markets. Using Michael Porter's (1985) Five Forces framework, the market or industry environment can be described in terms of such competitive dynamics as the firm's customers, suppliers (including suppliers of capital), current competitors, potential competitors, and product or service substitutes. This framework may be modified to include other factors, such as the degree of unionization, the severity of governmental regulation, and the impact of global influences (e.g., fluctuations in exchange rates) (Figure 4-3).

The required data include the following: (1) types of products and services, (2) market share in terms of dollars and units, (3) pricing, (4) selling and distribution channels and associated costs, (5) type, location, and age of production facilities, (6) product quality metrics, (7) customer service metrics, (8) compensation by major labor category, (9) research and development (R&D) expenditures, (10) supplier performance metrics, and (11) financial performance in terms of growth and profitability. These data must be collected on all significant competitors in the firm's chosen markets.

Customers

The firm must understand the key reasons its customers make buying decisions and rank order them from the most to the least important. Key reasons could include price, quality, service, convenience, or some combination. Market surveys can be conducted to determine how sensitive customers are to changes in these factors. Failure to understand even subtle differences in customer motivations can lead to a significant loss of business in highly competitive markets. For example, companies lending to consumers and businesses rely heavily on information supplied by the major credit reporting companies, such as Experian, Equifax, Trans-Union, and Dun & Bradstreet, for information to make credit-granting decisions. Although lenders require accurate, complete, and timely data, small differences in

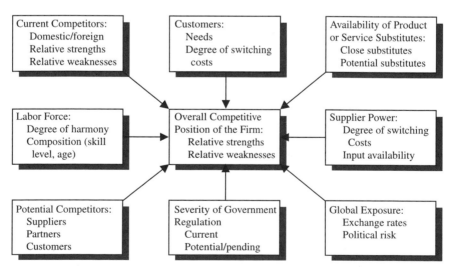

FIGURE 4-3.   Defining market/industry competitive dynamics (modified Porter competitive framework).

price will cause lenders to switch suppliers or renegotiate contracts with existing suppliers as soon as the current contracts expire.

Suppliers

The firm needs to determine the number and reputation for quality and reliability of critical suppliers. A single or a small number of relatively low-quality or unreliable suppliers may pose a significant threat to a firm attempting to expand its market share. Moreover, reliance on a single or a small number of suppliers shifts pricing power from the buyer to the seller. Examples include Intel's global dominance of the microchip market and Microsoft's worldwide supremacy in the market for personal computer operating systems. Suppliers also can make the products and services provided by former customers obsolete, as evidenced by Dell Computer's strategy of selling directly to customers (Case Study 4-1).

CASE STUDY 4-1: DELL COMPUTER'S DRIVE TO ELIMINATE THE MIDDLEMAN

Historically, personal computers were sold either through a direct sales force to businesses (e.g., IBM), through company-owned stores (e.g., Gateway), or through independent retail outlets and distributors to both businesses and consumers (e.g., CompUSA). Retail chains and distributors constituted a large percentage of the customer base of other PC manufacturers such as Compaq and Gateway. Consequently, most PC manufacturers were saddled with the large overhead expense associated with a direct sales force, a chain of company-owned stores, a demanding and complex distribution chain contributing a substantial percentage of revenue, or some combination of all three.

Michael Dell, the founder of Dell Computer, saw an opportunity to take cost out of the distribution of PCs by circumventing the distributors and selling directly to the end user. Dell Computer introduced a dramatically new business model for selling personal computers. By starting with this model when the firm was formed, Dell did not have to worry about being in direct competition with its distribution chain. Historically, this concern has limited the extent to which other major PC manufacturers such as Compaq and Hewlett- Packard felt they could sell directly to end users.

Dell also has changed the basis of competition in the PC industry by shifting much of its direct order business to the Internet and by introducing made-to-order personal computers. Businesses and consumers can specify online the features and functions of a PC and pay by credit card. Dell assembles the PC only after the order is processed and the customer's credit card has been validated. This has the effect of increasing both customer choice and convenience as well as dramatically reducing Dell's costs of carrying inventory.

Throughout 2001, there were on average just 4 days of stock in Dell's warehouse, down from an average of 7 days during the prior year. Moreover, Dell has developed 22,000 "Premier Pages" or Websites that allow businesses to order computers directly from the company.

The success of Michael Dell's business model is evident as Dell's share of the global PC market has increased from 4.2% in 1994 to 10% in 2001, making it the market leader. Dell currently sells about $22 million a day in computers on the Internet. This amounts to about 35% of its annual revenue. Competitors are trying to imitate the Dell model but continue to move slowly for fear of alienating wholesale and retail customers. In contrast to Dell, Hewlett-Packard currently has only 800 specialized Websites for their customers to order directly from the company. IBM is talking about having 1000 in place by the end of 2001.

Case Study Discussion Questions

1. In your opinion, what market need was Dell able to satisfy better than his competition?
2. To what do you attribute Dell's success in its market segment?

Current Competitors

An analysis of competitors, both domestic and foreign, should reveal the factors contributing to their overall financial performance. Although it is easiest to examine financial performance such as revenue and earnings growth, overall profit margins, and market value, the factors that should be examined are those ultimately driving financial performance. These factors include such considerations as product line breadth, consistent quality, efficient product distribution, low-cost production, or key patents. In the late 1960s and through most of the 1970s, it was widely believed that mini-mills (i.e., nonintegrated steel mills), which did not own their own coal and iron ore supplies, could not compete in the flat-rolled steel markets because the limitations of their technology. However, by the late 1970s, such companies as Nucor Steel and Florida Steel were able to achieve major cost advantages by adopting continuous casting technologies, which enabled them to make significant inroads into the lucrative flat-rolled steel markets.

Potential Competitors

Potential competitors include firms (both domestic and foreign) in the current market, those in related markets, current customers, and current suppliers. During the late 1990s, Amazon.com expanded well beyond its original product offering of books by moving into the sale of compact discs, pharmaceuticals, and consumer electronics. The stated goal was to become the Wal-Mart of the Internet. Other firms, already established in these markets, saw Amazon.com as a potential threat by enabling their customers to order these products in a new way over the Internet. However, the combination of huge investments in developing warehouse and distribution capabilities in concert with the 2001–2002 economic slowdown caused Amazon.com's management to narrow the firm's product focus considerably.

Product or Service Substitutes

What we don't know can hurt us. Examples include the shift of many products formerly ordered through traditional brick and mortar retail outlets to the Internet such as books, compact discs, and airline tickets; e-mail and faxes as substitutes for letters; and the replacement of the electric typewriter by the word processor.

Labor Force

Work stoppages create opportunities for competitors to gain market share. Customers are forced to satisfy their product and service needs elsewhere. Whereas in some cases the loss of customers may be temporary, it may be permanent if the customer finds that another firm's product or service is equal to or superior to what it had been purchasing. Frequent work stoppages also may have long-term impacts on productivity and production costs as a result of a less motivated labor force and increased labor turnover. High turnover can be particularly insidious as firms incur substantial search and retraining expenses to fill positions.

Government Regulation

Estimates of the total cost of complying with U.S. federal government regulations vary from about $200 to $700 billion annually (Hopkins, 1996). State and local regulations would add to this cost considerably. Regulations create barriers to both entering an industry and exiting an industry. Companies wishing to enter the pharmaceutical industry must have the capabilities to produce and test new drugs to the satisfaction of the Food and Drug Administration. Companies with large unfunded or underfunded pension liabilities may find exiting an industry impossible until they have met their pension obligations to the satisfaction of the U.S. Pension Benefit Guaranty Corporation.

Global Exposure

Global exposure refers to the extent to which participation in an industry necessitates having a multinational presence. For example, the automotive industry is widely viewed as a global industry in which participation requires having assembly plants and distribution networks in major markets throughout the world. As the major auto assemblers move abroad, they also are requiring their parts suppliers to build nearby facilities to ensure "just-in-time" delivery of parts. Global exposure introduces the firm to significant currency risk as well as political risk that could result in the confiscation of the firm's properties.

INTERNAL ANALYSIS

The primary output of the internal analysis is the determination of the firm's strengths and weaknesses. What are the firm's critical strengths and weaknesses as compared with the competition? Can the firm's critical strengths be easily duplicated and surpassed by the competition? Can these critical strengths be used to gain strategic advantage in the firm's chosen market? Can the firm's key weaknesses be exploited by competitors? These questions must be answered as objectively as possible for the information to be useful in formulating a viable business strategy. Management may benefit by utilizing consultants knowledgeable in the target market to assist in developing credible answers. The objectivity of existing management may be clouded. Current managers may be comfortable with the way they have been doing things in the past, they may be defensive about a loss of market share, or they may possess limited understanding of developments in markets related to the target market.

Business Attractiveness Matrix

Competing successfully ultimately means satisfying the firm's targeted customers' needs better than competitors can. Conducting a self-assessment consists of identifying those strengths or competencies necessary to compete successfully in the firm's chosen market. These strengths often are referred to as *success factors*. Examples of success factors could include the following: high market share compared with the competition, product line breadth, cost-effective sales distribution channels, age and geographic location of production facilities, relative product quality, price competitiveness, R&D effectiveness, customer service effectiveness, corporate culture, and profitability.

Once identified for the firm's target market, success factors are weighted to reflect their relative importance in determining the firm's probable degree of success in its target market. When success factors do not apply or are relatively insignificant in a specific market, they should be given a zero weight. The firm's competitive position with respect to each success factor is ranked relative to its primary competitors. A 5 ranking means that the firm is highly competitive with respect to a specific success factor when compared with the competition. A ranking of 1 indicates a very poor competitive position. The Business Attractiveness Matrix, shown in Table 4-3, illustrates how the firm's overall attractiveness in its chosen market is determined.

The weighted average score of 3.00 out of a possible score of 5.00 suggests that the firm's overall competitive position is somewhat favorable when compared with its primary competitor. This same matrix can be constructed for other competitors to compile a subjectively determined assessment of the firm's competitive position against other major competitors.

Core Competencies

Gary Hamel and C. K. Prahalad (1994) argue that a firm's strategy should be based on core competencies, which represent bundles of skills that can be applied to extend a firm's product offering in new areas. For example, Honda Motor Corporation traditionally has had a reputation for being able to manufacture highly efficient internal combustion engines. In addition to cars, these skills

TABLE 4-3   Business Attractiveness Matrix

Success Factor	Weight	Compared to Primary Competitor	
		Ranking (5 = highly favorable; 1 = highly unfavorable)	Weighted Score
Market share: Firm's current market share?	.20	3	.60
Product line breadth: Does firm offer a broad or limited product line?	0.0	3	.00
Sales distribution: Are firm's distribution channels cost effective?	.15	4	.60
Price competitiveness: Are firm's prices high or low compared to the competition?	.10	2	.20
Age and location of facilities: Are firm's facilities properly located and new?	.05	2	.10
Production capacity: Can customer demand be served?	.05	3	.15
Relative product quality: How does the firm's product quality compare with the competition?	.15	4	.60
R&D: Is the firm a product innovator or follower?	.10	3	.30
Customer service: How does it compare with the competition?	.03	3	.09
Corporate culture: Is the firm's culture suitable for the industry?	.02	3	.06
Profitability: Can the firm attract capital and funds needed for investments?	.15	2	.30
Total	1.00		3.00

have been applied to lawnmowers and snowblowers. The expansion into these product areas has met with considerable success. Similarly, Hewlett-Packard was able to utilize its skills in producing highly precise measurement instruments to move successfully into calculators and later into PCs.

In identifying core competencies, management should take great care in how they are defined. If they are defined too broadly, they provide little practical guidance in formulating business strategy; if they are defined too narrowly, significant opportunities may be overlooked. Honda could have viewed its core competency as the ability to provide efficient transportation, which is so broad as to be functionally meaningless, or so narrowly (e.g., applied to specific functions of the internal combustion engine) as to exclude logical extensions of its product line based on its core skills.

Can these core competencies be used to gain and sustain strategic advantage in the firm's chosen market? This question really addresses the extent to which the firm's core competencies enable it to provide a product or service that is highly valued in the marketplace better than the competition. For example, an ability to mass produce analog cellular phones more efficiently than the competition provides little advantage to the firm if its customers are shifting to digital cellular phones. Moreover, if a company is able to achieve a competitive edge by leveraging its core competencies, it may be able to sustain this advantage only through continuous innovation (Case Study 4-2).

CASE STUDY 4-2: IS SUSTAINABLE COMPETITIVE ADVANTAGE POSSIBLE?

Can the firm's core competencies be easily duplicated and surpassed by the competition? In the early 1980s, Apple Computer introduced an icon-based screen for its Macintosh operating system, which allowed them to sell Macintoshes at a premium price. However, with the introduction of Microsoft's Windows operating system, the perceived advantage in terms of ease of use of the Macintosh system diminished. There were such great similarities that Apple sued Microsoft for its alleged plagiarism of the Mac's "look and feel," but Apple lost in court. Similarly, Apple Computer sued a competitor for allegedly stealing the design of its enormously popular, highly stylish iMac computer.

The Netscape browser software improved substantially earlier versions of the software, which enables users to access information in a multimedia environment on the Web, only to be surpassed by Microsoft's Internet Explorer browser. The direct competition between the two companies resulted in a dramatic compression of the software product development cycle from what had been as long as several years to as little as 4–6 months for new versions of the browser.

Case Study Discussion Questions

1. In your opinion, how can a firm's competitive advantage be extended?
2. Cite examples of firms that have extended their competitive advantages.

DEFINING THE MISSION STATEMENT

At a minimum, a corporate mission statement seeks to describe the corporation's purpose for being and where the corporation hopes to go. The mission statement should not be so general as to provide little practical direction. A good mission statement should include references to such areas as the firm's targeted markets, product or service offering, distribution channels, and management beliefs with respect to the firm's primary stakeholders. Ultimately, the market targeted by the firm should reflect the fit between the corporation's primary strengths and competencies and its ability to satisfy customer needs better than the competition. The product and service offering should be relatively broadly defined so as to allow for the introduction of new products, which can be derived from the firm's core competencies. Distribution channels address how the firm chooses to distribute its products (e.g., through a direct sales force, agents, distributors, resellers, the Internet, or some combination of all of these methods). Customers are those targeted by the firm's products and services. Management beliefs establish the underpinnings of how the firm intends to behave with respect to its stakeholders.

SETTING STRATEGIC OR LONG-TERM BUSINESS OBJECTIVES

Business objectives are defined as what is to be accomplished within a specific time period. A good objective is measurable and has a time frame in which it is to be realized. Typical corporate objectives include revenue growth rates, minimum acceptable financial returns, and market share. A good objective might state that the firm seeks to increase revenue from $1 billion currently to $5 billion by the year 20??. A poorly written objective would be that the firm seeks to increase revenue substantially.

Common Business Objectives

Return: The firm seeks to achieve a rate of return that will equal or exceed the return required by its shareholders (cost of equity), lenders (cost of debt), or the combination of the two (cost of capital).

Size: The firm seeks to achieve the critical mass defined in terms of sales volume to realize economies of scale.

Growth:

— Accounting objectives: The firm seeks to grow earnings per share (EPS), revenue, or assets at a specific rate of growth per year.

— Valuation objectives: Such objectives may be expressed in terms of the firm's common stock price per share divided by earnings per share, book value, cash flow, or revenue.

Diversification: The firm desires to sell current products in new markets, new products in current markets, or new products in new markets.

Flexibility: The firm desires to possess production facilities and distribution capabilities that can be shifted rapidly to exploit new opportunities as they arise. This has become increasingly important in the global economy. The major automotive companies have moved toward standardizing parts across car and truck platforms. This reduces the time required to introduce new products and facilitates the companies' ability to shift production from one region to another.

Technology: The firm desires to possess capabilities in core or rapidly advancing technologies. Firms desirous of staying on or ahead of the rapidly changing technology curve frequently place a high priority on owning or having access to the latest technologies. Microchip and software manufacturers, as well as defense contractors, are good examples of industries in which staying abreast of new technologies is a prerequisite for survival.

SELECTING THE APPROPRIATE
CORPORATE-LEVEL STRATEGY

Corporate-level strategies are adopted at the corporate or holding company level and may include all or some of the business units, either wholly or partially, owned by the corporation. A *growth strategy* entails a focus on accelerating the firm's consolidated revenue, profit, and cash-flow growth. This strategy may be implemented in many different ways. This will be described in more detail later in this chapter in the discussion of implementation strategies. A *diversification strategy* involves a decision at the corporate level to enter new businesses. These businesses may be either related or totally unrelated to the corporation's existing business portfolio. See Chapter 1 for a more detailed discussion of diversification. An *operational restructuring strategy*, sometimes referred to as a turnaround or defensive strategy, usually refers to the outright or partial sale of companies or product lines, downsizing by closing unprofitable or nonstrategic facilities, obtaining protection from creditors in bankruptcy court, or liquidation. A *financial restructuring strategy* describes actions by the firm to change its total debt and equity structure. The motivation for this strategy may entail better utilization of corporate cash balances in excess of the level required for financing normal operations through share-repurchase programs, reducing the firm's cost of capital by increasing leverage, or increasing management's control by acquiring publicly traded company shares through a management buyout. The later strategy is discussed in more detail in Chapter 11.

SELECTING THE APPROPRIATE
BUSINESS LEVEL STRATEGY

A firm should choose that business strategy from among the range of reasonable alternatives that enables it to achieve its stated objectives in an acceptable time period subject to resource constraints. Resource constraints include limitations on the availability of management talent and funds. Gaining access to highly competent management talent is frequently the more difficult of the two to over-come. Strategies can be reduced to one of four basic categories: (1) price or cost leadership, (2) product differentiation, (3) focus or niche strategies, and (4) hybrid strategies.

Price or Cost Leadership

The price or cost leadership strategy reflects the influence of a series of tools introduced and popularized by the Boston Consulting Group (BCG). These tools include the experience curve, the product life cycle, and portfolio balancing techniques (Boston Consulting Group, 1985). Cost leadership is designed to make a firm the cost leader in its market by constructing efficient production facilities, tightly controlling overhead expense, and eliminating marginally profitable customer accounts. The experience curve postulates that as the cumulative historical volume of a firm's output increases, cost per unit of output decreases geometrically as the firm becomes more efficient in producing that product. Therefore, the firm with the largest historical output also should be the lowest cost producer. The implied strategy for this firm should be to enter markets as early as possible and to reduce product prices aggressively to maximize market share (Marrus, 1984).

Experience Curve

The applicability of the experience curve varies across industries. It seems to work best for largely commodity-type industries in which scale economies can lead to substantial reductions in per unit production costs. Examples include the manufacturing of PCs or cell-phone handsets. The strategy of continuously driving down production costs may make most sense for the existing industry market share leader. If the leader already has a cost advantage over its competitors because of its significantly larger market share compared with its competitors, it may be able to improve its cost advantage by more aggressively pursuing market share through price cutting. This strategy may be highly destructive if pursued concurrently by a number of firms with approximately the same market share in an industry whose customers do not see measurable differences in the products or services offered by the various competitors. Under such circumstances, repetitive price-cutting by firms within the industry is likely to drive down profitability for all firms in the industry. Industry profitability can continue to fall precipitously for many years, if the least profitable firms cannot exit the industry as a result of high fixed obligations in the form of long-term leases, leverage, or worker pension and health insurance obligations.

Product Life Cycle

BCG's second major contribution is the product life cycle, which characterizes a product's evolution in four stages: embryonic, growth, maturity, and decline. Strong sales growth and low barriers to entry characterize the first two stages. However, over time entry becomes more costly as early entrants into the market accumulate market share and experience lower per unit production costs as a result of the effects of the experience curve. New entrants have substantially poorer cost positions as a result of their small market shares when compared with earlier entrants and cannot catch up to the market leaders as overall market growth slows. During the later phases characterized by slow market growth, falling product prices force marginal firms and unprofitable firms out of the market or to consolidate with other firms.

Management can obtain insight into the firm's probable future cash requirements by determining its position in its industry's product life cycle. During the high-growth phase, firms in the industry normally have high investment requirements associated with capacity expansion and increasing working capital needs. Operating cash flow is normally negative. During the mature and declining growth phases, investment requirements are lower and cash flow becomes positive. Although the phase of the product life cycle provides insights into current and future cash requirements for both the acquiring and target companies, determining the approximate length of each phase can be challenging. The introduction of significant product innovation can reinvigorate industry growth and extend the length of the current growth phase. This is particularly true in such industries as microchip, PC, and cellular (Moore, 1991).

In addition to its applicability to valuing the firm, the product life cycle also can be useful in selecting the appropriate business strategy for the firm. In the early stages of the product life cycle, the industry tends to be highly fragmented, with many participants having very small market shares. Often firms in the early stages adopt a niche strategy in which they focus their marketing efforts on a relatively small and homogeneous customer group. If economies of scale are possible, the industry will begin to consolidate as firms aggressively pursue cost leadership strategies. As the industry becomes increasingly mature, the level of consolidation becomes very high as firms achieve increasingly larger market shares. Under these circumstances, firms increasingly pursue differentiation strategies, in which customers perceive them to be somehow different from their competitors based on such factors as service and quality.

Share-Growth Matrix

The final BCG innovation, *portfolio balance theory*, reflects the movements of products and firms through the product life cycle. Portfolio balance theory dictates that companies should fund high-growth, cash-poor businesses or product lines with cash provided by the more mature cash-generating businesses. Businesses in the growth phase of the product life cycle have low market share but substantial cash needs, and those in the mature or declining growth phase have higher market share. Note that this tool can be used to develop strategy at the corporate level, where the portfolio consists of operating units, or at the business level, where the portfolio may consist only of specific product lines.

Businesses in a firm's portfolio having high market share and high growth rates relative to the industry's growth rate and excellent profit potential are referred to as **stars**. The high-growth potential of the **stars** means they also have high reinvestment requirements. As the industry moves through its product life cycle and reaches the maturity stage, the stars begin to generate cash flow well in excess of their reinvestment requirements. As their potential growth rate slows, management may reclassify such businesses as cash cows. This excess cash flow generated by these *cash cows* can be used by the firm to fund other stars within the firm's portfolio or to acquire new or related businesses that appear to have the potential to become stars. Businesses that have low growth and market share are deemed to be either *question marks* or *dogs* and frequently are candidates for divestiture. High-growth, low-market-share question marks may be the next stars or dogs. Question marks use up more cash than they generate and may become liabilities if they cannot be transformed into market leaders. Most companies cannot afford to fund all of their stars and question marks; consequently, some are likely to be divested, spun off to shareholders, or combined with other businesses in a joint venture operation.

Product Differentiation

Differentiation represents a range of strategies in which the product or service offered is perceived to be slightly different by customers from other product or service offerings in the marketplace. Differentiation can be accomplished through brand image, technology features, or through alternative distribution channels, such as the ability to download products via the Internet. Examples of product differentiation strategies abound. Some firms attempt to compete by offering customers a range of features or functions. For example, many banks issue credit cards such as MasterCard or Visa. Each bank tries to differentiate its card by offering a higher credit line, a lower interest rate, or annual fee or by providing prizes. Software companies justify charging for upgrades based on additional features to word-processing or spreadsheet programs, which are not found on competing software packages. Other firms compete on the basis of consistent product quality by providing excellent service. Today, Dell Computer is perceived to be a strong competitor by providing both excellent quality and service, which in certain cases allows the firm to charge a slightly higher price for its PCs. Other firms attempt to compete by offering their customers excellent convenience. Amazon.com falls in this category by offering consumers the opportunity to buy books whenever and from wherever they choose.

Focus or Niche Strategies

Firms adopting these types of strategies tend to concentrate their efforts by selling a few products or services to a single market and compete primarily on the basis of understanding their customers' needs better than the competition does. In this strategy, the firm seeks to carve a specific niche with respect to a certain group of customers, a narrow geographic area, or a particular use of a product. Examples include the major airlines, airplane manufacturers (e.g., Boeing), and major defense contractors (e.g., Lockheed-Martin). Many companies that start with a single focus later diversify to broaden their revenue base. Recent examples include Yahoo and AOL, which started as an Internet search engine and

TABLE 4-4   Hybrid Strategies

	Cost Leadership	Product Differentiation
Niche focus approach	Cisco Systems WD-40	Coca-Cola McDonald's
Multimarket approach	Wal-Mart Oracle	America Online Microsoft

a consumer Internet access and content provider, respectively. Currently they are widely viewed as emerging multimedia or network companies.

Hybrid Strategies

Hybrid strategies involve some combination of the previously mentioned strategies (Table 4-4). For example, Coca-Cola pursues both a differentiated and highly market-focused strategy. Coca-Cola derives the bulk of its revenues by focusing on the worldwide soft drink market. Its product is differentiated in that consumers perceive it to have a distinctly refreshing taste. Moreover, consumers can expect the taste to be consistently the same. Other companies that pursue focused yet differentiated strategies include fast-food industry giant McDonald's, which competes on the basis of providing fast food of a consistent quality in a clean, comfortable environment.

As is always true, there are examples of highly successful companies that simply do not fit neatly into any model. These are the result of creative people daring to think the unthinkable. The Williams Companies, a large oil and gas transmission pipeline company, conceived of the idea of running fiber-optic cable through their extensive natural gas pipeline network. In doing so, they did not have to devote considerable sums of money to acquiring the right of way through extensive geographic areas. Wiltel, the subsidiary of The Williams Companies responsible for this fiber-optic network, later was sold and eventually became the telecommunications company WorldCom.

Business-Market Attractiveness Matrix

The business-market attractiveness matrix matches the attractiveness of markets with a firm's capabilities (Table 4-5). McKinsey & Company and General Electric Corporation introduced this analytical tool, which incorporates the results of internal and external analyses, as a means of summarizing the competitive position of all of a firm's lines of business. This matrix can be constructed from information obtained from the Industry/Market Attractiveness Matrix (Table 4-1) and the Business Attractiveness Matrix (Table 4-3) for each line of business (LOB) in the firm's business portfolio. Each LOB is positioned in the Business-Market Attractiveness Matrix by using as coordinates the weighted average numerical scores from its Industry/Market Attractiveness and Business Attractiveness Matrices.

TABLE 4-5   Business-Market Attractiveness Matrix

		Market Attractiveness		
		High	Average	Low
Business strengths	High	Invest or acquire		
	Average			
	Low			Divest or manage for cash

The Business-Market Attractiveness matrix displays what the firm believes to be those LOBs that are most attractive in terms of the firm's strengths and in terms of the characteristics of the marketplace. The strategic implications of this planning tool are that a firm should invest or acquire in that market which has favorable growth and profit potential and in which the firm is likely to satisfy customer needs better than other competitors in the market. The firm should divest those LOBs in those markets that are viewed as unattractive and in which the firm has a weak overall competitive position. As noted earlier, market attractiveness may be defined in terms of such factors as size, growth rate, price sensitivity of customers, degree of regulation, global exposure, and degree of unionization. Business strengths, relative to the competition, could include market share or cost, quality (real or perceived), and customer service advantages. Those LOBs with the highest scores fall in the upper left-hand quadrant (high market attractiveness and business strengths) and those with the lowest fall in the lower right-hand quadrant.

SELECTING THE APPROPRIATE IMPLEMENTATION STRATEGY

Once a firm has determined the appropriate business strategy (i.e., price–cost leadership, differentiation, focus or niche, or a hybrid strategy), attention must be turned to deciding the best means of implementing the desired strategy. Implementation involves selecting the right option from the range of reasonable options. Generally, a firm has five choices: (1) solo venture or build (i.e., implement the strategy based solely on internal resources), (2) partner, (3) invest, (4) acquire, or (5) swap assets. Each option has significantly different implications. Table 4-6 provides a comparison of the different options in terms of their advantages and disadvantages. In theory, the decision to choose among alternative options should be made based on the discounting of the cash-flow stream to the firm resulting from each option. In practice, there are many other considerations at work.

TABLE 4-6   Strategy Implementation—Solo Venture, Partner, Invest, Acquire, or Swap

Basic Options	Advantages	Disadvantages
Solo venture or build (organic growth)	—Control	—Capital/expense requirements —Speed
Partner (Shared growth/shared control) —Marketing/distribution alliance —Joint venture —License —Franchise	—Limits capital and expense investment requirements —May be precursor to acquisition	—Lack of or limited control —Potential for diverging objectives —Potential for creating a competitor
Invest (e.g., minority investments in other firms)	—Limits initial capital/expense requirements	—High risk of failure —Lack of control —Time
Acquire or merge	—Speed —Control	—Capital/expense requirements —Potential earnings dilution
Swap assets	—Limits use of cash —No earnings dilution —Limits tax liability if basis in assets swapped remains unchanged	—Finding willing parties —Reaching agreement on assets to be exchanged

The Role of Intangible Factors

Although financial analyses are conducted to evaluate the various options, the option chosen ultimately may depend on such nonquantifiable factors as the senior manager's risk profile, patience, and ego. The degree of control offered by the various alternatives displayed in Table 4-6 is often the central issue confronted by senior management in choosing among the various options. Although the solo venture and acquisition options offer the highest degree of control, they are often among the most expensive but for very different reasons. Typically a build strategy will take considerably longer to realize key strategic objectives, and it may, depending on the magnitude and timing of cash flows generated from investments, have a significantly lower net present value than the alternatives. In contrast, gaining control through acquisition also can be very expensive because of the substantial premium the acquirer normally has to pay to gain a controlling interest in another company.

The joint venture may represent a practical alternative to either a build or acquire strategy by giving a firm access to such factors as skills, product distribution channels, proprietary processes, and patents at a lower initial expense than might be involved otherwise. The joint venture is frequently a precursor to an acquisition because it gives both parties time to determine if their respective corporate cultures and strategic objectives are compatible (see Chapter 12).

Asset swaps may represent an attractive alternative to the other options, but they are generally very difficult to establish in most industries unless the assets involved are substantially similar in terms of physical characteristics and use. The best example of an industry in which this practice is relatively common is in commercial and industrial real estate. The cable industry is another example of how asset swaps can be used to achieve strategic objectives. In recent years, the cable industry has been swapping customers in different geographic areas to allow a single company to dominate a specific geographic area and to realize the full benefits of economies of scale. An interesting recent asset swap involved Cox Communications Inc. and AT&T, in which Cox swapped its 1.4% stake in AT&T, valued at $2.8 billion, for 495,000 AT&T cable TV customers and $750 million in cash. Cox's objective was to strengthen its cable customer base in such areas as Oklahoma, Arkansas, Louisiana, Texas, and New Mexico. Following the transaction, Cox will serve about 5.5 million customers nationwide.

Accounting Considerations

Table 4-6 distinguishes between capital investment and expense investment. Although both types of investment have an immediate impact on actual cash flow, they have substantially different effects on accounting or reported profits. The impact of capital spending affects reported profits by adding to depreciation expense. This effect is spread over the accounting life of the investment. In contrast, *expense investment* refers to expenditures made on such things as application software development or database construction. Although it may be possible to capitalize and to amortize some portion of these investments over several years, they usually are expensed in the year in which the monies are spent. Firms with publicly traded stocks may base strategic investment decisions on accounting considerations (e.g., the preservation of earnings per share) rather than on purely economic considerations. Consequently, a publicly traded company may be inclined to purchase a very expensive piece of depreciable equipment rather than develop a potentially superior piece of equipment internally through R&D expenditures, which may have to be expensed.

Analyzing Assumptions

To assist in the selection of the appropriate option, it is crucial to clearly state explicit and implicit assumptions. Assumptions will fall into two categories: those that are common to each option considered and those that are unique to a specific option. Assumptions common to all options (i.e., solo venture, partner, invest, acquire, or swap) include market assumptions such as the market's rate of growth, customer needs, and factors affecting customer buying decisions. Assumptions that will vary from one option to another include the amount and timing of investments and financing requirements. Competitors also may react quite differently depending on which option the firm selects. An acquisition strategy may be viewed by the competition as very aggressive; consequently, such a strategy may elicit a far more aggressive response from competitors than a more benign approach involving making minority investments in a number of different firms. Therefore, assumptions made with respect to competitors also may vary depending on the option selected.

With the assumptions displayed, the reasonableness of the various options can be compared more readily. The option with the highest net present value is not necessarily the preferred strategy if the assumptions underlying the analysis strain credulity. Understanding clearly stated assumptions underlying the chosen strategy and those underlying alternative strategies forces senior management to make choices based on a discussion of the reasonableness of the assumptions associated with each option. This is preferable to placing a disproportionately high level of confidence in the numerical output of computer models.

FUNCTIONAL STRATEGIES

Functional strategies are focused on short-term results and generally are developed by functional areas; they also tend to be very detailed and highly structured. Such strategies will result in a series of concrete actions for each function or business group, depending on the company's organization. It is common to see separate plans containing specific goals and actions for such functions as marketing, manufacturing, R&D, engineering, and financial and human resources. Functional strategies should include clearly defined objectives, actions, timetables for achieving those actions, resources required, and the individual responsible for ensuring that the actions are completed on time and within budget.

Specific functional strategies could read as follows:

- Set up a product distribution network in the northeastern United States capable of handling a minimum of 1 million units of product annually by 12/31/20??. (Individual responsible: Oliver Tran; estimated budget: $2 million.)
- Develop and execute an advertising campaign to support the sales effort in the northeastern United States by 10/31/20??. (Individual responsible: Maria Gomez; estimated budget: $.5 million.)
- Hire a logistics manager to administer the distribution network by 9/15/20??. (Individual responsible: Patrick Petty; estimated budget: $100,000.)
- Acquire a manufacturing company with sufficient capacity to meet the projected demand for the next 3 years by 6/30/20?? at a purchase price not to exceed $100 million. (Individual responsible: Chang Lee.)

The relationship between the business mission, business strategy, implementation strategy, and functional strategies can be illustrated for an application software company, which is targeting the credit card industry.

- Mission: To become recognized by its customers as the leader in providing accurate high-speed, high-volume transactional software for processing credit card remittances by 20??.

- Business Strategy: Upgrade the firm's current software by adding the necessary features and functions to differentiate the firm's product and service offering from its primary competitors and to satisfy projected customer requirements through 20??.
- Implementation Strategy: Purchase a software company at a price not to exceed $400 million capable of developing "state-of-the-art" remittance processing software by 12/21/20?? (Individual responsible: Donald Stuckee.) Note that this assumes that the firm has completed an analysis of available options including internal development, partnering, licensing, or acquisition.
- Functional Strategies to Support Implementation Strategy:

  — Research & Development: Identify and develop new applications for remittance processing software.
  — Marketing & Sales: Assess impact of new product offering on revenue generated from current and new customers.
  — Human Resources: Determine appropriate staffing requirements to support the combined firms (i.e., the acquirer and target firms).
  — Finance: Identify and quantify potential cost savings generated from improved productivity as a result of replacing existing software with the newly acquired software and from the elimination of duplicate personnel in acquirer and target companies. Evaluate the impact of the acquisition of on the combined companies financial statements.
  — Legal: Ensure that all target company customers have valid contracts and that such contracts are transferable to the acquirer without penalty. Also, ensure that the acquirer will have unlimited rights to use the remittance processing software.
  — Tax: Assess the tax impact of the acquisition of acquiring company operating cash flow.

STRATEGIC CONTROLS

Strategic controls consist of both incentive and monitoring systems. *Incentive systems* include bonus, profit sharing, or other performance-based payments made to motivate both acquirer and target company employees to work to implement the acquirer's business strategy or a business strategy for the combined firms. Such a strategy normally would have been agreed to during negotiation. Incentives often include *retention bonuses* made to key employees of the target firm, if they remain with the combined companies for a specific period following completion of the transaction. *Monitoring systems* are implemented to track the actual performance of the combined firms against the business plan. Such systems can be accounting based (and monitor such financial measures as revenue, profits, and cash flow) or activity based. Activity-based systems monitor variables, which drive financial performance. Such variables include customer retention, average revenue per customer, employee turnover, and revenue per employee.

THE BUSINESS PLAN AS A COMMUNICATION DOCUMENT

The necessary output of the planning process is a document designed to communicate effectively with key decisionmakers and stakeholders. Although there are many ways to develop such documents, Exhibit 4-1 outlines the key features that should be addressed in a good business plan (i.e., one that is so well-reasoned and compelling to cause decisionmakers to accept its recommendations). A good business plan should be short, focused, compelling, and well documented. Supporting documentation should be referred to in the text but placed primarily in appendixes to the business plan. The executive summary may be the most important and difficult piece of the business plan to write. It must communicate succinctly and compellingly what is being proposed, why it is being proposed, how it is to be achieved, and by when. It also must identify the major resource requirements and risks associated with the critical assumptions underlying the plan. The executive summary is often the first and only portion of the business plan that is read by the time-constrained chief executive officer (CEO), lender, or venture capitalist. As such, it may represent the first and last chance to catch the attention of the key decision maker.

EXHIBIT 4-1. TYPICAL BUSINESS UNIT LEVEL BUSINESS PLAN FORMAT

1. Executive Summary: In 1–2 pages, describe what you are proposing to do, why, how it will be accomplished, by what date, critical assumptions, risks, and major resource requirements.
2. Industry/market definition: Define the industry/market in which the firm competes in terms of size, growth rate, product offering, and other pertinent characteristics.
3. External analysis: Describe industry/market dynamics in terms of customers, competitors, potential entrants, product/service substitutes, and suppliers (e.g., Porter Framework). Discuss major opportunities and threats that exist because of the industry's competitive dynamics. Be sure that you can show how these threats to or opportunities for the firm are a consequence of the industry/market dynamics.
4. Internal analysis: Describe the company's strengths and weaknesses and how they compare with the competition. Identify which of these

strengths and weaknesses are important to the firm's targeted customers, and explain why.

5. Business mission/vision statement: Describe the purpose of the corporation, what it intends to achieve, and how it wishes to be perceived by its stakeholders. For example, an automotive parts manufacturer may envision itself as being perceived by the end of the decade as the leading supplier of high-quality automotive components worldwide by its customers and as fair and honest by its employees, the communities in which it operates, and its suppliers.

6. Quantified strategic objectives (including completion dates): Indicate both financial (e.g., rates of return, sales, cash flow, share price) and nonfinancial (e.g., market share, being perceived by customers or investors as number one in the targeted market in terms of market share, product quality, price, innovation) goals.

7. Business strategy: Identify how the mission and objectives will be achieved (e.g., become a cost leader, adopt a differentiation strategy, focus on a specific market segment, or some combination of these strategies). Show how the chosen business strategy satisfies a key customer need or builds on a major strength possessed by the firm. For example, a firm whose targeted customers are highly price sensitive may pursue a cost leadership strategy to enable it to lower selling prices and to increase market share and profitability. Alternatively, a firm with a well-established brand name may choose to pursue a differentiation strategy by adding features to its product that are perceived by its customers as valuable.

8. Implementation strategy: From a range of reasonable options (solo venture or "go it alone" strategy, partner via a joint venture or less formal business alliance, license, minority investment, and acquisition/merger), indicate which option would enable the firm to best implement its chosen business strategy. Indicate why the chosen implementation strategy is superior to alternative options. For example, an acquisition strategy may be appropriate if the perceived "window of opportunity" is believed to be brief. Alternatively, a solo venture may be preferable if there are few attractive acquisition opportunities or if the firm believes that it has the necessary resources to develop the needed processes or technologies.

9. Functional tactical strategies: Identify plans and resources required by each major functional area including manufacturing, engineering, sales and marketing, research and development, finance, legal, and human resources.

10. Business plan financials and valuation: Provide projected 5-year income, balance sheet, and cash-flow statements for the company and estimate the firm's value based on the projected

cash flows. State key forecast assumptions underlying the projected financials and the valuation.

11. Risk assessment: Evaluate the potential impact on valuation by changing selected key assumptions one at a time. Briefly identify contingency plans (i.e., alternative ways of achieving the firm's mission and objectives) that would be undertaken if critical assumptions prove to be inaccurate. Identify specific events that, if they occur, would trigger the firm to pursue a contingency plan. Such "trigger points" could include deviations in revenue growth of more than $x\%$ or the failure to acquire or develop a needed technology within a specific time period.

PHASE 2: BUILDING THE MERGER/ ACQUISITION IMPLEMENTATION PLAN

If it is determined following an analysis of available options that an acquisition or merger is necessary to implement the business strategy, a merger/acquisition plan is required. (The merger/acquisition implementation plan subsequently will be referred to as the "acquisition plan.") The acquisition plan is a specific type of implementation strategy. The acquisition plan focuses on short-term rather than strategic or longer-term issues. It consists of management objectives, a resource assessment, a market analysis, clearly specified actions, a timetable for completing the acquisition, and the name of the individual responsible for making it all happen. The acquisition plan communicates to those charged with acquiring a company the preferences of senior management. These are expressed in terms of management objectives and tactics defined in the plan. The objectives specify management's expectations for the acquisition, and the tactics provide guidance on how the acquisition process should be managed. This guidance could include the specification of the criteria for selecting potential acquisition targets and willingness to engage in a hostile takeover. Moreover, tactics also could indicate management's choice of the form of payment (stock, cash, or debt), willingness to accept temporary earnings per share dilution, preference for a stock or asset purchase, and limitations on contacting competitors.

MANAGEMENT OBJECTIVES

The acquisition plan's stated objectives and tactics should be completely consistent with the firm's strategic objectives. Objectives include both financial and nonfinancial considerations.

Financial Objectives

Financial objectives in the acquisition plan could include a minimum rate of return or operating profit, revenue, and cash-flow targets to be achieved within a specified time period. Minimum or required rates of return targets may be substantially higher than those specified in the business plan, which relates to the required return to shareholders or to total capital. The required return for the acquisition may reflect a substantially higher level of risk as a result of the perceived variability of the amount and timing of the expected cash flows resulting from the acquisition.

Basic financial theory teaches that the goal of the managers of the firm should be to maximize the wealth of the owners of the firm (i.e., the shareholders) (Gitman, 1998). The presumption is that managers should accept only those investments contributing to shareholder wealth. Although shareholder wealth maximization is widely viewed as the primary goal, many firms have added to this overarching objective the desire to meet the needs of other stakeholders. In addition to shareholders, stakeholder groups include employees, customers, suppliers, creditors, communities, and regulatory agencies.

Recognizing the needs of the other stakeholders while diligently pursuing the goal of maximizing shareholder wealth makes good business sense. Failure to make good-faith efforts to meet the reasonable needs of the other stakeholders may seriously impede the firm's ability to satisfy its shareholders. Examples of failures to satisfy reasonable stakeholder demands include plant closures as a result of protracted strikes; increasing government-imposed rules such as health, safety, and environmental regulations; and failure to receive regulatory or shareholder approval to complete the proposed transaction.

Nonfinancial Objectives

Nonfinancial objectives address the motivations for making the acquisition that support the achievement of the financial returns stipulated in the business plan. In many instances, such objectives provide substantially more guidance for those responsible for managing the acquisition process than financial targets. Nonfinancial objectives in the acquisition plan could include the following:

1. Obtain rights to products, patents, copyrights or brand names.
2. Provide growth opportunities in the same or related markets.
3. Develop new distribution channels in the same or related markets.
4. Obtain additional production capacity in strategically located facilities.
5. Add R&D capabilities.
6. Obtain access to proprietary technologies, processes, and skills.

MARKET ANALYSIS

Assuming the proposed acquisition is in the firm's target market, there is no need to conduct a separate external or internal assessment, which was completed as part of the business plan. If the market to be entered is new to the firm, a complete market assessment is required. Market assessments were discussed earlier in this chapter under the modified Porter Competitive Framework (see Figure 4-3).

RESOURCE AVAILABILITY

Early in the acquisition process it is important to determine the maximum amount of the firm's available resources that senior management will commit to a merger or acquisition. This information is used when the firm develops target selection criteria before undertaking a search for potential target firms. Financial resources that are potentially available to the acquirer include those provided by internally generated cash flow in excess of normal operating requirements plus funds from the equity and debt markets. If the target firm is known, the potential pool of funds includes funds provided by the internal cash flow of the combined companies in excess of normal operating requirements, as well as the capacity of the combined firms to issue equity or increase leverage.

Financial theory suggests that a firm always will be able to attract sufficient funding for an acquisition if the acquiring firm can demonstrate that it can earn its cost of capital. In practice, senior management's risk tolerance plays an important role in determining what the acquirer believes it can afford to spend on a merger or acquisition. Consequently, risk-adverse management may be inclined to commit only a small portion of the total financial resources potentially available to the firm.

Determining Affordability

Three basic types of risk confront senior management considering making an acquisition. These risks affect how they feel about the affordability of an acquisition opportunity. These include operating risk, financial risk, and overpayment risk. How managers perceive these risks will determine how much of their potential available resources they will be willing to commit to making an acquisition.

Operating Risk

Operating risk addresses the ability of the buyer to manage the acquired company. It generally is perceived to be higher for M&As in markets that are unrelated to the acquirer's core business. The limited understanding of managers in the acquiring company of the competitive dynamics of the new market and the inner workings of the target firm may negatively affect the postmerger integration effort as well as the ongoing management of the combined companies. As noted in Chapter 1, this perception is supported by empirical studies.

Financial Risk

Financial risk refers to the buyer's willingness and ability to leverage a transaction as well as the willingness of shareholders to accept near-term earnings per share dilution. Management's tolerance of financial risk can be measured in part by the credit rating the acquiring firm attempts to maintain. To retain a specific credit rating, the acquiring company must maintain certain levels of financial ratios such as debt to equity and interest coverage (i.e., earnings before interest expense divided by interest expense). A firm's incremental debt capacity can be approximated by comparing the relevant financial ratios to those of comparable firms in the same industry that are rated by the credit rating agencies. The difference represents the amount they theoretically could borrow without jeopardizing their current credit rating. Senior management could also gain insight into how much EPS dilution equity investors may be willing to tolerate through informal discussions with Wall Street analysts and an examination of recent comparable transactions financed by issuing stock.

Overpayment Risk

Overpayment risk involves the dilution of EPS or a reduction in its growth rate resulting from paying significantly more than the economic value of the acquired company. The effects of overpayment on earnings dilution can last for years. To illustrate the effects of overpayment risk, assume the acquiring company's shareholders are satisfied with the company's projected annual average increase in EPS of 20% annually for the next 5 years. The company announces that it will be acquiring another company and that a series of "restructuring" expenses will slow EPS growth in the coming year to 10%. However, management argues that the savings resulting from combining the two companies will raise the combined companies' EPS growth rate to 30% in the second through fifth year of the forecast. The risk is that the savings cannot be realized in the time frame assumed by management and the slowdown in earnings extends well beyond the first year. Failure to achieve the EPS growth rates promised investors is likely to result in a substantial deterioration in the new firm's share price.

TACTICS

Acquisition tactics should reflect senior management's preferences for conducting the acquisition process. To ensure that the process is managed in a manner consistent with management's risk tolerance and biases, management must provide guidance to those responsible for finding and valuing the target, as well as negotiating the transaction, in the following areas:

1. Determining the criteria used to evaluate prospective candidates (e.g., size, price range, current profitability, growth rate, or geographic location)
2. Specifying methods for finding candidates (e.g., soliciting board members; analyzing competitors; and contacting brokers, investment bankers, lenders, law firms, and the trade press)
3. Establishing roles and responsibilities of the acquisition team, including the use of outside consultants and defining the team's budget

4. Identifying acceptable sources of financing (e.g., equity issues, bank loans, unsecured bonds, seller financing, or asset sales)
5. Preferences for an asset or stock purchase and form of payment (cash, stock, or debt)
6. Tolerance for goodwill
7. Openness to partial rather than full ownership
8. Willingness to launch an unfriendly takeover
9. Setting affordability limits (such limits can be expressed as a maximum price to earnings, book earnings before interest and taxes, or cash flow multiple or a maximum dollar figure)
10. Desire for related or unrelated acquisitions

Substantial upfront participation by management will help dramatically in the successful implementation of the acquisition process. Unfortunately, senior management frequently avoids providing significant input early in the process, despite recognizing the value of communication. Management's reticence to get involved early in the process may reflect a very demanding schedule or uneasiness with the proceedings. In either case, limited participation by management inevitably leads to miscommunication, confusion, and poor execution later in the process by those charged with making it happen.

SCHEDULE

The final component of a properly constructed acquisition plan is a schedule that recognizes all of the key events that must take place throughout the acquisition process. Each event should be characterized by beginning and ending milestones or dates as well as the name of the individual responsible for ensuring that each milestone is achieved. The timetable of events should be aggressive but realistic. The timetable should be sufficiently aggressive to motivate all participants in the process to work as expeditiously as possible to meet the management objectives established in the acquisition plan. However, an overly optimistic timetable may prove to be demotivating to those involved because uncontrollable or unforeseen circumstances may delay reaching certain milestones.

Exhibit 4-2 outlines the contents of a typical acquisition plan as discussed in this chapter. The linkage between the acquisition plan and business plan is that the former describes how the firm will realize the business strategy, whose execution is believed to require an acquisition or merger. Note the same logic would apply if the implementation of the firm's business required some other business combination such as a joint venture or business alliance (see Chapter 12). Exhibit 4-3 provides a number of examples of how carefully crafted acquisition plan objectives can be linked directly to specific business plan objectives.

EXHIBIT 4-2. ACQUISITION PLAN
FOR THE ACQUIRING FIRM

1. Plan objectives: Identify the specific purpose of the acquisition. This should include what specific goals are to be achieved (e.g., cost reduction, access to new customers, distribution channels or proprietary technology, expanded production capacity) and how the achievement of these goals will better enable the acquiring firm to implement its business strategy (see Exhibit 4-1).

2. Timetable: Establish a timetable for completing the acquisition, including integration if the target firm is to be merged with the acquiring firm's operations.

3. Resource/capability evaluation: Evaluate the acquirer's financial and managerial capability to complete an acquisition. Identify affordability limits in terms of the maximum amount the acquirer should pay for an acquisition. Explain how this figure is determined.

4. Tactics: Indicate the acquirer's preferences for a "friendly" acquisition; controlling interest; using stock, debt, cash, or some combination; etc.

5. Search plan: Develop screening criteria for identifying potential target firms and explain plans for conducting the search, why the target ultimately selected was chosen, and how you will make initial contact with the target firm.

6. Negotiation strategy: Identify key buyer/seller issues. Recommend a deal structure that addresses the primary needs of all parties involved. Comment on the characteristics of the deal structure. Such characteristics include the proposed acquisition vehicle (i.e., the legal structure used in acquiring the target firm), the postclosing organization (i.e., the legal framework used to manage the combined businesses following closing), and form of payment (i.e., cash, stock, or some combination). Other characteristics include the form of acquisition (i.e., whether assets or stock are being acquired) and tax structure (i.e., whether it is a taxable or a nontaxable transaction). Indicate how you might "close the gap" between the seller's price expectations and the offer price. These considerations will be discussed in more detail in Chapters 5 and 10.

7. Determine initial offer price: Provide projected 5-year income, balance sheet, and cash-flow statements for the acquiring and target firms individually and for the consolidated acquirer and target firms with and without the effects of synergy. Develop a preliminary minimum and maximum purchase price range for the target. List key forecast assumptions. Identify an initial offer price, the composition (i.e., cash, stock, debt, or some combination) of the offer price, and

why you believe this price is appropriate in terms of meeting the primary needs of both target and acquirer shareholders. The appropriateness of the offer price should reflect your preliminary thinking about the deal structure. See Chapter 10 for a detailed discussion of the deal structuring process.

8. Financing plan: Using the combined/consolidated financial statements, determine if the proposed offer price can be financed without endangering the combined firm's credit worthiness or seriously eroding near-term profitability and cash flow. For publicly traded firms, pay particular attention to the near-term impact of the acquisition on the earnings per share of the combined firms. For a rigorous explanation of M&A financial modeling, see Chapter 8.

9. Integration plan: Identify potential integration challenges and possible solutions. (See Chapter 6 for a detailed discussion of how to develop integration strategies.) For financial buyers, identify an "exit strategy." Highly leveraged transactions are discussed in detail in Chapter 11.

THINGS TO REMEMBER

The success of an acquisition is frequently dependent on the focus, understanding, and discipline inherent in a thorough business plan. There are four overarching questions that must be addressed in developing a viable business plan. These include the following:

1. Where should the firm compete?
2. How should the firm compete?
3. How can the firm satisfy customer needs better than the competition?
4. Why is the chosen strategy preferable to other reasonable options?

To answer these questions, the business planning process should consist of a thorough analysis of customers and their needs and an intensive analysis of the firm's strengths and weaknesses compared with the competition. In addition, the planning process should result in a clearly articulated mission and set of quantified objectives with associated time frames and individuals responsible for meeting these objectives by the targeted dates. Using this information, a strategy is selected from a range of reasonable options. The assumptions underlying the strategy and supporting financial statements should be identified clearly. This last step is crucial because the reasonableness of any business strategy is solely dependent on the credibility of its underlying assumptions.

An acquisition is only one of many options available for implementing a business strategy. The decision to pursue an acquisition often rests on the desire to achieve control and a perception that the acquisition will result in achieving the desired objectives more rapidly than other options. Firms all too often pay far

EXHIBIT 4-3. EXAMPLES OF LINKAGES BETWEEN BUSINESS AND ACQUISITION PLAN OBJECTIVES

Business Plan Objective	Acquisition Plan Objective
Financial: The firm will 　Achieve rates of return that will equal or 　　exceed its cost of equity or capital by 20?? 　Maintain a debt/total capital ratio of $x\%$	Financial returns: The target firm should have 　A minimum return on assets of $x\%$ 　A debt/total capital ratio $\leq y\%$ 　Unencumbered assets of \$ z million 　Cash flow in excess of operating 　　requirements of \$$x$ million
Size: The firm will 　Be the number one or two market share 　　leader by 20?? 　Achieve revenue of \$$x$ million by 20??	Size: The target firm should be at least 　\$$x$ million in revenue
Growth: The firm will achieve through 20?? 　annual average 　Revenue growth of $x\%$ 　Earnings per share growth of $y\%$ 　Operating cash-flow growth of $z\%$	Growth: The target firm should 　Have annual revenue, earnings, and 　　operating cash-flow growth of 　　at least $x\%$ 　Provide new products and markets 　Possess excess annual production capacity 　　of x million units
Diversification: The firm will reduce earnings 　variability by $x\%$	Diversification: The target firm's earnings 　should be largely uncorrelated with the 　acquirer's earnings
Flexibility: The firm will achieve flexibility in 　manufacturing and design	Flexibility: The target firm should use flexible 　manufacturing techniques
Technology: The firm will be recognized by its 　customers as the industry's technology leader	Technology: The target firm should possess 　important patents, copyrights, and other 　forms of intellectual property
Quality: The firm will be recognized by its 　customers as the industry's quality leader	Quality: The target firm's product defects 　must be $<x$ per million units manufactured
Service: The firm will be recognized by its 　customers as the industry's service leader	Warranty record: The target firm's customer 　claims per million units sold should be not 　greater than x
Cost: The firm will be recognized by its 　customers as the industry's low-cost provider	Labor costs: The target firm should be 　nonunion and not subject to significant 　government regulation
Innovation: The firm will be recognized by its 　customers as the industry's innovation leader	R&D capabilities: The target firm should 　have introduced at least x new products in 　the last 12 months

too much for control. Alternative options may prove to be less risky. A firm may choose to implement what amounts to a phased acquisition by first entering into a joint venture with another company before acquiring it at a later date.

Once a firm has decided that an acquisition is key to realizing the strategic direction defined in the business plan, a merger/acquisition plan should be developed. The acquisition plan provides the detail needed to implement effectively the firm's business strategy. The acquisition plan defines the specific objectives management hopes to achieve by completing an acquisition, addresses issues of resource availability, and identifies the specific tactics management chooses to use to complete a transaction. The acquisition plan also establishes a schedule of milestones to keep the process on track and clearly defines the authority and responsibilities of the individual charged with managing the acquisition process.

CHAPTER DISCUSSION QUESTIONS

4-1. Why is it important to think of an acquisition or merger in the context of a process rather than as a series of semi-related, discrete events?

4-2. How does planning facilitate the acquisition process?

4-3. What are the major activities that should be undertaken in building a business plan?

4-4. What is market segmentation and why is it important?

4-5. What are the basic types of strategies that companies commonly pursue and how are they different?

4-6. What is the difference between a business plan and an acquisition plan?

4-7. What are the advantages and disadvantages of using an acquisition to implement a business strategy as compared with a joint venture?

4-8. Why is it important to understand the assumptions underlying a business plan or an acquisition plan?

4-9. Why is it important to get senior management heavily involved early in the acquisition process?

4-10. In your judgment, which of the acquisition plan tactics discussed in this chapter are the most important and why?

CHAPTER BUSINESS CASE

CASE STUDY 4-3: CONSOLIDATION IN THE GLOBAL PHARMACEUTICAL INDUSTRY CONTINUES—THE GLAXO WELLCOME AND SMITHKLINE BEECHAM EXAMPLE

Background

During the 1970s and 1980s, pharmaceuticals were sold largely through massive sales and marketing forces who made "detailing" calls on as many points of contact as possible. These points of contact included physicians' offices, hospitals, and pharmacies. During these sales calls, the company representatives would explain new drugs that have been developed to treat specific conditions. Once a drug became popular, drug development costs often would escalate as companies introduced "me-too" drugs.

Changing Market Dynamics

By the mid-1980s, demands from both business and government were forcing pharmaceutical companies to change the way they did business. Increased government intervention, lower selling prices, increased competition from generic drugs, and growing pressure for discounting from managed care organizations such as health maintenance and preferred provider organizations began to squeeze drug company profit margins. The number of contact points between the sales force and the customer shrank dramatically as more drugs were being purchased through managed care organizations and pharmacy benefit managers. Drugs commonly were sold in large volumes and often at heavily discounted levels as a result of discussions between senior managers of the buying and selling companies.

The demand for generic drugs also was declining. The use of formularies, drug lists from which managed care doctors are required to prescribe, gave doctors less choice and made them less responsive to direct calls from the sales force. The situation was compounded further by the ongoing consolidation in the hospital industry. Hospitals began centralizing purchasing and using stricter formularies, allowing physicians virtually no leeway to prescribe unlisted drugs. The growing use of formularies resulted in buyers needing fewer drugs and sharply reduced the need for similar drugs.

The First Merger Wave Among Pharmaceutical Firms

The industry's first major wave of consolidations took place in the late 1980s, with such mergers as SmithKline and Beecham and Bristol Myers and Squibb. This wave of consolidation was driven by increased scale and scope economies largely realized through the combination of sales and marketing staffs. Horizontal consolidation represented a considerable value creation opportunity for those companies able to realize cost synergies. In analyzing the total costs of pharmaceutical companies, William Pursche (1996) argued that the range of savings that could be achieved based on the mergers of the late 1980s was substantial. Potential savings could range from 15–25% of total R&D spending, 5–20% of total manufacturing costs, 15–50% of marketing and sales expenses, and 20–50% of overhead costs.

Continued consolidation seemed likely, enabling further cuts in sales and marketing expenses. Formulary-driven purchasing and declining overall drug margins spurred pharmaceutical companies to take action to increase the return on their R&D investments. Because development costs are not significantly lower for generic drugs, it became increasingly difficult to generate positive financial returns from marginal products. Duplicate overhead offered another opportunity for cost savings through consolidation because combining companies could eliminate redundant personnel in such support areas as quality assurance, manufacturing management, information services, legal services, accounting, and human resources.

The Second Merger Wave

The second merger wave began in the late 1990s. The sheer magnitude and pace of activity is striking. Of the top-20 companies in terms of global pharmaceutical sales in 1998, one-half either have merged or announced plans to do so. More are expected as drug patents expire for a number of companies during the next several years and the cost of discovering and commercializing new drugs continues to escalate.

The current round of consolidation is tied to the great strides that have been made by modern science in unlocking the secrets of the human genome. These genetic discoveries have yielded more than 10,000 viable biological targets around which to develop new medicines, but it will take billions of dollars to convert these discoveries into new drugs. The consolidation that is under way in the industry will enable companies to more readily pay for the expensive clinical trials that are necessary to exploit the countless opportunities emerging from gene sequencing. Consolidation also will enable companies to utilize new technologies such as bioinformatics, which uses new computer software to find similarities among gene sequences.

A New Industry Leader Emerges

On January 17, 2000, British pharmaceutical giants Glaxo Wellcome PLC and SmithKline Beecham PLC agreed to merge to form the world's largest drug company. The merger was valued at $76 billion. The resulting company would be called Glaxo SmithKline and have annual revenue of $25 billion and a market value of $184 billion. The combined companies also would have a total R&D budget of $4 billion and a global sales force of 40,000. Total employees would number 105,000 worldwide. Although stressed as a merger of equals, Glaxo shareholders will own about 59% of the shares of the two companies. The combined companies would have a market share of 7.5% of the global pharmaceutical market. The companies expect annual pretax cost savings of about $1.76 billion after 3 years. The cost savings will come primarily from job cuts among middle management and administration over the next 3 years (Bloomberg.com, 2000; *Business Week*, 2000; Pursche, 1996).

Case Study Discussion Questions

1. What drove change in the pharmaceutical industry in the late 1990s?
2. In your judgment, what are the likely strategic business plan objectives of the major pharmaceutical companies and why are they important?
3. What are the alternatives to mergers available to the major pharmaceutical companies? What are the advantages and disadvantages of each alternative?

4. How would you classify the typical drug company's strategy in the 1970s and 1980s: cost leadership, differentiation, focus, or hybrid? Explain your answer. How have their strategies changed in recent years?

5. What do you think was the major motivating factor behind the Glaxo SmithKline merger and why was it so important?

Solutions to these questions are found in the Appendix at the end of this book.

CHAPTER BUSINESS CASE

CASE STUDY 4-4: PEPSI BUYS QUAKER OATS IN A HIGHLY PUBLICIZED FOOD FIGHT

Food Fight

On June 26, 2000, Phillip Morris, which owned Kraft Foods, announced its planned $15.9 billion purchase of Nabisco, ranked seventh in the United States in terms of sales in 2000. By combining Nabisco with its Kraft operations, ranked number one in the United States, Philip Morris created an industry behemoth. Not to be outdone, Unilever, the jointly owned British–Dutch giant, which ranked fourth in sales, purchased Bestfoods in a $20.3 billion deal. Midsized companies such as Campbell's could no longer compete with the likes of Nestle, which ranked number three; Proctor & Gamble, which ranked number two; or Phillip Morris. Consequently, these midsized firms started looking for partners. Other companies were cutting back. The U.K.'s Diageo, one of Europe's largest food and beverage companies, announced the restructuring of its Pillsbury unit by cutting 750 jobs— 10% of its workforce. PepsiCo, ranked sixth in U.S. sales, spun off in 1997 its Pizza Hut, KFC, and Taco Bell restaurant holdings. Also, eighth-ranked General Mills spun off its Red Lobster, Olive Garden, and other brand-name stores in 1995. In 2001, Coca-Cola announced a reduction of 6000 in its worldwide workforce.

As one of the smaller firms in the industry, Quaker Oats faced a serious problem: it was too small to acquire other firms in the industry. As a result, they were unable to realize the cost reductions through economies of scale in production and purchasing that their competitors enjoyed. Moreover, they did not have the wherewithal to introduce rapidly new products and to compete for supermarket shelf space. Consequently, their revenue and profit growth prospects appeared to be limited.

The Quaker Quandary

Despite its modest position in the mature and slow-growing food and cereal business, Quaker Oats had a dominant position in the sports drink marketplace. As the owner of Gatorade, it controlled 85% of the U.S. market for sports drinks. However, its penetration abroad was minimal. Gatorade was the company's cash cow. Gatorade's sales in 1999 totaled $1.83 billion, about 40% of Quaker's total revenue. Cash flow generated from this product line was being used to fund its food and cereal operations. Gatorade's management recognized that it was too small to buy other food companies and therefore could not realize benefits of consolidation.

After a review of its options, Quaker's board decided that the sale of the company would be the best way to maximize shareholder value. This alternative presented a serious challenge for management. Most of Quaker's value was in its Gatorade product line. It quickly found that most firms wanted to buy only this product line and leave the food and cereal businesses behind. Quaker's management reasoned that it would be in the best interests of its shareholders if it sold the total company rather than to split it into pieces. That way they could extract the greatest value and then let the buyer decide what to do with the non-Gatorade businesses. In addition, if the business remained intact, management would not have to find some way to make up for the loss of Gatorade's substantial cash flow.

Quaker announced that it was for sale for $15 billion. Potential suitors viewed the price as very steep for a firm whose businesses, with the exception of Gatorade, had very weak competitive positions. Pepsi was the first to make a formal bid for the firm, quickly followed by Coca-Cola and Danone.

The Beverage Wars Begin

By November 21, 2000, Coca-Cola and PepsiCo were battling to acquire Quaker. Their interest stemmed from the slowing sales of carbonated beverages. They couldn't help noticing the explosive growth in sports drinks. Not only would either benefit from the addition of this rapidly growing product, but they also could prevent the other from improving its position in the sports drink market. Both Coke and PepsiCo could boost Gatorade sales by putting the sports drink in vending machines across the country and selling it through their worldwide distribution network.

PepsiCo's $14.3 billion fixed exchange stock bid consisting of 2.3 shares of its stock for each Quaker share in early November was the first formal bid Quaker received. However, Robert Morrison, Quaker's CEO, dismissed the offer as inadequate unless it were accompanied by a price collar. Morrison argued that the collar would allow for an increase in the number of PepsiCo shares exchanged for each share of Quaker stock if PepsiCo's share price declined in value before the deal closed.

Quaker also was expecting to get a higher bid from Coke, which seemed at the time to be in a better financial position than PepsiCo to pay a higher purchase price. Investors were expressing concerns about rumors that Coke would pay more than $15 billion for Quaker and seemed to be relieved that PepsiCo's offer had been rejected. Coke's share price was falling and PepsiCo's was rising as the drama unfolded. In the days that followed, talks between Coke and Quaker broke off, with Coke's board unwilling to support a $15.75 billion offer price.

Could the Third Time Be a Charm?

Reflecting considerable disappointment with the loss of the Coca-Cola deal valued at $115 per share, Quaker shares fell more than 8% to $87. After failing to strike deals with the world's two largest soft drink makers, Quaker turned to Danone, the manufacturer of Evian water and Dannon yogurt. Much smaller than Coca-Cola or PepsiCo, Danone was hoping to hype growth in its healthy nutrition and beverage business. Gatorade would complement Danone's bottled-water brands. Moreover, Quaker's cereals would fit into Danone's increasing focus on breakfast cereals. However, few investors believed that the diminutive firm could finance a purchase of Quaker. Danone proposed using its stock to pay for the acquisition, but the firm noted that the purchase would sharply reduce earnings per share through 2003. Danone backed out of the talks only 24 hours after expressing interest, when its stock got pummeled on the news.

PepsiCo Shows Renewed Interest

Nearly 1 month after breaking off talks to acquire Quaker Oats because of disagreements over price, PepsiCo once again approached Quaker's management. Its second proposal was the same as its first. PepsiCo was in a much stronger position this time, especially because Quaker had run out of suitors. However, this time Quaker's board was willing to accept the bid without a price collar if PepsiCo would accept Quaker's right to "walk away" if the stock swap bid fell below $92 per share. This means that either party could call the deal off if PepsiCo's shares fell below $40 per share (i.e., 2.3 × 40 = 92) for a period of 10 random days in the month before closing (Deogun and McKay, 2000). If PepsiCo's share price did slip below the $40 floor, it would have to increase the share exchange ratio to keep the transaction alive.

Quaker Oats would be liable for a $420 million breakup fee if the deal was terminated, either because its shareholders didn't approve the deal or the company entered into a definitive merger agreement with an alternative bidder. Quaker also granted PepsiCo an option to purchase 19.9% of Quaker's stock, exercisable only if Quaker is sold to another bidder (U.S. Securities and Exchange Commission, 2000). Such a tactic sometimes is used in conjunction with a breakup fee to discourage other suitors from making a bid for the target firm.

Pepsi Wins the Day

With the purchase of Quaker Oats, PepsiCo became the leader of the sports drink market by gaining the market's dominant share. With more than four-fifths of the market, PepsiCo dwarfs Coke's position of about 11% penetration. The assumption of this leadership position is widely viewed as giving PepsiCo, whose share of the U.S. carbonated soft drink market is 31.4% as compared with Coke's 44.1%, a psychological boost in its quest to accumulate a portfolio of leading brands.

Case Study Discussion Questions

1. What factors were driving consolidation within the food manufacturing industry? Name other industries that are currently undergoing consolidation.

2. Why did food industry consolidation prompt Quaker to announce that it was for sale?
3. Why do you think Quaker wanted to sell its consolidated operations rather than to divide the company into the food/cereal and Gatorade businesses?
4. Under what circumstances might the Quaker shareholder have benefited more if Quaker had sold itself in pieces (i.e., food/cereal and Gatorade) rather than in total?
5. Do you think PepsiCo may have been willing to pay such a high price for Quaker for reasons other than economics? Do you think these reasons make sense? Explain your answer.

Appendix A

Common Sources of Economic, Industry, and Market Data

ECONOMIC INFORMATION

Business Cycle Development (U.S. Department of Commerce)
U.S. Census Bureau publications on population, transportation, and housing
    Current Business Reports (U.S. Department of Commerce)
Economic Indicators (U.S. Joint Economic Indicators)
Economic Report of the President to the Congress (United States)
Long-Term Economic Growth (U.S. Department of Commerce)
Regional statistics and forecasts from large commercial banks
Monthly Labor Review (U.S. Department of Labor)
Monthly Bulletin of Statistics (United Nations)
Overseas Business Reports (By country, published by U.S. Department of
    Commerce)
World Trade Annual (United Nations)
U.S. Industrial Outlook (U.S. Department of Commerce)
Survey of Current Business (U.S. Department of Commerce)
Statistical Yearbook (United Nations)
Statistical Abstract of the United States (U.S. Department of Commerce)

INDUSTRY INFORMATION

Forbes (Mid-January issues provide performance data on firms in
    various industries)
Business Week (provides weekly economic and business information, and
    quarterly profit and sales rankings of corporations)

Fortune (each April issue includes listings of financial information on corporations within selected industries)

Industry Survey (Published quarterly by Standard and Poor's Corporation)

Industry Week (March/April issue provides information on 14 industry groups)

Inc. (May and December issues give information on Entrepreneurial firms)

Directory of National Trade Associations

Encyclopedia of Associations

Funk and Scott's Index of Corporations and Industries

Thomas' Register of American Manufacturers

Wall Street Journal Index

REFERENCES

Almaney, A. J., *Strategic Management: A Framework for Decision Making and Problem Solving*, Shelfield Publishing Company, 1992.

Bloomberg.com, "Glaxo, SmithKline Agree to Merge," January 18, 2000.

Boston Consulting Group, *The Strategy Development Process*, Boston: The Boston Consulting Group, 1985.

Business Week, "Burying the Hatchet Buys a Lot of Drug Research," January 31, 2000, p. 43.

Chung, Mary and Alistair Davidson, "Business Experts," *PC AI*, Summer 1987, pp. 16–21.

Deogun, Nikhil and Betsy McKay, "PepsiCo Revives Discussions on Takeover of Quaker Oats," Dow Jones News Service, *Wall Street Journal*, November 30, 2000, p. C6.

Gitman, Lawrence J., *Principles of Managerial Finance*, Brief Edition, New York: Addison-Wesley, 1998, p. 22.

Hamel, Gary C. and C. K. Prahalad, *Competing for the Future*, Cambridge, MA: Harvard Business School Press, 1994.

Hill, Charles W. L. and Gareth R. Jones, *Strategic Management: An Integrated Approach* (5th ed.), Boston: Houghton-Mifflin, 2001, pp. 158–233.

Hopkins, Thomas D., "Regulatory Costs in Profile," Center for the Study of American Business, Washington University, 1996.

James, Robert M., Henry Mintzberg, and James Brian Quinn, *The Strategy Process*, Englewood Cliffs, New Jersey: Prentice-Hall, 1988.

Marrus, Stephanie K., *Building the Strategic Plan: Find, Analyze and Present the Right Information*, New York: John Wiley & Sons, 1984, pp. 23–28.

Moore, Geoffrey A., *Crossing the Chasm*, Harper Business, 1991.

Porter, Michael E., *Competitive Advantage*, New York: The Free Press, 1985.

Pursche, William A., "Pharmaceuticals—The Consolidation Isn't Over," *The McKinsey Quarterly*, 2, 1996, pp. 110–119.

Stryker, Steven C., *Plan to Succeed: A Guide to Strategic Planning*, Princeton, NJ: Petrocelli Books, 1986.

U.S. Securities and Exchange Commission, PepsiCo, 8K Filing for Business Combinations, December 7, 2000.

Waterman, Robert H., Jr., *The Renewal Factor*, New York: Bantam Books, 1987.

5

IMPLEMENTATION

SEARCH THROUGH
CLOSING—PHASES 3–10

Say no, then negotiate.

—Anonymous

"Well, do we have a deal or not?" the lead negotiator for Timco demanded. Her patience strained by the seemingly endless negotiations that had been under way for more than 2 months, LeAnn leaned forward in her chair as if to underscore that she was no longer willing to accept the buyer's tendency to focus on details while avoiding the big issues. Delay was no longer acceptable. She wanted a straight answer and she wanted it now.

As part of their initial agreement they had set a time limit of 90 days in which the buyer was to complete their review of Timco's plants and decide if they would close the deal. But they seem to have spent countless hours discussing the condition of the firm's warehouses in Memphis, the increase in employee turnover at a plant in Baton Rouge, and the age of high-speed extrusion machines at the firm's facility in Dallas. After all this time, she realized that they had not yet put a firm offer on the table. They seemed to be accumulating reasons for lowering their initial offer.

As the "drop dead" date approached, she felt increasingly uneasy. It seemed that this is precisely what they were about to do. Timco had a lot at stake. Word had leaked to their employees, customers, and suppliers that they were for sale. Their customers were calling almost daily now for a reassurance that there would be no disruption in shipments if Timco were sold. Employees grumbled that they were being kept in the dark. Suppliers were concerned that any change in ownership could imperil their position with Timco. A lot was on the line, and the buyer knew it.

Carla had represented the buyer in these types of negotiations many times in recent years. She knew that stall tactics would no longer work. She also knew that Timco wanted to sell. She braced herself in her chair as she prepared to respond. "Yes," Carla said slowly, "but only if certain changes in the initial terms and conditions are made. These include . . . "

OVERVIEW

The firm's business plan sets the overall direction for the business. It defines where the firm has chosen to compete (i.e., target market) and how the firm has chosen to compete (i.e., through price–cost leadership, differentiation, or a focused strategy). A merger/acquisition implementation plan (subsequently referred to as the "acquisition plan") is required if the firm decides that an acquisition is needed to execute the firm's business strategy. The acquisition plan delineates key management objectives for the takeover that support specific strategic objectives in the business plan, resource constraints, appropriate tactics for implementing the proposed transaction, and a timetable in which to complete the transaction. An acquisition plan furnishes the appropriate guidance to those charged with success-fully completing the transaction by providing critical input into all subsequent phases of the acquisition process.

The acquisition plan communicates to those charged with acquiring a com-pany the preferences of senior management. It ensures that the acquisition team conducts itself in a manner consistent with management's risk tolerance. The acquisition plan defines the criteria, such as size, profitability, industry, and growth rate, used to select potential acquisition candidates. It may specify the degree of relatedness to the acquiring firm's current businesses and define the types of firms that should not be considered (e.g., current competitors). The plan also stipulates the roles and responsibilities of team members, including outside consultants, and sets the team's budget. Moreover, the plan indicates manage-ment's preference for the form of payment (stock, cash, or debt), for acquiring stock or assets, and for partial or full ownership. It may preclude any hostile takeover attempts or indicate a desire to limit goodwill. It also may specify management's desire to minimize the impact of the acquisition on the earnings per share of the combined companies immediately following closing. Finally, the acquisition plan may establish limits on what the acquiring firm is willing to pay for any acquisition by setting a ceiling on the purchase price in terms of a maximum price-to-earnings multiple or multiple of some other measure of value.

This chapter starts with the presumption that a firm has developed a viable business plan that requires an acquisition to realize the firm's strategic direction. Whereas Chapter 4 addressed the creation of business and acquisition plans (Phases 1 and 2), this chapter focuses on Phases 3–10 of the acquisition process, including search, screen, first contact, negotiation, integration planning, closing, integra-tion implementation, and evaluation. The negotiation phase is the most complex aspect of the acquisition process, involving refining the preliminary valuation, deal structuring, due diligence, and developing a financing plan. It is in the negotiation phase that all elements of the purchase price are determined.

PHASE 3: THE SEARCH PROCESS

INITIATING THE SEARCH

Initiating the search for potential acquisition candidates involves a two-step procedure. The first step is to establish the primary screening or selection criteria. At this stage of the search process it is best to use a relatively small number of criteria. The primary criteria should include the industry and size of the transaction. It also may be appropriate to add a geographic restriction. The size of the transaction is best defined in terms of the maximum purchase price a firm is willing to pay. This can be expressed as a maximum price-to-earnings, book, cash flow, or revenue ratio or a maximum purchase price stated in terms of dollars.

For example, an acute-care private hospital holding company wants to buy a skilled nursing facility within a range of 50 miles of its largest acute-care hospital in Allegheny County, Pennsylvania. Management believes that it cannot afford to pay more than $25 million for the facility. Its primary selection criteria could include the following: an industry (skilled nursing), location (Allegheny County), and maximum price (five times cash flow not to exceed $25 million). Similarly, a Texas-based manufacturer of patio furniture with manufacturing operations in the southwestern United States is seeking to expand its sales in California by purchasing a patio furniture manufacturer in the far western United States for an amount not to exceed $100 million. Its primary selection criteria could include an industry (outdoor furniture), a location (California, Arizona, and Nevada), and a maximum purchase price (15 times after-tax earnings not to exceed $100 million).

The second step is to develop a search strategy. Such strategies normally entail using computerized databases and directory services such as Disclosure, Dun & Bradstreet, Standard & Poor's *Corporate Register*, or Thomas' *Register* and *Million Dollar Directories* to identify qualified candidates. Firms also may query their law, banking, and accounting firms to identify other candidates. Investment banks, brokers, and leveraged buyout firms are also fertile sources of candidates, although they are likely to require an advisory or finder's fee. The Internet makes research much easier than in the past. Today the analyst has much more information at their fingertips. Such services as Yahoo! Finance, Hoover's, or EDGAR Online enable researchers to quickly gather data about competitors and customers. These sites provide easy access to a variety of public documents filed with the Securities and Exchange Commission (SEC). Exhibit 5-1 provides a comprehensive listing of sources of information that can be highly useful in conducting a search for prospective acquisition candidates.

EXHIBIT 5-1. INFORMATION SOURCES ON INDIVIDUAL COMPANIES

SEC Filings (Public Companies Only)

10-K: Provides detailed information on a company's annual operations, business conditions, competitors, market conditions, legal proceedings, risk factors in holding the stock, and other related information.

10-Q: Updates investors about the company's operations each quarter.

S-1: Filed when a company wants to register new stock. Can contain information about the company's operating history and business risks.

S-2: Filed when a company is completing a material transaction such as a merger or acquisition. Provides substantial detail underlying the terms and conditions of the transaction, the events leading up to completing the transaction, and justification for the merger or acquisition.

8-K: Filed when a company faces a "material event" such as a merger.

Schedule 14A: A proxy statement. Gives details about the annual meeting and biographies of company officials and directors including stock ownership and pay.

Websites

www.sec.gov
www.edgar-online.com
www.freeedgar.com
www.quicken.com
www.hooversonline.com
www.aol.com
http://finance.yahoo.com
www.bizbuysell.com
www.dialog.com
www.lexisnexis.com
www.mergernetwork.com
www.mergers.net
www.washingtonresearchers.com
www.twst.com
www.worldm-anetwork.com

Organizations

Value Line Investment Survey: Information on public companies
Directory of Corporate Affiliations: Corporate affiliations
Lexis/Nexis: Database of general business and legal information
Thomas Register: Organizes firms by products and services
Frost & Sullivan: Industry research
Findex.com: Financial information

Competitive Intelligence Professionals: Information about industries
Dialog Corporation: Industry databases
Predicasts: Provides databases through libraries
Business Periodicals Index: Business and technical article index
Dun & Bradstreet Directories: Information about private and public
    companies
Experian: Information about private and public companies
Nelson's Directory of Investment Research: Wall Street Research
    Reports
Standard and Poor's Publications: Industry surveys and corporate
    records
Harris Infosource: Information about manufacturing companies
Hoover's Handbook of Private Companies: Information on large
    private firms
Washington Researchers: Information on public and private firms,
    markets, and industries
The Wall Street Journal Transcripts: Wall Street research reports

If confidentiality is not an issue, a firm may seek to advertise its interest in acquiring a particular type of firm in the *Wall Street Journal* or the trade press. Although this is likely to generate substantial interest, it is less likely to generate high-quality prospects. Considerable time is wasted sorting through responses from those interested in getting a free estimate of their own company to those responses from brokers claiming their clients fit the buyer's criteria as a ruse to convince the buyer that they need the broker's services.

Finding reliable information about privately owned firms is a major problem. Often by using sources such as Dun & Bradstreet or Experian, an analyst is able to accumulate fragmentary data. Nonetheless, it is possible to use publicly available information to obtain additional detail. For example, industry surveys provided by trade associations or U.S. Census data often provide such data as average sales per employee for specific industries. A private firm's sales can be estimated by multiplying an estimate of its workforce by the industry average ratio of sales per employee. An estimate of the private firm's workforce may be obtained by searching the firm's product literature Website, or trade show speeches or even by counting the number of cars in the firm's parking lot.

BROKERS AND FINDERS

Employing Brokers and Finders in the Search Process

Brokers or so-called finders may be used to supplement your search process. A broker has a fiduciary responsibility to either the potential buyer or seller. The broker is not permitted to represent both parties. The broker is compensated by his or her client. In some states, the government licenses brokers. In contrast, a finder is someone who introduces both parties, without representing either one. The finder does not have a fiduciary responsibility to either party and is compensated by either party or both. Generally, finders are not regulated; consequently, they do not require a license. The line between whether the agent is a broker or a finder is often fuzzy. Courts often determine a finder to be a broker if the finder discusses price or any significant terms of the transaction. Brokers and finders are regulated at the state or local level—not by the federal government.

Fees Paid to Brokers and Finders

As a note of caution, it is important to always respond in writing if you receive a solicitation from a broker or finder. This is particularly important if you reject their services. If you at a later date acquire the firm they claim to have represented, the broker or finder may sue your firm for compensation. If you choose to use the broker or finder, make sure that the fees and terms are clearly stipulated in writing. It also is advisable to keep a written record of all telephone conversations and meetings with the finder or broker. These may at a later date be used in court if the broker or finder sues for fees that may be in dispute.

Actual fee formulas are based on the purchase price. The so-called Lehman formula was at one time a commonly used fee structure in which broker or finder fees would be equal to 5% of the first million dollars of the purchase price, 4% of the second, 3% of the third, 2% of the fourth, and 1% of the remainder. Today, this formula often is ignored in favor of a negotiated fee structure. A common fee structure consists of a basic fee, a closing fee, and an "extraordinary" fee. A basic fee or retainer is paid regardless of whether the deal is consummated. The closing fee is an additional amount paid on closing. Finally, the "extraordinary" fee is paid under unusual circumstances, which may delay eventual closing, such as gaining antitrust approval or a hostile takeover.

PHASE 4: THE SCREENING PROCESS

The screening process is a refinement of the search process. It starts with a pruning of the initial list of potential candidates created by applying such primary criteria as the type of industry and the maximum size of the transaction. Because relatively few primary criteria are used, the initial list of potential acquisition candidates may be lengthy. Additional or secondary selection criteria may be used to shorten the list.

Care should be taken to limit the number of secondary criteria used. An excessively long list of selection criteria will severely limit the number of candidates that will pass the screening process. Whenever possible, the selection criteria should be quantified. In addition to the maximum purchase price, industry, or geographic location criteria used to develop the initial list, secondary selection criteria may include a specific market segment within the industry or a specific product line within a market segment. Other measures often include the firm's profitability, degree of leverage, and market share.

MARKET SEGMENT

The search process involved the specification of the target industry. It is now necessary to identify the target segment in the industry. For example, a steel fabrication company may decide to diversify by acquiring a manufacturer of aluminum flat-rolled products. A primary search criterion would include only firms in the aluminum flat-rolled products industry. Subsequent searches may involve a further segmenting of the market to identify only those companies that manufacture aluminum tubular products.

PRODUCT LINE

The product line criterion identifies a specific product line within the target market segment. The steel fabrication company in the previous example may decide to focus its search on companies manufacturing aluminum tubular products used in the manufacturing of lawn and patio furniture.

PROFITABILITY

The profitability criterion should be defined in terms of the percentage return on sales, assets, or total investment. This enables a more accurate comparison among candidates of different sizes. A firm with after-tax earnings of $5 million on sales of $100 million may be less attractive than a firm earning $3 million on sales of $50 million because the latter firm may be more efficient.

DEGREE OF LEVERAGE

Debt-to-equity or debt-to-total capital ratios often are used to measure the level of indebtedness. The acquiring company may not want to purchase a company whose heavy debt burden may cause the acquiring company's leverage ratios to exceed targeted levels and jeopardize the acquirer's credit rating.

MARKET SHARE

The acquiring firm may be interested only in firms that are number one or number two in market share in the targeted industry or in firms whose market share is some multiple (e.g., 2 × the next largest competitor). Firms having substantially greater market share than their competitors often are able to achieve lower cost positions than their competitors because of economies of scale and experience curve effects.

PHASE 5: FIRST CONTACT

ALTERNATIVE APPROACH STRATEGIES

The approach suggested for initiating contact with a target company depends on the size of the company and if it is publicly or privately held.

Small Companies

For small companies (<$25 million in sales) in which the buyer has no direct contacts, a vaguely worded letter expressing interest in a joint venture or marketing alliance and indicating that you will follow up with a telephone call is often all that is necessary. During the follow-up call, be prepared to discuss a range of options with the seller, including the possibility of acquisition.

Preparation before the first telephone contact is essential. If possible, script your comments. Get to the point quickly but indirectly. Identify yourself, your company, and its strengths. Demonstrate your understanding of the contact's business and how an informal partnership could make sense. Be able to quickly and succinctly explain the benefits of your proposal to the contact. If the opportunity arises, propose a range of options, including an acquisition. Listen carefully to the contact's reaction. If the contact is willing to entertain the notion of an acquisition, request a face-to-face meeting. Choose a meeting place that affords sufficient privacy so that each party can be assured that confidentiality can be maintained. Create a written agenda for the meeting after soliciting input from all prospective meeting participants. The meeting should start with a review of your company and your perspective on the outlook for the industry. Encourage the potential target firm to provide information on its own operations and its outlook for the industry. Request information from the potential target firm to fill in any gaps you may have in your knowledge of the firm.

Medium-Sized Companies

For medium-sized companies (between $25 and $100 million) or a division of a larger company, make contact through an intermediary. Intermediaries can be less intimidating than a direct approach from the potential suitor. Intermediaries could include members of the acquirer's board of directors or the firm's outside legal counsel, accounting firm, lender, broker/finder, or investment banker.

Large Companies

For large, publicly traded companies, contact also should be made through an intermediary; however, in this instance, it is critical to make contact at the highest level possible. Discretion is extremely important because of the target's concern about being "put into play." Even rumors of an acquisition can have substantial, adverse consequences for the target. Current or potential customers may express concern about the uncertainty associated with a change of ownership. A change in ownership could imply changes in product or service quality, reliability, and the level of service provided under product warranty or maintenance contracts. Suppliers worry about possible disruptions in their production schedules as the transition to the new owner takes place. Employees worry about possible layoffs or changes in compensation. Competitors will do what they can to fan these concerns to persuade current customers to switch and potential customers to defer buying decisions; key employees will be encouraged to defect to the competition. Shareholders may experience a dizzying ride as arbitrageurs buying on the rumor bid up the price of the stock only to bail out if denial of the rumor appears credible.

DISCUSSING VALUE

Getting the contact at the target to provide a value for their business can be a daunting task. Neither the buyer nor seller has an incentive to be the first to provide an estimate of value. Getting a range may be the best you can do. This may be accomplished by discussing values for recent acquisitions of similar businesses. Listen carefully to the contact's reasons for wanting to sell so that any proposal made can be structured to satisfy as many of the seller's primary needs as possible. With the agreement of the seller, establish a timeline consisting of next steps to be taken and stick to it.

PRELIMINARY LEGAL DOCUMENTS

A common first step in many transactions is to negotiate a confidentiality agreement and letter of intent (LOI). Usually all parties to the deal desire to have a confidentiality agreement. This may not be true for a LOI. The LOI is useful in that it generally stipulates the initial areas of agreement and the rights and privileges of all parties to the transaction and contains certain provisions protecting the interests of both the buyer and seller. However, the LOI could result in some legal risk to either the buyer or seller if the deal is not consummated. The LOI may create legal liabilities if one of the parties is later accused of not negotiating in "good faith." This is frequently the basis for many lawsuits that are filed when transactions are undertaken but not completed as a result of disagreements that emerge during lengthy and often heated negotiations.

Confidentiality Agreement

A confidentiality agreement is generally mutually binding in that it covers all parties to the transaction. In negotiating the confidentiality agreement, the buyer requests as much audited historical data and supplemental information as the seller is willing to provide. The prudent seller requests similar information about the buyer to assess the buyer's financial credibility. It is important for the seller to determine the buyer's credibility early in the process to not waste time with a potential buyer incapable of raising the financing to complete the transaction. The agreement should cover only information that is not publicly available and should have a reasonable expiration date.

Letter of Intent

The LOI often is useful in identifying early in the process areas of agreement and disagreement. However, it may delay the signing of a definitive agreement of purchase and sale or, in the case of a public company, necessitate a public announcement to be in compliance with securities laws if it is likely to have a "material" impact on the buyer or seller. Depending on how it is written, it may or may not be legally binding.

The LOI formally stipulates the reason for the agreement, major terms and conditions, the responsibilities of both parties while the agreement is in force, a reasonable expiration date, and how all fees associated with the transaction will be paid. Major terms and conditions include a brief outline of the structure of the transaction, which may entail the payment of cash or stock for certain assets and the assumption of certain target company liabilities. The letter also may specify certain conditions such as an agreement that selected personnel of the target will not compete with the combined companies for some time period if they should leave. Another condition may indicate that a certain portion of the purchase price will be allocated to the *noncompete agreement*. Such an allocation of the purchase price is in the interests of the buyer because the amount of the allocation can be amortized over the life of the agreement and taken as a tax-deductible expense, but it may constitute taxable income for the seller. The agreement also may indicate a desire to place a portion of the purchase price in escrow.

The proposed purchase price may be expressed as a specific dollar figure, as a range, or as a multiple of some measure of value such as operating earnings or cash flow. The LOI also specifies the types of data to be exchanged and the duration and extent of the initial due diligence. The LOI usually will terminate if the buyer and the seller do not reach agreement by a certain date. The buyer usually demands a *no-shop provision*, preventing the seller from sharing the terms of the buyer's proposal with other potential buyers with the hope of instigating an auction environment. Legal, consulting, and deed transfer fees may be paid for by the buyer or seller, or they may be shared. As discussed in Chapter 3, buyers are sometimes able to negotiate break-up fees and options to purchase target stock or selected assets if the deal is not completed. These features may be part of the LOI or the agreement of purchase and sale.

A well-written LOI usually contains language that limits the extent to which the agreement binds the two parties. Price or other provisions are generally subject to *closing conditions*. Such conditions could include the buyer having full access to all of the seller's books and records; having completed due diligence; obtaining financing; and having received approval from both boards of directors, stockholders, and regulatory bodies. Other standard conditions include the requirement for signed employment contracts for key executives of the selling company and the completion of all necessary merger and acquisition documents. Failure to satisfy any of these conditions will invalidate the agreement.

A well-written LOI also should describe the due diligence process in some detail. It should stipulate how the potential buyer should access the potential seller's premises, the frequency and duration of such access, and how intrusive such activities should be. The LOI also should indicate how the buyer should meet and discuss the deal with the seller's employees, customers, and suppliers. Sometimes the provisions of a standard confidentiality agreement are negotiated as part of the LOI.

PHASE 6: NEGOTIATION

Phases 1–5 of the acquisition process could be viewed as discrete activities or events. Unlike the previous phases, the negotiation phase is an interactive, iterative process with many activities conducted concurrently by various members of the acquisition team. The actual purchase price paid for the acquired business is determined during this phase and frequently will be considerably different from the valuation of the target company made before due diligence and based on sketchy publicly available information.

Negotiating Strategy

Negotiating is essentially a process in which two or more parties, representing different interests, attempt to achieve a consensus on a particular issue. A useful starting point in any negotiation is to determine the areas of disagreement as soon as possible. This may be achieved by having the parties review and agree on the facts pertaining to the deal. In general, parties will be able to reach agreement on most facts relatively easily. By doing so early in the process, the negotiations gain momentum and enable the participants to focus their efforts on the most contentious areas.

Once such a list of areas of disagreement is compiled, each party determines if the list contains any "deal breakers." *Deal breakers* refer to issues that a party to the negotiation feels cannot be conceded without making the deal unattractive. Good negotiators make concessions on issues not considered deal breakers, but only if they receive something in return. The easiest areas of disagreement should be resolved first until only a few remain on the list. By this point, all parties to the negotiation have invested a great deal of money, time, and emotional commitment to the process. All parties generally will be looking forward to a near-term resolution of the remaining issues. Skilled negotiators will have taken great pains to establish trust between themselves and the other parties. All arguments should be explained in as logical a matter as possible. Unreasonable demands at this point in the negotiation are likely to evoke frustration by the other party and encourage them to end discussions. If the parties can reach a point where one side or the other is willing to state at least a price range, reaching the final agreement is in sight.

DEFINING THE PURCHASE PRICE

There are three commonly used definitions of purchase price. These include the total consideration, the total purchase price or enterprise value, and the net purchase price. Each definition serves a different purpose.

Total Consideration

In the agreement of purchase and sale, the **total consideration** consists of cash (C), stock (S), new debt issues (D), or some combination of all three. It is a term commonly used in legal documents to reflect the different types of remuneration received by target company shareholders. Note that the remuneration can include both financial and nonfinancial assets such as real estate. Nonfinancial compensation sometimes is referred to as *payment-in-kind*. The debt counted in the total consideration is what the target company shareholders receive as payment for their stock, along with any cash or acquiring company stock. Each component of the total consideration may be viewed in present value terms; therefore, the total consideration is itself expressed in present value terms (PV_{TC}). The present value of cash is its face value. The stock component of the total consideration would be the current value (PV_S) of future dividends or net cash flows or the acquiring firm's stock price per share times the number of shares to be exchanged for each outstanding share of the seller's stock. New debt issued by the acquiring company as part of the compensation paid to shareholders can be expressed as the present value (PV_{ND}) of the cumulative interest payments plus principal discounted at some appropriate market rate of interest.

Total Purchase Price (Enterprise Value)

The **total purchase price** or **enterprise value** (PV_{TPP}) of the target firm consists of the total consideration (PV_{TC}) plus the market value of the target firm's debt (PV_{AD}) assumed by the acquiring company. The enterprise value of the firm often is quoted in the financial press and other media as the purchase price because it is most visible to those not familiar with the details to the transaction. It is important to analysts and shareholders alike because it approximates the total investment made by the acquiring firm to purchase the target firm. It is an approximation because it does not necessarily measure liabilities the acquirer is assuming that are not visible on the target firm's balance sheet. Nor does it reflect the potential for recovering a portion of the total consideration paid to target company shareholders by selling undervalued or redundant assets.

Net Purchase Price

The **net purchase price** (PV_{NPP}) is the total purchase price plus other assumed liabilities (PV_{OAL}) less the proceeds from the sale of discretionary or redundant target assets (PV_{DA}) on or off the balance sheet. PV_{OAL} are those assumed liabilities not fully reflected on the target firm's balance sheet or in the estimation of the economic value of the target firm. Other assumed liabilities and discretionary assets will be explained in more detail later.

The net purchase price is the most comprehensive measure of the actual price paid for the target firm. It includes all known cash obligations assumed by the acquirer as well as any portion of the purchase price that is recovered through the sale of assets. It may be larger or smaller than the total purchase price. The various definitions of price can be summarized as follows:

Total Consideration: $PV_{TC} = C + PV_S + PV_{ND}$
Total Purchase Price/
    Enterprise Value: $PV_{TPP} = PV_{TC} + PV_{AD}$
Net Purchase Price: $PV_{NPP} = PV_{TPP} + PV_{OAL} - PV_{DA}$
$$= (C + PV_S + PV_{ND} + PV_{AD})$$
$$+ PV_{OAL} - PV_{DA}$$

Although the total consideration is most important to the target company's shareholders as a measure of what they receive in exchange for their stock, the acquirer's shareholders tend to focus on the total purchase price or enterprise value as the actual amount paid for the target firm. The total purchase price tends to be most visible to the acquirer's shareholders. However, the total purchase price tends to ignore other adjustments that should be made to determine actual or pending "out-of-pocket" cash spent by the acquirer. The net purchase price reflects the relevant adjustments to the total purchase price and is a much better indicator of whether the acquirer overpaid (i.e., paid more than its economic value including synergy) for the target firm. The application of the various definitions of the purchase price is addressed in more detail in Chapter 8.

Other Assumed Liabilities

The adjustment to the total purchase price referred to as other assumed liabilities consists of items that are not adequately accounted for on the target's balance sheet. If all of the target firm's balance sheet reserves reflected accurately all known future obligations, and if there were no significant potential off-balance sheet liabilities, there would be no need to adjust the purchase price for assumed liabilities other than for short- and long-term debt assumed by the acquiring company. Earnings and book value per share would accurately reflect the expected impact of known liabilities. Operating cash flows, which reflect both earnings and changes in items on the balance sheet, would also accurately reflect future liabilities. Therefore, valuations based on a multiple of earnings, book value, or discounted cash flow would accurately reflect the economic value of the business.

In practice, this is rarely the case. Reserves are often inadequate to satisfy pending claims. This is particularly true if the selling company attempts to improve current earnings performance by understating reserves. Common examples include underfunded or underreserved employee and health care obligations and uncollectable receivables, as well as underaccrued vacation and holidays, bonuses, and deferred compensation, such as employee stock options. Other examples include product warranties, environmental liabilities, pending lawsuits, severance expenses, maintenance and service agreements, and any other obligations of the selling company accepted by the buyer at closing. To the extent that such factors represent a future use of cash, the present value of their future impact, to the extent possible, should be estimated. Case Study 5-1 illustrates how these liabilities can add substantially to the actual out-of-pocket cost of an acquisition.

CASE STUDY 5-1: THE CASH IMPACT OF PRODUCT WARRANTIES

Reliable Appliances, a leading manufacturer of washing machines and dryers, acquired a marginal competitor, Quality-Built, which had been losing money during the last several years. To help minimize losses, Quality-Built reduced its quality-control expenditures and began to purchase cheaper parts. Quality-Built knew that this would hurt business in the long run, but it was more focused on improving its current financial performance to increase the firm's prospects for eventual sale. Reliable Appliances saw an acquisition of the competitor as a way of obtaining market share quickly at a time when Quality-Built's market value was the lowest in 3 years. The sale was completed quickly at a very small premium to the current market price.

Quality-Built had been selling its appliances with a standard industry 3-year warranty. Claims for the types of appliances sold tended to increase gradually as the appliance aged. Quality-Built's warranty claims' history was in line with the industry experience and did not appear to be a cause for alarm. Not surprisingly, in view of Quality-Built's cutback in quality-control practices and downgrading of purchased parts, warranty claims began to escalate sharply within 12 months of Reliable Appliances's acquisition of Quality-Built. Over the next several years, Reliable Appliances paid out $15 million in warranty claims. The intangible damage may have been much higher because Reliable Appliances's reputation had been damaged in the marketplace.

Discussion Questions

1. Should Reliable Appliances have been able to anticipate this problem from its due diligence of Quality-Built? Explain how this might have been accomplished.
2. How could Reliable have protected itself from the outstanding warranty claims in the agreement of purchase and sale?

Discretionary Assets

Discretionary assets are undervalued or redundant assets not required to run the acquired business and that can be used by the buyer to recover some portion of the purchase price. Such assets include land valued at its historical cost on the balance sheet, inventory and equipment whose resale value exceeds its fully depreciated value, cash balances in excess of normal working capital needs, and product lines or operating units considered nonstrategic by the buyer. The sale of discretionary assets are not considered in the calculation of the economic value of the target firm because economic value is determined by future operating cash flows before consideration is given to how the transaction will be financed.

CONCURRENT ACTIVITIES

The negotiation phase consists of four concurrent activities: (1) refining valuation, (2) deal structuring, (3) due diligence, and (4) developing a financing plan. Refining the preliminary valuation based on new information uncovered during due diligence provides the starting point for negotiating the agreement of purchase and sale. Deal structuring involves meeting the needs of both parties by addressing issues of risk and reward by constructing an appropriate set of compensation, legal, tax, and accounting structures. Due diligence provides additional information enabling the buyer to better understand the nature of the liabilities the buyer is being asked to assume and to confirm perceived sources of value. Finally, the financing plan provides a reality check on the buyer because it defines the maximum amount the buyer can reasonably expect to finance and in turn pay for the target company.

Refining Valuation

The first activity within the negotiation phase of the acquisition process deals with updating the preliminary target company valuation based on new information. At this stage, the buyer requests and reviews at least 5 years of historical financial data. Although it is highly desirable to examine data that have been audited in accordance with Generally Accepted Accounting Principals (GAAP), such data may not be available for small, privately owned companies. In fact, small companies rarely hire outside accounting firms to conduct expensive audits unless they are required to do so as part of a loan agreement.

The 5 years of historical data should be *normalized* or adjusted for nonrecurring gains, losses, or expenses. Nonrecurring gains or losses can result from the sale of land, equipment, product lines, patents, software, or copyrights. Nonrecurring expenses include severance, employee signing bonuses, and settlement of litigation. These adjustments are necessary to allow the buyer to smooth out irregularities in the historical information and to better understand the underlying dynamics of the business.

Once the data have been normalized, each major expense category should be expressed as a percentage of revenue. By observing year-to-year changes in these ratios, sustainable trends in the data are more discernable. For example, sellers may temporarily improve operating profits by postponing normal maintenance expenses. A decline in the ratio of capital spending, research and development, training, and advertising expenditures to sales from their historical average may indicate deliberate underinvestment in the business. An increase in the average time to collect receivables may suggest growing financial problems among the seller's customers. If the number of times inventory is being replaced each year is declining (i.e., slowing inventory turnover), the seller may be facing decelerating sales as a result of a loss of market share or simply capacity constraints, which limit the firm's ability to build inventory.

The normalized historical data will help the buyer project a minimum of 5 years of cash flows and adjust the projected cash flows for the amount and timing of anticipated synergy. The assumptions underlying the projections should be stated clearly. The buyer should discount heavily any projections provided by the seller. The process of refining valuations using standard financial modeling techniques is described in more detail in Chapter 8.

Deal Structuring

In purely financial terms, deal structuring involves the allocation of cash-flow streams (with respect to amount and timing); the allocation of risk; and, therefore, the allocation of value between different parties to the transaction. In terms of the personalities of the parties involved, deal structuring entails much more. It is the process of identifying and satisfying as many of the highest priority objectives of the parties involved in the transaction subject to their tolerance for risk.

In practice, deal structuring is about understanding the potential sources of disagreement from a simple argument over basic facts to substantially more complex issues, such as the form of payment, legal, accounting, and tax structures. It also requires understanding the potential conflicts of interest that can influence the outcome of the discussions. For example, when a portion of the purchase price depends on the long-term performance of the acquired business, the management of the business, often the former owner, may not behave in a manner that is in the best interests of the acquirer. The deal-structuring process also embodies feedback effects in which one element of the process such as the nature of payment, including amount, timing, and risk, may affect tax and accounting treatments.

Moreover, decisions made throughout the deal-structuring process influence various attributes of the deal. These attributes include, but are not limited to, how ownership is determined, how assets are transferred, how ownership is protected (*governance*), and how risk is apportioned among parties to the transaction. Other attributes include the type, number, and complexity of the documents required for closing; the types of approvals required; and the time needed to complete the transaction. These decisions also will influence how the combined companies will be managed, the amount and timing of resources committed, and the magnitude and timing of current and future tax liabilities (McCarthy, 1998;

Tillinghast, 1998). See Exhibit 5-2 for a listing of the characteristics of successful business deals.

Reflecting this complexity, the deal-structuring process should be viewed as consisting of a number of interdependent components. At a minimum, these include the acquisition vehicle, the postclosing organization, the legal form of the selling entity, the form of payment, the form of acquisition, and tax structure. The process starts with the determination by each party of their initial negotiating positions, potential risks, options for managing risk, levels of tolerance for risk, and conditions under which either party will "walk away" from the negotiations. The acquisition vehicle refers to the legal structure (e.g., corporate or partnership) used to acquire the target company. The postclosing organization is the organizational and legal framework used to manage the combined businesses following the completion of the transaction. The legal form of the selling entity refers to whether the seller is a C, S, or limited liability corporation or a partnership. These considerations will affect both the tax structure of the deal and form of payment. The form of payment may consist of cash, common stock, debt, or some combination of all three. Some portion of the payment may be deferred or dependent on the future performance of the acquired entity. The form of acquisition reflects both what is being acquired (e.g., stock or assets) and the form of payment. Consequently, the form of acquisition largely determines the tax structures. How and why these things happen are discussed in substantial detail in Chapter 10.

EXHIBIT 5-2. CHARACTERISTICS OF SUCCESSFUL DEALS

According to a Harvard University study, business deals—including mergers, acquisitions, joint ventures, and alliances—that have proven successful over a long period tend to have the following characteristics:

1. They are simple.
2. They do not fall apart when there are minor deviations from projections.
3. They may be changed.
4. They consider the incentives of each party to the deal under a variety of circumstances.
5. They provide mechanisms for communication and interpretation.
6. They are based primarily on trust rather than contract law.
7. They are not patently unfair to any party.
8. They do not make it too difficult to raise additional capital.

9. They match the needs of the parties involved.
10. They reveal information about each party (e.g., their faith in their ability to deliver on promises).
11. They allow for new information before financing is required.
12. They rely on incentives to ensure that the objectives of owners and managers are consistent.
13. They take into account the time required to raise additional capital.
14. They improve the chances for success for the venture.

Source: Harvard Business School, 1989.

Conducting Due Diligence

The parties to any transaction always should conduct their own due diligence to obtain the most accurate assessment of potential risks and rewards. Although some degree of protection is achieved through a well-written contract, legal agreements should never be viewed as a substitute for conducting formal due diligence. See Appendix A in this chapter for a detailed preliminary due diligence question list.

Buyer Due Diligence

Buyer due diligence is the process of validating assumptions underlying valuation. The primary objectives are to identify and confirm "sources of value" and to mitigate real or potential liability by looking for fatal flaws that reduce value. Due diligence involves three primary reviews: (1) a strategic/operational/marketing review conducted by senior operations and marketing management; (2) a financial review directed by financial and accounting personnel; and (3) and a legal review conducted by the buyer's legal counsel. A rigorous due diligence requires the creation of comprehensive checklists.

The strategic and operational review questions focus on the seller's management team, operations, and sales and marketing strategies. The financial review questions focus on the accuracy, timeliness, and completeness of the seller's financial statements. Finally, legal questions deal with corporate records, financial matters, management and employee issues, tangible and intangible assets of the seller, and material contracts and obligations of the seller such as litigation and claims. Interviews with key management provide invaluable sources of information (Krallinger, 1997).

Case Study 5-2 illustrates the importance of doing a thorough due diligence. Note how swiftly shareholders abandoned the company once its fraudulent accounting practices were uncovered, resulting in a dramatic loss of shareholder value.

CASE STUDY 5-2: McKESSON
HBOC RESTATES REVENUE

McKesson Corporation, the nation's largest drug wholesaler, acquired medical software provider HBO & Co. in a $14.1 billion stock deal in early 1999. The transaction was touted as having created the country's largest comprehensive health care services company. McKesson had annual sales of $18.1 billion in fiscal year 1998, and HBO & Co. had fiscal 1998 revenue of $1.2 billion. HBO & Co. makes information systems that include clinical, financial, billing, physician practice, and medical records software. Charles W. McCall, the chair, president, and chief executive of HBO & Co., was named the new chair of McKesson HBOC.

HBO was the leader in selling hospitals and doctors software to track financial and clinical data. As one of the decade's hottest stocks, it had soared 38-fold since early 1992. McKesson's first attempt to acquire HBO in mid-1998 collapsed following a news leak. However, McKesson's persistence culminated in a completed transaction in January 1999. In its haste, McKesson closed the deal even before an in-depth audit of HBO's books had been completed. In fact, the audit did not begin until after the close of the 1999 fiscal year. McKesson was so confident that its auditing firm, Deloitte & Touche, would not find anything that it released unaudited results that included the impact of HBO shortly after the close of the 1999 fiscal year on March 31, 1999. Within days, indications that contracts had been backdated began to surface.

By May, McKesson hired forensic accountants skilled at reconstructing computer records. By early June, the accountants were able to reconstruct deleted computer files, which revealed a list of improperly recorded contracts. This evidence underscored HBO's efforts to deliberately accelerate revenues by backdating contracts that weren't final. Moreover, HBO shipped software to customers that they had not ordered, while knowing that it would be returned. In doing so, they were able to boost reported earnings, the company's share price, and ultimately the purchase price paid by McKesson.

In mid-July, McKesson announced that it would have to reduce revenue by $327 million and net income by $191.5 million for the past 3 fiscal years to correct for accounting irregularities. The company's stock had fallen by 48% since late April when it first announced that it would have to restate earnings.

McKesson's senior management had to contend with rebuilding McKesson's reputation, resolving more than 50 lawsuits, and attempting to recover $9.5 billion in market value lost since the need to restate earnings was first announced. When asked how such a thing could happen,

McKesson spokespeople said they were intentionally kept from the due diligence process before the transaction closed. Despite not having adequate access to HBO's records, McKesson decided to close the transaction anyway (Bloomberg.com, 1999a).

Discussion Questions

1. Why do you think McKesson may have been in such a hurry to acquire HBO without completing an appropriate due diligence?
2. McKesson, a drug wholesaler, acquired HBO, a software firm. How do you think the fact that the two firms were in essentially different businesses may have contributed to what happened?

Selecting the Due Diligence Team

One of the most important aspects of performing due diligence is knowing the right questions to ask. This comes with experience in having performed due diligence numerous times and from having in-depth knowledge of the industry and the operations to be reviewed. Teams should include those with the required specialized expertise to address environmental, legal, and technical issues. This often necessitates the use of consultants.

Limiting Due Diligence

Due diligence is an expensive and exhausting process. The buyer frequently will want as much time as necessary to complete due diligence. In contrast, the seller frequently will want to limit the length and scope as much as possible. By its nature, due diligence is highly intrusive and places substantial demands on managers' time and attention. Due diligence rarely works to the advantage of the seller because a long and detailed due diligence is likely to uncover items that the buyer will use as an excuse to lower the purchase price. Consequently, sellers may seek to terminate due diligence before the buyer feels it is appropriate. In the interests of maintaining a cooperative relationship during negotiations, it is almost always in the best interests of the buyer to conduct a thorough due diligence in the shortest time possible so as not to disrupt the business and alienate the seller.

In some instances, buyers and sellers may agree to an abbreviated due diligence period. The theory is that the buyer can be protected in a well-written agreement of purchase and sale. In the agreement, the seller is required to make certain representations and warrant that they are true. Such "reps and warranties" could include the seller's acknowledgement that they own all assets listed in the agreement "free and clear" of any liens or attachments. If the representation is breached (found not to be true), the agreement generally will include a mechanism for compensating the buyer for any material loss. What constitutes material loss is defined in the contract. Relying on reps and warranties as a substitute for a thorough due diligence is rarely a good idea (Case Study 5-3).

CASE STUDY 5-3: WHEN "REPS AND WARRANTIES" DON'T PROVIDE ADEQUATE PROTECTION

A large financial services firm in the mid-1990s acquired a small database company that provided data supporting the lending process. The seller signed a contract with all the necessary reps and warranties that all their computer systems were fully operational and in compliance with prevailing laws. The buyer also withheld about 20% of the purchase price in the event that the operational effectiveness of the systems was not at the level specified in the contract. It became apparent almost immediately after closing that the seller had misstated dramatically the viability of his business. The buyer had to eventually shut down the business and write off the full extent of the purchase price. The buyer also had to submit to binding arbitration to recover that portion of the purchase price that had been placed in escrow. The buyer had virtually no recourse to the seller who had few assets in his own name and who may have moved the bulk of the cash received for his stock to banks that were beyond the jurisdiction of the U.S. legal system.

Discussion Question

1. Comment on the statement that there is no substitute for thorough due diligence.

A *data room* is another method commonly used by sellers to limit due diligence. This amounts to the seller sequestering the acquirer's team in a single room to complete due diligence. Typically, the data room consists of a conference room filled with file cabinets and boxes of documents requested by the buyer's due diligence team. Formal presentations by the seller's key managers are given in the often cramped conditions of the data room. Not surprisingly, the data room is a poor substitute for a tour of the seller's facilities.

Seller's Due Diligence

Although the bulk of due diligence is performed by the buyer on the seller, the prudent seller also should perform due diligence on the buyer and on themselves. In doing so, the seller can determine if the buyer has the financial wherewithal to finance the purchase price. In addition, a seller, as part of its own due diligence process, frequently will require all of its managers to sign documents stating that to the "best of their knowledge" what is being represented in the contract that pertains to their area of responsibility is indeed true. By conducting an internal investigation of their own operations, the seller hopes to mitigate liability stemming from inaccuracies in the seller's representations and warranties made in the agreement of purchase and sale.

Developing the Financing Plan

The final activity of the negotiation phase is to develop balance sheet, income, and cash-flow statements for the combined firms, in accordance with GAAP. Unlike the financial projections of cash flow made to value the target, these statements should include the expected cost of financing the transaction. This activity is a key input into the determination of the purchase price because it places a practical limitation on the amount of the purchase price the buyer can offer the seller. According to capital budgeting theory, an investment should be funded as long as its net present value (NPV) is greater than or equal to zero. The same concept could be applied to an acquisition. The buyer should be able to finance a purchase price (P_{TPP}) up to the present value of the target company as an independent or standalone entity (PV_I) plus synergy (PV_{SYN}) created by combining the acquiring and target companies discounted at the acquirer's cost of capital.

$$NPV = (PV_I + PV_{SYN}) - P_{TPP} \geq 0$$

The financing plan is appended to the acquirer's business and acquisition plans and is used to obtain financing for the transaction. No matter what size the transaction, lenders and investors will want to see a coherent analysis explaining why the proposed transaction is a good investment opportunity for them. Regardless of the intended audience, the financing plan largely is used as a marketing or sales document to negotiate the best possible terms for financing the proposed transaction. See Chapters 8 and 11 for a more detailed discussion of developing the financing plan.

Obtaining Bridge or Interim Financing

For an all-cash transaction, the buyer will go to the traditional sources of financing. These include banks, insurance companies, investment bankers and underwriters, venture capitalists and leveraged buyout funds, and the seller. Banks commonly are used to provide temporary or *bridge* financing to pay all or a portion of the purchase price and to meet possible working capital requirements until permanent financing is found. Bank lending is normally asset based, for which the collateral may consist of such tangible assets as accounts receivable, inventory, land, or fixed equipment.

Buyers usually seek more long-term sources of financing to replace bank debt because of the onerous covenants that restrict how the buyer may operate the combined firms. *Covenants* are promises made by the borrower that certain acts will be performed and others will be avoided. Covenants are designed to protect the lender's interests and may require the borrower to maintain a certain ratio of working capital to sales, debt-to-equity ratio, and credit rating. Covenants also may limit the amount of dividends the borrower can pay and future acquisitions or divestitures.

The nominal or stated rate on bank loans is generally significantly less than unsecured bond financing, reflecting differences in maturity and the underlying collateral. However, the actual cost of the bank loan is much higher than the stated rate because banks usually require the borrower to maintain large, low-yielding "compensating balances" with the bank. In addition, banks frequently demand warrants or rights to buy equity in the combined companies at some specified future date and price. When these warrants are exercised, there may be significant erosion of shareholder value, as new shares are issued at a price less than the prevailing share price.

Case Study 5-4 describes how acquiring companies arrange interim financing to meet immediate cash requirements at closing. These cash requirements consist of the need to pay target company shareholders the cash portion of the total consideration as well as the payment of cash for fractional shares. For large transactions, banking syndicates will include many banks to spread the risk of the transaction. These bank loans are usually short term in nature and are either "rolled over" at the prevailing rate of interest or refinanced using long-term debt.

CASE STUDY 5-4: VODAFONE FINANCES THE ACQUISITION OF AIRTOUCH

In April 1999, Vodafone Group PLC reached an agreement with 11 banks to underwrite and arrange the "facility" or line of credit for financing the merger with AirTouch Communications, Inc. Under the terms of the transaction, AirTouch common shareholders would receive five Vodafone AirTouch ADSs (equivalent to five Vodafone AirTouch ordinary shares) plus $9 in cash. The transaction closed in July 1999 and was valued at $55 billion.

The banking syndicate consisted of Bank of America, Barclay's, Banque Nationale de Paris, Citibank, Deutsche Bank, Goldman Sachs, HSBC, ING Barings, National Australia Bank, NatWest, and WestLB. The total facility, or amount that could be borrowed, was set at between $10 and $13 billion. The actual amount required could not be determined until the closing, when a more precise estimate of cash requirements could be determined.

The term of the major part of the facility is for 364 days, with the remaining balance multiyear. The initial borrowing rate is to be 60–70 basis points (six-tenths of 1%) above the London Interbank Overnight Rate. The actual spread will vary with the tranche (term) selected, utilization level (amount borrowed), and guarantee structure (the credit-worthiness of those banks issuing letters of credit).

Following completion of the merger, a substantial part of the facility will be refinanced in the bond and commercial paper markets through the banks, which have arranged the facility. The long-term financing consisted of a medium-term Euro note and U.S. commercial paper. These programs were not activated until after the merger was completed (Bloomberg.com, 1999b).

Discussion Questions

1. Why is short-term bank financing often used to finance an acquisition?
2. Why did Vodafone seek to convert the short-term bank financing to longer-term debt?

Mezzanine Financing

Mezzanine financing refers to capital that in liquidation has a repayment priority between senior debt and common stock. Although mezzanine financing may take the form of redeemable preferred stock, it generally is subordinated debt, with warrants convertible into common stock. It generally is unsecured, with a fixed coupon rate and a maturity of 5–10 years. Mezzanine investors usually look for firms with revenues in excess of $10 million. Such investors focus on a broad spectrum of businesses rather than on a single industry such as high-tech firms. Specialty retailing, broadcasting, communications, environmental services, distributors, and consumer or business service industries have tended historically to be more attractive to mezzanine investors (Remey, 1993).

Permanent Financing

"Permanent" financing usually consists of long-term unsecured debt. Such debt is generally not rated by the major credit-rating agencies, such as Standard & Poor's and Moody's services, and may be referred to as junk bond financing. Such financing may be obtained by investment bankers or underwriters raising funds by a "private placement" of all or a portion of the bond issue with investors willing to hold the bonds for long periods. These investors include insurance companies and pension funds, which are interested in matching their investment income stream with their obligations to policyholders and pensioners. Such debt is usually subordinate to bank debt if the firm is forced into bankruptcy. In addition, junk bonds may be sold to mutual funds or directly to the public. If a significant percentage of the debt is to be sold to the public, raising permanent financing will require many months to satisfy SEC requirements for full disclosure of risks associated with the bond issue.

Venture Capital Firms

Venture capitalists (VCs) are also a significant source of funds for financing both start-ups and acquisitions. VC firms identify and screen opportunities, transact and close deals, monitor and add value, and raise additional capital. General partners receive a 2–3% fee and 15–25% of capital gains from initial public offerings and mergers. The remaining 75–85% of capital gains plus a return of principal goes back to investors in the VC fund (Bygrave and Timmons, 1992). Only 2–4% of the firms contacting VC firms actually receive funding (Vachon, 1993; Wetzel, 1984). VCs sometimes are willing to lend when the more traditional sources, such as banks, insurance companies, and pension funds, are not. VCs usually demand a large equity position in the firm in exchange for their paying the firm a relatively low price per share. Consequently, the firm's owners are ceding a significant percentage of their ownership position for what could appear to be very high-cost financing in the future if the firm is successful in ultimately enhancing its market value. VC firms generally require a 60–70% return on their investments.

Seller Financing

Seller financing represents a highly important source of financing for buyers. Seller financing is a euphemism for the seller's willingness to defer receiving a portion of the purchase price until some future date. The advantages to the buyer include a lower overall risk of the transaction because of the need to provide less capital at the time of closing and the shifting of operational risk to the seller if the buyer ultimately defaults on the loan to the seller.

The "Road Show"

To arrange both bridge and permanent financing, the buyer will develop elaborate presentations to take on a "road show" to convince potential lenders of the attractiveness of the debt. It is referred to as a "road show" for good reason—immaculately dressed borrowers passionately display confidence in their business plan through carefully rehearsed and choreographed multimedia presentations in stuffy conference rooms throughout the country. It represents an opportunity for potential lenders to see management and to ask the "tough questions." If the "road show" is successful, at least several lenders will compete for all or a portion of the bond issue. Lender competition will result in lower stated rates on the loans as well as less onerous loan covenants.

As a cautionary note, taking management on the road to convince lenders that they should lend money is an exhausting exercise and represents a major distraction from day-to-day operations. It is common for the short-term performance of the target and the buyer companies to suffer as they spend more and more time dealing with due diligence and financing activities. Highly acquisitive companies run the risk of exhausting operating management through frequent presentations to external groups.

Selecting Alternative Financial Structures

The various methods of financing the transaction include cash, cash and notes, stock, and all debt. The latter option usually requires the presence of substantial amounts of unencumbered assets and a consistently strong operating cash flow. In practice, the total consideration paid to the seller often is financed using some

TABLE 5-1   Financing Mergers and Acquisitions

	Debt	Equity
Alternative Types		
Asset Based Lending	Tangible Assets Accounts Receivable Revolving Credit Lines Term Loans Sale/Lease-Back	
Cash-Flow Based	Projected Cash Flow	
Seller Financing	Deferred Payments Earnouts Installment Sales	Common Stock Preferred Stock
Public Offering and Private Placements	Senior Convertible Subordinated	Common Stock Preferred Stock
Alternative Sources	Commercial Banks Insurance Companies Pension Funds Investment/Merchant Banks	Buyout Funds Venture Capital Strategic Investors Individual Investors ("Angels")

of these alternative sources of funds. Table 5-1 summarizes the various types and sources of financing.

Computer models, which simulate the financial impact of various financial structures on the combined firms, are excellent tools for determining the appropriate capital structure (see Chapter 8). Although leverage raises the potential rate of return to equity investors, it also adds to risk. Increasing credit obligations to lenders implies increasing fixed interest expense, which raises the point at which the firm's revenue covers its costs (i.e., its breakeven point). An unanticipated downturn in the economy or aggressive pricing actions by competitors can erode cash flow and the firm's ability to meet its interest expense. This ultimately could lead to bankruptcy. This risk can be measured by creating various scenarios, each representing a different capital structure and determining the impact of lower-than-expected sales growth.

Financing Contingencies

Most well written agreements of purchase and sale contain a financing contingency. The buyer is not subject to the terms of the contract if the buyer cannot obtain adequate funding to complete the transaction. As previously discussed, breakup fees can be particularly useful to ensure that the buyer will attempt to obtain financing as aggressively as possible. In some instances, the seller may require the buyer to put a nonrefundable deposit in escrow to be forfeited if the buyer is unable to obtain financing to complete the transaction.

PHASE 7: DEVELOPING
THE INTEGRATION PLAN

The euphoria that surrounds the successful completion of a transaction erodes quickly once the challenges of making the combined firms perform in line with the predictions laid out in the business and acquisition plans become apparent. It is surprising how little effort goes into planning for these inevitable challenges before the agreement of purchase and sale is signed. Once the documents are signed the buyer has lost most, if not all, leverage over the seller.

EARNING TRUST

Decisions made before closing affect postclosing integration activity. Benefits packages, employment contracts, and bonuses to retain key employees (i.e., retention bonuses) normally are negotiated before closing. Contractual covenants and conditions also affect integration. Earnouts, payments to the seller based on future performance, and deferred purchase price mechanisms, involving the placement of some portion of the purchase price in escrow until certain contractual conditions have been realized, can limit the buyer's ability to effectively integrate the target into the acquirer's operations. Successfully integrating firms requires getting employees in both firms to work toward achieving common objectives. This comes about through building credibility and trust, not through superficial slogans, pep talks, and empty promises. Trust comes from people cooperating and experiencing mutual success.

EARNOUTS

Earnouts are generally very poor ways to create trust and often represent major impediments to the integration process. The two firms generally are kept physically separate. Accounting and management reporting systems are not merged immediately, data centers remain separate, and sales forces remain largely independent. The buyer's concern is that the effort to integrate the firms as soon as possible after closing will make tracking the financial progress of the acquired company toward meeting its earnout goals difficult. Moreover, the merging of facilities and sales forces could create a highly contentious situation once the earnout period has elapsed if the acquired company did not meet the earnout goals.

Employees covered by the earnout could plead in court that they were prevented from doing so by not being allowed by the buyer to implement the business plan on which the earnout was based. The hazards of earnouts are illustrated in Case Study 5-5. See Chapter 10 for a discussion of how to calculate earnout payments.

CASE STUDY 5-5:
THE DOWNSIDE OF EARNOUTS

In the mid-1980s, a well-known aerospace conglomerate acquired a high-growth systems integration company by paying a huge multiple of earnings. The purchase price ultimately could become much larger if certain earnout objectives were achieved during the 4 years following closing. However, the buyer's business plan assumed close cooperation between the two firms, despite holding the system integrator as a wholly owned but largely autonomous subsidiary. The dramatic difference in the cultures of the two firms was a major impediment to building trust and achieving the cooperation necessary to make the acquisition successful. Years of squabbling over policies and practices tended to delay the development and implementation of new systems. The absence of new systems made it difficult to gain market share.

Moreover, because the earnout objectives were partially defined in terms of revenue growth, many of the new customer contracts added substantial amounts of revenue but could not be completed profitably under the terms of these contracts. The buyer was slow to introduce new management into its wholly owned subsidiary for fear of violating the earnout agreement. Finally, market conditions changed, and what had been the acquired company's unique set of skills became commonplace. Eventually, the aerospace company wrote off most of the purchase price and merged the remaining assets of the acquired company into one of its other product lines after the earnout agreement expired.

Discussion Question

1. Describe conditions under which an earnout might be most appropriate.

CHOOSING THE INTEGRATION MANAGER

Great care should be taken before closing in the selection of the integration manager. This person should have excellent interpersonal and project management skills. During the integration phase, the skills of being able to get along with others are frequently more important than professional and technical skills. The buyer must determine what is critical for continuation of the acquired company's success during the first 12–24 months following closing. Critical activities include the identification of key managers, vendors, and customers and what is needed to retain these valued assets. The preclosing integration planning activity also should include the determination of operating norms or standards required for continued operation of the businesses. These include executive compensation, labor contracts, billing procedures, product delivery times, and quality metrics. Finally, a communication plan must be designed for all stakeholders to be implemented immediately following closing (Porter and Wood, 1998). Preclosing planning and postclosing integration are discussed in considerable detail in Chapter 6.

PHASE 8: CLOSING

The closing phase of the acquisition process consists of obtaining all necessary shareholder, regulatory, and third-party consents (e.g., customer and vendor contracts), as well as completing the definitive agreement. Like all other phases, this activity requires significant planning at the outset if it is to go smoothly. Unfortunately, this is frequently impractical in view of all the activities that are under way during the acquisition process. All such activities tend to converge on the closing date.

ASSIGNING CUSTOMER AND VENDOR CONTRACTS

Aside from errors of omission or last-minute changes in negotiating strategy, there are many daunting logistical challenges that must be overcome before closing can take place. In a purchase of assets, many customer and vendor contracts cannot be assigned to the buyer without receiving written approval from the other parties. Although this may be a largely mechanical process, both vendors and customers may view this as an opportunity to attempt to negotiate more favorable terms. Licenses also must receive approval from the licensor, and they also can be a major impediment to a timely closing if not properly planned for well in advance. For example, a major software vendor demanded a substantial increase in royalty payments before they would transfer the license to the buyer. The vendor knew that the software was critical for the ongoing operation of the business's data center. The exorbitant increase in the fee had a significant adverse impact on the economics of the transaction from the buyer's viewpoint and almost caused the deal to collapse.

A number of transitional issues also must be addressed before closing. These include continued payroll processing support by the seller on behalf of the buyer until the buyer is able to assume this function and the return of checks received by the seller from customers continuing to send checks to the seller's bank accounts after closing. Similarly, the buyer will want to be reimbursed by the seller for payments made by the buyer to vendors for materials supplied or services provided before closing but not paid until after closing.

GAINING THE NECESSARY APPROVALS

The buyer's legal counsel labors endlessly to ensure that the transaction is in full compliance with securities laws, antitrust laws, and state corporation laws.

Significant planning before closing is again crucial to minimizing roadblocks that a target company may place before the buyer. As noted in Chapter 3, target companies can be highly skilled at using prevailing laws as antitakeover measures. Great care must be exercised to ensure that all of the filings required by law have been made with the Federal Trade Commission and the Department of Justice. Noncompliance can delay or prevent a merger or acquisition (see Chapter 2). Finally, many transactions require approval by the shareholders of both the acquiring and target companies before ownership can be transferred legally.

COMPLETING THE DEFINITIVE AGREEMENT

The cornerstone of the closing documents is the definitive agreement of purchase and sale, which indicates all of the rights and obligations of the parties both before and after closing. The length of the definitive agreement depends on the complexity of the transaction. The major segments of an asset purchase agreement are outlined in the following sections (Sherman, 1998).

Purpose of Acquisition

In an asset sale, the purpose of acquisition section of the agreement specifies the specific assets or the shares to be acquired. It also stipulates the assets to be excluded from the transaction.

Price

The purchase price or total consideration may be fixed at the time of closing, subject to future adjustment, or it may be contingent on future performance. The purchase price may be initially fixed based on the seller's representations of the firm's total assets, total book value, tangible book value, or some other measure of value. However, the agreed-upon price may be adjusted following a postclosing audit. An independent auditing firm typically does such audits. In asset transactions, cash on the target's balance sheet frequently is excluded from the transaction; the price paid for noncurrent assets such as plant and intangible assets will be fixed, but the price for current assets will depend on their levels at closing. Contingent purchase prices or earnouts may be used if the seller does not have any current earnings or if the seller represents the accuracy of its forecasted cash flows.

Allocation of Price

The buyer typically has an incentive to allocate as much of the purchase price to depreciable assets such as fixed assets, customer lists, and noncompete agreements, which will shelter future income from taxes. In contrast, the seller may not want to allocate any portion of the purchase price to noncompete agreements. Such an allocation would constitute taxable income to the seller. Both parties should agree on how the purchase price should be allocated to the various assets acquired in an asset transaction before closing. This eliminates the chance that the parties involved will take different positions for tax purposes. Despite agreement between the parties, the Internal Revenue Service may challenge the appropriateness of any positions taken.

Payment Mechanism

Payment may be made at closing by wire transfer or cashier's check. The buyer may defer the payment of a portion of the purchase price by issuing a promissory note to the seller. The buyer and seller also may agree to put the unpaid portion of the purchase price in escrow. This will facilitate the settlement of claims that might be made in the future.

Assumption of Liabilities

The assets to be accepted by the buyer are identified in considerable detail in an asset deal. The seller retains those liabilities not assumed by the buyer. In instances such as environmental liabilities, unpaid taxes, and inadequately funded pension obligations, the courts may go after the buyer and seller. In contrast, the buyer assumes all known and unknown liabilities in a merger or purchase of shares.

Representations and Warranties

"Reps and warranties" are intended to provide for full disclosure of all information germane to the transaction. They typically cover the areas of greatest concern to both parties.

Covenants

Covenants cover the obligations of both parties between the signing of the definitive agreement and closing. A prime example is the requirement that the seller continues to conduct business in the usual and customary manner. The seller often will be required to seek approval for all expenditures that may be considered out of the ordinary, such as one-time dividend payments or sizeable increases in compensation.

Conditions for Closing

Closing cannot take place until certain conditions have been satisfied. These conditions could include the continued accuracy of the seller's representations and warranties and extent to which the seller is living up to their obligations under the covenants. Other examples include obtaining all necessary legal opinions, the execution of other agreements such as promissory notes, and the absence of any "material adverse change" in the condition of the target company.

Indemnification

The definitive agreement will require the seller to indemnify or absolve the buyer of liability in the event of misrepresentations or breaches of warranties or covenants. Similarly, the buyer usually agrees to indemnify the seller. Both parties generally want to limit the period during which the indemnity clauses remain in force. At least 1 full year of operation and a full audit is necessary to identify claims. Some claims such as environmental claims extend beyond the survival period of the indemnity clause. Usually, neither party can submit claims to the other until some minimum threshold, expressed in terms of the number or dollar size of claims, has been exceeded.

Merger Agreements

A merger is structurally simpler than an asset agreement because it does not require the stipulation of assets being transferred to the buyer and liabilities assumed by the buyer. Although it may take less time to negotiate and draft than an asset agreement, it may take longer to complete. A merger with a public company requires approval of the target companies' shareholders and must comply with the full public disclosure and filing requirements of both federal and state securities laws (see Chapter 2).

OTHER CLOSING DOCUMENTS

In addition to resolving the issues outlined above, closing may be complicated by the number of and complexity of the documents required to complete the transaction. In addition to the agreement of purchase and sale, the more important documents could include the following (Sherman, 1998):

a. Patents, licenses, royalty agreements, trade names, and trademarks
b. Labor and employment agreements
c. Leases
d. Mortgages, loan agreements, and lines of credit
e. Stock and bond commitments and details
f. Supplier and customer contracts
g. Distributor and sales representative agreements
h. Stock option and employee incentive programs
i. Health and social benefit plans (must be in place at closing to eliminate lapsed coverage)
j. Complete description of all foreign patents, facilities, and investments
k. Intermediary fee arrangements
l. Insurance policies, coverage, and claims pending
m. Litigation pending for and against each party
n. Environmental compliance issues resolved or on track to be resolved
o. Seller's corporate minutes of the board of directors and any other significant committee information
p. Articles of incorporation, bylaws, stock certificates, and corporate seals

IS CLOSING EVER SIMPLE?

The closing experience runs the gamut from mind-numbing routine to bombastic confrontation. How smoothly the process goes depends on its overall complexity and the level of trust among the parties involved. The size of the transaction is not a good indicator of complexity. Small transactions in terms of revenue or purchase price can be horrifically complicated where multiple parties are involved, significant off-balance sheet liabilities are suspected, or multiple levels of regulatory approval are required. Even when it appears that both parties have reached agreement on the major issues, what were previously minor issues seem to resurface on a grander, more complex scale. Sometimes this happens because the parties did not realize the significance of an item until the last minute; other times, one party intentionally takes a hard line on an issue as the closing date approaches in the hope of gaining a negotiating advantage. In one instance, a buyer of a computer maintenance business sat in the seller's mahogany-filled boardroom just minutes before the closing documents were to be signed and began to enumerate concerns he had with the deal. Tempers began to flare. Only after the seller threatened to walk away from the transaction did the buyer relent and the transaction closed. This strategy is ill advised. It amounts to playing Russian roulette and is ethically questionable.

Although closing normally involves one central location, offsite locations may be needed if documents for transferring deeds and titles to assets must be signed and filed from remote locations. Remote signings may be completed by having power of attorney for the buyer and seller transferred to local attorneys at each remote site. It is also a good idea to have separate conference rooms for the buyer and seller to ensure privacy and another room in which the parties meet to execute the documents. Finally, lenders should be kept separate from each other to minimize any exchange of information during closing that might cause them to reopen discussions between the buyer and the lender about the terms and conditions of loans.

For small, uncomplicated transactions, the closing can consist of a simple faxing back and forth of documents between the buyer and seller to ensure that there is complete agreement on the closing documents. Signature pages then are signed by one party and sent via overnight mail to the other party for their signature. However, other situations are far less mechanical. Case Study 5-6 illustrates the circus-like atmosphere that characterizes some closings.

CASE STUDY 5-6: SLEEPLESS IN PHILADELPHIA: A DRAMATIC CLOSING

Closings can take on a somewhat surreal atmosphere. In one transaction valued at $20 million, the buyer intended to finance the transaction with $10 million in secured bank loans, a $5 million loan from the seller, and $5 million in equity. However, the equity was to be provided by wealthy individual investors in amounts of $100,000 each. The closing took place in Philadelphia around a long conference room table in the law offices of the firm hired by the buyer, with lawyers and business people representing the buyer, the seller, and the several banks reviewing the final documents. Throughout the day and late into the evening, wealthy investors (some in chauffeur-driven limousines) and their attorneys would stop by to provide cashiers' checks, mostly in $100,000 amounts, and to sign the appropriate legal documents. The sheer number of people involved created an almost circus-like environment. Because of the lateness of the hour, it was not possible to deposit the checks on the same day. The next morning a briefcase full of cashiers' checks was taken to the local bank.

Discussion Question

1. What do you think are the major challenges faced by the buyer in financing a transaction in this manner?

PHASE 9: IMPLEMENTING POSTCLOSING INTEGRATION

The postclosing integration activity is widely viewed as among the most important phase of the acquisition process. Postclosing integration will be discussed in considerable detail in Chapter 6. What follows is a discussion of those activities required immediately following closing. Such activities fall into five categories: (1) implementing an effective communication plan, (2) retaining key managers, (3) identifying immediate operating cash-flow requirements, (4) employing the best practices of both companies, and (5) addressing cultural issues.

COMMUNICATION PLANS

Implementing an effective communication plan immediately following closing is crucial for purposes of retaining employees of the acquired firm and maintaining or boosting morale and productivity. The plan should address employee, customer, and vendor concerns. The message always should be honest and consistent. Employees need to understand how their compensation, including benefits, might change under new ownership. Employees may find a loss of specific benefits palatable if they are perceived as offset by improvements in other benefits or working conditions. Customers will want reassurance that there will not be any deterioration in product or service quality or delivery time during the transition from old to new ownership. Vendors also will be very interested in understanding how the change in ownership will affect their sales to the new firm. Whenever possible, communication is best done on a face-to-face basis. Senior officers of the acquiring company can be sent to address employee groups (on site, if possible). Senior officers also should contact key customers preferably in person or at least by telephone to provide the needed reassurances. Meeting these reasonable requests for information from employees, customers, and vendors immediately following closing with complete candor will contribute greatly to the sense of trust among stakeholders that is necessary for the ultimate success of the acquisition.

EMPLOYEE RETENTION

Retaining middle-level managers should be a top priority during this phase of the acquisition process. Frequently, senior managers of the target company that the buyer chooses to retain are asked to sign employment agreements as a condition of closing. Without these signed agreements, the buyer would not have completed the transaction. Although senior managers provide overall direction for the firm, middle-level managers execute the day-to-day operations of the firm. Plans should be in place to minimize the loss of such people, many of whom are likely to be receiving offers of employment from competitors once the transaction has been publicly announced. Bonuses, stock options, and enhanced sales commission schedules are commonly put in place to keep such managers.

SATISFYING CASH-FLOW REQUIREMENTS

Invariably, operating cash-flow requirements are higher than expected, despite having completed a thorough due diligence before closing. Conversations with middle-level managers following closing often reveal areas in which maintenance expenditures have been deferred. Customer disputes may result in invoices going unpaid for long periods. Receivables, previously thought to be collectable, may have to be written off. Production may be disrupted as employees of the acquired firm find it difficult to adapt to new practices introduced by the acquiring company's management or if inventory levels are inadequate to maintain desired customer delivery times. Finally, more customers than had been anticipated may be lost to competitors, which use the change in ownership as an opportunity to woo them away with various types of incentives.

EMPLOYING BEST PRACTICES

An important motivation for takeovers is to realize specific operating synergies, which result in improved operating efficiency, product quality, customer service, and on-time delivery. Both parties in a transaction are likely to excel in different areas. An excellent way for the combined companies to take advantage of the strengths of both companies is to use the "best practices" of both. However, in some areas, neither company may be employing what its customers believe to be the best practices in the industry. In these circumstances, management should look beyond its own operations to accept the practices of other companies that customers find preferable to what either company had been doing before the takeover.

CULTURAL ISSUES

Corporate cultures reflect the set of beliefs and behaviors of the management and employees of a corporation. In some instances, these belief systems and desired behaviors are codified in the firm's mission statement. Beliefs and desired behaviors may include acting with integrity, being nimble with respect to decision making, having a strong customer service orientation, and understanding customer needs.

Many behaviors may be implicit. Some corporations are very paternalistic, and others are very "bottom-line" oriented. Some empower employees, whereas others believe in highly centralized control. Some promote problem solving by applying employee teams; others promote individual performance. Inevitably different corporate cultures will impede postacquisition integration efforts. The key to success is to be sensitive to these differences and to take the time to explain to all employees of the new firm what is expected and why these beliefs and behaviors are desired in the new company. Once again, communication of desired beliefs and consistent practice of these beliefs from senior management on down the organization chart is necessary to overcome the stickiest of challenges.

PHASE 10: CONDUCTING A POSTCLOSING EVALUATION

The primary reasons for conducting a postclosing evaluation of all acquisitions are to determine if the acquisition is meeting expectations, to determine corrective actions if necessary, and to identify what was done well and what should be done better in future acquisitions.

DON'T CHANGE PERFORMANCE BENCHMARKS

Once the acquisition appears to be operating normally, evaluate the actual performance to that projected in the acquisition plan. This is an important step in measuring success. Success should be defined in terms of actual to planned performance. All too often, management simply ignores the performance targets stipulated in the acquisition plan and accepts less than plan performance to justify the acquisition. In some instances, this may be appropriate if circumstances beyond the firm's control cause a change in the operating environment. Examples include a recession, which slows the growth in revenue, or changing regulations, which preclude the introduction of a new product.

ASK THE DIFFICULT QUESTIONS

An introspective analysis of an acquisition should address as objectively as possible a series of targeted questions. The types of questions asked should vary depending on the elapsed time since closing. After 6 months, what has the buyer learned about the business? Were the original valuation assumptions reasonable? If not, what did the buyer not understand about the target company and why? What did the buyer do well? What should have been done differently? What can be done to ensure that the same mistakes are not made in future acquisitions? After 12 months, is the business meeting expectations? If not, what can be done to put the business back on track? Is the cost of fixing the business offset by expected returns? Are the right people in place to manage the business for the long term? After 24 months, does the acquired business still appear attractive? If not, should it be divested? If yes, when and to whom?

LEARN FROM MISTAKES

Although sometimes embarrassing, it always pays to take the time to identify lessons learned from each transaction. This is often a neglected exercise and results in firms repeating the same mistakes. This occurs even in the most highly acquisitive firms because those involved in the acquisition process may change from one acquisition to another. Lessons learned in an acquisition completed by the management of one of the firm's product lines may not be readily communicated to those about to undertake acquisitions in other parts of the company. Highly acquisitive companies can benefit greatly by dedicating certain legal, human resource, marketing, financial, and business development resources to support acquisitions made throughout the company. In doing so, the company minimizes the chance that the same mistakes will be made twice.

THINGS TO REMEMBER

The acquisition process consists of 10 identifiable phases. During the first phase, the business plan defines the overall direction of the business. If an acquisition is believed necessary to implement the firm's business strategy, an acquisition plan is developed during the second phase and defines the key objectives, available resources, and tactics for completing an acquisition. The next phase consists of the search for appropriate acquisition candidates. To initiate this phase, selection criteria need to be developed. At this stage, selection criteria should be relatively few in number and, whenever possible, should be quantified. At a minimum, criteria should include the industry and size (e.g., maximum price or revenue). The screening phase is a refinement of the search phase and entails applying more criteria to reduce the list of candidates surfaced during the search process. Key criteria in this phase may include profitability, market segment, product line, degree of leverage, and market share.

How the potential acquirer initiates first contact depends on the size of the target and the availability of intermediaries with highly placed contacts within the target firm. If the target is interested in proceeding, a LOI formally defining the reasons for the agreement, responsibilities of the two parties while the agreement is in force, and the expiration date is negotiated. Confidentiality agreements covering both parties also should be negotiated. If the target rebuffs overtures from the suitor, a tender offer may ensue to circumvent management and go straight to the target's shareholders.

The negotiation phase is an interactive, iterative process with many activities conducted concurrently. Such activities include refining valuation, structuring deals, conducting due diligence, and developing a financing plan. The actual amount and composition of the purchase price is determined during this phase.

The total purchase price or enterprise value of the target consists of the total consideration (cash, stock, debt, or some combination) received by the shareholder plus assumed debt currently on the target's books. The net purchase price includes the total purchase price plus other assumed liabilities that were not completely taken into account in estimating the economic value of the target's future cash flows less the proceeds from the sale of discretionary assets.

There is no substitute for performing a complete due diligence on the target company. Many activities under way during the negotiation phase are affected by the findings of due diligence. Refining valuation based on new information uncovered during due diligence affects the determination of the total consideration to be paid to the seller. New information also will affect how risks and liabilities are shared by the buyer and seller during the deal-structuring process. The financing plan may be affected by the discovery during due diligence of assets that can be sold to pay off debt accumulated to finance the transaction. Due diligence is not limited to the buyer. The seller should perform due diligence on the buyer to ensure that it will be able to finance the purchase price. Moreover, the seller also should perform due diligence on its own operations to ensure that its representations and warranties in the definitive agreement are accurate.

Integration planning is a highly important aspect of the acquisition process that must be done before closing. Once closing occurs, the acquiring company loses much of the leverage it may have had before the transaction was completed. Without adequate planning, integration is unlikely to provide the synergies anticipated by, at the cost included in, and on the timetable provided in the acquisition plan. Successful integration ultimately arises from building trust among all parties involved, which comes from people working cooperatively and experiencing mutual success. The closing phase goes well beyond organizing, finalizing, and signing all the necessary legal documents. It includes wading through the logistical quagmire of getting all the necessary third-party consents and regulatory and shareholder approvals. The postclosing integration phase consists of communicating effectively with all stakeholders, retaining key employees, and identifying and resolving immediate cash-flow needs.

The postclosing evaluation phase is the most commonly overlooked phase. Although many acquiring companies do closely monitor the performance of the acquisition to plan, many stop short of formally questioning how effective they were in managing the acquisition process. Such lessons sometimes can be embarrassing, but they are always instructive. Unfortunately, without identifying and communicating lessons learned to those involved in making future acquisitions, we are likely to relive our past mistakes.

CHAPTER DISCUSSION QUESTIONS

5-1. What resources are commonly used to conduct a search for potential acquisition targets?

5-2. Identify at least three criteria that might be used to select a manufacturing firm as a potential acquisition candidate. A financial services firm? A high technology firm?

5-3. Identify alternative ways to make "first contact" with a potential acquisition target. Why is confidentiality important? Under what circumstances might a potential acquirer make its intentions public?

5-4. What are the advantages and disadvantages of a letter of intent?

5-5. How do the various activities that are undertaken concurrently as part of the negotiation phase affect the determination of the purchase price?

5-6. What are the differences between total consideration, total purchase price/enterprise value, and net purchase price? How are these different concepts used?

5-7. What is the purpose of the buyer and seller performing due diligence?

5-8. What is the purpose of a financing plan?

5-9. Why is preclosing integration planning important?

5-10. What are the key activities that comprise a typical closing?

CHAPTER BUSINESS CASE

CASE STUDY 5-7: WHEN COMPANIES OVERPAY— MATTEL ACQUIRES THE LEARNING COMPANY

Background

Mattel, Inc., is the world's largest designer, manufacturer, and marketer of a broad variety of children's products selling directly to retailers and consumers. Most people recognize Mattel as the maker of the famous Barbie, the best-selling fashion doll in the world, generating sales of $1.7 billion annually. The company also manufactures a variety of other well-known toys and owns the primary toy license for the most popular kids educational program "Sesame Street." In 1988, Mattel revived its previous association with The Walt Disney Company and signed a multiyear deal with them for the worldwide toy rights for all of Disney's television and film properties. Under this agreement, Mattel has the right to Disney's characters including the following: Mickey and Minnie Mouse, Goofy, Donald Duck, and Winnie the Pooh. Mattel also has the rights to film characters from such popular movies as The Lion King, Beauty and the Beast, A Bug's Life, Aladdin, and Mulan.

Business Plan

Mission Statement and Strategy

Mattel's mission is to maintain its position in the toy market as the largest and most profitable family products marketer and manufacturer in the world. Mattel will continue to create new products and innovate in their existing toy lines to satisfy the constant changes of the family-products market. Its business strategy is to diversify Mattel beyond the market for traditional toys at a time when the toy industry is changing rapidly. This will be achieved by pursuing the high-growth and highly profitable children's technology market, while continuing to enhance Mattel's popular toys to gain market share and increase earnings in the toy market. Mattel believes that its current software division, Mattel Interactive, lacks the technical expertise and resources to penetrate the software market as quickly as the company desires. Consequently, Mattel seeks to acquire a software business that will be able to manufacture and market children's software that Mattel will distribute through its existing channels and through its Website (Mattel.com).

Defining the Marketplace

The toy market is a major segment within the leisure time industry. Included in this segment are many diverse companies, ranging from amusement parks to yacht manufacturers. Mattel is one of the largest manufacturers within the toy segment of the leisure time industry. Other leading toy companies are Hasbro, Nintendo, and Lego. Annual toy industry sales in recent years have exceeded $21 billion. Approximately one-half of all sales are made in the fourth quarter, reflecting the Christmas holiday.

Customers   Mattel's major customers are the large retail and e-commerce stores that distribute their products. These retailers and e-commerce stores in 1999 included Toys "R" Us Inc., Wal-Mart Stores Inc., Kmart Corp., Target, Consolidated Stores Corp., E-toys, ToyTime.com, Toysmart.com, and Toystore.com. The retailers are Mattel's direct customers; however, the ultimate buyers are the parents, grandparents, and children who purchase the toys from these retailers.

Competitors   The two largest toy manufacturers are Mattel and Hasbro, which together account for almost one-half of industry sales. In the past few years, Hasbro has acquired several companies whose primary products include electronic or interactive toys and games. On December 8, 1999, Hasbro announced a major restructuring in which it would cut 2200 jobs, close two plants, and shift its focus to software and other electronic toys. Traditional games, such as Monopoly, would be converted into software.

Potential Entrants   Potential entrants face substantial barriers to entry in the toy business. Current competitors, such as Mattel and Hasbro, already have secured distribution channels for their products based on longstanding relationships with key customers such as Wal-Mart and Toys "R" Us. It would be costly for new entrants to replicate these relationships. Moreover, brand recognition of such toys as Barbie, Nintendo, and Lego makes it difficult for new entrants to penetrate certain product segments within the toy market. Proprietary knowledge and patent protection provide additional barriers to entering these product lines. The large toymakers have licensing agreements that grant them the right to market toys based on the products of the major entertainment companies. For example, Mattel's licensing agreement with Disney guarantees access to a continuous flow of new product lines based on Disney's animated feature films and television programs.

Product Substitutes   One of the major substitutes for traditional toys such as dolls and cars are video games and computer software. In 1999, video games saw an increase of 45% in dollar sales and 62% in unit sales. Consumer demand continued strong for both the Nintendo 64 and Sony PlayStation video game systems. Even traditional toy product lines such as Mattel's famous Barbie doll have taken on electronic elements. CD-ROM titles for Barbie have been released that allow children to style Barbie's hair on screen. Other product substitutes include virtually all kinds of entertainment including books, athletic wear, tapes, and TV. However, these entertainment products are less of a concern for toy companies than the Internet or electronic games because they are not direct substitutes for traditional toys.

Suppliers   An estimated 80% of toy production is manufactured abroad. Both Mattel and Hasbro own factories in the Far East and Mexico to take advantage of low labor costs. Parts, such as software and microchips, often are outsourced to non-Mattel manufacturing plants in other countries and then imported for the assembly of such products as Barbie within Mattel-owned factories. Although outsourcing has resulted in labor cost savings, it also has resulted in inconsistent quality. Frequently, toys or parts imported from other countries must be reworked to comply with U.S. safety regulations.

Opportunities and Threats

Opportunities

New Distribution Channels   Mattel.com represents 80 separate toy and software offerings. Mattel hopes to spin this operation off as a separate company when it becomes profitable. Mattel.com lost about $70 million in 1999. The other new channel for distributing toys is directly to consumers through catalogs.

The so-called direct channels offered by the Internet and catalog sales help Mattel reduce its dependence on a few mass retailers.

Aging Population   Grandparents accounted for 14% of U.S. toy purchases in 1999. The number of grandparents is expected to grow from 58 million in 1999 to 76 million in 2005.

Interactive Media   As children have increasing access to computers, the demand for interactive computer games is expected to accelerate. The "high-tech" toy market segment is growing 20% annually, compared with the modest 5% growth in the traditional toy business.

International Growth   In 1999, 44% of Mattel's sales came from its international operations. Mattel already has redesigned its Barbie doll for the Asian and the South American market by changing Barbie's face and clothes.

Threats

Decreasing Demand for Traditional Toys   Children's tastes are changing. Popular items are now more likely to include athletic clothes and children's software and video games rather than more traditional items such as dolls and stuffed animals.

Distributor Returns   Toys found to be unsafe or unpopular may be returned by distributors. A quality problem with the Cabbage Patch Doll could cost Mattel more than $10 million in returns and in settling lawsuits.

Shrinking Target Market   Historically, the toy industry has considered their prime market to be children from birth to age 14. Today, the top toy-purchasing years for a child range from birth to age 10.

Just-In-Time Inventory Management   Changing customer inventory practices make it difficult to accurately forecast reorders, which has resulted in lost sales as unanticipated increases in orders could not be filled from current manufacturer inventories.

Internal Assessment

Strengths

Mattel's key strengths lie in its relatively low manufacturing cost position, with 85% of its toys manufactured in low-labor-cost countries like China and Indonesia, and its established distribution channels. Moreover, licensing agreements with Disney enable Mattel to add popular new characters to its product lines. These factors are believed to give Mattel a significant competitive edge over many of its smaller competitors.

Weaknesses

Mattel's Barbie and Hot Wheels product lines are mature, but the company has been slow to reposition these core brands. The lack of technical expertise to create software-based products limits Mattel's ability to exploit the shift away from traditional toys to video or interactive games. In addition, Mattel's board of directors has lost confidence in senior management because of their inability to achieve financial targets communicated to the investment community during the last 2 years.

Acquisition Plan

Objectives and Strategy

Mattel's corporate strategy is to diversify Mattel beyond the mature traditional toys segment into high-growth segments. Mattel believed that it had to acquire a recognized brand identity in the children's software and entertainment segment of the toy industry, sometimes called the "edutainment" segment, to participate in the rapid shift to interactive, software-based toys that are both entertaining and educational. Mattel believed that such an acquisition would remove some of the seasonality from sales and broaden their global revenue base. Key acquisition objectives included building a global brand strategy, doubling international sales, and creating a $1 billion software business by January 2001.

Defining the Target Industry

The "edutainment" segment has been experiencing strong growth predominantly in the entertainment segment. Parents are seeing the importance of technology in the workplace and want to familiarize their children with the technology as early as possible. In 1998, more than 40% of households had computers and, of those households with children, 70% had educational software. One-fourth of preschool and kindergarten classrooms are equipped with two-to-four personal computers loaded with children's software programs. As the number of homes with PCs continues to increase worldwide and with the proliferation of video games, the demand for educational and entertainment software is expected to accelerate.

Tactics

Mattel was looking for an independent children's software company with a strong brand identity and more than $400 million in annual sales. Mattel preferred not to acquire a business that was part of another competitor (e.g., Hasbro Interactive). Mattel's management stated that the target must have brands that complement Mattel's business strategy and the technology to support their existing brands, as well as to develop new brands. Mattel preferred to engage in a stock-for-stock exchange in any transaction to maintain manageable debt levels and to ensure that it preserved the rights to all software patents and licenses.

Moreover, Mattel reasoned that such a transaction would be more attractive to potential targets because it would enable target shareholders to defer the payment of taxes.

Potential Targets

Mattel selected Goldman Sachs to undertake a target search and initiate contact. Game and edutainment development divisions are often part of software conglomerates, such as Cendant, Electronic Arts, and GT Interactive, which produce software for diverse markets including games, systems platforms, business management, home improvement, and pure educational applications. Other firms may be subsidiaries of large book, CD-ROM, or game publishers. The parent firms showed little inclination to sell these businesses at what Mattel believed were reasonable prices. Therefore, Mattel focused on five publicly traded firms: Acclaim Entertainment, Inc., Activision, Inc., Interplay Entertainment Corp, The Learning Company, Inc. (TLC), and Take-Two Interactive Software. Of these, only Acclaim, Activision, and The Learning Company had their own established brands in the games and edutainment sectors and the size sufficient to meet Mattel's revenue criterion (Acclaim Entertainment, 1999; Activision, 1999; Mattel, 1999).

In 1999, TLC was the second largest consumer software company in the world, behind Microsoft. TLC was the leader in educational software, with a 42% market share, and in-home productivity software (i.e., home improvement software), with a 44% market share. The company has been following an aggressive expansion strategy, having completed 14 acquisitions since 1994. At 68%, TLC also had the highest gross profit margin of the target companies reviewed. TLC owned the most recognized titles and appeared to have the management and technical skills in place to handle the kind of volume that Mattel desired. Their sales were almost $1 billion, which would enable Mattel to achieve its objective in this "high-tech" market. Thus, TLC seemed the best suited to satisfy Mattel's acquisition objectives.

Completing the Acquisition

Despite disturbing discoveries during due diligence, Mattel acquired TLC in a stock-for-stock transaction valued at $3.8 billion on May 13, 1999. Mattel had determined that TLC's receivables were overstated because product returns from distributors were not deducted from receivables and its allowance for bad debt was inadequate. A $50 billion licensing deal also had been prematurely put on the balance sheet. Finally, TLC's brands were becoming outdated. TLC had substantially exaggerated the amount of money put into research and development for new software products. Nevertheless, driven by the appeal of rapidly becoming a big player in the children's software market, Mattel closed on the transaction aware that TLC's cash flows were overstated.

Epilogue

Mattel's profits during the third quarter of 1999, the first full quarter following consolidation of TLC with Mattel, fell $50 million short of expectations because of asset write-offs and questionable accounting practices. Consolidated net income for the third quarter was $135.3 million, as compared with $168.7 million during the same period in 1998. Profits were affected negatively by TLC distributor and retailer returns and an increase in bad debt reserves of $56 million, of which $35 million related to one of TLC's major distributors. Mattel also decided not to complete a significant TLC licensing agreement, which was expected to generate approximately $60 million in pretax earnings. For all of 1999, TLC represented a pretax loss of $206 million. After restructuring charges, Mattel's consolidated 1999 net loss was $82.4 million on sales of $5.5 billion. TLC's top executives left Mattel and sold their Mattel shares in August, just before the third quarter's financial performance was released. Mattel's stock fell by more than 35% during 1999 to end the year at about $14 per share. On February 3, 2000, Mattel announced that its chief executive officer (CEO), Jill Barrad, was leaving the company.

On September 30, 2000, Mattel virtually gave away The Learning Company to rid itself of what had become a seemingly intractable problem. This ended what had become a disastrous foray into software publishing that had cost the firm literally hundreds of millions of dollars. Mattel, which had paid $3.5 billion for the firm in 1999, sold the unit to an affiliate of Gores Technology Group for rights to a share of future profits (White, 2000). Essentially, the deal consisted of no cash upfront and only a share of potential future revenues. In lieu of cash, Gores agreed to give Mattel 50% of any profits and part of any future sale of TLC.

In a matter of weeks, Gores was able to do what Mattel could not do in a year. Gores restructured TLC's seven units into three, set strong controls on spending, sifted through 467 software titles to focus on the key brands, and repaired relationships with distributors. Gores also has sold the entertainment division and is seeking buyers for the remainder of TLC (Creswell, 2001).

Case Study Discussion Questions

1. Why was Mattel interested in diversification?
2. What alternatives to acquisition could Mattel have considered? Discuss the pros and cons of each alternative.
3. How might the Internet affect the toy industry? What potential conflicts with customers might be created?
4. What are the primary barriers to entering the toy industry?
5. What could Mattel have done to protect itself against risks uncovered during due diligence?

Solutions to this case study are provided in the Appendix at the back of the book.

CHAPTER BUSINESS CASE

CASE STUDY 5-8: FIRST UNION BUYS WACHOVIA
BANK—A MERGER OF EQUALS?

Background

First Union announced on April 17, 2001, that an agreement had been reached to acquire Wachovia Corporation for about $13 billion in stock, thus uniting two fiercely independent rivals. With total assets of about $324 billion, the combination created the fourth largest bank in the United States behind Citigroup, Bank of America, and J.P. Morgan Chase. The combined banks have 2900 branches and 90,290 employees. The merger also represents the joining of two banks with vastly different corporate cultures. Because both banks have substantial overlapping operations and branches in many southeastern U.S. cities, the combined banks are expected to be able to add to earnings in the first 2 years following closing. Hoping to reduce expenses by $890 million a year, the new bank plans to cut 7000 jobs over a 3-year period. Wachovia, which is much smaller than First Union, agreed to the merger for only a small 6% premium.

A Merger of Equals?

The deal is being structured as a merger of equals. That is a rare step given that the merger of equals framework usually is used when two companies are similar in size and market capitalization. L. M. Baker, chair and CEO of Wachovia, will be chair of the new bank and G. Kennedy Thompson, First Union's chair and CEO, will be CEO and president. The name Wachovia will survive. Of the other top executives, six will be from First Union and four from Wachovia. The board of directors will be evenly split, with nine coming form each bank. Wachovia shareholders own about 27% of the combined companies and received a special one-time dividend of $.48 per share because First Union recently had slashed its dividend.

To discourage a breakup, First Union and Wachovia used a fairly common mechanism called a "cross option," which gives each bank the right to buy a 19.9% stake in the other using cash, stock, and other property including such assets as distressed loans, real estate, or less appealing assets. (At less than 20% ownership, neither bank would have to show the investment on its balance sheet for financial reporting purposes.) Thus, the bank exercising the option would not only be able to get a stake in the merged bank but also would be able to unload its least attractive assets. A hostile bidder would have to deal with the idea that another big bank owned a chunk of the stock and that it might be saddled with unattractive assets.

The deal structure also involved an unusual fee if First Union and Wachovia parted ways. Each bank is entitled to 6% of the $13 billion merger value, or about $780 million in cash and stock. The 6% is about twice the standard breakup fee.

The cross-option and 6% fee were intended to discourage other last-minute suitors from making a bid for Wachovia.

A Last-Minute Suitor Shows Up

According to a First Union filing with the Securities and Exchange Commission (First Union, 2001), Wachovia rebuffed an overture from an unidentified bank just 24 hours before accepting First Union's offer. Analysts identified the bank as SunTrust Bank. SunTrust had been long considered a likely buyer of Wachovia after having pursued Wachovia unsuccessfully in late 2000. Wachovia's board dismissed the offer as not being in the best interests of the Wachovia's shareholders.

A Tale of Two Cultures

The transaction brings together two regional banking franchises. In the mid-1980s, First Union was much smaller than Wachovia. That was to change quickly, however. In the late 1980s and early 1990s, First Union went on an acquisition spree that made it much larger and better known than Wachovia. Under the direction of now-retired CEO Edward Crutchfield, First Union bought 90 banks. Mr. Crutchfield became known in banking circles as "fast Eddie." However, acquisitions of the Money Store and CoreStates Financial Corporation hurt bank earnings in late 1990s, causing First Union's stock to fall from $60 to less than $30 in 1999. First Union had paid $19.8 billion for CoreStates Financial in 1998 and then had trouble integrating the acquisition. Customers left in droves. Ill, Mr. Crutchfield resigned in 2000 and was replaced by G. Kennedy Thompson. He immediately took action to close the Money Store operation and exited the credit card business, resulting in a charge to earnings of $2.8 billion and the layoff of 2300 in 2000.

In contrast, Wachovia assiduously avoided buying up its competitors and its top executives frequently expressed shock at the premiums that were being paid for rival banks. Wachovia had a reputation as a cautious lender.

Whereas big banks like First Union did stumble mightily from acquisitions, Wachovia also suffered during the 1990s. Although Wachovia did acquire several small banks in Virginia and Florida in the mid-1990s, it remained a mid-tier player at a time when the size and scope of its bigger competitors put it at a sharp cost disadvantage. This was especially true with respect to credit cards and mortgages, which require the economies of scale associated with large operations. Moreover, Wachovia remained locked in the Southeast. Consequently, it was unable to diversify its portfolio geographically to minimize the effects of different regional growth rates across the United States.

The Demise of the Big Bank Premium

In the past, big bank deals prompted a rash of buying of bank stocks, as investors bet on the next takeover in the banking sector. Banks such as First Union, Bank of America (formerly NationsBank), and Bank One acquired midsize regional banks at lofty premiums, expanding their franchises. They rationalized these premiums by noting the need for economies of scale and bigger branch networks. Many mid-size banks that were obvious targets refused to sell themselves without receiving premiums bigger than previous transactions. But things have changed.

Back in 1995 buyers of banks paid 1.94 times book value and 13.1 times after-tax earnings. By 1997, these multiples rose to 3.4 times book value and 22.2 times after-tax earnings. However, by 2000, buyers paid far less, averaging 2.3 times book value and 16.3 times earnings. First Union paid 2.47 times book value and 15.7 times after-tax earnings (Deogun and Brown, 2001). The declining bank premiums reflect the declining demand for banks. Most of the big acquirers of the 1990s (e.g., Wells Fargo, Bank of America, and Bank One) now feel that they have reached an appropriate size. Some are still working through problems from past deals. Moreover, few banks wanted to take responsibility for another's problem loans during the slowing economy of 2000–2001.

Banking went through a wave of consolidation in the late 1990s, but many of the deals did not turn out well for the acquirers' shareholders. Consequently, most buyers were unwilling to pay much of a premium for regional banks unless they had some unique characteristics. The First Union–Wachovia deal is remarkable in that it showed how banks that were considered prized entities in the late 1990s could barely command any premium at all by early 2001.

Case Study Discussion Questions

1. In your judgment was this merger a true merger of equals? Why might this framework have been used in this instance? Do you think it was a fair deal for Wachovia stockholders? Explain your answer.
2. Do you believe the cross option and unusual fee structure in this transaction were in the best interests of Wachovia? Explain your answer.
3. How did big banks during the 1990s justify paying lofty premiums for smaller, regional banks? Why do you think their subsequent financial performance was hurt by these acquisitions?
4. What integration challenges do you believe these two banks will encounter as they attempt to consolidate operations?
5. Speculate on why Wachovia's management rebuffed the offer from SunTrust Bank with the ambiguous statement that it was not in the best interests of Wachovia's shareholders?

Appendix A

Legal Due Diligence Preliminary Information Request

The following list applies mainly to transactions involving large public companies. For smaller, privately owned target firms, the list may be substantially more focused. Normally the length and complexity of a "due diligence question list," submitted by the acquiring firm to the target firm's management, is determined through negotiation. The management of the target firm normally would view a lengthy list as both intrusive and costly to complete. Consequently, the target firm's management often will try to narrow both the number and breadth of the questions included in the initial request for information. The request for such a list often is included as part of the letter of intent signed by the acquirer and target firms.

The acquirer typically attempts to protect itself either through an exhaustive review of the target's records and facilities (i.e., due diligence), extensive representations and warranties (i.e., claims and promises made by the seller), or some combination of the two. If the target firm is successful in reducing the amount of information disclosed to the target firm, it can expect to be required to make more representations and warranties as to the accuracy of its claims and promises in the agreement of purchase and sale. This will no doubt add to the time required to negotiate such a document. Notwithstanding the intrusiveness of the following due diligence question list, the buyer is well advised to rely more on an on-site review of facilities and records and personnel interviews than it would be to rely on the seller's contract obligations. If the seller declares bankruptcy, cannot be found, or moves assets to offshore accounts, receiving remuneration for breach of contract may be impossible. Note that all references to the Company in the following due diligence question list refer to the target.

CONTENTS

A. Corporate Matters

1. Furnish a list of all Company subsidiaries, affiliates, joint ventures, partnerships or other such investments of the Company, including for each such entity or investment the name, jurisdiction of incorporation or establishment, address of the principal location, and ownership of capital stock or other interests.

2. Furnish copies of these Company documents: permanent corporate and/or organizational records and business licenses, certifications, permits, or similar authorizations (including authority to use assumed or fictitious name).

3. Furnish access to (with selective copies on request) all agreements executed since 20xx pertaining to the acquisition and divestiture of material Company investments, including subsidiaries, affiliates, joint ventures and partnerships, and operating assets and liabilities, including agreements or other commitments to make additional investments or to sell any current investments.

4. Furnish a list setting forth for the Company (including for each subsidiary, affiliate, joint venture, partnership, or other investments) all states and countries in which the Company is qualified to do business.

5. Furnish copies of all press releases issued for the period 1/1/20xx (or as far back as available) through the present that were issued by the Company or, if pertinent to the Company, by any of the Company's affiliates.

6. Identify and provide full information (including copies of any agreements) that may give rise to a finder's fee or broker's claim in respect to the contemplated transaction between the acquiring company and the Company.

7. Provide a list identifying all currently effective powers of attorney executed by the Company and furnish a copy or describe the term and significant provisions of each.

B. Securities Matters

8. Furnish the number of shares currently authorized and the number issued and outstanding; the name and address of each shareholder of the Company, the number of shares held and any officer or director position in the Company held by such shareholder; and the extent to which outstanding shares are held by employee plans in which employees of the Company participate such as employee stock ownership plans (ESOPs) or stock purchase plans and the number of shares held by such plans.

9. Furnish copies, including amendments and exhibits, of all registration statements covering the issuance or resale of equity or debt securities or rights or options, employee stock options, bonus, purchase, or similar plans to purchase such securities.

10. Furnish access to (with selective copies on request) of all annual, quarterly, and special reports to Company shareholders and/or to corporate authority (e.g., divisional and parent company level) for any period from 20xx through the present. Focus on operational performance, excluding strategic plans and forecasts.

11. Provide a list identifying, and furnish copies of, all options (including employee stock purchase and option plans), warrants, pledges, contracts, plans, investment letters, arrangements or commitments relating to the stock of the Company, whether authorized and unissued, treasury, or outstanding.

C. Tax Matters

12. Furnish copies of all federal income tax returns of the Company for 20xx through the most recent year available.
13. Furnish copies of all state and local income tax, sales and use tax, real estate tax, employment tax, and other state and local tax returns of the Company for 20xx through the most recent year available.
14. Make available copies of all foreign income tax returns of the Company for 20xx through the most recent year available.
15. Furnish copies of receipts or other evidence of payments of taxes by or on behalf of the Company for all open years.
16. Furnish copies of any correspondence or other documentation since 20xx pertaining to any tax deficiencies proposed or assessed or any waivers or any statute of limitations on assessment or collection of any tax, which the Company has executed.
17. Identify and describe any pending tax audits and furnish estimated assessments with respect to such audits, including but not limited to sales tax, income tax, gross receipts tax, franchise tax, use and occupancy taxes, personal and real property taxes, payroll and unemployment taxes, workers' compensation, and customs and duty audits.
18. Furnish copies of any tax opinions received by the Company relating to the greater of all open years or since 20xx from outside advisors such as attorneys and accountants.
19. Provide full information on unemployment tax experience ratings and reserves.

D. Financial and Accounting Matters

20. Furnish copies, with detail by business unit, of the Company balance sheet and year-end financial statements since 20xx, and make available for inspection all financial/accounting books, records, accounts, and journals of the Company, including all monthly internal financial statements from 20xx to the present.
21. Provide a listing of inventory.
22. Provide a listing of accrued expenses in excess of $5000.
23. Provide a schedule of deferred revenue items in excess of $5000.
24. Provide a listing of other assets.
25. Provide a list of journal entry payables.
26. Provide a list of insurance accruals by policy.
27. Provide details supporting vacation and sick pay accruals.
28. Provide a reconciliation of intangible assets.

29. Identify the sales and cost of sales by product. Describe the fixed versus variable components.

30. Provide a list of all Company debt securities or instruments, notes or accounts payable, financial or performance guarantees, and loan or credit agreements involving the Company. Provide a list of all mortgages, liens, pledges, indemnifications, and UCC (Uniform Commercial Code) filing statements by or against the Company. Provide a list of charges or encumbrances of any nature whatsoever to which any of the properties or assets of the Company are subject. Provide a list, to the best of the Company's knowledge, of pending, potential, and contingent claims or charges or encumbrances of any nature whatsoever to which any of the properties or assets of the Company may be subject. Furnish copies of all pertinent documents.

31. Provide a statement of the Company's common accounting practices, including the timing of revenue and expense recognition, depreciation, inventory valuation, and contingency reserve policies. Provide copies of opinions and/or reports of the Company's independent auditors for the fiscal year(s) ending 20xx through 20yy. Make available for inspection the work papers of the Company's independent auditors and internal auditors for the fiscal year(s) ending 20xx through 20yy.

32. Furnish a list identifying any account payable of more than $5000 included in the Company's balance sheet that is at least sixty (60) days overdue, for which a dispute exists, or which was incurred outside of the ordinary course of business. Identify separately any account payable owing to or note or account receivable collectible from a related party and included in the balance sheet.

33. To the extent not disclosed elsewhere, identify and describe any (a) contingent liabilities not reflected in the balance sheet, (b) monetary reserves established for specific risk situations, and (c) disagreements with the Company's independent auditors and internal auditors concerning financial statements prepared during the last three (3) accounting years.

34. Furnish a summary of all accounts receivables and terms and provide a list identifying any account receivable included in the balance sheet that is not current and collectible or that is or may be subject to any defense or offset.

35. Identify and describe any extraordinary charges and credits, "catch-up" adjustments, prior period adjustments, and other nonrecurring or unusual charges and credits since 20xx.

36. Furnish a list of the names and locations of all banks utilized by the Company, including full information on the accounts maintained by the Company in each bank and the names and positions of persons authorized to draw thereon.

E. Risk-Management Matters

37. Provide a list and describe all liability and property insurance and risk-management policies and programs of the Company, which includes, but is not limited to, policies for general liability, product liability, professional errors and

omissions liability, directors' and officers' liability, fiduciary liability, environmental liability, aircraft liability, umbrella liability, product recalls, workers' compensation, automobile liability, first-party property damage, business interruption, crime/fidelity, and employee medical. Describe the nature of funding of each policy/program (e.g., guaranteed cost insurance, self-insurance, retrospective charge-backs, deductibles). Identify for each policy/program if coverage is afforded on an occurrence or claims-made basis. Include in such descriptions, for each type of coverage, limit, deductible, annual premium, carrier, and expiration date. Provide copies of all such policies/programs.

38. Furnish a listing of all claims submitted under each policy/program—except under employee medical—from 20xx to the present, including all currently outstanding claims and the status thereof.

39. Provide a list and copies (or representative copies) of all warranties extended by the Company to its customers to the extent applicable to its products and services. Provide claims experience.

40. Describe the procedures used for reviewing the Company's costs and policies regarding warranties of its products and services and with respect to any pertinent costs provided for in the balance sheet. Identify by type and amount all product warranty reserves established.

F. Assets, Real Property, and Personal Property Matters

41. Provide a list of all domestic and foreign facilities owned, leased, or used (including second-party facilities such as distributors) by the Company, setting forth for each such facility the following: the complete address; the type of facility and its use(s); total square feet; whether the facility is owned, leased, or otherwise used; the annual rent, operating expenses, term, and landlord if leased; the book value and annual operating expenses if owned; and the number of employees.

42. Identify any options, easements, encumbrances, mortgages, liens, zoning, or other restrictions on any of the real property used by the Company.

43. Furnish copies of all deeds, title certificates, mortgages, leases, and other material documents and agreements relating to the ownership and/or use of the real property used by the Company.

44. Furnish a list identifying and describing all items of machinery and equipment, furniture and fixtures, and other items of personal property owned, used, or leased by the Company having an original value in excess of $15,000.

45. Identify separately any real, personal, tangible, or intangible property owned by a related party and leased or used by the Company.

G. Conduct of Business Matters

46. Furnish a list of and describe for each of the Company's business units their currently marketed products and services, indicating for each whether it is or will be entirely performed by the Company or whether all or part is purchased or subcontracted and, if so, from or to whom.

47. For each of the past 3 accounting years, and through the current month of the current accounting year, furnish a breakdown of the Company's sales by major product/service line, including second-party distributions, city or county and state market, and customer segment or type.

48. For each of the past 3 years, furnish a list of the ten (10) largest customers of the Company for each of its business units, indicating the types of products/services and amounts purchased in each year by each such customer.

49. For each of the past 3 years, furnish a list of the ten (10) largest suppliers to the Company indicating the types of products/services and amounts purchased in each year from each such supplier and terms for each.

50. Provide copies of representative Company product/service catalogs, descriptions, specifications, etc., as well as any collateral promotional materials. Furnish access to all and representative copies of price lists and discount schedules. Describe pricing policies and practices, including discriminatory practices. Identify the major categories of advertising spending and associated dollar amounts spent quarterly for fiscal year 20xx through 20yy.

51. Furnish a list of the Company's principal competitors and principal potential competitors by major product/service lines, identifying for each their estimated percentage share of the applicable market.

52. For each of the last 3 fiscal years, furnish a breakdown of the Company's research and development (R&D) expenses by major development project, and provide a summary description of each current R&D project.

53. Provide copies of the Company's standard forms of contractual documents, including purchase orders, sales quotations, sales order forms, leases, and licenses.

54. Provide a list of all current open purchase orders, agreements, or commitments in excess of $10,000, setting forth the name of the vendor, the amount of the obligation outstanding, and the date such obligation will be satisfied.

55. Make available or provide copies of all purchase orders, agreements, or commitments in excess of $10,000; purchase orders, agreements, or commitments over one (1) year; all commitments to purchase all or any specific percentage of a vendor's output or all commitments of a vendor to sell all or a specific percentage of its output to the Company; all nonassignable purchase orders, agreements, or commitments; and all purchase orders, agreements, or commitments for any purchased services or utilities.

56. Provide for each business unit or product line a list of all sales representatives (with their names and territories, but excluding personal contact information), distributors, dealers, agents, franchisees, consignees, and service representatives of the Company and any other third parties to whom the Company pays a sales or similar commission and describe the relationship, including compensation, duties, territories, term, and termination. Furnish copies of all agreements relating to such arrangements.

57. Provide access to customer lists and provide summary breakdowns (numbers of, dollar amounts related to) of such lists (e.g., by type of product/service, market, type of customer, i.e., business or consumer list). Provide a list of all current

open leases of Company property or products/services, setting forth for each type of lease the total number of such leases, the total and average value, the lease term, and any standard or nonstandard material terms. Indicate for each type of lease whether assignable. Provide access to pertinent records and documentation.

58. With respect to any of the above purchase, sale, or lease contracts or similar documents, identify any of such under which a dispute, breach, or default has occurred; is likely to occur; or is claimed to have occurred or under which premature termination is pending or anticipated or under which a loss to the Company is expected to result or on which the Company is or may become liable for penalties or assessments.

H. Intellectual Property Matters

59. Furnish a list identifying all U.S. and foreign patents and applications owned and/or used by the Company in the course of business, and make available or provide copies of all such patents and applications.

60. Furnish a list identifying all common law and/or registered U.S. and/or foreign trademarks, service marks or trade names, or pending applications therefor owned and/or used by the Company in the course of business, and make available or provide copies of all such trademarks, service marks, trade names, and applications.

61. Furnish a list identifying or describing all copyrights and pending applications owned and/or used by the Company in the course of business, and make available or provide copies of all such copyrights and applications.

62. Furnish a list identifying and describing all patents, patent applications, trademarks, service marks, trade names and copyrights, and applications therefor, trade secrets, know-how, rights to inventions or other proprietary information, including any and all related licenses, owned or held, directly or indirectly, by any related party or affiliate of the Company and relating to or used in the Company's business.

63. Furnish a list identifying and describing any claims made or pending from 1/20xx to the present to the effect that the Company's business or products/services infringe or dilute the rights of others or to the effect that the business, products, or services of others infringe or dilute the rights of the Company.

I. Management, Labor, and Personnel Matters

64. Describe the management organization of the Company, listing the names and titles of all officers, directors, and key managers. Provide job descriptions where available. Provide copies of all Company organization charts (showing, among other things, reporting relationships). List the names of the five (5) most highly compensated employees of the Company during each of the last three (3) fiscal years. Indicate the total amount of compensation received by each such person during each such period.

65. Furnish a list of all employees of the Company, organized by business unit and departments within each. For each employee, list name, title, work location,

date of hire, union membership (if applicable), and current annual compensation. Indicate separate components of compensation (e.g., base salary, bonus, commissions) where applicable. Describe employee turnover history by Company business unit and facility during each of the last three (3) fiscal years.

66. Describe any transactions between the Company and any related party or any Company transactions in which a related party has a beneficial interest, any borrowings from the Company by related parties, and any purchases by the Company of goods or services from related parties (other than in their capacity as employees). Further, identify and describe all transactions where related parties or others have guaranteed or endorsed any Company obligation, or vice versa, and make available or furnish copies of all documentation related thereto.

67. Furnish copies of all written, and provide particulars on any oral, employment agreements, retirement agreements, consulting agreements, and other agreements existing or proposed between the Company and any present or former (*with some time limitation*) officer, director, shareholder, and employee.

68. Furnish a list of all collective bargaining agreements setting forth and identifying the union, bargaining unit, and expiration date of each agreement. Make available copies of all such agreements.

69. Furnish a summary of union history, if any, indicating the dates of any union elections, organizational activities, strikes, or work stoppages involving the Company in the past five (5) years and any anticipated or threatened union elections, organizational activities, and states of work stoppages.

70. Describe any instances in which the Company has been subject to any charges or investigations relating to noncompliance with labor laws since 1/20*xx*.

71. Identify and furnish copies of all pension, retirement, profit sharing, deferred compensation, bonus, stock savings or other savings programs, agreements or plans, or related future or contingent commitments of the Company concerning employee benefits. If not in written form (i.e., if oral), provide descriptions and other particulars.

72. Identify all other Company fringe benefits not set forth elsewhere, including but not limited to insurance (life, disability income, medical, dental, vision, automobile), vacation, sick pay, and company car programs. Describe how each benefit is funded (insured or self-insured) and who administers claims. Furnish copies of all written agreements and other material documentation pertaining thereto, including summary plan descriptions and the latest ERISA (Employee Retirement Income Security Act) Form 5500 for each plan. If not in written form (i.e., if oral), provide descriptions and other particulars.

73. Furnish copies of the current Company audit reviews. Indicate the date of the last audit compliance review, if any. Describe what happened during the review and results thereof. Describe any conciliation agreements or cause notices and furnish copies of same. Describe the Company's program for self-audit and compliance review.

74. Furnish copies of all standard Company personnel practices, procedures, and forms, such as, without limitation, hourly wage scales, salaried compensation practices, vacation and holiday policies, expense guidelines and expense account or travel/entertainment reimbursement, employment applications, relocation policies and agreements, confidentiality agreements, noncompetition agreements, avoidance of conflict of interest, assignment of inventions, grievance procedures, scheduled and unscheduled salary, and performance reviews.

J. Legal Compliance Matters

75. Furnish copies of any Company statements and standard policies and procedures relating to legal and ethical conduct, including but not limited to compliance with laws, conduct of business, gifts and contributions, investigations, entertainment, and conflicts of interest.

76. Describe fully any present and prior circumstances in which the Company or its officers, employees, or agents are making or made any payments to obtain business, domestic or foreign, and any practices, policies, or procedures relating to such payments including the manner in which such payments are or were controlled or recorded for tax and financial accounting purposes.

77. Identify and furnish copies of any Company, affiliated company, or governmental study or investigation known to Company management concerning the Company's: (i) eligibility for government contracting; (ii) use of lobbyists or consultants for lobbying purposes; (iii) payment of gratuities; (iv) time charging, mischarging, or cross charging; (v) entertainment; and (vi) other fraud, waste, and abuse issues.

78. If not otherwise provided in response to any of the preceding questions, furnish a list of all governmental permits, approvals, licenses, etc., which the Company currently holds or has applied for.

79. Describe the Company's pricing policies and procedures. Further, describe any programs of the Company for obtaining competitors' pricing information or for providing the Company's pricing information to competitors.

80. Describe the Company's policies and procedures for compliance with environmental and occupational health and safety laws, including any Company programs, policy statements, and guides thereto.

81. Describe any instances in which the Company has been, currently is, or is threatened to be the subject of any governmental inquiry or investigation concerning its compliance with environmental laws or occupational health and safety laws.

82. Identify and describe any known legal issues under past operations from 20xx to the present or under present operations or under contracts with respect to the following: (a) hazardous activities, (b) use and disposal of hazardous materials and waste, and (c) compliance with environmental laws.

83. Identify and describe any known legal issues under past operations from 20xx to the present or under present operations or under contracts with respect

to the following: (a) federal or state antitrust or similar laws and (b) export and import laws.

K. Litigation, Disputes, and Claims Matters

84. Provide a list identifying and describing all currently pending or threatened litigation, claims, protests, actions, or proceedings, whether judicial, arbitral, or administrative, brought by the Company (or by an affiliate of the Company in which the Company is a party) or brought against the Company (or against an affiliate of the Company in which the Company is a party), which affects or may affect the Company's contracts, employment obligations, assets, patents and intellectual property, property, or business. For each such matter, identify the nature of the claim, the amount claimed and the amount reserved, the jurisdiction, and the name of the counsel representing the Company. Provide comparable particulars for each such matter pending at any time from 20xx to the present, including a description of the disposition of each such matter. Make available access to, and on request, copies of pertinent documentation.

85. Provide a list identifying and describing all outstanding or prospective judgments, writs, injunctions, decrees or orders of any court, administrative tribunal, or other governmental authority against the Company.

86. Provide a list identifying and describing all outstanding or anticipated notices of any actual or alleged violation of any zoning requirement, building code, environmental, pollution control, occupational safety, or other federal, state, or local statutes, ordinances or regulations relating to the contracts, property, or business of the Company or the health and safety of its employees.

L. Information Systems Matters

87. Provide summary level information regarding the Company's information processing systems, operations, procedures, etc., including:

a. General

1. Copy of current Information Systems (IS) plan
2. Current year and future operating budgets
3. Actual expenses by category for fiscal years 20xx to 20yy
4. List of capital expenditures anticipated in the next 12–36 months
5. Description of facilities utilized by IS organization
6. Copy of current disaster recovery plan
7. Service level measurement criteria

b. People

1. Functional organization chart
2. Staff numbers by job class

     3. Staffing level forecasts

     4. Contract personnel usage

  c. Hardware

     1. Depreciation schedules of major computer and communications assets

     2. Lease schedules of major computer and communications assets

     3. List of current maintenance agreements

     4. Copy of resource utilization reports (specify type of equipment)

     5. Number and types of PCs/workstations deployed

  d. Software

     1. List of software products utilized with associated depreciation and/or lease schedules

     2. List of maintenance agreements in effect

     3. Copy of third-party license agreements

  e. Network (voice, data, local and wide area networks)

     1. Network diagrams or configuration with line speeds

     2. Traffic volumes

     3. Number of telephones and terminals supported by location

  f. Applications

     1. List of production systems and the associated technical environment

     2. Description and status of current development and enhancement projects

     3. Plans for future development and enhancement projects

     4. Description of user change request backlog

REFERENCES

Acclaim Entertainment, *Annual Report*, www.reportgallery.com, and 10K, www.sec.gov/edgarhp/htm, 1999.

Activision, *Annual Report*, www.reportgallery.com, and 10K, www.sec.gov/edgarhp.htm, 1999.

Bloomberg.com, "McKesson Revises Earnings," July 17, 1999a.

Bloomberg.com, "Vodafone Secures Financing for Air Touch Merger," May 14, 1999b.

Bygrave, William D. and Jeffrey A. Timmons, *Venture Capital at the Crossroads*, Boston: Harvard Business School Press, 1992.

Creswell, Julie, "Would You Give This Man Your Company?" *Fortune*, May 28, 2001, pp. 127–129.

Deogun, Nikhil and Ken Brown, "The Incredible Shrinking Bank Premium: Wachovia Deal Illustrates the Mood of Caution," *The Wall Street Journal*, Section C, April 17, 2001, p. 1.

First Union, S8 Filing on Business Combinations, Securities & Exchange Commission, April 26, 2001.

Harvard Business School, "Notes on Financial Contracting: Deals," *Cases and Reviews*, 9-288-014, June 22, 1989, p. 34.

Krallinger, Joseph, *Mergers & Acquisitions: Managing the Transaction*, New York: McGraw-Hill, 1997, pp. 94–116.

Mattel, *Annual Report*, www.reportgallery.com,and 10K, www.sec.gov/edgarhp.htm, 1999.

McCarthy, Paul, "Legal Aspects of Acquiring U.S. Enterprises," in David J. BenDaniel and Arthur H. Rosenbloom, eds., *International M&A, Joint Ventures & Beyond: Doing the Deal*, Wiley & Sons, 1998, pp. 27–57.

Porter, Richard and Cynthia N. Wood, "Post-merger Integration," in David J. BenDaniel and Arthur H. Rosenbloom, eds., *International M&A, Joint Ventures & Beyond: Doing the Deal*, Wiley & Sons, 1998, pp. 459–457.

Remey, Donald P., "Mezzanine Financing: A Flexible Source of Growth Capital," in D. Schutt, ed., *Pratt's Guide to Venture Capital Sources*, New York: Venture Economics Publishing, 1993, pp. 84–86.

Sherman, Andrew, *Mergers and Acquisitions from A to Z: Strategic and Practical Guidance for Small- and Middle-Market Buyers and Sellers*, New York: AMACOM, 1998, pp. 171–218.

Tillinghast, David R., "Tax Aspects of Inbound Merger and Acquisition and Joint Venture Transactions," in David J. BenDaniel and Arthur H. Rosenbloom, eds., *International M&A, Joint Ventures & Beyond: Doing the Deal*, New York: Wiley & Sons, 1998, pp. 151–172.

Vachon, Michael, "Venture Capital Reborn," *Venture Capital Journal*, January 1993, p. 32.

Wetzel, William H., Jr., "Angels and Risk Capital," *Sloan Management Review*, 24 (4), Summer1984, pp. 23–34.

White, Michael, "Learning Company Hard Lesson for Mattel," *The Associated Press, Orange County Register*, Business Section, September 30, 2000, p. 3.

6

INTEGRATION

MERGERS, ACQUISITIONS, AND BUSINESS ALLIANCES

What could be worse than being without sight?
Being born with sight and no vision.

—Helen Keller

Unlike most gossip around the water cooler, the conversation appeared to be unusually urgent between an engineer and draftsman employed by an engineering services company, which recently had been taken over by its competitor. "Do you think there will be substantial layoffs?" one worried engineer asked, shaking his head in dismay. The draftsman nodded somberly, noting that not only had terminations been announced immediately following the last two acquisitions in the industry but also that there had been some loss of employer-paid benefits for most of the workforce. Concern seemed to turn to anger as they discussed the windfall that some senior managers were likely to receive when they exercised their stock options. "I think it's obscene that some of the brass is already out buying new cars . . . you would think they could just wait until, well, until the other shoe dropped."

The intensity of their conversation caught the attention of others in nearby cubicles, who set aside their work to join in the conversation. Normally conscientious employees were increasingly oblivious to project deadlines when their only source of information seemed to come from the "gossip mill." No one really knew if the rumors that circulated were accurate, but the more often they were repeated the more they were believed. A tide of paranoia swept through the office, engulfing all but a few at the top who actually knew what was going to happen.

OVERVIEW

As noted in Chapter 1, motives for purchasing a company vary widely. Acquirers tend to fall into two broad categories: strategic buyers and financial buyers. Financial buyers are typically those who buy a business for eventual resale. In general, they do not intend to integrate the acquired business into another entity. Moreover, instead of managing the business, they are inclined to monitor the effectiveness of current management, intervening only if there is a significant and sustained deviation between actual and projected performance. In contrast, strategic buyers are interested in making a profit by managing a business for an extended period. The strategic buyer may choose to manage the acquisition as a separate subsidiary in a holding company or merge it into another business. These choices influence greatly the extent of and speed with which integration takes place.

This chapter assumes that integration is the goal of the acquirer immediately after the transaction closes. The chapter begins by stressing the importance of the integration phase of the acquisition process in contributing to the eventual success of the merger or acquisition. As noted in Chapter 1, ineffective integration is the second most commonly cited factor contributing to the failure of mergers and acquisitions (M&As) to meet or exceed expectations.

If done correctly, the integration process can help to mitigate the loss of key talent or managers and the potential deterioration in employee morale and productivity. The potential loss of this "human capital" is perhaps one of the greatest risks associated with (M&As). Although key talent and managers do not represent the only value in most acquisitions, it is widely recognized as among the most important. In a recent survey of 190 chief executive officers (CEOs) and chief financial officers (CFOs) from companies with M&A experience, more than three-fourths of the respondents cited the retention of key talent and managers as critical to the eventual success of a merger or acquisition (Watson Wyatt Worldwide, 1999).

The factors critical to the success of any integration activity are addressed in this chapter. These include careful premerger planning, candid and continuous communication, the pace at which the businesses are combined, the appointment of an integration manager and team with clearly defined goals and lines of authority, and making the difficult decisions early in the process. This chapter views integration as a process consisting of six activities: planning, developing communication plans, creating a new organization, developing staffing plans, implementing functional integration, and integrating corporate cultures. This chapter concludes with a discussion of how to overcome some of the unique obstacles encountered in integrating business alliances.

THE ROLE OF INTEGRATION IN SUCCESSFUL MERGERS AND ACQUISITIONS

In a global study of 100 acquisitions, each of which is valued at more than $500 million, Andersen Consulting (1999) concluded that integration is an exceedingly important factor contributing to successful M&As. Moreover, the study suggested that integration must be done quickly to achieve proper staffing requirements, eliminate redundant assets, and generate the financial returns expected by shareholders and Wall Street analysts. The study concludes that, if done well, most postmerger activities are completed within 6 months to 1 year. For some companies, horizontal acquisitions (i.e., mergers between competitors) may be the best source of creating shareholder wealth in the short run. In an assessment of the pharmaceutical industry, one study found that the range of actual cost savings achieved has been 15–25% on research and development (R&D), 5–20% on manufacturing, 15–20% on marketing and sales, and 20–50% on administration. The savings vary according to differences in the extent of geographic, product, and R&D overlap. In the aggregate, these savings can amount to 30–40% of the acquired company's total cost base (Pursche, 1996).

THE IMPORTANCE OF RAPID INTEGRATION

For our purposes, the term rapid is defined as relative to the pace of normal operations for a firm. The importance of rapid integration can be demonstrated using a simple numerical example. Suppose a firm has a current market value of $100 million and this value accurately reflects the firm's future cash flows discounted at its cost of capital. Assume an acquirer is willing to pay a $25 million control premium for this firm, believing that it can recover the control premium by realizing cost savings resulting from integrating the two firms. The amount of cash the acquirer will have to generate to recover the premium will increase the longer it takes to integrate the target company. If the cost of capital is 10% and integration is completed by the end of the first year, the acquirer will have to earn $27.5 million by the end of the first year to recover the control premium plus its cost of capital (i.e., $25 + $25 × .10). If integration is not completed until the end of the second year, the acquirer will have to earn incremental cash flow of $30.25 million (i.e., $27.5 + $27.5 × .10).

Numerous studies also support the conclusion that rapid integration efforts are more likely to result in mergers that achieve the acquirer's expectations (*Business Week*, 1995; Coopers & Lybrand, 1996; Marks, 1996; McKinsey Company, 1987). However, the pace of integration, although among the most commonly cited factors, is certainly not the only factor contributing to the success or failure of M&As. Overly optimistic assessments of potential synergies resulting in overpayment for the target firm and poor strategy are also among the most common explanations for the failure of M&As.

THE IMPACT OF EMPLOYEE TURNOVER

Although there is little evidence that firms necessarily experience an actual reduction in their total workforce following an acquisition, studies do show that turnover among management and key employees does increase after a corporate takeover (Hayes, 1979; Shivdasani, 1993; Walsh, 1989; Walsh and Ellwood, 1991). Some loss of managers is intentional as part of an effort to eliminate redundancies and overlapping positions, whereas others quit during the turmoil of integration. Flanagan and O'Shaughnessy (1998) found that layoffs were announced about the same time as mergers about 50% of the time.

What is difficult to measure in any of these studies is whether the employees that leave represent a significant "brain drain" or loss of key managers. For many acquisitions, talent and management skills represent the primary value of the target company to the acquirer. This is especially true in high technology and service companies for which assets are largely the embodied knowledge of their employees (Lord and Ranft, 2000). Consequently, the loss of key employees rapidly degrades the value of the target company, thereby making the recovery of any premium paid to target shareholders increasingly difficult for the buyer.

The cost of employee turnover does not stop with the loss of key employees. The loss of any significant number of employees can be very costly. Current employees already have been recruited and trained. Firms will incur both recruitment and training costs again when equally qualified employees are hired to replace those lost. Moreover, the loss of employees is likely to reduce the morale of those who remain and add to benefit claims. Studies by the American Management Association and CIGNA Corporation show that employees, whether they leave or stay with the new firm, file more disability claims for longer time periods after downsizing (*Wall Street Journal*, November 21, 1996).

INTEGRATION OFTEN MISMANAGED

Companies involved in integrating acquisitions frequently botch "people" issues. In a survey of 179 mergers since 1995, Right Management Consultants (1999) found that only 30% of the executives surveyed said they had successfully integrated the workforces and combined the cultures of the two companies. These results are striking particularly when we take into account that more than four-fifths of the survey responses came from companies at least 1 year after the acquisition had been completed. With respect to integrating the workforces, just 33% said they had effectively redeployed management talent, and only 34% reported good employee morale through the transition period. In terms of success in combining cultures, only one-fifth of the executives surveyed said that the career objectives of the employees of the acquired company were in synch with the combined companies' goals.

KEY FACTORS CONTRIBUTING TO
SUCCESSFUL INTEGRATION

Perhaps the best way to retain employees is for the acquiring company to maintain a reputation as a great place to work. Following an acquisition, the new owner must demonstrate to employees at all levels that the future is promising.

Through clear and continuous communication, the acquirer must provide answers to questions that are on employees' minds—the so-called "me-issues." These include questions about pay, benefits, job security, relocation, corporate direction, and their future role in the combined company. Despite immediate and compelling communication, employees of both the acquiring and target companies are likely to resist change in the wake of a corporate takeover. Differences in the way the management of the acquiring and target companies make decisions, the pace of decision making, perceived values, as well as the frequency and content of communication can result in major differences in corporate cultures. These differences can be overcome by applying time and transaction-tested techniques for integrating businesses (Exhibit 6-1).

EXHIBIT 6-1. INTEGRATION
SUCCESS FACTORS

1. **Plan carefully, act quickly**. Fast change limits uncertainty and deteriorating productivity. Before closing the transaction, make sure that specific goals for integration have been established, that someone is in charge of the integration activity, and that lines of authority have been delineated clearly.

2. **Introduce project management**. Integration should be managed as a fully coordinated project, with objectives well understood by all involved in the integration process, supporting timetables, and individuals responsible for achieving each objective.

3. **Communicate from the top of the organization**. Tell people as much as you can as soon as you can. Address the "me-issues."

4. **Provide clear leadership**. Define and communicate the future direction of the combined companies. Do not exaggerate or overcommit. Make sure that you meet or exceed all your commitments.

5. **Focus on customers**. Mergers can result in lost sales and deteriorating customer service. Actions to raise sales and service must be planned carefully but executed quickly.

6. **Make the tough decisions as soon as possible**. Decide on the organizational structure, reporting relationships, spans of control, people selection, roles and responsibilities, and workforce reductions as early as possible during the integration phase.

7. **Focus on the highest leverage issues**. Prioritize objectives carefully and concentrate resources on achieving those offering the greatest payoff first.

Source: Adapted from Marks, Mitchell L., *Joining Forces: Making One Plus One Equal Three in Mergers, Acquisitions and Alliances*, Jossey-Bass, 1998.

VIEWING INTEGRATION AS A PROCESS

The activities involved in integrating an acquired business into the acquirer's business do not fall neatly into a well-defined process. Some activities fall into a logical sequence, whereas others are continuous and in some respects unending. The major activities fall loosely into the following sequence: premerger planning, resolving communication issues, defining the new organization, developing staffing plans, integrating functions and departments, and building a new corporate culture. In practice, communicating with all major stakeholder groups and developing a new corporate culture are largely continuous activities, running through the integration period and beyond. Each of these six activities will be discussed in the coming sections of this chapter in the sequence outlined in Figure 6-1.

INTEGRATION PLANNING

Thinking about how the postmerger integration may be implemented should begin before the deal is completed. However, assumptions made before the closing based on information accumulated during due diligence must be reexamined once the transaction is consummated to ensure their validity. For an excellent discussion of postmerger integration challenges, see Reed-Lajoux (1998) and Schweiger (2002).

Premerger Integration Planning: Begin Planning Before Closing

Initiating the integration planning before closing is intended to accomplish a number of important objectives. The process enables the acquiring company to refine further its original estimate of the value of the target company and to deal with transition issues in the context of the agreement of purchase and sale. Furthermore, the buyer has an opportunity to insert into the agreement the appropriate representations (claims) and warranties (promises), as well as conditions of closing that facilitate the postmerger integration process. Finally, the planning process creates a postmerger integration organization to expedite the integration process following closing.

Refining Valuation Doing Due Diligence

Part of the integration planning process involves the preclosing due diligence activity. One responsibility of the due diligence team is to identify ways in which assets, processes, and other resources can be combined to realize cost savings, productivity improvements, or other perceived synergies. This information is also essential for refining the valuation process by enabling planners to better understand the necessary sequencing of events and the resulting pace at which the expected synergies may be realized. Consequently, understanding how and over what time period the integration will be implemented is important in determining the magnitude and timing of the cash flows of the combined companies used in making the final assessment of value.

Integration Planning	Developing Communication Plans	Creating a New Organization	Developing Staffing Plans	Functional Integration	Building a New Corporate Culture
Premerger Planning: – Refine valuation – Resolve transition issues – Negotiate contract assurances	Stakeholders: – Employees – Customers – Suppliers – Investors – Communities (including regulators)	Learn from the past	Determine personnel requirements for the new organization	Revalidate due diligence data	Identify cultural issues through profiling
		Business needs drive organizational structure	Determine resource availability	Conduct performance bench-marking	Integrate through shared: – Goals – Standards – Services – Space
		Integrate corporate structures	Establish staffing plans & timetables	Integrate functions: – Operations – Information technology – Finance – Sales – Marketing – Purchasing – R&D – Human resources	
			Develop compensation strategy		
			Create supporting information systems		

FIGURE 6-1.   Viewing merger integration as a process.

Contract-Related Transition Issues: Resolve Before Closing

Integration planning also involves addressing human resource, customer, and supplier issues that overlap the change of ownership. These issues should be resolved as part of the agreement of purchase and sale. For example, the agreement may stipulate how target company employees will be paid and how their benefit claims will be processed. Payroll systems must be in place to ensure that employees of the acquired company continue to be paid without disruption. For a small number of employees this may be accommodated easily by loading the acquirer's payroll computer system with a computer tape containing the necessary salary and personal information before closing or by having a third-party payroll processor perform these services. For larger operations or where employees are dispersed geographically, the target's employees may continue to be paid using the target's existing payroll system.

Employee health care or disability claims tend to escalate just before a transaction closes. This is especially true if the target's employees believe that the benefits to be provided by the acquirer are likely to be less attractive than their current benefit coverage. The sharp increase in such expenses can pose an unexpected financial burden for the acquirer if the responsibility for payment of such claims has not been addressed in the merger agreement. For example, the agreement may read that all claims incurred within a specific number of days before closing, but not submitted by employees for processing until after closing, will be reimbursed by the seller after the closing. Alternatively, such claims may be paid from an escrow account containing a portion of the purchase price set aside to cover these types of expenses.

Similar timing issues exist for target company customers and suppliers. For example, the merger agreement should specify how the seller should be reimbursed for products shipped or services provided by the seller before closing but not paid for by the customer until after closing. A prudent buyer typically would be the recipient of such payments because the seller's previous lockboxes (i.e., checking accounts) would have been closed and replaced by the buyer's. Likewise, the buyer will want to be reimbursed by the seller for monies owed to suppliers for products or services provided to the seller before closing but not billed until after closing. The merger agreement may indicate that both parties will keep track of customer and supplier invoices paid during the 60–90 days following closing and will submit them for reimbursement to the other party at the end of that period.

Contract Assurances: Never a Substitute for Thorough Due Diligence

At a minimum, the agreement of purchase and sale will contain basic assurances that the seller is what it claims to be and that the seller has a right to sell the business. Similar assurances will apply to the acquiring company. For example, the buyer must assert that it has the right and the financial capacity to buy the target firm. A comprehensive set of "reps and warranties" may be viewed as a due diligence checklist for the buyer. The "reps and warranties" provide the buyer with recourse to the seller if any of these claims or promises are untrue.

A prudent buyer will want to include certain assurances in the agreement of purchase and sale to limit its postclosing risk. Most seller representations and warranties made to the buyer refer to the past and present condition of the seller's business. Such "reps and warranties" usually pertain to such items as the ownership of securities; real and intellectual property; current levels of receivables, inventory, and debt; and pending lawsuits, worker disability, customer warranty claims, and that the target's accounting practices are strictly in accordance with Generally Accepted Accounting Principles. Although "reps and warranties" apply primarily to the past and current state of the seller's business, they do have ramifications for the future. For example, if a seller claims that there are no lawsuits pending and a lawsuit is filed shortly after closing, the buyer may seek to recover damages from the seller.

Moreover, sellers commonly provide potential acquirers with financial projections The seller may have an incentive to provide an overly optimistic forecast to inflate the purchase price. To minimize this possibility, the prudent buyer will demand that the seller represent the reasonableness of the assumptions underlying the forecast and the accuracy of the data used in making the projections. If the acquired company's financial performance deteriorates following closing, the acquirer may be able to recover damages by claiming breach of contract. For this reason, sellers normally vigorously oppose providing any warranty for financial projections.

The buyer also may insist that certain conditions must be satisfied before closing can take place. Common conditions include employment contracts, agreements not to compete, financing, and regulatory and shareholder approval. The buyer usually will insist that key target company employees sign contracts obligating them to remain with the newly formed company for a specific period. The former owners, managers, and other key employees also are asked to sign agreements precluding them from going into any business that would directly compete with the new company during the duration of the noncompete agreement. Financial buyers in particular usually will require that they have firm commitments from lenders before completing the transaction. Finally, the buyer will want to make the final closing contingent on receiving approval from the appropriate regulatory agencies and shareholders of both companies before any money changes hands.

Postmerger Integration Organization

A postmerger integration organization with clearly defined goals and responsibilities should be in place before closing. For friendly mergers, the organization, including supporting work teams, should consist of individuals from both the acquiring and target companies who have a vested interest in the newly formed company. The extent to which such an organization can be assembled during a hostile takeover is problematic given the lack of trust that may exist between the parties to the transaction. In such circumstances, the acquiring company is likely to find it difficult to gain access to the necessary information and to get the involvement of the target company's management in the planning process before the transaction actually closes.

Postmerger Integration Organization: Composition and Responsibilities

The postmerger integration organization should consist of a management integration team (MIT) and a series of integration work teams. Each work team is focused on implementing a specific portion of the integration plan.

Management Integration Team: Consists of Acquirer and Target Managers

The MIT consists of senior managers from the two merged organizations and is charged with delivering on sales and operating synergies identified during the preclosing due diligence. The composition of the work teams also should reflect employees from both the acquiring and target companies. Other team members might include outside advisors, such as investment bankers, accountants, attorneys, and consultants. The MIT's emphasis during the integration period should be on those activities creating the greatest value for shareholders. The MIT's primary responsibility is to focus on key concerns such as long-term revenue, cost, and cash-flow performance targets, as well as product and customer strategies. Exhibit 6-2 summarizes the key tasks that should be performed by the MIT to realize anticipated synergies.

EXHIBIT 6-2. KEY MANAGEMENT INTEGRATION TEAM RESPONSIBILITIES

1. Build a master schedule of what should be done by whom and by what date.
2. Determine the required economic performance for the combined entity.
3. Establish work teams to determine how each function and business unit will be combined (e.g., structure, job design, and staffing levels).
4. Focus the organization on meeting ongoing business commitments and operational performance targets during the integration process.
5. Create an early warning system consisting of performance indicators to ensure that both integration activities and business performance stay on plan.
6. Monitor and expedite key decisions.
7. Establish a rigorous communication campaign to aggressively and repeatedly support the integration plan. Address both internal (e.g., employees) and external (e.g., customers, suppliers, and regulatory authorities) constituencies.

Integration Work Teams

Although the MIT cannot do everything, it is responsible for making sure that everything gets done. Dedicated integration work teams perform the detailed integration work. In addition to driving the integration effort, the MIT ensures that the managers not involved in the integration effort remain focused on running the business. The MIT allocates dedicated resources to the integration effort and clarifies nonteam membership roles and enables day-to-day operations to continue at premerger levels. The MIT should be careful to give the work teams not only the responsibility to do certain tasks but also the authority to get the job done. The teams should be encouraged to inject ideas into the process to foster creativity by encouraging solutions rather than by dictating processes and procedures. To be effective, the work teams must have access to accurate, timely information and should receive candid, timely feedback. The teams also should be given adequate resources to do the task they have been asked to do and should be kept informed of the broader perspective of the overall integration effort so that they will not become too narrowly focused.

Institutionalizing the Integration Process

In recognition of the importance of integration, firms that frequently acquire companies in the same industry often have staffs fully dedicated to managing the integration process. The presumption is that integration is likely to proceed more smoothly and rapidly if those guiding the process have substantial experience in integrating certain types of businesses. It is ironic that some firms can have such discipline when it comes to postacquisition integration but display such poor judgment by consistently overpaying for acquisitions. By overpaying for the target firm, the acquirer is implicitly assuming that all anticipated synergies used to justify the exorbitant purchase price can be realized in a reasonable time period following completion of the acquisition (Case Study 6-1). Thus, overpayment leaves little room for errors during the integration process.

CASE STUDY 6-1: M&A GETS OUT OF HAND AT CISCO

An Acquisition Machine

Cisco Systems, the Internet infrastructure behemoth, provides the hardware and software to support efficient traffic flow over the Internet. Between 1993 and 2000, Cisco completed 70 acquisitions using its high-flying stock as its acquisition currency (Frank and Sidel, 2002). With engineering talent in short supply and a dramatic compression in product life cycles, Cisco turned to acquisitions to expand existing product lines and to enter new businesses. The firm's track record during this period in acquiring and absorbing these acquisitions was impressive. In fiscal year 1999, Cisco acquired 10 companies. During the same period, its sales and operating profits soared by 44% and 55%, respectively. In view of its pledge not to layoff any employees of the target companies, its turnover rate among employees acquired through acquisition was 2.1%, versus an average of 20% for other software and hardware companies.

"Institutionalizing" the Integration Process at Cisco

Cisco's strategy for acquiring companies is to evaluate its targets' technologies, financial performance, and management talent with a focus on ease of integrating the target into Cisco's operations. Cisco tends to target small companies having a viable commercial product or technology. Cisco believes that larger, more mature companies tend to be more difficult to integrate because they have entrenched beliefs about technologies, hardware and software solutions, and product development processes. Cisco often acquires a minority ownership position before attempting to takeover a firm.

The frequency with which Cisco makes acquisitions has caused the firm to "institutionalize" the way in which it integrates acquired companies. The integration process is tailored for each acquired company and is implemented by an integration team of 12 professionals. Newly acquired employees receive an information packet including descriptions of Cisco's business strategy, organizational structure, benefits, a contact sheet if further information is required, and an explanation of the strategic importance of the acquired firm to Cisco. On the day the acquisition is announced, teams of Cisco human resources people travel to the acquired firm's headquarters and meet with small groups of employees to answer questions.

Working with the newly acquired firm's management, integration team members help place newly acquired employees within Cisco's workforce. Generally, product, engineering, and marketing groups are kept independent, whereas sales and manufacturing functions are merged into existing Cisco departments. Cisco payroll and benefits systems are updated to reflect information about the new employees, who are quickly given access to Cisco's online employee information systems. Cisco also offers customized orientation programs intended to educate managers about Cisco's hiring practices, salespeople about Cisco's products, and engineers about the firm's development process. The entire integration process generally is completed in 4–6 weeks. This lightning-fast pace is largely the result of Cisco's tendency to purchase small, highly complementary companies; to leave much of the acquired firm's infrastructure in place; and to dedicate a staff of human resource and business development people to facilitate the process (Cisco Systems, 1999 and Goldblatt, 1999).

The Great Ride Ends

Cisco was unable to avoid the devastating effects of the explosion of the dot.com bubble and the 2001–2002 recession in the United States. Corporate technology buyers, who used Cisco's high-end equipment, stopped making purchases because of economic uncertainty. Moreover, Internet service providers and telephone carriers, which had been the mainstay of Cisco's long-term growth, also cut back their purchases. Consequently, Cisco was forced to repudiate its no-layoff pledge and announced a workforce reduction of 8500, about 20% of its total employees, in early 2001.

Despite its concerted effort to retain key employees from previous acquisitions, Cisco's turnover began to soar. Some high-priced talent simply walked away shortly after the deals were completed. Companies that had been acquired at highly inflated premiums during the late 1990s lost much of their value as the loss of key talent delayed new product launches. In one instance, the Monterey acquisition, Cisco was forced to shut it down, although Monterey had not yet put out a single new product after having been owned for more than a year. By the time a product was ready, the market opportunity was no longer there because of the rapid rate of change in Cisco's targeted markets.

By mid-2001, the firm had announced inventory and acquisition-related write-downs of more than $2.5 billion. The precipitous drop in its share price made growth through acquisition much less attractive than during the late 1990s, when its stock traded at lofty price-to-earnings ratios. Thus, Cisco was forced to abandon its previous strategy of growth through acquisition to one emphasizing improvement in its internal operations. Some analysts have complained that it is difficult to determine how profitable Cisco actually was during the 1990s. After spending billions of dollars on buying companies, Cisco routinely wrote off massive amounts of acquisition-related charges. Such charges totaled $5.4 billion in the 5 years ending 2001 (*Business Week*, January 21, 2002).

Case Study Discussion Questions

1. Describe how Cisco "institutionalized" the integration process. What are the advantages and disadvantages to the approach adopted by Cisco?
2. Why did Cisco have a "no layoff" policy? How did this contribute to maintaining or increasing the value of the companies it acquired?
3. What evidence do you have that the high price-to-earnings ratio associated with Cisco's stock during the late 1990s caused the firm to overpay for many of its acquisitions? How might overpayment have complicated the integration process at Cisco?

COMMUNICATING TO KEY STAKEHOLDER GROUPS

Before there is any public announcement of an acquisition, the acquiring company should have prepared a communication plan. The plan should be developed jointly by the MIT and the public relations (PR) department or outside PR consultant. It should contain key messages and specify target stakeholders and appropriate media for conveying the messages to each group. The major stakeholder groups should include employees, customers, suppliers, investors, communities, and regulators. Regulatory agencies often become key stakeholders in highly regulated industries or whenever a pending transaction is viewed as potentially anticompetitive (see Chapter 2).

Employees: Address the "Me Issues" Immediately

As noted earlier, target company employees typically represent a substantial portion of the value of the acquired business. This is particularly true for technology and service-related businesses having few tangible assets. These types of businesses comprise an increasingly larger share of the number of transactions consummated each year. Therefore, preserving the value of an acquisition requires that companies must be highly sensitive to when and how something is communicated to employees and to the accuracy of its content.

When to Communicate

Communication, particularly during crisis periods, should be as frequent as possible. A report of "nothing to report" can be comforting. It is better to report that there is no change than to remain silent. Silence breeds uncertainty, which adds to stress associated with what constitutes a major life change for most people. Stress engendered by transition from one corporate parent to another can undermine morale and endanger productivity. Deteriorating job performance, absences from work, fatigue, anxiety, and depression are clear signs of workforce stress.

How to Communicate

The CEO should lead the effort to communicate to employees at all levels through employee meetings on site or via teleconferencing. Many companies find it useful to create a single source of information accessible to all employees. This may be an individual whose job it is to answer questions or a menu-driven automated phone system programmed to respond to commonly asked questions. The best forum for communication in a crisis is through regularly scheduled employee meetings. All external communication in the form of press releases should be coordinated with the PR department to ensure that the same information is released concurrently to employees. This minimizes the likelihood that employees will learn about important developments second hand. Internal e-mail systems, voice-mail, or intranets may be used to facilitate employee communications. In addition, personal letters, question-and-answer sessions, newsletters, or videotapes are highly effective ways of delivering the desired messages.

What to Communicate

Employees are highly interested in any information pertaining to the merger and, more importantly, how it will affect them. They will want to know how changes will affect the overall strategy, business operations, job security, working conditions, and total compensation. The human resources (HR) staff plays an important role in communicating to employees. HR representatives must learn what employees know and want to know, what the prevailing rumors are, and what employees find most disconcerting. This can be achieved through surveys, interviews, focus groups, or employee meetings.

Customers: Undercommit and Overdeliver

To minimize customer attrition, the newly merged firm must commit to customers that it will maintain or improve product quality, on-time delivery, and customer service. The commitments should be realistic in terms of what needs to be accomplished during the integration phase. Despite these efforts some attrition related to the acquisition is inevitable. The firm continuously must communicate to customers realistic benefits associated with the merger. From the customer's perspective, the merger can increase the range of products or services offered or provide lower selling prices as a result of economies of scale and new applications of technology. However, the firm's actions must support its talk. Under the best of circumstances the firm should exceed the product quality, customer service, and on-time delivery commitments made following closing.

Case Study 6-2 illustrates the negative effects of failure to meet customer commitments in a timely manner. History shows that companies are vulnerable particularly to market share loss immediately following mergers. Competitors use these periods to sow doubt among the firm's customers about its ability to achieve and sustain acceptable product quality and customer service as well as on-time delivery. Deterioration in any one of these areas is often all that is needed to lose even the most historically loyal customers. In this case study, the protracted integration clearly is eroding the value of the deal as the overall competitive position of CNH Corporation continues to deteriorate.

CASE STUDY 6-2: CASE CORPORATION LOSES SIGHT OF CUSTOMER NEEDS IN INTEGRATING NEW HOLLAND CORPORATION

Farm implement manufacturer Case Corporation acquired New Holland Corporation in a $4.6 billion transaction in 1999. Overnight, its CEO, Jean-Pierre Rosso, had engineered a deal that put the combined firms, with $11 billion in annual revenue, in second place in the agricultural equipment industry just behind industry leader John Deere. The new firm was named CNH Global (CNH). Although Rosso proved adept at negotiating and closing a substantial deal for his firm, he was markedly less agile in meeting customer needs during the protracted integration period.

Bigger Isn't Necessarily Better

Today, CNH is a poster child of what can happen when managers become so preoccupied with the details of combining two big operations that they neglect external issues such as the economy and competition. Since the merger in November 1999, CNH has posted five straight quarterly losses totaling $400 million. Annual revenues in 2000 fell by $2.5 billion from their 1999 level. Although some of the revenue loss was a result of weakness in the economy, the cyclical slowdown didn't tell the whole story. CNH began losing market share to John Deere and other rivals across virtually all of its product lines almost from the day the takeover was announced. This market erosion continued well after closing. CNH clearly had dropped the ball with respect to staying focused on satisfying its customers' needs.

Too Little, Too Late

Rosso remained preoccupied in negotiating with antitrust officials about what it would take to get regulatory approval. Once achieved, CNH was slow to complete the last of its asset sales as required under the consent decree with the FTC. The last divestiture was not completed until late January 2001, more than 20 months after the deal had been announced. This delay forced Rosso to postpone cost cutting and to slow their new product entries. This spooked farmers and dealers who could not get the firm to commit to telling them which products would be discontinued and which the firm would continue to support with parts and service. Fearful that CNH would discontinue duplicate Case and New Holland products, farmers and equipment dealers switched brands. The result was that John Deere became more dominant than ever. CNH was slow to reassure customers with tangible actions and to introduce new products competitive with Deere. This gave Deere the opportunity to fill the vacuum in the marketplace.

Moreover, in an attempt to avert a price war, Rosso waited a full year after the merger was announced to counter Deere's equipment price reductions. Deere seized this opportunity with a marketing campaign directed at Case and New Holland's current customers. Deere offered them low interest rates to finance their equipment purchases plus $5,000 in cash if they swapped their current agricultural machinery for new Deere equipment.

Integration Efforts Continue at a Snail's Pace

Rosso stepped aside as CEO to Paolo Monferino in November 2000 but retained his position as president of CNH. Monferino initiated a program that resulted in CNH continuing to operate Case and New Holland dealerships separately. CNH combined assembly at a single plant for each product line, building Case and New Holland equipment on common platforms. This was expected to reduce operating expense and to help trim its 31,000 workforce worldwide while enhancing its ability to wring cost savings from suppliers. CNH expected to realize annual savings of about $600 million by 2004. Moreover, it attempted to counter Deere's incentive program with one of its own (*Business Week*, February 5, 2001).

Assuming the current integration plans remained on schedule, the elapsed time to complete the integration of the Case and New Holland operations would be 4 years. Despite this lengthy delay, no one seemed to be worried. Despite the deterioration in CNH's overall competitive position, Fiat, which owns 84% of CNH, said it would guarantee CNH's debt through at least 2003 and continued to support CNH management. The risk is that the longer the integration takes to complete, the greater the loss of market share to Deere, which has continued to aggressively roll out new products. As a sign of how painful the integration could be, CNH was laying workers off as Deere was hiring to keep up with the strong demand for its products. Deere also appeared to be ahead in moving toward common global platforms and parts to take fuller advantage of economies of scale.

Case Study Discussion Questions

1. Why is rapid integration important? Illustrate with examples from the case study.
2. What could CNH have done differently to slow or reverse its loss of market share?
3. How did Fiat aid and abet CNH's management negligence?

Acquisition-Related Customer Attrition

During normal operations, businesses can expect a certain level of churn in their customer list. Depending on the industry, normal churn as a result of competitive conditions can be anywhere from 20–40%. A newly merged company will experience a loss of another 5–10% of its existing customers as a direct result of the merger (Down, 1995). The loss of customers may reflect uncertainty about on-time delivery and product quality as well as more aggressive pricing by competitors following the merger. Moreover, many companies lose revenue momentum as they concentrate on realizing expected cost synergies.

The loss of customers may continue well after closing. A McKinsey study of 160 acquisitions by 157 publicly traded firms in 11 different industries in 1995 and 1996 found that on average these firms grew 4 percentage points less than their peers during the 3 years following closing. Moreover, 42% of the sample actually lost ground. It is interesting that the size and experience of the acquiring firm did not seem to matter. Only 12% of the sample showed revenue growth significantly ahead of their peers (Bekier, Bogardus, and Oldham, 2001).

Meeting Commitments to Current Customers

The buyer always should be aware of the set of explicit (contractual) or implicit (handshake) agreements that the target company has made to its customers. To fulfill commitments to wholesalers and distributors, the integration team needs to review all of the legal agreements the new company has inherited from the target company. In fulfilling commitments to customers buying directly or indirectly, the new company must be aware of promises, such as slogans used in advertising or product warranties, the target company has made publicly. Current customers are often worth more than new ones because the cost of maintaining an existing relationship is usually less expensive than acquiring a new one. This is recognized in the process of allocating purchase price to customer lists. Customers with a known value and life, usually those with contracts, receive a much larger allocation than the assignment of value to future customer relationships.

Suppliers: Develop Long-Term Vendor Relationships

Just as a current customer is often worth more than a new one, a current supplier with a proven track record also may be worth more than a new one. It is a buyer's market following an acquisition, so the new company should approach its suppliers carefully. Although substantial cost savings are possible by "managing" suppliers, the new company should be seeking a long-term relationship rather than simply a way to reduce costs. Suppliers should be viewed as partners rather than adversaries. Aggressive negotiation can get high-quality products and services at lower prices in the short run, but it may be transitory if the new company is a large customer of the supplier and if the supplier's margins are squeezed continuously. The supplier's product or service quality will suffer, and the supplier eventually may exit the business. Ways to effectively manage the supply chain following an acquisition will be discussed later in this chapter.

Investors: Maintain Shareholder Loyalty

The new firm must be able to present a compelling vision of the future to investors. In a share-for-share exchange, there are compelling reasons for appealing to current investors of both the acquirer and target companies. Target shareholders will become shareholders in the newly formed company. Loyal shareholders tend to provide a more stable ownership base, and they may contribute to lower share price volatility.

All firms attract particular types of investors—some with a preference for high dividends and others for capital gains. The acquisition of Time Warner by America Online in January 2000 illustrated the potential clash between investor preferences. The combined market value of the two firms lost 11% in the 4 days following the announcement, as investors puzzled over what had been created. The selling frenzy following the announcement may have involved different groups of investors who bought Time Warner for its stable growth and American Online for its meteoric growth rate of 70% per annum. The new company may not have met the expectations of either group.

Communities: Build Strong, Credible Relationships

Companies should communicate plans to build or keep plants, stores, or office buildings in a community as soon as they can be confident that these actions will be implemented. These pronouncements translate readily into new jobs and increased taxes for the community. Good working relations with surrounding communities are simply good public relations. A community that views a firm as a partner is more prone to making changes in zoning restrictions and in offering tax incentives. However, the company must be prepared to satisfy commitments to invest in the community. It is ethically correct and ensures that the company will not be subject to lawsuits by communities seeking to recover any expenses they incurred in demolishing and clearing sites on behalf of the firm.

CREATING A NEW ORGANIZATION

Business Needs Drive Structure

Organization or structure traditionally is defined in terms of titles and reporting relationships. For the purpose of this chapter, we will follow this definition. A properly structured organization should support, not retard, the acceptance of a culture in the new company that is desired by top management. An effective starting point in setting up a structure is to learn from the past and to recognize that the needs of the business drive structure and not the other way around.

Learn from the Past

Building new reporting structures for combining companies requires knowledge of the target company's prior organization, some sense as to the effectiveness of this organization in the decision-making process, and the future business needs of the newly combined companies. Therefore, in creating the new organization, it is necessary to start with previous organization charts. They provide insights into how individuals from both the target and acquiring companies will interact within the new company because they reveal the past experience and future expectations of individuals with regard to reporting relationships.

Structure Facilitates Decision Making, Provides Internal Controls, and Promotes Behaviors

The next step is to move beyond the past and into the future by creating a structure that focuses on meeting the business needs of the combined companies rather than attempting to make everyone happy. All corporations require some degree of structure to facilitate decision making, provide internal controls, and promote behaviors consistent with the mission and principles of the new company. Often, acquiring companies simply impose their reporting structures on the target company. This is particularly true if the acquirer is much larger than the target. By ignoring the target's existing organizational structure, the acquiring company is in effect ignoring the expectations of the target's employees. Unfulfilled expectations will demotivate target company employees. No structure guarantees behavior; it only makes it easier or more difficult to get things accomplished (Lajoux, 1998, pp. 175–214).

Basic Organizational Structures

There are three basic types of structures: functional, product or service, and divisional. The functional tends to be the most centralized, and the divisional tends to be the most decentralized.

In a functional organization, people are assigned to specific groups or departments such as accounting, engineering, marketing, sales, distribution, customer service, manufacturing, or maintenance. This type of structure tends to be highly centralized and is becoming less common. In a product or service organization, functional specialists are grouped by product line or service offering. Each product line or service offering has its own accounting, human resources, sales, marketing, customer service, and product development staffs. These types of organizations tend to be somewhat decentralized. Individuals in these types of organizations often have multiple reporting relationships, such as a finance manager reporting to a product line manager and the firm's CFO. Divisional organizations continue to be the dominant form of organizational structure, in which groups of products are combined into independent divisions or "strategic business units." Such organizations have their own management teams and tend to be highly decentralized. Divisional structures may be the most complex of the various types of structures, with product–service line or functional organizational structures often existing within each division. Divisional structures often are used in this manner because each division can stand alone while containing other types of organizational structures (A. T. Kearney Inc., 1998).

Decentralized versus Centralized Structures

The popularity of decentralized versus centralized management structures varies with the state of the economy. During recessions when top management is under great pressure to cut costs, companies often tend to move toward centralized management structures, only to decentralize when the economy recovers. Highly decentralized authority can retard the pace of integration because there is no single authority to resolve issues or determine policies. In contrast, a centralized structure may make postmerger integration much easier. Senior management can dictate policies governing all aspects of the combined companies, centralize all types of functions providing support to operating units, and resolve issues among the various operating units.

Although centralized control does provide significant advantages during postmerger integration, it also can be highly detrimental if the policies imposed by the central headquarters are simply not appropriate for the operating units. Highly centralized parent company management may destroy value by imposing too many rigid controls, by focusing on the wrong issues, by hiring or promoting the wrong managers, or by monitoring the wrong performance measures. Moreover, highly centralized parent companies often have multiple layers of management to link multiple operating units and centralized functions providing services to the operating units. The parent companies pass the costs of centralized management and support services on to the operating units. There are a number of studies that suggest that the costs of this type of structure outweigh the benefits (Alexander, Campbell, and Gould, 1995; Campbell, Sadler, and Koch, 1997; Chakrabarti, 1990).

The right structure may be an evolving one. The substantial benefits of a well-managed, rapid integration of the two businesses suggest a centralized management structure initially with relatively few layers of management. This does not mean that all integration activities should be driven from the top without any input from middle managers and supervisors of both companies. It does mean taking decisive and timely action based on the best information available. Once the integration is viewed as relatively complete, the new company should move to a more decentralized structure in view of the well-documented explicit and implicit costs of centralized corporate organizations.

Integrating Corporate Structures: Balance Need for Control with Need for Flexibility

A corporate hierarchy often is associated with slow decision making and unfair pay scales. During the 1990s, companies modified corporate hierarchies to reflect different levels of business rather than management. At the corporate level, managers set strategy and determine corporate policies; managers at the business-unit level focus on strategy execution. Finally, within each business unit, work teams focus on improving efficiency, product quality, and customer service.

Merging Corporate Boards: Outsiders Improve Effectiveness

Mergers can have significant effects on the boards of the two companies. What happens depends largely on the type of transaction. In a merger of companies of comparable size, often referred to as a merger of equals, the members of both boards are merged into the board of the newly formed company. Downsizing the board comes through attrition, retirement policies, and director term limits. In some cases, a planned reduction in the size of the board of the combined company is made part of the merger agreement. In a merger in which the participants are markedly different in terms of size, the smaller company's board will generally not be included in the new company's board if the acquired company is to be fully integrated into the acquirer. However, if the acquired company is to be operated as a subsidiary of the parent, its board may remain in place.

Incumbent board members may be encouraged to leave to achieve an appropriate size or to make room for new directors with the desired skills and experience to improve the board's effectiveness. A poll of 99 representatives from the largest pension funds and money managers in the United States determined that the attributes of an effective corporate board included quality, independence, and accountability (*Business Week*, 2000). Respondents indicated that the quality of a board should be measured by the extent to which board meetings included open discussion among members who truly understood the issues being addressed. Independence was measured by a virtual absence of members who were close associates of the CEO. Respondents indicated that key committees, such as audit and compensation, should include only "outside directors." Finally, accountability reflected the extent to which board members held significant equity positions in the company and were willing to challenge the CEO about the company's underperformance.

Integrating Senior Management

A review of the historical performance of both companies and their respective organizations by the MIT will provide crucial insight into the selection of the best candidates for senior management positions in the new company. An external facilitator may be used to break deadlocks. The team should agree on the new strategy for the combined companies and subsequently select people who are best suited to implement this strategy.

Integrating Middle Management

Once senior managers have been selected, they should be given full responsibility for selecting their direct reports. As is true for senior managers, jobs for middle-level and supervisory positions should go to those with the superior integration skills.

DEVELOPING STAFFING PLANS

Staffing plans should be formulated as soon as possible in the integration process. In friendly acquisitions, the process should begin before closing. The early development of such plans provides an opportunity to include the key personnel from both firms in the integration effort. Other benefits from early planning include the increased likelihood of retaining those with key skills and talents, maintaining corporate continuity, and team building. Figure 6-2 describes the logical sequencing of staffing plans and the major issues addressed in each segment.

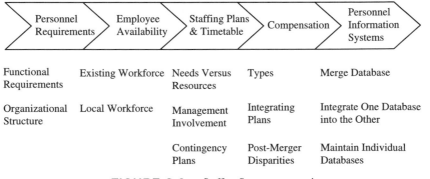

FIGURE 6-2.   Staffing Strategy sequencing.

Personnel Requirements

The appropriate organizational structure is one able to meet the current functional requirements or needs of the business and flexible enough to be expanded to satisfy future business requirements. The process for creating such a structure should involve input from all levels of management, should be consistent with the combined firm's business strategy, and should reflect expected sales growth.

Functional Requirements

Before establishing the organizational structure, the integration team should agree on what specific functions are needed to run the combined businesses. These discussions should reflect a clear understanding of the specific roles and responsibilities of each function.

Organizational Structure

Once the necessary functions have been identified, the effort to project personnel requirements by function should start with each functional department describing the ideal structure to meet the roles and responsibilities assigned by senior management. By asking for department input, department personnel are involved in the process, can communicate useful insights, and can contribute to the creation of a consensus for changing the organization.

Employee Availability

Availability refers to the number of each type of employee required by the new organization that can be identified in the new company's existing workforce and in the local communities in which the new company has operations. The skills of the existing workforce should be documented and compared with the current and future functional requirements of the new company. An examination of the current workforce also should involve a demographic profile in terms of sex and ethnic makeup to ensure that the new organization is in compliance with prevailing regulations. The local labor pool can be used to augment the existing workforce. These workers represent potential new hires for the combined firms. Data should be collected on the educational levels, skills, and demographic composition of the local workforce, as well as prevailing wage rates by skill category.

Staffing Plans and Timetable

Following the determination of the appropriate organizational structure and the pool of current and potential employees available to staff the new organization, a detailed staffing plan can be developed.

Staffing Needs versus Employee Availability

By matching the number of workers and skills required to support current and future business requirements with the current workforce, gaps in the firm's workforce needing to be filled from recruiting outside the company can be readily identified. The effort to recruit externally should be tempered by its potentially adverse impact on current employee morale. The filling of gaps should be prioritized and phased in over time in recognition of the time required to fill certain types of positions and the impact of major hiring programs on local wage rates in communities with relatively small labor pools.

Management Involvement

Once management positions have been filled, the managers should be enlisted to interview, evaluate, and select new employees to fill job openings in their departments and operations. Senior management should stress that filling job openings should be given top priority, particularly when the skills required are crucial to successfully completing the integration of the acquired business. During the integration period, managers are under the enormous stress of having to continue to conduct normal business operations as well as to integrate portions of the acquired business. In view of the increased workload, it is common for managers to defer the time-consuming hiring process by assuming multiple responsibilities. This hurts the manager's morale and health and the completion of the integration process because many of these managers are insufficiently trained to handle many responsibilities they assumed.

Contingency Plans

As noted previously, key employees inevitably will be lost to the new company. Other employees should be trained to fill positions considered critical to the long-term viability of the organization. This can be accomplished by developing job descriptions that clearly identify the skills required to fill the position and then by cross-training other workers in the position.

Compensation

Merging compensation plans can be one of the most challenging activities of the integration process. Such activities must be conducted in compliance with prevailing regulations and with a high degree of sensitivity.

Types of Compensation

Total compensation consists of base pay, bonuses or incentive plans, benefits, and special contractual agreements. Bonus or incentive pay is compensation designed to encourage employees to meet predetermined performance targets. Bonuses may take the form of a lump sum of cash or stock paid to an employee for meeting or exceeding these targets. Special contractual agreements may consist of noncompete agreements in which key employees, in exchange for an agreed on amount of compensation, sign agreements not to compete against the newly formed company if they should leave . Special agreements also may take the form of golden parachutes for senior management the new firm wishes to retain and severance agreements to compensate employees in the event of job loss. Finally, retention bonuses often are given to employees if they agree to stay with the new company for a specific time period.

Integrating Compensation Plans

The extent to which compensation plans are integrated depends on whether the two companies are going to be managed separately or integrated. Financial acquirers may be intent on reselling the acquired business in a few years; as such, they may choose to keep compensation plans separate. The strategic acquirer also may keep the plans separate especially if it is moving into an industry in which compensation differs from that prevailing in its current industry. In instances in which the parent chooses to combine plans, the design of the new plan generally is done in consultation with the acquired unit's management. The parent will set guidelines, such as how much stock senior executives should own (e.g., a percentage of base pay) and how managers will receive the stock (e.g., whether they will be awarded stock or will have to buy it at a discount from its current market price). The parent also will set guidelines for base pay. For example, the parent may decide that base pay will be at market, below market, or above market adjusted for regional differences in the cost of living. Moreover, the parent may also decide on how bonuses will be paid, and the operating unit will determine who receives them. Finally, the parent will determine the benefits policy and plans. Such plans normally require specialized expertise to administer and must be in compliance with the prevailing regulations.

Postmerger Disparities

Base pay for employees may differ by geographic area and industry for similar jobs. Bonuses may differ widely for firms acquired in different industries. In recent years, commercial banks have acquired investment banks and brokerage firms where bonuses may be four or five times base salary levels. Bonuses also may be linked to different performance measures, such as sales and market share for high-growth subsidiaries, and to operating profit or cash flow for mature businesses. Benefits also may differ for acquired firms in different industries to reflect the incentives required to attract and to retain employees in that industry.

Personnel Information Systems

The acquiring company may choose to merge all personnel data into a new database, to merge one corporate database into another, or to maintain the personnel databases of each business. A single database enables authorized users to more readily access employee data, to more efficiently plan for future staffing requirements, and to conduct analyses and print reports. Maintenance expense associated with a single database also may be lower. The decision to keep personnel databases separate may reflect plans to divest the unit at some time in the future.

FUNCTIONAL INTEGRATION

Previous activities within the integration process dealt primarily with planning for the actual integration of the acquired business into the acquirer's business. Functional integration refers to the actual execution of the plans.

The first consideration of the MIT is to determine the extent to which the two companies' operations and support staffs are to be centralized or decentralized. The main areas of focus should be information technology (IT), manufacturing operations, sales, marketing, finance, purchasing, R&D, and the requirements to staff these functions. However, before any actual integration takes place, it is crucial to revalidate data collected during due diligence and to benchmark all operations by comparing them to industry standards, whenever available.

Due Diligence Data Revalidation: Verify Assumptions

Data collected during due diligence should be revalidated immediately after closing. In theory, this should not be necessary if a thorough due diligence is conducted. In practice, it is highly unlikely that the necessary in-depth analyses actually were completed. The pressure exerted by both the buyer and the seller to complete the transaction often results in a haphazard preclosing review. For example, in an effort to compress the time devoted to due diligence, sellers often allow buyers access to senior managers only. Middle-level managers, supervisory personnel, and equipment operators often are excluded from the interview process. For similar reasons, site visits by the buyer often are limited to only those with the largest concentrations of employees, thus ignoring the risks and opportunities that might exist at sites not visited. The buyer's legal and financial reviews normally are conducted only on the largest customer and supplier contracts, promissory notes, and operating and capital leases. Receivables are evaluated and physical inventory is counted using sampling techniques. The effort to determine if intellectual property has been properly protected, with key trademarks or service marks properly registered and copyrights and patents filed, is often spotty.

Although some of these exposures can be limited by including the appropriate "reps and warranties" in the agreement of purchase and sale, buyer efforts to recover damages as a result of breaches of contract may require extended and expensive legal battles. Moreover, an abbreviated due diligence also limits the opportunity to understand the potential synergies between the two businesses and the actual cost of integrating the acquired business. Exxon's merger with Mobil demonstrates how revalidation of earlier due diligence findings resulted in an approximate 26% upward revision in expected pretax cost savings as a result of personnel reductions (Case Study 6-3). In contrast, Albertson's acquisition of American Stores shows the downside of inadequate due diligence, which resulted in seriously underestimating actual integration costs (Case Study 6-4).

CASE STUDY 6-3: EXXON-MOBIL—
A STUDY IN COST CUTTING

Having obtained access to more detailed information following consummation of the merger, Exxon-Mobil announced dramatic revisions in its estimates of cost savings. The world's largest publicly owned oil company would cut almost 16,000 jobs by the end of 2002 (Bloomberg.com, December 16, 1999). This was an increase from the 9000 cuts estimated when the merger was first announced in December 1998. Of the total, 6000 would come from early retirement. Estimated annual savings are expected to reach $3.8 billion by 2003, up by more than $1 billion from when the merger originally was announced.

As time passed, the Exxon-Mobil merger looked more and more like the proverbial marriage made in heaven. The companies seemed to have become a highly focused, smooth-running machine remarkably efficient at discovering, refining, and marketing oil and gas. An indication of this is the fact that the firm spent less per barrel to find oil and gas in 2000 than at almost any time in history. With revenues of $210 billion, Exxon-Mobil surged to the top of the Fortune 500 in 2000 (Taylor, 2001).

Case Study Discussion Question

1. In your judgment, are acquirers more likely to under- or overestimate anticipated cost savings? Explain your answer.

CASE STUDY 6-4: ALBERTSON'S ACQUIRES
AMERICAN STORES—UNDERESTIMATING
THE COSTS OF INTEGRATION

In 1999, Albertson's acquired American Stores for $12.5 billion, making it the nation's second largest supermarket chain, with more than 1000 stores. The corporate marriage stumbled almost immediately. Escalating integration costs resulted in a sharp downward revision of its fiscal year 2000 profits. In the quarter ended October 28, 1999, operating profits fell 15% to $185 million, despite an increase in sales of 1.6% to $8.98 billion. Albertson proceeded to update the Lucky supermarket stores that it had acquired in California and to combine the distribution operations of the two supermarket chains. It appears that Albertson's substantially underestimated the complexity of integrating an acquisition of this magnitude. Albertson's spent about $90 million before taxes to convert more than 400 stores to its information and distribution systems as well as to change the name to Albertson's.

Albertson's share price fell 11% following the announcement of the lower earnings outlook, its biggest 1-day drop in more than 3 years. By the end of 1999, Albertson's stock had lost more than one-half of its value (Bloomberg.com, November 1, 1999).

Case Study Discussion Questions

1. In your judgment, do you think acquirers' commonly understate integration costs? Why or why not?
2. Cite examples of expenses you believe are commonly incurred in integrating target companies.

Performance Benchmarking

Benchmarking important functions such as the acquirer's and the target's manufacturing and IT operations and processes is a useful starting point for determining how to integrate these activities. Standard benchmarks include the International Standards Organization's (ISO) 9000 Quality Systems-Model for Quality Assurance in Design, Development, Production, Installation, and Servicing. The ISO is a worldwide standard-setting organization that has achieved global acceptance in a variety of industries. Other benchmarks that can be used include the U.S. Food and Drug Administration's Good Manufacturing Practices and the Department of Commerce's Malcolm Baldridge Award. Sanderson and Uzumeri (1997, p. 135) provide a comprehensive list of standards-setting organizations.

Manufacturing and Operations

The data revalidation process for integrating and rationalizing facilities and operations requires in-depth discussions with key target company personnel and on-site visits to all facilities. The objective should be to reevaluate overall capacity, the potential for future cost reductions, the age and condition of facilities, adequacy of maintenance budgets, and compliance with environmental laws. Careful consideration should be given to manufacturing capabilities that duplicate those of the acquirer. The integration team also needs to determine if the duplicate facilities are potentially more efficient than those of the buyer. As part of the benchmarking process, the operations of both the acquirer and the target company should be compared with industry standards to properly evaluate their efficiency.

Manufacturing Processes

Process effectiveness is an accurate indicator of overall operational efficiency (Porter and Wood, 1998). The four processes that should be examined include planning, materials ordering, order entry, and quality control. For example, production planning is often a very inaccurate exercise, particularly when the operations are relatively inflexible and require long-term forecasts of sales. The production planning and materials ordering functions need to work closely together because the quantity and composition of the materials ordered depends on the accuracy of sales projections. Inaccurate projections result in shortages or costly excess inventory accumulation.

The order entry activity may offer significant opportunities for cost savings. Companies building to stock and subsequently satisfying orders from finished product inventories frequently have huge working capital requirements. For this reason, companies such as personal computer manufacturers are building inventory according to orders received to minimize finished product inventories. A key indicator of the effectiveness of quality control is the percentage of products that go through the manufacturing process without being inspected. Companies whose "first run yield" is in the 70–80% range may have serious quality problems.

Facility Consolidation

Plant consolidation starts with the adoption of a common set of systems and standards for all manufacturing activities. Such standards include cycle time between production runs, cost per unit of output, first-run yield, and scrap rates. Links between the different facilities then are created by sharing information management and processing systems, inventory control, supplier relationships, and transportation links. Vertical integration can be achieved by focusing on different stages of production. Different facilities specialize in the production of selected components, which then are shipped to other facilities to assemble the finished product. Finally, a company may close certain facilities whenever there is excess capacity.

Information Technology

IT spending constitutes an ever-increasing share of most businesses' budgets. In view of this trend, it is crucial that IT operations be monitored not only by technical people but also by general managers. Studies have shown that about 80% of software projects have failed to meet their performance expectations or deadlines (*Financial Times*, 1996). Almost one-half are scrapped before they are completed, and about one-half cost two or three times their original budgets and take three times as long as expected to complete (*Wall Street Journal*, November 18, 1996). Studies conclude that managers tend to focus too much on technology and not enough on the people and processes that will use it. If the buyer intends to operate the target company independently, the information systems of the two companies may be kept separate as long as communications links between the two companies' systems can be established. However, if the buyer intends to integrate the target, the process can be daunting. To implement full integration, the new IT systems usually must be combined into a new operation. Studies show that nearly 70% of buyers choose to combine their information systems immediately after closing. Almost 90% of acquirers eventually combine these operations (Cossey, 1991).

Finance

Some target companies will be operated as standalone operations, whereas others will be completely merged with the acquirer's existing business. Many international acquisitions involve companies in areas that are geographically remote from the parent company and operate largely independently from the parent. Such situations require a great deal of effort to ensure that the buyer can monitor the financial results of the new business's operations from a distance, even if the parent has its representative permanently on site. This monitoring requires reliable financial reporting.

Implementing Internal Controls and Financial Reporting

The acquirer should establish a budgeting process and signature approval levels to control spending. Signing authority levels refer to levels of expenditures that must be approved in writing by a designated manager. The magnitude of approval levels will vary by the size of the firm. At a minimum, the budget should require projections of monthly cash inflows and outflows for the coming year. The budget projection will be used to monitor the firm's actual progress against forecast.

Implementing External Financial Reporting

In the United States, certain companies must file annual and quarterly reports with the Securities and Exchange Commission (see Chapter 2). These reports include balance sheets as of the end of the most recent and prior fiscal years. Comparative income statements and statements of cash flows must be included for the most recent and preceding 2 fiscal years. Notes to the financial statements are required for the most recent 2 fiscal years. Although annual financial statements must be audited, quarterly statements need not be. Returns must be filed annually with the Internal Revenue Service and in compliance with the rules and regulations included in the Internal Revenue Code.

Sales: It Is Often Hard to Teach an Old Dog New Tricks

The extent to which the sales forces of the two firms are combined depends on their relative size, the nature of their products and markets, and their geographic location. Based on these considerations, the sales forces may be wholly integrated or operated separately. A relatively small sales force may be readily combined with the larger sales force if the products they sell and the markets they serve are sufficiently similar. In contrast, the sales forces may be kept separate if the products they sell require in-depth understanding of the customers' needs and a detailed knowledge of the product. For example, firms using the "consultative selling" approach employ highly trained specialists to advise current or potential customers on how the firm's product and service offering can be used to solve particular customer problems. Consequently, a firm may have a separate sales force for each product or service sold to specific markets. Sales forces in globally dispersed businesses often are kept separate to reflect the uniqueness of their markets except for certain support activities such as training or technical support. These activities often are centralized and used to support sales forces in several different countries. Geographically dispersed sales forces may be linked by reporting relationships to regional or other centralized sales management structures.

The benefits of integrating sales forces include significant cost savings by eliminating duplicate sales representatives and related support expenses such as travel and entertainment expenses, training, and management. A single sales force also may minimize potential confusion by enabling customers to deal with a single sales representative in the purchase of multiple products and services. Moreover, an integrated sales force may facilitate product cross-selling (i.e., the sale of one firm's products to the other firm's customers).

Marketing: Avoid Brand Confusion

Enabling the customer to see a consistent image in advertising and promotional campaigns is often the greatest challenge facing the integration of the marketing function. For example, the acquired company may be offering an explicit or implied warranty that the acquirer finds unacceptable. However, ensuring consistency should not result in confusing the customer by radically changing a product's image or how it is sold.

The location and degree of integration of the marketing function depends on the global nature of the business, the diversity or uniqueness of product lines, and the pace of change in the marketplace. A business with operations worldwide often is inclined to decentralize marketing to the local countries to increase awareness of local laws and cultural patterns. Companies with a large number of product lines, which can be grouped into logical categories or which require extensive product knowledge, may opt to disperse the marketing function to the various operating units. Finally, if the market for a product or set of products is changing rapidly, it is crucial that the marketing function be kept as close to the customer as possible. This expedites the inclusion of changing customer requirements into product development cycles and changes in the advertising and promotional campaigns needed to support the sale of these products.

Purchasing

According to an analysis of 50 M&As, managing the merged firm's purchasing function efficiently can reduce the total cost of goods and services purchased by merged companies by 10–15%. Companies in this sample have been able to recover at least half of the premium paid for the target company by moving aggressively to manage their purchasing activities (Chapman, Dempsey, Ramsdell, and Bell, 1998). For firms in this sample, purchased goods and services, including office furniture, raw materials, and outside contractors, constituted up to 75% of the firms' total spending.

The opportunity to reap substantial savings from suppliers comes immediately following closing of the transaction. A merger creates uncertainty among both companies' suppliers, particularly if they might have to compete against each other for business with the combined firms. Many will offer cost savings and new partnership arrangements, given the merged organization's greater bargaining power to renegotiate contracts. The newly combined company may choose to realize savings by reducing the number of suppliers. The first step is for both the acquirer and the acquired company to identify their critical suppliers. This should have been done as part of the premerger due diligence. The list should be kept relatively short. The focus should be on those accounting for the largest share of purchased materials expenses. These suppliers should be subject to a certification program, which companies use to approve suppliers.

Research and Development

The role of R&D is an extremely important source of value in many M&As. Often the buyer's and seller's organizations are either working on duplicate projects or projects not germane to the buyer's long-term strategy. Consequently, such activities need to be rationalized. The integration team responsible for managing the integration of R&D activities needs to define future areas of R&D collaboration and set priorities for future R&D research subject to senior management approval.

Barriers to R&D integration include the differing research time frames of different projects and of the personnel involved in conducting research. For example, some scientists and engineers may feel that their current projects require at least 10 years of continuing research, whereas others are looking for results in a much shorter time frame. Another obstacle is that some personnel stand to lose in terms of titles, prestige, and power if they collaborate. Finally, the acquirer's and the target's R&D financial return expectations may be different. The acquirer may wish to give R&D a higher or lower priority in the combined operation of the two companies. A starting point for integrating R&D is to have researchers from both companies make presentations of their work to each other, meet with each other, and co-locate. Work teams also can follow a balanced scorecard approach for obtaining funding for their projects. In this process, R&D projects are scored according to their impact on key stakeholders, such as shareholders and customers. Those projects receiving the highest scores are funded, and others are deferred or eliminated.

Human Resources

Traditionally, HR departments have been highly centralized and have been responsible for conducting opinion surveys, assessing managerial effectiveness, developing hiring and staffing plans, and providing training. HR departments are often instrumental in conducting strategic reviews of the strengths and weaknesses of potential target companies, integrating the acquirer's and target's management teams, recommending and implementing pay and benefit plans, and disseminating information about acquisitions. More recently, the trend has been to disperse the HR function to the operating unit. Highly centralized HR functions have been found to be very expensive and not responsive to the local needs of the operating units. Hiring and training often can be more effectively done at the operating unit level. Most of the traditional HR activities are conducted at the operating units with the exception of the administration of benefit plans, management of HR information systems, and in some cases organizational development (Porter & Wood, 1998).

INTEGRATING CORPORATE CULTURES

Culture refers to a common set of values, traditions, and beliefs that influence behavior. Large, diverse businesses have an overarching culture and a series of subcultures that reflect local conditions. When two companies with different cultures merge, the newly formed company will take on a new culture that may be quite different from either the acquirer's or the target's culture. Cultural differences are not inherently bad or good. They can instill creativity in the new company or create a contentious environment.

Cultural Issues

Cultural issues can run the gamut from dress codes to compensation. They differ by size and maturity of the company, by industry, and by geographic location. Maturity is defined by the number of years in business.

Company Size and Maturity

Start-up companies are usually highly unstructured and informal in terms of dress and decision making. Compensation may consist largely of stock options and other forms of deferred income. Benefits, beyond those required by state and federal law, and other "perks," such as company cars, are largely nonexistent. Company policies are frequently either nonexistent, not in writing, or made up as needed. Internal controls covering items such as employee expense accounts are often minimal. In contrast, larger, mature companies are frequently more highly structured with well-defined internal controls, compensation structures, benefits packages, and employment policies. Such firms have grown too large and complex to function in an orderly manner without some structure in the form of internal policies and controls. Employees usually have clearly defined job descriptions and career paths. Decision making can be either decentralized at the operating unit level or centralized within a corporate office. In either case, the process for decision making often is well defined. Decision making may be ponderous, requiring consensus within a large management bureaucracy.

Industry Differences

Industry and geographic differences create another set of challenges. High-technology companies, no matter what the size, are often far more informal in terms of dress codes and working hours. In contrast, companies dealing directly with the public, such as banks and retailers, often have formal dress codes and require a high level of decorum to instill a sense of confidence and trust in the public.

International Considerations

Language barriers and different customs, working conditions, work ethics, and legal structures create an entirely new set of challenges in integrating cross-border transactions. If cultures are extremely different, integration may be inappropriate. For this reason, acquiring and acquired companies in international transactions frequently maintain separate corporate headquarters, stock listings, and CEOs for an extended period (*Wall Street Journal*, September 26, 1996).

In choosing how to manage the new acquisition, a manager with an in-depth knowledge of the acquirer's priorities, decision-making processes, and operations is appropriate in entering a new country where the acquirer expects to make very large new investments. However, when the acquirer already has existing operations within the country, a manager with substantial industry experience in the country is generally preferable because of their cultural sensitivity and knowledge of local laws and regulations. Local managers are especially helpful when foreign customer requirements are substantially different from domestic customers or when all production is done within the foreign country.

Case Study 6-5 illustrates how the acquirer's sensitivity to potential cultural conflicts helps maintain the value of the target company. Note how Allianz AG attempted to minimize cultural conflict by keeping Pimco's operations largely intact and allowing a high level of local autonomy. Allianz recognized that the real value in this acquisition is in the expertise and reputation of Pimco's money managers. To retain key personnel, Allianz offered operational independence, employment contracts, and very lucrative deferred compensation packages. Allianz also recognized that the highly successful portfolio management techniques used by Pimco's money managers could best be applied to managing customer accounts in Europe by transferring selected Pimco personnel to their European operations.

CASE STUDY 6-5: OVERCOMING CULTURE CLASH—ALLIANZ AG BUYS PIMCO ADVISORS LP

On November 7, 1999, Allianz AG, the leading German insurance conglomerate, acquired Pimco Advisors LP for $3.3 billion. The Pimco acquisition boosts assets under management at Allianz from $400 billion to $650 billion, making it the sixth largest money manager in the world. The acquisition gives the firm the critical mass to compete against Citigroup, Axa, and other financial service giants. The transaction also gives Allianz a foothold in the U.S. money management business to help offset fluctuations in Allianz's income generated in other geographic areas.

The cultural divide separating the two firms represented a potentially daunting challenge. Allianz's management was well aware that firms distracted by culture clashes and the morale problems and mistrust they breed are less likely to realize the synergies and savings that caused them to acquire the company in the first place. Allianz was acutely aware of the potential problems as a result of difficulties they had experienced following the acquisition of Firemen's Fund, a major U.S.-based property–casualty company. A major motivation for the acquisition was to obtain the well-known skills of the elite Pimco money managers to broaden Allianz's financial services product offering.

Although retention bonuses can buy loyalty in the short run, employees of the acquired firm need much more than money in the long term. Pimco's money managers stated publicly that they wanted Allianz to let them operate independently, the way Pimco existed under their former parent, Pacific Mutual Life Insurance Company. Allianz had decided not only to run Pimco as an independent subsidiary but also to move $100 billion of Allianz's assets to Pimco. Bill Gross, Pimco's legendary bond trader, and other top Pimco money managers now collect about one-fourth of their compensation in the form of Allianz stock. Moreover, most of the top managers have been asked to sign long-term employment contracts and have received retention bonuses.

Historically, Pimco's bond fund managers have outperformed their counterparts both in the United States and Europe. Allianz wanted to spread these skills throughout the Allianz organization. To achieve this objective, several top investment managers at Pimco were transferred from Orange County, California, to Germany to teach Allianz their money-management techniques.

Joachim Faber, chief of money management at Allianz, played an essential role in smoothing over cultural differences. Led by Faber, top Allianz executives had been visiting Pimco for months and having quiet dinners with top Pimco fixed income investment officials and their families. The intent of these intimate meetings was to reassure these officials that their operation would remain independent under Allianz's ownership. The perceived value in this merger is clearly the acquisition of investment talent. Faber noted, "There's not one penny of savings from synergies in this deal" (Lansner, 1999).

Case Study Discussion Questions

1. How did Allianz attempt to retain key employees? In the short run? In the long run?
2. How did the potential for culture clash affect the way Alliance acquired Pimco?

Characteristics of the New Corporate Culture

When two separate corporate cultures combine, it is crucial to realize from the outset that the combined companies will create a new culture that in some respects may be distinctly different from the two previous cultures. Moreover, it may be impossible to predict the distinguishing features of the new culture. In general, cultural issues are going to be less in mergers taking place between companies in the same industry (except perhaps for firms that had been virulent competitors) and of comparable size than in cross-industry or cross-border transactions or those involving companies substantially different in size and maturity. Because a company's culture is something that evolves over a long time, it is wishful thinking that changing the culture can be managed carefully. A more realistic expectation is that employees in the new company can be encouraged to take on a shared vision, set of core values, and behaviors deemed important by senior management. However, getting to the point at which employees wholly embrace management's desired culture may take years and may be unachievable in practice. What follows is a process intended to expedite the acceptance of the desired vision, values, and behaviors by the new corporate culture.

Cultural Profiling

The first step in integrating cultures is to develop a cultural profile of both the acquirer and the acquired companies. The information may be obtained from employee surveys and interviews and by observing management styles and practices in both companies. The information then is used to show how the two cultures are alike or different and what are the comparative strengths and weaknesses of each culture. Common differences may include having one culture value individualism and the other value teamwork. Following a review of this information, senior management must decide those characteristics of both cultures that should be emphasized in the new business's culture.

Techniques for Integrating Corporate Cultures

Sharing common goals, standards, services, and space can be a highly effective and practical way to integrate disparate cultures (Lajoux, 1998, pp. 187–191; Malekzadeh and Nahavandi, 1990).

Shared Goals

Common goals serve to drive different units to cooperate. For example, at the functional level, setting exact timetables and procedures for new product development can drive the different units of the organization to work together as project teams to launch the product by the target date. At the corporate level, a multiyear plan to improve the stock price can drive collective performance for the duration of the plan. Although it is helpful in the integration process to have shared or common goals, individuals still must have specific goals to minimize the tendency of some to underperform while benefiting from the collective labors of others.

Shared Standards

Shared standards or practices enable the adoption of the "best practices" found in one unit or function by another entity. Standards include operating procedures, technological specifications, ethical values, internal controls, employee performance measures, and comparable reward systems throughout the combined companies.

Shared Services

Some functional services can be logically centralized. The centralized functions then provide services to the operating units. Commonly centralized services include accounting, legal, PR, internal audit, and information processing. The most common way to share services is to use a common staff. Alternatively, a firm can create a support services unit and allow operating units to purchase services from it or to buy similar services outside the company.

Shared Space

Isolating target company employees in a separate building or even a floor of the same building will impair the integration process. Mixing offices or even locating acquired company employees in space adjacent to the parent's offices is a highly desirable way to improve communication and idea sharing. Sharing laboratories, computer rooms, or libraries also can facilitate communication and cooperation.

Case Study 6-6 illustrates the many gut wrenching challenges that must be overcome in integrating two highly similar yet complex businesses.

CASE STUDY 6-6: AVOIDING THE MERGER BLUES—AMERICAN AIRLINES INTEGRATES TWA

TWA on the Brink

Trans World Airlines (TWA) had been tottering on the brink of bankruptcy for several years, jeopardizing a number of jobs and the communities in which they are located. American's proposed buyout of TWA in 2000 was at first met with great skepticism by regulators who feared that the resulting increase in market share in certain airline hubs would seriously erode competition and lead to higher fares. Notwithstanding this concern, approval to acquire TWA was granted largely on the basis of the "failing company doctrine." This doctrine suggested that two companies should be allowed to merge despite an increase in market concentration if one of the firms can be saved from liquidation.

American, now the world's largest airline, has struggled to assimilate such smaller acquisitions as AirCal in 1987 and Reno Air in 1998. Now, in trying to meld together two major carriers with very different and deeply ingrained cultures, a combined workforce of 113,000 and 900 jets serving 300 cities, American faced even bigger challenges. For example, because switches and circuit breakers are in different locations in TWA's cockpits than in American's, the combined airlines must spend millions of dollars to rearrange cockpit gear and to train pilots how to adjust to the differences. TWA's planes also are on different maintenance schedules than American's jets. For American to see any savings from combining maintenance operations, it gradually must synchronize those schedules. Moreover, TWA's workers have to be educated in American's business methods, and the carrier's reservations have to be transferred to American's computer systems. Planes will have to be repainted, and seats will have to be rearranged (McCartney, 2001).

Despite these challenges, American Airlines moved to systematically integrate the new company into its own operations in early 2001. American's management studied the airline mergers of the past in an effort to try to avoid the mistakes of others.

The Northwest Fiasco

Combining airline operations always has proved to be a huge task. American has studied the problems that plagued other airline mergers, such as Northwest, which moved too quickly to integrate Republic Airlines in 1986. This integration proved to be one of the most turbulent in history. The computers failed on the first day of merged operations. Angry workers vandalized ground equipment. For 6 months, flights were delayed and crews did not know where to find their planes. Passenger suitcases were misrouted. Former Republic pilots complained that they were being demoted in favor of Northwest pilots. Friction between the two groups of pilots continued for years. Travelers began calling the carrier "Northworst."

In contrast, American has adopted a more moderately paced approach as a result of the enormity and complexity of the tasks involved in putting the two airlines together. The model they followed was Delta Airline's acquisition of Western Airlines in 1986. Delta succeeded by methodically addressing every issue, although the mergers were far less complex because they involved merging far fewer computerized systems.

Even Delta had its problems, however. In 1991, Delta purchased Pan American World Airways' European operations. Pan Am's international staff found little common ground with Delta's largely domestic-minded workforce, creating a tremendous cultural divide in terms of how the combined operations should be managed. In response to the 1991–1992 recession, Delta scaled back some routes, cut thousands of jobs, and reduced pay and benefits for workers who remained. As recently as 1996, Delta was able to win concessions from its pilots' union that remain a sore point in labor relations even today.

Planning Is Undertaken before the Closing

Before closing, American had set up an integration management team of 12 managers, six each from American and TWA. An operations czar, who was to become the vice chair of the board of the new company, directed the team. The group met daily by phone for as long as 2 hours, coordinating all merger-related initiatives. American set aside a special server to log the team's decisions. The team concluded that the two lynchpins to a successful integration process were successfully resolving labor problems and meshing the different computer systems. To ease the transition, William Compton, TWA's CEO, agreed to stay on with the new company through the transition period as president of the TWA operations.

Integration Starts Immediately Following Closing

The day after closing the team empowered 40 department managers at each airline to get involved. Their tasks included replacing TWA's long-term airport leases with short-term ones, combining some cargo operations, changing over the automatic deposits of TWA employees' paychecks, and implementing American's environmental response program at TWA in case of fuel spills. Work teams, consisting of both American and TWA managers, identified more than 10,000 projects that must be undertaken before the two airlines can be fully integrated.

Complexity Proved Daunting

Project planning requires prioritizing activities that must be undertaken. This becomes increasingly complicated whenever actions taken to complete one project affect a number of others. For example, if the airline were to change the food served on former TWA planes to American's standard fare before converting TWA to American's computerized provisioning system, chaos would ensue. Differing dimensions of the two carriers' galleys require different size food carts. This resulted in American having to replace the galleys on all 173 of the TWA aircraft.

Managers Heartened by Early Successes

American, which had revenue in 2000 of $16.4 billion, expected to get a substantial boost in revenue with the addition of TWA. Some immediate cost savings were realized as American was able to negotiate new lease rates on TWA jets that are $200 million a year less than what TWA was paying. These savings were a result of the increased credit rating of the combined companies. However, other cost savings were expected to be modest during the 12 months following closing as the two airlines were operated separately.

TWA's union workers, who would have lost their jobs had TWA shut down, have been largely supportive of the merger. American has won a tentative agreement from its own pilots' union on a plan to integrate the carriers' cockpit crews. Seniority issues proved to be a major hurdle. Getting the mechanics' and flight attendants' unions on board required substantial effort. All of TWA's licenses had to be switched to American. These ranged from the Federal Aviation Administration operating certificate to TWA's liquor license in all the states.

Like most airline mergers during the last 20 years, the American and TWA merger promises to be a difficult ride for passengers, employees, and shareholders alike. Nonetheless, the potential cost savings by combining the two and the preservation of jobs that may have been lost at TWA without the merger seems likely to make this one of the industry's success stories.

Case Study Discussion Questions

1. In your opinion, what are the advantages and disadvantages of moving to integrate operations quickly? What are the advantages and disadvantages of moving more slowly and deliberately?
2. Why did American choose to use managers from both airlines to direct the integration of the two companies?
3. How did the interests of the various stakeholders to the merger affect the complexity of the integration process?

INTEGRATING BUSINESS ALLIANCES

Business alliances, particularly those created to consolidate resources such as manufacturing facilities or sales forces, also must pay close attention to integration activities. Unlike M&As, alliances usually involve shared control. Successful implementation requires maintaining a good working relationship between venture partners. When partners cannot maintain a good working relationship, the alliance is destined to fail. The breakdown in the working relationship is often a result of an inadequate integration (Lynch, 1993, pp. 189–205).

INTEGRATING MECHANISMS

Robert Porter Lynch suggests six integration mechanisms to apply to business alliances: (1) leadership, (2) teamwork and role clarification, (3) control by coordination, (4) policies and values, (5) consensus decision making, and (6) resource commitments.

Leadership

Although the terms *leadership* and *management* often are used interchangeably, there are critical differences. A leader sets direction and makes things happen, whereas a manager follows through and ensures that things continue to happen. Leadership involves vision, drive, enthusiasm, and strong selling skills; management involves communication, planning, delegating, coordinating, problem solving, making choices, and clarifying lines of responsibility. Successful alliances require the proper mix of both sets of skills. The leader must provide clear direction, values, and behaviors to create a culture that focuses on the alliance's strategic objectives as its top priority. Managers foster teamwork and promote long-term stability in the shared control environment of the business alliance.

Teamwork and Role Clarification

Teamwork is the underpinning that makes alliances work. Teamwork comes from trust, fairness, and discipline. Teams reach across functional lines and often consist of diverse experts or lower-level managers with critical problemsolving skills. The team provides functional managers with the broader, flexible staffing to augment their own specialized staff. Teams tend to create better coordination and communication at lower levels of the alliance, as well as between partners in the venture. Because teams represent individuals with varied backgrounds and possibly conflicting agendas, they may foster rather than resolve conflict. The alliance manager must be diligent in clarifying what behaviors will not be tolerated. Problems must be confronted openly and resolved amicably, even if it involves changing the composition of the team.

Coordination

In contrast to an acquisition, no one company is in charge. Alliances do not lend themselves to control through mandate; rather, in the alliance, control is best exerted through coordination. The best alliance managers are those who coordinate activities through effective communication. When problems arise, the manager's role is to manage the decision-making process, not necessarily to make the decision.

Policies and Values

Alliance employees need to understand how decisions are made, what the priorities are, who will be held accountable, and how rewards will be determined. When people know where they stand and what to expect, they are better able to deal with ambiguity and uncertainty. This level of clarity can be communicated through a distinct set of policies and procedures that are well understood by joint venture or partnership employees. The extent to which the partners can agree on policies depends to a great extent on the degree of trust between partners. Formal policies serve as a substitute for the traditional corporate hierarchy.

Consensus Decision Making

Consensus decision making does not mean that decisions are based on unanimity. Rather, decisions are based on the premise that all participants have had an opportunity to express their opinions and that they are willing to accept the final decision even though they may not be in complete agreement. Like any other business, operating decisions must be made within a reasonable time frame. The formal decision-making structure will vary with the type of legal structure. Joint ventures often have a board of directors and a management committee, which meet quarterly and monthly, respectively. Projects normally are governed by steering committees.

Resource Commitments

Many alliances are started to take advantage of complementary skills or resources available from alliance participants. The alliance can achieve its strategic objective only if all parties to the alliance live up to the resources they agreed to commit. The failure of one party to meet its commitments will erode trust, undermine teamwork, and limit the alliance's ability to meet its objectives. Meeting resource commitments also means contributing high-quality resources, such as a partner's best managers or most highly skilled employees. Personnel contributed to the alliance by a partner should be those whose goals and skills match the needs of the venture.

THE PACE OF INTEGRATION FOR BUSINESS ALLIANCES

Although M&As focus on speed, most business alliances tend to phase their integration efforts over time. A period of rapid consolidation of facilities and staff takes place at the outset of the alliance formation. However, subsequent integration activity tends to slow dramatically. Once the business alliance has been formed, the pace and extent of integration is largely determined by the relative bargaining power of the parents. Many business alliances require resource contributions from their parents throughout the life of the venture. Efforts to integrate additional resources often are slowed by the parents' efforts to understand the impact their own contributions can have on their potential bargaining power within the alliance (Andersen Consulting, 1999). Resource contributions, which augment a parent's bargaining power the most, are those that are integral to the success of the alliance and are easy for the contributor to withdraw.

THINGS TO REMEMBER

Postclosing integration is a critical phase of the M&A process. Integration itself can be viewed in terms of a process consisting of six activities: integration planning, developing communication plans, creating a new organization, developing staffing plans, functional integration, and integrating corporate cultures. Both communication and cultural integration extend beyond what normally is considered the conclusion of the integration period. Combining companies must be done quickly (i.e., 6–12 months) to achieve proper staffing levels, eliminate redundant assets, and generate the financial returns expected by shareholders. Delay contributes to employee anxiety and accelerates the loss of key talent and managers; delay also contributes to the deterioration of employee morale among those that remain. The loss of key talent and managers often is viewed as the greatest risk associated with the integration phase. This is especially true for high-technology and services companies with few tangible assets. Nevertheless, although speed is important to realize immediate cost savings and retain key employees, highly complex operations must be integrated in a more deliberate and systematic fashion to minimize long-term problems.

Successfully integrated M&As are those that demonstrate leadership by candidly and continuously communicating a clear vision, a set of values, and unambiguous priorities to all employees. Successful integration efforts are those that are well planned, that appoint an integration manager and a team with clearly defined lines of authority, and that make the tough decisions early in the process. These decisions include organizational structure, reporting relationships, spans of control, people selection, roles and responsibilities, and workforce reduction. Throughout the integration process, all effort is focused on those issues having the greatest near-term impact.

Unlike M&As, the integration of business alliances tends to be phased. Resources are contributed at the outset to enable the formation of the alliance. Subsequent resource contributions are subject to a lengthy negotiation process in which the partners are trying to get the most favorable terms. Because alliances involve shared control, the integration process requires good working relationships with the other participants. Successful integration also requires leadership capable of defining a clear sense of direction and well-defined priorities and managers who accomplish their objectives as much by coordinating activities through effective communication as by unilateral decision making. Like M&As, cross-functional teams are used widely to achieve integration. Finally, the successful integration of business alliances, as well as M&As, demands that the necessary resources, in terms of the best people, the appropriate skills, and sufficient capital, be committed to the process.

CHAPTER DISCUSSION QUESTIONS

6-1. Why is the integration phase of the acquisition process considered so important?

6-2. Why should acquired companies be integrated quickly? What are the risks to rapid integration?

6-3. Why might the time required to integrate acquisitions vary by industry?

6-4. What are the costs of employee turnover?

6-5. Why is candid and continuous communication so important during the integration phase?

6-6. What are the messages that might be communicated to the various audiences or stakeholders of the new company?

6-7. What are examples of difficult decisions that should be made early in the integration process?

6-8. What are some of the contract-related "transition issues" that should be resolved before closing?

6-9. How does the process for integrating business alliances differ from that of integrating an acquisition? How are they similar?

CHAPTER BUSINESS CASE

CASE STUDY 6-7: DAIMLER ACQUIRES CHRYSLER—ANATOMY OF A CROSS-BORDER TRANSACTION

In 1998, when Daimler-Benz took over Chrysler Corporation to form DaimlerChrysler, Chrysler earned more on each vehicle than any other major car-maker. It also had a well-deserved reputation for eye-catching designs. Four years later, it was bleeding cash—losing more than $2 billion in 2001. Since the merger, its market share has fallen from 16.2% to 13.9% (*Business Week*, September 17, 2001). Although the merger did not precipitate this sorry situation, it is likely that it aggravated Chrysler's problems. For Daimler, the acquisition has proved very costly. In 2000, Chrysler's operating profit collapsed by 90% to $500 million on sales of $64.2 billion. Reflecting this debacle, Daimler's profits plunged to $4.9 billion, one-half of what they were in the prior year, on sales of $152 billion. Shareholders have seen the value of their holdings drop by more than 60% since the merger. Only the combined firm's cash hoard of more than $11 billion seems to be keeping the firm afloat.

It Seemed to Make Sense at the Time

The combination of Chrysler and Daimler created the third largest auto manu-facturer in the world, with more than 428,000 employees worldwide. Conceptually, the strategic fit seemed obvious. German engineering in the automotive industry was highly regarded and could be used to help Chrysler upgrade both its prod-uct quality and production process. In contrast, Chrysler had a much better track record than Daimler in getting products to market rapidly. Daimler's distribution network in Europe would give Chrysler products better access to European mar-kets; Chrysler could provide parts and service support for Mercedes-Benz in the United States. With greater financial strength, the combined companies would be better able to make inroads into Asian and South American markets.

Daimler's product markets were viewed as mature, and Chrysler was under pressure from escalating R&D costs and retooling demands in the wake of rapidly changing technology. Both companies watched with concern the growing excess capacity of the worldwide automotive manufacturing industry. Daimler and Chrysler had been in discussions about doing something together for some time. They initiated discussions about creating a joint venture to expand into Asian and South American markets, where both companies had a limited presence. Despite the termination of these discussions as a result of disagreement over responsibili-ties, talks were renewed in February 1998. Both companies shared the same sense of urgency about their vulnerability to companies such as Toyota and Volkswagen. The transaction was completed in April 1998 for $36 billion.

Enjoying a robust auto market, starry-eyed executives were touting how the two firms were going to save billions by using common parts in future cars and trucks and by sharing research and technology. In a press conference to announce the merger, Jurgen Schrempp, CEO of DaimlerChrysler, beamed at the formation of the new automotive powerhouse. The merger was described as highly complementary in terms of product offerings and the geographic location of many manufacturing operations of the two firms. It also was described to the press as a merger of equals. Schrempp told everyone that "This is not a merger where you close factories and cut jobs" (Tierney, 2000). On the surface, it all looked so easy.

The Looming Cultural Clash

The limitations of cultural differences became apparent during efforts to integrate the two companies. Daimler had been run as a conglomerate, in contrast to Chrysler's highly centralized operations. Daimler managers were accustomed to lengthy reports and meetings to review the reports. Under Schrempp's direction, many top management positions in Chrysler went to Germans. Only a few former Chrysler executives reported directly to Schrempp. Made rich by the merger, the potential for a loss of American managers within Chrysler was high. Chrysler managers were accustomed to a higher degree of independence than their German counterparts. Mercedes dealers in the United States balked at the thought of Chrysler's trucks still sporting the old Mopar logo delivering parts to their dealerships. All the trucks had to be repainted.

Implementing Cost Savings Strategies

Charged with the task of finding cost savings, the integration team identified a list of hundreds of opportunities, offering billions of dollars in savings. For example, Mercedes dropped its plans to develop a battery-powered car in favor of Chrysler's electric minivan. The finance and purchasing departments were combined worldwide. This would enable the combined company to take advantage of savings on bulk purchases of commodity products such as steel, aluminum, and glass. In addition, inventories could be managed more efficiently because surplus components purchased in one area could be shipped to other facilities in need of such parts. Long-term supply contracts and the dispersal of much of the purchasing operations to the plant level meant that it could take as long as 5 years to fully integrate the purchasing department.

The time required to integrate the manufacturing operations could be significantly longer because both Daimler and Chrysler had designed their operations differently and are subject to different union work rules. Changing manufacturing processes will require renegotiating union agreements as the multiyear contracts expire. All of this must take place without causing product quality to suffer.

To facilitate this process, Mercedes issued very specific guidelines for each car brand pertaining to R&D, purchasing, manufacturing, and marketing.

DaimlerChrysler Faced Tough Times from the Outset

Although certainly not all of DaimlerChrysler's woes can be blamed on the merger, it clearly accentuated problems associated with the cyclical economic slowdown during 2001 and the stiffened competition from Japanese automakers. The firm's top management has reacted, perhaps somewhat belatedly to the downturn, by slashing production and eliminating unsuccessful models. Moreover, the firm has pared its product development budget from $48 billion to $36 billion and eliminated more than 26,000 jobs, or 20% of the firm's workforce, by early 2002. Six plants in Detroit, Mexico, Argentina, and Brazil are scheduled for closure by the end of 2002. The firm is also in the process of cutting back the number of U.S. car dealerships bearing the firm's logo.

In a stunning and unusual expression of candor, Schrempp admitted publicly that he had never really intended for the combined auto giant to be a "merger of equals," as stated when the merger was first announced in 1998. He also stated that he intended to be misleading for psychological reasons, noting that the merger would not have taken place if he had been honest. Chrysler workers said morale has plummeted—employees have posted Schrempp's remarks on bulletin boards throughout the company (McNatt, 2000).

With the benefit of hindsight, it is possible to note a number of missteps DaimlerChrysler has made that are likely to haunt the firm for years to come. These include paying too much for some parts, not updating some vehicle models sooner, falling to offer more high-margin vehicles that could help ease current financial strains, not developing enough interesting vehicles for future production, and failing to be completely honest with Chrysler employees. Daimler needed to continue to do what Chrysler always had done well and that was to be innovative (Bott, 2001). Although Daimler managed to take costs out, it also managed to alienate the workforce. The failure to build strong management–labor relations may haunt the company for years to come.

Case Study Discussion Questions

1. Identify ways in which the merger combined companies with complementary skills and resources.
2. What are the major cultural differences between Daimler and Chrysler?
3. What were the principal risks to the merger?
4. Why might it take so long to integrate manufacturing operations and certain functions such as purchasing?
5. How might Daimler have better managed the postmerger integration period?

Solutions to these questions are found in the Appendix at the back of this book.

CHAPTER BUSINESS CASE

CASE STUDY 6-8: THE TRAVELERS AND
CITICORP INTEGRATION EXPERIENCE

Getting the Deal Done is Only Half the Battle

Billed as a merger of equals, the merger of Travelers and Citicorp to form Citigroup illustrates many of the problems encountered during postmerger integration. At $73 billion, the merger between Travelers and Citicorp was the second largest merger in 1998 and is an excellent example of how integrating two businesses can be far more daunting than consummating the transaction. Their experience demonstrates how everything can be going smoothly in most of the businesses being integrated, except for one, and how this single business can sop up all of management's time and attention to correct its problems. In some respects, it highlights the ultimate challenge of every major integration effort: getting people to work together, despite coming from distinctly different corporate cultures. It also spotlights the complexity of managing large, intricate businesses when authority at the top is divided among several managers. Citicorp was widely regarded as a very strong marketing and planning organization, but it was viewed as weak operationally and on execution of business plans.

Motivation for the Merger

The strategic rationale for the merger relied heavily on cross-selling the financial services products of both corporations to the other's customers. The combination would create a financial services giant capable of making loans, accepting deposits, selling mutual funds, underwriting securities, selling insurance, and dispensing financial planning advice. Citicorp had relationships with thousands of companies around the world. In contrast, Travelers' Salomon Smith Barney unit dealt with relatively few companies. It was believed that Salomon could expand its underwriting and investment banking business dramatically by having access to the much larger Citicorp commercial customer base. Moreover, Citicorp lending officers, who frequently had access only to midlevel corporate executives at companies within their customer base, would have access to more senior executives as a result of Salomon's investment banking relationships.

Co-CEO Arrangements Often Lack Well-Defined Lines of Authority

At the time, Citicorp-Travelers was faced with the challenge of either changing current law or selling off large portions of Travelers' insurance business. Under new financial service legislation, such combinations are now legal. Although the characteristics of the two businesses seemed to be complementary, motivating all parties to cooperate proved a major challenge. Because of the combined firm's co-CEO arrangement, the lack of clearly delineated authority exhausted management time and attention without resolving major integration issues. This was particularly true in the Global Corporate Business product area.

Some decisions proved to be relatively easy. Others were not. Citicorp, in stark contrast to Travelers, was known for being highly bureaucratic with marketing, credit, and finance departments at the global, North American, and business unit levels. North American departments were eliminated quickly. Salomon was highly regarded in the fixed income security area, so Citicorp's fixed income operations were folded into Salomon. Citicorp received Salomon's foreign exchange trading operations because of their premerger reputation in this business. However, both the Salomon and Citicorp derivatives business tended to overlap and compete for the same customers. Each business unit within Travelers and Citicorp had a tendency to believe they "owned" the relationship with their customers and were hesitant to introduce others that might ultimately assume control over this relationship. Pay constituted a very thorny issue. Investment banker salaries in Salomon Smith Barney tended to dwarf those of Citicorp middle-level managers. When it came time to cut costs, issues arose around who would be terminated.

Organizational Issues Quickly Surface

Citicorp was organized along three major product areas: global corporate business, global consumer business, and asset management. The merged companies' management structure consisted of three executives in the global corporate business area and two in each of the other major product areas. Each area contained senior managers from both companies. Moreover, each area reported to the co-chairs and CEOs John Reed and Sanford Weill, former CEOs of Citicorp and Travelers, respectively. Of the three major product areas, the integration of two was progressing well, reflecting the collegial atmosphere of the top managers in both areas. However, the global business area was well behind schedule, beset by major riffs among the three top managers. Travelers' corporate culture was characterized as strongly focused on the bottom line, with a lean corporate overhead structure and a strong predisposition to impose its style on the Citicorp culture. In contrast, Citicorp, under John Reed, tended to be more focused on the strategic vision of the new company rather than on day-to-day operations.

During 1998, Travelers was subject to sizable fixed-income trading losses at its Salomon Smith Barney operations; both Citicorp and Travelers sustained huge losses when Russia defaulted on its debt. Although these problems occurred independently of the merger, they compounded efforts to support the stock price while the two businesses were being integrated. The organizational structure coupled with personal differences among certain key managers ultimately resulted in the termination of James Dimon, who had been a star as president of Travelers before the merger, leaving each major product area co-CEOs. On July 28, 1999, the co-chair arrangement was dissolved. Sanford Weill assumed responsibility for the firm's operating businesses and financial function, and John Reed became the focal point for the company's Internet, advanced development, technology, human resources, and legal functions. This change in organizational structure was intended to help clarify lines of authority and to overcome some of the obstacles in managing a large and complex set of businesses that result from split decision-making authority. On February 28, 2000, John Reed formally retired.

Although the power sharing arrangement may have been necessary to get the deal done, Reed's leaving certainly made it easier for Weill to manage the business. The co-CEO arrangement had contributed to an extended period of indecision, resulting in part to their widely divergent views. Reed wanted to support Citibank's Internet efforts with substantial and sustained investment, whereas the more bottom-line-oriented Weill wanted to contain costs.

Postmerger Results Look Promising

With its $112 billion in annual revenue in 2000, Citigroup ranked sixth on the Fortune 500 list. Its $13.5 billion in profit was second only to Exxon-Mobil's $17.7 billion. The combination of Salomon Smith Barney's investment bankers and Citibank's commercial bankers is working very effectively. In a year-end 2000 poll by Fortune magazine of the Most Admired U.S. companies, Citigroup was the clear winner. Among the 600 companies judged by a poll of executives, directors, and securities analysts, it ranked first for using its assets wisely and for long-term investment value (Loomis, 2001).

This success has taken its toll on management. Of the 15 people initially on the management committee, only five remain in addition to Weill. Among those that have left are all those that were with Citibank when the merger was consummated. The only exception is Victor Menezes, head of Citigroup's emerging markets operations. Sandy Weill, Citigroup's current CEO, expects to continue to grow the company through acquisition. For the faint of heart, this may be a chilling prospect in view of the increasingly global complexity of this behemoth. However, the last thing anyone will ever call Sandy Weill is faint of heart.

Case Study Discussion Questions

1. Why did Citibank and Travelers resort to a co-CEO arrangement? What are the advantages and disadvantages of such an arrangement?
2. Describe the management challenges you think may face Citigroup's management team as a result of the increasing global complexity of Citigroup?
3. Identify the key differences between Travelers' and Citibank's corporate cultures. Discuss ways you would resolve such differences.
4. In what sense is the initial divergence in Travelers' operational orientation and Citigroup's marketing and planning orientation an excellent justification for the merger? Explain your answer.
5. One justification for the merger was the cross-selling opportunities it would provide. Comment on the challenges that might be involved in making such a marketing strategy work.

REFERENCES

Alexander, Marcus, Andrew Campbell, and Michael Gould, "Parenting Advantage," *Prism*, Arthur D. Little, Incorporated, Second Quarter 1995, pp. 23–33.

Anderson Consulting, *Global Survey Acquisition and Alliance Integration*, 1999, www.ac.com/overview.

A.T. Kearney Inc., *Shaping the Organizational Future*, Special Report Series, 45, 1998.

Bekier, Matthias M., Anna J. Bogardus, and Tim Oldham, "Why Mergers Fail," *The McKinsey Quarterly*, 4, 2001, p. 3.

Bloomberg.com, "Profit Improvement at Exxon-Mobil," December 16, 1999.

Bloomberg.com, "Albertson's and American Stores: A Marriage in Trouble," November 1, 1999.

Bott, Jennifer, "Trimming the Ranks," Knight Ridder Newspapers, *Orange County Register*, Business, January 30, 2001, p. 3.

Business Week, "The Case against Mergers," October 31, 1995, pp. 122–125.

Business Week, "Making Corporate Boards Effective," January 24, 2000, pp. 142–152.

Business Week, "A Merger's Bitter Harvest," February 5, 2001, p. 112.

Business Week, "Cisco: Behind the Hype," January 21, 2002, pp. 55–59.

Business Week, "Chrysler?" September 17, 2001, pp. 87–91.

Campbell, Andrew, David Sadler, and Richard Koch, *Breakup! When Companies are Worth More Dead than Alive*, Oxford: Capstone, 1997.

Chakrabarti, Alok, "Organizational Factors in Post-Acquisition Performance," *IEEE Transactions in Engineering Management*, 37 (4), November 1990, pp. 259–266.

Chapman, Timothy L., Jack J. Dempsey, Glenn Ramsdell, and Trudy E. Bell, "Purchasing's Big Moment—After a Merger," *The McKinsey Quarterly*, 1, 1998, pp. 56–65.

Cisco Systems, "Annual Report, 1999," www.reportgallery.com.

Coopers & Lybrand, "Most Acquisitions Fail, C&L Study Says," *Mergers & Acquisitions Report 7*, (47), November 18, 1996, pp. 2–4.

Cossey, Bernard, "Systems Assessment in Acquired Subsidiaries," *Accountancy*, January 1991, pp. 98–99.

Down, James W., "The M&A Game is Often Won or Lost after the Deal," *Management Review Executive Forum*, November 1995, p. 10.

Financial Times, "Bugged by Failures," November 29, 1996, p. 8.

Flanagan, David J. and K. C. O'Shaughnessy, "Determinants of Layoff Announcements Following Mergers and Acquisitions: An Empirical Investigation," *Strategic Management Journal*, 19 (10), October 1998, pp. 989–999.

Frank, Robert and Robin Sidel, "Firms that Lived by the Deal in the 1990s Now Sink by the Dozens," *Wall Street Journal*, June 6, 2002, p. A1.

Goldblatt, Henry, "Merging at Internet Speed," *Fortune*, November 8, 1999, pp. 164–165.

Hayes, Robert H., "The Human Side of Acquisitions," *Management Review*, November 1979, p. 41.

Lajoux, Alexandra Reed, *The Art of M&A Integration*, New York, McGraw-Hill, 1998.

Lansner, Jonathan, "Common Ground Was Key," *Orange County Register*, November 1, 1999, p. 4.

Loomis, Carol J., "Sandy Weill's Monster," *Fortune*, April 16, 2001, pp. 107–110.

Lord, Michael D. and Annette L. Ranft, "Acquiring New Knowledge: The Role of Retaining Human Capital in Acquisitions of High Tech Firms," *Journal of High Technology Management Research*, 11 (2), Autumn 2000, pp. 295–320.

Lynch, Robert P., *Business Alliances Guide: The Hidden Competitive Weapon*, John Wiley & Sons, 1993.

Malekzadeh, Ali R., and Nahavandi, Afsaneh, "Making Mergers Work by Managing Cultures," *Journal of Business Strategy*, 11 (3), May/June 1990, pp. 55–57.

Marks, Mitchell L., *From Turmoil to Triumph: New Life after Mergers, Acquisitions, and Downsizing*, Lexington Books, 1996.

Marks, Mitchell L., *Joining Forces: Making One Plus One Equal Three in Mergers, Acquisitions and Alliances*, Jossey-Bass, 1998.

McCartney, Scott, "Flying Lessons," *Wall Street Journal*, April 20, 2001, p. 1.

McNatt, Robert, "Chrysler Not Quite So Equal," *Business Week*, November 13, 2000.

McKinsey & Company, "Creating Shareholder Value through Merger and/or Acquisition: A McKinsey & Company Perspective, April 1987, cited in Tom Copeland, Tim Koller, and Jack Murrin (eds.), *Valuation: Measuring and Managing the Value of Companies*, New York, John Wiley & Sons, 1990, p. 321.

Porter, Richard and Cynthia N. Wood, "Post-Merger Integration," in David J. BenDaniel and Arthur H. Rosenbloom (eds.), *International M&A: Joint Ventures and Beyond*, New York, John Wiley & Sons, 1998, pp. 459–497.

Pursche, William R., "Pharmaceuticals—The Consolidation Isn't Over," *The McKinsey Quarterly*, (2), 1996, pp. 110–119.

Right Management Consultants, *Lessons Learned from Mergers & Acquisitions: Best Practices in Workforce Integration*, 1999, www.right.com.

Sanderson, Susan and Mustafa Uzumeri, *The Innovative Imperative: Strategies for Managing Products, Models, and Families*, Burr Ridge, IL, Irwin Professional, Publishing, 1997.

Schweiger, David M., *M&A Integration: Framework for Executives and Managers*, New York, McGraw-Hill, 2002.

Shivdasani, Anil, "Board Composition, Ownership Structure, and Hostile Takeovers," *Journal of Accounting and Economics*, 16, 1993, pp. 167–198.

Taylor, Alex, "Oil, Oil Everywhere," *Fortune*, April 16, 2001, pp. 149–151.

Tierney, Christine, "Can Schrempp Stop the Careening at Chrysler?," *Business Week*, December 4, 2000, p. 40.

Wall Street Journal, "When Things Go Wrong," November 18, 1996, p. R-25.

Wall Street Journal, "Disability Claims Mirror Rising Job Cuts," November 21, 1996, p. A-2.

Wall Street Journal, "Together but Equal," September 26, 1996, p. R-20.

Walsh, James P., "Doing a Deal: Merger and Acquisition Negotiations and Their Impact Upon Target Company Top Management Turnover," *Strategic Management Journal*, 10 (4), July/August 1989, pp. 307–322.

Walsh, James P. and John W. Ellwood, "Mergers, Acquisitions, and the Pruning of Managerial Deadwood," *Strategic Management Journal*, 12 (3), March 1991, pp. 201–217.

Watson Wyatt Worldwide, *Assessing and Managing Human Capital—A Key to Maximizing the M&A Deal*, 1998/99 Mergers and Acquisitions Survey, December 1999, www.watsonwyatt.com.

MERGER AND ACQUISITION TOOLS AND CONCEPTS

7

A PRIMER ON MERGER AND ACQUISITION VALUATION

Happiness is positive cash flow.

—*Fred Adler*

As the chief financial officer for her firm, Sara Bertram poured over reams of computer printouts provided by her subordinates. Clearly, considerable effort had been expended to develop a preliminary estimate of the value of a potential acquisition target. As a publicly traded company, substantial financial detail on the target was available. Four financial analysts had labored feverishly through the weekend to collect the data necessary to project cash flows. These cash flows, along with other measures of value, were used to determine the "economic value" of the target firm. By all accounts, the analysis seemed rigorous and complete. She should have been satisfied. Yet something was lacking.

Sara was having considerable difficulty understanding why projected revenue for the target firm was expected to grow at more than twice the pace of working capital. Similarly, forecasts of capital spending seemed to lag the expected robust growth of the potential acquisition target. Moreover, operating margins were growing throughout the forecast period. The combination of these factors caused the target's projected cash flow to escalate at an unprecedented rate. Were sales growing because of an anticipated improvement in market share? Perhaps improved inventory controls were contributing to a reduction in working capital per dollar of sales during the forecast period. Moreover, it wasn't clear why capital spending should not at least grow at its historical rate. Could expected improvements in productivity account for the improvement in operating profit margins? Frustrated, Sara summoned the financial analysts to a meeting to explain the assumptions they made in generating the forecast. While expressing appreciation for their substantial effort, she admonished them to be more careful in clearly stating their assumptions. "After all," she said, "the credibility of any forecast is solely dependent on the reasonableness of its underlying assumptions." Sheepishly, the analysts agreed to redo the financial statements to reflect what Sara believed were more realistic assumptions.

OVERVIEW

The purpose of this chapter is to provide an overview of the basics of valuing mergers and acquisitions (M&As). The chapter assumes the reader has a working knowledge of elementary finance and begins with a brief review of rudimentary finance concepts including measuring risk and return, the capital asset pricing model (CAPM), the effects of leverage on risk and return, and calculating present and future values of cash flow. The cash-flow definitions, free cash flow to equity and to the firm, discussed in this chapter will be used in valuation problems in subsequent chapters. The distinction between these cash-flow definitions will be particularly relevant for the discussion of leveraged buyouts in Chapter 11. Five basic methods of valuation are addressed, including the income or discounted cash flow, market-based, asset-oriented, replacement cost, and weighted-average methods. The chapter concludes with a discussion of the valuation of nonoperating assets such as excess cash and marketable securities, investments in other firms, unutilized and pension fund assets, and intangible assets in recognition of the increasingly important role of technology, knowledge-based, and service-oriented businesses in the global economy. For more exhaustive analyses of valuation, see Damodaran (2001) and Copeland, Koller, and Murrin (2000). For those seeking a more rigorous quantitative approach to valuation, see Abrams (2001).

REQUIRED RETURNS

Investors require a minimum rate of return on an investment to compensate them for the perceived level of risk associated with that investment. The required rate of return must be at least equal to what the investor can receive on alternative investments exhibiting a comparable level of perceived risk. For an excellent discussion of basic concepts of finance, see Gitman (2000), Lasher (2000), and Moyer, McGuigan, and Kretlow (1998).

COST OF EQUITY

The cost of equity (k_e) is the rate of return required to induce investors to purchase a firm's equity. The cost of equity also can be viewed as an *opportunity cost* (i.e., a foregone opportunity) because it represents the rate of return investors could earn by investing in equities of comparable risk. The cost of equity can be estimated by using the CAPM, which measures the relationship between expected risk and expected return. It postulates that investors require higher rates of return for accepting higher levels of risk. It also states that the investor's required return is equal to the risk-free rate of return, such as the interest rate on 10-year U.S. Treasury securities, plus a risk premium. Treasury securities are used to approximate the risk-free rate because of the excellent credit worthiness of the U.S. government. The *risk premium* refers to the additional rate of return in excess of the risk-free rate that investors require to purchase a firm's equity. Of the various Treasury debt issues, the 10-year bond rate often is used as a proxy for the risk-free rate because it commonly is used as a benchmark for pricing other securities, it is among the most highly liquid debt markets, and it is less volatile than Treasury issues of a shorter maturity.

$$\text{CAPM: } k_e = R_f + \beta(R_m - R_f),$$

where R_f = risk free rate of return
    β = beta
    R_m = the expected rate of return on equities
    $R_m - R_f$ = 5.5% (i.e., its geometric mean between January 1,
                      1962 and December 31, 2000; Ibbotson, 2000)[1]

PRETAX COST OF DEBT

The cost of debt represents the cost to the firm of borrowed funds. It reflects the current level of interest rates and the level of default risk as perceived by investors. Interest paid on debt is tax deductible by the firm. In bankruptcy, bondholders are paid before shareholders as the firm's assets are liquidated. Default risk can be measured by the firm's credit rating. Default rates vary from an average of .52% of AAA-rated firms for the 15-year period ending in 2001 to 54.38% for those rated CCC by Standard and Poor's Corporation (Burrus and McNamee, April 8, 2002).

For nonrated firms, the analyst may estimate the pretax cost of debt by comparing commonly used measures of a firm's leverage and ability to satisfy interest expense and principal repayments with those of similar firms that have been rated. Such standard measures include debt-to-equity or total capital ratios, interest coverage ratios, and operating margins. Alternatively, the analyst may use the

[1]The geometric mean is used to reflect the compounding effect of interest being earned on interest during this period. Some may argue that this "risk premium" should be changed to reflect fluctuations in the stock market. However, history shows that such fluctuations are relatively short term in nature. Consequently, the risk premium should reflect more long-term considerations such as the expected holding period of the investor or acquiring company. Therefore, for the strategic or long-term investor or acquirer, the risk premium should approximate the 5.5% long-term historical geometric average.

firm's interest rate paid on recently borrowed funds. Much of this information can be found in local libraries in such publications as Moody's *Company Data*; Standard & Poor's Corporation's *Descriptions, The Outlook,* and *Bond Guide*; and Value Line's *Investment Survey.*

COST OF PREFERRED STOCK

Preferred stock exhibits some of the characteristics of long-term debt in that its dividend is generally constant and preferred stockholders are paid before common shareholders in the event the firm is liquidated. Unlike interest payments on debt, preferred dividends are not tax deductible. Because preferred stock is riskier than debt but less risky than common stock in bankruptcy, the cost to the company to issue preferred stock should be less than the cost of equity but greater than the cost of debt. Viewing preferred dividends as paid in perpetuity, the cost of preferred stock can be calculated as dividends per share of preferred stock divided by the market value of the preferred stock.

COST OF CAPITAL

The weighted average cost of capital (WACC) is a broader measure than the cost of equity and represents the return that a firm must earn to induce investors to buy its stock and bonds. The WACC is calculated using a weighted average of the firm's cost of equity and cost of debt.

$$\text{WACC} = k_e \times \frac{E}{D + E} + i \times (1 - t) \times \frac{D}{D + E}$$

where $E =$ the market value of equity

$D =$ the market value of debt

$i \ =$ the interest rate on debt

$t \ =$ the firm's marginal tax rate.

A portion of interest paid on borrowed funds is recoverable by the firm because of the tax deductibility of interest. Therefore, the actual cost of borrowed funds to the firm is estimated by multiplying the pretax interest rate, i, by $(1 - t)$. Furthermore, note that $[E/(D + E)]$ and $[D/(D + E)]$, the weights associated with the cost of equity and debt, reflect the firm's *target* capital structure or capitalization. These are targets in the sense that they represent the capital structure the firm hopes to achieve and sustain in the future. It is important to remember that these are targets and not the current actual values. The actual market value of equity and debt as a percentage of total capitalization may differ from the targets. Market values rather than book values are used because WACC measures the cost of issuing debt and equity securities. Such securities are issued at market and not book value. The cost of capital formula can be generalized to include other sources of funds available to firms such as preferred stock.

Note that noninterest-bearing liabilities such as accounts payable are excluded from the estimation of the cost of capital for the firm to simplify the calculation of WACC. Although such liabilities do have an associated cost of capital, it is assumed to have been included in the price paid for the products and services whose purchase generated the accounts payable. Consequently, the cost of capital associated with these types of liabilities affects free cash flow through its inclusion in operating expenses.

ANALYZING RISK

Risk is the degree of uncertainty associated with the outcome of an investment. It takes into consideration the probability of a loss as well as a gain on an investment. Risk consists of a *diversifiable* component-such as strikes, defaulting on debt repayments, and lawsuits-and a *nondiversifiable* component-such as inflation and war-that affects all firms. A *beta coefficient* (β) is a measure of nondiversifiable risk or the extent to which a firm's (or asset's) return changes because of a change in the market's return. It is a measure of the risk of a stock's financial returns, as compared with the risk of the financial returns to the general stock market. $\beta = 1$ means that the stock is as risky as the general market; $\beta < 1$ means the stock is less risky, whereas $\beta > 1$ means that the stock is more risky than the overall stock market.

β may be estimated by applying linear regression analysis to explain the relationship between the dependent variable, stock returns (R_j), and the independent variable, market returns (R_m). The intercept or constant term of the regression equation provides a measure of R_j's performance as compared with the general market during the regression period. The following equations express R_j as defined by the linear regression model and R_j as defined by the CAPM.

$$R_j = \alpha + \beta R_m \text{ (regression equation formulation)}$$
$$R_j = R_f + \beta(R_m - R_f)$$
$$= R_f + \beta R_m - \beta R_f$$
$$= R_f(1 - \beta) + \beta R_m \text{ (CAPM formulation)}$$

If α is greater than $R_f(1 - \beta)$, this particular stock's rate of return, R_j, performed better than would have been expected using the CAPM during the same time period. The cumulative daily difference between α and $R_f(1 - \beta)$ is a measure of "abnormal or excess return" for a specified number of days often used in empirical studies assessing the impact of acquisitions on the shareholder value of both acquiring and target companies (Exhibit 7-1).

EXHIBIT 7-1. ESTIMATING β FOR PUBLICLY TRADED COMPANIES

Calculate the return to the jth company's shareholders as capital gains (or losses) plus dividends paid during the period adjusted for stock splits that take place in the current period. Regress this adjusted return against a similarly defined return for a broadly defined market index.

$$\frac{SP \times P_{jt} - P_{jt-1} + SP \times \text{Dividends}}{P_{jt-1}}$$

$$= \alpha + \beta \frac{(\text{S\&P500}_t - \text{S\&P500}_{t-1}) + \text{Dividends}}{\text{S\&P500}_{t-1}}$$

[1]SP is equal to 2 for a two-for-one stock split, 1.5 for a three-for-two split, and 1.33 for a four-for-three split. If we do not adjust for stock splits that may take place in the current period, the stock price will drop, resulting in a negative return.

[2]Betas for public companies can be obtained from estimation services such as Value Line, Standard & Poor's, Ibbotson, Bloomberg, and Barra. Betas for private companies can be obtained by substituting a beta for comparable publicly traded companies.

EFFECTS OF LEVERAGE ON BETA

The presence of debt magnifies financial returns to shareholders. A firm whose total capital consists of $1 million in equity generates a return to shareholders of 10% if its after-tax profits are $100,000. A firm whose total capital is $1 million, consisting of $500,000 in equity and $500,000 in debt, will achieve a 20% return ($100,000/$500,000) to the shareholder on the same level of after-tax profits.

In the absence of debt, β measures the volatility of a firm's financial return to changes in the general market's overall financial return. Such a measure of volatility or risk is called an *unlevered* β and is denoted as β_u. Increasing leverage will raise the level of uncertainty of shareholder returns and increase the value of β. However, this will be offset to some extent by the tax deductibility of interest, which reduces shareholder risk by increasing after-tax cash flow available for shareholders. A beta reflecting the effects of both the increased volatility of earnings and the tax-shelter effects of leverage is called a *leveraged* or *levered* β and is denoted as β_l (Exhibit 7-2).

These relationships can be expressed as follows:

$$\beta_l = \beta_u[1 + (1 - t)(D/E)] \quad \text{and}$$
$$\beta_u = \beta_l/[1 + (1 - t)(D/E)]$$

EXHIBIT 7-2. CALCULATING A LEVERED β

Company X has no debt, a tax rate of .4, and an unlevered beta of 1.2. It is considering borrowing up to 50% of its equity value in 2000 and up to 75% in 2003. What would be the impact of this decision on its unlevered beta?

$$\beta_{l,2000} = \beta_u[1 + (1 - t)(D/E)_{2000}]$$
$$= 1.2[1 + (1 - .4)(.5)] = 1.2(1.30) = 1.56$$
$$\beta_{l,2003} = \beta_u[1 + (1 - t)(D/E)_{2003}]$$
$$= 1.2[1 + (1 - .4)(.75)] = 1.2(1.45) = 1.74$$

CALCULATING FREE CASH FLOWS

An increase in the amount of cash flow generated by an asset tends to raise the value of that asset, unless it is offset by increasing risk and an increasing discount rate associated with that cash flow. Conversely, decreases in cash flow tend to reduce the value of the asset for a given level of risk and discount rate. Generally speaking, a firm's operating, investment, and financing activities generate its cash flow. The difference between cash inflows and cash outflows often is referred to as *free cash flow*. Such cash flow is free or discretionary in that it can be either reinvested in the firm or distributed to shareholders. Note that this difference can be positive or negative, resulting in an increase or decrease in the firm's cash balances between the beginning and end of the accounting period. Several different definitions of free cash flow are discussed in this chapter. These include free cash flow to the firm (FCFF), often referred to as enterprise cash flow, and free cash flow to equity investors (FCFE) (i.e., equity cash flow). Although the more inclusive free cash flow to the firm definition is more widely used for valuation, free cash flow to equity investors is best suited for special situations such as for valuing financial institutions and leveraged buyouts. For an excellent discussion of cash-flow concepts, see Damodaran (1997).

FREE CASH FLOW TO THE FIRM
(ENTERPRISE CASH FLOW)

Free cash flow to the firm represents cash available to satisfy all investors holding claims against the firm's resources. These claim holders include common stockholders, lenders, and preferred stockholders. FCFF can be calculated in two ways. First, FCFF can be calculated by adding up cash flows to all of a firm's claim holders:

$$FCFF = FCFE + Interest\ Expense(1 - Tax\ Rate) + Principal\ Repayments$$
$$- New\ Debt/Equity\ Issues + Preferred\ Dividends$$

Second, FCFF can be calculated by adjusting operating earnings before interest and taxes (EBIT):

$$FCFF = EBIT(1 - Tax\ Rate) - (Gross\ Capital\ Expenditures - Depreciation)$$
$$- \Delta\ Net\ Working\ Capital$$

In the formulation beginning with EBIT, there is no effort to adjust for payments of interest or preferred dividends because this measure of cash flow is calculated before any consideration is given to how expenditures will be financed. Under this definition, only cash flow from operating and investment activities, but not financing activities, is included. The tax rate refers to the firm's marginal tax rate. Depreciation expense used in all the formulae used in this book is assumed to include all amortization expense.

Differences between FCFE and FCFF are the result of debt-related cash flow plus nonequity claims. Interest expense is multiplied by $(1 - tax\ rate)$ to adjust FCFF for that portion of interest paid to bondholders that is not recoverable by shareholders as a result of the tax deductibility of interest. The effects of tax savings already are included in net income.

Note that the calculation of FCFF based on EBIT is frequently the preferred methodology for valuation purposes because it does not require an analyst to estimate future debt repayment schedules to project principal repayments. This methodology is most helpful when a firm's level of future borrowing is expected to change substantially during the forecast period, thereby making the estimation of debt repayment schedules very difficult. However, the estimation of FCFF starting with EBIT does require assumptions about the acquiring firm's target debt-to-equity ratio to calculate the firm's weighted average cost of capital.

Adjusting EBIT for Operating Lease Expense

For many firms, future operating lease commitments are substantial. As noted later in this chapter, future lease commitments should be discounted to the present at the firm's pretax cost of debt (i) and included in the firm's total debt outstanding. Once operating leases are converted to debt, operating lease expense (OLE_{EXP}) must be added to EBIT because it is a financial expense. Depreciation expense associated with the leased asset (DEP_{OL}) then must be deducted from EBIT, as is depreciation expense associated with other fixed assets owned by the firm, to calculate an "adjusted" EBIT ($EBIT_{ADJ}$). $EBIT_{ADJ}$ then is used to calculate free cash flow to the firm. EBIT may be adjusted as follows:

$$EBIT_{ADJ} = EBIT + OLE_{EXP} - DEP_{OL}$$

Alternatively, if the depreciation on the leased asset is assumed to approximate the principal portion of the debt being repaid, adjusted EBIT may be calculated by adding back the imputed interest, i, on the debt value of the operating lease (PV_{OL}). Depreciation expenses associated with the leased assets need not be deducted from EBIT because free cash flow to the firm is calculated before financing considerations. Consequently, adjusted EBIT ($EBIT_{ADJ}$) also may be shown as follows:

$$EBIT_{ADJ} = EBIT + PV_{OL} \times i$$

FREE CASH FLOW TO EQUITY INVESTORS
(EQUITY CASH FLOW)

Free cash flow to equity investors is the cash flow remaining for paying dividends to common equity investors or for reinvesting in the firm after the firm satisfies all obligations (Damodaran, 1997). These obligations include debt payments, capital expenditures, changes in net working capital, and preferred dividend payments.

Income and cash-flow statements differ in terms of how they treat depreciation. The income statement amortizes the cost of capital equipment over its depreciable accounting life and deducts depreciation expense from revenue. Depreciation is an expense item that does not actually involve an outlay of cash by the firm. Although depreciation reduces income, it does not reduce cash flow. In calculating FCFE, depreciation is added back to net income. Net income plus depreciation often is referred to as a measure of the firm's ability to generate funds from internal operations. FCFE can be defined as follows:

FCFE = Net Income + Depreciation − Gross Capital Expenditures

$\quad\quad$ − Δ Net Working Capital + New Debt/Equity Issues

$\quad\quad$ − Principal Repayments − Preferred Dividends

$\quad$ = Net Income − (Gross Capital Expenditures − Depreciation)

$\quad\quad$ − Δ Net Working Capital + New Debt/Equity Issues

$\quad\quad$ − Principal Repayments − Preferred Dividends

Gross capital expenditures less depreciation represents that portion of capital spending that cannot be financed from internal cash flow. Other expense items that do not involve an actual expenditure of cash that should be added back to net income in the calculation of free cash flow include the amortization expense associated with such items as goodwill or capitalized software. See Exhibit 7-3

for a simple hypothetical numerical example of how to calculate free cash flow to
the firm and free cash flow to equity investors.

EXHIBIT 7-3. CALCULATING
FREE CASH FLOWS

The market served by Cash Cow Corporation (CCC) has matured. CCC
has the dominant market share in the industry and is the recognized leader
in product quality. The company is spending very little to modernize or
expand its production capacity or on research and development. Efficient
inventory control and cash management systems have helped to minimize
working capital requirements. High barriers to entry limit the number of
direct competitors. Gross capital expenditures in 2003 are $600 million,
about the same as their year-earlier level. The firm's 2003 principal repayment is $75 million on $1.2 billion in short- and long-term debt, and the firm's
combined federal, state, and local tax rate is .40. The firm also issued $50
million in subordinated debt in 2003. Annual dividends on preferred stock
total $10 million. Total working capital is $95 million and $115 million in
2002 and 2003, respectively. Revenue and expenses are given in the following table for 2002 and 2003. What is CCC's equity cash flow (FCFE) and
enterprise cash flow (FCFF) in 2003?

	2002	2003
Revenue	$4200	$4400
Less Operating Expenses	2730	2900
Less Depreciation	500	505
Equal EBIT	970	995
Less Interest Expense	100	102
Less Taxes	348	357
Equal Net Income	522	536

FCFE (Equity Cash Flow) = $536 + $505 − $600 − $20 + $50 − $75 − $10 = $386
FCFF (Enterprise Cash Flow) = $995(1 − .4) − $600 + $505 − $20 = $482

Exhibit 7-4 illustrates the calculation of free cash flow to equity investors
(equity cash flow) and free cash flow to the firm (enterprise cash flow) using
real data on IBM. The example clearly delineates the difference between equity
and enterprise cash flow. The former reflects operating, investment, and financing
activities, whereas the latter excludes cash flow from financing activities. The
calculation of equity cash flow follows a typical consolidated statement of cash
flows found in the firm's annual report and 10K. The only difference between the
typical consolidated statement of cash flows and Exhibit 7-4 is that equity cash
flow is determined before cash dividends to common shareholders. The deduction

of cash dividends to common shareholders, as well as an adjustment for exchange rate changes, results in the net change in cash and cash equivalents, which measures the change in IBM's cash balances between the beginning and the end of the year.

EXHIBIT 7-4. IBM'S EQUITY AND ENTERPRISE CASH FLOWS (2000)

Line Item	Equity Cash Flow	Line Item	Enterprise Cash Flow
Cash Flow from Operating Activities		**Cash Flow from Operating Activities**	
Net Income	8093	Earnings Before Interest and Taxes	12,251
+Depreciation	4513	−Earnings Before Interest & Taxes × Tax Rate[1]	12,251 × .4
+Amortization of Software	482	+Depreciation	4513
+Deferred Taxes	29	+Amortization of Software	482
+Net Gain on the Disposition of Fixed Assets	(792)	+Net Gain on the Disposition of Fixed Assets	(792)
+Other Changes That (Use)/Provide Cash Flow:		+Other Changes that (use)/provides cash flow:	
Receivables	(4720)	Receivables	(4720)
Inventories	(55)	Inventories	(55)
Other Assets	(643)	Other Assets	(643)
Accounts Payable	2245	Accounts Payable	2245
Other Liabilities	122	Other Liabilities	122
Net Cash Flow from Operating Activities	9274	Net Cash Flow from Operating Activities	8503
Cash Flow from Investing Activities		**Cash Flow from Investing Activities**	
Plant & Equipment (P&E) Spending	(5616)	Plant & Equipment (P&E) Spending	(5616)
Proceeds from the Disposition of P&E	1619	Proceeds from the Disposition of P&E	1619
Investment in Software	(565)	Investment in Software	(565)
Purchases of Marketable Securities	(1079)	Purchases of Marketable Securities	(1079)
Sales of Marketable Securities	1393	Sales of Marketable Securities	1393
Net Cash Flow from Investing Activities	(4248)	Net Cash Flow from Investing Activities	(4248)
		Enterprise Cash Flow[3]	4255

Cash Flow from Financing Activities	
Proceeds from New Debt Issues	9604
Short-Term (Repayments)/ Borrowings <90 Days	(1400)
Principal Repayments	(7561)
Preferred Stock Transactions (Net)	0
Common Stock Transactions (Net)	(6073)
Cash Dividends Paid on Preferred Stock	(20)
Net Cash Flow from Financing Activities	(5450)
Equity Cash Flow[2]	(424)
Effect of Exchange Rate Changes on Cash and Cash Equivalents	(147)
Cash Dividends Paid on Common Stock	(909)
Net Change in Cash & Cash Equivalents	(1480)
Cash & Cash Equivalents (January 1)	5043
Cash & Cash Equivalents (December 31)	3563

[1] Note that $EBIT - EBIT \times t = EBIT\,(1 - t)$. The marginal tax rate is assumed to be 40%, including federal, state, and local taxes.

[2] Equity cash flow or free cash flow to equity investors equals the sum of cash flow from operating, investment, and financing activities.

[3] Enterprise cash flow or free cash flow to the firm equals the sum of cash flow from operating and investment activities only.

TIME VALUE OF MONEY

This concept rests on the basic premise that money received today is worth more than the same sum received tomorrow because it can be invested at the current rate of interest. Moreover, the growth in the money received today and reinvested will be equal to the amount of interest income earned on the initial investment plus the interest earned on that interest income.

FUTURE VALUE

Future value (FV) compounding refers to the value of an initial investment, after a specified time period, at a specific rate of interest (Exhibit 7-5). This can be expressed as follows:

Future Value (FV) of $1 invested at interest rate i for 1 year $-$ $1 \times (1 \mid i)$

Future Value (FV) of $1 invested at interest rate i for 2 years $= \$1 \times (1 + i)$

$$\times (1 + i)$$

Future Value (FV) of $1 invested at interest rate i for n years $= \$1 \times (1 + i)^n$

This formula can be generalized for an amount A invested for n periods at an interest rate i and written as follows:

$$\text{Future Value (FV)} = A \times (1 + i)^n$$

EXHIBIT 7-5. FUTURE VALUE COMPOUNDING

What is the future value of $100 deposited for 2 years earning 10% per year?

$$FV = \$100(1.10)(1.10) = \$100(1.10)^2$$
$$= \$100(FVIF_{2,10}) = \$100(1.21)$$
$$= \$121$$

where $FVIF_{2,10}$ is the future value interest factor for 2 years at 10% annually. $FVIF_{2,10}$ may be found on a future value interest table.

What is the future value of $100 deposited for 3 years at 10% for the first 2 years and 5% for the third year?

$$FV = \$100(1.10)(1.10)(1.05)$$
$$= \$127$$

Note: This sometimes is referred to as cumulative compounding when the interest rate differs from one period to the next.

Continuous compounding represents an extreme case in which interest is compounding over all time periods, no matter how small. In this instance, the equation for future value compounding would approach infinity. The future value equation can be rewritten as follows:

$$FV = A \times e^{i \times n}, \quad \text{where } e \text{ is the exponential function whose value is 2.7183.}$$

PRESENT VALUE

PV of future returns refers to the cash value, today, of future returns after adjustments are made for the time value of money (Exhibit 7-6).

$$PV = \frac{FV}{(1+i)^n}$$

EXHIBIT 7-6. PRESENT VALUE OF FUTURE RETURNS

What is the PV of $150 received 2 years from now discounted at 10%?

$$PV = \$150/(1 + .10)^2$$
$$= \$150/1.21$$
$$= \$123.97$$

Note that the present value of an amount invested using continuous compounding is the reciprocal of the FV calculation and can be written as follows:

$$PV = A \times e^{-i \times n}, \quad \text{where } e \text{ is the exponential function whose value is } 2.7183.$$

ANNUITIES

An annuity is a series of equal payments, or receipts, made at any regular interval of time.

Future Value of an Annuity

The FV of an annuity (FVA) for equal payments, A, made at n regular intervals, and invested at an interest rate, i, can be written as follows (Exhibit 7-7):

$$FVA = A \times \frac{[(1+i)^n - 1]}{i}$$

Present Value of an Annuity

The present value of an annuity (PVA) can be calculated by discounting each cash flow to the present and then adding up the discounted values. Alternatively, PVA for equal payments, A, made for n time periods, at an interest rate (i) can be written as follows (Exhibit 7-8):

$$PVA = A \left[\frac{1 - (1/(1+i)^n)}{i} \right]$$

EXHIBIT 7-7. FUTURE VALUE OF ANNUITIES

Find the total future value of payments for a $100 annuity payment made once a year over a period of 4 years. Assume a 10% compound rate of interest.

$$\text{FVA} = \$100 \times \frac{(1 + .10)^4 - 1}{.10}$$

$$= \$100(4.641)$$

$$= \$464.10$$

EXHIBIT 7-8. PRESENT VALUE OF ANNUITIES

Find the present value of a stock that will return $100 annually for 4 years. Assume a 10% discount rate.

$$\text{PVA} = \$100 \left[\frac{1 - (1/(1 + .10)^4)}{.10} \right]$$

$$= \$100(3.169)$$

$$= \$316.90$$

ALTERNATIVE APPROACHES TO VALUATION

There are a variety of ways that are commonly used to value firms. These include the income or discounted cash-flow, market-based, asset-oriented, replacement cost, and weighted-average valuation methods. These methods provide estimates of the economic value of a company, which do not need to be adjusted if the intent is to acquire a small portion of the company. However, if the intention is to obtain a controlling interest in the firm, a control premium must be added to the estimated economic value of the firm to determine the purchase price. A controlling interest generally is considered more valuable to an investor than a minority interest because the investor has the right to final approval of important decisions affecting the business. These methods are explained in more detail later in this chapter.

INCOME OR DISCOUNTED CASH-FLOW METHOD

The income method focuses on some measure of cash flow or income. Valuation may be based on historical or projected data. Cash flow can be defined as FCFE or

FCFF and income may be defined as after-tax (NI); operating earnings or earnings before interest and taxes (EBIT); or earnings before interest, taxes, depreciation and amortization (EBITDA).

During the late 1980s and throughout the 1990s, EBITDA had been a popular measure of cash flow for valuing cable and telecommunications companies, which had argued that their networks were likely to hold value or even appreciate. Following the WorldCom scandal of 2002, the shortcomings of EBITDA became apparent. WorldCom had incorrectly capitalized $3.8 billion in expenditures that should have been expensed. While this resulted in an improvement in the firm's net income, it had a much greater impact on EBITDA, because this cash flow measure is calculated before depreciation. Consequently, the entire $3.8 billion was excluded. In the future, the prudent analyst is more likely to use more inclusive measures, such as free cash flow, for valuation purposes than the more narrowly defined EBITDA.

A commonly used technique to value a company's cash flow or income stream is the *discounted cash flow* (DCF) method. The DCF approach involves forecasting year-by-year results and then converting these annual projections into their present value or PV by dividing each annual figure by a discount rate. The *discount or capitalization rate* reflects the investor's required return to purchase an asset exhibiting a specific level of risk. The term capitalization rate commonly is used by professional appraisers, business brokers, valuation experts, and other M&A practitioners. At the end of the forecast period, a final estimation is made to determine the *terminal, sustainable, or continuing growth value*, which represents the estimated value of future cash flows at that point. The terminal value then is discounted to the present and added to the sum of the discounted values of the annual cash flow or income projections. The PV of the firm calculated in this manner sometimes is referred to as the *intrinsic value* of the firm. If the DCF method is applied to free cash flows to the firm, it is referred to as the *enterprise method*; if it is applied to free cash flows to shareholders, it is called the *equity method*. As will be discussed later in this chapter, the DCF model may be applied to cash flows that are not expected to grow or to grow at either a constant or variable rate.

MARKET-BASED OR RELATIVE VALUE METHODS

This method assumes that markets are efficient in that the current values of businesses determined in the marketplace embody all the information currently available about the business. Current values represent what a willing buyer and seller, having access to the same information, would pay for the business. Using this approach, value is determined by multiplying market-determined value measures (e.g., price-to-earnings [P/E], price-to-book, or price-to-sales ratios of other firms in the same industry, comparable industries, or comparable recent sales of similar firms) by the earnings, book value, or sales of the firm to be valued. The resulting calculation provides an estimate of the PV or current value of the firm.

ASSET-ORIENTED METHODS

Asset-oriented approaches, such as tangible book, liquidation, and breakup values, are useful in highly specialized situations. The calculation of tangible book value per share, book value less goodwill, may be useful in valuing financial services and distribution companies because highly liquid assets often comprise a large percentage of the total assets of such firms. The liquidation value of a firm is the current market value of the firm's assets as if it is going out of business less the cash value of its liabilities and costs incurred to liquidate the firm. Alternatively, a diversified firm consisting of multiple operating units or product lines can be valued by summing the PVs of each operating unit or product line as if they are operated independently. In a manner similar to calculating liquidation value, the breakup value of the firm is determined by estimating the after-tax proceeds from the sale of the firm's operating units and deducting the PV of the firm's liabilities and costs incurred in selling the company in pieces. Asset-oriented approaches ignore potential synergies that might exist among the various operations comprising the business.

REPLACEMENT COST METHOD

The cost approach estimates what it would cost to replace the target firm's assets at current market prices using professional appraisers less the PV of the firm's liabilities. The difference provides an estimate of the market value of equity. This approach does not take into account the *going concern value* of the company, which reflects how effectively the assets are being used in combination (i.e., synergies) to generate profits and cash flow. Valuing the assets separately in terms of what it would cost to replace them may seriously understate the firm's true going concern value. This approach also may be inappropriate if the firm has a significant amount of intangible assets on its books as a result of the difficulty in valuing such assets. For these reasons, the discussion in this chapter will focus on the income, market, and asset-oriented approaches. See Exhibit 7-9 for a summary of alternative valuation methods and Table 7-1 for a listing of the advantages and disadvantages of each approach.

EXHIBIT 7-9. SUMMARIZING COMMONLY USED METHODS TO VALUE FIRMS

1. Enterprise (FCFF) and Equity (FCFE) Discounted Cash-Flow Methods

   a. Zero-Growth Model
   b. Constant-Growth Model
   c. Variable-Growth Model

2. Market-Based Methods

  a. Comparable Companies

  b. Comparable Transactions

  c. Same Industry or Comparable Industry

3. Asset-Oriented Methods

  a. Tangible Book Value

  b. Liquidation Value

  c. Breakup Value

4. Replacement Cost Method (Cost to replace the target firm's assets)
5. Weighted Average Method (Uses an average of alternative valuation methods adjusted to reflect the analyst's confidence in the relative importance of each method)

APPLYING INCOME OR DISCOUNTED CASH-FLOW METHODS

The various DCF models used to value acquisitions are special cases of the conventional capital budgeting process. Capital budgeting is the process for evaluating and comparing alternative investment opportunities to ensure the best long-term financial return for the firm. In the capital budgeting process, cash flows are projected over the expected life of the project and discounted to the present at the firm's cost of capital. The resultant PV then is subtracted from the initial investment required to generate the cash-flow stream in order to calculate net present value (NPV) for the project. In this manner, NPV of each alternative project is calculated and ranked from the highest to the lowest in terms of dollar value. The firm then can maximize the value of the firm by first undertaking the project with the highest NPV, then the project with the second highest NPV, and so forth, until the firm has exhausted its available financial resources. M&As can be viewed as one of the alternative investment opportunities available to the firm.

ENTERPRISE DISCOUNTED CASH-FLOW MODEL (ENTERPRISE OR FCFF METHOD)

The enterprise valuation or FFCF approach discounts the after-tax free cash flow available to the firm from operations at the weighted average cost of capital to obtain the estimated enterprise value. The firm's estimated common equity value then is determined by subtracting the market value of the firm's debt and other investor claims on cash flow such as preferred stock from the enterprise value.

TABLE 7-1 Comparison of Alternative Valuation Techniques

	Strengths	Weaknesses
Income Approach		
Discounted Cash Flow	• Considers differences in the magnitude/timing of cash flows • Adjusts for risk • Requires a clear statement of valuation assumptions	• Requires forecasting of cash flows for each period, a terminal value, and discount or capitalization rate(s), using limited or unreliable data • Highly sensitive to the accuracy of income or cash flow and discount rate estimates • Terminal value may constitute a disproportionate share of the total value
Market Approach		
Comparable Companies	• Utilizes market-based price-to-earnings, sales, or book value for substantially similar companies	• Truly comparable public companies rarely exist • Valuations must be adjusted to reflect control premiums • Reflects accounting-based historical data • May be distorted because of current market psychology
Comparable Transactions	• Uses the most accurate market-based valuation at a point in time	• May be few in number or not current • Limited availability of specific transaction related data
Same or Comparable Industry	• Provides additional valuation for comparative purposes	• Assumes industry average valuation multiples are applicable to a specific company • Industry information often nonexistent
Replacement Cost Approach	• Applicable whenever the DCF or market approaches are unsuitable because of limited information	• May be of limited use when a large share of the firm's assets are intangible or if the target firm is highly profitable • Requires use of appraisers with specialized knowledge • Ignores value created by operating the assets as a going concern
Asset Oriented Approach		
Tangible Book Value	• Useful for financial services and distribution companies where assets tend to be highly liquid	• Book value may not equate to market value • Limited availability of required data
Breakup Value	• May unlock value in operating subsidiaries whose actual value cannot be determined easily by analysts outside the company	• Assumes that individual businesses can be sold quickly without any material loss of value • Available markets often highly illiquid
Liquidation Value	• Provides estimate of minimum value of a firm	• Frequently assumes that an "orderly" liquidation is possible • Available markets often highly illiquid

The estimate of equity derived in this manner will equal the value of equity determined by discounting the cash flow available to the firm's shareholders at the cost of equity. This assumes that the discount rates used to calculate the present values of the firm's debt and other investor claims reflect accurately the risk associated with each cash-flow stream. The enterprise approach is consistent with the capital budgeting process in that value is determined independently of how the business is financed. Moreover, it can be applied to individual business units or the parent firm in precisely the same manner. For example, for multiunit businesses, the value of equity using this method is equal to the sum of the value of each individual business unit owned by the parent firm plus excess cash balances less the present value of corporate overhead, debt, and preferred stock.

EQUITY DISCOUNTED CASH-FLOW MODEL
(EQUITY OR FCFE METHOD)

The equity valuation or FCFE approach discounts the after-tax cash flows available to the firm's shareholders at the cost of equity. This approach is used primarily in special situations such as for valuing highly leveraged transactions in which the capital structure is changing frequently and for financial services firms in which the cost of capital for various operations within the firm may be very difficult to estimate. For example, a retail commercial banking operation typically finances its operations using noninterest-bearing checking accounts. Determining the actual cost of acquiring such accounts is often quite arbitrary. By focusing on FCFE, the analyst only needs to estimate the financial services firm's cost of equity. The enterprise or FCFF method and the equity or FCFE method are illustrated in the following sections of this chapter using three different cash-flow growth scenarios: zero-growth, constant-growth, and variable growth rates.

ZERO-GROWTH VALUATION MODEL

This model assumes that free cash flow is constant in perpetuity. The value of the firm at time zero (P_0) is the discounted or capitalized value of its annual cash flow. In this instance, the discount rate and the capitalization rate are the same (Exhibit 7-10). The subscript FCFF or FCFE refers to the definition of cash flow used in the valuation.

$P_{0,\text{FCFF}} = \text{FCFF}_0/\text{WACC}$,   where FCFF_0 is free cash flow to the firm at time zero and WACC is the cost of capital.

$P_{0,\text{FCFE}} = \text{FCFE}_0/k_e$,   where FCFE_0 is free cash flow to equity investors at time zero and k_e is the cost of equity.

EXHIBIT 7-10. ZERO-GROWTH VALUATION MODEL

1. What is the enterprise value of a firm whose annual $FCFF_0$ of \$1 million is expected to remain constant in perpetuity and whose cost of capital is 12%?

$$P_{0,FCFF} = \$1/.12 = \$8.3 \text{ million}$$

2. Calculate the weighted average cost of capital and the enterprise value of a firm whose capital structure consists only of common equity and debt. The firm desires to limit its leverage to 30% of total capital. The firm's marginal tax rate is .4 and its beta is 1.5. The corporate bond rate is 8% and the 10-year U.S. Treasury bond rate is 5%. The expected annual return on stocks is 10%. Annual FCFF is expected to remain at \$4 million indefinitely.

$$k_e = .05 + 1.5(.10 - .05) = .125 \times 100 = 12.5\%$$
$$\text{WACC} = .125 \times .7 + .08 \times (1 - .4) \times .3 = .088 + .014$$
$$= .102 \times 100 = 10.2\%$$
$$P_{0,FCFF} = \$4/.102$$
$$= \$39.2 \text{ million}$$

CONSTANT-GROWTH VALUATION MODEL

The constant growth model is applicable for firms in mature markets, characterized by a moderate and somewhat predictable rate of growth. Examples of such industries include beverages, cosmetics, prepared foods, and cleaning products. To project growth rates, extrapolate the industry's growth rate over the past 5–10 years.

The constant-growth model frequently is referred to as the Gordon model (Gordon, 1962). The constant-growth model assumes that cash flow grows at a constant rate, g, that is less than the required return, k_e. The assumption that k_e is greater than g is a necessary mathematical condition for deriving the model (Gitman, 2000). In this model, next year's cash flow to the firm ($FCFF_1$) or the first year of the forecast period is expected to grow at the constant rate of growth g. Therefore, $FCFF_1 = FCFF_0(1 + g)$.

$$P_{0,FCFF} = FCFF_1/(\text{WACC} - g),$$
$$P_{0,FCFE} = FCFE_1/(k_e - g), \quad \text{where } FCFE_1 = FCFE_0(1 + g)$$

In this instance, the capitalization rate (CR) is equal to the difference between the cost of capital (WACC) or equity (k_e) and the expected growth rate g.

Note that this simple valuation model also provides a means of estimating the risk premium component of the cost of equity as an alternative to relying on historical information as is done in the capital asset pricing model. The Gordon model was developed originally to estimate the value of stocks in the current period (P_0) using the level of expected dividends (d_1) in the next period. This formulation provides an estimate of the present value of dividends growing at a constant rate forever. Assuming the stock market values stocks correctly and we know P_0, d_1, and g, we can estimate k_e. Therefore:

$$P_0 = d_1/(k_e - g) \quad \text{and} \quad k_e = (d_1/P_0) + g$$

This expression suggests that increases in a firm's share price relative to earnings (i.e., increases in its P/E ratio) lowers the firm's required return on acquisitions financed by issuing stock. This explains why high levels of M&A activity frequently coincide with booming stock markets. For example, if d_1 is $1, g is 10%, and $P_0 = \$10$, k_e is 20%. However, if P_0 increases to $20 and g and d_1 remain the same, k_e declines to 15%. Note that an increase in P_0 without an increase in earnings growth, g, implies a higher P/E ratio for the firm (Exhibit 7-11).

EXHIBIT 7-1 1. CONSTANT-GROWTH MODEL

1. Determine the enterprise value of a firm whose projected free cash flow to the firm next year is $1 million, WACC is 12%, and expected annual cash-flow growth rate is 6% is

$$P_{0,\text{FCFF}} = \$1/(.12 - .06) = \$16.7 \text{ million}$$

2. Estimate the equity value of a firm (P_0) whose cost of equity is 15% and whose free cash flow to equity holders is projected to grow 20% next year and then at a constant 10% annual rate thereafter. The current year's free cash flow to equity holders is $2 million.

$$P_{0,\text{FFCF}} = (2.0 \times 1.2)/(.15 - .10) = \$48.0 \text{ million}$$

3. Assume the expected dividend yield on the Standard & Poor 500 Index is 1.5% and that the expected growth in earnings and dividends is 8% annually. Estimate the equity value of a firm whose free cash flow to equity holders is $4.5 million in the current year. The firm's FCFE is expected to grow by 10% next year and 8% thereafter.

Estimate the value of the firm ($P_{0,\text{FCFE}}$).

$$k_e = d_1/P_0 + g = .015 + .08 = .095$$

$$P_{0,\text{FCFE}} = [\$4.5 \times (1.1)]/(.095 - .08) = \$4.95/.015$$

$$= \$330 \text{ million}$$

VARIABLE GROWTH VALUATION MODEL

Many firms experience periods of high growth followed by a period of slower, more stable growth. Examples of such industries include cellular phones, personal computers, and cable TV. Firms within such industries routinely experience double-digit growth rates for periods of 5–10 years because of low penetration of these markets in the early years of the product's life cycle. As the market becomes saturated, growth inevitably slows to a rate more in line with the overall growth of the economy or the general population. The PV of such firms is equal to the sum of the PV of the discounted cash flows during the high-growth period plus the discounted value of the cash flows generated during the stable growth period. In capital budgeting terms, the discounted value of the cash flows generated during the stable growth period is called the *terminal, sustainable, or continuing growth value*.

The terminal value may be estimated using the Gordon growth model. Free cash flow during the first year beyond the *nth* or final year of the forecast period, FFCF_{n+1}, is divided by the difference between the assumed cost of capital and the expected cash-flow growth rate beyond the *nth* year forecast period. The terminal value is the value in the *nth* year of all future cash flows beginning in the *nth* year and beyond. Consequently, to convert the terminal value to its value in the current year, it is necessary to discount the terminal value by using the discount rate used to convert the *nth* year value to a present value.

Although there are other ways to calculate the terminal value, the use of the Gordon model provides consistency in estimating the value of the firm created beyond the end of the forecast period. It enables the application of discounted cash-flow methodology in estimating value during both the variable and stable growth periods. However, the selection of the earnings growth rate and cost of capital must be done very carefully. Small changes in assumptions can result in dramatic swings in the terminal value and, therefore, in the valuation of the firm. Table 7-2 illustrates the sensitivity of a terminal value of $1 million to different spreads between the cost of capital and the stable growth rate. Note that using the Gordon constant-growth model formula, the terminal value declines dramatically as the spread between the cost of capital and expected stable growth for cash flow increases by one percentage point.

Note that the expected stable growth rate in cash flow can be either positive or negative. The use of a positive growth rate suggests that the firm is expected to continue forever. This assumption is not as bizarre as it may seem because

TABLE 7-2 Impact of Changes in Assumptions on a Terminal Value of $1 Million

Difference Between Cost of Capital and Cash-Flow Growth Rate	Terminal Value ($ Millions)
3%	33.3[1]
4%	25.0
5%	20.0
6%	16.7
7%	14.3

[1]$1.0/.03.

companies frequently are acquired or liquidated, enabling the investor to earn a premium on their investment or to recover at least some portion of their original investment. In contrast, the use of a negative growth rate implies that the firm will shrink each year until it eventually disappears. Therefore, we may use the Gordon model to estimate the terminal value of a firm that we do not expect to last forever.

There are numerous other ways terminal values can be estimated. The price-to-earnings, price-to-cash flow, or price-to-book techniques value the target as if it is sold at the end of a specific number of years. At the end of the forecast period, the terminal year's earnings, cash flow, or book value is projected and multiplied by a P/E, cash flow, or book value believed to be appropriate for that year. The terminal value also may be estimated by assuming the firm's cash flow or earnings in the last year of the forecast period will continue in perpetuity. This is equivalent to the zero-growth valuation model discussed previously.

Using the definition of free cash flow to the firm and assuming the actual cash balances are at required levels, P_0 can be estimated using the variable growth model as follows (Exhibit 7-12):

$$P_{0,\text{FCFF}} = \sum_{t=1}^{n} \frac{\text{FCFF}_0 \times (1 + g_t)^t}{(1 + \text{WACC})^t} + \frac{P_n}{(1 + \text{WACC})^n}$$

where $P_n = \dfrac{\text{FCFF}_n \times (1 + g_m)}{(\text{WACC}_m - g_m)}$

FCFF_0 = FCFF in year 0
WACC = Weighted average cost of capital through year n
WACC_m = Cost of capital assumed beyond year n
P_n = Value of the firm at the end of year n (terminal value)
g_t = Growth rate through year n
g_m = Stabilized or long-term growth rate beyond year n

After having determined the value of the firm using free cash flow to the firm, the value of the firm to equity investors can be estimated as follows:

$$P_{0,FCFE} = \sum_{t=1}^{n} \frac{FCFE_0 \times (1 + g_t)^t}{(1 + k_e)^t} + \frac{P_n}{(1 + k_e)^n}$$

where $\quad P_n \quad = \dfrac{FCFE_n \times (1 + g_m)}{(k_{em} - g_m)}$

$FCFE_0$ = FCFE in year 0
k_e = Cost of equity through year n
k_{em} = Cost of equity used to determine terminal value

EXHIBIT 7-12. VARIABLE-GROWTH VALUATION MODEL

Estimate the enterprise value of a firm (P_0) whose free cash flow is projected to grow at a compound annual average rate of 35% for the next 5 years. Growth then is expected to slow to a more normal 5% annual growth rate. The current year's cash flow to the firm is $4 million. The firm's cost of capital during the high-growth period is 18% and 12% beyond the fifth year, as growth stabilizes. The firm's cash in excess of normal operating balances is assumed to be zero. Therefore, the present value of cash flows during the forecast period:

$$PV_{1-5} = \frac{4.00 \times 1.35}{(1.18)} + \frac{4.00 \times (1.35)^2}{(1.18)^2} + \frac{4.00 \times (1.35)^3}{(1.18)^3}$$

$$+ \frac{4.00 \times (1.35)^4}{(1.18)^4} + \frac{4.00 \times (1.35)^5}{(1.18)^5}$$

$$= 5.40/1.18 + 7.29/(1.18)^2 + 9.84/(1.18)^3$$

$$+ 13.29/(1.18)^4 + 17.93/(1.18)^5$$

$$= 4.58 + 5.24 + 5.99 + 6.85 + 7.84 = 30.50$$

Calculation of terminal value:

$$PV_5 = \frac{[(4.00 \times (1.35)^5 \times 1.05)]/(.12 - .05)}{(1.18)^5}$$

$$= \frac{18.83/.07}{2.29} = 117.65$$

$$P_{0,FCFF} = PV_{1-5} + PV_5 = 30.50 + 117.65 = 148.15$$

DETERMINING GROWTH RATES

The key premise of the variable growth discounted cash-flow model is that the value of the firm can be represented by the sum of the high-growth period(s) plus a stable or sustainable growth period extending indefinitely into the future. A key risk is the sensitivity of the terminal values to the choice of assumptions about the stable growth period, such as the cash-flow growth rate and the discount rate associated with that period.

Growth rates can be readily calculated based on the historical experience of the firm or industry. The average annual growth rate, g, for a time series extending from t_1 to t_n can be calculated by solving the following equation:

$$g = (t_n/t_1)^{1/n} - 1$$

Care should be taken to discard aberrant data points resulting from infrequent or nonrecurring events such as labor stoppages and droughts. Such data points will result in a distortion of the growth rate.

Duration of High-Growth Period

Determining the appropriate length of time for the high-growth period can be elusive. There are no compelling rules. However, intuition suggests that the length of the high-growth period should be longer the greater the current growth rate of a firm's cash flow when compared with the stable growth rate. This is particularly true when the high-growth firm has a relatively small market share and there is little reason to believe that its growth rate will slow in the foreseeable future. For example, if the industry is expected to grow at 5% annually and the target firm, which has only a negligible market share, is growing at three times that rate, it may be appropriate to assume a high-growth period of 5–10 years. Moreover, if the terminal value comprises a substantial percentage (e.g., three-fourths) of total PV, the forecast period should be extended beyond the customary 5 years to at least 10 years. The extension of the time period reduces the impact of the terminal value in determining the market value of the firm. High-growth rates usually are associated with increased levels of uncertainty. In applying discounted cash-flow methodology, risk is incorporated into the discount rate. Consequently, the discount rate during the high-growth (i.e., less predictable) period or periods should generally be higher than during the stable growth period.

More sophisticated forecasts of growth rates involve an analysis of the firm's customer base. Annual revenue projections are made for each customer or product and summed to provide an estimate of aggregate revenue. A product or service's life cycle (see Chapter 4) is a useful tool for making such projections. In some industries, a product's life cycle may be a matter of months (e.g., software) or years (e.g., an automobile). This information is readily available by examining the launch dates of new products and services in an industry in publications provided by the industry's trade associations. By determining where the firm's products are in their life cycle, the analyst can project annual unit volume by product.

Stable or Sustainable Growth Rate

The stable growth rate generally is going to be less than or equal to the overall growth rate of the industry in which the firm competes or the general economy. Stable growth rates in excess of these levels implicitly assume that the firm's output eventually will exceed that of its industry or the general economy. Similarly, for multinational firms, the stable growth rate should not exceed the projected growth rate for the world economy or for a particular region of the world.

ESTIMATING THE MARKET VALUE OF THE FIRM'S DEBT

In the previous sections, we estimated the equity value of the firm by discounting the projected free cash flows to equity investors by the firm's cost of equity. Alternatively, the equity value may be estimated by subtracting the market value of the firm's debt from the firm's estimated enterprise value. In some instances, the analyst may not know the exact principal repayment schedule for the largest firm's debt. To determine the market value of debt, treat the book value of all of the firm's debt as a conventional coupon bond in which interest is paid annually or semiannually and the principal is repaid at maturity. The coupon is the interest on all of the firm's debt, and the principal at maturity is a weighted average of the maturity of all of the debt outstanding. The weighted average principal at maturity is the sum of the amount of debt outstanding for each maturity date multiplied by its share of total debt outstanding. The estimated current market value of the debt then is calculated as the sum of the annuity value of the interest expense per period plus the present value of the principal. The only debt that must be valued is the debt outstanding on the valuation date. Future borrowing is irrelevant if we assume that cash inflows generated from investments financed with future borrowings are sufficient to satisfy interest and principal payments associated with these borrowings.

Both capital and operating leases also should be counted as outstanding debt of the firm. When a lease is classified as a capital lease, the present value of the lease expenses is treated as debt. Interest is imputed on this amount that corresponds to debt of comparable risk and maturity. This imputed interest is shown on the income statement. Although operating lease expenses are treated as operating expenses on the income statement, they are not counted as part of debt on the balance sheet for financial reporting purposes. For valuation purposes, operating leases should be included in debt because failure to meet lease payments will result in the loss of the leased asset, which is contributing in some capacity to generating operating cash flows. Future operating lease expenses are shown in financial statement footnotes. These future expenses should be discounted at an interest rate comparable to current bank lending rates for unsecured assets. The discount rate may be approximated using the firm's current pretax cost of debt. The pretax cost of debt is used to reflect the market rate of interest lessors would charge the firm (Exhibit 7-13). If future operating lease expenses are not available, the analyst can approximate the principal amount of the operating leases by discounting the current year's operating lease payment as a perpetuity using the firm's cost of debt.

EXHIBIT 7-13. ESTIMATING THE MARKET VALUE OF A FIRM'S DEBT

According to its 10K report, Gromax, Inc. has two debt issues outstanding, with a total book value of $220 million. Annual interest expense on the two issues totals $20 million. The first issue, whose current book value is $120 million, matures at the end of 5 years; the second issue, whose book value is $100 million, matures in 10 years. The average maturity of the two issues is 7.27 years (i.e., $5 \times (120/220) + 10 \times (100/220)$). The current cost of debt maturing in 7–10 years is 8.5%. The firm's 10K also shows that the firm has annual operating lease expenses of $2.1, $2.2, $2.3, and $5.0 million in the fourth year and beyond (the 10K indicated the firm's cumulative value in the fourth year and beyond to be $5.0). (For our purposes, we may assume that the $5.0 million is paid in the fourth year.) What is the total market value of the firm's total long-term debt (MV_{TD}), including conventional debt (MV_D) and operating leases (MV_{OL})?

$$MV_D = \$20 \times \frac{[(1 - (1/(1.085)^{7.27})]}{.085} + \frac{\$220}{(1.085)^{7.27}}$$

$$= \$105.27 + \$121.55$$

$$= \$226.82$$

$$MV_{OL} = \frac{\$2.1}{(1.085)} + \frac{\$2.2}{(1.085)^2} + \frac{\$2.3}{(1.085)^3} + \frac{\$5.0}{(1.085)^4}$$

$$= \$1.94 + \$1.87 + \$1.80 + \$3.61$$

$$= \$9.22$$

$$MV_{TD} = \$226.82 + \$9.22 = \$236.04$$

Capitalizing operating lease payments requires that the cost of capital incorporates the effects of this source of financing and that operating income must be adjusted to reflect lease expenses, as discussed earlier in this chapter. Finally, to calculate the value of the firm's equity, both debt and the capitalized value of operating leases must be subtracted from the estimated enterprise value of the firm (FCFF).

The Enron bankruptcy in late 2001 highlighted the importance of incorporating off-balance sheet financing into the calculation of the firm's total leverage. Such financing often takes the form of so-called *synthetic-lease arrangements* in which a financial institution sets up a *special purpose entity* that borrows money to finance new construction or equipment purchases. The entity holds the title and leases it to the firm for the term of the lease, typically 3–7 years with an option to renew. During the lease term, the firm is allowed to deduct interest payments and depreciation of the property's value for tax purposes; however, for financial reporting purposes, the arrangement is treated as a standard operating lease in which both the leased property and associated debt is kept off the balance sheet. In early 2002, the Financial Accounting Standards Board announced that new rules were being considered that would require that such special purpose entities be shown on the firm's balance sheet (Urban, 2002). If the rulings become effective, the problem of off-balance sheet financing may be less pronounced in the future.

Once we have estimated the market value of a firm's debt, the firm's equity value can be estimated by deducting the market value of the firm's debt from the enterprise value of the firm, which includes both the value of equity and debt (Exhibit 7-14).

EXHIBIT 7-14. ESTIMATING EQUITY VALUE BY DEDUCTING THE MARKET VALUE OF DEBT FROM THE ENTERPRISE VALUE

The enterprise value of a firm is estimated to be $1,500,000. The book value of the firm's debt is $1 million, with annual interest expense of $80,000 and term to maturity of 4 years. The debt is a conventional "interest only" note with a repayment of principal at maturity. The firm does not have any operating leases; there is no excess cash balance. The firm's current cost of debt is 10%. What is the value of the firm to equity investors?

$$MV_0 = \$80,000 \times \left[\frac{1 - (1/1.10)^4}{.10}\right] + \frac{\$1,000,000}{1.10^4}$$

$$= \$80,000(\text{PVIFA}_{4,10}) + \$1,000,000(\text{PVIF}_{4,10})$$

$$= \$80,000(3.17) + \$1,000,000(.683)$$

$$= \$253,600 + \$683,000$$

$$= \$936,600$$

$$P_{0,\text{FCFE}} = \$1,500,000 - \$936,600$$
$$= \$563,400$$

Notes:

1. The formula for the PV of an annuity is used to calculate the market value of debt (MV_0) because of the four equal interest payments made during the remaining term to maturity. PVIFA is the present value interest factor associated with a 4-year annuity at a 10% interest rate.
2. The firm's current cost of debt of 10% is higher than the implied interest rate of 8% ($\$80,000/\$1,000,000$) on the loan currently on the firm's books. This suggests that the market rate of interest has increased since the firm borrowed the $1 million "interest only" note.

APPLYING MARKET-BASED (RELATIVE VALUE) METHODS

Market-based methods assume a firm's market value can be approximated by a measure of value for comparable companies, comparable transactions, or comparable industry averages. Measures of value could include the firm's earnings, cash flow, sales, or book value. Because of the requirement for positive current or near-term earnings or cash flow, market-based methods are meaningful only for companies with a positive, stable earnings or cash flow stream. If comparable companies are available, the market value of a target firm T (MV_T) can be estimated by solving the following equation:

$$MV_T = (MV_C/I_C) \times I_T,$$

where MV_C = Market value of the comparable company C
        I_C = Measure of value for comparable company C
        I_T = Measure of value for firm T
      (MV_C/I_C) = Market value multiple for the comparable company

For example, if the P/E ratio for the comparable firm is equal to 10 (MV_C/I_C) and the after-tax earnings of the target firm is $2 million ($I_T$), the market value of the target firm is $20 million ($MV_T$).

Market-based or relative value methods are popular for three reasons. First, such methods are relatively simple to calculate and require far fewer assumptions than discounted cash-flow techniques. Second, relative valuation is far easier to explain than DCF methods. Finally, the use of market-based techniques is more likely to reflect current market demand and supply conditions.

COMPARABLE COMPANIES METHOD

Applying the comparable companies approach requires that the analyst identify companies that are substantially similar to the target firm (see Table 7-3). The primary advantage of this approach is that it uses market-based values rather than assumption-driven discounted cash flow-based valuations. Moreover, it can be used to establish valuations for companies that are not publicly traded. Consequently, this approach is used widely in so-called "fairness opinions," which investment bankers frequently are asked to give before a request for shareholder approval of an acquisition. Because it frequently is viewed as more objective than alternative approaches, the comparable companies method also enjoys widespread use in legal cases.

This approach has a number of limitations. First, the difficulty in obtaining truly comparable companies can result in widely divergent ratios and values. In practice, it is frequently difficult to find companies that are substantially similar to the target

TABLE 7-3 Valuing a Target Company Using Comparable Companies

An analyst selects two companies that are believed to be quite similar to the target company that she wishes to value. Three indicators of value are selected for the valuation of the target company. These include revenue, operating cash flow, and net income. The market value for each comparable company is given in row (1). The dollar value of each measure of value is given in rows (2)–(4). Market value multiples are given in rows (5)–(7). These multiples are calculated by dividing market value by the dollar value of each measure of value. Note that the market value to net income is equivalent to the price-to-earnings ratio. Estimated values of the target firm are obtained by multiplying column (3) by column (4). A single value of the target is determined by averaging the estimates in column (5).

Measure of Value	Comparable Company 1 (1)	Comparable Company 2 (2)	Comparable Company Average (3)	Target Company Projections (Millions) (4)	Estimated Value of Target (Millions) (5)
Measures of Value (Millions)					
(1) Market Value	$120	$80	$100		
(2) Revenue	$100	$57	$78.5		
(3) Operating Cash Flow	$10	$7	$8.5		
(4) Net Income	$7	$4	$5.5		
Market Value Multiples					
(5) Revenue	1.2	1.4	1.3	$150	$195
(6) Operating Cash Flow	12	11.4	11.7	$23	$269.1
(7) Net Income	17.1	20	18.6	$15	$279
			Average Estimated Value of Target		$247.7

in terms of markets served, product offering, degree of leverage, and size. Even when companies appear to be substantially similar, there are likely to be significant differences in these ratios at any one moment in time. These differences may result from investor overreaction to one-time events, which quickly abate with the passage of time. Consequently, comparisons made at different times can provide distinctly different results. By taking an average of multiples over 6 months or 1 year, these differences may be minimized. Second, the use of market-based methods can result in significant under- or overvaluation during periods of declining or rising stock markets because this method reflects the current market psychology more readily than does the DCF method. Finally, market-based methods can be manipulated easily because the methods do not require a clear statement of assumptions with respect to risk, growth, or the timing or magnitude of cash flows.

When using the this approach to valuation, it is critical to remember that the "comparable" companies used to value a target will generally not reflect a premium paid over the prevailing market price to gain a controlling interest in the target company. Consequently, the comparable company approach to valuation is only a starting point for valuation. An appropriate premium generally must be added to the estimated market value of the firm. The premium generally will be determined as a result of the negotiation process and should reflect premiums paid of recent acquisitions of similar firms.

The analyst should be careful not to mechanically add an acquisition premium to the target firm's estimated value based on the comparable companies' method if there is evidence that the market values of these "comparable firms" already may reflect the effects of acquisition activity elsewhere in the industry. For example, rival firms' share prices will rise in response to the announced acquisition of a competitor, regardless of whether the proposed acquisition is ultimately successful or unsuccessful (Song and Walkling, 2000). Akhigbe, Borde, and Whyte (2000) find that the increase in rivals' share prices may be even greater if the acquisition attempt is unsuccessful because investors believe that the bidder will attempt to acquire other firms in the same industry.

COMPARABLE TRANSACTIONS METHOD

The comparable transactions approach is conceptually similar to the comparable companies approach. Multiples used to estimate the value of the target are based on purchase prices of comparable companies that recently were acquired. P/E, sales, cash flow, and book value are calculated using the purchase price for the recent transaction. Earnings, sales, cash flow, and book value for the target subsequently are multiplied by these ratios to obtain an estimate of the market value of the target company. This estimated value of the target firm obtained by using recent comparable transactions already reflects a purchase price premium, unlike the comparable companies approach to valuation. The obvious limitation to the comparable transactions method is the difficulty in finding truly comparable, recent transactions.

SAME OR COMPARABLE INDUSTRY METHOD

In the same or comparable industry method, the target company's earnings, revenue, cash flow, and book value are multiplied by the ratio of the market value of shareholders' equity to earnings, revenue, cash flow, and book value for the average company in the target firm's industry or for a comparable industry (Exhibit 7-15). Such information can be obtained from Standard & Poor's, Value Line, Moody's, Dun & Bradstreet, and Wall Street analysts. The primary advantage of this technique is the ease of use. Disadvantages include the presumption that industry multiples are actually comparable and that analysts' projections are unbiased.

EXHIBIT 7-15. VALUING A TARGET COMPANY USING THE SAME OR COMPARABLE INDUSTRIES

Industry analysts estimate a firm's earnings per share (E/S) for the coming year to be $3.00. The firm has 1 million shares of common stock outstanding. The industry in which the firm competes currently has an average price-to-earnings ratio (P/E) of 20. What is the firm's estimated price per share (P/S) and market value (MV)?

$$P/S = (E/S) \times (P/E) = \$3.00 \times 20 = \$60$$

$$MV = \$60 \times 1,000,000 = \$60,000,000$$

VALUE DRIVER-BASED VALUATION

In the absence of earnings, other factors that drive the creation of value for a firm may be used for valuation purposes. Such factors commonly are used to value start-up companies and initial public offerings, which often have little or no earnings performance records. Measures of profitability and cash flow are simply manifestations or measures of value. These measures are dependent on factors both external and internal to the firm. Value drivers exist for each major functional category of the firm including sales, marketing and distribution; customer service; operations and manufacturing, and purchasing.

There are both micro value drivers and macro value drivers. *Micro value drivers* are those that directly influence specific functional aspects of the firm. Micro value drivers for sales, marketing, and distribution could include product quality measures such as part defects per 100,000 units sold, on-time delivery, the number of multiyear subscribers, and the ratio of product price to some measure of perceived quality. Customer service drivers could include average waiting time on the telephone, the number of billing errors, and the time required to correct such errors. Operational value drivers include average collection period, inventory turnover, and the number of units produced per manufacturing employee hour. Purchasing value drivers include average payment period, on-time vendor delivery, and the quality of purchased materials and services. *Macro value drivers* are more encompassing than micro value drivers in that they may affect all aspects of the firm. Examples of macro value drivers include market share, overall customer satisfaction measured by survey results, total asset turns (sales to total assets), and revenue per employee.

Using value drivers to value businesses is straightforward. First, the analyst needs to determine the key determinants of value or value drivers for the target. Second, the market value for comparable companies is divided by the value driver selected for the target to calculate the dollars of market value per unit of value driver. Third, multiply this figure by the same indicator or value driver for the target company. For example, assume that the primary macro value driver or determinant of a firm's market value in a particular industry is market share. How investors value market share can be estimated by dividing the market leader's market value by its market share. If the market leader has a market value and market share of $300 million and 30%, respectively, the market is valuing each percentage point of market share at $10 million (i.e., $300 million/30). If the target company in the same industry has a 20% market share, the market value of the target company is $200 million (20 points of market share times $10 million per market share point).

Similarly, the market value of comparable companies could be divided by other known value drivers. Examples include the number of visitors or page views per month for an Internet content provider, the number of subscribers to a magazine, and the number of households with TVs in a specific geographic area for a cable TV company. Using this method, AT&T's acquisitions of the cable companies TCI and Media One in the late 1990s would appear to be a "bargain." AT&T spent an average of $5000 per household (the price paid for each company divided by the number of customer households acquired) in purchasing these companies' customers. In contrast, Deutsche Telekom and Mannesmann spent $6000 and $7000 per customer, respectively, in buying mobile phone companies One 2 One and Orange Plc (*Business Week*, 2000).

The major advantage of this approach is its simplicity. Its major disadvantages include the assumption that a single value driver or factor is representative of the total value of the business. The recent bankruptcy of many dotcom companies illustrates how this valuation technique can be misused. Many of these firms had never shown any earnings, yet they exhibited huge market valuations. Investors often justified these lofty valuations by using page views and subscribers of supposedly comparable firms to value any firm associated with the Internet. These proved to be very poor indicators of the firm's ability to generate earnings. What actually determined these firms' share prices was investor fascination with Internet stocks at that time rather that the assumed value drivers.

APPLYING ASSET-ORIENTED METHODS

TANGIBLE BOOK VALUE OR EQUITY
PER SHARE METHOD

Book value is a much-maligned indicator of value because book asset values rarely reflect actual market values (Exhibit 7-16). They may over- or understate market value. For example, the value of land frequently is understated on the balance sheet, whereas inventory often is overstated if it is old or obsolete. The applicability of this approach varies by industry. Although book values generally do not mirror actual market values for manufacturing companies, they may be more accurate for distribution companies with high inventory turnover rates. Examples of such companies include pharmaceutical distributor Bergen Brunswick and personal computer distributor Ingram Micro. Book value is also widely used for valuing financial services companies, where tangible book value is primarily cash or liquid assets. Tangible book value is book value less goodwill.

EXHIBIT 7-16. VALUING COMPANIES
USING BOOK VALUE

Target Company has total assets (TA) of $15 million, of which goodwill (GW) accounts for $2 million. Total liabilities (TL) are $9 million. Total shares outstanding (S) are 2 million. Estimate tangible book value per share (BVS).

$$\text{BVS} = (\text{TA} - \text{TL} - \text{GW})/S = (\$15 - \$9 - \$2)/2 = \$2$$

Another firm in the same industry as Target Company and of approximately the same size, customer base, and profitability recently was sold at a price that equated to five times its book value per share. Estimate the implied market value of Target Company using BVS as a measure of value.

$$\text{Market Value Per Share} = 5 \times \$2 = \$10$$

LIQUIDATION OR BREAKUP VALUE

The terms liquidation and breakup value often are used interchangeably. However, there are subtle distinctions. *Liquidation* or *breakup value* is the projected price of the firm's assets sold separately less its liabilities. Liquidation may be involuntary as a result of bankruptcy or voluntary if a firm is viewed by its owners as worth more in liquidation than as a going concern. The *going concern* value of a company may be defined as the firm's value in excess of the sum of the value of its parts. The breakup value of the firm is synonymous with its voluntary liquidation value. Liquidation and breakup strategies will be explored in more detail in Chapter 13.

During the late 1970s and throughout most of the 1980s, highly diversified companies routinely were valued by investors in terms of their value if broken up and sold as discrete operations as well as their going concern value as a consolidated operation. Companies lacking real synergy among their operating units or sitting on highly appreciated assets often were viewed as more valuable when broken up. For example, natural resource companies such as Weyerhauser, a leading forest products company and owner of enormous tracts of timberland, or Mobil Oil, a global energy giant possessing vast amounts of oil and gas reserves, often were valued in terms of their book value per share. Investors reasoned that during periods of inflation, the value of their tangible assets would appreciate. If the tangible book value per share exceeded their current market value per share for any significant period, they could become acquisition candidates and subsequently be dismembered for sale in discrete pieces. FEDCO, the creator of the large warehouse-discount store concept, determined in 1999 that its shareholders would be better served if the board of directors liquidated the firm rather than spent the money necessary to refurbish the firm's stores. The value of the firm's real estate exceeded the value that could be created by continuing to operate the firm.

In practice, the calculation of liquidation value, voluntary or otherwise, requires a concerted effort by appraisers, who are intimately familiar with the operations to be liquidated. In some instances, the expenses incurred in terms of legal, appraisal, and consulting fees may constitute a large percentage of the dollar proceeds of the sale of the firm's assets. Guidelines do exist for the probable liquidation value of various types of assets. However, they will differ dramatically from one industry to another. They also depend on the condition of the economy and on whether the assets must be liquidated in a hurry to satisfy creditors.

Analysts frequently estimate the liquidation value of a target company to determine the minimum value of the company in the worst-case scenario of bankruptcy. They make a simplifying assumption that the assets can be sold in an orderly fashion, which is defined as a reasonable amount of time to solicit bids from qualified buyers. "Orderly fashion" often is defined as 9–12 months. Under these circumstances, high-quality receivables typically can be sold for 80–90% of book value. Inventories might realize 80–90% of book value depending on the condition and the degree of obsolescence. More rapid liquidation might reduce the value of inventories to 60–65% of book value. The liquidation value of equipment will vary widely depending on the age and condition.

Inventories need to be reviewed in terms of obsolescence, receivables in terms of collectability, equipment in terms of age and effectiveness, and real estate in terms of true market value. Equipment such as lathes and computers with a

TABLE 7-4   Calculating Liquidation Value

Titanic Corporation has declared bankruptcy and the trustee has been asked by its creditors to estimate its liquidation value assuming orderly sale conditions. Note that this example does not take into account legal fees, taxes, management fees, and contractually required employee severance expenses. In certain cases, these expenses can comprise a substantial percentage of the proceeds from liquidation.

Balance Sheet Item	Book Value ($)	Orderly Sale Value ($)
Cash	100	100
Receivables	500	450
Inventory	800	720
Equipment (After Depreciation)	200	60
Land	200	300
Total Assets	1800	1630
Total Liabilities	1600	1600
Shareholders' Equity	200	30

zero book value may have a significant economic market value (i.e., useful life). Land can be a hidden source of value because it frequently is undervalued on generally accepted accounting principles balance sheets. Prepaid assets such as insurance premiums sometimes can be liquidated with a portion of the premium recovered. The liquidation value will be reduced dramatically if the assets have to be liquidated in "fire sale" conditions under which assets are sold to the first rather than the highest bidder (Table 7-4).

Table 7-5 illustrates a hypothetical estimation of the breakup value of a firm consisting of multiple operating units. The assumption is that the interdependencies among the four operating units are limited such that they can be sold separately without a significant degradation of the value of any individual unit.

VALUING THE FIRM USING THE
WEIGHTED AVERAGE METHOD

Weights reflect the analyst's relative confidence in the various methodologies. Valuations of multiples based on recent comparable transactions frequently are given the greatest weight, followed by discounted cash-flow calculations. Liquidation values generally are given the smallest weight because they generally represent the worst-case scenario (Exhibit 7-17).

As mentioned earlier, Table 7-1 summarizes the primary strengths and weaknesses of the alternative valuation methodologies discussed in this chapter. The methodologies actually used may vary from situation to situation depending on the circumstances.

TABLE 7-5   Calculating Breakup Value

Sea Bass Inc. consists of four operating units. The value of operating synergies among the units is believed to be minimal. All but $10 million in debt can be allocated to each of the 4 units. Such debt is associated with financing the needs of the corporate overhead structure. Legal, consulting, and investment banking fees, as well as severance expenses associated with terminating corporate overhead personnel, amount to $10 million. What is the breakup value of Sea Bass Inc.?

Operating Unit	Estimated Equity Value ($ Millions)
Unit 1	100
Unit 2	125
Unit 3	50
Unit 4	75
Total Equity Value	350
Less any unallocated liabilities held at the corporate level, corporate overhead expense, and costs associated with the breakup.	20
Total Breakup Value	330

EXHIBIT 7-17. WEIGHTED AVERAGE VALUATION OF ALTERNATIVE METHODOLOGIES

An analyst has estimated the value of a company using multiple valuation methodologies. The discounted cash-flow value is $220 million, the comparable transactions value is $234 million, the P/E-based value is $224 million, and the liquidation value is $150 million. The analyst has greater confidence in certain methodologies than others. Estimate the weighted average value of the firm using all valuation methodologies and the weights or relative importance the analyst gives to each methodology.

Estimated Value ($ Millions)	Relative Weight (As Determined by Analyst)	Weighted Average ($ Millions)
220	.30	66.0
234	.40	93.6
224	.20	44.8
150	.10	15.0
	1.00	219.4

VALUING NONOPERATING ASSETS

Operating cash flow is generated from operating assets. The cost of capital measures the cost of financing these assets. The value of such assets is calculated by discounting projected operating cash flows to the present. However, other assets, which are not directly used in operating the firm, also may provide substantial value. Examples of such nonoperating assets include cash in excess of normal operating requirements, investments in other firms, and unused or underutilized assets. The value of such assets should be added to the value of the discounted cash flows from operating assets to determine the total value of the firm.

CASH AND MARKETABLE SECURITIES

Cash and short-term marketable securities, held in excess of the firm's normal operating requirements, represent value that should be added to the present value of operating assets to determine the value of the firm. The amount of cash a firm actually requires to satisfy normal working capital needs varies by size and type of firm. Small retailers whose transactions consist primarily of cash transactions may require more cash on hand than larger retailers dependent on credit card transactions. Large firms, with sophisticated cash management systems, may require very little cash for operating purposes because cash receipts mailed to lock boxes are frequently "swept" into interest-bearing accounts. These accounts consist of marketable securities such as U.S. Treasury securities, federal funds, and high-grade commercial paper.

The challenge is to determine what constitutes excess cash balances. Holdings of cash and short-term marketable securities can fluctuate as a result of seasonal changes in revenue; business cycle fluctuations; and nonrecurring gains, losses, or expenses. Although some of these changes in cash balances are predictable (e.g., seasonal variation or nonrecurring gains/losses), changes related to the business cycle or management decisions to enhance cash flow by deferring needed expenditures may not be.

Some analysts are inclined to simply add the firm's holdings of cash and short-term marketable securities to the value of the firm's operating assets to determine the firm's value. The implicit assumption is that projected operating cash flows accurately reflect all future sources and uses of cash. However, this assumption often is incorrect. Consequently, adding cash and marketable securities to the value of operating assets may seriously overstate the firm's value if some portion of these balances should really be considered as part of the firm's future working capital and therefore as part of operating assets. Invariably, some portion of investments in short-term marketable securities really represents cash required for working capital purposes. Such cash may be invested overnight as federal funds or for a few days in the form of security repurchase arrangements. The timing of such investments is to coincide with anticipated cash needs.

This problem becomes more pronounced during slow growth periods. Firms often improve short-term cash flow at the expense of long-term performance by postponing maintenance and research and development (R&D) outlays, as well as delaying vendor payments and training, safety, and advertising expenditures. To accurately determine firm value, the analyst needs to include such items in projected cash flow, which would tend to reduce the present value of operating assets.

To avoid this pitfall, the firm's normal cash balances should be estimated by calculating the ratio of total cash and marketable securities to sales during the last 3–5 years for the target firm, or for a comparable firm if the target firm has insufficient history. Whether the target firm has sufficient, excess, or deficient cash balances may be determined by multiplying this ratio by the target firm's current sales and comparing this estimate of normal cash balances with the firm's actual cash balances at the end of the current period. Although excess cash and marketable securities should be added to the present value of operating assets, any cash deficiency should be subtracted from the value of operating assets to determine the value of the firm. This reduction in the value of operating assets will reflect the need for the acquirer to invest additional working capital to make up any deficiency.

INVESTMENTS IN OTHER FIRMS

Many target firms will have investments in other firms. These investments generally have value and need to be included in any valuation of the target's nonoperating assets. Such investments for financial reporting purposes may be classified as minority passive investments, minority active investments, or majority investments. These investments need to be valued individually and added to the firm's nonoperating assets, which subsequently are added to the present value of the firm's operating assets to determine the total value of the firm. Table 7-6 describes their accounting treatment and valuation methodology.

UNUTILIZED AND UNDERVALUED ASSETS

Many firms have assets that may not be contributing anything to operating cash flows. Such assets could include both tangible and intangible assets. Real estate on the books of the target firm at historical cost may have an actual market value substantially in excess of the value stated on the balance sheet. In other cases, a firm may have more assets on hand to satisfy future obligations than it currently might need. An illustration of such an asset would be an overfunded pension fund. Examples of intangible assets include such patents, copyrights, licenses, and trade names. Intangible assets, so-called intellectual property, are becoming increasingly important for high technology and service firms. Intangible assets may represent significant sources of value on a target firm's balance sheet. However, they tend to be difficult to value. Furthermore, it is difficult to determine whether investors

TABLE 7-6 Investments in Other Firms

Percent Ownership of Other Firm	Accounting Treatment	Valuation Methodology
Minority, Passive Investments (Investment < 20% of other firm)	• Assets held to maturity are carried at book value with interest/dividends shown on income statement • Investments available for sale are carried at market value with unrealized gains/losses included as equity and not as income • Trading investments are shown at market value with unrealized gains/losses shown on the income statement	For investments recorded on investing firm's balance sheet at book value • Value firm in which investment held • Multiply the firm's value by the proportionate share held by the investing firm to determine the investment's value • Add the investment's value to the value of the investing firm's nonoperating assets For investments recorded at market value, add to the investing firm's nonoperating assets
Minority, Active Investments—Equity Method (investment is between 20% and 50% of the other firm's value)	• Initial acquisition value is adjusted for proportional share of subsequent profits/losses • Market value estimated on liquidation and gain/loss reported on income statement	• Value the firms in which the investments are held • Add the resulting estimated value to the firm's nonoperating assets
Majority Investments (Investment > 50% of other firm's value)	• Requires consolidation of both firms' balance sheets[1] • Shares held by other investors are shown as a minority interest on the liability side of the balance sheet	• If the parent owns 100% of the subsidiary, value the two on a consolidated basis[2] • If the parent owns less than 100%, value the parent and subsidiary on a consolidated basis and subtract the market value of minority interest shown as a liability item on the parent's balance sheet[3]

[1] A firm may be required to consolidate both firms' balance sheets even if it owns less than 50%, if its ownership position gives it effective control of the other firm.

[2] If the subsidiary is in a different industry from the parent, a weighted average cost of capital reflecting the different costs of capital for the two businesses should be used to discount cash flows generated by the consolidated businesses.

[3] If a subsidiary is valued at $500 million and the parent owns 75% of the subsidiary, the value of the subsidiary to the parent is $375 million (i.e., $500 million −.25 × $500 million to reflect the value owned by minority shareholders).

have access to the necessary information to accurately include the value of such assets in the firm's share price.

AOL Time Warner's primary assets are its subscriber base and Time Warner content, yet their value is not fully reflected on the firm's balance sheet. Similarly, the true value of Coca Cola's brand name and its highly effective distribution system are not carried as specific assets on the balance sheet. The balance sheets of Microsoft and Dell also are understated to the extent that they do not reflect their brand images, the knowledge of their workers, and the presence of online ordering and customer service systems. If the markets are truly efficient, investors should be able to understand the impact of these intangible factors in generating future earnings and build these factors into the price of the stock. A study by Chan, Lakonishok, and Sougiannis (1999) provides evidence that the value of intangible spending such as R&D expenditures is indeed factored into a firm's current share price. Despite this evidence, it is doubtful that intellectual property rights such as patents, which a firm may hold but not currently use, contribute anything to the firm's current share price. Such patents may have substantial value to another firm that has the financial resources, production capacity, or distribution channel to realize the full value of the patent.

Patents

A patent is a grant of some privilege by the government to someone to exclude others from making, selling, or using one's invention and includes the right to license others to make, use, or sell the invention. At the time of an acquisition, the value of the patent generally is based on some measure of the future after-tax cash flows that can reasonably be expected to result from the use or licensing of the patent. In the absence of a predictable cash-flow stream, the cost of developing a comparable invention or technology may be used to estimate the value of a patent.

Patents without Applications

Many firms have patents for which no current application within the firm has yet been identified. However, the patent may have value to an external party. Before closing, the buyer and seller may negotiate a value for a patent that has not yet been licensed to a third party based on the cash flows that can reasonably be expected to be generated over its future life. In cases where the patent has been licensed to third parties, the valuation is based on the expected future royalties that are to be received from licensing the patent over its remaining life.

Patents Linked to Existing Products or Services

When a product is used internally to produce a product, it is normally valued based on the "avoided cost" method. This method uses market-based royalty rates (RR) paid on comparable patents multiplied by the projected future stream of revenue (REV) from the products whose production depends on the patent discounted to its present value. The present value of the patent, the tax rate, and the cost of capital are PV_{pat}, t, and WACC, respectively.

$$PV_{pat} = \sum_{i=1}^{n} \frac{REV_i \times RR(1-t)}{(1+WACC)^n}$$

Note that patents still may have value even after their protection expires. This occurs when the presence of the patent creates a continuing business opportunity beyond the life of the patent protection. Although the cash flow generated by the patent or products based on the patent may decline as competitors copy the patent, additional patents may emerge that relate to the original product and extend the original life of the invention far beyond its inception.

Patent License Agreements

A firm may receive an exclusive right to an invention in return for helping the inventor develop the invention, developing and marketing products based on the invention, and paying the inventor a royalty on future sales. The patent license agreement is valued as if the licensee owns the patent. Cash flows generated, as a result of the patent, are reduced by any lump-sum or royalty payments made in accordance with the license agreement.

Patent Portfolios

Products and services often depend on a number of patents. This makes it exceedingly difficult to determine the amount of the cash flow generated by the sale of the products or services to be allocated to each patent. In this case, the patents are grouped together as a single portfolio and valued as a group using a single royalty rate applied to a declining percentage of the company's future revenue and then discounting this cash-flow stream to its present value. Using a declining percentage of revenue reflects the probable diminishing value of the patents with the passage of time.

Using Real Options to Value Intellectual Property

Patents and licenses owned by a target company may appear to have little value, particularly if they have never been used. As noted earlier in this chapter, they can be valued and added to the total present value of the target by applying conventional capital budgeting techniques. This involves discounting projected cash flows generated from products based on the patent and deducting the resulting present value from the cost of developing the technology, process, or product. Even if the NPV is negative, the patent or license owned by the target still may have significant value. The acquiring company ordinarily will gain access to the patents and licenses owned by the target. The acquirer may choose to provide whatever funds are necessary to exploit the patents or licenses. Alternatively, the acquiring company may choose to transfer ownership by selling the patent or license to another party, who may choose to fund implementation of the patent or license. If we think of the ownership rights to the unused or underutilized patent or license as essentially an unexploited opportunity, such ownership rights can be viewed as call options.

An option is the exclusive right, but not the obligation, to buy (i.e., call option), sell (i.e., put option), or utilize property for a specific time period in exchange for an agreed-on sum of money. The owner of the call option has the right to exercise the option at a predetermined price. The right expires at a specific time in the future, when the patent or license expires. Options that are traded on financial exchanges, such as puts and calls, are called financial options. Options that are not publicly traded, such as licenses, copyrights, trademarks, and patents, are called real options. Other examples of real options include the right to buy land, commercial property, and equipment. Options to assets whose cash flows have large variances and that have a long time before they expire are typically more valuable than those with smaller variances and less time remaining. The greater variance and time to expiration increases the chance that the factors affecting cash flows will change a project from one with a negative NPV to one with a positive NPV. Option pricing theory that traditionally has been applied to valuing financial options (i.e., the Black and Scholes Option Pricing Model [Black and Scholes, 1989]) also can be applied to value real options. For an excellent discussion of how to apply real options methodology to value intellectual property and other types of real assets, see Damodaran (2001).

Trademarks and Service Marks

A trademark is the right to use a name associated with a company, product, or concept; a service mark is the right to use an image associated with a company, product, or concept. Trademarks and service marks have recognition value. Examples include Bayer Aspirin or Kellogg's Corn Flakes. For these firms and others like them, name recognition reflects the firm's longevity, cumulative advertising expenditures, the overall effectiveness of their marketing programs, and the consistency of perceived product quality. Although we know there is value in the trademark or service mark, the challenge is to estimate it in terms of dollars. There are four commonly used methods for doing so: cost avoidance, comparable firms, recent transactions, and focus groups and surveys.

Cost-Avoidance Approach

The underlying assumption in applying the cost-avoidance approach to the valuation of trademarks and service marks is that cumulative advertising and promotion campaigns build brand recognition and association with certain desirable characteristics such as consistent quality or value (i.e., high quality at a reasonable price). The initial outlays for promotional campaigns are the largest and tend to decline as a percentage of sales over time as the brand becomes more recognizable. Consequently, the valuation of a trademark associated with a specific product or business involves multiplying projected revenues by a declining percentage to reflect the reduced level of spending, as a percentage of sales, that is required to maintain brand recognition. These projected expenditures then are adjusted for taxes (because marketing expenses are tax deductible) and discounted to the present at the acquiring firm's cost of capital.

Comparable Firm Approach

Assume that we have two firms, F1 and F2, which have similar cost structures. However, F1 is able to command significantly higher product selling prices than F2 because of its greater brand recognition. As such, F1 also will have significantly higher operating margins than F2. If the firms are growing at approximately the same rate and have similar risk characteristics, F1 should have a significantly higher market value than F2. The difference between the market value of the two firms reflects the dollar value of the brand recognition. However, such situations are relatively hard to find in practice.

Recent Transactions

Companies may license the right to use a trademark or service mark. The acquiring company may apply the license rate required to obtain the rights to comparable trademarks and service marks and apply it as a percentage of the cash flows that reasonably can be expected to be generated by selling the products or services under the licensed trademark or service mark during the remaining term of the license. The resulting cash flows then are discounted to the present using the acquiring company's cost of capital.

Alternatively, a value may be determined by examining recent outright purchases of comparable trademarks or, in the case of the Internet, Web addresses or domain names. For example, in early 2000, Bank of America revealed that it had purchased the rights to the Loans.com Web address for $3 million in an on-line auction. The largest payment for a domain name occurred in 1999 when eCompanies, a venture capital firm, purchased the www.business.com address for $7.5 million (*Orange County Register*, 2000).

Focus Groups and Surveys

Estimating the value of such an intangible asset may be accomplished indirectly through such techniques as customer surveys or an analysis of product selling prices. The key question is how much more would consumers be willing to pay for a widely recognized brand-name product than for a generic product. Focus groups may be used to determine how a representative sample of the consumers of a specific product would respond to this question. Alternatively, the percentage difference between the selling prices of branded products and generic products may serve as a reasonable proxy for the value of the brand name to the firm selling the branded products. For example, if these surveys and analyses of selling prices reveal that consumers are willing to pay 20% more for the branded product, an analyst may attribute 20% of the firm's market value to its brand recognition. Similarly, an acquiring company may believe that 20% of its proposed purchase price for this same firm is attributable to the firm's brand name.

Overfunded Pension Plans

Defined benefit pension plans require firms to accumulate an amount of financial assets to enable them to satisfy estimated future employee pension payments. During periods of rising stock markets such as during the 1990s, firms with defined benefit pension plans routinely accumulated assets in excess of the amount required to meet expected obligations. As owners of the firm, shareholders have the legal right to these excess assets. In practice, if such funds are liquidated and paid out to shareholders, the firm will have to pay taxes on the pretax value of these excess assets. Therefore, the after-tax value of such funds may be added to the present value of projected operating cash flows.

ADJUSTING THE TARGET FIRM'S EQUITY VALUE FOR NONOPERATING ASSETS AND LIABILITIES

In general, the value of a firm's equity is the value of the firm's operating cash flows plus the terminal or residual value less the market value of the firm's long-term debt. This assumes that the cash-flow impact of all nonoperating assets and liabilities, assumed by the acquiring firm, is reflected in the target's projected operating cash flows. Under ideal conditions, the actual price paid by the acquirer for the target firm's equity would fully reflect these considerations. However, this is often not the case because the actual price paid reflects the relative bargaining strength of the acquiring and target firms, which may involve the acquirer receiving valuable nonoperating assets or assuming significant off-balance sheet liabilities that are not fully reflected in the purchase price.

The value of the firm's equity may be understated or overstated if the estimated value provided by discounting operating cash flows is not adjusted for the existence of nonoperating assets and liabilities assumed by the acquirer. Examples of nonoperating assets include cash and marketable securities in excess of minimum working capital requirements, unused patents or copyrights, facilities leased at below prevailing market lease rates, and land or buildings not used for current operations. Nonoperating liabilities include potential litigation, potential environmental clean-up expenses, and possible warranty claims from discontinued product lines. Exhibit 7-18 illustrates how the value of the firm may be adjusted for these factors to provide a more accurate estimate of the equity value of the firm.

EXHIBIT 7-18. ADJUSTING FIRM VALUE

A target firm (which sells washing machines) initially is estimated to have a present value (PV) of annual cash flows for the next 5 years of $20 million and a terminal value of $34 million. The target firm has 2 million common shares outstanding, and the current market value of its long-term debt (LTD) and preferred stock are $12 million and $1 million, respectively. The acquirer is willing to assume this debt. During due diligence, it is determined that the firm currently has excess operating cash balances of $2 million, unused patents that could be used by the acquiring firm with a present value of $3 million, and unused commercial property with an estimated market value of $3 million. Because of the depressed nature of the current commercial real estate market, it is expected to take 18–24 months to dispose of the property. Consequently, the PV of the surplus property is estimated to be $2.5 million. However, it also is discovered that a product line consisting of several different models of washing machines had been discontinued the year before because of quality problems. Potential warranty claims are estimated to have a PV of $2 million. Finally, potential litigation with several customers could result in judgments against the target firm between $5 to $10 million over the next 4 years. The PV of these judgments is $7 million. Note that the cash-flow impact of pending warranty claims and potential litigation expenses were not included in the projection of the target firm's future cash flows. Calculate the adjusted equity value of the target firm as well as the equity value per share.

PV of cash flow from operations during the next 5 years	$20.0
PV of Terminal Value	$34.0
Total PV (Market Value of Firm — Equity + Debt)	$54.0
Plus Nonoperating Assets	
Excess Operating Cash & Short-Term Marketable Securities	2.0
PV of Surplus Commercial Property	2.5
PV of Unused Process Patents (Valued as a Call Option)	3.0
Total Nonoperating Assets	7.5
Total Value of the Firm	$61.5
Less Nonoperating and Non-LTD Liabilities (not included in operating cash flows)	
PV of Warranty Claims	2.0
PV of Judgments	7.0
Total Nonoperating Liabilities	9.0
Less Long-Term Debt (including operating leases in present value terms)	12.0
Less: Preferred Stock	1.0
Equity Value	$39.5
Equity Value Per Share	$19.75

THINGS TO REMEMBER

The CAPM is used widely to estimate the cost of equity. The cost of equity also can be estimated from the firm's dividend yield plus its earnings growth rate. The pretax cost of debt for nonrated firms can best be approximated by comparison with similar firms, whose debt is rated by the major credit-rating agencies or by looking at interest rates on debt currently on the firm's books. Weights for the firm's cost of capital should be calculated using market rather than book values and reflect the acquiring firm's target capital structure.

FCFF, free cash flow to the firm, is used widely as a measure of cash flow for valuing an acquisition target because it does not require an estimate of the firm's debt-repayment schedule during the forecast period. FCFF generally is defined for valuation purposes as follows:

$$FCFF = EBIT\,(1 - \text{tax rate}) - (\text{Gross Cap. Exp.} - \text{Depreciation}) - \Delta\,WC$$

FCFE, free cash flow to equity investors, is defined as follows:

$$FCFE = \text{Net Income} - (\text{Gross Capital Expenditures} - \text{Depreciation})$$
$$- \Delta\,\text{Net Working Capital} + \text{New Debt Issues} - \text{Principal Repayments}$$
$$- \text{Preferred Dividends}$$

The resulting value estimated using FCFF often is referred to as the enterprise value of the firm. Valuation based on FCFE commonly is called the equity method or equity value. Equity value also can be calculated by deducting the market value of the target firm's long-term debt (including operating leases expressed in present value terms) from the enterprise value.

Discounted cash-flow valuation is far more an art than a science. It is highly sensitive to the choice of the discount rate as well as the magnitude and timing of future cash flows. Despite its shortcomings, it is essential to determining a preliminary or baseline valuation. Other valuation techniques should be used to provide additional credibility for the estimate provided by the discounted cash-flow method. In the constant-growth model, free cash flow to the firm is expected to grow at a constant rate. This model commonly is used in the calculation of terminal values.

$$P_0 = FCFF_1/(WACC - g), \quad \text{where } FCFF_1 = FCFF_0(1 + g)$$

In the variable-growth model, cash flow exhibits both a high and a stable growth period. Total PV in this case represents the sum of the discounted value of the cash flows over both periods.

$$\text{FCFF: } P_0 = \sum_{t=1}^{n} \frac{\text{FCFF}_0 \times (1 + g_t)^t}{(1 + \text{WACC})^t} + \frac{P_n}{(1 + \text{WACC})^n}$$

where

$$P_n = \frac{\text{FCFF}_n \times (1 + g_m)}{(\text{WACC}_m - g_m)}$$

The cost of capital during the stable growth period should be lower than during the high-growth period to reflect the reduced rate of uncertainty associated with the slower rate of growth of cash flow. The terminal value frequently accounts for most of the total PV calculation and is highly sensitive to the choice of the growth rate of free cash flow and discount rate during the stable growth period. If the terminal value accounts for a large percentage of the total PV (e.g., more than three-fourths), the conventional 5-year projection of future cash flows should be extended to at least 10 years. In any valuation exercise, assumptions always should be stated clearly. The credibility of any valuation is ultimately dependent on the credibility of its underlying assumptions.

Market-based valuation techniques offer a variety of alternatives to discounted cash-flow estimates. The comparable companies approach entails the multiplication of certain measures of value for the target such as earnings by the appropriate valuation multiple for comparable companies. Similarly, the comparable transactions method involves the multiplication of the target's earnings by the same valuation multiple for recent, similar transactions. However, unlike the comparable companies method, the estimated value of the target firm obtained by using the comparable transactions method includes the value of the purchase price or control premium. If available, similar transactions are generally the most reliable of these market-based valuation methods. The comparable industry approach applies industry average multiples to earnings, cash flow, book value, or sales. Asset-oriented methods, such as tangible book value, are very useful for valuing financial services companies and distribution companies. Liquidation or breakup value is the projected price of the firm's assets sold separately less its liabilities. Liquidation may be involuntary as a result of bankruptcy or voluntary if a firm is viewed by its owners as worth more in liquidation than as a going concern.

The target firm's equity value should be adjusted for the value of nonoperating assets and liabilities not on the balance sheet. Such factors can materially enhance or degrade the value of the target firm. This value also is called the adjusted equity value. Thus, the equity value of the target firm is ultimately the sum of the firm's operating cash flows, terminal value, and nonoperating assets less the current market value of long-term debt and nonoperating liabilities not accurately reflected on the balance sheet.

CHAPTER DISCUSSION QUESTIONS

7-1. What is the significance of the weighted average cost of capital? How is it calculated? Do the weights reflect the firm's actual or target debt to total capital ratio? Why?

7-2. What does a firm's β measure? What is the difference between an unlevered and levered β? Why is this distinction significant?

7-3. What are the primary differences between FCFE and FCFF?

7-4. Explain the primary differences between the income (discounted cash flow), market-based, and asset-oriented valuation methods?

7-5. Which discounted cash-flow valuation methods require the estimation of a terminal value? Why?

7-6. Do small changes in the assumptions pertaining to the estimation of the terminal value have a significant impact on the calculation of the total value of the target firm? If so, why?

7-7. In your judgment, does valuing a firm using the weighted average valuation method make sense? If yes, why? If no, why not?

7-8. Why do increasing P/E ratios increase the attractiveness of stock-for-stock exchanges for acquiring companies?

7-9. How is the liquidation value of the firm calculated? Why is the assumption of orderly liquidation important?

7-10. Explain how you would value a patent under the following situations: a patent without any current application, a patent linked to an existing product, and a patent portfolio.

CHAPTER PRACTICE PROBLEMS

7-11. ABC Incorporated shares are currently trading for $32 per share. The firm has 1.13 billion shares outstanding. In addition, the market value of the firm's outstanding debt is $2 billion. The 10-year Treasury bond rate is 6.25%. ABC has an outstanding credit record and has earned a AAA rating from the major credit rating agencies. The current interest rate on AAA corporate bonds is 6.45%. The historical risk premium over the risk-free rate of return is 5.5 percentage points. The firm's beta is estimated to be 1.1 and its marginal tax rate, including federal, state, and local taxes, is 40%.

a. What is the cost of equity?

b. What is the after-tax cost of debt?

c. What is the cost of capital?

Answers:

a. 12.3%

b. 3.9%

c. 11.9%

7-12. HiFlyer Corporation does not currently have any debt. Its tax rate is .4 and its unlevered beta is estimated by examining comparable companies to be 2.0. The 10-year bond rate is 6.25%, and the historical risk premium over the risk-free rate is 5.5%. Next year, HiFlyer expects to borrow up to 75% of its equity value to fund future growth.

a. Calculate the firm's current cost of equity.

b. Estimate the firm's cost of equity after it increases its leverage to 75% of equity.

Answers:

a. 17.25%

b. 22.2%

7-13. Abbreviated financial statements are given for Fletcher Corporation in the following table:

	2001	2002
Revenues	$600.0	$690.0
Operating expenses	520.0	600.0
Depreciation	16.0	18.0
Earnings before interest and taxes	64.0	72.0
Less interest expense	5.0	5.0
Less taxes	23.6	26.8
Equals: net income	35.4	40.2
Addendum:		
Yearend working capital	150	200
Principal repayment	25.0	25.0
Capital expenditures	20	10

Yearend working capital in 2000 was $160 million and the firm's marginal tax rate is 40% in both 2001 and 2002. Estimate the following for 2001 and 2002:

a. Free cash flow to equity.

b. Free cash flow to the firm.

Answers:

a. $16.4 million in 2001 and $26.8 million in 2002

b. $44.4 million in 2001 and $1.2 million in 2002

7-14. No Growth Incorporated had operating income before interest and taxes in 2002 of $220 million. The firm was expected to generate this level of operating income indefinitely. The firm had depreciation expense of $10 million that same year. Capital spending totaled $20 million during 2002. At the end of 2001 and 2002, working capital totaled $70 million and $80 million, respectively. The firm's combined marginal state, local, and federal tax rate was 40%, and its debt outstanding had a market value of $1.2 billion. The 10-year Treasury bond rate is 5%, and the borrowing rate for companies exhibiting levels of creditworthiness similar to No Growth is 7%. The historical risk premium for stocks over the risk-free rate of return is 5.5%. No Growth's beta was estimated to be 1.0. The firm had 2,500,000 common shares outstanding at the end of 2002.

a. Estimate free cash flow to the firm in 2002.
b. Estimate the firm's cost of capital.
c. Estimate the enterprise value of the firm (i.e., includes the value of equity and debt) at the end of 2002, assuming that it will generate the value of free cash flow estimated in (a) indefinitely.
d. Estimate the value of the equity of the firm at the end of 2002.
e. Estimate the value per share at the end of 2002.

Answers:

a. $112 million
b. 8.61%
c. $1,380.8 million
d. $100.8 million
e. $40.33

7-15. Sematech has achieved a dominant market position in its targeted market. Its huge market share makes it unlikely that the firm can grow faster than the growth rate of the overall market, which is expected to be 8% annually through the foreseeable future. Its net income in 2002 was $15 million. Depreciation expense and capital expenditures were $5 million and $10 million, respectively. The annual change in working capital was minimal. The 10-year Treasury bond rate was 5%, and the firm's beta was estimated to be 1.3. The historical risk premium on stocks was 5.5%.

a. Calculate Sematech's discount rate.
b. Calculate the firm's free cash flow in 2002.
c. Estimate the value of Sematech at the end of 2002.

Answers:

a. 12.2%

b. $10 million

c. $257.1 million

7-16. Carlisle Enterprises, a specialty pharmaceutical manufacturer, has been losing market share for 3 years since several key patents have expired. The free cash flow to the firm in 2002 was $10 million. This figure is expected to decline rapidly as more competitive generic drugs enter the market. Projected cash flows for the next 5 years are $8.5 million, $7.0 million, $5.0 million, $2.0 million, and $.5 million. Cash flow after the fifth year is expected to be negligible. The firm's board has decided to sell the firm to a larger pharmaceutical company interested in using Carlisle's product offering to fill gaps in its own product offering until it can develop similar drugs. Carlisle's cost of capital is 15%. What purchase price must Carlisle obtain to earn its cost of capital?

Answer:

$17.4 million

7-17. Ergo Unlimited's current year's free cash flow is $10 million. It is projected to grow at 20% per year for the next 5 years. It is expected to grow at a more modest 5% beyond the fifth year. The firm estimates that its cost of capital is 12% during the next 5 years and then will drop to 10% beyond the fifth year as the business matures. Estimate the firm's current market value.

Answer:

$358.30

7-18. BigCo's chief financial officer is trying to determine a fair value for PrivCo, a nonpublicly traded firm that BigCo's is considering acquiring. Several of PrivCo's competitors, Ion International and Zenon, are publicly traded. Ion and Zenon have P/E ratios of 20 and 15, respectively. Moreover, Ion and Zenon's shares are trading at a multiple of earnings before interest, taxes, depreciation, and amortization (EBITDA) of 10 and 8, respectively. BigCo estimates that next year PrivCo will achieve net income and EBITDA of $4 million and $8 million, respectively. To gain a controlling interest in the firm, BigCo expects to have to pay at least a 30% premium to the firm's market value. What should BigCo expect to pay for PrivCo?

a. Based on P/E ratios?

b. Based on EBITDA?

Answers:

a. $91 million

b. $93.6 million

7-19. LAFCO Industries believes that its two primary product lines, automotive and commercial aircraft valves, are becoming obsolete rapidly. Its free cash flow is diminishing quickly as it loses market share to new firms entering its industry. LAFCO has $200 million in debt outstanding. Senior management expects the automotive and commercial aircraft valve product lines to generate $25 million and $15 million, respectively, in earnings before interest, taxes, depreciation, and amortization next year. The operating liabilities associated with these two product lines are minimal. Senior management also believes that they will not be able to upgrade these product lines because of declining cash flow and excessive current leverage. A competitor to its automotive valve business last year sold for 10 times EBITDA. Moreover, a company that is similar to its commercial aircraft valve product line sold last month for 12 times EBITDA. Estimate LAFCO's breakup value before taxes.

Answer:

$230 million

7-20. Siebel Incorporated, a nonpublicly traded company, has 2002 earnings before interest of $33.3 million, which is expected to grow at 5% annually into the foreseeable future. The firm's combined federal, state, and local tax rate is 40%; capital spending will equal the firm's rate of depreciation; and the annual change in working capital is expected to be minimal. The firm's beta is estimated to be 2.0, the 10-year Treasury bond is 5%, and the historical risk premium of stocks over the risk-free rate is 5.5%. Rand Technology, a direct competitor of Siebel's, recently was sold at a purchase price 8 times 2002 current EBITDA. Siebel's equity owners would like to determine what it might be worth if they were to attempt to sell the firm in the near future. They have chosen to value the firm using the discounted cash flow and comparable recent transactions methods. They believe that either method would provide an equally valid estimate of the firm's value.

a. What is the value of Siebel using the DCF method?
b. What is the value using the comparable recent transactions method?
c. What would be the value of the firm if we combine the results of both methods?

Answers:

a. $190.7 million
b. $160.0 million
c. $175.4 million

7-21. In the year before going public, a firm has revenues of $20 million and net income after taxes of $2 million. The firm has no debt, and revenue is expected to grow at 20% annually for the next 5 years and 5% annually thereafter. Operating margins are expected to remain constant throughout. Capital expenditures are expected to grow in line with depreciation, and the change in working capital requirements is minimal. The average beta of a publicly traded company in this industry is 1.50 and the average debt/equity ratio is 20%. The firm is managed very conservatively and does not intend to borrow through the foreseeable future. The Treasury bond rate is 6%, and the tax rate is 40%. The normal spread between the return on stocks and the risk-free rate of return is believed to be 5.5%. Reflecting the slower growth rate in the sixth year and beyond, the discount rate is expected to decline by 3 percentage points. Estimate the value of the firm's equity.

Answer:

$63.41 million

7-22. Titanic Corporation has reached agreement with its creditors to voluntarily liquidate its assets and to use the proceeds to pay off as much of its liabilities as possible. The firm anticipates that it will be able to sell off its assets in an orderly fashion, realizing as much as 70% of the book value of its receivables, 40% of its inventory, and 25% of its net fixed assets (excluding land). However, the firm believes that the land on which it is located can be sold for 120% of book value. The firm has legal and professional expenses associated with the liquidation process of $2.9 million. The firm has only common stock outstanding. Estimate the amount of cash that would remain for the firm's common shareholders once all assets have been liquidated.

Balance Sheet Item	Book Value of Assets	Liquidation Value
Cash	$10	
Accounts receivable	$20	
Inventory	$15	
Net fixed assets excluding land	$8	
Land	$6	
Total assets	$59	
Total liabilities	$35	
Shareholders' equity	$24	

Answer:

$1.3 million

7-23. The following information is available for two different common stocks: Company A and Company B.

	Company A	Company B
Free cash flow per share at the end of year 1	$1.00	$5.00
Growth rate in cash flow per share	8%	4%
Beta	1.3	.8
Risk-free return	7%	7%
Expected return on all stocks	13.5%	13.5%

a. Estimate the cost of equity for each firm.

b. Assume that the companies' growth rates will continue at the same rate indefinitely. Estimate the per share value of each companies common stock.

Answers:

a. Company A = 15.45%; Company B = 12.2%

b. Company A = $13.50; Company B = $61

7-24. You have been asked to estimate the beta of a high-technology firm that has three divisions with the following characteristics.

Division	Beta	Market Value ($ Million)
Personal computers	1.6	100
Software	2.00	150
Computer mainframes	1.2	250

a. What is the beta of the equity of the firm?

b. If the risk-free return is 5% and the spread between the return on all stocks is 5.5%, estimate the cost of equity for the software division.

c. What is the cost of equity for the entire firm?

d. Free cash flow to equity investors in the current year (FCFE) for the entire firm is $7.4 million and for the software division is $3.1 million. If the total firm and the software are expected to grow at the same 8% rate into the foreseeable future, estimate the market value of the firm and of the software division.

Answers:

a. 1.52

b. 16%

c. 13.4%

d. PV (total firm) = $147.96; PV (software division) = $41.75

7-25. Financial Corporation wants to acquire Great Western Inc. Financial has estimated the enterprise value of Great Western at $104 million. The market value of Great Western's long-term debt is $15 million, and cash balances in excess of the firm's normal working capital requirements are $3 million. Financial estimates the present value of certain licenses that Great Western is not currently using to be $4 million. Great Western is the defendant in several outstanding lawsuits. Financial Corporation's legal department estimates the potential future cost of this litigation to be $3 million, with an estimated present value of $2.5 million. Great Western has 2 million common shares outstanding. What is the value of Great Western per common share?

Answer:

$46.75/share

CHAPTER BUSINESS CASE

CASE STUDY 7-1: THE HUNT FOR ELUSIVE SYNERGY—@HOME ACQUIRES EXCITE

Background Information

@Home Network announced its merger with Excite Inc. in January 1999 for $6.7 billion. Before the announcement, Excite's market value was about $3.5 billion. The transaction closed in May 1999. The announced purpose of the transaction was to create a new media company capable of providing home and business customers with high-speed, 24-hour access to personalized services from their PCs, pagers, cellular phones, and television sets. The new company combined the search engine capabilities of one of the best known brands on the Internet, Excite, with @Home's agreements with 21 cable companies worldwide. @Home gains access to the nearly 17 million households that are regular users of Excite. At the time, this transaction constituted the largest merger of Internet companies ever. As of July 1999, the combined companies displayed a P/E ratio in excess of 260 based on the consensus estimates for the year 2000 of $.21 per share. The firm's market value was $18.8 billion, 270 times sales. Investors had great expectations for the future performance of the combined firms, despite their lackluster profit performance since their inception.

Founded in 1995, @Home provides interactive services to home and business users over its proprietary network, over telephone company circuits, and through the cable companies' infrastructure. Cable hookups provide connections at more than 100 times the speed of dial-up services. @Home also provides branded content in this broadband environment. Subscribers paid $39.95 per month for the service.

Assumptions

- Excite is properly valued immediately before announcement of the transaction.
- Annual customer service costs equal $50 per customer.
- Annual customer revenue in the form of @Home access charges and ancillary services equals $500 per customer. This assumes that declining access charges in this highly competitive environment will be offset by increases in revenue from the sale of ancillary services.
- None of the current Excite user households are current @Home customers.
- New @Home customers acquired through Excite remain @Home customers in perpetuity.
- @Home converts immediately 2% or 340,000 of the current 17 million Excite user households. A 2% response rate is typical of both online and direct mail solicitations.
- @Home's cost of capital is 20% during the growth period and drops to 10% during the slower, sustainable growth period; its combined federal and state tax rate is 40%.
- Capital spending equals depreciation; current assets equal current liabilities.
- FCFF from synergy increases by 15% annually for the next 10 years and 5% thereafter. Its cost of capital after the high-growth period drops to 10%.
- The maximum purchase price @Home should pay for Excite equals Excite's current market price plus the synergy that results from the merger of the two businesses.

Case Study Discussion Questions

1. Did @Home overpay for Excite?
2. What other assumptions might you consider?
3. What are the limitations of the valuation method used in this case?
4. What alternative valuation techniques could you use?

Solutions to these questions are found in the Appendix at the back of this book.

REFERENCES

Abrams, Jay B., *Quantitative Business Valuation: A Mathematical Approach for Today's Professionals*, McGraw-Hill: New York, 2001.

Akhigbe, Aigbe, Stephen F. Borde, and Anne Marie Whyte, "The Source of Gains to Targets and Their Industry Rivals: Evidence Based on Terminated Merger Proposals," *Financial Management*, 29 (4), Winter 2000, pp. 101–118.

Black, Fischer and Myron Scholes, "The Pricing of Options and Corporate Liabilities," *Journal of Applied Corporate Finance*, 1 (4), Winter 1989, pp. 67–73.

Burrus, Amy and Mike McNamee, "Evaluating the Rating Agencies," *Business Week*, April 8, 2002, pp. 39–40.

Business Week, "What's a Cell-Phone User Worth?" February 21, 2000, p. 60.

Chan, Louis K. C., Josef Lakonishok, and Theodore Sougiannis, "Investing in High R&D Stocks," *Business Week*, October 11, 1999, p. 28.

Copeland, Tom, Tim Koller, and Jack Murrin, *Valuation: Measuring, and Managing the Value of Companies* (3rd ed.), John Wiley & Sons: New York, 2000.

Damodaran, Aswath, *Corporate Finance: Theory and Practice*, New York: John Wiley & Sons, 1997, pp. 160–193.

Damodaran, Aswath, *The Dark Side of Valuation: Valuing Old Tech, New Tech, and New Economy Companies*, Prentice-Hall: New York, 2001.

Gitman, Lawrence J., *Principles of Managerial Finance* (9th ed.), New York: Addison-Wesley, 2000.

Gordon, Myron, *The Investment, Financing, and Valuation of the Modern Corporation*, Homewood, IL: Irwin, 1962.

Ibbotson, Roger, *Stocks, Bonds, Bills, and Inflation Yearbook*, Chicago: Ibbotson Associates, 1999, www.ibbotson.com

Lasher, William R., *Practical Financial Management* (2nd ed.), Cincinnati: Southwestern College Publishing, 2000.

Moyer, R. Charles, James R. McGuigan, and William J. Kretlow, *Contemporary Financial Management* (7th ed.), Cincinnati: Southwestern College Publishing, 1998.

Orange County Register, "B of A Buys Loans.com Domain Name," February 7, 2000, Business Section, p. 2.

Song, M.H. and R.A. Walkling, "Abnormal Returns to Rivals of Acquisition Targets: A Test of the Acquisition Probability Hypothesis," *Journal of Financial Economics*, 55 (2), 2000, pp. 143–171.

Urban, Rob, "Rules for Debt Disclosure May Soon Change," *Bloomberg News* as reported in the Business Section of the *Orange County Register*, February 28, 2002, p. 8.

8

APPLYING FINANCIAL MODELING TECHNIQUES TO VALUE AND STRUCTURE MERGERS AND ACQUISITIONS

If you don't agree with me, it means you haven't been listening.

—Sam Markewich

It was crunch time. Both parties to the negotiation were in heated discussions to resolve several key sticking points. The seller was insisting on a higher price for certain assets that the buyer simply could not justify paying. Nonetheless, the buyer was a seasoned veteran and realized that as long as both parties were motivated a deal was still possible. To bridge the gap between what the seller was demanding and what the buyer was willing to pay, the buyer would have to be creative to meet the seller's needs. However, the proposed changes to the terms of the transaction clearly would have implications for the combined companies' taxes, leverage, compliance with loan covenants, and EPS.

The buyer turned to a financial model he had constructed of the combined firms to assess the impact of various changes in the terms of the transaction. After changing certain assumptions that had been used to generate the initial offer, the buyer was able to estimate the potential risk to the combined companies if the buyer made the changes demanded by the seller. The model's results were pleasantly surprising to the buyer. The impact of the changes on variables the buyer considered critical was much less than had been imagined. Armed with this information, the buyer returned to the negotiating table optimistic that an agreement could be reached.

OVERVIEW

Financial modeling refers to the application of spreadsheet software to define simple arithmetic relationships among variables within the firm's income, balance sheet, and cash-flow statements and to define the interrelationships among the various financial statements. Examples of simple relationships within individual financial statements include the effects of price, quantity, and product mix on revenue and profitability on the income statement and the relationship between shareholders' equity and total assets and liabilities on the balance sheet. Common interrelationships among the financial statements include the link between net income less dividends and the change in retained earnings as well as the link between net income and the change in cash flow.

The primary objective in applying financial modeling techniques is to create a computer-based model, which facilitates the acquirer's understanding of the affect of changes in certain operating variables on the firm's overall performance and valuation (Benninga, 2000). Examples include the effects of product selling prices and volume levels on the firm's break-even point and increasing leverage on the firm's financial returns. Once in place, these models can be used to simulate alternative valuation scenarios to determine which one enables the acquirer to achieve its financial objectives without violating identifiable and measurable constraints. Financial objectives could include earnings per share (EPS) for publicly traded firms, return on total capital for privately held firms, or return on equity for leveraged buyout firms. Typical constraints include Wall Street analysts' expectations for the firm's EPS, the acquirer's leverage compared with other firms in the same industry, and loan covenants limiting how the firm uses its available cash flow and currently unencumbered assets as collateral for new borrowing. Another important constraint is the risk tolerance of the acquiring company, which could be measured by the acquirer's target debt-to-equity ratio.

The models can be used to answer several different sets of questions. The first set pertains to valuation. How much is the target company worth without the effects of synergy? What is the value of expected synergy? What is the maximum price that the acquiring company should pay for the target? The second set of questions pertains to financing. Can the maximum price be financed? What combination of potential sources of funds, both internally generated and external sources, provides the lowest cost of funds for the acquirer, subject to known constraints? The final set of questions pertains to deal structuring. What is the impact on the acquirer's financial performance if the deal is structured as a taxable rather than a nontaxable transaction? What is the impact on financial performance and valuation if the acquirer is willing to assume certain target company liabilities? Deal structuring considerations are discussed in more detail in Chapter 10.

The objectives of this chapter are to emphasize the limitations of financial data used in the valuation process and to provide a procedure for building a financial model in the context of a merger or acquisition. The procedure allows the analyst to determine the minimum and maximum prices for a target firm and the initial offer price. The chapter contains numerous examples of how these techniques may be applied. Finally, simple formulae for calculating share-exchange ratios and assessing the impact on postmerger EPS are provided. These can be included in models used to evaluate the impact of various scenarios on EPS.

THE LIMITATIONS OF FINANCIAL DATA

There are several major sources of error in any valuation methodology. These include the conceptual limitations of the valuation methodology described in Chapter 7, the difficulty in predicting the magnitude and the timing of projected earnings or cash flows, and the inaccuracies inherent in the published data used to apply the various valuation tools. Data limitations can result in severe distortions in any of the valuation techniques used.

MANAGING EARNINGS

Daily gyrations in the stock prices of publicly traded companies underscore the importance of meeting or exceeding investor expectations. Acutely aware of the potentially catastrophic consequences of disappointing investors, corporate managers have for many years attempted to smooth earnings fluctuations and hopefully fluctuations in the share price of their corporation. The effort to "manage earnings" has in some cases required the use of certain accounting artifices. These include the alleged misuse of restructuring charges, acquisition accounting adjustments, reserves, and revenue recognition.

THE IMPORTANCE OF GENERALLY
ACCEPTED ACCOUNTING PRINCIPLES

The output of models is only as good as the accuracy and timeliness of the numbers that are used to create them and the quality of the assumptions used in making projections. Consequently, analysts must understand on what basis numbers are collected and reported. Consistency and adherence to uniform standards become exceedingly important. However, imaginative accounting tricks threaten to undermine an analyst's ability to properly understand a firm's underlying dynamics. Although accounting distortion is not new, with roots as far back as the halcyon days of the junk bond and leveraged buyouts during the 1980s, it reemerged with a vengeance during the Internet speculative bubble. Recent examples of inordinate accounting abuses include WorldCom, Tyco, Enron, Sunbeam, Waste Management, and Cendant. The Enron case is discussed in substantial detail in Chapter 13.

Generally Accepted Accounting Principles

Generally accepted accounting principles (GAAP) financial statements are those prepared in accordance with guidelines established by the Financial Accounting Standards Board. GAAP provides specific guidelines as to how to account for specific events, although some require judgment calls. Few would argue that GAAP ensures that all transactions are accurately recorded; nonetheless, the scrupulous application of GAAP does ensure consistency in comparing one firm's financial performance to another. It is customary for definitive agreements of purchase and sale to require that a target company represent that its financial books are kept in accordance with GAAP. Consequently, the acquiring company at least understands how the financial numbers were assembled. During due diligence, the acquirer can look for discrepancies between the target's reported numbers and GAAP practices. Such discrepancies are often indications of potential problems. It is comforting to know that the target firm's financial statements used for a preliminary valuation of the business were compiled in accordance with GAAP. Unfortunately, this may provide a false sense of security.

Pro Forma Accounting

In recent years, there has been a trend toward using *pro forma financial statements*, which present financial statements in a way that purports to more accurately describe a firm's current or projected performance. Because there are no accepted standards for pro forma accounting, pro forma statements may deviate substantially from standard GAAP statements. Pro forma statements frequently are used to show what an acquirer's and target's combined financial performance would look like if they were merged. When one company acquires another, year over year earnings comparisons for the acquiring firm make little sense. Consequently, the acquirer simply adds the target's revenues and profits to its own and then calculates period over period changes in financial performance. This is pro forma accounting at its purest and is the least controversial.

Potential Abuse

Although public companies still are required to file their financial statements with the Securities and Exchange Commission in accordance with GAAP, companies increasingly are using pro forma statements to portray their financial performance in what they argue is a more realistic (and usually more favorable) manner. Companies maintain that such statements provide investors with a better view of a company's core performance than reporting that strictly adheres to GAAP. Although pro forma statements do provide useful insight into how a proposed combination of businesses might look, such liberal accounting techniques easily can be abused so as to hide a company's poor performance.

In January 1999, Yahoo! reported earnings that were 35% better than GAAP by excluding a variety of costs related to buying Internet companies. In the first quarter of 2000, it excluded other costs including the payment of payroll taxes on stock options exercised by its employees. Amazon.com even uses different definitions of "pro forma operating losses," declaring that "pro forma numbers are how we think about our business and how Wall Street analysts follow it." Using this logic, from its first quarter 2001 earnings Amazon.com excluded from pro forma operating losses such items as net interest expense of $24 million and a $114 million charge for closing a warehouse (Henry, 2001). When Broadcom Corporation booked a "pro forma net loss" of $41.1 million during the second quarter of 2001, it excluded the "effects of acquisition-related expenses, payroll taxes it paid as employees exercised stock options, and certain other non-recurring charges and related income tax effects." The firm's quarterly loss prepared in accordance with GAAP showed a $436.6 million loss, more than 10 times larger than the pro forma loss (Kelleher, 2001). Another firm, Conexant, in reporting its second quarter 2001 earnings, made things even more confusing when it prepared two pro forma statements, one showing a $220 million net loss and the other showing a $112 million net loss using another tax rate. According to GAAP, its loss was $745 million, which was available in the firm's 10Q.

Implications of Recurring "Nonrecurring Expenses"

The elimination of nonrecurring items is useful if they are truly nonrecurring, such as a restructuring charge related to weakness in the economy. But when such charges occur repeatedly, they should tell the analyst a great deal about both the quality of a firm's management and its so-called business model (i.e., its business strategy). Acquisition write-downs reflect management having overpaid for an acquired company. Write-downs of other assets such as equipment, inventory, and facilities may also reflect poor management decisions. Consequently, if such write-downs become a relatively common occurrence, it says something about management's competence, the validity of the firm's strategy, or both. Empirical studies seem to support this conclusion. Contrary to frequent comments in the popular press, restructuring that reduces reported earnings generally are associated with negative excess returns. Moreover, the larger the size of the restructure, the more negative the stock price reaction (Durtschi, Poon, Newbould, 2001). In reconstructing a target firm's financial performance, the analyst should be careful to add back expenses that logically could be considered a cost of doing business. For example, technology companies increasingly exclude the payment of payroll taxes on employee stock options. Such expenses could be considered a normal cost of doing business in view of the importance of granting options to attract and retain employees.

THE FINDINGS OF SECURITY AND EXCHANGE
COMMISSION INVESTIGATIONS

Without credible data, the range of potential error in efforts to value target companies expands considerably. Hence, the analyst should never become so preoccupied with the choice and application of the valuation methodology that he or she overlooks the need to understand the limitations of the data. Exhibit 8-1 suggests some ways in which an analyst can tell if a firm is engaging in inappropriate accounting practices. For a more detailed discussion of these issues, see Sherman and Young (2001).

EXHIBIT 8-1. ACCOUNTING
DISCREPANCY RED FLAGS

1. The source of the revenue is questionable. Beware of revenue generated by selling to an affiliated party or by selling something to a customer in exchange for something other than cash or by recording as revenue investment income or cash received from a lender.

2. Income is inflated by nonrecurring gains. Gains on the sale of assets may be inflated by an artificially low book value of the assets sold.

3. Deferred revenue shows an unusually large increase. Deferred revenue increases as a firm collects money from customers in advance of delivering its products. It is reduced as the products are delivered. A jump in this balance sheet item could mean that the firm is having trouble delivering its products.

4. Reserves for bad debt are declining as a percentage of revenue. Also a balance sheet item, this could suggest that a firm is boosting revenue by not reserving enough to cover probable losses from customer accounts that cannot be collected.

5. Growth in accounts receivable exceeds substantially the increase in revenue growth or inventory. This may mean that a firm is having difficulty in selling its products (inventories are accumulating) or that it is having difficulty collecting what it is owed.

6. The growth in net income is significantly different from the growth in cash from operations. Because it is more difficult to "manage" cash flow (a measure of cash coming in or flowing out) than net income, which is distorted easily because of improper revenue recognition, this could indicate that net income is being deliberately distorted. Potential distortion may be particularly evident if the analyst adjusts end-of-period cash balances by deducting cash received from financing activities and adding back cash used for investment purposes. Consequently, changes in the adjusted cash balances should reflect changes in reported net income.

Revenue Recognition a Common Source of Abuse

The most widespread abuse of GAAP occurs when the decision is made to count a sale to a customer as revenue. In a recent study, improper revenue recognition was found to be the most common form of financial reporting fraud, with about 50% resulting from revenue having been stated incorrectly (Committee of Sponsoring Organizations of the Treadway Commission, 1999). GAAP is very specific about when a sale should be counted as revenue. Revenue can be recognized when the product or service provided by the firm has been received by the customer or performed in full and the firm providing the product or service either has received cash or a receivable that is both observable and measurable. Expenses that are tied directly to the generation of that revenue must be recognized in the same period in which the revenue is recognized.

Long-Term Contracts

For long-term contracts spanning multiple accounting periods, revenue is recognized on the basis of the percentage of the contract completed. When there is considerable uncertainty about the customer's ability to pay, the firm may recognize revenue only when it receives portions of what it is owed on an installment basis.

False Invoices

Well-publicized abuses of revenue recognition include Al "Chain-Saw" Dunlap, the former chief executive officer (CEO) of Sunbeam, who allegedly recorded the sale of goods, despite having not yet shipped them to customers. In other instances, firms have been caught creating false invoices or holding the accounting period open beyond the end of the quarter to boost revenue.

Vendor Financing

In recent years, a number of high-tech firms have effectively inflated their revenues by extending extremely favorable payment terms to their customers— in effect becoming lenders. Although it can be an effective selling tool if done in moderation, it can be disastrous if it becomes excessive. At the end of 2000, telecommunication equipment suppliers were collectively owed more than $15 billion by their customers—25% more than in the prior year (Henry, 2001, p. 102.). Revenue and earnings were being overstated because they were buying their own products with their own money.

Restructuring Reserves Often Used to Smooth Earnings

Firms sometimes set up reserves to smooth fluctuations in earnings. According to GAAP, firms intending to undertake a restructuring of their operations are required to estimate the costs they will eventually incur, such as severance expenses, and to charge them against current earnings. A reserve liability is set up on the balance sheet to reflect these anticipated expenses. The actual cash outlay may not occur for several years or perhaps not at all. Firms may reverse or eliminate the reserve at a later time. This has the effect of increasing earnings at the time the reserve is reversed. Some firms build reserves when taxable income is high and later reverse those reserves when income is less robust. Examples of expenses that should not be included in the estimate of reserves include legal and accounting fees, investment banking fees, special bonuses, and training expenses. GAAP states that reserves cannot be established for contingencies because such costs cannot be predicted. Contingent events should impact the income statement in the period in which they occur.

In Process Research and Development Write-Offs Often Inflate Future Earnings

Merger accounting also has been a source of abuse in those industries that rely heavily on research and development (R&D) to introduce new products. An acquiring company must assign values to all the assets it has purchased, record them on the balance sheet, and write them off in future years. In-process R&D can be written off immediately because GAAP states that in-process R&D expenditures refer to spending on largely untested rather than proven technology. Acquiring companies have an incentive to assign a high value to R&D assets and then to write them off immediately to avoid charges against future earnings.

THE MODEL-BUILDING PROCESS

The merger and acquisition (M&A) model-building process for valuing and structuring a transaction involves four discrete steps. First, value the acquiring and target firms as standalone businesses. A standalone business is one whose financial statements reflect all the costs of running the business and all of the revenues generated by the business. Second, value the consolidated acquirer and target firms including the effects of synergy. Third, determine the initial offer price for the target firm. Fourth, determine the acquirer's ability to finance the purchase using an appropriate financial structure (Figure 8-1). The appropriate financial structure (debt-to-equity ratio) is that which satisfies certain predetermined criteria. The appropriate financial structure can be determined from a range of different scenarios created by making small changes in selected value drivers. Value drivers are factors such as product volume, selling price, and cost of sales that have a significant impact on the value of the firm whenever they are altered (see Chapter 7).

STEP 1: VALUE ACQUIRER (Pv_a) AND TARGET FIRM (Pv_t) AS STANDALONE BUSINESSES

The following discussion applies to both the acquiring and target firms. The analyst should apply as many valuation methods as data availability and common sense will allow. These include income, market-based, and asset-oriented methods.

Step 1 Value Acquirer & Target as Standalone Firms	Step 2 Value Acquirer & Target Firms Including Synergy	Step 3 Determine Initial Offer Price for Target Firm	Step 4 Determine Combined Firms' Ability to Finance the Transaction
1. Understand specific firm and industry competitive dynamics	1. Estimate a. Sources and destroyers of value b. Implementation costs incurred to realize synergy	1. Estimate minimum & maximum purchase price range	1. Estimate impact of alternative financing stuctures
2. Normalize 3–5 years of historical financial data	2. Consolidate the acquirer and target standalone values including the effects of synergy	2. Determine amount of synergy willing to share with target shareholders	2. Select financing structure that a. Meets acquirer's required financial returns b. Meets target's primary needs c. Does not raise cost of debt or violate loan covenants d. Minimizes EPS dilution and short-term reduction in financial returns
3. Project normalized cash flow based on expected market growth and competitive industry dynamics	3. Estimate value of net synergy (Consolidated incl. synergy less stand-alone values of acquirer and target)	3. Determine appropriate composition of offer price	

← Key assumptions made for each step should be clearly stated. →

FIGURE 8-1. The Mergers and Acquisition Model-Building Process. NPV, net present value; EPS, earnings per share.

The estimates resulting from the various methods then can be averaged to arrive at a single valuation estimate.

Understand Specific Firm and Industry Competitive Dynamics

The accuracy of any valuation is heavily dependent on understanding the historical competitive dynamics of the industry, the historical performance of the company within the industry, and the reliability of the data used in the valuation. A careful examination of historical information can provide insights into key relationships among various operating variables and represents the first step in the process for modeling both the acquirer and the target companies. Examples of relevant historical relationships include seasonal or cyclical movements in the data, the relationship between fixed and variable expenses, and the impact on revenue of changes in product prices and unit sales. If these relationships can reasonably be expected to continue through the forecast period, they can be used to project the earnings and cash flows that will be used in the valuation process.

Normalizing Historical Data

To ensure that these historical relationships can be accurately defined, it is necessary to cleanse the data of anomalies, nonrecurring changes, and questionable accounting practices. For example, cash flow may be adjusted by adding back unusually large increases in reserves or by deducting large decreases in reserves from free cash flow to the firm. Similar adjustments can be made for significant nonrecurring gains or losses on the sale of assets or for nonrecurring expenses such as those associated with the settlement of a lawsuit or warranty claim. Monthly revenue may be aggregated into quarterly or even annual data to minimize period-to-period distortions in earnings or cash flow resulting from inappropriate accounting practices. Ideally, at least 3–5 years of historical data should be normalized.

Common-Size Financial Statements

Common-size financial statements are among the most frequently used tools to uncover data irregularities. These statements may be constructed by calculating the percentage each line item of the income statement, balance sheet, and cash-flow statement is of annual sales for each quarter or year for which historical data are available. Common-size financial statements are useful for comparing businesses of different sizes in the same industry at a specific moment in time. Such analyses are called *cross-sectional comparisons*. By expressing the target's line-item data as a percentage of sales, it is possible to compare the target company with other companies' line item data expressed in terms of sales to highlight significant differences. For example, a cross-sectional comparison may indicate important differences in the ratio of capital spending to sales between the target firm and other firms in the industry. This discrepancy may simply reflect "catch-up" spending under way at the target's competitors, or it may suggest a more troubling development in which the target is deferring necessary plant and equipment spending. To determine which is the case, it is necessary to calculate common-size financial statements for the target firm and its primary competitors over a number of consecutive periods. This type of analysis is called a *multi-period comparison*. Comparing companies in this manner will help to confirm whether the target simply has completed a large portion of capital spending that others in the industry are undertaking currently or whether the target is woefully behind in making necessary expenditures.

Even if it is not possible to collect sufficient data to undertake cross-sectional and multi-period comparisons of both the target firm and its direct competitors, constructing common-size statements for the target firm only will provide useful insights. Abnormally large increases or decreases in these ratios from one quarter or 1 year to the next highlight the need for further examination to explain why these fluctuations occurred. If it is determined that they are likely to be one-time events, these fluctuations may be eliminated by averaging the data immediately preceding and following the period in which these anomalies occurred. The anomalous data then are replaced by the data created through this averaging process. Alternatively, anomalous data can be completely excluded from the analysis. In general, non-recurring events affecting more than 10% of the net income or cash flow for a specific period should be "smoothed" or discarded from the data to allow for a clearer picture of trends and relationships in the firm's historical financial data.

Financial Ratio Analysis

Financial ratio analysis is the calculation of performance ratios from data in a company's financial statements to identify the firm's financial strengths and weaknesses. Such analysis helps in identifying potential problem areas that may require further examination during due diligence. Because ratios adjust for the size of the firm, they enable the analyst to compare a firm's ratios with industry averages. Appendix A to this chapter lists commonly used formulas for financial ratios, how they are expressed, and how they should be interpreted. The analyst need not describe all the ratios listed; instead, only those that appear to have an impact on the firm's performance need be analyzed. These ratios should be compared with industry averages to discover if the company is out of line with others in the industry. A successful competitor's performance ratios may be used if industry average data is not available. Industry average data commonly is found in such publications as *Almanac of Business and Industrial Financial Ratios* (Prentice Hall), *Annual Statement Studies* (Robert Morris Associates), *Dun's Review* (Dun and Bradstreet), *Industry Norms and Key Business Ratios* (Dun and Bradstreet), and *Value Line Investment Survey for Company and Industry Ratios*.

Project Normalized Cash Flow

Normalized cash flows should be projected for at least 5 years and possibly more until they turn positive. Projections should reflect the best available information about product demand growth, future pricing, technological changes, new competitors, new product and service offerings from current competitors, potential supply disruptions, raw material and labor cost increases, and possible new product or service substitutes. Projections also should include the revenue and costs associated with known new product introductions and capital expenditures required to maintain or expand operations by the acquiring and target firms during the forecast period.

A simple model to project cash flow involves the projection of revenue and cost of sales to obtain earnings before interest and taxes (EBIT). Cost of sales, depreciation, gross capital spending, and the change in working capital then are estimated as a percentage of projected revenue. What percentage is applied to projected revenue for these components of free cash flow to the firm may be determined by calculating their historical ratio to revenue. In this simple model, revenue drives cash-flow growth. Therefore, special attention must be given to project revenue by forecasting unit growth and selling prices, the product of which provides estimated revenue. As suggested in Chapters 4 and 7 of this book, the product life cycle concept may be used to project unit growth and prices.

The most common forecasting technique used by firms to project revenue is trend extrapolation (Klein and Linneman, 1984). This entails extending present trends into the future using historical growth rates or more sophisticated techniques such as multiple regression. The second most common forecasting method is to use scenario analysis. The scenario may involve simply a description of the future expressed in terms of key variables or issues.

Needed Adjustments When Acquirer or Target Is Part of a Larger Firm

If the acquirer or target is part of a larger firm, the projected cash flows must be adjusted to reflect all costs and revenue associated with the acquirer's or target's operation. The failure to make the proper adjustments can result in an over- or understatement of value.

Accounting for Administrative Expenses

As an operating unit within a larger company, administrative costs such as legal, tax, audit, benefits, and treasury may be heavily subsidized or even provided without charge to the subsidiary. Alternatively, these services may be charged to the subsidiary as part of an allocation equal to a specific percentage of the subsidiary's sales or cost of sales. If these expenses are accounted for as part of an allocation methodology, they may substantially overstate the actual cost of purchasing these services from outside parties. Such allocations are often ways for the parent to account for expenses incurred at the level of the corporate headquarters but that have little to do with the actual operation of the subsidiary. Such activities may include the expense associated with maintaining the corporation's headquarters building and airplanes.

If the cost of administrative support services are provided for free or are heavily subsidized by the parent, the subsidiary's reported profits should be reduced by the actual cost of providing these services. If the cost of such services is measured by using some largely arbitrary allocation methodology, the subsidiary's reported profits may be increased by the difference between the allocated expense and the actual cost of providing the services.

Accounting for Intercompany Revenue

When the target is an operating unit of another firm, it is common for its reported revenue to reflect sales to other operating units of the parent firm. Unless the parent firm contractually commits as part of the divestiture process to continue to buy from the divested operation, such revenue may evaporate as the parent firm satisfies its requirements from other suppliers. Moreover, intercompany revenue may be overstated because the prices paid for the target's output reflect artificially high internal transfer prices rather than market prices. The parent firm may not be willing to continue to pay the inflated transfer prices following the divestiture.

STEP 2: VALUE ACQUIRER AND TARGET
FIRMS INCLUDING SYNERGY (PV$_{atns}$)

Synergy generally is considered to consist only of those factors or sources of value adding to the economic value of the combined firms. However, factors that destroy value also should be considered in the estimation of the economic value of the combined firms. Net synergy (NS) is the difference between estimated sources of value and destroyers of value. The present value of net synergy can be estimated in either of two ways. The common approach is to subtract the sum of the present values of the acquirer and target firms on a standalone basis from the present value of the consolidated acquirer and target firms including the estimated effects of synergy. Alternatively, the present value of net synergy can be estimated by calculating present value of the difference between sources and destroyers of value. The first approach is illustrated in this chapter.

Sources of Value

Look for quantifiable sources of value and destroyers of value while conducting due diligence. The most common include the potential for cost savings resulting from shared overhead, duplicate facilities, and overlapping distribution channels. Potential sources of value also include assets not recorded on the balance sheet at fair value and off-balance sheet items. Common examples include land, "obsolete" inventory and equipment, patents, licenses, and copyrights. Underutilized borrowing capacity also can make an acquisition target more attractive. The addition of the acquired company's assets, low level of indebtedness, and strong cash flow from operations could enable the buyer to increase substantially the borrowing levels of the combined companies. Other sources of value could include access to new customers, intellectual property (i.e., patents, trade names, and rights to royalty streams), and new technologies and processes. Income tax loss carry forwards and tax credits also may represent an important source of value for an acquirer seeking to shelter significant amounts of pretax income.

Destroyers of Value

Factors that can destroy value include poor product quality, wage and benefit levels above comparable industry levels, and high employee turnover. A lack of customer contracts or poorly written contracts often result in customer disputes about the terms and conditions of a contract and what amounts actually are owed. Verbal agreements made with customers by the seller's sales representatives also may become obligations for the buyer. These are particularly onerous because commissioned sales forces frequently make agreements that are not profitable for their employer. Nonexistent or poorly written contracts are commonplace among large as well as small companies. Environmental issues, product liabilities, unresolved lawsuits, and other current or pending liabilities are also major potential destroyers of value for the buyer. These also serve as ticking time bombs because the actual liability may not be apparent for years following the acquisition. Moreover, the magnitude of the liability actually may force a company into bankruptcy. In the 1980s, a major producer of asbestos, Johns Manville Corporation, was forced into bankruptcy because of the discovery that certain types of asbestos, used for decades for insulating buildings, could be toxic.

Net Synergy

To the extent possible, known sources and destroyers of value should be quantified in terms of their cash inflows or outflows. Careful consideration should be given to the timing of such cash flows. This information then should be used to estimate the present value of sources of value and destroyers of value. The present value of net synergy is equal to the difference between the present values of the sources and destroyers of value.

Implementation Costs Often Overlooked

In calculating net synergy, it is important to include the costs associated with recruiting and training, realizing cost savings, achieving productivity improvements, and exploiting revenue opportunities. No matter how much care is taken to minimize employee attrition following closing, some employees will be lost. Often these are the most skilled. Once a merger or acquisition is announced, target company employees start to circulate their resumes. The best employees start to receive job solicitations from competitors or executive search firms. Consequently, the costs associated with replacing employees who leave following closing can escalate sharply. Not only will the firm incur recruitment costs; the firm also will incur the cost of training the new hires. Moreover, the new hires are not likely to reach the productivity levels of those they are replacing for some time.

Cost savings are likely to be greatest when firms with similar operations are consolidated and redundant or overlapping positions are eliminated. Many analysts take great pain to estimate savings in terms of wages, salaries, benefits, and associated overhead, such as support staff and travel expense, without accurately accounting for severance expenses associated with layoffs. How a company treats its employees during layoffs will have a significant impact on the morale of those that remain. Consequently, severance packages should be constructed as fairly as possible.

Realizing productivity improvements frequently will require additional spending in new structures and equipment, retraining employees that remain with the combined companies, or redesigning workflow. Such spending may be sizable. Similarly, exploiting revenue-raising opportunities may require substantial training of the sales force of the combined firms in selling each firm's products or services and additional advertising expenditures to inform current or potential customers of what has taken place.

STEP 3: DETERMINE INITIAL OFFER
PRICE (PV$_{IOP}$) FOR TARGET FIRM

Estimate Minimum and Maximum Offer Price Range

The initial offer price for the target firm lies between the minimum and maximum offer prices. The minimum offer price may be defined as the target's standalone or present value (PV$_T$) or its current market value (MV$_T$) (i.e., the target's current stock price times its shares outstanding). The maximum price is the sum of the minimum price plus the present value of net synergy (PV$_{NS}$). Note that the maximum price may be overstated if the current market value of the target firm reflects investor expectations of an impending takeover. As such, the current market value may reflect some portion of future synergies. Consequently, simply adding the present value of net synergy to the current market value of the target firm can result in double counting some portion of future synergy. The initial offer price (PV$_{IOP}$) is the sum of both the minimum purchase price and some percentage between 0 and 1 of the PV of net synergy (Exhibit 8-2).

EXHIBIT 8-2. DETERMINING THE
INITIAL OFFER PRICE FOR THE
TARGET FIRM'S EQUITY

Step 1: Estimate PV$_A$ and PV$_T$, the present values of the acquiring and target firms' equity, respectively. These may be estimated by subtracting the market value of each firm's long-term debt from the total market or enterprise value of each firm.

Step 2: Estimate PV$_{ATNS}$ = PV$_A$ + PV$_T$ + PV$_{NS}$, where PV$_{ATNS}$ is the present value of the acquirer and target firms including synergy and PV$_{NS}$ is the present value of net synergy resulting from combining the target and acquiring firms.

Step 3: Estimate the initial offer price (PV$_{IOP}$)

a. PV$_{MIN}$ = PV$_T$ or MV$_T$, whichever is greater. MV$_T$ is the target firm's current share price times the number of shares outstanding

b. PV$_{MAX}$ = PV$_{MIN}$ + PV$_{NS}$, where PV$_{NS}$ = PV$_{ATNS}$ − (PV$_A$ + PV$_T$)

c. PV$_{IOP}$ = PV$_{MIN}$ + αPV$_{NS}$, where $0 \leq \alpha \leq 1$

d. Offer price range for the target firm = (PV$_T$ or MV$_T$) < PV$_{IOP}$ < (PV$_T$ or MV$_T$) + PV$_{NS}$

Determine Synergy Distribution

In determining the initial offer price, the acquiring company must decide how much of anticipated synergy it is willing to share with the target firm's shareholders.

It is logical that the offer price should fall between the minimum and maximum prices for two reasons. First, it is unlikely that the target company can be purchased at the minimum price because the acquiring company normally will have to pay a premium to the current market value to induce target shareholders to transfer control to another firm. Second, at the maximum end of the range, the acquiring company would be ceding all of the net synergy value created by the combination of the two companies to the target company's shareholders. Moreover, it is prudent to pay significantly less than the maximum price because the amount of synergy actually realized tends to be less than the amount anticipated.

The acquirer's initial offer generally will be at the lowest point in the range between the minimum and maximum prices consistent with the acquirer's perception of what constitutes an acceptable price to the target firm. If the target's financial performance is remarkable, the target firm will command a high premium and the final purchase price will be close to the maximum price. Moreover, the acquirer may make a bid close to the maximum price to preempt other potential acquirers from having sufficient time to submit competing offers. However, hubris on the part of the acquirer's management or an auction environment may push the final negotiated purchase price to or even above the maximum economic value of the firm.

Adjusting Projections for Synergy

Broadly speaking, there are two general categories of synergy: revenue-related and cost savings-related synergy. Revenue-related synergy arises from sales and marketing opportunities that can be realized as a result of the combining of the target and acquiring firms. Similarly, cost savings-related synergy refers to the opportunities for the elimination of duplicate operations, processes, and personnel resulting from the combination of the two firms.

Revenue-Related Synergy

The customer base for the target and acquiring firms can be segmented into four categories: (1) those served only by the target, (2) those served only by the acquirer, (3) those served by both firms, and (4) those served by neither firm (Exhibit 8-3). The first two segments may represent revenue enhancement opportunities by enabling the target or the acquirer to sell its current products into the other's current customer base. The third segment could represent a net increase or decrease in revenue for the new firm. Incremental revenue may result from new products that could be offered only as a result of exploiting the capabilities of the target and acquiring firms in combination. However, revenue may be lost as some customers choose to have more than one source of supply. The last segment represents prospective customers who neither firm has been able to capture with its existing product offering but who may become customers for products that can be offered only as a result of combining the capabilities of the acquiring and target firms. The analysis is made simpler by focusing on the largest customers because it is generally true that 80% of a company's revenues come from about 20% of its customers.

**EXHIBIT 8-3. COMBINED FIRM CUSTOMER
BASE SEGMENTATION ANALYSIS**

Segment: Customers served by:	Segment: Represents potential
Target only	New customers for acquirer products
Acquirer only	New customers for target products
Both firms	Net gain or loss equal to
	—Gain from sale of new firm's products less
	—Loss from existing customers seeking to diversify suppliers
Neither firm	Prospective customers for new firm's combined product offering

---

Cost Savings-Related Synergies

The cost of sales for the combined firms may be adjusted for cost savings resulting from such factors as the elimination of redundant jobs and bulk purchases of raw materials. Direct labor refers to those employees directly involved in the production of goods and services. Indirect labor refers to supervisory overhead. A distinction needs to be made because of likely differences in average compensation for direct and indirect labor. Sales, general, and administrative expenses (S,G,&A) may be reduced by the elimination of overlapping jobs and the closure of unneeded sales offices (Table 8-1). To realize these savings, the combined firms will experience certain one-time expenses as severance associated with layoffs and the cost of buying out leases for sales offices that are to be closed. Severance expenses are often equal to several months of salary, including benefits, for each employee that is terminated. Other one-time expenses could include such items as retraining expenses and the cost of facility, equipment, technology, and process upgrades. The cost of sales and S,G,&A expenses including synergy then are used to calculate operating income (EBIT), which results in a higher free cash-flow number as a result of the effects of anticipated synergy (Table 8-2). Note that operating earnings, including synergy, in Table 8-2 are calculated from the line items in bold type.

Determine Appropriate Composition of Offer Price

The purchase price offered to the target company could consist of the acquirer's stock, debt, cash, or some combination of all three. The actual composition of the purchase price depends on what is acceptable to the target and acquiring companies and what the financial structure of the combined companies can support. Consequently, the acquirer needs to determine the appropriate financing or capital

TABLE 8-1   Estimating Synergy

	Year 1		Year 2	
	Head Count Reduction		Head Count Reduction	
	Staff Reduction	Dollar Savings	Staff Reduction	Dollar Savings
Cost of Sales				
Direct Labor[1]	65	4,057,143	129	8, 845, 714
Indirect Labor[2]	24	2,228,571	59	5, 478, 571
Total	89	6,285,714	188	14, 324, 285
Purchased materials[3]		3,160,000		3, 360, 000
S,G,&A				
Direct Sales[4]	10	1,071,421	25	2, 678, 571
Sales Administration[5]	5	285,714	10	571, 429
Total	15	1,357,135	30	3, 250, 000
Lease Buyouts		765,000		382, 197

[1] Average direct annual salary of $48,000. Benefits equal 30% of annual salary.
[2] Averge indirect annual salary of $65,000. Benefits equal 30% of annual salary.
[3] Volume discount of 5% on total dollar value of purchased materials. Purchased materials equal to 40% of cost of sales. Therefore, the dollar value of purchased materials savings increase each year.
[4] Average direct sales annual salary of $75,000. Benefits equal 30% of annual salary.
[5] Average sales administration salary of $40,000. Benefits equal 30% of annual salary.

structure of the combined companies, including debt, common equity, and preferred equity. In this chapter, the initial offer price is the market value or economic value (i.e., present value of the target firm defined as a standalone business) plus some portion of projected net synergy. In Chapter 5, the offer or purchase price was defined in a different context as total consideration, total purchase price or enterprise value, and net purchase price. These definitions were provided with the implicit assumption that the acquiring company had determined the economic value of the firm on a standalone basis and the value of net synergy. Economic value is determined before any consideration is given to how the transaction will be financed.

STEP 4: DETERMINE COMBINED FIRMS'
ABILITY TO FINANCE THE TRANSACTION

Estimate Impact of Alternative Financing Structures

The consolidated target and acquiring firms' financial statements, adjusted to reflect the net effects of synergy, are run through a series of scenarios to determine the impact on such variables as earnings, leverage, covenants, and borrowing costs. For example, each scenario could represent different amounts of leverage as measured by the firm's debt-to-equity ratio.

TABLE 8-2 Adjusting the Combined Acquirer and Target Company Projections for the Estimated Value of Synergy

	Forecast Period (Millions of Dollars)				
	Year 1	Year 2	Year 3	Year 4	Year 5
Revenue[1]	198	210	222	236	250
Revenue-Related Synergy:					
—Target Customers	4	6	8	12	12
—Acquirer Customers	2	4	6	10	10
—Both Firms	(4)	0	3	4	8
—Neither Firm	0	0	2	2	6
Total	2	10	19	28	36
Revenue (Including Synergy)	**200**	**220**	**241**	**264**	**286**
Cost of Sales	158	168	178	189	200
Cost of sales-related synergy:					
—Direct labor	4	8	8	8	8
—Indirect labor	2	5	5	5	5
—Purchased materials	3	3	4	4	4
Total	9	16	17	17	17
Cost of sales (Including Synergy)	**149**	**152**	**161**	**172**	**183**
S,G,&A Expenses	20	21	22	24	25
S,G,&A-Related Synergy	2	3	3	3	3
S,G,&A Expenses (Including Synergy)	**18**	**18**	**19**	**21**	**22**
Implementation Expenses	**3**	**4**			
Operating Earnings (EBIT) (Including Synergy)	**30**	**46**	**61**	**71**	**81**
Addendum:					
Cost of Sales/Revenue (%)	80	80	80	80	80
Cost of Sales (Including Net Synergy)/Revenue (Including Synergy) (%)	75	69	67	65	64
S,G,&A/Revenue (%)	10	10	10	10	10
S,G,&A (Including Synergy)/ Revenue (Including Synergy) (%)	9	8	7	8	8

[1]Revenue of the combined firms before the effects of synergy is projected to grow at an annual rate of 6% during the forecast period.

Select Appropriate Financing Structure

The appropriate financing structure is that which satisfies certain predetermined selection criterion. These selection criteria should be determined as part of the process of developing the acquisition plan (see Chapter 4). For a public company, the appropriate capital structure could be that scenario whose debt-to-equity ratio results in the highest net present value for cash flows generated by the combined businesses, the least near-term EPS dilution, no violation of loan covenants, and no significant increase in borrowing costs. Excluding EPS considerations, private companies could determine the appropriate capital structure in the same manner. In effect, the acquirer should select the financing structure that enables the following criteria to be satisfied:

1. The acquirer is able to achieve its financial return objectives for the combined companies.
2. The primary needs of the target firm's shareholders are met.
3. There is no significant increase in the cost of debt or violation of loan covenants.
4. For public companies, EPS dilution, if any, is minimized and any reduction in reported financial returns is temporary.

For publicly traded companies, financial return objectives often are couched in terms readily understood by investors, such as earnings per share. Acquiring companies must be able to convince investors that any EPS dilution is temporary and that the long-term EPS growth of the combined companies will exceed what the acquirer could have achieved without the acquisition. Financial returns for both public and private companies also may be described as the firm's estimated cost of capital or in terms of the return on total capital, assets, or equity. Moreover, the combined companies' cash flow must be sufficient to meet any incremental interest and principal repayments resulting from borrowing undertaken to finance all or some portion of the purchase price without violating existing loan covenants or deviating from debt service ratios typical for the industry. If loan covenants are violated, lenders may require the combined companies to take immediate remedial action or be declared in technical default and forced to repay the outstanding loans promptly. Moreover, if the combined firms' interest coverage or debt-to-equity ratios deviate significantly from what is considered appropriate for similar firms in the same industry, borrowing costs may escalate sharply.

THE IMPORTANCE OF STATING ASSUMPTIONS

The credibility of any valuation ultimately depends on the validity of its underlying assumptions. Valuation-related assumptions tend to fall into five major categories: (1) market, (2) income statement, (3) balance sheet, (4) synergy, and (5) valuation. Note that implicit assumptions about cash flow already are included in assumptions made about the income statement and changes in the balance sheet, which together drive changes in cash flow. *Market assumptions* are generally those that relate to the growth rate of unit volume and product price per unit. *Income statement assumptions* include the projected growth in revenue, the implied market share, and the growth in the major components of cost in relation to sales. *Balance sheet assumptions* may include the growth in the primary components of working capital and fixed assets in relation to the projected growth in sales. *Synergy assumptions* relate to the amount and timing associated with each type of anticipated synergy, including cost savings from workforce reductions, productivity improvements as a result of the introduction of new technologies or processes, and revenue growth as a result of increased market penetration. Finally, examples of important *valuation assumptions* include the acquiring firm's target debt-to-equity ratio used in calculating the cost of capital, the discount rates used during the forecast and stable growth periods, and the growth assumptions used in determining the terminal value.

FACTORS AFFECTING POSTMERGER SHARE PRICE

The stock market often is viewed as an efficient mechanism for determining whether an acquiring company has overpaid for an acquisition. Frequently, the price of both the acquirer's and the target's stock will adjust immediately following the announcement of a pending acquisition. The target's current stock price will increase by somewhat less than the announced purchase price as arbitrageurs buy the target's stock in anticipation of a completed transaction. The difference between what they pay and the announced purchase price is their potential profit. The current stock price of the acquiring company may decline, reflecting a potential dilution of its EPS or a growth in EPS of the combined companies that is somewhat slower than the growth rate investors had anticipated for the acquiring company without the acquisition. For these reasons, immediately following the acquisition announcement, investors may place a somewhat lower price-to-earnings (P/E) ratio on the acquiring company's EPS and later on the combined companies' EPS than had prevailed for the acquiring company before the announcement of the acquisition.

SHARE-EXCHANGE RATIOS

For public companies, the exchange of the acquirer's shares for the target's shares requires the calculation of the appropriate exchange ratio. The share-exchange ratio (SER) indicates the number of shares of the acquirer's stock to be exchanged for each share of the target's stock. SER is equal to the ratio of the target's stock price (P_T), including any premium, to the acquirer's stock price (P_A). The SER is calculated by the following equation:

$$SER = P_T/P_A$$

The SER can be less than, equal to, or greater than one, depending on the value of the target's shares relative to the acquirer's shares on the date set during the negotiation for valuing the transaction. Exhibit 8-4 illustrates how the SER is calculated.

EXHIBIT 8-4. CALCULATING SERs

The price offered and accepted by the target company is $40 per share, and the acquiring company's share price is $60. What is the SER?

$$SER = \$40/\$60 = .6667$$

Implication: To complete the merger, the acquiring company will give .6667 shares of its own stock for each share of the target company.

ESTIMATING POSTMERGER EARNINGS PER SHARE

The critical "go, no go" decision variable for senior management of many publicly traded acquiring companies is the impact of the acquisition on EPS following the acquisition. This measure is perhaps the simplest summary measure available of the economic impact of an acquisition or merger on the acquirer. As such, it is among the most widely followed indicators by market analysts and investors. Earnings dilution, although temporary, can cause a dramatic loss of market value for the acquiring company.

As illustrated in Exhibit 8-5, the calculation of postmerger EPS reflects the EPS of the combined companies, the price of the acquirer's stock, the price of the target's stock, and the number of shares of acquirer and target stock outstanding (Moyer, McGuigan, and Kretlow, 1998).

$$\text{Postmerger EPS} = \frac{E_{T\&A}}{N_A + [N_T \times (P_T/P_A)]}$$

E_{T+A} = the sum of the current earnings of the target and acquiring companies plus any earnings increase as a result of synergy

N_A = the acquiring company's outstanding shares

P_T = price offered for the target company

N_T = number of target company's outstanding shares

P_A = current price of the acquiring company's stock

EXHIBIT 8-5. CALCULATING POSTMERGER EPS

The acquiring company's share price is $40 and the price offered to the target, including an appropriate premium, is $20. The combined earnings of the two companies, including estimated synergies, are $1,000,000. If the acquiring company has 200,000 shares outstanding and the target company has 100,000 shares outstanding, what is the postmerger EPS for the combined companies?

$$\text{Postmerger EPS} = \frac{\$1,000,000}{200,000 + [100.000 \times (\$20/\$40)]}$$

$$= \frac{\$1,000,000}{250,000}$$

$$= \$4.00$$

ESTIMATING POSTMERGER SHARE PRICE

The share price of the combined firms following an acquisition reflects both the anticipated EPS for the combined firms and the P/E ratio investors are willing to pay for the anticipated per-share earnings. Exhibit 8-6 provides an example of how this process works for a share-for-share exchange, for an all-cash purchase, and for a transaction whose purchase price includes a combination of stock and cash. The exhibit illustrates how the postmerger share price may be determined by multiplying the postmerger EPS by an appropriate P/E ratio. For simplicity, the prevailing postmerger P/E is assumed to be the acquiring firm's premerger P/E.

EXHIBIT 8-6. CALCULATING THE POSTMERGER SHARE PRICE

Share-for-Share Exchange

The acquiring company is considering the acquisition of Target Company in a stock-for-stock transaction in which Target Company would receive $84.30 for each share of its common stock. The acquiring company does not expect any change in its P/E multiple after the merger and chooses to value the target company conservatively by assuming no earnings growth due to synergy. We have the following data on the companies:

	Acquiring Company	Target Company
Earnings available for common stock	$281,500	$62,500
Number of shares of common outstanding	112,000	18,750
Market price per share	$56.25	$62.50

1. Purchase price premium = Offer price for target company stock/Target Company market price per share

$$= \$84.30/\$62.50$$
$$= 1.35 \text{ or } 35\% \text{ (i.e., } 1.35 - 1.00)$$

2. Exchange ratio = Price per share offered for Target Company/Market price per share for the Acquiring Company

$$= \$84.30/\$56.25$$
$$= 1.5 \text{ (i.e., Acquiring Company issues 1.5 shares of stock for each share of Target Company's stock)}$$

3. New shares issued by Acquiring Company = 18,750 (shares of Target Company) × 1.5 (Exchange ratio) = 28,125

4. Total shares outstanding of the combined companies
$$= 112,000 + 28,125 = 140,125$$
5. Postmerger EPS of the combined companies

$$= (\$281,500 + \$62,500)/140,125$$
$$= \$344,000/140,125$$
$$= \$2.46$$

6. Premerger EPS of Acquiring Company $= \$281,500/112,000 = \$2.51$
7. Premerger P/E $=$ Premerger price per share/premerger earnings per share

$$= \$56.25/\$2.51$$
$$= 22.4$$

8. Postmerger share price $=$ Postmerger EPS $\times$ Premerger P/E

$$= \$2.46 \times 22.4$$
$$= \$55.10 \text{ (as compared with \$56.25 premerger)}$$

9. Postmerger equity ownership distribution:

$$\text{Target Company} = 28,125/140,125 = \quad 20.1\%$$
$$\text{Acquiring Company} = 100 - 20.1 = \frac{79.9}{100.0\%}$$

Implications: The acquisition results in an $1.15 reduction in the share price of the acquiring company as a result of a $.05 decline in the EPS of the combined companies. (Recall that the acquiring company assumed no gains in earnings of the combined companies due to synergy.) Whether the acquisition is a poor decision depends on what happens to the earnings of the combined companies over time. If the combined companies' earnings grow more rapidly than Acquiring Company's earnings would have in the absence of the acquisition, the acquisition may contribute to the market value of Acquiring Company.

All-Cash Purchase: Instead of a share for share exchange, Target Company agrees to an all-cash purchase of 100% of its outstanding stock for $84.30 for each of its 18,750 shares of common stock outstanding. When the transaction is closed, the 18,750 shares of Target Company's stock are retired. The acquiring company believes that investors will apply its premerger P/E to determine the postmerger share price. Moreover, the acquiring company finances the purchase price by using cash balances on hand in excess of its normal cash requirements.

1. Postmerger EPS of the combined companies
   $= (\$281{,}500 + \$62{,}500)/112{,}000 = \$3.07$
2. Postmerger share price $=$ Postmerger EPS $\times$ Premerger P/E
   $= \$3.07 \times 22.4$
   $= \$68.77$ (as compared with $56.25 premerger)

Implications: The all-cash acquisition results in a $12.52 increase in the share price of the combined companies. This is a result of a $.56 improvement in the EPS of the combined companies as compared with the $2.51 premerger EPS of the acquiring company. In practice, the improvement in EPS would not have been as dramatic if the earnings of the combined companies had been reduced by accrued interest on the excess cash balances of the acquirer or by interest expense if the acquirer had chosen to finance the transaction using debt.

Combination Cash and Stock: If the offer price for the target firm consists of one share of acquirer stock valued at $56.25 (given in the problem) and $28.05 in cash ($84.30 offer price $-$ $56.25), calculate the postmerger earnings per share and share price.

1. Postmerger EPS $= (\$281{,}500 + \$62{,}500)/(112{,}000 + 18{,}750) = \$2.63$
2. Postmerger share price $= 22.4 \times \$2.63 = \$58.91$

Implications: The combination cash and stock offer increases the share price of the combined firms by somewhat more than the all-stock offer, which actually results in some destruction of value but far less than the increase in shareholder value provided by the all-cash offer. Moreover, as with the all-cash offer, the combined firms' EPS must be adjusted to reflect the loss of interest earnings on any excess cash balances used by the acquirer to buy the target firm or interest expense if the acquirer borrowed to pay the cash portion of the purchase price.

KEY M&A MODEL FORMULAS

Each component of cash flow used to value the acquiring and target firms individually (Step 1) and the consolidated acquirer and target firms including the effects of synergy (Step 2) is estimated by projecting the appropriate line items of the firm's income statement and balance sheet. Often many of the financial statement line items are forecast by calculating each item as a percentage of sales based on the last 3–5 years of historical information and then applying these historical percentages to projections of sales. This method is intuitively appealing because sales are normally the principal determinant of changes in cash flow over long time periods. This method also is simple to apply. Of course, the implicit assumptions are that all financial statement line items that are projected in this manner grow at the same rate as sales over time and that the historical relationship between these line items and sales will continue to apply to the forecast period. All financial statement line items need not or conceptually should not be expressed as a function of sales. These include such line items as depreciation and amortization expense, interest income and expense, and borrowing. Exhibit 8-7 lists the key formulas used to create the M&A model outlined in Steps 1–4 and illustrated in Case Study 8-1.

EXHIBIT 8-7. KEY FINANCIAL MODELING RELATIONSHIPS

Projected financial data may be based on historical relationships observed in the normalized data.

1. Net sales equal net sales in the prior year $\times (1 + g)$, where g is the expected sales growth rate.
2. Variable component of cost of sales and S,G,&A determined as a percentage of sales.
3. Depreciation and amortization determined as a percentage of gross fixed assets (GFA).
4. Gross profit equals net revenue less variable component of cost of sales, depreciation and amortization, lease expense, and other expenses that might be allocated to production activities.
5. Operating profit (EBIT) equals gross profit less S,G,&A.
6. Interest income equals the interest rate $\times$ cash and marketable securities.
7. Interest expense equals cost of borrowed funds $\times$ yearend debt outstanding.
8. Before-tax profit equals EBIT plus interest income less interest expense.
9. Tax liability equals before tax profits $\times$ marginal tax rate (federal, state, and local $= .4$)
10. Net profits equal before-tax profits less tax liability.
11. Other current assets (e.g., receivables, inventories, and prepaid assets) determined as a percentage of sales.
12. Cash and marketable securities (used as balancing item) $=$ long-term debt $+$ current liabilities $+$ shareholders' equity $-$ other current assets $-$ net fixed assets.[1]

13. Gross fixed assets determined as a percentage of sales.
14. Accumulated depreciation and amortization equals current depreciation and amortization plus accumulated depreciation and amortization in the prior year.
15. Net fixed assets (NFA) equal GFA less accumulated depreciation and amortization.
16. Total assets = Cash and marketable securities plus other current assets + NFA.
17. Current liabilities determined as a percentage of net sales.
18. Long-term debt (LTD) equal to the difference between uses and sources of funds.

    a. If "a" × net sales + other current assets + net fixed assets − current liabilities − shareholders' equity > 0, LTD = "a" × net sales + other current assets + net fixed assets − current liabilities − shareholders' equity

    b. If "a" × net sales + other current assets + net fixed assets − current liabilities − shareholders' equity < 0, LTD = 0, where "a" = minimum percentage of net sales that must be held as cash to meet working capital requirements[2]

19. Retained earnings equal net income after tax plus retained earnings in the prior year. Shareholders' equity equals common stock (including earned surplus) plus retained earnings.
20. Total liabilities and shareholders' equity equal current liabilities plus LTD plus shareholders' equity.
21. Working capital equals current assets less current liabilities.[3]
22. Change in working capital equals working capital in the current year less working capital in the prior year.
23. Capital spending equals the actual change in gross fixed assets whenever the current year's sales growth exceeds some predetermined number; otherwise, it equals depreciation and amortization expense.[4]
24. Free cash flow (to the firm) equals EBIT $\times (1 - t)$ plus depreciation and amortization less capital expenditures less the change in working capital.

[1] If long-term debt + current liabilities + shareholders' equity (i.e., sources of funds) > other current assets + net fixed assets (i.e., uses of funds), cash and marketable securities increases by the difference between (long-term debt + current liabilities + shareholders' equity) and (other current assets + net fixed assets) to ensure that total assets equal total liabilities plus shareholders' equity. In contrast, cash and marketable securities will decline by the difference between sources and uses of funds if uses of funds exceeds sources of funds.

[2] The Microsoft Excel spreadsheet formula for estimating long-term debt is expressed as follows:
= IF (0.12 ∗ B26 + B47 + B51 − B53 − B57 > 0, 0.12 ∗ B26 + B47 + B51 − B53 − B57, 0),

where B26 refers to the spreadsheet cell containing 1998 sales and .12 ∗ B26 is the minimum cash balance management desires to maintain; B47 contains other current assets, B51 net fixed assets, B53 current liabilities, and B57 shareholders' equity.

[3]The cash and short-term marketable securities component of working capital can be divided into two categories: (1) minimum cash needed to meet working capital requirements equal to "a" times net sales (see item 18 above) and (2) investments in short-term marketable securities. For purposes of calculating the working capital component of free cash flows used for valuation, current assets may be defined as minimum cash balances needed to meet working capital requirements (i.e., "a" times net sales) plus other current assets.

[4]If sales grow at less than some predetermined rate, capital spending equals depreciation and amortization expenses, a proxy for the required level of maintenance spending. If sales growth exceeds that predetermined rate, the firm must add to its capacity. Therefore, capital spending equals the change in gross fixed assets, which reflects both spending for additional capacity and maintenance spending.

Note: In solving the model using Microsoft Excel, the analyst should make sure the iteration command is turned on. Iteration is the recalculation of the worksheet until certain conditions are reached. Excel will recalculate the model the maximum number of times specified or until the results between the calculations change by less than the amount specified in the maximum change box. To turn on the iteration command, on the menu bar click on Tools > > > Options > > > Calculation. Select iteration and specify the maximum number of iterations and amount of maximum change.

CASE STUDY 8-1: DETERMINING THE INITIAL OFFER PRICE—THE GEE WHIZ MEDIA AND GO GO TECHNOLOGY SAGA

Background: Gee Whiz Media (GWM) is a leader in the electronic publishing industry, focused on the conversion of text, video, and music to an electronic medium such as CD-ROMs. Despite owning relatively little content, GWM was able to secure significant market share growth by licensing content from others and then providing it on a CD-ROM in a highly creative way. The firm's business model involves putting well-known artists on CD-ROMs and then distributing these products through nationally known online and "brick and mortar" outlets. However, by the late 1990s, it soon became apparent that continued growth would require substantially more resources than were currently available to the firm. GWM's senior management believed that they would have to acquire another firm in the industry that possessed, or had access to, an extensive content library, a first-rate software development staff, and distribution channels not currently used by GWM. In late 1999, after an extensive review of potential target firms, GWM's management decided to approach Go Go Technology (GGT), a firm that satisfied most of their important selection criteria.

GWM's management understood that a successful acquisition would be one that would create more shareholder value at an acceptable level of risk than if the firm retained its current "go it alone" strategy. Consequently, GWM valued their own business on a standalone basis, GGT's business, and then combined the two and included the effects of potential synergy. The difference between the combined valuation with synergy and the sum of the two businesses valued as standalone operations provided an estimate of the potential incremental value that could be created from the acquisition of GGT. GWM's management also understood the importance of not paying too much for GGT, while offering enough to make GGT management take the bid seriously. Thus, the challenge was to determine the initial GGT offer price.

Analysis: Tables 8-3 to 8-6 provide pro forma financial output from a M&A model used to determine the initial GGT offer price. Each table corresponds to one step in the four-step process outlined in this chapter. The total value created by combining GWM and GGT is summarized in Table 8-7.

• Table 8-3: Based on management's best estimate of future competitive dynamics and the firm's internal resources, GWM devised a business plan that suggested that, if GWM continued its current strategy, GWM would be worth about $97 million. Reflecting limited data provided by GGT's management and publicly available information, GWM normalized GGT's historical financial statements by eliminating nonrecurring gains, losses, or expenses. This provided GWM with a better understanding of GGT's sustainable financial performance. Future performance was determined by adjusting the firm's past performance to reflect what GWM's management thought was possible. Despite its significantly smaller size in terms of revenue, GGT's market value was estimated to be about $103 million—about $6 million more than GWM's standalone market value.

• Table 8-4: By consolidating the two firms and estimating potential synergy, GWM believed that together they could achieve about $118 million in additional shareholder value. This incremental value was to result from sustainable revenue increases of as much as $15 million annually as a result of improved product quality, a broader product offering, and cross-selling activities, as well as cost savings resulting from economies of scale and scope and the elimination of duplicate jobs.

• Table 8-5: After an extensive review of the data, GWM's management proposed to GGT's CEO the acquisition of 100% of the firm's outstanding 3 million shares for $50.20 per share—a 46% premium over the current GGT share price. The initial offer consisted of 1.14 GWM shares plus $12.55 in cash for each GGT share. If accepted, GGT shareholders would own about 77% of the stock of the combined firms.

• Table 8-6: It appeared that the combined firms would be able to finance the transaction without violating covenants on existing debt. Despite $40 million in additional borrowing to finance the transaction, the key credit ratios for the combined firms remained attractive relative to industry averages. This may enable the new firm to borrow additional funds to exploit selected future strategic opportunities as they arise. Finally, the after-tax return on total capital for the combined firms exceeds by 2003 what GWM could have achieved on a standalone basis.

- Table 8-7: The estimated equity value for the combined firms is $251.7 million. This reflects the enterprise or total present value of the new firm, including synergy, adjusted for long-term debt and excess cash balances. The estimated posttransaction price per share is $56.95—$23.95 above GWM's pretransaction share price.

KEY ISSUES

Note the key issues or questions raised in Case Study 8-1 are those that have been discussed in this chapter and include the following:

- What is the standalone value of the acquiring firm? From the viewpoint of the acquirer's shareholders, an acquisition makes sense only if the per share value of the combined firm is higher than that of the standalone value of the acquiring firm.
- What is the standalone value of the target firm? This figure, or the firm's current public market value, establishes the logical minimum offer price for the target firm.
- What is the potential value that can be created (i.e., synergy) for shareholders in the new firm by combining the target and acquirer firms?
- How rapidly can the potential synergy be realized?
- How much will have to be spent to realize the potential synergy?
- How much of the synergy must be shared with the target firm's shareholders to offer a price that will induce target shareholders to surrender control?
- What portion of the new firm's equity will be held by acquirer shareholders and what portion will be held by target shareholders.
- Can the proposed purchase price for the target firm be financed by the aggregate resources of the combined firms without violating existing loan covenants?
- Are the key assumptions underlying the model realistic?

ARE COMPLEX MODELS NECESSARILY
MORE ACCURATE THAN SIMPLE MODELS?

In the author's opinion, the answer to the question, "Are complex models necessarily more accurate than simple models?" should depend primarily on practical considerations. Efforts to make models more realistic often add substantial

TABLE 8-3 "Step 1" Acquiring Company—GWM

Forecast Assumptions (2001–2005)	2001	2002	2003	2004	2005
Net Sales Growth Rate	1.25	1.20	1.15	1.15	1.15
Cost of Sales (Variable)/Sales (%)	0.65	0.65	0.65	0.65	0.65
Dep. & Amort./Gross Fixed Assets (%)	0.1	0.1	0.1	0.1	0.1
Selling Expense/Sales (%)	0.09	0.09	0.09	0.09	0.09
General & Admin. Expense/Sales (%)	0.07	0.07	0.07	0.07	0.07
Interest on Cash/Marketable Sec.	0.04	0.04	0.04	0.04	0.04
Interest Rate on Debt (%)	0.1	0.1	0.1	0.1	0.1
Marginal Tax Rate	0.4	0.4	0.4	0.4	0.4
Other Assets/Sales (%)	0.3	0.3	0.3	0.3	0.3
Gross Fixed Assets/Sales (%)	0.4	0.4	0.4	0.4	0.4
Minimum Cash Balances/Sales (%)	0.12	0.12	0.12	0.12	0.12
Current Liabilities/Sales (%)	0.1	0.1	0.1	0.1	0.1
Common Shares Outstanding (Mil.)	1	1	1	1	1
Discount Rate (2001–2005) (%)	0.15				
Discount Rate (Terminal Period) (%)	0.10				
Sustainable Cash-Flow Growth Rate	1.06				
Sustainable Cash-Flow Rate as %	0.06				
Market Value of Long-Term Debt[1]	23.8				

(Continued)

TABLE 8-3 (Continued)

Gee Whiz Media Standalone Income, Balance Sheet, and Cash-Flow Statements

Valuation Analysis	Historical Financials						Projected Financials			
	1996	1997	1998	1999	2000	2001	2002	2003	2004	2005
Income Statement ($ Mil.)										
Net Sales	27.4	31.5	41.0	53.3	66.6	83.2	99.8	114.8	132.0	151.9
Less: Cost of Sales										
Variable	17.8	20.5	26.6	34.6	43.3	54.1	64.9	74.6	85.8	98.7
Depreciation & Amortization	1.1	1.3	1.6	2.1	2.7	3.3	4.0	4.6	5.3	6.1
Lease Expense	0.4	0.4	0.6	0.7	0.8	1.0	1.2	1.2	1.3	1.3
Total Cost of Sales	19.3	22.1	28.9	37.4	46.7	58.4	70.1	80.4	92.4	106.1
Gross Profit	8.1	9.4	12.1	15.8	19.8	24.8	29.8	34.4	39.6	45.8
Less: Sales, General & Admin. Exp.										
Selling Expense	2.5	2.8	3.7	4.8	6.0	7.5	9.0	10.3	11.9	13.7
General and Admin. Expense	1.9	2.2	2.9	3.7	4.7	5.8	7.0	8.0	9.2	10.6
Total S,G&A	4.4	5.0	6.6	8.5	10.7	13.3	16.0	18.4	21.1	24.3
Operating Profits (EBIT)	3.7	4.3	5.5	7.3	9.2	11.5	13.8	16.0	18.5	21.5
Plus: Interest Income	0.2	0.2	0.2	0.3	0.4	0.4	0.5	0.6	0.6	0.7
Less: Interest Expense	1.5	1.5	1.8	2.1	2.4	2.7	2.8	2.6	2.3	1.9
Net Profits Before Taxes	2.4	3.0	4.0	5.5	7.2	9.2	11.4	14.0	16.9	20.3
Less: Taxes	0.9	1.2	1.6	2.2	2.9	3.7	4.6	5.6	6.7	8.1
Net Profits After Taxes	1.4	1.8	2.4	3.3	4.3	5.5	6.9	8.4	10.1	12.2
Earnings per Share ($/Share)	1.4	1.8	2.4	3.3	4.3	5.5	6.9	8.4	10.1	12.2

Balance Sheet (12/31)

Current Assets										
Cash & Mkt. Securities[2]	3.3	3.8	4.9	6.4	8.0	10.0	12.0	13.8	15.8	18.2
Other Current Assets	8.2	9.5	12.3	16.0	20.0	25.0	30.0	34.4	39.6	45.6
Total Current Assets	11.5	13.2	17.2	22.4	28.0	34.9	41.9	48.2	55.5	63.8
Gross Fixed Assets	11.0	12.6	16.4	21.3	26.6	33.3	39.9	45.9	52.8	60.7
Less: Accumulated Deprec. & Amort.	0.6	1.9	3.5	5.6	8.3	11.6	15.6	20.2	25.5	31.6
Net Fixed Assets	10.4	10.7	12.9	15.7	18.3	21.7	24.3	25.7	27.3	29.2
Total Assets	21.9	24.0	30.1	38.0	46.3	56.6	66.3	73.9	82.8	93.0
Current Liabilities	2.7	3.2	4.1	5.3	6.7	8.3	10.0	11.5	13.2	15.2
Long-Term Debt[3]	15.1	15.0	17.8	21.2	23.8	26.9	28.1	25.9	22.9	18.9
Common Stock[4]	2.0	2.0	2.0	2.0	2.0	2.0	2.0	2.0	2.0	2.0
Retained Earnings	2.0	3.8	6.2	9.5	13.8	19.3	26.2	34.6	44.7	56.9
Shareholders' Equity	4.0	5.8	8.2	11.5	15.8	21.3	28.2	36.6	46.7	58.9
Total Liabilities + Shareholders' Equity	21.9	24.0	30.1	38.0	46.3	56.6	66.3	73.9	82.8	93.0

Free Cash Flow ($ Mil.)

EBIT (1 − t)	2.2	2.6	3.3	4.4	5.5	6.9	8.3	9.6	11.1	12.9
Plus: Depreciation & Amortization	1.1	1.3	1.6	2.1	2.7	3.3	4.0	4.6	5.3	6.1
Less: Capital Expenditures[5]	1.2	1.3	3.8	4.9	5.3	6.7	4.0	4.6	5.3	6.1
Less: Change in Working Capital	0.4	1.3	3.0	3.9	4.3	5.3	5.3	4.8	5.5	6.3
Equals: Free Cash Flow[6]	1.7	1.3	−1.8	−2.3	−1.4	−1.8	2.9	4.8	5.6	6.5
PV (2001–2005) @15%	10.3									
PV of Terminal Value @ 10%	86.3									
Total PV (Market Value of the Firm)	96.6									

(Continued)

423

TABLE 8-3 (Continued)

	Gee Whiz Media Standalone Income, Balance Sheet, and Cash-Flow Statements									
	Historical Financials						Projected Financials			
Valuation Analysis	1996	1997	1998	1999	2000	2001	2002	2003	2004	2005
Plus: Excess Cash Balances	0.0									
Less: Mkt. Value of Long-Term Debt	23.8									
Equity Value ($ Millions)	72.8									
Equity Value Per Share ($/Share)	72.8									

[1]PV of GWM's debt = $C * \text{PVIFA}_{i,n} + P * \text{PVIF}_{i,n}$, where C is the average coupon rate in dollars on GWM's debt at an interest rate, I, for the average remaining maturity on the debt, n. P is the principal in dollars. PVIFA is the present value interest factor for an annuity and PVIF is the present value interest factor for a single value.

[2]Cash & marketable securities = long-term debt + current liabilities + shareholders' equity − other current assets − net fixed assets.

[3]If .12 × net sales + other current assets + net fixed assets − current liabilities − shareholders' equity > 0, long-term debt = .12 × net sales + other current assets + net fixed assets − current liabilities − shareholders' equity. Otherwise, if 12 × net sales + other current assets + net fixed assets − current liabilities − shareholders' equity < 0, debt = 0.

[4]Common stock includes both stock issued at par plus additional paid in capital (i.e., premium paid to the firm over par or stated value of the stock).

[5]Capital spending is undertaken to maintain existing and to provide additional capacity. Additions to capacity come at periodic intervals related to the level of utilization of existing production facilities. Consequently, capital spending equals the actual change in gross fixed assets (GFA) only if the current year's percentage change in sales exceeds 20% (a measure of facility utilization); otherwise, capital spending equals depreciation.

[6]Free cash flow equals after-tax EBIT + depreciation & amortization − capital expenditures − the change in working capital.

424

"Step 1" Target Company—GGT

Forecast Assumptions (2001–2005)	2001	2002	2003	2004	2005
Net Sales Growth Rate	1.4	1.35	1.3	1.3	1.2
Cost of Sales (Variable)/Sales (%)	0.60	0.60	0.60	0.60	0.60
Dep. & Amort./Gross Fixed Assets (%)	0.1	0.1	0.1	0.1	0.1
Selling Expense/Sales (%)	0.08	0.08	0.08	0.08	0.08
General & Admin. Expense/Sales (%)	0.06	0.06	0.06	0.06	0.06
Interest on Cash/Marketable Sec.	0.04	0.04	0.04	0.04	0.04
Interest Rate on Debt (%)	0.1	0.1	0.1	0.1	0.1
Marginal Tax Rate	0.4	0.4	0.4	0.4	0.4
Other Assets/Sales (%)	0.3	0.3	0.3	0.3	0.3
Gross Fixed Assets/Sales (%)	0.35	0.35	0.35	0.35	0.35
Minimum Cash Balances/Sales (%)	0.12	0.12	0.12	0.12	0.12
Current Liabilities/Sales (%)	0.1	0.1	0.1	0.1	0.1
Common Shares Outstanding (Mil.)	3	3	3	3	3
Discount Rate (2001–2005) (%)	0.15				
Discount Rate (Terminal Period) (%)	0.1				
Sustainable Cash-Flow Growth Rate	1.06				
Sustainable Cash-Flow Rate as %	0.06				
Market Value of Long-Term Debt[1]	3.1				

(Continued)

TABLE 8-3 (Continued)

Go Go Technology Income, Balance Sheet, and Cash-Flow Statements

Valuation Analysis	Historical Financials					Projected Financials				
	1996	1997	1998	1999	2000	2001	2002	2003	2004	2005
Income Statement ($ Mil.)										
Net Sales	10.4	12.0	16.1	21.8	28.3	39.7	53.6	69.6	90.5	108.6
Less: Cost of Sales										
Variable	6.2	7.2	9.7	13.1	17.0	23.8	32.1	41.8	54.3	65.2
Depreciation and Amortization	0.4	0.4	0.6	0.8	1.0	1.4	1.9	2.4	3.2	3.8
Lease Expense	0.4	0.4	0.6	0.7	0.8	1.0	1.2	1.2	1.3	1.3
Total Cost of Sales	7.0	8.0	10.9	14.5	18.8	26.2	35.2	45.4	58.8	70.3
Gross Profit	3.4	4.0	5.3	7.3	9.5	13.5	18.3	24.2	31.7	38.3
Less: Sales, General & Admin. Exp.										
Selling Expense	0.8	1.0	1.3	1.7	2.3	3.2	4.3	5.6	7.2	8.7
General and Admin. Expense	0.6	0.7	1.0	1.3	1.7	2.4	3.2	4.2	5.4	6.5
Total S,G,&A	1.5	1.7	2.3	3.1	4.0	5.6	7.5	9.7	12.7	15.2
Operating Profits (EBIT)	1.9	2.3	3.0	4.2	5.6	7.9	10.8	14.5	19.1	23.1
Plus: Interest Income	0.1	0.1	0.1	0.1	0.2	0.2	0.3	0.3	0.4	0.6
Less: Interest Expense	0.3	0.2	0.2	0.3	0.3	0.5	0.6	0.6	0.5	0.0
Net Profits Before Taxes	1.7	2.2	2.9	4.0	5.4	7.6	10.5	14.2	19.0	23.7
Less: Taxes	0.7	0.9	1.2	1.6	2.2	3.1	4.2	5.7	7.6	9.5
Net Profits After Taxes	1.0	1.3	1.7	2.4	3.3	4.6	6.3	8.5	11.4	14.2
Earnings per Share ($/Share)	0.3	0.4	0.6	0.8	1.1	1.5	2.1	2.8	3.8	4.7

Balance Sheet (12/31)

Current Assets										
Cash & Marketable Securities[2]	1.2	1.4	1.9	2.6	3.4	4.8	6.4	8.4	10.9	13.8
Other Current Assets	3.1	3.6	4.8	6.5	8.5	11.9	16.1	20.9	27.2	32.6
Total Current Assets	4.4	5.0	6.8	9.2	11.9	16.7	22.5	29.2	38.0	46.4
Gross Fixed Assets	3.6	4.2	5.7	7.6	9.9	13.9	18.7	24.4	31.7	38.0
Less: Accumulated Deprec. & Amort.	0.4	0.8	1.4	2.1	3.1	4.5	6.4	8.8	12.0	15.8
Net Fixed Assets	3.2	3.4	4.3	5.5	6.8	9.4	12.3	15.5	19.7	22.2
Total Assets	7.6	8.4	11.0	14.6	18.7	26.0	34.8	44.8	57.7	68.6
Current Liabilities	1.0	1.2	1.6	2.2	2.8	4.0	5.4	7.0	9.1	10.9
Long-Term Debt[3]	2.6	1.9	2.4	3.0	3.1	4.7	5.9	5.7	5.1	0.0
Common Stock[4]	2.0	2.0	2.0	2.0	2.0	2.0	2.0	2.0	2.0	2.0
Retained Earnings	2.0	3.3	5.0	7.5	10.7	15.3	21.6	30.2	41.6	55.8
Shareholders' Equity	4.0	5.3	7.0	9.5	12.7	17.3	23.6	32.2	43.6	57.8
Total Liabilities + Shareholders' Equity	7.6	8.4	11.0	14.6	18.7	26.0	34.8	44.8	57.7	68.6

Free Cash Flow ($ Mil.)

EBIT (1 − t)	1.2	1.4	1.8	2.5	3.3	4.8	6.5	8.7	11.4	13.9
Plus: Depreciation & Amortization	0.4	0.4	0.6	0.8	1.0	1.4	1.9	2.4	3.2	3.8
Less: Capital Expenditures[5]	1.2	0.4	1.5	2.0	1.0	4.0	4.9	2.4	3.2	3.8
Less: Change in Working Capital	0.4	0.5	1.3	1.8	2.1	3.6	4.4	5.1	6.7	6.6
Equals: Free Cash Flow[6]	−0.1	0.9	−0.4	−0.5	1.3	−1.5	−0.9	3.5	4.8	7.3

(Continued)

TABLE 8-3 (Continued)

Go Go Technology Income, Balance Sheet, and Cash-Flow Statements

	Historical Financials				Projected Financials				
Valuation Analysis	1996	1997	1998	1999	2000	2001	2002	2003	2004	2005
PV (2001–2005) @ 15%	6.7									
PV of Terminal Value @ 10%	96.0									
Total PV (Market Value of the Firm)	102.7									
Plus: Excess Cash Balances	0.0									
Less: Mkt. Value of Long-Term Debt	3.1									
Equity Value ($ Millions)	99.6									
Equity Value Per Share ($/Share)	33.2									

[1]PV of GGT's debt = C * PVIFA$_{i,n}$ + P * PVIF$_{i,n}$, where C is the average coupon rate in dollars on GGT's debt at an interest rate, I, for the average remaining maturity on the debt, n. P is the principal in dollars. PVIFA is the present value interest factor for an annuity and PVIF is the present value interest factor for a single value.

[2]Cash & marketable securities = long-term debt + current liabilities + shareholders' equity − other current assets − net fixed assets.

[3]If .12 × net sales + other current assets + net fixed assets − current liabilities − shareholders' equity > 0, long-term debt = .12 × net sales + other current assets + net fixed assets − current liabilities − shareholders' equity. Otherwise, if .12 × net sales + other current assets + net fixed assets − current liabilities − shareholders' equity < 0, debt = 0.

[4]Common stock includes both stock issued at par plus additional paid-in capital (i.e., premium paid to the firm over par or stated value of the stock).

[5]Capital spending equals the actual change in gross fixed assets if the percentage change in sales is greater than 30%; otherwise, capital spending is equal to depreciation and amortization.

[6]Free cash flow equals after-tax EBIT + depreciation & amortization − capital expenditures − the change in working capital. For purposes of calculating the working capital component of free cash flows used for valuation, current assets may be defined as minimum cash balances needed to meet working capital requirements (i.e., the minimum fraction of net sales that must be maintained in cash) plus other current assets.

TABLE 8-4 "Step 2" Acquirer/Target Consolidation

Forecast Assumptions (2001–2005)

	2001	2002	2003	2004	2005
Sales-Related Synergy ($ Mil.)	2	10	15	15	15
Variable COS/Sales (%)	0.63	0.63	0.63	0.63	0.63
Selling Expense/Sales (%)	0.085	0.08	0.08	0.08	0.08
General & Admin./Sales (%)	0.055	0.05	0.05	0.05	0.05
Integration Expenses	−5	−3			
Discount Rate (2001–2005)	0.15				
Discount Rate (Terminal Period)	0.1				
Sustainable Cash-Flow Growth Rate	1.065				
Sustainable Cash-Flow Rate as %	0.065				
Market Value of Long-Term Debt	26.9				

Consolidated GWM and GGT Income, Balance Sheet, and Cash-Flow Statements Including Synergy

Valuation Analysis	Historical Financials					Projected Financials				
	1996	1997	1998	1999	2000	2001	2002	2003	2004	2005
Income Statement ($ Mil.)										
Net Sales	37.8	43.5	57.1	75.0	94.9	122.9	153.4	184.4	222.6	260.5
Sales-Related Synergy[1]						2.0	10.0	15.0	15.0	15.0
Total Net Sales	37.8	43.5	57.1	75.0	94.9	124.9	163.4	199.4	237.6	275.5
Less: Cost of Sales										
Variable[2]	24.1	27.7	36.3	47.7	60.3	78.7	102.9	125.7	149.7	173.5

(Continued)

TABLE 8-4 (*Continued*)

Consolidated GWM and GGT Income, Balance Sheet, and Cash-Flow Statements Including Synergy

	Historical Financials				Projected Financials				
Valuation Analysis	1996	1997	1998	1999	2000	2001	2002	2003	2004	2005
Depreciation & Amortization	1.5	1.7	2.2	2.9	3.7	4.7	5.9	7.0	8.4	9.9
Lease Expense	0.8	0.8	1.2	1.4	1.6	2.0	2.4	2.4	2.6	2.6
Total Cost of Sales	26.3	30.1	39.7	52.0	65.5	85.4	111.2	135.1	160.7	186.0
Gross Profit	11.5	13.3	17.4	23.1	29.4	39.5	52.2	64.4	76.8	89.4
Less: Sales, General & Admin. Exp.										
Selling Expense	3.3	3.8	5.0	6.5	8.3	10.6	13.1	16.0	19.0	22.0
General and Admin. Expense	2.5	2.9	3.8	5.0	6.4	6.9	8.2	10.0	11.9	13.8
Total S,G&A[3]	5.8	6.7	8.8	11.6	14.6	17.5	21.2	25.9	30.9	35.8
Integration Expenses[4]						−5.0	−3.0	0.0	0.0	0.0
Operating Profits (EBIT)	5.7	6.6	8.6	11.5	14.8	17.0	27.9	38.4	46.0	53.6
Plus: Interest Income	0.2	0.3	0.3	0.5	0.6	0.6	0.7	0.9	1.1	1.3
Less: Interest Expense	1.8	1.7	2.0	2.4	2.7	3.2	3.4	3.2	2.8	1.9
Net Profits Before Taxes	4.1	5.2	6.9	9.5	12.6	14.4	25.3	36.2	44.2	53.0
Less: Taxes	1.6	2.1	2.8	3.8	5.1	5.8	10.1	14.5	17.7	21.2
Net Profits After Taxes[5]	2.5	3.1	4.1	5.7	7.6	8.7	15.2	21.7	26.5	31.8

Balance Sheet (12/31)

Current Assets										
Cash & Marketable Securities	4.5	5.2	6.9	9.0	11.4	14.7	18.4	22.1	26.7	32.1
Other Current Assets	11.3	13.0	17.1	22.5	28.5	36.9	46.0	55.3	66.8	78.1
Total Current Assets	15.9	18.3	24.0	31.5	39.9	51.6	64.4	77.5	93.5	110.2
Gross Fixed Assets	14.6	16.8	22.0	28.9	36.5	47.2	58.7	70.3	84.5	98.8
Less: Accumulated Depreciation	1.0	2.7	4.9	7.8	11.4	16.1	22.0	29.0	37.5	47.4
Net Fixed Assets	13.6	14.1	17.2	21.2	25.1	31.0	36.7	41.3	47.0	51.4
Total Assets	29.5	32.4	41.1	52.7	65.0	82.6	101.1	118.7	140.5	161.6
Current Liabilities	3.8	4.3	5.7	7.5	9.5	12.3	15.3	18.4	22.3	26.0
Long-Term Debt	17.7	16.9	20.2	24.2	26.9	31.7	33.9	31.5	28.0	18.9
Common Stock	4.0	4.0	4.0	4.0	4.0	4.0	4.0	4.0	4.0	4.0
Retained Earnings	4.0	7.1	11.3	17.0	24.5	34.6	47.8	64.8	86.3	112.7
Shareholders' Equity	8.0	11.1	15.3	21.0	28.5	38.6	51.8	68.8	90.3	116.7
Total Liabilities + Shareholders' Equity	29.5	32.4	41.1	52.7	65.0	82.6	101.1	118.7	140.5	161.6
Free Cash Flow ($ Mil.)										
EBIT $(1 - t)$	3.4	4.0	5.1	6.9	8.9	10.2	16.8	23.1	27.6	32.2
Plus: Depreciation & Amortization	1.5	1.7	2.2	2.9	3.7	4.7	5.9	7.0	8.4	9.9
Less: Capital Expenditures	2.4	1.7	5.2	6.9	6.3	10.6	8.9	7.0	8.4	9.9
Less: Change in Working Capital	0.8	1.8	4.4	5.7	6.4	9.0	9.8	9.9	12.2	12.9

(Continued)

TABLE 8-4 *(Continued)*

Consolidated GWM and GGT Income, Balance Sheet, and Cash-Flow Statements Including Synergy										
	Historical Financials					Projected Financials				
Valuation Analysis	1996	1997	1998	1999	2000	2001	2002	2003	2004	2005
Equals: Free Cash Flow to the Firm	1.7	2.2	–2.3	–2.8	–0.2	–4.7	4.0	13.1	15.4	19.2
PV (2001–2005) @ 15%	26.0									
PV of Terminal Value @ 10% (8)	291.2									
Total PV (Market Value of the Firm)	317.2									
Plus: Excess Cash Balances	0.0									
Less: Mkt. Value of Long-Term Debt	26.9									
Equity Value ($ Millions)	290.2									
Equity Value Per Share ($/Share)	77.3									

[1] Revenue increases as a result of improved product quality, a broader product offering, and cross-selling to each firm's customers.

[2] Production cost-related savings are realized as a result of economies of scale (i.e., better utilization of existing facilities) and scope (i.e., existing operations are used to produce a broader product offering) and the elimination of duplicate jobs.

[3] Selling expenses and administrative overhead savings result from the elimination of duplicate jobs.

[4] Integration expenses include severance, training, marketing, and advertising expenses, as well as production, process, and technology upgrades.

[5] EPS is not shown because the consolidated valuation does not consider how the acquisition will be financed. The use of stock to finance a portion of the offer price would affect the estimation of the EPS of the combined companies by affecting the number of shares outstanding.

TABLE 8-5 "Step 3" Offer Price Determination

Forecast Assumptions

Acquirer (GWM) Share Price[1]	$33.00
Target (GGT) Share Price[2]	$34.50
% Synergy Shared with Target[3]	0.4
Target Firm Shares Outstanding (Mil.)	3
Acquirer Shares Outstanding (Mil.)	1
Cash Portion of Offer Price (%)[4]	0.25

	Standalone Value		Consolidated GWM & GGT		Value of Synergy
	GWM (1)	GGT (2)	Without Synergy (3) $(1) + (2)$	With Synergy (4)	PV_{NS} $(4) - (3)$
Financing Metrics			**$ Millions**		
Valuations (See PV in Tables 8-3–8-4)	72.8	99.6	172.4	290.2	117.9
Minimum Offer Price (PV_{MIN}) ($ Mil.)	103.5				
Maximum Offer Price (PV_{MAX}) ($ Mil.)	221.4				
Initial Offer Price ($ Mil.)	150.6				
Initial Offer Price Per Share ($)	50.2				
Purchase Price Premium Per Share	0.46				
Cash Per Share ($)[5]	12.55				
Share-Exchange Ratio[6]	1.14				
New Shares Issued by GWM	3.42				

(Continued)

TABLE 8-5 (Continued)

Financing Metrics	Standalone Value		Consolidated GWM & GGT		Value of Synergy
	GWM (1)	GGT (2)	Without Synergy (3) (1) + (2)	With Synergy (4)	PV$_{NS}$ (4) − (3)
			$ Millions		
Total Shares Outstanding (GWM/GGT)	4.42				
Ownership Distribution in New Firm					
GWM Shareholders (%)	0.23				
GGT Shareholders (%)	0.77				
Offer Price Composition					
Offer Price Incl. Assumed GGT Debt[7]	153.8				

[1] GWM share price at the close of business the day before the offer is presented to GGT management. Note that GWM's market value estimated by GWM management is substantially higher than that implied by its current share price, reflecting their greater optimism than investors.

[2] GGT share price at the close of business the day before the offer is received from GGT management.

[3] This fraction represents the share of net synergy GWM's management is willing to share initially with GGT shareholders.

[4] GWM management desired to limit the amount of borrowing associated with the transaction to 25% of the purchased price.

[5] Cash portion of the offer price equals .25 × $50.20.

[6] ($50.20 − .25 × $50.20)/$33.00 = ($50.20 − $12.55)/$33.00 = 1.14 GWM shares for each GGT share. Note that $12.55 is the cash portion of the purchase price GWM management is willing to pay GGT shareholders.

[7] GWM's management is willing to assume GGT's long-term debt outstanding of $3.1 million at the end of 2000.

1.14 shares of GWM stock + $12.55 for each share of GGT stock outstanding.

434

TABLE 8-6 "Step 4" Financing Feasibility Analysis

Forecast Assumptions (2001–2005)	
New Transaction-Related Borrowing:	
Principal ($ Mil.)[1]	40
Interest (%)	0.11
Loan Covenants on Existing Debt	
Debt/Total Capital	<1.0
Fixed Payment Coverage Ratio	>1.0
Current Assets/Current Liabilities	>2.0
New GWM Shares Issued (Millions)	3.42

Consolidated GWM and GGT Financial Statements Including Synergy & Financing Effects

Financial Reporting	Projected Financials					Forecast Comments
	2001	2002	2003	2004	2005	Data from Tables 8-3 and 8-4 unless otherwise noted
Income Statement ($ Millions)						
Net Sales	124.9	163.4	199.4	237.6	275.5	
Less: Cost of Sales	85.4	111.2	135.1	160.7	186.0	
Gross Profit	39.5	52.2	64.4	76.8	89.4	
Less: Sales, General & Admin. Exp.	17.5	21.2	25.9	30.9	35.8	
Integration Expenses	−5.0	−3.0	0.0	0.0	0.0	
Operating Profits (EBIT)	17.0	27.9	38.4	46.0	53.6	
Plus: Interest Income	0.6	0.7	0.9	1.1	1.3	
Less: Interest Expense	7.6	7.7	7.3	6.8	5.7	Includes interest on current and transaction related debt
Net Profits Before Taxes	10.0	21.0	32.1	40.3	49.3	
Less: Taxes	4.0	8.4	12.8	16.1	19.7	
Net Profits After Taxes	6.0	12.6	19.2	24.2	29.6	
Earnings Per Share ($/Share)	1.4	2.9	4.3	5.5	6.7	Includes 1 million existing and 3.42 million newly issued GWM shares

(*Continued*)

435

TABLE 8-6 (Continued)

Consolidated GWM and GGT Financial Statements Including Synergy & Financing Effects

Financial Reporting	2001	2002	2003	2004	2005	Forecast Comments
		Projected Financials				Data from Tables 8-3 and 8-4 unless otherwise noted
Balance Sheet (12/31)						
Current Assets						
Cash & Marketable Securities	53.5	55.9	58.1	61.0	64.6	
Other Current Assets	36.9	46.0	55.3	66.8	78.1	
Total Current Assets	90.4	101.9	113.4	127.8	142.7	
Gross Fixed Assets	47.2	58.7	70.3	84.5	98.8	
Less: Accumulated Depreciation	16.1	22.0	29.0	37.5	47.4	
Net Fixed Assets	31.0	36.7	41.3	47.0	51.4	
Total Assets	121.4	138.6	154.7	174.8	194.1	
Current Liabilities	12.3	15.3	18.4	22.3	26.0	
Long-Term Debt	38.8	37.6	36.1	34.5	32.8	
Existing Debt	31.7	33.9	31.5	28.0	18.9	
Transaction-Related Debt	38.8	37.5	36.0	34.3	32.5	$40 million, 15 year loan at 11% per annum
Total Long-Term Debt	70.5	71.4	67.5	62.3	51.4	
Common Stock	4.0	4.0	4.0	4.0	4.0	
Retained Earnings	34.6	47.8	64.8	86.3	112.7	
Shareholders' Equity	38.6	51.8	68.8	90.3	116.7	
Total Liabilities + Shareholders' Equity	121.4	138.6	154.7	174.8	194.1	
Addendum						
Lease Payments	2.0	2.4	2.4	2.6	2.6	
Principal Repayments	5.6	5.6	5.6	5.6	5.6	[1]$40 million, 15 year loan at 11% per annum
Financial Scenario Selection Criteria						
After-Tax Return on Capital-Combined Firms (%)	9.7	13.7	16.7	17.7	20.7	[Net Income + (Interest and Lease Expense) × (1 − .4)]/ Shareholders' Equity + Long-Term Debt + PV of Operating Leases

436

After-Tax Return on Capital-GWM (%)	12.6	14.4	15.1	15.6	16.2	Same
Key Combined Firm Credit Ratios & Performance Measures						
Debt to Total Capital	0.65	0.58	0.50	0.41	0.31	Total Long-term Debt/(Total Long-term Debt + Equity)
Fixed-Payment Coverage Ratio	1.01	1.56	2.15	2.60	3.20	(EBIT + Lease Payments)/(Interest Expense + Lease Payment + Principal Repayment $\times [1/(1 - .40)]$
Current Assets/Current Liabilities	7.36	6.64	6.15	5.74	5.48	
Return on Equity	15.5	24.3	27.9	26.8	25.4	
Key Industry Average Credit Ratios & Performance Measures						
Debt to Total Capital	.72					
Fixed-Payment Coverage Ratio	.92					
Current Assets/Current Liabilities	3.15					
Return on Equity	16.4					

[2]Level payment loan

Year	2001	2002	2003	2004	2005	2006	2007	2008	2009	2010	2011	2012	2013	2014	2015
Annual Payment[3]	5.6	5.6	5.6	5.6	5.6	5.6	5.6	5.6	5.6	5.6	5.6	5.6	5.6	5.6	5.6
Interest[4]	4.4	4.3	4.1	4.0	3.8	3.6	3.4	3.1	2.8	2.5	2.5	1.8	1.4	.9	.4
Principal[5]	1.2	1.3	1.5	1.6	1.8	2.0	2.2	2.5	2.8	3.1	3.4	3.8	4.2	4.7	5.2
Ending Balance[6]	38.8	37.5	36.0	34.3	32.5	30.5	28.2	25.7	23.0	19.9	16.5	12.7	8.5	3.8	−1.4

[1]The $40 million in new debt borrowed to finance the cash portion of the purchase price is equal to $12.55 (i.e., the cash portion of the offer price per share) times 3 million GGT shares outstanding plus $2.35 million to cover anticipated acquisition related investment banking, legal, and consulting fees.

[3]Equal annual payments including principal and interest are calculated by solving $PVA = PMT - PVIAF_{11,15}$ (i.e., future value interest factor for 11% and 15 years) for PMT.

[4]Loan balance times annual interest rate.

[5]Annual payment less interest payment.

[6]Beginning loan balance less principal payment.

TABLE 8-7   Equity Value of the Combined Companies (GWM/GGT)

	($ Millions)	Comments
Enterprise Value of the Combined Companies	317.20	Total PV of free cash flow to the firm from Table 8-4.
Less: Transaction-Related Debt	40.00	GWM's incremental borrowing to finance the cash portion of the purchase price from Table 8-6.
GWM's Pretransaction Debt	23.80	GWM's long-term debt at closing from Table 8-3 at yearend 2000.
GGT's Pretransaction Debt	3.10	GGT's long-term debt at closing from Table 8-3 at yearend 2000.
Total Debt of the Combined Companies	66.90	
Plus: Excess Cash Balances	1.40	• Minimum desired operating cash balances for the combined companies are estimated to be 8% of 2001 net sales. This is less than the 12% held previously by each firm as a result of the presumed increase in operating efficiencies of the combined firms. • Excess cash balances equal total cash and marketable securities of $11.4 million at the end of 2000 from Table 8-4 less .08 times net sales of $124.9 million in 2001 from Table 8-6.
Equals: Equity Value of the Combined Firms	251.70	
Estimated Combined Company Price Per Share Following Acquisition ($/Share)	56.95	$251.7/4.42 (total shares outstanding of the combined firms from Table 8-5). Note that this share price compares quite favorably with the pretransaction share price of $33 for GWM.

additional complexity without necessarily adding to their accuracy or reliability. Additional complexity often makes the interpretation of a model's output increasingly difficult. In view of these considerations, the optimal model may well be the one that includes as much realism as possible without generating spurious results.

MAINTAINING SHAREHOLDER VALUE IN A STOCK-FOR-STOCK EXCHANGE

A *fixed SER*, share-exchange ratio, is one in which the number of acquirer's shares exchanged for each target share does not change between the agreement date, when the SER is agreed on, and the actual closing date. However, the value of the shares of the acquiring and target companies may in fact change between the agreement and closing dates. This problem may be remedied by using a *floating SER*, in which the SER is allowed to float until a specific time, which may be at closing or a day just before closing.The actual exchange ratio at that time then is used to calculate the number of acquirer's shares that will be exchanged for each target share outstanding. The risk of a completely floating SER is that the actual purchase price for the target company cannot be determined at the time shareholders are asked to approve a proposed merger. Consequently, transactions involving fully floating SERs may be unattractive to target shareholders, particularly if the time between the agreement date and closing is lengthy because of the requirement for shareholder or regulatory approval. Moreover, the acquiring firm will find it difficult to estimate potential earnings dilution as a result of the acquisition because it will be unclear precisely how many new shares it will have to issue to complete the transaction.

Share-exchange transactions can be made more attractive to target and acquiring firm shareholders by limiting the extent of the fluctuation in the actual SER before the agreed on ratio is adjusted. One commonly used method of preserving value is to employ a *collar agreement*. A typical agreement states that, if the actual SER calculated from the share prices of the two stocks on the closing date goes above or below a specific value, there will be an adjustment of the previously agreed on SER. The agreement protects the acquiring firm from "overpaying" in the event that its share price is higher or the target firm's share price is lower on the closing date than it was on the day the actual agreement on the SER was finalized. Similarly, the target shareholders are protected from receiving less than the originally agreed on purchase price if the acquirer's stock declines in value by the closing date. In essence, a collar agreement involves the preservation of a fixed price for the target stock within a specific price range for the acquirer's stock and helps the acquirer to estimate the range of new shares to be issued within the limits set by the collar. This process is illustrated in Northrop Grumman's bid for TRW (Case Study 8-2).

CASE STUDY 8-2: NORTHROP GRUMMAN MAKES A BID FOR TRW—HOW COLLAR ARRANGEMENTS AFFECT SHAREHOLDER VALUE

On March 5, 2002, Northrop Grumman initiated a tender offer for 100% of TRW's common shares by offering to exchange $47.00 in market value of Northrop Grumman common stock for each share of TRW common stock. The tender offer would expire at the end of the month. Northrop implicitly was offering to exchange .4352 (i.e., $47/$108) of its own common shares (based on its March 5th share price of $108.00) for each share of TRW stock. However, the actual share-exchange ratio would be based on the average Northrop share price during the last 5 business days of the month. The $47 offer price is assured within a narrow range to TRW shareholders by placing a collar of plus 5% ($113.40) or minus 5% ($102.60) around the $108 Northrop share price on the tender offer announcement date. The range of share-exchange ratios implied by this collar is as follows:

.4581 (i.e., $47/$102.60) < .4352 (i.e., $47/$108) < .4145($47/$113.40)

The .4581 and .4145 share-exchange ratios represent the maximum and minimum fraction of a share of Northrop stock that would be offered for each TRW share during this tender offer period. The collar gave TRW shareholders some comfort that they would receive $47 per share and enabled Northrop to determine how many shares of its stock it would have to issue within a narrow range to acquire TRW and in turn the potential impact on the EPS of the combined firms.

An increase in Northrop's share price to $117.40 on April 10, 2002, enabled Northrop to increase its offer price to $53 per share of TRW stock outstanding on April 15, 2002 without issuing more than the maximum number of shares they were willing to issue in their March 5 offer. This could be accomplished because the maximum share-exchange ratio of .4581 would not be exceeded as long as the share price of Northrop stock remained above $115.75 per share (i.e., .4581 × $115.75 = $53).

In an effort to boost its share price, TRW repeatedly rejected Northrop's offers as too low and countered with its own restructuring plan. This plan would split the firm into separate defense and automotive parts companies while selling off the aeronautical systems operation. TRW also moved aggressively to solicit bids from other potential suitors. TRW contended that its own restructuring plan was worth as much as $60 per share to its shareholders. In June, TRW reached agreement with Goodrich Corporation to sell the aeronautical systems unit for $1.5 billion.

Northrop Grumman and TRW finally reached an agreement on July 1, 2002. Under the terms of the agreement, Northrop would acquire all of TRW's outstanding common stock for $60 per share in a deal valued at approximately $7.8 billion. Northrop also agreed to assume approximately $4 billion of TRW's debt. Moreover, Northrop withdrew its original tender offer. The actual share exchange ratio will be determined by dividing the $60 offer price by the average of the reported prices per share of Northrop common stock on the five consecutive trading days prior to the closing date. Under a revised collar arrangement, the exchange ratio will not be less than .4348 or more than .5357 of Northrop's shares. After completion of the merger, Northrop plans to sell or spin-off TRW's automotive business to Northrop shareholders. The merger makes Northrop Grumman the second largest U.S. defense contractor, behind Lockheed Martin Corporation.

Case Study Discussion Questions

1. Would TRW shareholders have been better or worse off had Northrop used an unrestricted floating share-exchange ratio rather than a collar? What would have been the implications for TRW shareholders had a fixed exchange ratio been used? Explain your answer.

2. Would the use of an unrestricted floating share-exchange ratio have positively or negatively affected Northrop's shareholders? Explain your answer. Consider the implications for Northrop shareholders had a fixed exchange ratio been used.

THINGS TO REMEMBER

Financial modeling in the context of M&As facilitates the process of valuation, deal structuring, and selection of the appropriate financial structure. The process outlined in this chapter entails a four-step procedure.

1. Value the acquirer and target firms as standalone businesses. All costs and revenues associated with each business should be included in the valuation. Understand industry and company competitive dynamics. This requires normalizing the components of historical valuation cash flow. Aberrations in the data should be omitted. Common-size financial statements applied at a point in time, over a number of periods, and compared with other companies in the same industry provide useful insights into how to properly value the target firm. This normalized information can be used to understand both industry and company competitive dynamics. Multiple valuation methods should be used and the results should be averaged to increase confidence in the accuracy of the estimated value.

2. Value the combined financial statements of the acquirer and target companies including the effects of anticipated synergy. Ensure that all costs that are likely to be incurred in realizing synergy are included in the calculation of net synergy. All key assumptions should be stated clearly to provide credibility for the valuation and to inject a high degree of discipline into the valuation process.

3. Determine the initial offer price for the target firm. Define the minimum and maximum offer price range.

$$(PV_T \text{ or } MV_T) < P_{IOP} < (PV_T \text{ or } MV_T + PV_{NS})$$

where PV_T and MV_T are the economic value of the target as a standalone company and the market value of the target, respectively. PV_{NS} is the present value of net synergy, and P_{IOP} is the initial offer price for the target.

4. Determine the combined companies' ability to finance the transaction. The appropriate capital structure of the combined businesses is that which enables the acquirer to meet or exceed its required financial returns, satisfies the seller's price

expectations, does not significantly raise borrowing costs, and does not violate any significant financial constraints. Examples of financial constraints include loan covenants and prevailing industry average debt service ratios.

CHAPTER DISCUSSION QUESTIONS

8-1. Why are financial modeling techniques used in analyzing M&As?

8-2. Give examples of the limitations of financial data used in the valuation process.

8-3. Why is it important to analyze historical data on the target company as part of the valuation process?

8-4. Explain the process of normalizing historical data and why it should be done before undertaking the valuation process.

8-5. What are common-size financial statements, and how might they be used to analyze a target firm?

8-6. Why should a target company be valued as a standalone business? Give examples of the types of adjustments that might have to be made if the target company is part of a larger company.

8-7. Define the minimum and maximum purchase price range for a target company.

8-8. What are the differences between the final negotiated price, total consideration, total purchase price, and net purchase price?

8-9. Can the initial offer price ever exceed the maximum purchase price? If yes, why? If no, why not?

8-10. Why is it important to clearly state assumptions underlying a valuation?

CHAPTER PRACTICE PROBLEMS

8-1. Acquiring Company is considering the acquisition of Target Company in a stock-for-stock transaction in which Target Company would receive $50.00 for each share of its common stock. The Acquiring Company does not expect any change in its P/E multiple after the merger.

	Acquiring Co.	Target Co.
Earnings available for common stock	$150,000	$30,000
Number of shares of common stock outstanding	60,000	20,000
Market price per share	$60.00	$40.00

Using the information provided above on these two firms, showing your work calculate the following:

a. Purchase price premium: Answer: 25%

  b. Share-exchange ratio: Answer: .8333

  c. New shares issued by Acquiring Company:

   Answer: 16,666

  d. Total shares outstanding of the combined companies:

   Answer: 76,666

  e. Postmerger EPS of the combined companies: Answer: $2.35

  f. Premerger EPS of Acquiring Company: Answer: $2.50

  g. Postmerger share price: Answer: $56.40 (as compared with $60.00 premerger)

8-2. Acquiring Company is considering buying Target Company. Target Company is a small biotechnology firm that develops products that are licensed to the major pharmaceutical firms. Development costs are expected to generate negative cash flows during the first 2 years of the forecast period of $(10) and $(5) million, respectively. Licensing fees are expected to generate positive cash flows during years 3 through 5 of the forecast period of $5 million, $10 million, and $15 million, respectively. Because of the emergence of competitive products, cash flow is expected to grow at a modest 5% annually after the fifth year. The discount rate for the first 5 years is estimated to be 20% and then to drop to 10% beyond the fifth year. Also, the present value of the estimated synergy by combining Acquiring and Target companies is $30 million. Calculate the minimum and maximum purchase prices for Target Company. Show your work.

Answer: Minimum price = $128.5 million
Maximum price = $158.5 million

8-3. Company A offers to acquire 100% of Company B's stock for $50 a share (a $10 premium to the current price). Company A's stock currently is selling for $100 per share. Show your work.

  a. How many new shares of A's stock would have to be issued for each share of B's stock? Answer: .5

  b. What is the dollar value of A's shares exchanged for 100 shares of B's stock? Answer: $5000

Suppose Company A's share price falls to $75 before the transaction is consummated. B's shareholders are protected if Company B has negotiated a fully flexible or floating exchange ratio of Company B's stock in terms of Company A's stock.

  a. Calculate the new exchange ratio. Answer: .66

  b. What is the dollar value of A's shares received by a holder of 100 shares of B's stock? Answer: $5000

CHAPTER BUSINESS CASE

CASE STUDY 8-3: TRIBUNE COMPANY ACQUIRES THE TIMES MIRROR CORPORATION IN A TALE OF CORPORATE INTRIGUE

Background: Oh What Tangled Webs We Weave . . .

CEO Mark Willes had reason to be optimistic about the future. Operating profits had grown at a double-digit rate, and earnings per share had grown at a 55% annual rate between 1995 to 1999. Many shareholders appeared to be satisfied. However, some were not. Although pleased with the improvement in profitability, they were concerned about the long-term growth prospects of the firm. Reflecting this disenchantment, Times Mirror's largest shareholder, the Chandler family, was contemplating the sale of the company and along with it the crown jewel *Los Angeles Times*. It had been assumed for years that the Chandler family trusts made a sale of Times Mirror out of the question. The Chandler's super voting stock (i.e., stock with multiple voting rights) allowed them to exert a disproportionate influence on corporate decisions. The Chandler Trusts controlled more than two-thirds of voting shares, although the family owned only about 28% of the total shares of the outstanding stock.

In May 1999 the Tribune Chair John Madigan contacted Willes and made an offer for the company, but Willes, with the help of his then-chief financial officer (CFO), Thomas Unterman, made it clear to Madigan that the company was not for sale. What Willes did not realize was that Unterman soon would be serving in a dual role as CFO and financial adviser to the Chandlers and that he would eventually step down from his position at Times Mirror to work directly for the family. In his dual role, he worked without Willes' knowledge to structure the deal with the Tribune.

Following months of secret negotiations, the Chicago-based Tribune Company and the Times Mirror Corporation announced a merger of the two companies in a cash and stock deal valued at approximately $7.2 billion, including $5.7 billion in equity and $1.5 billion in assumed debt. The transaction, announced March 13, 2000, created a media giant that has national reach and a major presence in 18 of the nation's top 30 U.S. markets, including New York, Los Angeles, and Chicago. The combined company has 22 television stations, four radio stations, and 11 daily newspapers—including the *Los Angeles Times*, the nation's largest metropolitan daily newspaper and flagship of the Times Mirror chain.

Transaction Terms: Tribune Shareholders Get Choice of Cash or Stock

The Tribune agreed to buy 48% of the outstanding Times Mirror stock, about 28 million shares, through a tender offer. After completion of the tender offer, each remaining Times Mirror share would be exchanged for 2.5 shares of Tribune stock.

TABLE 8-8   Times Mirror Transaction Terms

	As of June 12, 2000	Transaction Value
Times Mirror Shares Outstanding @ 3/13/00	59,700,000	
No. of Times MirrorShares Exchanged for 2.5 Shares of Tribune Stock	27,238,253	$2,587,634,035[1]
No. of Times Mirror Shares Exchanged for Cash	10,648,318	$1,011,536,968[2]
Times Mirror Shares Outstanding after Tender Offer	21,813,429	
No. of New Tribune Shares Issued for Remaining Times Mirror Shares	54,533,573[5]	$2,072,275,774[3]
Equity Value of Offer	$5,671,446,777	
Market Value of Times Mirror on Merger Announcement Date		$2,805,900,000[4]
Premium		102%

[1] 27,238,253 × 2.5 × $38/share of Tribune stock.

[2] $41.70 in cash + 1.4025 shares of Tribune stock × $38 per share for each Times Mirror share remaining × 10,648,318.

[3] Equals 2.5 shares × 21,813,429 × $38 per Tribune share.

[4] Times Mirror share price on announcement date of $47 times 59,700,000.

[5] The total number of new Tribute shares issued equals 27,238,318 × 2.5 + 10,648,318 × 2.5 + 54,533,573 or 137,537,013.

Under the terms of the transaction, Times Mirror shareholders could elect to receive $95 in cash or 2.5 shares of Tribune common stock in exchange for each share of Times Mirror stock. Holders of 27.2 million shares of Times Mirror stock elected to receive Tribune stock, whereas holders of 10.6 million elected to receive cash (Tribune Company, June 28, 2000). Because the amount of cash offered in the merger was limited and the cash election was oversubscribed, Times Mirror shareholders electing to receive cash actually received a combination of cash and stock on a pro rata basis (Table 8-8).

Newspaper Advertising Revenues Continue to Shrink

Most U.S. newspapers are mired in the mature or declining phase of their product life cycle. For the past half-century newspapers have watched their portion of the advertising market shrink as a result of increased competition from radio and television. By the early 1990s, all major media began taking a significant hit in their advertising revenue streams as businesses discovered that direct mail could target their message more precisely. Moreover, consolidation among major retailers further reduced the size of advertising dollar pool. The same has happened with numerous large supermarket chain mergers. Newspaper advertising revenues also have been threatened by increasing competition from advertising and editorial content delivered on the Internet. Finally, newspapers simply have become less attractive places to advertise as readership continues to decline as a result of an aging population and new generations that do not see newspapers as relevant.

Times Mirror: A Largely Traditional Business Model

As essentially a traditional newspaper, Times Mirror publishes five metropolitan and two suburban daily newspapers, a variety of magazines, and professional information such as flight maps for commercial airline pilots. The *Los Angeles Times*, a southern California institution founded in 1881, is Times Mirror's largest holding and operates some two dozen expensive foreign news bureaus—more than any other newspaper in the country. The *Los Angeles Times* has more than 1200 *Los Angeles Times* reporters and editors around the world (CNNfn, March 13, 2000).

Tribune Company Profile: The Face of New Media?

Unlike the Times Mirror, Tribune has built its strategy around four business groups: broadcasting, publishing, education, and interactive. The Tribune is also an equity investor in America Online and other leading Internet companies, underscoring the company's commitment to new-media technologies. Applying leading-edge new-media technology has allowed the Tribune to transform they way it does business, and the technology commitment creates the opportunity for future growth. The Internet has been the greatest driver for change, and the Tribune's interactive business group continues to focus on capitalizing on emerging Web technologies. Throughout the company, new technologies have been applied aggressively to create new products, improve existing products, and make operations more efficient. The Tribune's nonnewspaper revenues accounted for more than half of its earnings by 2000 (White, 2000).

Anticipated Synergy

Cost Savings: Opportunities Abound

Cost savings are expected as a result of the closing of selected foreign and domestic news bureaus, a reduction in the cost of newsprint through greater volume purchases, the closing of the Times Mirror corporate headquarters, and elimination of corporate staff. Such savings are expected to reach $200 million per year (Table 8-9).

Revenue: Great Potential . . . But Is It Achievable?

The combined companies will have a major presence in 18 of the nation's top 30 U.S. advertising markets, including New York, Los Angeles, and Chicago (Hofmeister and Shaw, 2000). The combined companies provide unprecedented opportunities for advertisers to reach major market consumers in any media form— broadcast, newspapers, or interactive. In addition, the combined companies will benefit consumers by giving them rich and diverse choices for obtaining the news, information, and entertainment they want anytime, anywhere. These factors provide an increased ability to capture national advertising in the most important U.S. population centers. The significantly greater breadth of the combined firm's geographic coverage is expected to boost advertising revenues from about 3% to 6% annually.

TABLE 8-9   Annual Merger-Related Cost Savings

Source of Value	Annual Savings
Bureau Closings[1]	$73,000,000
Newsprint Savings[2]	$93,000,000
Other Office Closings (e.g., Times Mirror	$34,000,000
Corporate Office in Los Angeles)[3]	
Total Annual Savings	$200,000,000

[1]Assumes Tribune will close overlapping bureaus in United States (9) and most of the Times Mirror's foreign bureaus (21 abroad).

[2]As a result of bulk purchasing and more favorable terms with different suppliers, 15% of the newsprint expense of the combined companies is expected to be saved.

[3]Layoffs of 120 L.A. Times Mirror Corporate Office personnel at an average salary of $125,000 and benefits equal to 30% of base salaries. Total payroll expenses equal $19,500,000 (i.e., $125,000 × 1.3 × 120). Lease, travel and entertainment, and other support expenses added another $14.5 million.

Source: Moore, Kathryn, Tim Schnabel, and Mark Yemma, "A Media Marriage," paper prepared for Chapman University, EMBA 696, May 18, 2000, p. 9.

Integration Challenges: Cultural Warfare?

Based on the current, traditional culture found at the *Los Angeles Times* and other Times Mirror properties, integration following the merger was likely to be slow and painful. Concerns among journalists about spreading their talents thin across three or four media—print, television, online, and radio—in the course of a day's work raised the stress level. Although the Tribune has been able to make the transition to a largely multimedia company more rapidly than the more traditional newspapers, it has been costly. For example, development losses in 1999 were $30–35 million at Chicagotribune.com and an estimated $45 million in 2000 (Tribune Company, June 12, 2000). The bleeding was expected to continue for some time and to constitute a major distraction for the management of the new company.

Financial Analysis

The present values of the Tribune, Times Mirror, and the combined firms are $8.5 billion, $2.4 billion, and $16.5 billion, respectively; the estimated present value of synergy is $5.6 billion (Table 8-10). This assumes that pretax cost savings are phased in as follows: $25 million in 2000, $100 million in 2001, and $200 million thereafter. The cost savings are net of all expenses related to realizing such savings such as severance, lease buyouts, and legal fees. Table 8-11 describes how the initial offer price could have been determined and the postmerger distribution of ownership between Times Mirror and Tribune shareholders.

Epilogue

The Tribune was granted early termination of the Hart–Scott–Rodino (HRS) waiting period in the tender offer for Times Mirror shares. The HSR Antitrust Improvement Act requires a 30-day waiting period that allows the Federal Trade Commission and the Justice Department to review the proposed acquisition.

TABLE 8-1O Merger Evaluation

	1997	1998	1999	2000	2001	2002	2003	2004	2005
Tribune					($ Millions)				
Sales	2891.5	2980.9	3221.9	3261.5	3473.5	3699.3	3939.7	4195.8	4468.5
Operating Expenses	2232.5	2279.0	2451.0	2283.1	2431.4	2589.5	2757.8	2937.1	3128.0
EBIT	659.0	701.9	770.9	978.5	1042.0	1109.8	1181.9	1258.7	1340.6
EBIT $(1 - t)$	395.4	421.1	462.5	587.1	625.2	665.9	709.2	755.2	804.3
Depreciation	172.5	195.5	221.1	212.0	225.8	240.5	256.1	272.7	290.5
Gross Plant & Equipment	103.8	139.7	134.7	163.1	173.7	185.0	197.0	209.8	223.4
Change in Working Capital	−47.7	49.0	1107.0	260.9	243.1	258.9	275.8	293.7	312.8
Free Cash Flow to Firm	511.8	427.9	−558.1	375.1	434.2	462.4	492.5	524.5	558.6
PV (2001–2005) @ 8.5	51.5								
PV (Terminal Value) @ 8.5	11144.2								
Total Present Value	11195.7								
Less: Long-Term Debt	2694.2								
Plus: Excess Cash Balances	0								
Equity Value	8501.5								
Shares Outstanding	237.4								
Equity Value Per Share	35.81								
Times Mirror					($ Millions)				
Sales	2728.2	2783.9	3029.2	3140.0	3297.0	3461.9	3634.9	3816.7	4007.5
Operating Expenses	2337.0	2380.5	2558.7	2449.2	2571.7	2700.2	2835.3	2977.0	3125.9
EBIT	391.2	403.4	470.5	690.8	725.3	761.6	799.7	839.7	881.7
EBIT $(1 - t)$	234.7	242.0	282.3	414.5	435.2	457.0	479.8	503.8	529.0
Depreciation	133.4	152.1	166.4	188.4	197.8	207.7	218.1	229.0	240.5
Gross Plant & Equipment	173.4	131.5	113.0	125.6	131.9	138.5	145.4	152.7	160.3
Change in Working Capital	199.2	551.1	−791.1	251.2	257.2	270.0	283.5	297.7	312.6

($ Millions)								
Free Cash Flow to Firm	−4.5	−288.5	1126.8	226.1	244.0	256.2	269.0	282.4	296.6
PV (2001–2005) @ 9.5%	25.8								
PV (Terminal Value) @ 9.5%	3937.2								
Total Present Value	3963.0								
Less: Long-Term Debt[1]	1562.2								
Plus: Excess Cash Balances	0								
Equity Value	2375.0								
Shares Outstanding	59.7								
Equity Value Per Share	39.8								

Combined Firms

					($ Millions)				
Sales	5619.7	5764.8	6251.1	6401.5	6770.5	7161.1	7574.7	8012.5	8476.1
Operating Expenses	4569.5	4659.5	5009.7	4732.3	5003.1	5289.7	5593.1	5914.1	6253.8
Synergy				25.0	100.0	200.0	200.0	200.0	200.0
EBIT	1050.2	1105.3	1241.4	1694.3	1867.4	2071.4	2181.6	2298.4	2422.2
EBIT $(1-t)$	630.1	663.2	744.8	1016.6	1120.4	1242.8	1309.0	1379.0	1453.3
Depreciation	305.9	347.6	387.5	400.4	423.6	448.2	474.2	501.7	530.9
Gross Plant & Equipment	277.2	271.2	247.7	288.7	305.6	323.4	342.4	362.5	383.7
Change in Working Capital	151.5	600.1	315.9	512.1	500.3	529.0	559.3	591.4	625.4
Free Cash Flow to Firm	507.3	139.5	568.7	616.2	738.2	838.6	881.5	926.9	975.1
PV (2001–2005) @ 9.5%	88.1								
PV (Terminal Value) @ 9.5%	22805.6								
Total Present Value	22893.8								
Less: Long-Term Debt	4256.4								
Less: Acquisition-Related Debt	2193.7								
Plus: Excess Cash Balances	0								
Equity Value	16443.7								
Shares Outstanding	374.9								
Equity Value Per Share	43.9								

[1] Book values for long-term debt may be used if the coupon rate on the debt approximates competitive market rates.

The waiting period was scheduled to expire on April 26, but the early termination was granted on April 6. Closing took place June 12, 2000. Since the closing, the Tribune sold a number of Times Mirror assets, which generated pretax proceeds of $2.75 billion to reduce the Tribune's overall level of indebtedness (Tribune Company, October 20, 2000).

Only time will tell if actual returns to shareholders in the combined Tribune and Times Mirror company exceed the expected financial returns provided in the valuation models in this case study. Times Mirror shareholders earned a substantial 102% purchase price premium over the value of their shares on the day the merger was announced. Some portion of those undoubtedly "cashed out" of their investment following receipt of the new Tribune shares. However, for those former Times Mirror shareholders continuing to hold their Tribune stock and for Tribune shareholders of record on the day the transaction closed, it is unclear if the transaction made good economic sense.

Case Study Discussion Questions

1. In your judgment, did it make good strategic sense to combine the Tribune and Times Mirror corporations? Why or why not?
2. Using the Merger Evaluation Table (Table 8-10) given in the case, determine the estimated equity values of Tribune, Times Mirror, and the combined firms. Why is long-term debt deducted from the total present value estimates to obtain the estimated equity values?
3. Despite the merger having closed in mid-2000, the full effects of synergy may not be realized until 2002. Why? What factors could account for the delay?
4. The estimated equity value for the Times Mirror Corporation on the day the merger was announced was about $2.8 billion. However, as shown in the offer price determination table (Table 8-11), the equity value estimated

TABLE 8-11   Offer Price Determination

	Tribune	Times Mirror	Combined Incl. Synergy	Value of Synergy
Equity Valuations	8501.5	2375.0	16443.7	5567.3
Minimum Offer Price[1]		2805.9		
Maximum Offer Price		8373.2		
Actual Offer Price		5671.4		
% Maximum Offer Price		67.7%		
Purchase Price Premium		1.02		
New Tribune Shares Issued		137.50		
Ownership Distribution				
TM Shareholders		0.37		
Tribune Shareholders		0.63		

[1] Market value of Times Mirror on the merger announcement date.

using discounted cash-flow analysis is given as $2.4 billion. What factors might explain this difference? Why is the minimum offer price shown as $2.8 billion rather than the lower $2.4 billion figure? How is the maximum offer price determined in the offer price determination table? How much of the estimated synergy value generated by combining the two businesses is being transferred to the Times Mirror shareholders? Why?

5. Does the Times Mirror-Tribune Corporation merger create value? If so, how much? What percentage of this value goes to Times Mirror shareholders and what percentage to Tribune shareholders? Why?

Solutions to these questions appear at the back of this book.

CHAPTER BUSINESS CASE

CASE STUDY 8-4: FORD ACQUIRES VOLVO'S PASSENGER CAR OPERATIONS

The case illustrates how the dynamically changing worldwide automotive market is spurring a move toward consolidation among automotive manufacturers. The Volvo financials used in the valuation are for illustration only—they include revenue and costs for all of the firm's product lines. For purposes of exposition, we shall assume that Ford's acquisition strategy with respect to Volvo was to acquire all of Volvo's operations and later to divest all but the passenger car and possibly the truck operations. Note that synergy in this business case is determined by valuing projected cash flows generated by combining the Ford and Volvo businesses rather than by subtracting the standalone values for the Ford and Volvo passenger car operations from their combined value including the effects of synergy. This was done because of the difficulty in obtaining sufficient data on the Ford passenger car operations.

Background

By the late 1990s, excess global automotive production capacity totaled 20 million vehicles, and three-fourths of the auto manufacturers worldwide were losing money. Consumers continued to demand more technological innovations, while expecting to pay lower prices. Continuing mandates from regulators for new, cleaner engines and more safety measures added to manufacturing costs. With the cost of designing a new car estimated at $1.5 billion to $3 billion, companies were finding mergers and joint ventures an attractive means to distribute risk and maintain market share in this highly competitive environment (Welch and Howes, 1999).

Ford's Merger Strategy

By acquiring Volvo, Ford hoped to expand its 10% worldwide market share with a broader line of near-luxury Volvo sedans and station wagons as well as to strengthen its presence in Europe. Ford saw Volvo as a means of improving its product weaknesses, expanding distribution channels, entering new markets, reducing development and vehicle production costs, and capturing premiums from niche markets. Volvo Cars is now part of Ford's Premier Automotive Group, which also includes Aston Martin, Jaguar, and Lincoln.

Ford Motor Company Profile

The Ford Motor Company is the second largest automobile manufacturer in the world. It offers a highly diverse and extensive line of vehicles under six major brands. These include the Aston Martin, Ford, Jaguar, Lincoln, Mazda, and Mercury. Each of these brands has been defined to appeal to a specific market segment to minimize market overlap. Ford in Europe is very strong in the small-to-medium-sized European car market. The Ford product line consists of small-to-medium-sized cars, the Ford Explorer sport utility vehicle, and a minivan. Ford has had difficulty moving into the luxury car market because it is not perceived as a luxury brand. Ford's strength is its dominant position in the booming U.S. truck market. Other areas of strength include customer loyalty and satisfaction, global brand leverage, and relatively low total production costs (Ford Motor Company, 1999). Although Ford has been riding high on the success of its truck business, its domestic passenger car line has experienced product and positioning difficulties, which have led to disappointing sales. Regaining its position as a leader in passenger car sales is one of the highest priorities for Ford executives.

Volvo Company Profile

Between 1987 and 1998, Volvo posted operating profits amounting to 3.7% of sales. Excluding the passenger car group, operating margins would have been 5.3%. To stay competitive, Volvo would have to introduce a variety of new passenger cars over the next decade. Volvo viewed the capital expenditures required to develop new cars as overwhelming for a company the size of Volvo. Historically, Volvo has filled a small niche in the marketplace by appealing to safety-conscious family-oriented buyers who can afford a European-made automobile. Unfortunately, Volvo does not have the necessary sales volume to support the enormous cost of developing new cars. The company made it clear that they were interested in a buyer in an effort to keep the company viable over the long run. (Volvo, 1999). Volvo has a relatively limited product line that includes a sporty coupe, mid-sized sedans, and station wagons that compete in the luxury segment of the market. Volvo's major source of value is its brand name and close association with producing safe, reliable passenger cars.

Historical and Projected Data

The initial review of Volvo's historical data suggests that cash flow is highly volatile. However, by removing nonrecurring events, it is apparent that Volvo's cash flow is steadily trending downward from its high in 1997. Table 8-12 displays

TABLE 8-12 Volvo Common-Size Normalized Income Statement, Balance Sheet, and
Cash-Flow Statement (Percentage of Net Sales)

	1993	1994	1995	1996	1997	1998	1999	2000	2001	2002	2003	2004
						Income Statement						
Net Sales	1.000	1.000	1.000	1.000	1.000	1.000	1.000	1.000	1.000	1.000	1.000	1.000
Cost of Goods Sold	.772	.738	.749	.777	.757	.757	.757	.757	.757	.757	.757	.757
Operation Expense	.167	.101	.120	.077	.119	.133	.132	.131	.129	.128	.127	.126
Depreciation	.034	.033	.033	.034	.029	.038	.038	.039	.040	.040	.041	.042
EBIT	.027	.128	.098	.112	.088	.073	.073	.074	.074	.074	.075	.075
Interest on Debt	.050	.023	.022	.021	.015	.023	.023	.022	.021	.021	.020	.020
Earnings Before Taxes	.024	.017	.076	.091	.072	.049	.051	.052	.053	.054	.055	.056
Income Taxes	.004	.018	.022	.012	.015	.014	.014	.015	.015	.015	.015	.016
Net Income	.028	.087	.054	.079	.057	.035	.036	.037	.038	.039	.040	.040
						Balance Sheet						
Current Assets	.632	.503	.444	.524	.497	.500	.500	.500	.500	.500	.500	.500
Current Liabilities	.596	.400	.283	.298	.304	.350	.350	.350	.350	.350	.350	.350
Working Capital	.036	.103	.161	.226	.192	.150	.150	.150	.150	.150	.150	.150
Total Assets	1.21	.889	.809	.905	.889	.906	.880	.858	.839	.822	.808	.795
Long-Term Debt	.371	.211	.227	.236	.256	.234	.215	.196	.180	.165	.151	.307
Equity	.244	.278	.299	.371	.329	.321	.316	.312	.309	.308	.307	.307
					Selected Valuation Cash-Flow Items							
EBIT $(1 - t)$	.022	.150	.126	.126	.105	.093	.094	.094	.095	.095	.096	.096
Capital Expenditures	.031	.027	.033	.053	.054	.061	.069	.078	.088	.099	.112	.126
Δ Working Capital	.025	.077	.068	.049	.000	.017	.020	.020	.020	.020	.020	.020
Free Cash Flow to the Firm (FCFF)	.047	.079	.053	.059	.088	.087	.044	.036	.027	.017	.005	(.008)

a common-sized, normalized income statement, balance sheet, and cash-flow statement for Volvo, including both the historical period from 1993 through 1999 and a forecast period from 2000 through 2004. Although Volvo has managed to stabilize its cost of goods sold as a percentage of net sales, operating expenses as a percentage of net revenue have escalated in recent years. Operating margins have been declining since 1996. To regain market share in the passenger car market, Volvo would have to increase substantially its capital outlays. The primary reason valuation cash flow turns negative by 2004 is the sharp increase in capital outlays during the forecast period. Ford's acquisition of Volvo will enable volume discounts from vendors, reduced development costs as a result of platform sharing, access to wider distribution networks, and increased penetration in selected market niches because of the Volvo brand name. Savings from synergies are phased in slowly over time, and they will not be fully realized until 2004. There is no attempt to quantify the increased cash flow that might result from increased market penetration.

Determining the Initial Offer Price

Table 8-13 provides the data and the underlying assumptions used in estimating Volvo's value on a standalone basis at $15 billion. The present value of anticipated synergy is $1.1 billion. This suggests that the purchase price for Volvo should lie

TABLE 8-13 Volvo Normalized Income, Balance Sheet, and Cash-Flow Statement; Valuation; and Purchase Price Range Determination

Income Statement ($ Millions)

	1993	1994	1995	1996	1997	1998	1999	2000	2001	2002	2003	2004
Net Sales	76,659	107,494	118,283	107,628	126,638	145,634	167,479	192,600	221,491	254,714	292,921	336,859
Cost of Goods Sold	(59,200)	(79,374)	(88,641)	(83,620)	(95,855)	(110,233)	(126,768)	(145,784)	(167,651)	(192,799)	(221,719)	(254,977)
Operation Expense	(12,814)	(10,814)	(14,156)	(8,266)	(15,114)	(19,352)	(22,061)	(25,150)	(28,671)	(32,685)	(37,261)	(42,477)
Depreciation	(2,605)	(3,522)	(3,901)	(3,690)	(4,687)	(5,484)	(6,416)	(7,507)	(8,783)	(10,276)	(12,023)	(14,067)
EBIT	2,039	13,783	11,586	12,051	10,982	10,564	12,233	14,160	16,386	18,955	21,919	25,339
Interest on Debt	(3,861)	(2,488)	(2,591)	(2,256)	(1,895)	(3,404)	(3,782)	(4,210)	(4,694)	(5,244)	(5,868)	(6,577)
Earning Before Taxes	(1,822)	11,295	8,995	9,795	9,087	7,161	8,451	9,950	11,691	13,710	16,051	18,762
Income Taxes	(323)	(1,919)	(2,580)	(1,259)	(1,866)	(2,045)	(2,366)	(2,786)	(3,274)	(3,839)	(4,494)	(5,253)
Net Income (NI)	(2,145)	9,376	6,415	8,537	7,221	5,116	6,085	7,164	8,418	9,872	11,557	13,509

Balance Sheet ($ Millions)

	1993	1994	1995	1996	1997	1998	1999	2000	2001	2002	2003	2004
Current Assets	48,452	54,051	52,511	56,406	62,890	72,817	83,739	96,300	110,745	127,357	146,461	168,430
Current Liabilities	45,666	43,038	33,460	32,036	38,536	50,972	58,618	67,410	77,522	89,150	102,522	117,901
Working Capital	2,787	11,013	19,051	24,370	24,354	21,845	25,122	28,890	33,224	38,207	43,938	50,529
Total Assets	92,770	95,574	95,654	97,351	112,617	131,900	147,439	165,300	185,835	209,446	236,599	267,827
Long-Term Debt	28,423	22,652	26,884	25,401	32,405	34,122	35,931	37,835	39,840	41,952	44,175	46,517
Equity	18,681	29,884	35,310	39,914	41,690	46,806	52,891	60,055	68,473	78,344	89,901	103,410
Shares	78	444	464	464	442	442	442	442	442	442	442	442

Valuation Cash Flow ($ Millions)

	1993	1994	1995	1996	1997	1998	1999	2000	2001	2002	2003	2004
EBIT (1 − t)	1,678	16,126	14,909	13,600	13,237	13,581	15,658	18,125	20,974	24,262	28,056	32,434
Depreciation	2,605	3,522	3,901	3,690	4,687	5,484	6,416	7,507	8,783	10,276	12,023	14,067
Capital Expenditures	(2,390)	(2,948)	(4,477)	(5,655)	(6,802)	(8,843)	(11,495)	(14,944)	(19,427)	(25,256)	(32,832)	(42,682)
Change in Working Capital	1,930	(8,226)	(8,038)	(5,319)	16	2,509	(3,277)	(3,768)	(4,334)	(4,984)	(5,731)	(6,591)
Valuation Cash Flow	3,824	8,474	6,296	6,316	11,137	12,731	7,302	6,919	5,995	4,298	1,516	(2,772)
NPV (WACC = 11.54%) 1999 ∼ 2004	18,644											
Terminal Value (2004∼)	(3,652)											
Total NPV	14,992											

Purchase Price Range ($ Millions)

Lower Range	14,992
Lower Range + 25% of Synergy	15,273
Lower Range + Synergy	16,117

within a range of $15 million to about $16 billion. Although the potential synergies appear to be substantial, savings due to synergies will be phased in gradually between 2000 and 2004. In 1998, Volvo had rejected an approximate $7 billion bid by Renault for the car and truck operations. By late 1998, there were no other immediate bidders for Volvo. The absence of other current bidders for the entire company and Volvo's urgent need to fund future capital expenditures in the passenger car business enabled Ford to set the initial offer price at the lower end of the range. Consequently, the initial offer price could be conservatively set at about $15.25 billion, reflecting only about one-fourth of the total potential synergy resulting from combining the two businesses. Other valuation methodologies tended to confirm this purchase price estimate. The market value of Volvo was $11.9 billion on January 29, 1999. To gain a controlling interest, Ford had to pay a premium to the market value on January 29, 1999. Applying the 26% premium Ford paid for Jaguar, the estimated purchase price including the premium is $15 billion, or $34 per share. This compares to $34.50 per share estimated by dividing the initial offer price of $15.25 billion by Volvo's total common shares outstanding of $442 million. Thus, the initial offer price can be reasonably set at between $34.00 and $34.50 per share.

Determining the Appropriate Financing Structure

Ford had $23 billion in cash and marketable securities on hand at the end of 1998 (Naughton, 1999). This amount of cash is well in excess of its normal cash operating requirements. The opportunity cost associated with this excess cash is equal to Ford's cost of capital, which is estimated to be 11.5%—about three times the prevailing interest on short-term marketable securities at that time. By reinvesting some portion of these excess balances to acquire Volvo, Ford would be adding to shareholder value because the expected return, including the effects of synergy, exceeds the cost of capital. Moreover, by using this excess cash, Ford also is making itself less attractive as a potential acquisition target. The acquisition is expected to increase Ford's EPS. The loss of interest earnings on the excess cash balances would be more than offset by the addition of Volvo's pretax earnings. Furthermore, severance expenses and one-time write-offs at closing are expected to be modest.

Epilogue

Seven months after the megamerger between Chrysler and Daimler-Benz in 1998, Ford Motor Company announced that it was acquiring only Volvo's passenger-car operations. Ford acquired Volvo's passenger car operations on March 29, 1999, for $6.45 billion. At $16,000 per production unit, Ford's offer price was considered generous when compared with the $13,400 per vehicle that Daimler-Benz AG paid for Chrysler Corporation in 1998. The sale of the passenger car business allows Volvo to concentrate fully on its truck, bus, construction equipment, marine engine, and aerospace equipment businesses. (Note that the standalone value of Volvo in the case was estimated to be $15 billion. This included Volvo's trucking operations.)

Case Study Discussion Questions

1. What is the purpose of the common-size financial statements developed for Volvo (see Table 8-13)? What insights does this table provide about the historical trend in Volvo's historical performance? Based on past performance, how realistic do you think the projections are for 2000–2004?

2. Ford anticipates substantial synergies from acquiring Volvo. What are these potential synergies? As a consultant hired to value Volvo, what additional information would you need to estimate the value of potential from each of these areas?

3. In your judgment, do the assumptions implicit in Tables 8-12 and 8-13 seem realistic? Why or why not?

4. How was the initial offer price determined according to this case study? Do you find the logic underlying the initial offer price compelling? Explain your answer.

5. What was the composition of the purchase price? Why was this composition selected according to this case study?

Appendix A: Commonly Used Financial Ratios

Financial Ratio (How Measured)	Formula	Interpretation
Liquidity Ratios		
Current Ratio (Decimal)	Current Assets/Current Liabilities	Indicator of firm's ability to pay its short-term liabilities
Quick (Acid-Test) Ratio (Decimal)	$\dfrac{\text{Current Assets} - \text{Inventory}}{\text{Current Liabilities}}$	Measures firm's ability to pay off short-term debt liabilities from current assets excluding inventories
Profitability Ratio		
Net Profit Margin (%)	Net Profits After Taxes/Net Sales	Indicates after-tax profits produced by each dollar of sales
Gross Profit Margin (%)	$\dfrac{\text{Net Sales} - \text{Cost of Sales}}{\text{Net Sales}}$	Margin available to cover expenses other than the cost of sales while still providing a profit
Return on Investment (%)	Net Profit After Taxes/Total Assets	Indicates return on the firm's total assets; it shows how efficiently the firm is using its assets regardless of how they are financed
Return on Equity (%)	Net Profit After Taxes/Shareholders' Equity	Measures return on book value of shareholders' total investment in the firm
Earnings Per Share (Dollars Per Share)	$\dfrac{\text{Net Profit After Taxes} - \text{Preferred Dividends}}{\text{Average Number of Common Shares}}$	Measures after-tax earnings produced for each share of common stock outstanding
Activity Ratios		
Inventory Turnover (Decimal)	Net Sales/Inventory	Indicates number of times average inventory is sold during a particular period

(Continued)

Appendix A (*Continued*)

Appendix A: Commonly Used Financial Ratios

Financial Ratio (How Measured)	Formula	Interpretation
Days in Inventory (Days)	$\dfrac{\text{Inventory}}{(\text{Cost of Goods Sold}/365)}$	Indicates number of days of inventory a firm has on hand at a particular time
Asset Turnover (Decimal)	Net Sales/Total Assets	Measures firms utilization of its assets and net sales generated by each dollar of assets
Average Collection Period (Days)	$\dfrac{\text{Accounts Receivable}}{(\text{Annual Sales}/365)}$	Average number of days a firm must wait to receive payment after a sale is made
Accounts Payable (Days)	$\dfrac{\text{Accounts Payable}}{(\text{Annual Purchases}/365)}$	Indicates average length of time in days the firm takes to pay its suppliers
Leverage Ratios		
Debt-to-Equity Ratio (%)	Total Debt/Shareholders' Equity	Measures funds provided by creditors versus those provided by shareholders
Long-Term Debt to Total Capital (%)	$\dfrac{\text{Long-Term Debt}}{\text{Shareholders' Equity} + \text{Long-Term Debt}}$	Measures share of total financing received from long-term creditors
Times Interest Earned (Decimal)	$\dfrac{\text{Earnings Before Taxes} + \text{Interest Expense}}{\text{Interest Expense}}$	Measures firm's capacity to pay its interest expense
Fixed Charge Coverage Ratio (Decimal)	$\dfrac{(\text{Profit Before Taxes} + \text{Interest Expense})}{[\text{Profit Before Taxes} + \text{Interest Expense} + \text{Principal Repayment} \times (1/(1 - \text{Tax Rate}))]}$	Indicates firm's ability to repay all fixed obligations

REFERENCES

Benninga, Simon, *Financial Modeling*, MIT Press: Cambridge, MA, 2000.

CNNfn, "Tribune, Times Mirror Deal," http://cnnfn.cnn.com/2000/03/13/deal/tribune, March 13, 2000.

Committee of Sponsoring Organizations of the Treadway Commission, 1998. Cited in Loomis, C. J., "Lies, Damned Lies, and Managed Earnings," *Fortune*, 140 (3), 1999, p. 75.

Durtschi, Cindy, Percy S. Poon, and Gerald D. Newbould, "Market Reactions to Corporate Restructurings," *Review of Quantitative Finance and Accounting*, 16 (3), May 2001, pp. 269–290.

Ford Motor Company, "Ford Completes Acquisition of Volvo Cars," Press Release, March 31, 1999.

Henry, David, "The Numbers Game," *Business Week*, May 14, 2001, pp. 100–103.

Hofmeister, Sallie and David Shaw, "Times Mirror Agrees to Merger with Tribune Company," latimes.com, www.latimes.com/business/updates/lat_times000313.html, March 13, 2000.

Kelleher, James B., "The Numbers Racket," *Orange County Register*, Your Money Section, p. 1.

Klein, H.E. and R. E. Linneman, "Environmental Assessment: An International Study of Corporate Practices," *Journal of Business Strategy*, Summer 1984, p. 72.

Moore, Kathryn, Tim Schnabel, and Mark Yemma, "A Media Marriage," paper prepared for Chapman University, EMBA 696, May 18, 2000.

Moyer, Charles R., James R. McGuigan, and William J. Kretlow, *Contemporary Financial Management*, Cincinnati: South Western College Publishing, 1998, pp. 810–811.

Naughton, Keith, "The Global Six," *Business Week*, January 25, 1999, pp. 68–72.

Sherman, David H. and S. David Young, "Tread Lightly Through These Accounting Minefields," *Harvard Business Review*, July–August, 2001, pp. 129–137.

CNNfn, Tribune Company, "Tribune and Times Mirror: A Winning Combination," Press Release, http://www.tribune.com/overview/qa.html, June 12, 2000.

Tribune Company, "Tribune Reports Merger Election Results," Press Release, www.tribune.com/about/news/2000/election.htm, June 28, 2000.

Tribune Company, "Tribune to Sell Times Mirror Magazines for $475 Million," Press Release, www.tribune.com/about/nes/2000/magazinesale.htm., October 20, 2000.

Volvo, "Volvo Enters into Agreement with Ford to Sell Volvo Cars and Concentrate on Commercial Products," Press Release, January 23, 1999.

Welch, David and Daniel Howes, "Ford Buyout will Save Volvo, Shareholders Told," *Detroit News*, February 24, 1999.

White Michael, "Tribune to Buy Times Mirror," Associated Press, ABCNews.com, http://archive.abcnews.go.com/sections.business/dailynews/merger000313.html, March 13, 2000.

9

ANALYSIS AND VALUATION
OF PRIVATELY HELD
COMPANIES

*Maier's Law: If the facts do not conform to the theory, they
must be disposed of.*

Things just didn't seem to add up. Alan had led due diligence teams for his
firm before. He was well aware that the reliability of the financial data provided
by the 30-year-old family-owned microfiche company, Imaging Services, was
not consistent with generally accepted accounting standards and that some of
the firm's practices would have to change if the company were acquired.
Although impressed with some of the family members on the payroll, he
wasn't yet convinced that they were all contributing as much as they could
to the overall operation of the firm. The "handshake agreements" the owners
had with several large customers reflected the informal practices of many
small companies. The absence of detailed travel expense accounts also was
troubling.

Despite these observations, a restatement of the firm's historic profitability
to eliminate certain anomalies indicated that the firm clearly had been consistently profitable for the last 5 years. Moreover, the firm's cash flow had shown a
strong upward trend during this period. A survey of customers indicated substantial satisfaction with product quality and turnaround time—factors that
were highly valued by the firm's clientele. Because of these considerations,
customers were willing to pay a premium to have their paper records converted
to microfilm by Imaging Services.

Alan was puzzled by the relatively small expense entry recorded for disposal of silver nitrate, a highly toxic chemical that is used in the conversion
of paper to microfilm. The owners assured him that such chemicals had been
disposed of properly and that they had negotiated favorable terms with a local

waste disposal company. Alan decided to crosscheck this explanation by interviewing several employees, who had been with the firm for a number of years and who were not family members or shareholders. During these interviews, Alan learned that chemicals often were dumped down the drain rather than into barrels that were to be emptied by the local waste disposal company. The drain emptied into a grassy area behind the building. An environmental consultant was hired to evaluate the toxicity of the property and confirmed Alan's worst fears. It would cost at least $500,000 to make the property compliant with both state and federal environmental standards.

Alan confronted the owners with an ultimatum. Accept a reduction in the purchase price or he would recommend that his firm not complete the acquisition. The owners relented. Imaging Services was acquired but at a much lower price.

OVERVIEW

If you own an interest in a privately held business, you cannot simply look in the *Wall Street Journal* to see what your investment is worth. This is the situation with the vast majority of the nation's businesses. Publicly traded businesses comprise a miniscule .003 of 1% of all businesses that file tax returns with the Internal Revenue Service. The absence of an easy and accurate method of valuing your investment can create significant financial burdens for both investors and business owners. Investors and business owners may need a valuation as part of a merger or acquisition, for settling an estate, or because employees wish to exercise their stock options. Employee stock ownership plans (ESOPs) also may require periodic valuations. In other instances, shareholder disputes, court cases, divorce, or the payment of gift or estate taxes may necessitate a valuation of the business.

In addition to the absence of a public market, there are other significant differences between publicly traded versus privately held companies. The availability and reliability of data for public companies tends to be much greater than for small private firms. Moreover, in large publicly traded corporations and large privately held companies, managers are often well versed in contemporary management practices, accounting, and financial valuation techniques. This is frequently not the case for small privately owned businesses. Finally, managers in large public companies are less likely to have the same level of emotional attachment to the business than frequently is found in family-owned businesses.

A private corporation is a firm whose securities are not registered with state or federal authorities. Consequently, they are prohibited from being traded in the public securities markets. Buying a private firm is easier than buying a public firm because there are generally fewer shareholders; however, the lack of publicly available information and the lack of public markets in which to value their securities provides formidable challenges. Most acquisitions of private firms are friendly takeovers. However, in some instances, a takeover may occur despite opposition from certain shareholders. To circumvent such opposition, the acquirer seeks the cooperation of the majority shareholders, directors, and management because only they have access to the information necessary to properly value the business.

The intent of this chapter is to discuss how the analyst deals with these problems. Issues concerning making initial contact and negotiating with the owners of privately held businesses were addressed in Chapter 5. Consequently, this chapter will focus on the challenges of valuing private or closely held businesses. Specifically, this chapter begins with a detailed discussion of the hazards of dealing with both limited and often unreliable data associated with privately held firms. The chapter then focuses on how to properly adjust questionable data as well as how to select the appropriate valuation methodology and discount or capitalization rate. The chapter also includes a discussion of how corporate shells, created through reverse mergers, and leveraged ESOPs are used to acquire privately owned companies.

The information in this chapter is decidedly practical, based more on actual experience than theoretical concepts. Unfortunately, the amount of empirical research in applying valuation techniques to privately held firms is highly limited as a result of the paucity of reliable data. Although the same tools and financial modeling techniques discussed in earlier chapters still apply, their reliability is likely to be less as a result of the limited, inconsistent, and possibly erroneous information that the analyst must use to analyze privately owned businesses. Investment bankers and business brokers have long recognized these limitations and have introduced numerous clever adjustments that allegedly make the valuations more accurate. Adjustments to data, like medieval efforts to convert base metals into gold, do not necessarily make it more valuable. A propensity to overadjust data may change the fundamental nature of the data and further reduce its reliability. In this regard, the valuation of privately held firms becomes far more an art than a science.

CHALLENGES OF VALUING PRIVATELY HELD COMPANIES

Because of the need to satisfy both the demands of stockholders and regulatory agencies, public companies need to balance the desire to minimize taxes with the goal of achieving quarterly earnings levels consistent with investor expectations. Failure to do so frequently results in an immediate loss in the firm's market value. The presence of such regulatory agencies as the Securities and Exchange Commission (SEC) limits the ability of public companies to manipulate financial information. In contrast, private companies have much more opportunity to do so, particularly when they are not widely followed by investment analysts or subject to ongoing regulation and periodic review. The anonymity of many privately held firms, the potential for manipulation of information, problems specific to small firms, and the tendency of owners of private firms to manage in a way to minimize tax liabilities creates a number of significant valuation risks. These issues are addressed in the next sections of this chapter.

LACK OF EXTERNALLY GENERATED INFORMATION

There is generally a lack of analyses of private firms generated by sources outside of the company. There is little incentive for outside analysts to cover these firms because of the absence of a public market for their securities; consequently, there are few forecasts of their performance other than those provided by the firm's management. Press coverage is usually quite limited, and what is available is again often based on information provided by the firm's management. Even highly regarded companies purporting to offer demographic and financial information on small privately held firms use largely superficial and infrequent telephone interviews with the management of such firms as their primary source of such information.

LACK OF INTERNAL CONTROLS AND INADEQUATE REPORTING SYSTEMS

Private companies are generally not subject to the same level of rigorous controls and reporting systems as are public companies. Public companies are required to prepare audited financial statements for their annual reports. The SEC enforces the accuracy of these statements under the authority provided by the Securities and Exchange Act of 1934. The use of audits is much more rigorous and thorough than other types of reports known as accounting reviews and compilations. Although accounting reviews are acceptable for quarterly 10Q reports, compilation reports are not acceptable for either 10Ks or 10Qs. The *audit* consists of a professional examination and verification of a company's accounting documents and supporting data for the purpose of rendering an opinion as to their fairness, consistency, and conformity with generally accepted accounting principles.

Although reporting systems in small firms are generally poor or nonexistent, the lack of formal controls, such as systems to monitor how money is spent and an approval process to ensure that funds are spent appropriately, invites fraud and misuse of company resources. Documentation is another formidable problem. Intellectual property is a substantial portion of the value of many private firms. Examples of such property include system software, chemical formulae, and recipes. Often only one or two individuals within the firm know how to reproduce these valuable intangible assets. The lack of documentation can destroy a firm if such an individual leaves or dies. Moreover, customer lists and the terms and conditions associated with key customer relationships also may be largely undocumented, creating the basis for customer disputes on a change in ownership. Moreover, as is explained in the next section of this chapter, both revenue and costs may be manipulated to minimize the firm's tax liabilities or to make the business more attractive for sale.

FIRM-SPECIFIC PROBLEMS

There are also a number of factors that may be unique to the private firm that make valuation difficult. The company may lack product, industry, and geographic diversification. There may be insufficient management talent to allow the firm to develop new products for its current markets or to expand into new markets. The company may be highly sensitive to fluctuations in demand because of significant fixed expenses. Its small size may limit its influence with regulators and unions. The company's size also may limit its ability to gain access to efficient distribution channels and leverage with suppliers and customers. Finally, the company may have an excellent product but very little brand recognition. Such considerations normally tend to reduce the standalone value of the business because of the uncertainty associated with efforts to forecast future cash flows. However, these considerations also present an opportunity for a shrewd buyer to realize synergy by merging firms with complementary strengths.

COMMON FORMS OF MANIPULATING REPORTED INCOME

Overstating Revenue

Revenue may be over- or understated depending on the owner's objectives. If the intent is tax minimization, businesses operating on a cash basis may opt to report less revenue because of the difficulty outside parties have in tracking transactions. Although illegal, it is a major factor in the growth of the so-called "underground economy."

Private business owners intending to sell a business may be inclined to inflate revenue if the firm is to be sold. Common examples include manufacturers, which rely on others to distribute their products. These manufacturers can inflate revenue in the current accounting period by booking as revenue products shipped to resellers without adequately adjusting for probable returns. Membership or subscription businesses, such as health clubs and magazine publishers, may inflate revenue by booking the full value of multiyear contracts in the current period rather than prorating the payment received at the beginning of the contract period over the life of the contract. Such booking activity results in a significant boost to current profitability because not all of the costs associated with multiyear contracts, such as customer service, are incurred in the period in which the full amount of revenue is booked.

If the buyer believes that revenue has been overstated in a specific accounting period by the seller, the buyer can reconstruct revenue by examining usage levels, in the same accounting period, of the key inputs (e.g., labor and materials) required to produce the product or service. Although not necessarily precise, examining activity or usage levels does tend to highlight discrepancies that might exist in the data provided by the seller. Case Study 9-1 illustrates how this might be done.

CASE STUDY 9-1: DUE DILIGENCE UNCOVERS MISSTATED REVENUE

The owner of a custom brass doorknob manufacturer states that 1 million doorknobs of a certain specification were produced during the last calendar year. During due diligence, the potential buyer learns that one skilled worker can produce 100 brass doorknobs in 1 hour. He also learns that there was no overtime last year and that hourly workers were paid for a standard 2080 hours (52 weeks per year times 40 hours per week) each during the year and accrued 2 weeks of paid vacation and holiday time. In addition, he discovers that, because there was no reduction in finished goods inventories during the year, all products reported sold during the year must have been produced during that same year.

The prospective buyer reasons that one worker could produce in 1 year, assuming an average of 2 weeks of vacation time, 200,000 doorknobs (100 doorknobs per hour × 2000 hours). Because there were only four skilled workers employed during the year, annual production of this particular specification could not have exceeded 800,000 doorknobs. Therefore, the sales figures reported by the owner appear to be overstated by as much as 200,000 units. The owner needs to explain what appears to be a logical discrepancy between the reported number and the theoretically determined number of doorknobs produced.

Case Study Discussion Question

1. How might the seller have rebuked the buyer's claims?

Manipulation of Operating Expenses

Owners of private businesses attempting to minimize taxes may overstate their contribution to the firm by giving themselves or family members unusually high salaries, bonuses, and benefits. Because the vast majority of all businesses are family owned, this is a widespread practice. The most common distortion of costs comes in the form of higher than normal salary and benefits provided to family members and key employees. Other examples of cost manipulation include extraordinary expenses that are really other forms of compensation for the owner, his family, and key employees, which may include the rent on the owner's summer home or hunting lodge and salaries for the pilot and captain for the owner's airplane and yacht. Current or potential customers sometimes are allowed to use these assets. Owners frequently argue that these expenses are necessary to maintain customer relationships or to close large contracts and are therefore legitimate business expenses. One way to determine if these are appropriate business expenses is to ascertain how often these assets are used for the purpose the owner claims they were intended.

Other areas that commonly are abused include travel and entertainment, personal insurance, and excessive payments to vendors supplying services to the firm. Due diligence frequently will uncover situations in which the owner or a family member is either an investor in or an owner of the vendor supplying the products or services.

Alternatively, if the business owner's objective is to maximize the selling price of the business, salaries, benefits, and other operating costs may be understated significantly. An examination of the historical trend in the firm's reported profitability may reveal that the firm's profits are being manipulated. For example, a sudden improvement in operating profits in the year in which the business is being offered for sale may suggest that expenses had been overstated, revenues understated, or both during the historical period. The onus of explaining this spike in profitability should be put on the business owner.

ADJUSTING THE INCOME STATEMENT

The purpose of adjusting the income statement is to provide an accurate estimate of the current year's operating income or earnings before interest and taxes (EBIT). In valuing private firms, it is likely that the historical financial information available to the buyer will be misstated. The common misconception is that costs will be overstated. Although this is frequently the case, it is by no means always true. A cost item, such as key employee salaries, may reflect the true value of services received by the firm. An analyst can seriously overstate profitability by ignoring areas in which the target firm's spending is inadequate. Competitive pressures may cause a firm to cut back on advertising, employee training, and safety and environmental compliance.

The key point is that the analyst always must make adjustments based on the best information available. It is often appropriate to hire subject matter experts to assist in making sizable adjustments to important data items. Adjustments should never be made based on preconceptions, personal biases, or emotion. In some instances, operating expenses may have to be adjusted upward, whereas others are reduced.

MAKING INFORMED ADJUSTMENTS

Owner/Officer's Salaries

Before drawing any conclusions, the analyst should determine the actual work performed by all key employees and the compensation generally received for performing the same or a similar job in the same industry. Comparative salary information can be obtained by employing the services of a compensation consultant familiar with the industry or simply by scanning "employee wanted" advertisements in the industry trade press and magazines and the "help wanted" pages of the local newspaper. Case Study 9-2 illustrates how the failure to complete this type of analysis can lead to a substantial disruption to the business following a change in ownership.

CASE STUDY 9-2: LOSS OF KEY EMPLOYEE CAUSES CARPET PADDING MANUFACTURER'S PROFITS TO GO FLAT

A manufacturer of carpet padding in southern California had devised a unique chemical process for converting such materials as discarded bedding and rags to high-quality commercial carpet padding. Over a period of 10 years, the firm established itself as the regional leader in this niche market. With annual sales in excess of $10 million, the firm consistently earned pretax profits of 18–20% of sales.

The owner and founder of the company had been trained as a chemist and developed the formula for decomposing the necessary raw materials purchased from local junkyards into a mixture to produce the foam padding. In addition, the owner routinely calibrated all of the company's manufacturing equipment to ensure that the machines ran at peak efficiency, without any deterioration in product quality. Over the years, the owner also had developed relationships with a network of local junk dealers to acquire the necessary raw materials. The owner's reputation for honesty and the firm's ability to produce consistently high-quality products ensured very little customer turnover. The owner was also solely responsible for acquiring several large accounts, which consistently contributed about 30% of annual revenue.

When the firm was sold, the owner's salary and benefits of $200,000 per year were believed to be excessive by the buyer. Efforts to reduce his total compensation caused him to retire. The new owner soon was forced to hire several people to replace the former owner, who had been performing the role of chemist, maintenance engineer, and purchasing agent. These were functions that did not appear on any organization chart when the buyer performed due diligence. Consequently, the buyer did not increase the budget for salaries and benefits to provide personnel to perform these crucial functions. This tended to overstate profits and inflated the purchase price paid by the buyer.

Replacing the owner required hiring a chemist, a machinist, a purchasing agent, and a salesperson at an annual cost in salary and benefits of more than $300,000. Despite the additional personnel, the new owner also found it necessary to hire the former owner under a consulting contract valued at $25,000 per year. To add insult to injury, because of the change in ownership the firm lost several large customers, who accounted for $2 million in annual sales.

> **Case Study Discussion Questions**
>
> 1. Explain how the buyer's inadequate due diligence contributed to its postclosing problems.
> 2. How could the buyer have retained the firm's president? Give several examples.

Benefits

Depending on the industry, benefits can range from 14–35% of an employee's base salary. Certain employee benefits, such as Social Security and Medicare taxes, are mandated by law and, therefore, are an uncontrollable cost of doing business. Other types of benefits may be more controllable. These include items such as pension contributions and life insurance coverage, which are calculated as a percentage of base salary. Consequently, efforts by the buyer to trim salaries, which appear to be excessive, also will reduce these types of benefits. Efforts to reduce such benefits also may contribute to higher overall operating costs in the short run. Operating costs may increase as a result of higher employee turnover and the need to retrain replacements, as well as the potential negative impact on the productivity of those that remain.

Travel and Entertainment

Travel and entertainment (T&E) expenditures tend to be one of the first cost categories cut when a potential buyer attempts to value a target company. The initial reaction is almost always that actual spending in this area is far in excess of what it needs to be. However, what may look excessive to one relatively unfamiliar with the industry may in fact be necessary for retaining current customers and acquiring new customers. Establishing, building, and maintaining relationships is particularly important for personal and business services companies, such as consulting and law firms. Account management may require consultative selling at the customer's site. A complex product like software may require onsite training. Indiscriminant reduction in the T&E budget could lead to a serious loss of customers following a change in ownership.

Auto Expenses and Personal Life Insurance

Before assuming auto expenses and life insurance are excessive, ask if they represent a key component of the overall compensation required to attract and retain key employees. This can be determined by comparing total compensation paid to employees of the target firm with compensation packages offered to employees in similar positions in the same industry. A similar review should be undertaken with respect to the composition of benefits packages. Depending on the demographics and special needs of the target firm's workforce, an acquirer may choose to alter the composition of the benefits package by substituting other types of benefits for those eliminated or reduced. By carefully substituting benefits that meet the specific needs of the workforce, such as onsite day-care services, the acquirer may be able to provide an overall benefits package that better satisfies the needs of the employees. Alternatively, the acquirer may find that administrative costs associated with reimbursable benefits such as car expenses may be reduced by simply offering a standard car allowance or by increasing the employees' salaries to compensate for anticipated car-related expenses.

Family Members

Similar questions need to be asked about family members on the payroll. Frequently, they do perform real services and tend to be highly motivated because of their close affinity with the business. If the business has been in existence for many years, the loss of key family members who have built relationships with customers over the years may result in a subsequent loss of key accounts. Moreover, family members may be those who possess proprietary knowledge necessary for the ongoing operation of the business.

Rent or Lease Payments in Excess of Fair Market Value

Check who owns the buildings housing the business or equipment used by the business. This is a frequent method used by the owner to transfer company funds to the owner in excess of their stated salary and benefits. However, rents may not be too high if the building is a "special-purpose" structure retrofitted to serve the specific needs of the tenant.

Professional Services Fees

Professional services could include legal, accounting, personnel, and actuarial services. This is an area that is frequently subject to abuse. Once again, check to see if there is any nonbusiness relationship between the business owner and the firm providing the service. Always consider any special circumstances that may justify unusually high fees. An industry that is subject to continuing regulation and review may incur what appear to be abnormally high legal and accounting expenses when compared with firms in other industries.

Depreciation Expense

Accelerated depreciation methodologies may make sense for tax purposes, but they may seriously understate current earnings. For financial reporting purposes, it may be appropriate to convert depreciation schedules from accelerated to straight-line depreciation if this results in a better matching of when expenses actually are incurred and revenue actually is received.

Reserves

Current reserves may be inadequate to reflect future events. An increase in reserves lowers taxable income, whereas a decrease in reserves raises taxable income. Collection problems may be uncovered following an analysis of accounts receivable. It may be necessary to add to reserves for doubtful accounts. Similarly, the target firm may not have adequately reserved for future obligations to employees under existing pension and health care plans. Reserves also may have to be increased to reflect known environmental and litigation exposures.

Accounting for Inventory

During periods of inflation, businesses frequently use the last-in, first-out (LIFO) method to account for inventories. This approach results in an increase in the cost of sales that reflects the most recent and presumably highest cost inventory; therefore, it reduces gross profit and taxable income. During periods of inflation, the use of LIFO also tends to lower the value of inventory on the balance sheet because the items in inventory are valued at the lower cost of production associated with earlier time periods. In contrast, the use of first-in, first-out (FIFO) accounting for inventory assumes that inventory is sold in the chronological order in which it was purchased. During periods of inflation, the FIFO method produces a higher ending inventory, a lower cost of goods sold, and higher gross profit. Although it may make sense for tax purposes to use LIFO, the buyer's objective for valuation purposes should be to obtain as realistic an estimate of actual earnings as possible in the current period. FIFO accounting would appear to be most logical for products that are perishable or subject to rapid obsolescence and, therefore, are most likely to be sold in chronological order. In an environment in which inflation is expected to remain high for an extended time period, LIFO accounting may make more sense.

AREAS COMMONLY UNDERSTATED

Projected increases in sales normally require more aggressive marketing efforts, more effective customer service support, and enhanced employee training. Nonetheless, it is common to see the ratio of annual advertising and training expenses to annual sales decline during the period of highest projected growth in forecasts developed by either the buyer or the seller. The seller has an incentive to hold costs down during the forecast period to provide the most sanguine outlook possible. The buyer simply may be overly optimistic about how much more effectively the business can be managed as a result of a change in ownership.

Other areas that are commonly understated in projections but that can never really be escaped include the expense associated with environmental clean-up, employee safety, and pending litigation. Even in an asset purchase, the buyer still may be liable for certain types of risks such as environmental problems, pension obligations, and back taxes. From a legal standpoint, both the buyer and the seller often are held responsible for these types of obligations. See Chapter 10 for a more detailed discussion of the implications of asset and stock purchases.

AREAS COMMONLY OVERLOOKED

Understandably, buyers find the valuation of tangible assets easier than intangible assets. Unfortunately, in many cases the value in the business is more in its intangible than tangible assets. The best examples include the high valuations placed on many Internet-related and biotechnology companies. The target's intangible assets may include customer lists, intellectual property, licenses, distributorship agreements, leases, regulatory approvals (e.g., U.S. Food and Drug Administration approval of a new drug), and employment contracts. An aggressive seller often attempts to "showcase" these items in an attempt to increase the buyer's perceived valuation of the firm. Valuing intangibles is often highly subjective. The prudent buyer should pay a professional appraiser with specific subject matter expertise to evaluate these items.

Table 9-1 illustrates how a target firm's financial reporting statements could be restated to reflect what the buyer believes to be a more accurate characterization of costs. Note that although some cost items are reduced, others are increased. The implications for other cost categories of cost reductions in one area must be determined. For example, rents are reduced by $100,000 as a result of the elimination of out-of-state sales offices. However, the sales and marketing-related portion of the T&E budget is increased by $50,000 to accommodate the increased

TABLE 9-1   Adjusting the Target's Financial Statements

	($ Thousands)			
	Target's Statements	Net Adjustment	Adjusted Statements	Explanation of Adjustment
Revenue	8000		8000	
Less: Cost of Sales (COS), including all direct costs	5000	(400)	4600	LIFO COS higher than FIFO cost; adjustment converts to FIFO costs
Equals: Gross Profit	3000		3400	
Less: Depreciation	100	(40)	60	Convert depreciation to straight line from accelerated on book and tax returns
Less: Selling				
Salaries & Benefits	1000	(100)	900	Eliminate part-time family members
Rent	200	(100)	100	Eliminate out-of-state sales offices
Insurance	20	(5)	15	Eliminate owner's life and car insurance
Advertising	20	10	30	Increase targeted advertising
Travel & Entertainment	150	50	200	Increase to support out-of-state customer accounts
All Other	100		100	
Total Selling	1490	(145)	1345	

(*Continued*)

TABLE 9-1 *(Continued)*

	($ Thousands)			
	Target's Statements	Net Adjustment	Adjusted Statements	Explanation of Adjustment
Less: Administration				
Salaries & Benefits	600	(100)	500	Reduce owner's salary and benefits
Rent	150	(30)	120	Reduce office space
Insurance	50		50	
Travel & Entertainment	150	(30)	120	
Director Fees	30	(30)	0	Remove family members as directors
Professional Fees	100	20	120	Increase training budget
All Other	50		50	
Total Admin	1130	(170)	960	
Equals: EBIT	280	(755)	1035	

travel that will be necessary to service out-of-state customer accounts once the regional offices are closed.

APPLYING VALUATION METHODOLOGIES TO PRIVATE COMPANIES

DEFINING VALUE

The most common generic definition of value used by valuation professionals is fair market value. Hypothetically, *fair market value* is the cash or cash-equivalent price that a willing buyer would propose and a willing seller would accept for a business if both parties have access to all relevant information. Furthermore, fair market value assumes that neither the seller nor the buyer is under any obligation to buy or sell. As described in Chapter 7, the income or market valuation approaches often are used to determine fair market value.

It is easier to obtain the fair market value for a public company because of the existence of public markets in which stock in the company is actively traded. The concept may be applied to privately held firms if similar publicly traded companies exist. However, because finding substantially similar companies is rare, valuation professionals have developed a related concept called fair value. *Fair value* is applied when no strong market exists for a business or it is not possible to identify the value of substantially similar firms. Fair value is by necessity more subjective because it represents the dollar value of a business based on an appraisal of the tangible and intangible assets of the business.

HIRING VALUATION PROFESSIONALS

The usefulness of valuation methodologies depends on the competence and experience of the analyst conducting the valuation. Thus, the two most important elements in selecting a valuation professional are experience and demonstrated ability in the industry in which the firm to be valued competes. In selecting valuation professionals, it is important to understand what the various certifications obtained by valuation professionals really mean. Historically, many individuals could enter the valuation field without much specialized or formal training. Consequently, the depth of experience and expertise varies widely.

The American Society of Appraisers (ASA) is one of the nation's oldest and most respected appraisal societies, and it generally is considered to be the leading accrediting body of business valuation professionals. The major business valuation firms require that their appraisers obtain an ASA certification. The requirements for the ASA's Accredited Senior Member certification include a minimum of 5 years of full-time business valuation experience and passing four courses in financial analysis and valuation techniques. Other certificates that are available include the Certified Business Appraiser, Certified Valuation Analyst, and Accredited in Business Valuation (ABV). Of these, only the ABV requires the candidate to have performed at least 10 valuations.

SELECTING THE APPROPRIATE VALUATION METHODOLOGY

Valuing private or closely held businesses involves three important steps. The first step involves the adjustment of data so that they accurately reflect the true profitability and cash flow of the firm. This was discussed at length previously in this chapter. The second and third steps entail the determination of the appropriate methodology for valuing the firm and the selection of the proper discount or capitalization rate. These steps are discussed in detail during the balance of this chapter.

The terms discount rate and capitalization rate often are used interchangeably. Whenever the growth rate of a firm's cash flows are projected to vary over time, the term *discount rate* generally refers to the factor used to convert the projected cash flows to present values. In contrast, if the cash flows of the firm are not expected to grow or are expected to grow at a constant rate indefinitely, the discount rate used by practitioners often is referred to as the *capitalization rate*.

As noted in Chapter 7, appraisers, brokers, and investment bankers generally classify valuation methodologies into four distinct approaches: income, market, replacement cost, and asset oriented. Table 9-2 summarizes the strengths and weaknesses of alternative valuation methodologies. Although the strengths noted for each valuation technique are also true when applied to publicly traded firms, the weaknesses tend to be most pronounced when applied to the valuation of private or closely held companies.

TABLE 9-2   Applying Alternative Valuation Methodologies to Privately Held Firms

	Strengths	Weaknesses
Income Approach		
Discounted Cash Flow	• Considers differences in the magnitude and timing of cash flows • Adjusts for risk	• Requires forecasting of cash flows for each period, a terminal value, and discount or capitalization rate(s), using limited or unreliable data • Highly sensitive to the accuracy of income or cash flow and capitalization rate estimates
Market-Based Approach		
Comparable Companies	• Utilizes market-based price-to-earnings, sales, or book value for substantially similar companies	• Truly comparable public companies rarely exist • Valuations must be adjusted to reflect control premiums • Reflects accounting-based historical data
Comparable Transactions	• Uses the most accurate market-based valuation at a point in time • Valuations include control premiums	• May be few in number or not current • Limited availability of specific transaction-related data
Same or Comparable Industry	• Provides additional valuation for comparative purposes	• Assumes industry average valuation multiples are applicable to a specific company • Industry information often nonexistent
Replacement Cost Approach		
Applied to Tangible Assets	• Applicable whenever the discounted cash flow or market approaches are unsuitable because of limited information	• May be of limited use if the target firm is highly profitable • Requires use of appraisers with specialized knowledge • Ignores value created by operating the assets in combination as a going concern
Applied to Intangible Assets	• Simplicity: relies on cumulative investment required to create intangible asset	• Assumes historical investment in intangible asset proxy for future cost of replacement
Asset-Oriented Approach		
Tangible Book Value	• Useful for financial services and distribution companies where assets tend to be highly liquid	• Book value may not equate to market value • Limited availability of required data

(Continued)

TABLE 9-2   (*Continued*)

	Strengths	Weaknesses
Breakup Value	• May unlock value in operating subsidiaries whose actual value cannot be determined easily by analysts outside the company	• Assumes that individual businesses can be sold quickly without any material loss of value • Available markets often highly illiquid
Liquidation Value	• Provides estimate of minimum value of a firm	• Frequently assumes that an "orderly" liquidation is possible • Available markets often highly illiquid

Income Approach

This method was discussed at length in Chapter 7. It requires projected cash flows for a specific number of periods plus a terminal value to be discounted to the present using an appropriate discount rate. The method is heavily dependent on the particular definition of income or cash flow, the timing of those cash flows, and the selection of an appropriate discount rate.

Capitalization is also the conversion of a future income stream into a present value. It generally applies when future income or cash flows are not expected to grow, or they are expected to grow at a constant rate. When no growth in future income or cash flows is expected, the capitalization rate is defined as the perpetuity growth model. When future cash flow or income is expected to grow at a constant rate, the capitalization rate commonly is defined as the difference between the discount rate and the expected growth rate (i.e., the constant growth or Gordon model). See Chapter 7.

Several alternative definitions of income or cash flow can be used in either the discounting or capitalization process. These include free cash flow to equity holders or to the firm; EBIT, earnings before taxes (EBT), or earnings after taxes (EAT or NI). The present value or capitalized value may vary widely depending on the definition of income or cash flow used.

Capitalized values and capitalization rates often are used in valuing small businesses because of their inherent simplicity. Many small business owners lack sophistication in financial matters. Consequently, a valuation concept, which is easy to calculate, understand, and communicate to the parties involved, may significantly facilitate completion of the transaction.

Market Approach

This approach is used widely in valuing private firms by business brokers or appraisers to establish a purchase price. The Internal Revenue Service (IRS) and the U.S. tax courts have encouraged the use of market-based valuation techniques. Therefore, in valuing private companies, it is always important to keep in mind what factors the IRS thinks are relevant to the process because the IRS may contest any sale requiring the payment of estate, capital gain, or unearned income taxes. The IRS's positions on specific tax issues can be determined by reviewing revenue rulings.

Revenue Rulings

A revenue ruling is an official interpretation by the IRS of the Internal Revenue Code, related statutes, tax treaties, and regulations. These rulings represent the IRS's position on how the law is applied to a specific set of circumstances and are published in the Internal Revenue Bulletin to assist taxpayers, IRS personnel, and other concerned parties in interpreting the Internal Revenue Code.

Revenue Ruling 59–60

Issued in 1959, Revenue Ruling 59–60 describes the general factors that the IRS and tax courts consider relevant in valuing private businesses. These factors include general economic conditions, the specific conditions in the industry, the type of business, historical trends in the industry, the firm's performance, and the firm's book value. In addition, the IRS and tax courts consider the ability of the company to generate earnings and pay dividends, the amount of intangibles such as goodwill, recent sales of stock, and the stock prices of companies engaged in the "same or similar" line of business.

In deference to Revenue Ruling 59–60, tax courts historically have supported the use of the comparable company method of valuing private businesses. However, they have differed on their interpretation of the notion of "same or similar." In one case, appraisers used companies that had similar capital structures and financial ratios to the company that was being valued. The court rejected the valuation because it argued that the companies selected were not in the same line of business as the company being valued (*Northern Trust Company v. Commissioner*, 1986). In contrast, the courts were willing to use companies in substantially different lines of business in settling an estate associated with Hallmark Cards, Inc. American Greetings was the only company found that was truly comparable to Hallmark. Appraisers were allowed to use other companies in very different lines of business, such as Coca-Cola, IBM, Anheuser-Busch, McDonald's, and Avon, because they exhibited financial structures, brand recognition, and dominant market share comparable to Hallmark (*Estate of James C. Hall v. Commissioner*, 1989).

Replacement Cost Approach

This approach states that the assets of a business are worth what it would cost to replace them. The approach is most applicable to businesses that have substantial amounts of tangible assets for which the actual cost to replace them can be determined easily. In the case of a business whose primary assets consist of intellectual property, it may be difficult to determine the actual cost of replacing the firm's intangible assets using this method. The accuracy of this approach is heavily dependent on the skill and specific industry knowledge of the appraisers employed to conduct the analyses.

Moreover, the replacement cost approach ignores the value created in excess of the cost of replacing each asset by operating the assets as a going concern. For example, an assembly line may consist of a number of different machines, each performing a specific task in the production of certain products. The value of the total production coming off the assembly line over the useful lives of the individual machines is likely to far exceed the sum of the costs to replace each machine. Consequently, the business should be valued as a going concern rather than the sum of cost to replace its individual assets.

The replacement cost approach sometimes is used to value intangible assets by examining the amount of historical investment associated with the asset. For example, the cumulative historical advertising spending targeted at developing a particular product brand or image may be a reasonable proxy for the intangible value of the brand name or image. However, because consumer tastes tend to change over time, applying historical experience to the future may be highly misleading.

Asset-Oriented Approach

Like the replacement cost approach, the accuracy of asset-oriented approaches depends on the overall proficiency of the appraiser hired to establish value and the availability of adequate information.

Tangible Book Value

Book value is an accounting concept and is generally not considered a good measure of market value because book values generally reflect historical rather than current market values. However, as noted in Chapter 7, tangible book value (i.e., book value less intangible assets) may be a good proxy for the current market value for both financial services and product distribution companies.

Breakup Value

Breakup value is an estimate of what the value of a business would be if each of its primary assets were sold independently. This approach may not be practical if there are few public markets for the firm's assets.

Liquidation Value

Liquidation value is a reflection of the firm under duress. A firm in liquidation normally must sell its assets within a specific time period. Consequently, the cash value of the assets realized is likely to be much less than their actual replacement value or value if the firm were to continue as a viable operation. Liquidation value is thus a good proxy for the minimum value of the firm.

DEVELOPING CAPITALIZATION RATES

The discount or capitalization rate can be derived from the capital asset pricing model (CAPM), cost of capital, accounting based returns, price-to-earnings (P/E) ratio, or the buildup method. These five methods are explored below.

Capital Asset Pricing Model

The CAPM method provides an estimate of the acquiring firm's cost of equity, which may be used as the discount or capitalization rate when no debt is involved in the transaction. However, the cost of equity may have to be adjusted to reflect risk specific to the target when it is applied to valuing a private or closely held company.

The Nature of Specific Business Risk

The CAPM may understate significantly the specific business risk associated with acquiring a privately held firm because it may not adequately reflect the risk associated with such firms. As noted earlier, private or closely held firms are often subject to risks not normally found with public firms. These include inconsistent or improperly stated financial information resulting in inaccurate financial statements, inadequate controls increasing the possibility of fraudulent activities, and potential "hidden" liabilities, such as noncompliance with Occupational Safety and Health Administration and Environmental Protection Agency regulations. Private or closely held firms also may be subject to significant commercial risk because of reliance on a few customers or suppliers or a narrow product offering. Consequently, it is appropriate to adjust the CAPM for the additional risks associated with private or closely held firms.

Adjusting the CAPM for Specific Business Risk

Recall that risk premiums for public companies are determined by examining the historical premiums earned by stocks over some measure of risk-free returns, such as 10-year treasury bonds. This same logic may be applied to calculating specific business risk premiums for small private firms. The specific business risk premium can be measured by the difference between the junk bond and risk-free rate or the return on comparable small stocks and the risk-free rate. Note that comparable companies are more likely to be found on the NASDAQ, OTC, or regional stock exchanges than on the New York Stock Exchange (NYSE).

For example, consider an acquiring firm that is attempting to value a small software company. If the risk-free return is 6%, the historical return on all stocks minus the risk-free return is 5.5%, and the historical return on OTC software stocks minus the risk-free return is 10%, the cost of equity (k_e) can be calculated as follows:

$$k_e = \text{Risk-Free Return} + \text{Market Risk Premium}$$
$$+ \text{Specific Business Risk Premium}$$
$$= 6\% + 5.5\% + 10\% = 21.5\%$$

Cost of Capital

In the presence of debt, the cost of capital method should be used to estimate the discount or capitalization rate. This method involves the calculation of a weighted average of the cost of equity and the after-tax cost of debt. The weights reflect the market value of the acquirer's target debt-to-equity ratio. See Chapter 7 for more detail.

Accounting-Based Returns

The return on equity (ROE) and the return on investment (ROI) sometimes are used as capitalization rates. ROE is the return to equity owners in the business. ROI measures the return on total capital, which includes both the debt and equity of the business. Although after-tax income normally is used to calculate these returns, pretax income should be used for private firms because of the unreliability of after-tax income for such companies (see Exhibit 9-1).

EXHIBIT 9-1. ACCOUNTING-BASED CAPITALIZATION RATES

Doors Unlimited, Inc., has pretax earnings of $1 million, debt of $5 million, and equity of $15 million.

$$ROE = \$1/\$15 = 6.7\%$$

$$ROI = \$1/\$20 = 5.0\%$$

The capitalized value of the business using ROE is $1/.067 = $14.93 million.

The capitalized value of the business using ROI is $1/.05 = $20 million.

Price-to-Earnings Ratio

The capitalization rate also can be measured by calculating the reciprocal of the P/E ratio (i.e., E/P). The P/E ratio used for this purpose can be for the current, the most recent, or a projected year. The P/E used for valuing a private firm should be selected from among the P/Es of comparable public companies adjusted to reflect risks specific to the target firm. Such adjustments are included in the so-called buildup method.

The Buildup Method

The buildup method attempts to compensate for some of the shortcomings associated with applying CAPM or accounting-based returns to evaluating private or closely held businesses. The buildup method involves the adjustment of the underlying discount rate to reflect risks associated with such businesses. Using this method, the capitalization rate (R_{cr}) can be expressed as follows:

$$R_{cr} = R_f + \beta(R_m - R_f) + (R_j - R_f) + R_{ji}$$

Where R_f = the risk-free rate of return

$$R_m = \text{the return on all stocks}$$

$$R_j = \text{the return on the } j\text{th stock}$$

$$(R_m - R_f) = \text{the market risk premium}$$

$$(R_j - R_f) = \text{the specific business risk premium}$$

$$R_{ji} = \text{the liquidity risk associated with } j\text{th stock}$$

$$\beta = \text{the beta associated with the } j\text{th stock}$$

The risk associated with an illiquid market for the specific stock (R_{ji}) often is referred to as the **marketability** or **liquidity** discount. Liquidity is the ease with which investors can sell their stock without a serious loss of value. An investor in a small company may find it difficult to quickly sell their shares because of limited interest in the company. Consequently, the investor may find it necessary to sell their shares at a significant discount from what they paid for the shares. R_f is free of default risk and is usually taken to be the rate on U.S. Treasury notes or bonds. The market risk premium, $R_m - R_f$, the difference between the return on stocks and the risk-free rate, has been averaging about 5.5% since 1926 (Ibbotson, 2002). The β for a private firm may be estimated by using the β for a comparable publicly traded firm or by using an industry-average β. The solution to the case study at the end of this chapter provides an example of how to approximate the β for a private firm if comparable publicly traded firms are available. In the absence of comparable publicly traded firms, analysts may use the buildup methodology by assuming a β of 1.

The specific business risk premium, $R_j - R_f$, the difference between the return on small company stocks and the risk-free rate, has been averaging about 9% since 1960. $R_j - R_f$ also can be measured using the difference between junk bond yields and the risk-free rate of return. Information on junk bonds and small stocks may be found in the financial press such as in the *Wall Street Journal*. Historical data are available through Ibbotson Associates (www.ibbotson.com).

Exhibit 9-2 summarizes the calculation of both the discount and capitalization rates using the buildup method. The risk-free return is assumed to be 6%, and the long-term rate of growth in earnings is estimated at 8.5%. For purposes of illustration, R_{ji}, the marketability or illiquidity discount, is assumed to be 33%. (How this discount is determined is discussed in considerable detail in the next section.) For purposes of illustration, the specific business risk premium, $R_j - R_f$, is estimated to be 9% based on the historical difference between the return on small company stocks and the risk-free rate of return.

In practice, the magnitude of the business-specific risk premium can vary widely depending on the perceived risk characteristics of the firm such as leverage, dependence on a single product, outstanding litigation, or environmental liabilities. For example, for a sample of 51 firms, Kaplan and Ruback (1995) estimated that the return required by investors to invest in highly leveraged transactions averages about 16–17%, almost twice the spread between the average return on small company stocks and the risk-free rate of return.

EXHIBIT 9-2. CALCULATING CAPITALIZATION RATES USING THE BUILDUP METHOD

Risk-Free Rate (R_f)	6.0
+ Market Risk Premium Required to Invest in Stocks $(R_m - R_f)^1$	5.5
+ Specific Business Risk Premium $(R_j - R_f)$	9.0
+ Marketability Discount (R_{ji})	33.0
= *Discount Rate* (zero earnings growth model)	53.5
− Long-Term Earnings Growth Rate	8.5
= *Capitalization Rate* (R_{cr}) (constant earnings growth model)	45.0

[1] The beta in this example is assumed to be one because, in this illustration, it is assumed that there are no publicly traded comparable firms.

ESTIMATING THE MARKETABILITY OR LIQUIDITY DISCOUNT

Measuring the cost of illiquidity associated with stocks lacking a ready resale market is a challenge. This is especially true for closely held companies such as family-owned firms. There is generally only a limited market for such stocks. The size of the illiquidity discount is determined largely by three factors: the size of the business, the type and quality of the firm's assets, and the magnitude and predictability of the firm's cash flows. The illiquidity discount should in practice be smaller for large firms because the continuing viability of the larger firm may be less in question. Firms with highly liquid assets, which can be sold to raise cash, also should exhibit less illiquidity risk. Finally, firms with a history of stable, large operating cash flows are easier to value accurately than those with erratic cash flows.

When family-owned businesses are sold, it is common to follow the guidelines suggested in Revenue Ruling 59–60 and to use the comparable companies' method to estimate the value of the subject firm. Valuation professionals frequently use P/E multiples and other indicators of value associated with publicly traded companies. The stock of such companies usually trades in more liquid markets than closely held companies. Consequently, estimates of the value of closely held companies based on the comparable companies' approach are likely to be overstated because they do not reflect the lower marketability of closely held shares. Numerous studies have been done to estimate the amount of the marketability discount. These include analyses of restricted stock, initial public offerings (IPOs), and option pricing.

Restricted Stock

Restricted stock, also called letter stock, is similar to other types of common stock except that its sale on the open market is prohibited for a period of time. Restricted stock is issued by a firm but not registered with the SEC. It can be sold through private placements to investors, but it cannot be resold to the public, except under provisions of the SEC's Rule 144, which allows limited amounts of the stock to be sold 2 years after the issuance date.

Differences between the value of restricted and unrestricted stock in the same firm are believed to be an accurate reflection of the marketability discount because the only difference between the two is the waiting period before the restricted stock can be sold. The results of numerous empirical studies of the difference between the value of restricted and unrestricted stock suggest that the average illiquidity discount is about 33% for private or closely held firms (Gelman, 1972; *Institutional Investor Study Report*, 1971; Maher, 1976; Silber, 1991; Trout, 1977). However, the size of the discount should be adjusted for the size of the firm, with a larger discount used for smaller firms and firms with uncertain cash flows and whose assets are largely illiquid.

Initial Public Offerings

An alternative to estimating marketability discounts is to compare the value of a company's stock that is sold before an IPO, largely through private placements, with the actual IPO offering price. Because the level of liquidity available to stockholders is substantially less before the IPO, the difference is believed to be an estimate of the marketability discount. In six separate studies of 173 companies over an 18-month period, Emory (1985) found an average discount of 47% between the pre-IPO transaction prices and the actual post-IPO prices.

Applying Marketability Discounts: Controlling Versus Minority Interests

The bulk of the estimates of marketability or illiquidity discounts seem to lie within a range of 33–50%. Given the wide variability of estimates, it should be evident that marketability discounts must be applied with care. Circumstances specific to the company's situation must be taken into account when determining the appropriate size of the discount. These circumstances include differences in the size of the interests being valued, the timing of the sale, the attractiveness of the firm to potential investors, and the size of the market for stocks of companies most similar to the subject company. The implication is that there is no such thing as a standard marketability discount.

Despite the subjective nature of these adjustments, some analysts argue that additional adjustments are required to reflect the size of the investor position in the privately held firm (Pratt, 1998; Pratt, Reilly, and Scheweihs, 1995). Intuitively, the size of the discount should vary with the size of the ownership position in the private firm. An investor holding a controlling interest in a company is better able to affect change in the company than is a minority shareholder. Control can include the ability to select management, determine compensation, set policy and change the course of the business, acquire and liquidate assets, award contracts, make acquisitions, sell or recapitalize the company, and register the company's stock for a public offering. Control also involves the ability to declare and pay dividends, change the articles of incorporation or bylaws, or block any of the aforementioned actions. Therefore, it may be argued that the marketability discount applied to the value of the stock for the investor with a controlling interest should be lower than that for the minority interest shareholder. The key question is how much lower.

A marketability discount in the range of 33–50% may be appropriate for many transactions, with the size of the discount varying with the size of the equity interest being valued. For example, the value of a 20% equity interest might be reduced by 50%, whereas the value of a 60% interest may be reduced by only 33%. In ether case, the investor should be wary because the adjustment remains quite arbitrary.

REVERSE MERGERS

Many small businesses fail each year. In a number of cases, all that remains is a business with no significant assets or operations. Such companies are referred to as *shell corporations*. Shell corporations also may be part of a deliberate business strategy in which a corporate legal structure is formed in anticipation of future financing, a merger, joint venture, spin-off, or some other infusion of operating assets.

THE VALUE OF CORPORATE SHELLS

Is there any value in shells resulting from corporate failure or bankruptcy? The answer may seem surprising, but it is a resounding yes. Merging with an existing corporate shell of a formerly publicly traded company may be a reasonable alternative for a firm wanting to go public that is unable to provide the 2 years of audited financial statements required by the SEC or unwilling to incur the costs of going public. Thus, merging with a shell corporation may represent an effective alternative to an IPO for a small firm (Case Study 9-3).

CASE STUDY 9-3: GHS HELPS
ITSELF BY AVOIDING AN IPO

In 1999, GHS, Inc., a little known supplier of medical devices, engineered a reverse merger to avoid the time-consuming, disclosure-intensive, and costly process of an initial public offering to launch its new Internet-based self-help Website. GHS spun off its medical operations as a separate company to its shareholders. The remaining shell is being used to launch a "self-help" Website, with self-help guru Anthony Robbins as its CEO. The shell corporation will be financed by $3 million it had on hand as GHS and will receive another $15 million from a private placement. With the inclusion of Anthony Robbins as the first among many brand names in the self-help industry that it hopes to feature on its site, its stock soared from $.75 per share to more than $12 between May and August 1999.

Robbins, who did not invest anything in the venture, has stock in the new company valued at $276 million. His contribution to the company is the exclusive online rights to his name, which it will use to develop Internet self-help seminars, chat rooms, and e-commerce sites (Bloomberg.com, 1999).

Case Study Discussion Question

1. Why is this type of transaction called a reverse merger?

AVOIDING THE COSTS OF GOING PUBLIC

Direct issuance costs associated with going public include the underwriter spread (i.e., the selling price to the public less the proceeds to the company) and administrative and regulatory costs. The underwriter spread can range from less than 1% of gross proceeds for a high-quality company to more than 8% for lower quality companies. Administrative and regulatory fees consist of legal and accounting fees, taxes, and the cost of SEC registration. For offerings less than $10 million in size, total direct issuance costs may exceed 10% of gross proceeds. For equity issues between $20 million and $50 million in size, these costs average less than 5% of gross proceeds and less than 3% for those issues larger than $200 million (Hansen, 1986).

Direct issuance costs are higher for common stock than for preferred stock issues, and direct costs of preferred issues are higher than those of debt issues. The difference in costs reflects the differences in risk to the underwriters. Investment bankers normally incur greater marketing expenses for common stock than for preferred stock or debt issues. Indirect costs include the cost of management time associated with new security offerings and the cost of underpricing a new equity issue below the current market value. The latter occurs because of the uncertainty surrounding its true value and the desire to ensure that the issue is a success. Underpricing results in significant amounts of money being "left on the table" (Ritter, 1987).

EXPLOITING INTANGIBLE VALUE

Shell corporations also may be attractive for investors interested in capitalizing on the intangible value associated with the existing corporate shell. This could include name recognition; licenses, patents, and other forms of intellectual properties; and underutilized assets such as warehouse space and fully depreciated equipment with some economic life remaining. Case Study 9-4 illustrates one such instance.

CASE STUDY 9-4: THE CORPORATE SHELL GAME

ShellCo, a company widely known for providing security, cleaning, and office plant maintenance services to businesses, sold substantially all of its operating assets for cash at a significant gain for its shareholders. With few earnings-generating assets remaining, the company was essentially a corporate shell. Its primary assets following the sale include its reputation, a small office building that it owns free and clear of any liens, office furniture and equipment, several trucks, and all the state and local licenses necessary to do business in its municipality. The firm's monthly payments on a long-term lease negotiated some years earlier on prime commercial warehouse space are two-thirds of the currently prevailing lease terms for comparable space. The company name is widely recognized in the local business community and is synonymous with quality and reliability. The company has cash balances in excess of working capital requirements of $50,000.

The firm's dilemma is that without sufficient revenue it will have to liquidate its operations and force existing stockholders to incur additional tax liabilities. As an alternative to liquidation, the firm hired a local business broker to solicit other companies that may have an interest in the corporate shell. The business broker is charged with the responsibility of finding potential buyers who see value in the firm's name and reputation, valuable lease terms, office building, trucks, furniture and fixtures, and licenses and regulatory approvals. The broker understands that, in any likely transaction, the excess cash would be distributed to current shareholders and would therefore have no value to potential acquirers. The broker develops a list of local firms in the same or similar business as the shell corporation. The list includes other commercial security, cleaning, pest control, food, custodial, and temporary employment services that might be interested in growing their existing businesses or expanding their service offering to their current customers or ShellCo's former customers.

The broker is optimistic that a suitable buyer can be found. The current ShellCo stockholders are very interested in minimizing tax liabilities and dispensing with the inconvenience and risk of liquidation, which would involve the sale of the building; subleasing of the leased commercial office space; and disposal of office furniture, fixtures, and other miscellaneous assets. Potential buyers will be interested in the opportunity to utilize ShellCo's brand name in the local community and to dispense with the expense and aggravation of obtaining licenses and other regulatory approvals. They also will like the favorable lease terms and the office building. The broker begins to make initial contacts of the potential interested parties with these factors woven into a compelling sales pitch.

Case Study Discussion Questions

1. How would you "position" this business if you were the business broker hired to sell this business? Consider its key attributes.
2. What other types of firms not listed in the case study might be potential buyers?

CALCULATING OWNERSHIP SHARE: THE VENTURE CAPITAL METHOD

Historically, venture capitalists (VCs) have been among the few willing to invest in firms that have no prospect of earnings for an extended period. The investment technique used by VCs to determine their appropriate share of equity involves estimating net income in the year in which the investor plans to suspend investment and harvest the business (see Exhibit 9-3). The VC calculates the terminal value at the "harvest" year by multiplying the projected net income for that year by the appropriate P/E, determined by studying current multiples of companies with similar characteristics. The terminal value then is discounted to the present using discount rates of 35–80%. The investor's required ownership percentage (IOR) is based on the initial investment and is calculated by dividing the initial investment by the estimated present value (Sahlman, 1988). The IOR equation for a terminal value n periods in the future can be shown as follows:

$$\text{IOR} = \frac{I_R}{[(P/E)_{TV} \times NI_{TV}]/(1 + i)^n}$$

where

IOR	= Investor's required ownership percentage
I_R	= Required initial investment in dollars
$(P/E)_{TV}$	= Projected price-to-earnings ratio for terminal year
NI_{TV}	= Terminal year's net income
i	= Venture capitalist's cost of capital or hurdle rate

EXHIBIT 9-3. CALCULATING OWNERSHIP SHARE: THE VENTURE CAPITAL METHOD

Assume a start-up company is seeking $3 million in initial financing from a venture capital group. The VC requires a 50 compound annual average return, expects to hold the investment for 7 years, and projects that the firm (which is currently losing money) will earn $3 million in net income in the seventh year. After looking at current multiples of net income for comparable firms, the VC estimates the P/E in the seventh year to be 30. What is the ownership position required (OP) by the VC?

$$OP = \frac{\$3}{(3 \times 30)/(1 + .5)^7}$$

$$= \frac{\$3}{90/17.09}$$

$$= .57$$

Implication: The venture capitalist will demand a 57% share of equity in the start-up business in exchange for $3 million. Note that a higher discount rate would result in a larger share of owner's equity demanded by the VC.

USING LEVERAGED EMPLOYEE STOCK OWNERSHIP PLANS TO BUY PRIVATE COMPANIES

An ESOP is a means whereby a corporation can make tax-deductible contributions of cash or stock into a trust. The assets are allocated to employees and are not taxed until withdrawn by employees. ESOPs generally are required to invest at least 50% of their assets in employer stock. There are three types of ESOPs recognized by the 1974 Employee Retirement Income Security Act: (1) leveraged (ESOP borrows to purchase qualified employer securities), (2) leverageable (ESOP is authorized but not required to borrow), and (3) nonleveraged (ESOP may not borrow funds).

FINANCIAL INCENTIVES

The incentives for firms, lenders, and employees to participate in ESOPs are substantial. Both the interest and principal of ESOP loans are tax deductible to the sponsoring firm. Dividends paid on stock contributed to ESOPs are also deductible if they are used to repay ESOP debt. Effective in 1983, tax credits equal to 0.5% of covered payroll can be used by the sponsoring firm if contributions in that amount are made to the ESOP. Banks, insurance companies, and investment companies can reduce their taxable income by 50% of their income earned on loans to ESOPs that own more than 50% of the sponsoring firm's stock. Employees accumulate on a tax-deferred basis common equity in the sponsoring firm. This may be helpful in attracting, retaining, and motivating employees.

THE PROCESS

Employees commonly use leveraged ESOPs to buy out owners of private companies, who have most of their net worth in the firm. The firm establishes an ESOP. The owner sells at least 30% of his stock to the ESOP, which pays for the stock with borrowed funds. The owner may invest the proceeds and defer taxes if the investment is made within 12 months of the sale of the stock to the ESOP, the ESOP owns at least 30% of the firm, and neither the owner nor his family participates in the ESOP. The firm makes tax-deductible contributions to the ESOP in an amount sufficient to repay interest and principal. Shares held by the ESOP are distributed to employees as the loan is repaid. As the outstanding loan balance is reduced, the shares are allocated to employees who eventually own the firm.

ANALYZING PRIVATE SHAREHOLDER RETURNS

In contrast to the mountain of empirical studies of the impact of M&A activity on public company shareholders, there are very few rigorous studies of privately held companies because of the limited availability of data. Chang (1998), in a study of the returns to public company shareholders when they acquire privately held firms, found an average positive 2.6% abnormal return for shareholders of bidding firms for stock offers but not for cash transactions. Chang's sample consisted of 281 transactions, of which 131 were cash offers, 100 were stock offers, and the remainder were a combination of stock and cash, from 1981 to 1992.

The finding of positive abnormal returns earned by buyers using stock to acquire private companies is in sharp contrast with the negative abnormal returns earned by bidders using stock to acquire publicly traded companies (see Chapter 1). Chang (1998) notes that ownership of privately held companies tends to be highly concentrated, such that a stock exchange tends to create a few very large stockholders. Close monitoring of management and the acquired firm's performance may contribute to abnormal positive returns experienced by firms bidding for private firms. This conclusion is consistent with studies of returns to companies that issue stock and convertible debt in private placements (Fields and Mais, 1991; Hertzel and Smith, 1993; Wruck, 1989). It generally is argued that in private placements large shareholders are effective monitors of managerial performance, thereby enhancing the prospects of the acquired firm (Demsetz and Lehn, 1996). Ang and Kohers (2001) also found positive excess returns to bidder shareholders and for private firm shareholders regardless of the form of payment.

THINGS TO REMEMBER

Valuing private companies tends to be more challenging than efforts to value public companies. The current value of a private company can be very difficult to obtain because of the absence of published price information that is readily available for publicly traded companies. The problem is made more difficult because there is generally very little published information about the firm produced by sources external to the privately held firm. The data provided by sources within the firm often are confusing and distorted. Substantial effort often is required to restate the data to determine actual current profitability.

The data that are available are often inaccurate and out-of-date and presented in an inconsistent manner because of poor reporting systems within private companies. The absence of internal controls in many private firms means that fraud or waste may go largely undetected. Private firms often face problems that may be unique to their size and market position. These include inadequate management talent; lack of sophistication; limited access to capital and distribution channels; and a limited ability to influence customers, suppliers, unions, and regulators.

Owners considering the sale of their firms may overstate revenue by inadequately adjusting for product returns. Other ploys used to inflate revenue include booking as revenue products not yet shipped or received by the customer and counting revenue as earned in the current accounting period that should have been spread over a number of periods. Costs also may be understated if owners are desirous of selling the business. However, in examining the historical performance of privately owned firms, there is a greater likelihood that profits will be understated to minimize tax liabilities by failing to report revenue fully and by inflating operating expenses. Common examples of overstatement include above-market salaries and benefits for family members and expenses paid by the firm for services largely enjoyed by the owner and his family. Notwithstanding this tendency to overstate costs, there are areas that frequently are understated. These include employee training, advertising, safety, and environmental clean-up.

Although many small businesses have few hard assets, they may have substantial intangible value in areas that commonly are overlooked. These areas include the following: customer lists, intellectual property, licenses and regulatory approvals, distributor agreements, franchises, supply contracts, leases, and employment contracts.

In view of these considerations, it is crucial to restate the firm's financial reports to determine the current period's actual profitability. Once this has been achieved, comparisons with similar publicly traded firms or projections of cash flow to determine value will be more meaningful.

Revenue Ruling 59–60 describes factors the IRS and the tax courts think are relevant in valuing privately held companies. They should be viewed largely as guidelines because they tend to be incomplete and in some instances of limited value. Nonetheless, in a court of law, the valuation professional may be called on to address these issues. Historically, the tax courts have applauded the use of the comparable companies' approach to valuation of private companies, but their interpretation of what constitutes a truly comparable company has varied.

Fair market value is the cash value that a willing buyer or seller would accept for a business assuming they both have access to all necessary information and that neither party is under duress. Fair value is a term applied whenever public markets for purposes of valuing the firm simply do not exist and the value is estimated based on the informed judgment of appraisers.

The capitalization rate is equivalent to the discount rate when the firm's earnings or cash flows are not expected to grow. When earnings or cash flow are expected to grow at a constant rate, the capitalization rate equals the difference between the discount rate and the projected constant rate of growth. The capitalization rate may be estimated using the CAPM, cost of capital, accounting returns, P/E ratio, and the buildup method. The latter equals the sum of the risk-free rate, the premium required to induce investors to invest in equities, the premium required to induce investment in a specific stock, and the marketability discount.

Empirical evidence suggests that marketability discounts generally lie in a range of 33–50%, although factors specific to the firm could result in discounts outside of this range. Although largely subjective, the discounts are estimated by looking at the difference between the prices of restricted and nonrestricted stock for comparable companies or the spread between the price of sales of the stock that took place before an IPO and the actual IPO price. The size of the adjustment should reflect the degree of control the equity interest has in the firm. The value of a controlling interest should be discounted less than that of a minority interest.

CHAPTER DISCUSSION QUESTIONS

9-1. Why is it more difficult to value privately held companies than those that are publicly traded?

9-2. What factors should be considered in adjusting target company data?

9-3. What is the capitalization rate, and how does it relate to the discount rate?

9-4. What are the common ways of estimating the capitalization rate?

9-5. What is the marketability discount, and what are common ways of estimating this discount?

9-6. Give examples of private company costs that might be understated, and explain why.

9-7. How can an analyst determine if the target firm's costs and revenues are understated or overstated?

9-8. What is the difference between the concept of fair market value and fair value?

9-9. What is the importance of Revenue Ruling 59–60?

9-10. Why might shell corporations have value?

CHAPTER BUSINESS CASE

CASE STUDY 9-5: VALUING A PRIVATELY HELD COMPANY

Background

BigCo is interested in acquiring PrivCo, whose owner desires to retire. The firm is 100% owned by the current owner. PrivCo has revenues of $10 million and an EBIT of $2 million in the preceding year. The market value of the firm's debt is $5 million; the book value of equity is $4 million. For publicly traded firms in the same industry, the average debt-to-equity ratio is .4 (based on the market value of debt and equity), and the marginal tax rate is 40%. Typically, the ratio of the market value of equity to book value for these firms is 2. The average β of publicly traded firms that are in the same business is 2.00.

Capital expenditures and depreciation amounted to $0.3 million and $0.2 million in the prior year. Both items are expected to grow at the same rate as revenues for the next 5 years. Capital expenditures and depreciation are expected to be equal beyond 5 years (i.e., capital spending will be internally funded). As a result of excellent working capital management practices, the change in working capital is expected to be essentially zero throughout the forecast period and beyond. The revenues of this firm are expected to grow 15% annually for the next 5 years and 5% per year after that. Net income is expected to increase 15% a year for the next 5 years and 5% thereafter. The 10-year U.S. Treasury bond rate is 6%. The pretax cost of debt for a nonrated firm is 10%. No adjustment is made in the calculation of the cost of equity for a marketability discount. Estimate the shareholder value of the firm.

A solution to this case is provided in the back of this book.

CHAPTER BUSINESS CASE

CASE STUDY 9-6: PACIFIC WARDROBE ACQUIRES SURFERDUDE APPAREL BY A SKILLFUL STRUCTURING OF THE TRANSACTION BUSINESS PLAN

Pacific Wardrobe (Pacific) is a privately owned California corporation that has annual sales of $20 million and pretax profits of $2 million. Its target market is the surfwear/sportswear segment of the apparel industry. The surfwear/sportswear market consists of two segments: cutting-edge and casual brands. The first segment includes high-margin apparel sold at higher-end retail establishments. The second segment consists of brands that sell for lower prices at retail stores such as Sears, Target, and J.C. Penney. Pacific operates primarily as a U.S. importer/distributor of mainly casual sportswear for young men and boys between 10–21 years of age. Pacific's strategic business objectives are to triple sales and pretax profits during the next 5 years. Pacific intends to achieve these objectives by moving away from the casual sportswear market segment and more into the high-growth, high-profit cutting-edge surfer segment. Because of the rapid rate at which trends change in the apparel industry, Pacific's management believes that it can take advantage of current trends only through a well-conceived acquisition strategy.

Pacific's Operations and Competitive Environment

Pacific imports all of its apparel from factories in Hong Kong, Taiwan, Nepal, and Indonesia. Its customers consist of major chains and specialty stores. Most customers are lower-end retail stores. Customers include J.C. Penney, Sears, Stein Mart, Kids "R" Us, and Target. No one customer accounts for more than 20% of Pacific's total revenue. The customers in the lower-end market are extremely cost sensitive. Customers consist of those in the 10–21 years of age range who want to wear cutting-edge surf and sport styles but who are not willing or able to pay high prices. Pacific offers an alternative to the expensive cutting-edge styles.

Pacific has found a niche in the young men's and teenage boy's sportswear market. The firm offers similar styles as the top brand names in the surf and sport industry, such as Mossimo, Red Sand, Stussy, Quick Silver, and Gotcha, but at a lower price point. Pacific indirectly competes with these top brand names by attempting to appeal to the same customer base. There are few companies that compete with Pacific at their level—low-cost production of "almost" cutting-edge styles. Furthermore, Pacific has access to resources that a new entrant would not. Potential entrants would include a company that has both the financial and production resources in place to be able to compete on quantity and price without sacrificing quality.

Pacific's Strengths and Weaknesses

Pacific's core strengths lie in their strong vendor support in terms of quantity, quality, service, delivery, and price/cost. Pacific's production is also scaleable and has the potential to produce at high volumes to meet peak demand periods. Additionally, Pacific also has strong financial support from local banks and a strong management team, with an excellent track record in successfully acquiring and integrating small acquisitions. Pacific also has a good reputation for high-quality products and customer service and on-time delivery. Finally, Pacific has a low cost of goods sold when compared with the competition. Pacific's major weakness is that it does not possess any cutting-edge/trendy labels. Furthermore, their management team lacks the ability to develop trendy brands.

Acquisition Plan

Objectives

Pacific's management objectives are to grow sales, improve profit margins, and increase its brand life cycle by acquiring a cutting-edge surfwear retailer with a trendy brand image. Pacific intends to improve its operating margins by increasing its sales of trendy clothes under the newly acquired brand name, while obtaining these clothes from its own low-cost production sources.

Tactics

Pacific would prefer to use its stock to complete an acquisition because it is currently short of cash and wishes to use its borrowing capacity to fund future working capital requirements. Pacific's target debt-to-equity ratio is 3 to 1. The firm desires a friendly takeover of an existing surfwear company to facilitate integration and avoid a potential "bidding war." The target will be evaluated on the basis of profitability, target markets, distribution channels, geographic markets, existing inventory, market brand recognition, price range, and overall "fit" with Pacific. Pacific will locate this surfwear company by analyzing the surfwear industry; reviewing industry literature; and making discrete inquiries relative to the availability of various firms to board members, law firms, and accounting firms. Pacific would prefer an asset purchase because of the potentially favorable impact on cash flow and because it is concerned about unknown liabilities that might be assumed if it acquired the stock.

Pacific's screening criteria for identifying potential acquisition candidates include the following:

1. Industry: Garment industry targeting young men, teens, and boys
2. Product: Cutting-edge, trendy surfwear product line
3. Size: Revenue ranging from $5 million to $10 million
4. Profit: Minimum of break-even on operating earnings for fiscal year 1999
5. Management: Company with management expertise in brand and image building
6. Leverage: Maximum debt-to-equity ratio of 3 to 1

After a review of 14 companies, Pacific's management determined that SurferDude best satisfied their criteria. SurferDude is a widely recognized brand in the surfer sports apparel line; it is marginally profitable, with sales of $7 million and a debt-to-equity ratio of 3 to 1. SurferDude's current lackluster profitability reflects a significant advertising campaign undertaken during the last several years. Based on financial information provided by SurferDude, industry averages, and comparable companies, the estimated purchase price ranges from $1.5 million to $15 million. The maximum price reflects the full impact of anticipated synergy. The price range was estimated using several valuation methods.

Valuation

On a standalone basis, sales for both Pacific and SurferDude are projected to increase at a compound annual average rate of 20% during the next 5 years. SurferDude's sales growth assumes that its advertising expenditures in 1998 and 1999 have created a significant brand image, thus increasing future sales and gross profit margins. Pacific's sales growth rate reflects the recent licensing of several new apparel product lines. Consolidated sales of the combined companies are expected to grow at an annual growth rate of 25% as a result of the sales and distribution synergies created between the two companies.

The discount factor was derived using different methods, such as the buildup method or the CAPM. Because this was a private company, the buildup method was utilized and then supported by the CAPM. At 12%, the specific business risk premium is assumed to be somewhat higher than the 9% historical average difference between the return on small stocks and the risk-free return as a result of the capricious nature of the highly style-conscious surfware industry. The marketability discount is assumed to be a relatively modest 20% because Pacific is acquiring a controlling interest in SurferDude. After growing at a compound annual average growth rate of 25% during the next 5 years, the sustainable long-term growth rate in SurferDude's standalone revenue is assumed to be 8%.

The buildup calculation included the following factors:

	%
Risk-Free Rate:	6.00
Market Risk Premium to Invest in Stocks:	5.50
Specific Business Risk Premium:	12.00
Marketability Discount:	20.00
Discount Rate	43.50
Long-Term Growth Rate	8.00
Capitalization Rate	35.50

The CAPM method supported the buildup method. One comparable company, Apparel Tech, had a ß estimated by Yahoo.Marketguide.com to be 4.74, which results in a k_e of 32.07 for this comparable company. The weighted average cost of capital using a target debt-to-equity ratio of 3 to 1 for the combined companies is estimated to be 26%.

The standalone values of SurferDude and Pacific assume that fixed expenses will decrease as a percentage of sales as a result of economies of scale. Pacific will outsource production through its parent's overseas facilities, thus significantly reducing the cost of goods sold. SurferDude's administrative expenses are expected to decrease from 25% of sales to 18% because only senior managers and the design staff will be retained.

The sustainable growth rate for the terminal period for both the standalone and the consolidated models is a relatively modest 8%. Pacific believes this growth rate is reasonable considering the growth potential throughout the world. Although Pacific and SurferDude's current market concentration resides largely in the United States, it is forecasted that the combined companies will develop a global presence, with a particular emphasis in developing markets. The value of the combined companies including synergies equals $15 million, with the terminal value representing 71.2% of the total value of the company.

Developing an Initial Offer Price

Using price-to-cash flow multiples to develop an initial offer price, the target was valued on a standalone basis using a multiple of 4.51 for a comparable publicly held company called Stage II Apparel Corp. The standalone valuation, excluding synergies, of SurferDude ranges from $621,000 to $2,263,000.

Negotiating Strategy

Pacific expects to initially offer $2.25 million and close at $3.0 million. Pacific's management believes that SurferDude can be purchased at a modest price when compared with anticipated synergy because an all-stock transaction would give SurferDude's management ownership of between 25% and 30% of the combined companies.

Integration

A transition team consisting of two Pacific and two SurferDude managers will be given full responsibility for consolidating the businesses following closing. A senior Pacific manager will direct the integration team. Once an agreement of purchase and sale has been signed, the team's initial responsibilities will be to first contact and inform employees and customers of SurferDude that operations will continue as normal until the close of the transaction. As an inducement to remain through closing, Pacific intends to offer severance packages for those SurferDude employees who will be terminated following the consolidation of the two businesses.

Source: Adapted from Contino, Maria, Domenic Costa, Lauri Deyhimy, and Jenny Hu, Loyola Marymount University, MBAF 624, Los Angeles, CA, Fall 1999.

Case Study Discussion Questions

1. What were the key assumptions implicit in Pacific Wardrobe's acquisition plan, with respect to the market, valuation, and integration effort? Comment on the realism of these assumptions.
2. Discuss some of the challenges that Pacific Wardrobe is likely to experience during due diligence.
3. Identify alternative deal structures Pacific Wardrobe might have employed in order to complete the transaction. Discuss why these might have been superior or inferior to the one actually chosen.

REFERENCES

Ang, James and Ninon Kohers, "The Takeover Market for Privately Held Companies: The U.S. Experience," *Cambridge Journal of Economics*, 25, 2001, pp. 723–748.
Bloomberg.com, "Self-Help Goes on the Internet," August 14, 1999.
Chang, Saeyoung, "Takeovers of Privately Held Targets, Methods of Payment, and Bidder Returns," *Journal of Finance*, 53 (3), June 1998.

Contino, Maria, Domenic Costa, Lauri Deyhimy, and Jenny Hu, Loyola Marymount University, MBAF 624, Los Angeles, CA, Fall 1999.

Demsetz, Harold and Kenneth Lehn, "The Structure of Corporate Ownership: Causes and Consequences," *Journal of Political Economy*, 93, 1996, pp. 1155–1177.

Emory, John D., "The Value of Marketability as Illustrated in Initial Public Offerings of Common Stock," *Business Valuation News*, September 1985, pp. 21–24.

Estate of James C. Hall v. Commissioner, 92 T.C. 19, 1989.

Fields, L. Paige and Eric L. Mais, "The Valuation Effects of Private Placements of Convertible Debt," *Journal of Finance*, 46, 1991, pp. 1925–1932.

Gelman, Martin, "An Economist-Financial Analyst's Approach to Valuing Stock of a Closely Held Company," *Journal of Taxation*, June 1972, pp. 46–53.

Hansen, Robert, "Evaluating the Costs of a New Equity Issue," *Midland Corporate Finance Journal*, Spring 1986, pp. 42–55.

Hertzel, Michael and Richard L. Smith, "Market Discounts and Shareholder Gains for Placing Equity Privately," *Journal of Finance*, 48, 1993, pp. 459–485.

Ibbotson, Roger, *Stocks, Bonds, Bills, and Inflation: Classic Edition Yearbook*, Ibbotson Associates: Chicago, Illinois, 2002, www.ibbotson.com

Institutional Investor Study Report, Securities and Exchange Commission, Washington, DC: U.S. Government Printing Office, Document No. 93–64, March 10, 1971.

Kaplan, Steven N. and Richard S. Ruback, "The Valuation of Cash Flow Forecasts," *Journal of Finance*, 50 (4), September 1995, pp. 1059–1094.

Maher, J. Michael, "Discounts for Lack of Marketability for Closely Held Business Interests," *Taxes*, 54 (9), September 1976, pp. 562–571.

Northern Trust Company v. Commissioner, 87 T.C. 349, 1986.

Pratt, Shannon, *Cost of Capital: Estimation and Applications*, New York: John Wiley & Sons, 1998.

Pratt, Shannon P., Robert F. Reilly (Contributor), and Robert P. Scheweihs (Contributor), *Valuing a Business: The Analysis and Appraisal of Closely Held Companies* (3rd ed.), Toronto: Irwin Professional Publishers, October 1995.

Ritter, J. B., "The Costs of Going Public," *Journal of Financial Economics*, December 1987, pp. 269–281.

Sahlman, A. L., "A Method for Valuing High Risk Long-Term Investments: The Venture Capital Method," Note 9-288-006, Harvard Business School, 1988, pp. 2–4.

Silber, W. L., "Discounts on Restricted Stocks: The Impact of Illiquidity on Stock Prices," *Financial Analysts Journal*, 47, 1991, pp. 60–64.

Trout, Robert R., "Estimation of the Discount Associated with the Transfer of Restricted Securities," *Taxes*, 55, June 1977, pp. 381–385.

Wruck, Karen H., "Equity Ownership Concentration and Firm Value: Evidence from Private Equity Financing," *Journal of Financial Economics*, 23, 1989, pp. 3–28.

10

STRUCTURING THE DEAL: PAYMENT, LEGAL, TAX, AND ACCOUNTING CONSIDERATIONS

If you can't convince them, confuse them.
—Harry S. Truman

It was apparent that the fast-paced, highly informal, and entrepreneurial environment of HiTech Corporation would not readily blend with the more structured and reserved environment of BigCo., Inc. Nonetheless, BigCo.'s senior management knew that they needed access to certain patents owned by HiTech to become more cost competitive in the firm's primary markets. Concerned about creating competitors, HiTech chose not to license its technologies to others. Consequently, BigCo. felt compelled to gain complete control of these patents and any further updates to this technology by acquiring HiTech.

As chief executive officer (CEO) of BigCo., Kristen Bailey and her staff studied the demographic profile of HiTech shareholders and employees. As a publicly traded company, considerable information was available through Securities and Exchange Commission (SEC) filings, newspaper articles, and presentations made by HiTech's senior managers at trade association meetings. She understood that almost one-half of the stock was held by the firm's founders, about one-fourth by employees whose average age was about 30, and the remainder by unaffiliated investors and institutions. At last year's stockholders' meeting, HiTech's management, while responding to questions from attendees, indicated that remaining independent would better serve the shareholders' interests at this stage of the firm's development. After all, the firm was less than 10 years old, and management believed they were on the verge of a technological breakthrough whose full commercial value could not yet be determined. Management did acknowledge that once the technology had been developed, they might consider being acquired or partnering with another firm that had excess manufacturing capacity and effective distribution channels that HiTech currently lacked.

Kristen believed that, once BigCo.'s bid for HiTech became public knowledge, BigCo.'s competitors were likely to make offers for HiTech. To preempt its competitors, Kristen reasoned that BigCo.'s initial offer would have to be structured to meet as many of the primary needs of HiTech's shareholders, managers, and employees as possible. By satisfying the concerns of management, BigCo. was more likely to gain their support in obtaining approval by HiTech's shareholders. Moreover, by meeting the needs of employees, BigCo. was more likely to minimize employee attrition once the transaction was closed.

Kristen recommended to her board of directors that BigCo. acquire all of the stock of HiTech to ensure that it would own the rights to the firm's existing and future intellectual property. She suggested that BigCo.'s stock be used as the primary form of payment. By combining BigCo.'s state-of-the-art manufacturing facilities, which were only 65% utilized, and highly effective sales force with HiTech's technology, she believed that HiTech's shareholders and senior managers could be persuaded that the combined companies would be able to grow more rapidly than if HiTech remained independent. Moreover, by accepting stock, HiTech shareholders could defer the payment of capital gains taxes. This would be highly attractive to the founders, whose average cost basis in the stock was very low. Moreover, in view of the relative youthfulness of the workforce, HiTech employees might jump at the chance to own an interest in the combined companies. Finally, BigCo. would assure HiTech managers that HiTech would be operated as a wholly owned subsidiary with minimal interference in its daily operations from BigCo.'s management.

Kristen received approval to proceed. Contact was made through a BigCo. board member who had served on an industry trade association board with HiTech's CEO. HiTech's CEO said that he was flattered by the proposal and would like to confer with his board before making a formal response. Kristen waited impatiently for the drama to unfold.

OVERVIEW

Once management has determined that an acquisition is the best way to implement the firm's business strategy, a target has been selected, the target's fit with the strategy is well understood, and the preliminary financial analysis is satisfactory, it is time to consider how to properly structure the transaction. The process of deal structuring involves identifying the primary goals of the parties involved, the risks associated with satisfying these goals, alternative ways to attain those goals, and how to share risks. The appropriate deal structure is that which satisfies, subject to an acceptable level of risk, as many of the primary objectives of the parties involved as necessary to reach overall agreement.

In this chapter, the deal-structuring process is described in terms of six interdependent components. These include the acquisition vehicle, the postclosing organization, the form of payment, the legal form of the selling entity, the form of acquisition, and tax structure. This chapter will briefly address the form of the acquisition vehicle, postclosing organization, and legal form of selling entity because these are discussed in some detail elsewhere in this book. The focus will be on the form of payment, form of acquisition, and tax structure and strategy. The chapter also will address the interrelatedness of payment, legal, and tax forms by illustrating how decisions made in one area affect other aspects of the overall deal structure. The chapter concludes with a discussion of how transactions are reported for financial reporting purposes. The chapter business cases provide recent illustrations of the role of the deal structuring process in recent successful (Vodafone–AirTouch) and unsuccessful (JDS Uniphase–SDL) mega-mergers.

THE DEAL-STRUCTURING PROCESS

The *deal-structuring process* is fundamentally about satisfying as many of the primary objectives of the parties involved and determining how risk will be shared. Risk sharing refers to the extent to which the acquirer assumes all, some, or none of the liabilities, disclosed or otherwise, of the target. The process may be highly complex in large transactions involving multiple parties, approvals, forms of payment, and sources of financing. Decisions made in one area inevitably affect other areas of the overall deal structure. Containing risk associated with a complex deal is analogous to catching a water balloon. Squeezing one end of the balloon simply forces the contents to shift elsewhere.

KEY COMPONENTS

Figure 10-1 summarizes the deal-structuring process. The process begins with addressing a set of key questions, whose answers greatly influence the primary components of the entire structuring process. Answers to these questions help to define initial negotiating positions, potential risks, options for managing risk, levels of tolerance for risk, and conditions under which the buyer or seller will "walk away" from the negotiations.

The *acquisition vehicle* refers to the legal structure created to acquire the target company. The *postclosing organization* or structure is the organizational and legal framework used to manage the combined businesses following the consummation of the transaction. Commonly used structures for both the acquisition vehicle and postclosing organization include the corporate or divisional, holding company, joint venture (JV), partnership, limited liability company (LLC), and employee stock ownership plan (ESOP) structures.

For transactions in which the target's shares are purchased using the acquirer's shares, the acquirer often creates a wholly owned *acquisition subsidiary* to transfer ownership. The transfer of ownership may be accomplished through a triangular forward three-party merger or a triangular reverse three-party merger. The *forward*

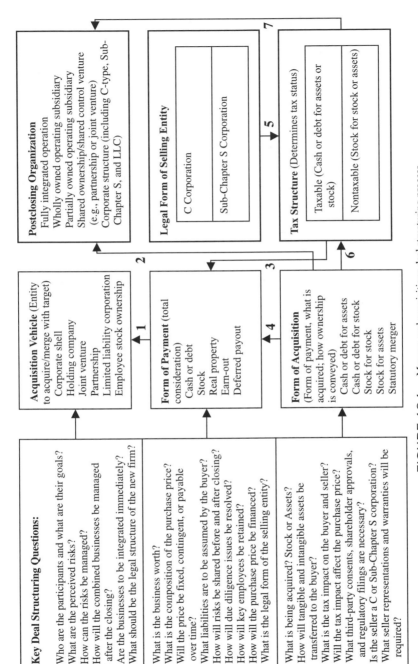

FIGURE 10-1. Mergers and acquisitions deal structuring process.

triangular merger involves the acquisition subsidiary being merged with the target firm and the acquiring subsidiary surviving. The *reverse triangular merger* entails the merger of the target with the acquiring subsidiary, with the target firm surviving. Because the surviving entity is owned entirely by the parent, the parent now indirectly owns the target's assets and liabilities. Such legal structures commonly are used to transfer ownership in stock-for-stock or stock-for-asset purchases.

Because forward and reverse mergers require the exchange of acquirer stock for either the stock or assets of the target firm, most transactions involve some mechanism other than triangular mergers to convey ownership because most transactions involve some form of payment other than acquirer stock. Cash typically accounts for about 45%, stock about 30%, and some combination about 20%, with the remainder accounted for by debt and contingent payouts (Applied Financial Information, 2001). Forward and reverse triangular mergers are used primarily in large transactions in which an exchange of stock is used because the acquirer is unable to finance the transaction through the use of debt. The advantages and disadvantages of the forward and reverse triangular mergers, along with other mechanisms for conveying ownership, are discussed later in this chapter.

Although the two structures are often the same before and after completion of the transaction, the postclosing organization may differ from the acquisition vehicle depending up the acquirer's strategic objectives for the combined firms. An acquirer may choose a corporate or divisional structure to purchase the target firm and to rapidly integrate the acquired business to realize synergies. Alternatively, the acquirer may opt to undertake the transaction using a JV or partnership vehicle to share risk. Once the operation of the acquired entity is better understood, the acquirer may choose to buy out its partners and to operate within a corporate or divisional structure. Similarly, the acquirer may complete the transaction using a holding company legal structure. The acquirer may operate the acquired firm as a wholly owned subsidiary to preserve the attractive characteristics of its culture for an extended time period and later move to a more traditional corporate or divisional framework.

The *form of payment* or total consideration may consist of cash, common stock, debt, or a combination of all three types. The payment may be fixed at a moment in time, contingent on the future performance of the acquired unit, or payable over time. The form of payment influences the selection of the appropriate form of acquisition. The *form of acquisition* reflects both what is being acquired (stock or assets) and the form of payment (cash, debt, or stock). As such, the form of acquisition largely determines the *tax structure* (taxable or nontaxable). A transaction usually is taxable to the target firm's shareholders if the firm's assets or stock are purchased with some form of payment other than the acquirer's stock. The form of acquisition also defines how the ownership of assets will be conveyed from the seller to the buyer, either by rule of law as in a merger or through transfer and assignment as in a purchase of assets. *The legal form of the selling entity* (i.e., whether it is a C or S chapter corporation, LLC, or partnership) also affects the tax structure and may affect the form of payment. These considerations are explored in considerably greater detail later in this chapter.

COMMON LINKAGES

For simplicity, many of the linkages or interactions that reflect how decisions made in one area affect other aspects of deal are not shown in Figure 10-1. Common linkages or interactions among various components of the deal structure are illustrated through examples described below. The numbers indicated in Figure 10-1 relate to the examples described below.

Form of Payment Influences Choice of Acquisition Vehicle and Postclosing Organization (1)

If the buyer and seller agree on a price, the buyer may offer a purchase price that is contingent on the future performance of the target. The buyer may choose to acquire and to operate the acquired company as a wholly owned subsidiary within a holding company structure during the term of the "earnout." This facilitates monitoring the operation's performance during the earnout period. The use of stock makes the actual return to the seller dependent on the future success of the combined businesses, whereas the use of cash reduces uncertainty. However, the use of cash has tax consequences for the seller's shareholders.

Form of Acquisition Affects Acquisition Vehicle and Postclosing Organization (2)

If the form of acquisition is a statutory merger, all known and unknown or contingent liabilities are transferred to the buyer. Under these circumstances, the buyer may choose to change the form of the acquisition vehicle to one better able to protect the buyer from the liabilities of the target, such as a holding company arrangement. Acquisition vehicles and postclosing organizations that facilitate a sharing of potential risk or of the purchase price include JV or partnership arrangements.

Tax Structure Affects the Amount and Composition of the Purchase Price (3)

If the transaction is taxable to the target's shareholders, it is likely that the purchase price will be increased to compensate the target's shareholders for their tax liability. The increase in the purchase price may affect the form of payment. The acquirer may maintain the present value of the total cost of the acquisition by deferring some portion of the purchase price by altering the terms to include more debt or installment payments.

Form of Acquisition Affects Form and Amount of Payment (4)

The assumption of all seller liabilities through a merger also may induce the buyer to change the form of payment to decrease the present value of the cost of the transaction. The buyer also may attempt to negotiate a lower overall purchase price.

Legal Form of Selling Entity Affects Tax Structure (5)

Because of the potential for deferring shareholder tax liabilities, target firms that qualify as C corporations often prefer share-for-share exchanges. In contrast, owners of S corporations and LLCs are indifferent as to whether the transaction is taxable or nontaxable.

Form of Acquisition Drives Tax Structure (6)

The use of anything other than stock to acquire the target's stock renders the transaction taxable.

Tax Structure Affects Selection of Postclosing Organization (7)

The decision as to what constitutes the appropriate organizational structure of the combined businesses is affected by several tax-related factors: the desire to minimize taxes and to pass through losses. The sub-chapter S corporation, LLC, and the partnership eliminate double taxation problems. Moreover, current operating losses, loss carry forwards or carry backs, or tax credits generated by the combined businesses can be passed through to the owners only if the postclosing organization is a partnership or LLC.

FORM OF ACQUISITION VEHICLE

The acquisition vehicle is the legal entity used to acquire the target and generally continues to own and operate the acquired company after closing. Which form of legal entity is used has markedly different risk and tax implications for the acquirer. The various forms of potential acquisition vehicles are discussed in detail in Chapters 1 and 12. They include the corporate/divisional structure, LLCs, JV corporations, holding companies, general and limited liability partnerships (LLPs), and ESOPs.

CORPORATION (INCLUDING LLCs AND JVs)

The major advantage of the corporation structure is that the stockholders' liability is limited to the extent of their investment in the corporation's shares. The corporation is a more permanent form of legal organization than other types of legal entities because the legal existence of the corporation is not affected by whether the stockholders sell their shares. The corporation also facilitates change of ownership because the corporation continues to exist in its original form after shares are sold. Finally, the corporation is able to raise large amounts of capital as a result of the limited liability of its shareholders. The major disadvantage of this structure is the potential for double taxation of dividends. The corporate structure or some variation is the most commonly used acquisition vehicle. In such an arrangement, the acquired company generally is integrated into an existing operating division or product line within the corporation.

An LLC avoids double taxation and allows flexibility in allocating profits and losses. This type of legal framework is particularly attractive in situations such as JVs in which the target is going to be owned by two or more unrelated parties. Used as an acquisition vehicle, the JV corporation offers a lower level of risk than a direct acquisition of the target firm by one of the JV corporate owners. By acquiring the target firm through the JV, the corporate investor limits the potential liability to the extent of their investment in the JV corporation.

A sub-chapter S corporation is defined as a corporation that has fewer than 76 shareholders, who must be U.S. residents, and who are unincorporated. This type of structure is limited to one class of stock, such that it could issue voting stock but could not have nonvoting common or preferred stock. The major advantages include the elimination of double taxation and limited liability. However, financing growth may be hampered severely by the requirement to pass 100% of earnings to shareholders, the limitation on the total number of shareholders, the inability to issue multiple classes of stock, and the inability to have corporate shareholders.

HOLDING COMPANY

A holding company does not have to own the majority of the stock in another company to gain control. However, it must own at least 80% of the subsidiary's voting stock to receive dividends made to the parent tax-free and to be allowed to consolidate operating losses for tax purposes. Non-U.S. buyers intending to make additional acquisitions may prefer a holding company structure. The advantages of this structure over a corporate merger are the ability to control other companies by only owning a small portion of the company's voting stock and to gain this control without getting shareholder approval. One major disadvantage is multiple taxation whenever less than 80% of the subsidiary's stock is owned. Moreover, the holding company may become excessively leveraged as a result of the pyramiding effects of holding debt at various levels of the holding company. See Chapter 1 for a more detailed discussion of holding company structures.

PARTNERSHIPS

Partnerships spread the risk of an acquisition over a number of partners, avoid double taxation, and achieve flexibility in distributing profits and losses. Partnerships may borrow to finance their activities and carry the debt on their books as long as no single partner has a controlling interest in the entity. Otherwise, the controlling partner must display the debt on their balance sheet. Recall that a controlling interest may be less than 51% ownership if the partner has the ability to make important strategic and operational decisions for the partnership. In 2002, critics alleged that debt held by Enron-affiliated partnerships should have been consolidated on the Enron balance sheet because Enron had control over these partnerships far in excess of their actual ownership interest. An important disadvantage of partnerships is that partnership interests are often highly illiquid. Moreover, they lack the continuity and financing flexibility of the corporate structure.

EMPLOYEE STOCK OWNERSHIP PLANS

Sellers may create an ESOP to buy all or substantially all of the company. As noted in Chapter 1, the leveraged ESOP uses borrowed funds either directly from the company or from a third-party lender based on a guarantee from the company, with the securities of the company used as collateral, to acquire the employer's securities. The ESOP repays the loan from employer and employee contributions, as well as from any dividends paid on the employer's securities. A nonleveraged ESOP may consist of a stock bonus plan that purchases the employer's securities with funds the employer otherwise would have paid as some other form of compensation to employees (Sherman, 1998).

POSTCLOSING ORGANIZATION

What form the postclosing structure takes depends largely on the objectives of the acquiring company. These objectives could include the following: (1) facilitating postclosing integration, (2) minimizing risk to owners from the known and unknown liabilities of the combined businesses, (3) minimizing taxes, and (4) passing through losses to shelter the owners' tax liabilities.

If the acquirer is interested in integrating the target business immediately following closing, the corporate or divisional structure may be most desirable because the acquirer is most likely to be able to gain the greatest control by using this structure. In other structures, such as JVs and partnerships, decision making may be slower or more contentious as a result of dispersed ownership. Decision making is more likely to depend on close cooperation and consensus building, which may slow efforts to rapidly integrate the acquired company (see Chapter 6).

In contrast, a holding company structure in which the acquired company is managed as a wholly owned subsidiary may be preferable when an earnout is involved, the target is a foreign firm, or the acquirer is a financial investor. In an earnout agreement, the acquired firm must be operated largely independently from other operations of the acquiring firm to minimize the potential for lawsuits. If the acquired firm fails to achieve the goals required to receive the earnout payment, the acquirer may be sued for allegedly taking actions that prevented the acquired firm from reaching the necessary goals. When the target is a foreign firm, it is often appropriate to operate it separately from the rest of the acquirer's operations because of the potential disruption from significant cultural differences. Prevailing laws in the foreign country may also affect the form of the organization.

Finally, a financial buyer may use a holding company structure because they have no interest in operating the target firm for any length of time.

A partnership or JV structure may be appropriate if the risk associated with the target firm is believed to be high. Consequently, partners or JV owners can limit their financial exposure to the amount they have invested in the partnership or JV. The acquired firm also may benefit from being owned by a partnership or JV because of the expertise that may be provided by the different partners or owners. The availability of such expertise actually may reduce the overall risk of managing the business. Finally, a partnership or LLC may be most appropriate for eliminating double taxation and passing through current operating losses, tax credits, and loss carry forwards and carry backs to the owners.

LEGAL FORM OF SELLING ENTITY

Whether the seller will care about the form of the transaction (i.e., whether stock or assets are sold) may depend on whether the seller is an S, limited liability, or a C corporation. As noted previously, C corporations are subject to double taxation, whereas owners of S corporations and LLCs are not. With S corporations and LLCs, income and losses pass through to the owners and thus avoid the double taxation of a C corporation. (Exhibit 10-1).

EXHIBIT 10-1. HOW LEGAL FORM OF SELLER AFFECTS FORM OF PAYMENT

Assume a business owner starting with an initial investment of $100,000 sells her business for $1,000,000. Different legal structures have different tax impacts.

1. After-tax proceeds of a stock sale: ($1,000,000 − $100,000) × (1 − .2) = $720,000. The C, S, or limited liability corporation shareholder holding shares for more than 1 year pays a capital gains tax equal to 20%, the current maximum capital gains tax on shares held for more than 1 year, of the gain on the sale.
2. After-tax proceeds from an asset sale: ($1,000,000 − $100,000) × (1 − .4) × (1 − .2) = $900,000 × .48 = $432,000. A C corporation pays tax equal to 40% and the shareholder pays a capital gains tax equal to 20%, resulting in double taxation of the gain on sale.

Implications:

1. C corporation shareholders generally prefer a stock-for-stock exchange to avoid double taxation.

2. S and limited liability corporation owners are indifferent to an assets sale or stock sale because 100% of the corporation's income passes through the corporation untaxed to the owners who are subject to their own personal tax rates. The S or limited liability corporation shareholders still may prefer a share-for-share exchange if they are interested in deferring their tax liability.

FORM OF PAYMENT OR TOTAL CONSIDERATION

Determining the proper form of payment can be a surprisingly complicated exercise. Each form of payment can have significantly different implications for the parties involved in the transaction. The use of cash is the simplest and most commonly used means of payment for acquiring shares or assets. Although cash payments generally will result in an immediate tax liability for the target company's shareholders, there is no ambiguity about the value of the transaction as long as no portion of the payment is deferred.

NONCASH FORMS OF PAYMENT

The use of common equity may involve certain tax advantages for the parties involved. This is especially true for the selling company. However, the use of shares is much more complicated than cash because it requires compliance with the prevailing security laws (see Chapter 2). Moreover, the acquirer's share price may suffer if investors believe that the newly issued shares will result in a long-term dilution in earnings per share (EPS) (i.e., a reduction in an individual shareholder's claim on future earnings and the assets that produce those earnings). The use of convertible preferred stock or debt can be attractive to both buyers and sellers. Convertible preferred stock provides some downside protection to sellers in the form of continuing dividends, while providing upside potential if the acquirer's common stock price increases above the conversion point. Acquirers find convertible debt attractive because of the tax deductibility of interest payments. The major disadvantage in using securities of any type is that the seller may find them unattractive. Debt instruments may be unacceptable because of the perceived high risk of default associated with the issuer. When offered common equity, shareholders of the selling company may feel the growth prospects of the acquirer's stock may be limited. Finally, debt or equity securities may be illiquid because of the small size of the resale market for these types of securities.

Other forms of payment include real property, rights to intellectual property, royalties, earnouts, and contingent payments. Real property consists of such things as a parcel of real estate. So-called "like-kind" exchanges or swaps may have favorable tax consequences. Real property exchanges are most common in commercial real estate transactions. Granting the seller access to valuable licenses or franchises limits the use of cash or securities at the time of closing; however, it does raise the possibility that the seller could become a future competitor. The use of debt or other types of deferred payments reduces the overall present value of the purchase price to the buyer by shifting some portion of the purchase price into the future.

CLOSING THE GAP ON PRICE

Balance sheet adjustments, earnouts, rights to intellectual property, licensing fees, and consulting agreements commonly are used to consummate the deal, when buyers and sellers cannot reach agreement on purchase price.

Balance Sheet Adjustments

Balance sheet adjustments most often are used in purchases of assets when the elapsed time between the agreement on price and the actual closing date is lengthy. This may be a result of the need to obtain regulatory or shareholder approvals or a result of ongoing due diligence. During this period, balance sheet items, particularly those related to working capital, may change significantly. As indicated in Table 10-1, to protect the buyer or seller, the buyer reduces the total purchase price by an amount equal to the decrease in net working capital or shareholders' equity of the target and increases the purchase price by any increase in these measures during this period. Buyers and sellers generally view purchase price adjustments as a form of insurance against any erosion or accretion in assets, such as receivables or inventories. Such adjustments protect the buyer from receiving a lower dollar value of assets than originally believed or the seller from transferring to the buyer more assets than expected. The actual payments are made between the buyer and seller after a comprehensive audit of the target's balance sheet by an independent auditor is completed some time after closing.

Earnouts

Earnouts are payments made subsequent to closing and are based on the achievement of agreed-on goals stipulated in the closing contract. Earnouts frequently are used whenever the buyer and seller cannot agree on the probable performance of the seller's business over some future period. The earnout normally requires that the acquired business be operated as a wholly owned subsidiary of the acquiring

TABLE 10-1   Balance Sheet Adjustments ($ Millions)

	Purchase Price		Purchase Price	
	At Time of Negotiation	At Closing	Reduction	Increase
If Working Capital Equals	110	100	10	
If Working Capital Equals	110	125		15

company under the management of the former owners or key executives of the business. Both the buyer and seller are well advised to keep the calculation of such goals and resulting payments as simple as possible because disputes frequently arise as a result of the difficulty in measuring actual performance to the goals.

Historically, earnouts have been considered contingent liabilities. Therefore, they did not appear on acquirer balance sheets. New accounting rules under consideration in the United States in 2002 may require that potential earnout payments be shown as debt.

Exhibit 10-2 illustrates how an earnout formula could be constructed. The purchase price consists of two components. At closing, the seller receives a lump-sum payment of $100 million. The seller and the buyer agree to a baseline projection for a 3-year period and agree that the seller will receive a fixed multiple of the average annual performance of the acquired business in excess of the baseline projection. Thus, the earnout provides an incentive for the seller to operate the business as effectively as possible. Normally, the baseline projection is what the buyer used to value the seller's business. Shareholder value for the buyer is created whenever the acquired business's actual performance exceeds the baseline projection and the multiple applied by investors at the end of the 3-year period exceeds the multiple used to calculate the earnout payment. This assumes that the baseline projection accurately values the business and that the buyer does not overpay. By multiplying the anticipated multiple investors will pay for operating cash flow at the end of the 3-year period by projected cash flow, it is possible to estimate the potential increase in shareholder value.

EXHIBIT 10-2. HYPOTHETICAL EARNOUT AS PART OF THE PURCHASE PRICE

Purchase Price:

1. Lump sum payment at closing: The seller receives $100 million.
2. Earnout payment: The seller receives four times the excess of the actual average annual net operating cash flow over the baseline projection at the end of 3 years.

Base Year (First Full Year of Ownership)	Year 1	Year 2	Year 3
Baseline Projection (Net Cash Flow)	$10	$12	$15
Actual Performance (Net Cash Flow)	$15	$20	$25

Earnout at the end of 3 years[1]:

$$\frac{(\$15 - \$10) + (\$20 - \$12) + (\$25 - \$15)}{3} \times 4 = \$30.67$$

Potential increase in shareholder value[2]:

$$\left\{ \frac{(\$15 - \$10) + (\$20 - \$12) + (\$25 - \$15)}{3} \times 10 \right\} - \$30.67 = \$46$$

[1] The cash flow multiple of four applied to the earnout is a result of negotiation before closing.

[2] The cash flow multiple of 10 applied to the potential increase in shareholder value for the buyer is the multiple the buyer anticipates that investors would apply to a 3-year average of actual operating cash flow at the end of the 3-year period.

Earnouts tend to shift risk from the acquirer to the seller or acquired firm in that a higher price is paid only when the seller or acquired firm has met or exceeded certain performance criteria. However, earnouts also may create some perverse results during implementation. Management motivation may be lost if the acquired firm does not perform well enough to achieve any payout under the earnout formula or if the acquired firm substantially exceeds the performance targets, effectively guaranteeing the maximum payout under the plan. Moreover, the management of the acquired firm may have an incentive to take actions not in the best interests of the acquirer. For example, management may cut back on certain expenses such as advertising and training to improve the operation's current cash-flow performance. In addition, management may make only those investments that improve short-term profits at the expense of investments that may generate immediate losses but favorably affect profits in the long term. As the end of the earnout period approaches, management may postpone any investments at all to maximize their bonus under the earnout plan.

In a study of 938 earnouts from 1984 to 1996, Kohers and Ang (2000) find that earnouts are more commonly used when the targets are private firms or subsidiaries of larger firms rather than for large, publicly traded firms. Contingent payout contracts are more easily written and enforced when there are relatively few share-holders. Earnouts tend to be most common in high tech industries and when the acquirer and target firms are in different industries and little integration will be attempted. The study also shows that earnouts, if fully realized, on average account for 45% of the total purchase price paid for private firms and 33% for subsidiary acquisitions. Moreover, target firm shareholders tend to realize about 62% of the potential earnout amount. Interestingly, in transactions involving earnouts, acquirers earn abnormal returns of 5.39% around the announcement date, in contrast to transactions not involving contingent payments in which abnormal returns to acquirers tend to be zero or negative. The authors argue that the positive abnormal returns to acquiring company shareholders are a result of investor perception that with an earnout the buyer is less likely to overpay and more likely to retain key target firm talent.

Rights, Royalties, and Fees

Other forms of payment that can be used to close the gap between what the buyer is willing to offer and what the seller expects include such things as the rights to intellectual property, royalties from licenses, and fee-based consulting or employment agreements. Having the right to use a proprietary process or technology for free or at a below market rate may be of interest to the former owners who are considering pursuing business opportunities in which the process or technology would be useful. Note that such an arrangement, if priced at below market rates or if free to the seller, would represent taxable income to the seller. Obviously, such arrangements should be coupled with reasonable agreements not to compete in the same industry as their former firm. Consulting or employment contracts are also widely used to provide ongoing or deferred payment to the former owners. Contracts may be extended to both the former owners and their family members. By spreading the payment of consulting fees or salary over a number of years, the seller may be able to reduce the income tax liability that might have resulted from receiving a larger lump-sum purchase price. Table 10-2 summarizes the various forms of payment in terms of their advantages and disadvantages. Note the wide range of options available to satisfy the various needs of the parties to the transaction.

FORM OF ACQUISITION

The form of acquisition describes the mechanism for conveying ownership of assets or stock and associated liabilities from the target to the acquiring firm. Although the form of acquisition may vary widely, the most commonly used methods include the following: asset purchases, stock purchases, statutory mergers, stock-for-stock purchases, and stock-for-assets purchases.

Asset purchases involve the acquiring company buying all or a portion of the target company's assets and assuming all, some, or none of the target's liabilities in exchange for cash or assets. *Stock purchases* involve the exchange of the target's stock for either cash, debt, or the stock of the acquiring company. A *statutory merger* involves the combination of the acquiring and target firms, in which one firm ceases to exist. The statutes of the state or states, in which the parties to the transaction are located, govern such transactions. State laws also provide for a streamlined procedure called a *short form merger*, in which a small group of investors control 90% or more of the voting stock of the selling firm. *Stock-for-stock* or *stock-for-assets* transactions represent alternatives to a merger. Table 10-3 highlights the primary advantages and disadvantages of these alternative forms of acquisition.

TABLE 1O-2 Form of Payment Risk Evaluation

Form of Payment	Advantages	Disadvantages
Cash (Including highly marketable securities)	*Buyer:* Simplicity *Seller:* Ensures payment if acquirer's creditworthiness questionable	*Buyer:* Must rely solely on protections afforded in contract to recover claims *Seller:* Creates immediate tax liability
Stock —Common —Preferred —Convertible Preferred	*Buyer:* High P/E relative to seller's P/E increases value of combined businesses *Seller:* Defers taxes and provides potential price increase. Retains interest in the business	*Buyer:* Adds complexity; potential EPS dilution *Seller:* Potential decrease in purchase price if the value of equity received declines. May delay closing because of registration requirements
Debt —Secured —Unsecured —Convertible	*Buyer:* Interest expense tax deductible *Seller:* Defers tax liability on principal	*Buyer:* Adds complexity and increases leverage *Seller:* Risk of default
Performance-Related Earnouts	*Buyer:* Shifts some portion of risk to seller *Seller:* Potential for higher purchase price	*Buyer:* May limit integration of businesses *Seller:* Increases uncertainty of sales price
Purchase Price Adjustments	*Buyer:* Protection from eroding values of working capital before closing *Seller:* Protection from increasing values of working capital before closing	*Buyer:* Audit expense. Buyer and seller often share audit costs *Seller:* Audit expense
Real Property —Real Estate —Plant and Equipment —Business or Product Line	*Buyer:* Minimizes use of cash; potentially tax free if exchange of substantially similar properties *Seller:* May minimize tax liability	*Buyer:* Opportunity cost *Seller:* Real property may be illiquid
Rights to Intellectual Property —License —Franchise	*Buyer:* Minimizes cash use *Seller:* Gains access to valuable rights and spreads taxable income over time	*Buyer:* Potential for setting up new competitor *Seller:* May be illiquid. Income taxed at ordinary rates
Royalties from —Licenses —Franchises	*Buyer:* Minimizes cash use *Seller:* Spreads taxable income over time	*Buyer:* Opportunity cost *Seller:* Income taxed at ordinary rates
Fee-Based —Consulting Contract —Employment Agreement	*Buyer:* Uses seller's expertise and removes seller as potential competitor for a limited time *Seller:* Augments purchase price and allows seller to stay with the business	*Buyer:* May involve demotivated employees *Seller:* Limits ability to compete in same line of business. Income taxed at ordinary rates

TABLE 10-3 Advantages and Disadvantages of Alternative Forms of Acquisition

Alternative Forms	Advantages	Disadvantages
Purchase of Assets		
—Buyer	• Allows targeted purchase of assets • Asset write-up • May renegotiate union and benefits agreements • May avoid need for shareholder approval • Maintains corporate existence and ownership of assets not acquired • Retains NOLs and tax credits	• Lose NOLs[1] and tax credits • Lose rights to intellectual property • May require consents to assignment of contracts • Potential double-taxation if shell liquidated • Subject to state transfer taxes • Necessity of disposing of unwanted residual assets
—Seller		• Responsible for known and unknown liabilities • No asset write-up unless 338 election taken by buyer[2] • Union and employee benefit agreements do not terminate • Potential for minority shareholders
Purchase of Stock		
—Buyer	• Assets transfer automatically • May avoid need to get consents to assignment for contracts • Less documentation • NOLs and tax credits pass to buyer • No state transfer taxes • Favorable tax treatment for target shareholders if stock received • Liabilities generally pass to the buyer	• Requires shareholder approval • Loss of NOLs and tax credits • Favorable tax treatment lost if buyer adopts 338 election
—Seller		
Statutory Merger	• Stock and assets transfer automatically • No state transfer taxes • No minority shareholders	• May have to pay dissenting shareholders' appraised value of stock • May be time consuming because of the need for shareholder approvals • Requires shareholder approval
Stock-for-Stock Transaction	• May operate target company as a subsidiary	• May postpone realization of synergies • Requires shareholder approval
Stock-for-Assets Transaction	• Favorable tax treatment for target shareholders	• May dilute acquiring shareholders' ownership position • Requires shareholder approval
Staged Transactions	• Provides greater strategic flexibility	• May postpone realization of synergies

[1] Net operating loss carry forwards or carry backs.

[2] In Section 338 of the U.S. tax code, the acquirer in a purchase of 80% or more of the stock of the target may elect to treat the acquisition as if it were an acquisition of the target's assets.

PURCHASE OF ASSETS

In an asset purchase, a buyer acquires all rights a seller has to an asset for cash, stock, or some combination. Such assets may be tangible or intangible. Ownership is transferred whenever the seller provides the buyer with documents that demonstrate that title has been transferred. Such documents include a bill of sale and a deed. Asset purchases are governed by the Uniform Commercial Code (UCC), a portion of which includes the bulk sales law. The bulk sales law focuses on inventory transfer to the buyer and requires that, if inventory ownership is transferred, notice of the transfer must be sent to creditors of the seller 10 days before the transfer takes place. Because such inventory may have been used for collateral, the notice must indicate whether the seller's obligation to the creditors will be satisfied before transferring title to the inventory.

Advantages: Buyer's Perspective

Buyers can be selective as to which assets of the target will be purchased. The buyer is generally not responsible for the seller's liabilities, unless specifically assumed under the contract. However, the buyer can be held responsible for certain liabilities such as environmental claims; property taxes; and, in some states, substantial pension liabilities and product liability claims. To protect against such risks, buyers usually insist on seller *indemnification* (i.e., the seller is held responsible for payment of damages resulting from such claims). Of course, such indemnification is worthwhile only as long as the seller remains solvent. (Note that in most agreements of purchase and sale buyers and sellers agree to indemnify each other from claims for which they are directly responsible. Liability under such arrangements usually is subject to specific dollar limits and is in force only for a specific time period.)

Acquired assets may be revalued to market value on the closing date under the purchase method of accounting. (Purchase accounting is a form of financial reporting of business combinations that is discussed in detail later in this chapter.) This increase or *step-up* in the tax basis of the acquired assets to fair market value provides for higher depreciation and amortization expense deductions for tax purposes. Such expense deductions are said to *shelter* pretax income from taxation. Buyers are generally free of any undisclosed or contingent liabilities. The asset purchase normally results in the termination of union agreements, thereby providing an opportunity to renegotiate agreements viewed as too restrictive. Benefit plans may be maintained or terminated at the discretion of the acquirer. The acquiring company frequently will terminate existing plans if it feels it can obtain comparable benefits from other providers on better terms. Failure by the acquiring company to provide comparable benefits can result in the loss of key employees. If the amount of the purchase falls within certain limits set by the firm's bylaws, the buyer may not be required to obtain shareholder approval.

Advantages: Seller's Perspective

Sellers are able to maintain their corporate existence and hence ownership of tangible assets not acquired by the buyer and of intangible assets such as licenses, franchises, and patents. The seller retains the right to use the corporate identity in subsequent marketing programs, unless ceded to the buyer as part of the transaction. The seller also retains the right to use all tax credits and accumulated net operating losses, which can be used to shelter future income from taxes.

Disadvantages: Buyer's Perspective

The buyer loses the seller's net operating losses and tax credits. Rights to assets such as licenses, franchises, and patents cannot be transferred to buyers. Such rights are viewed as belonging to the owners of the business (i.e., target stockholders). These rights sometimes can be difficult to transfer because of the need to obtain consent from the agency (e.g., U.S. Patent Office) issuing the rights. The buyer must seek the consent of customers and vendors to transfer existing contracts to the buyer. The transaction is more complex and costly because acquired assets must be listed on appendixes to the definitive agreement and the sale of and titles to each asset transferred must be recorded and state title *transfer taxes* must be paid. Such taxes must be paid whenever titles to assets are transferred. Moreover, a lender's consent may be required if the assets to be sold are being used as collateral for loans.

Disadvantages: Seller's Perspective

Taxes also may be a problem because the seller may be subject to double taxation. If the tax basis in the assets or stock is low, the seller may experience a sizable gain on the sale. In addition, if the corporation subsequently is liquidated, the seller may be responsible for the recapture of taxes deferred as a result of the use of accelerated rather than straight-line depreciation. If the number of assets transferred is large, the amount of state transfer taxes may become onerous. Whether the seller or the buyer actually pays the transfer taxes or they are shared is negotiable.

PURCHASE OF STOCK

Advantages: Buyer's Perspective

All assets are transferred with the target's stock, resulting in less need for documentation to complete the transaction. This sometimes enables the transaction to be completed more rapidly than a purchase of assets. State asset transfer taxes may be avoided with a purchase of shares. Net operating losses and tax credits pass to the buyer with the purchase of stock. The right of the buyer to use the target's name, licenses, franchises, patents, and permits also is preserved. Furthermore, the purchase of the seller's stock provides for the continuity of contracts and corporate identity. This obviates the need to renegotiate contracts and enables the acquirer to utilize the brand recognition that may be associated with the name of the target firm. However, some customer and vendor contracts, as well as permits, may stipulate that the buyer must gain their consent before the contract is transferred.

Advantages: Seller's Perspective

The seller is able to defer paying taxes. If stock is received from the acquiring company, taxes are paid by the target's shareholders only when the stock is sold. All obligations, disclosed or otherwise, transfer to the buyer. This advantage for the seller usually is attenuated by the insistence by the buyer that the seller indemnify the buyer from damages resulting from any undisclosed liability. The applicable tax is the more favorable capital gains rate. Finally, the seller is not left with the problem of disposing of assets that the seller does not wish to retain but that were not purchased by the acquiring company.

Disadvantages: Buyer's Perspective

The buyer is liable for all unknown, undisclosed, or contingent liabilities. The seller's tax basis is carried over to the buyer at historical cost, unless the seller consents to take certain tax code elections. These elections potentially can create a tax liability for the seller and, therefore, they rarely are used. Consequently, there is no step-up in the cost basis of assets and no tax shelter is created. Dissenting shareholders have the right to have their shares appraised, with the option of being paid the appraised value of their shares or remaining as minority shareholders. The purchase of stock does not terminate existing union agreements or employee benefit plans.

Disadvantages: Seller's Perspective

The seller cannot pick and choose the assets to be retained and loses all net operating losses and tax credits.

MERGERS

With a merger, two corporations are combined and one disappears. Mergers require approval from the target's board of directors and shareholders and a public filing with the state in which the merger is to be consummated. The purchase price can consist of cash, stock, or debt, giving the acquiring company more latitude in how it will pay for the purchase of the target's stock.

Advantages

The primary advantage is that the transfer of assets and the exchange of stock between the acquirer and the target happen automatically by "rule of law." (Rule of law refers to the accumulation of applicable federal and state laws and legal precedents established as a result of numerous court cases that establish when and how ownership is transferred.) Target company shareholders cannot retain their stock; however, as with the purchase of stock, dissenting shareholders have the right to have their shares appraised and to be paid the appraised value rather than what is being offered by the acquiring firm. Transfer taxes are not paid because there are no asset transfer documents. However, contracts, licenses, patents, and permits do not automatically transfer. This transfer can be accomplished by merging a subsidiary set up by the buyer with the target. The subsidiary can be merged with the parent immediately following closing.

Disadvantages

Mergers of public corporations can be costly and time consuming because of the need to obtain shareholder approval and to conform to proxy regulations (see Chapter 3). The resulting delay can open the door to other bidders, create an auction environment, and boost the final purchase price.

Statutory Mergers

Among the most common forms of acquisition, statutory mergers are governed by the statutory provisions of the state or states in which the parties to be merged are chartered. State statutes typically address considerations such as the percentage of the total voting stock that is required for approval of the transaction, who is entitled to vote, how the votes are counted, and the rights of the dissenting voters. The Delaware statute is typical of state merger statutes. According to this statute, the boards of both companies must first approve the transaction. It subsequently is submitted for ratification to the shareholders of each corporation, which must be approved by a majority of those holding stock with voting rights. Once the appropriate documents are filed with the states in which the buyer and seller are incorporated, the merger becomes legal. One corporation survives, whereas the other goes out of existence. The surviving corporation assumes the other corporation's assets, contract rights, and all disclosed and undisclosed liabilities, unless otherwise specified in the merger agreement.

Alternatives to Mergers

Stock-for-Stock Purchase

As an alternative to a merger or immediate combination of the acquiring and target firms into a single legal entity, the acquiring company exchanges its voting stock for the stock of the target company, and the target company then is managed as a wholly owned subsidiary of the acquirer. The acquirer may choose to merge the subsidiary into the parent at a later date. This is likely to be a nontaxable event for target shareholders. The motivation for a subsidiary structure is explained in more detail under the discussion of "staged transactions." The major disadvantage of a subsidiary structure is the postponement of any significant effort to integrate rigorously the acquired company into the acquirer's operations to realize the benefits of synergy. The use of voting stock may also seriously erode or dilute the ownership position of acquiring company shareholders.

Stock for Assets

The acquiring company exchanges its voting stock for all or substantially all of the target's assets. Although generally tax-free for the target shareholders, this transaction may become taxable if the target is forced to liquidate. The use of voting stock may reduce the ownership position of the acquirer's shareholders.

Staged Transactions

There are a number of motivations for a staged or multistep transaction. Staged transactions may be used to structure an earnout, to enable the target to complete the development of a technology or process, to await regulatory approval, to eliminate the need to obtain shareholder approval, and to minimize cultural conflicts with the target.

Supporting an Earnout Structure

As part of an earnout agreement, the acquirer may agree to allow the target to operate as a wholly owned but largely autonomous unit until the earnout period expires. This suggests that there will be little attempt to integrate facilities, overhead operations, and distribution systems during the earnout period.

Enable Completion of a Technology or Process

The value of the target may be greatly dependent on the target developing a key technology or production process, receiving approval from a regulatory authority such as the Federal Communications Commission (FCC), or signing a multiyear customer or vendor contract. The target's ability to realize these objectives may be enhanced if it is aligned with a larger company or receives a cash infusion to fund the required research. A potential acquirer may assume a minority investment in the target with an option to acquire the company at a later date. Similarly, the potential acquirer may provide support to the target via a strategic alliance or licensing arrangement, which provides funding for the target, potential revenues for the acquirer, and an opportunity to merge at a later time.

Awaiting Regulatory Approval

The target also may have reason to wait for certain events to occur before proceeding with a transaction. If the long-term value of the acquirer's stock offered to the target is dependent on the acquirer receiving approval from a regulatory agency, developing a new technology, or landing a key contract, the target may be well advised to wait. The two parties may enter into a letter of intent, with the option to exit the agreement without any liability to either party if certain key events are not realized within a stipulated time.

Eliminate Need for Shareholder Vote

Another motivation for staged transactions may be a desire to eliminate the need for a shareholder vote. This may be accomplished through a triangular merger in which the acquiring firm uses a relatively small percentage of its voting stock to purchase the target firm. The acquiring company may create a special merger subsidiary. The subsidiary subsequently is funded by the consideration to be used in the merger and the subsidiary and the target company merge. Because the acquirer is the sole shareholder in the operating subsidiary, the only approval required may be the board of directors of the subsidiary. This board may be essentially the same as that of the parent or acquiring company. However, this tactic may not work for stocks traded on some exchanges that still may require a shareholder vote under certain conditions.

Minimize Cultural Conflicts

Companies that acquire a foreign firm may choose to initially manage the acquired company as a subsidiary because of substantial cultural differences. Daimler-Benz managed Chrysler Corporation as a wholly owned subsidiary, even maintaining separately traded stocks, before merging the two corporations more than 1 year after closing.

TAX STRUCTURES AND STRATEGIES

Taxes are an important consideration in almost any transaction. However, taxes are seldom the primary motivation for an acquisition. The fundamental economics of the transaction always should be the deciding factor. Tax benefits accruing to the buyer should simply reinforce a purchase decision. Transactions may be non-taxable or entirely or partially taxable. These alternative structures are discussed in detail next. For a comprehensive discussion of these issues, see Scholes and Wolfson (1992) and Tillinghast (1998).

TAXABLE TRANSACTIONS

A transaction generally will be considered taxable if it involves the purchase of the target's stock or assets for cash, notes, or some other nonequity consideration. If the acquirer's stock is used, it is generally nontaxable.

Taxable Purchase of Assets

If a transaction involves a purchase of assets, the target company's tax cost or basis in the acquired stock or assets is increased or "stepped up" to their fair market value (FMV), which is equal to the purchase price paid by the acquirer. The resulting additional depreciation and amortization reduces the tax liability of the combined companies. To compensate the target company shareholders for any tax liability they may incur, the buyer usually will have to increase the purchase price. Buyers are willing to do this only if the present value of the tax savings resulting from the step-up of the target's assets is greater than the increase in the purchase price required to compensate the target's shareholders for the increase in their tax liability.

There is little empirical evidence that the tax shelter resulting from the ability of the acquiring firm to increase the value of acquired assets to their FMV is a highly important motivating factor for a takeover (Auerbach and Reishus, 1988, pp. 69–88). Nonetheless, tax considerations do provide some value to the acquiring company and are considered in undertaking transactions. Auerbach and Reishus found the gain from tax benefits averaged about 10.5% of the acquiring firm's FMV for a sample of 318 mergers and acquisitions (M&A) between 1968 and 1983. Most of the firms in the sample were in manufacturing and were substantially larger than the target companies (Auerbach and Reishus, 1988, pp. 300–313). Taxable transactions have been made somewhat more attractive since 1993, when a change in the legislation allowed acquirers to amortize intangible assets, including goodwill, over 15 years for tax purposes.

Taxable Purchase of Stock

Taxable transactions usually involve the purchase of stock because the purchase of assets automatically will trigger a taxable gain for the target if the FMV of the acquired assets exceeds the firm's tax basis in the assets. All stockholders are affected equally in a taxable purchase of assets because the target is paying the taxes. In contrast, in a taxable stock purchase, the affect of the potential tax liability will vary depending on the individual shareholder's tax basis in the stock. If the transaction involves a purchase of stock, the assets will not be automatically stepped up to FMV unless the acquirer adopts a special election. This is found in Section 338 of the U.S. tax code.

Section 338 Election

According to Section 338 of the U.S. tax code, a purchaser of 80% or more of the stock of the target may elect to treat the acquisition as if it were an acquisition of the target's assets. This enables the acquiring corporation to avoid having to transfer assets and obtain consents to assignment of all contracts, while still benefiting from the write-up of assets, assuming the FMV exceeds the book value of the acquired assets.

TAX-FREE TRANSACTIONS

As a general rule, a transaction is taxable if the target company's shareholders receive something other than the acquirer's stock and it is nontaxable if they receive the acquirer's stock. Transactions may be partially taxable if the target shareholders receive some nonequity consideration, such as cash or debt, in addition to the acquirer's stock. This nonequity consideration or **_boot_** is taxable either as a dividend, if all shareholders receive it pro rata, and taxed as ordinary income or as a capital gain to the extent it does not exceed the shareholder's overall gain as a result of the transaction. If the transaction is tax-free, the acquiring company is able to transfer or carry over the target's tax basis to its own financial statements. In the tax-free transaction, there is no increase or step-up in assets to FMV.

Continuity of Interests Requirement

Under the law, tax-free transactions contemplate substantial continuing involvement of the target company's shareholders. This continued involvement is intended to demonstrate a long-term or strategic commitment on the part of the acquiring company to the target. Nontaxable transactions usually involve mergers, with the acquirer's stock exchanged for the target's stock or assets. Nontaxable transactions also are called *tax-free reorganizations*.

Avoiding the Loss of Tax-Free Status

Tax-free reorganizations generally require that all or substantially all of the target company's assets or shares be acquired. The divestiture of a significant portion of the acquired company immediately following closing could jeopardize the tax-free status of the transaction. Such an action would run counter to the Internal Revenue Service's (IRS) notion that the acquirer is making a long-term strategic commitment to the entire business for the transaction to be tax-free. The loss of tax-free status can be avoided by spinning off the unwanted business to the target's shareholders in a tax-free exchange. The target then is merged into a subsidiary of the acquirer in a tax-free statutory merger. See Table 10-4 for a comparison of taxable and tax-free transactions.

Tax-free reorganizations also require that substantially all of the consideration received by the target's shareholders be paid in common or preferred stock. However, if the preferred stock is redeemable or has a dividend that is indexed to interest rates, the IRS could disallow the tax-free status. In this instance, the preferred stock will be viewed as debt rather than equity.

Alternative Tax-Free Reorganizations

The eight principal forms of tax-free reorganizations are described in Section 368 of the Internal Revenue Code. Three are excluded from our discussion. These include Type D, transfers between related corporations; Type E, the restructuring of a firm's capital structure; and Type F, a reorganization in which the firm's name or location is changed. What follows is a discussion of the Type A statutory merger, Type B stock-for-stock merger, and Type C stock-for-assets merger and the forward and reverse triangular subsidiary mergers in which the acquiring company creates a shell subsidiary as an intermediary to complete the transaction. Type A and B are the most common tax-free reorganizations for mergers in which a combination of stock, cash, or debt is used to acquire the target's stock or assets. Forward and reverse triangular mergers are used primarily when the acquirer stock is the predominate form of payment used to purchase the target's stock or assets.

TABLE 10-4   Key Characteristics of Taxable versus Tax-Free Transactions

Taxable Transactions[1]	Tax-Free Transactions[2]
Purchase of target stock or assets with cash, notes, or other nonequity consideration	Exchange of the acquirer's stock for the target's stock or assets
Purchase of assets for cash, notes, or other nonequity consideration	Exchange of the acquirer's stock for substantially all of the target's assets.
Acquiring Firm: 1. Stepped up basis for acquired assets 2. Loss of NOLs and tax credits	Acquiring Firm: 1. NOL carryover 2. Tax credit carryover
Target Firm: 1. Immediate recognition of gain by target shareholders 2. Recapture of tax credits and excess depreciation	Target Firm: 1. Deferred taxable gains for shareholders

[1]Taxable transactions are those in which the target shareholders have little continuing equity participation in the acquired firm.

[2]Tax-free transactions are those in which the target shareholders have a continuing direct or indirect interest in the acquired firm, enabling deferral by target shareholders of any gain.

The IRS views reorganizations as a continuation of interest in the original corporation in a reorganized form rather than as true sales. Thus, IRS requires that target shareholders must continue to hold a substantial equity interest in the acquiring company. The tax code defines what constitutes a substantial equity interest, and the definition varies with the type of tax-free reorganization used. Reorganizations under the tax code may be wholly (all stock) or partially tax-free (stock and other nonequity consideration). See Table 10-5 for a comparison of alternative tax-free structures.

Type A Reorganization

Type A reorganizations are statutory mergers or consolidations governed by state law. To qualify for a Type A reorganization, the transaction must be either a merger or a consolidation. There are no limitations on the type of consideration involved. Target company shareholders may receive cash, voting or nonvoting common or preferred stock, notes, or real property. The acquirer may choose not to purchase all of the target's assets. At least 50% of the purchase price must be in the stock of the acquiring company to ensure that the IRS's continuity of interests requirement is satisfied.

For target company shareholders receiving acquiring company shares, no taxable gain or loss is recognized at the time of the transaction, and the basis in the target shares carries over to the shares received from the acquiring company. Any taxable gain is deferred until the acquiring firm's shares are sold. At that time, the taxable gain is equal to the difference between the value of the acquirer's shares received at the time of the transaction less the target shareholder's original basis in the target's stock. This gain is taxed at the capital-gains rate. Nonequity remuneration received by target shareholders is taxed as ordinary income. This transaction is viewed as tax-free because the stockholders of the target firm retain title to the assets because they own shares of the acquiring firm.

Type A reorganizations are used widely because of their great flexibility. Because there is no requirement to use voting stock, acquiring firms enjoy more options. By issuing nonvoting stock, the acquiring corporation may acquire control over the target without diluting control over the combined or newly created company. Moreover, there is no stipulation as to the amount of target assets that must be acquired. Finally, there is no maximum amount of cash that may be used in the purchase price, and the limitations articulated by both the IRS and the courts allow significantly more cash than Types B or C reorganizations. Flexibility with respect to the amount of cash being used may be the most important consideration because it enables the acquirer to better satisfy the disparate requirements of the target's shareholders. Some will want cash, and some will want stock. The acquirer must be careful that not too large a proportion of the purchase price be composed of cash because this might not meet the IRS's requirement for continuity of interests of the target shareholders and disqualify the transaction as a Type A reorganization.

The acquirer normally requests an ***advance ruling*** from the IRS to ensure that they are not violating the continuity-of-interests requirement. The IRS takes the position on advance rulings that the continuity-of-interests requirement is satisfied if at least 50% of the total consideration consists of the acquirer's stock.

Type B Stock-for-Stock Reorganizations

The acquisition must be consummated using only the acquirer's voting stock for at least 80% of voting stock of the target company and at least 80% of the target's nonvoting shares. Any cash or debt will disqualify the transaction as a Type B reorganization. However, cash may be used to purchase fractional shares. Type B reorganizations are used as an alternative to a merger or consolidation. Following the merger, the target may be liquidated into the acquiring company or maintained as an independent operating subsidiary. The transaction also may be phased over a certain period. The target's stock may be purchased over 12 months or less as part of a formal acquisition plan. Only stock may be used to acquire the target, although the acquirer may have used cash to purchase some portion of the target's stock in the past as long as it was not part of the acquisition plan. Type B reorganizations may be appropriate if the acquiring company wishes to conserve cash or its borrowing capacity.

Type C Reorganization

A Type C reorganization is a stock-for-assets reorganization with the requirement that at least 80% of the FMV of the target's assets, as well as the assumption of certain specified liabilities, are acquired solely in exchange for voting stock. Cash may be used to purchase the remainder of the stock only if the assumed liabilities amount to less than 20% of the FMV of the acquired assets. As part of the plan of reorganization, the target subsequent to closing dissolves and distributes the acquirer's stock to the target's shareholders for the now-canceled target stock. The Type C reorganization is used when it is essential for the acquirer not to assume any undisclosed liabilities. It is technically more difficult than a merger because all of the acquired assets must be conveyed. In a merger, all assets (and liabilities) pass by operation of law. The requirement to use only voting stock is also a major deterrent to the use of this type of reorganization.

Forward Triangular Merger

A forward triangular merger is the most commonly used form of reorganization for tax-free asset acquisitions in which the form of payment is acquirer stock. It involves three parties: the acquiring firm, the target firm, and a shell subsidiary of the acquiring firm (Figure 10-2). The parent funds the shell corporation by buying stock issued by the shell with its own stock. All of the target's stock is acquired by the subsidiary with the stock of the parent, and the target's stock is canceled. The target company's assets and liabilities are merged into the acquirer's subsidiary in a statutory merger. The parent's stock may be voting or nonvoting, and the acquirer must purchase substantially all of the target's assets and liabilities. Substantially all is defined as 70% of fair market value of the target's gross assets and 90% of the fair market value of the target's net assets. The transaction qualifies as a Type A tax-free reorganization. The parent indirectly owns all of the target's assets and liabilities because it owns all of the subsidiary's voting stock.

The advantages of the forward triangular merger may include the avoidance of approval by the parent firm's shareholders. However, public exchanges on which the parent firm's stock trades still may require parent shareholder approval if the amount of the parent stock used to acquire the target exceeds some predetermined percentage of parent voting shares outstanding. Other advantages include the

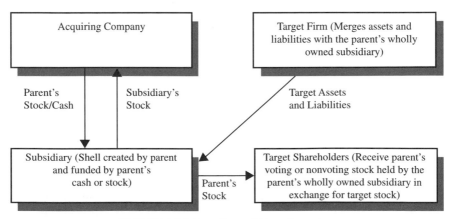

FIGURE 10-2.   Forward triangular merger.

possible insulation of the parent from the target's liabilities, which remain in the subsidiary, and the avoidance of asset recording fees and transfer taxes because the target's assets go directly to the parent's wholly owned subsidiary.

Reverse Triangular Merger

The reverse triangular merger most commonly is used to effect tax-free stock acquisitions in which the form of payment is predominately the acquirer's voting stock (Figure 10-3). The acquirer forms a new shell subsidiary, which is merged into the target in a statutory merger. The target is the surviving entity and must hold substantially all of the assets and liabilities of both the target and shell subsidiary. The target firm's shares are canceled. The target shareholders receive the acquirer's or parent's shares. Because all subsidiary stock may not have been exchanged from target stock, any remaining subsidiary stock is exchanged for new target firm stock. The parent, which owned all of the subsidiary stock, now owns all of the new target stock and indirectly all of the target's assets and liabilities. Target shareholders must exchange at least 80% of their stock for the parent's voting stock. This transaction qualifies as a Type B tax-free reorganization.

Although the reverse triangular merger is similar to a Type B reorganization in which the acquiring company purchases the target's stock in exchange for its stock, it permits the acquirer to use up to 20% cash. This could not be done in a pure Type B reorganization. The reverse merger also may avoid the need for parent company shareholder approval. Because the target firm remains in existence, the target can retain any nonassignable franchise, lease, or other valuable contract rights. Moreover, by avoiding the dissolution of the target firm, the acquirer avoids the possible acceleration of loans outstanding. Finally, insurance, banking, and public utility regulators may require the target to remain in existence in exchange for their granting regulatory approval.

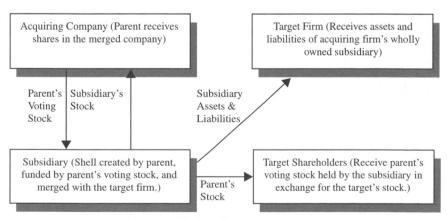

FIGURE 10-3.   Reverse triangular merger.

TABLE 10-5 Summary of Alternative Tax-Free Structures

Type of Reorganization	Maximum Cash Payment Requirement	Requirement to Purchase Substantially All the Assets	Type of Stock	Commonly Used When
A	50% under advance ruling from IRS	No	Voting or nonvoting	Substantial portion of purchase price is cash
B	0% for advance ruling	No	Voting only	Acquirer wants to limit use of cash or leverage
C	20% reduced by any target liabilities assumed by acquirer	Yes	Voting only	Acquirer wants to avoid undisclosed and contingent liabilities
Forward Triangular Merger	Same as Type A	Yes	Voting or nonvoting	Tax-free asset acquisitions
Reverse Triangular Merger	20%	Yes	Voting only	Tax-free stock acquisitions

Table 10-5 summarizes the five primary types of tax-free reorganizations in terms of their key characteristics and the conditions under which they are commonly used. Table 10-6 indicates the types of M&A legal structures that are consistent with certain tax-free reorganizations.

TAX REFORM ACT OF 1986

Many aspects of the 1986 Tax Reform Act affected corporate restructuring activities. The most significant areas included the treatment of net operating losses, corporate capital gain taxes, the introduction of the alternative corporate minimum tax, and the treatment of greenmail for tax purposes.

Net Operating Loss Carry Forwards

The Tax Reform Act introduced an annual limit on the use of net operating loss (NOL) carry forwards. The limit takes effect if there is a greater than 50% change in ownership in a corporation generating cumulative losses during the 3 years preceding the change in ownership. Such corporations are referred to as *loss corporation*s. The maximum amount of the NOL that can be used annually to offset earnings is limited to the value of the "loss corporation" on the date of the acquisition multiplied by the long-term tax-exempt bond rate. Furthermore, "loss corporations" cannot use a net operating loss carry forward unless they remain

TABLE 10-6　Relating Common M&A Legal Structures to Tax Free Reorganizations

Common Tax Free Reorganizations → Common M&A Legal Structures ↓	Type A	Type B	Type C
Statutory Merger[1]	X		
Consolidation[2]	X		
Stock-for-Stock Exchange[3]		X	
Stock for Assets Exchange[4]			X
Forward Triangular Merger[5]	X		
Reverse Triangular Merger[6]		X	

[1] Target shareholders exchange stock for acquirer's shares.

[2] Both target and acquirer's shareholders exchange their stock for stock in the newly created company.

[3] Target is either liquidated or maintained as a subsidiary of the acquiring firm.

[4] Target firm sells at least 80% of fair market value of its assets to acquirer and dissolves and distributes acquirer stock for target stock. The target stock then is cancelled.

[5] Parent creates a shell subsidiary that issues stock purchased by the parent with cash or its own stock. The target is acquired with cash or parent stock held by the subsidiary and merged with the subsidiary.

[6] Parent's subsidiary merged into target. Parent's stock held by the subsidiary is distributed by target shareholders in exchange for their target stock.

viable and in essentially the same business for at least 2 years following the closing of the acquisition.

Corporate Capital Gains Taxes

Before the 1986 act, corporate capital gains had been taxed at 28%. Effective July 1, 1987, both short-term and long-term corporate capital gains are taxed as ordinary income and are subject to a maximum corporate tax rate of 34%. This change in the law has increased the popularity of alternative legal structures having more favorable tax attributes, such as LLCs, master limited partnerships (MLP), and Sub-chapter S corporations. Profits distributed directly to MLP partners or to Sub-chapter S and LLC shareholders are taxed at their personal tax rates.

Alternative Corporate Minimum Tax

Before 1986, corporations paid a minimum tax on specific tax preference items that was added to its normal statutory tax rate. With the 1986 Tax Reform Act, this minimum tax was replaced by an alternative minimum flat rate tax of 20%. The introduction of the alternative minimum tax has proved to be particularly burdensome for leveraged buyouts (LBOs), which are by intent highly leveraged and have little if any taxable income because of their high annual interest expense. Consequently, the imposition of the alternative minimum tax reduced the potential returns to equity investors that could be achieved as a result of highly leveraged transactions.

Greenmail Payments

Greenmail refers to payments made to "corporate raiders" to buy back positions they had taken in target companies (see Chapter 3). Greenmail was made more expensive for corporations to pay as a result of the 1986 act, which sharply reduced the amount of such payments that could be deducted from before-tax profits.

NET OPERATING LOSSES

NOL carry forwards are provisions in the tax laws allowing firms to use NOLs generated in the past to offset future taxable income. Although the 1986 Tax Reform Act reduced the attractiveness of NOLs to acquirers, they still represent a potentially significant source of value to acquirers that should be considered during the process of valuing an acquisition target. Exhibit 10-3 illustrates how the analyst might value NOLs on the books of a target corporation.

EXHIBIT 10-3. VALUING NET OPERATING LOSSES

Acquiring Company is contemplating buying Target Company, which has a tax loss carry forward of $8000. Acquiring Company has a 40% tax rate. Assume the tax-loss carry forward is within the limits of the Tax Reform Act of 1986 and that the firm's cost of capital is 15%. The following information is given for the two firms:

Years Remaining in Loss Carry Forward	Amount ($)	Years After Acquisition	Earnings Before Tax ($)
1	2000	1	1800
2	2000	2	2000
3	800	3	1000
4	1200	4	1000
5	800	5	2000
Total	6800	Total	7800

Calculate Acquiring Company's tax payments without the acquisition.

Years	Tax Benefit
1	720
2	800
3	400
4	400
5	800

Calculate Acquiring Company's tax payment for each year with the proposed acquisition.

Years	Earnings Before Taxes ($)	Tax Loss ($)	Amount Carried Forward ($)	Use of Tax Loss ($)	Taxable Income ($)	Tax Payment ($)
1	1800	2000		1800	0	0
2	2000	2000	200	2000	0	0
3	1000	800	0	1000	0	0
4	1000	1200	200	1000	0	0
5	2000	800	0	1000	1000	400

What is the most the Acquiring company should pay for the Target Company if its only value is its tax loss?

Answer: The Acquiring Company should not pay more than the present value of the net tax benefit: $720, $800, $400, $400, and $400. The present value of the cumulative tax benefits discounted at a 15% cost of capital is $1921.58.

1. Tax benefits are equal to earnings before tax times the 40% marginal tax rate of the Acquiring Company. Therefore, the tax benefit in year 1 is $1800 × .4 = $720.2. The net tax benefit in the fifth year is equal to the $800 tax benefit less the $400 in tax payments required in the fifth year.

Although NOLs represent a potential source of value, their use must be monitored carefully to realize the full value resulting from the potential for deferring income taxes. An acquirer must be highly confident that expected future pretax income stream would be realized. Without the future income, the NOLs will expire worthless. Because the acquirer can never be certain that future income will be sufficient to fully realize the value of the NOLs, loss carry forwards alone rarely justify an acquisition. Studies show that it is easy to overstate the value of loss carry forwards because of the potential for them to expire before they can be fully used. Empirical analyses indicate that the actual tax savings realized from loss carry forwards tend to be about one-half of their expected value (Auerbach and Poterba, 1987).

FINANCIAL REPORTING OF BUSINESS COMBINATIONS

Historically, the two principal forms of accounting for financial reporting purposes for M&As were purchase accounting and the pooling of interests. In **purchase accounting** the excess of the purchase price paid over the book value of the target firm's equity is assigned first to depreciable assets, with the remainder going to goodwill. A *pooling of interests* was defined for financial reporting purposes as the representation of two formerly independent shareholder groups as a single group. Under a pooling of interests, the assets and liabilities of both companies were added together. To qualify for a pooling of interests, the transaction must satisfy 12 conditions, which defined the characteristics of the companies to be combined and the way in which they had to be combined and required an absence of any planned transactions. Any transaction that could not qualify as a pooling of interests had to be accounted for using the purchase method. For an excellent discussion of M&A accounting issues relating to the two forms of accounting treatment, see Pahler and Mori (1997).

Effective December 15, 2001, new accounting rules promulgated by the Financial Accounting Standards Board, an independent organization funded entirely by the private sector whose mission is to set accounting and reporting standards to protect users of financial information, changed the guidelines covering business combinations and the treatment of goodwill. All M&As had to be accounted for using the purchase method. Goodwill, the difference between the price of an acquisition and the "fair value" of the acquired firm's net assets, would have to be written off if it was found to be impaired. Firms must review annually all goodwill for impairment. This means that firms whose balance sheet value of the acquired assets far exceeds the fair market value of such assets may be required to write-off the entire value of goodwill. This constitutes a public admission by the firm's management of having substantially overpaid for the acquired assets.

While the write-off of a book asset like goodwill could have a substantial impact on current reported earnings, it would not have any impact on the firm's cash flow. Unlike prior accounting practices, goodwill no longer has to be amortized for financial reporting purposes. Therefore, the use of purchase accounting does not affect reported earnings, unless existing goodwill is determined to have been impaired.

PURCHASE ACCOUNTING

With purchase accounting, analysts and investors gain significant insight into the premium paid for a company because the purchase price is allocated to tangible assets and certain intangible assets such as customer lists, patents, franchises, and licenses. The balance then is entered as goodwill. All liabilities are transferred at the net present value of their future cash payments. Therefore, the difference in the shareholders' equity of the acquiring company before the transaction and the shareholders' equity of the combined companies immediately following the closing date equal the purchase price of the target company. Under purchase accounting, the cost of the acquired entity becomes the new basis for recording the acquirer's investment in the target's assets. If part of the purchase price consists of something other than cash, the cost of the assets is determined using either the fair market value of the assets acquired or the fair market value of the noncash component of the purchase price plus the cash portion of the purchase price.

Balance Sheet Considerations

For financial reporting purposes, the purchase price (PP) paid for the target company consists of three components: the book value of equity (BVE) of the target company, goodwill (GW), and the portion of the PP allocated to revalued acquired assets (RVA). The excess of the PP paid over the BVE of the target company is assigned to either acquired tangible or intangible assets up to their fair market value or to GW. Thus, RVA equals the difference between the FMV and the book value of the acquired assets (BVA). RVA can be either positive (i.e., FMV > BVA) or negative (i.e., FMV < BVA).

These relationships can be summarized as follows:

1. Distribution of purchase price: $PP = BVE + GW + RVA$
2. Excess of purchase price over book value of equity: $PP - BVE = GW + RVA$
3. Calculation of goodwill: $GW = PP - (BVE + RVA)$

From (2), it should be noted that as RVA increases, GW decreases. Also note that from (3) the calculation of goodwill can result in either a positive (i.e., $PP > (BVE + RVA)$), or negative (i.e., $PP < (BVE + RVA)$) number. Negative GW arises if the acquired assets are purchased at a discount to their FMV.

Under purchase accounting, the shareholders' equity accounts of the acquired company are eliminated to reflect the change in ownership. The total common stock account is calculated as the total number of shares multiplied by the par value per share. The total amount paid (total debit) less any additional credit to the common stock account is a balancing item credited to the paid-in capital account. The consolidated firm's retained earnings is the amount of retained earnings of the acquiring firm only. The specific methodology for valuing each major balance sheet category is discussed in Exhibit 10-4.

EXHIBIT 10-4. VALUATION METHODOLOGY FOR PURCHASE ACCOUNTING

1. Cash and accounts receivable, reduced for bad debt and returns, are valued at their values on the books of the target before the acquisition.
2. Marketable securities are valued at their realizable value after any transaction costs.
3. Inventories are broken down into finished goods and raw materials. Finished goods are valued at their liquidation value; raw material inventories are valued at their current replacement cost. Last-in, first-out inventory reserves maintained by the target before the acquisition are eliminated.

4. Property, plant, and equipment are valued at FMV.
5. Accounts payable and accrued expenses are valued at the levels stated on the target's books before the acquisition.
6. Notes payable and long-term debt are valued at their net present value of the future cash payments discounted at the current market rate of interest for similar securities.
7. Pension fund obligations are booked at the excess or deficiency of the present value of the projected benefit obligations over the present value of pension fund assets. This may result in an asset or liability being recorded by the consolidated firms.
8. All other liabilities are recorded at their net present value of future cash payments.
9. Intangible assets are booked at their appraised values.
10. Goodwill is the difference between the acquisition purchase price less the book value of the target's equity and revalued acquired tangible and intangible assets. Positive goodwill is recorded as an asset, whereas negative goodwill is allocated to all long-lived acquired assets other than marketable securities.

Many assets are not specifically identified on the firm's balance sheet. These intangible assets can be classified into three categories: operational intangibles, production or product intangibles, and marketing intangibles (Table 10-7). Operational intangibles have been defined as the ability of a business to continue to function and generate income without interruption because of a change in ownership. Production or product intangibles are values placed on the accumulated intellectual capital resulting from the production and product design experience of the combined entity. This experience gives the combined firm an ability to create a product or service that has a competitive advantage to other similar products or services. Marketing intangibles are those factors that help a firm to sell a product or service. For tax and financial reporting purposes, goodwill is a residual item equal to the difference between the purchase price for the target company and the FMV of tangible and intangible assets, including operational, production, and marketing intangible assets. In most cases, intangible assets, like tangible assets, have separately determinable values with limited useful lives. In certain cases, the useful lives are defined by the legal protection afforded by the agency issuing the protection, such as the U.S. Patent Office. In contrast, the useful life of such intangible assets as customer lists is more difficult to define. Examples of how some of these intangible items could be valued are described in the following sections. The concepts and methodologies discussed previously may be applied to many of the different types of intangible assets. Exhibit 10-5 illustrates the calculation of goodwill by allocating purchase price to both intangible and tangible assets.

TABLE 10-7   Intangible Asset Categories

Intangible Asset Categories	Examples
Operating Intangibles	Assembled and trained workforce Operating and administrative systems Corporate culture
Production or Product Intangibles	Patents Technological know-how Production standards Copyrights Software Favorable leases and licenses

Marketing Intangibles	Customer lists and relationships
	Price lists and pricing strategies
	Marketing strategies, studies,
	   and concepts
	Advertising and promotional
	   materials
	Trademarks and service marks
	Trade names
	Covenants not to compete
	Franchises

EXHIBIT 10-5. GOODWILL ESTIMATION

Assume that Acquiring Company pays $26 million for all of the outstanding stock in Target Company, whose book value of equity is $1.68 million. The portion of the purchase price allocated to Target Company's tangible assets is $9 million and to intangible assets is $5.32 million. Calculate the value of goodwill that must be shown on the balance sheet of the combined companies. (Hint: $GW = PP - (BE + RVA) = PP - BVE - RVA$).

Purchase Price	$26.00
Less: 100% interest in Target Company (book value of equity)	1.68
Equals: Purchase price over book value	$24.32

Less: Portion of purchase price allocated to tangible
   assets (e.g., receivables, inventory, and plant
   and equipment), i.e., revalued tangible assets
	9.00

Less: Portion of purchase price allocated to intangible
   assets (e.g., customer list, distributor contracts,
   copyrights, capitalized software, patents, and
   assembled workforce), i.e., revalued intangible assets
	5.32

Equals: Goodwill	$10.00

INCOME STATEMENT CONSIDERATIONS

For financial reporting purposes, an upward valuation of tangible and intangible assets, other than goodwill, raises depreciation and amortization expenses, which lowers operating and net income. For tax purposes, goodwill created after July 1993 may be amortized up to 15 years and is tax deductible. Goodwill booked before July 1993 is not tax deductible.

CASH-FLOW CONSIDERATIONS

Cash flow benefits from the tax deductibility of additional depreciation and amortization expenses that are written off over the useful lives of the assets. This assumes that the acquirer paid more than the net book value of the target's assets. Cash flow also benefits from the tax shelter effects of the amortization of goodwill created since 1993.

PURCHASE ACCOUNTING EXAMPLE

Exhibit 10-6 illustrates a simplified hypothetical purchase accounting transaction. See the notes to the exhibit for a detailed explanation. Recall that a debit is an entry on the left-hand side of an account constituting an addition to an expense or asset account or a deduction from revenue, a net worth, or a liability account. A credit is an entry on the right-hand side of an account constituting an addition to revenue, net worth, or a liability account and a deduction from an expense or asset account. Accounts payable and accrued expenses are included on the books of the acquirer at their values stated on the target's books before the acquisition; notes payable and long-term debt are valued at their net present value.

EXHIBIT 10-6. EXAMPLE OF PURCHASE ACCOUNTING ($000)

	Acquiring Firm	Target Firm	Adjustments		Consolidated
			Debit	Credit	
Current Assets	300	100			400
Land	200	100			300
Gross Plant and Equipment	500	200	1000	50	1650
Less: Depreciation	100	50		50	100
Net Plant and Equipment	400	150			1550
Goodwill			750		750
Total Assets	900	350			3000
Current Liabilities	200	60			260

(Continued)

	Acquiring Firm	Target Firm	Adjustments		Consolidated
			Debit	Credit	
Long-Term Debt	100	40			140
Total Liabilities	300	100			400
Common Stock	150	50	50	150	300
Paid-In-Surplus	250	150	150	1850	2100
Retained Earnings	200	50	50		200
Shareholders' Equity	600	250			2600
Total Liabilities + Shareholders' Equity	900	350	2050	2050	3000

ASSUMPTIONS AND ACCOUNTING PROCEDURE FOR EXHIBIT 10-6

Assumptions

1. The acquirer paid $50 per share for 40,000 target shares, or $2,000,000. This represents 100% of the target's shares.
2. The share exchange ratio is .75 shares of the acquirer's stock for each share of the target's stock.
3. The acquirer's shareholders' equity consists of 30,000 shares at a par value of $5 per share, or $150,000 in common stock. Paid-in-surplus and retained earnings are as shown. The acquirer issues another 30,000 shares at a par value of $5 per share to purchase the target. The composition of the target's shareholders' equity is as shown.
4. As a result of an appraisal of the target's assets, 57.14% percent of the excess of the purchase price over the target's shareholders' equity is allocated to plant and equipment, and the balance is allocated to goodwill.

Accounting Procedure

1. Calculate the excess of the purchase price over the target's shareholders' equity. The target's shareholders' equity is eliminated by subtracting the target's equity of $250,000 from the purchase price of $2,000,000. The difference of $1,750,000 is first allocated to fixed assets and then goodwill.
2. $1,000,000 (57.14%) of $1,750,000 is allocated (debited) to plant and equipment and the rest to goodwill in the "adjustments" column. Because the acquired assets are being revalued, the target's historical depreciation is eliminated with a debit and an offsetting credit of $50,000. Consolidated plant and equipment equals $500,000 + $200,000 + $1,000,000 − $50,000 = $1,650,000. The accumulated depreciation of $100,000 is the acquirer's depreciation. Therefore,

net plant and equipment is $1,550,000. Goodwill is debited by $750,000 (i.e., $2,000,000 − $250,000 − $1,000,000 = $750,000).

3. The target's equity accounts are eliminated by debiting the "adjustments" column by the amounts for the target's common stock, paid-in-surplus, and retained earnings.

4. Total debits are $2,050,000. A credit of $150,000 in the "adjustment's column" is made to common stock in an amount equal to the 30,000 new shares issued at a par value of $5. It is necessary to make an additional credit of $1,850,000 (i.e., $2.050,000 − $50 − $250) to paid-in surplus to ensure that the total debits and credits balance.

THINGS TO REMEMBER

The deal-structuring process addresses satisfying as many of the primary objectives of the parties involved and determining how risk will be shared. The process begins with addressing a set of key questions, whose answers help to define initial negotiating positions, potential risks, options for managing risk, levels of tolerance for risk, and conditions under which the buyer or seller will "walk away" from the negotiations. The deal-structuring process can be defined in terms of six major components. These components include the form of the acquisition vehicle, the postclosing organization, the form of payment, the form of acquisition, the legal form of the selling entity, and tax structure.

The form of the acquisition vehicle refers to the legal structure used to acquire the target. The postclosing organization is the legal framework used to manage the combined businesses following the consummation of the transaction. The post-closing organization may differ from the acquisition vehicle depending on the acquirer's strategic objectives for the combined firms. The form of payment or total consideration may consist of cash, common stock, debt, or some combination of all three. The form of acquisition reflects what is being acquired, the form of payment, and how the ownership of assets will be conveyed from the seller to the buyer. Finally, the form of acquisition drives the tax structure for the combined companies. Tax structure also is affected by the legal structure of the selling entity.

Commonly used structures for both the acquisition vehicle and the postclosing organization include the corporate, holding company, JV, partnership, LLC, and ESOP structures. The choice of the acquisition vehicle will depend largely on the strategic objectives of the acquiring company. The simplest form of payment is cash. The form of payment may be modified to reflect the requirements of the target's shareholders to include common and preferred equity, conventional and convertible debt, and nonequity considerations such as real estate. When buyers and sellers are unable to agree on price, different forms of payment such as earnouts, rights to intellectual property, license fees, employment agreements, and consulting contracts can be used to close the gap.

The form of acquisition describes the mechanism for conveying ownership of assets or stock and associated liabilities from the target to the acquiring firm. The most common forms of acquisition include asset purchases, stock purchases, statutory mergers, stock-for-stock purchases, and stock-for-assets purchases. For stock purchases, the primary advantages to the buyer include the preservation of tax benefits and certain rights to use items such as patents and licenses. However, the buyer is also responsible for all unknown and contingent liabilities. From the seller's perspective, the advantages include the deferral of taxes and favorable treatment afforded by capital gains taxes; however, the seller loses NOLs and tax credits, which pass to the buyer. For asset purchases, buyers benefit from additional tax shelter because of the write-up of assets to FMV, as well as protection from liabilities not assumed in the contract and, in general, undisclosed, unknown, and contingent liabilities. However, tax benefits and rights that would otherwise automatically transfer with the stock are lost. Sellers retain tax benefits and rights associated with the stock, but they may be subject to double taxation if forced to liquidate the remaining corporate assets.

The form of acquisition reflects what is being acquired and the form of payment. The form of acquisition drives the tax structure. Taxable transactions are those in which the target shareholders have little continuing equity participation in the acquired firm. Tax-free transactions are those in which the target shareholders have a continuing direct or indirect interest in the acquired firm, enabling deferral by target shareholders of any gain. Taxable transactions usually involve the purchase of stock or assets for cash, notes, or other nonequity consideration. Tax-free transactions entail the exchange of the acquirer's stock for the target stock or substantially all of the target's assets. The Type A tax-free reorganization is the most common form because there is no requirement to buy all of the target's assets and no restriction on the type of stock that may be used and because a substantial portion of the purchase price may be in cash.

For financial reporting purposes, all M&As must be accounted for using the purchase method. Under the purchase method of accounting, the excess of the purchase price over the target's book value of equity and revalued or restated values of acquired assets is treated as goodwill on the combined firm's balance sheet. If goodwill is found to be impaired, it must be written off. Although such a write-off does not affect cash flow, it does represent an admission by management that they had overpaid for certain previous acquisitions.

CHAPTER DISCUSSION QUESTIONS

10-1. Describe the deal-structuring process.

10-2. Provide two examples of how decisions made in one area of the deal-structuring process are likely to affect other areas.

10-3. What are some of the reasons acquirers may choose a particular form of acquisition vehicle?

10-4.   Describe techniques used to "close the gap" when buyers and sellers cannot agree on price.

10-5.   How does the purchase method of accounting affect the income statement, balance sheet, and cash-flow statements of the combined companies?

10-6.   What are the advantages and disadvantages of a purchase of assets from the perspective of the buyer and seller?

10-7.   What are the advantages and disadvantages of a purchase of stock from the perspective of the buyer and seller?

10-8.   What are the advantages and disadvantages of a statutory merger?

10-9.   What are the reasons some acquirers choose to undertake a staged or multistep takeover?

10-10. What are the primary conditions that must be satisfied for a transaction to be deemed nontaxable by the Internal Revenue Service?

CHAPTER BUSINESS CASE

CASE STUDY 10-1: CONSOLIDATION IN THE WIRELESS COMMUNICATIONS INDUSTRY— VODAFONE ACQUIRES AIRTOUCH

Deregulation of the telecommunications industry has resulted in increased consolidation. In Europe, rising competition is the catalyst driving mergers. In the United States, the break up of AT&T in the mid-1980s and the subsequent deregulation of the industry has led to key alliances, JVs, and mergers, which have created cellular powerhouses capable of providing nationwide coverage. Such coverage is being achieved by roaming agreements between carriers and acquisitions by other carriers. Although competition has been heightened as a result of deregulation, the telecommunications industry continues to be characterized by substantial barriers to entry. These include the requirement to obtain licenses and the need for an extensive network infrastructure. Wireless communications continue to grow largely at the expense of traditional landline services as cellular service pricing continues to decrease. Although the market is likely to continue to grow rapidly, success is expected to go to those with the financial muscle to satisfy increasingly sophisticated customer demands. What follows is a brief discussion of the motivations for the merger between Vodafone and AirTouch Communications. This discussion includes a chronology of events leading up to the merger and a description of the key elements of the deal structure that made the Vodafone offer more attractive than a competing offer from Bell Atlantic.

Vodafone

Company History

Vodafone is a wireless communications company based in the United Kingdom. The company is located in 13 countries in Europe, Africa, and Australia/New Zealand. Vodafone reaches more than 9.5 million subscribers. It has been the market leader in the United Kingdom since 1986 and as of 1998 had more than 5 million subscribers in the United Kingdom alone. The company has been very successful at marketing and selling prepaid services in Europe. In Europe, if a landline customer calls a mobile telephone, the landline party pays for the cellular phone call. This has made prepaid services enormously successful. Vodafone also is involved in a venture called Globalstar, LP, a limited partnership with Loral Space and Communications and Qualcomm, a phone manufacturer. "Globalstar will construct and operate a worldwide, satellite-based communications system offering global mobile voice, fax, and data communications in over 115 countries, covering over 85% of the world's population" (AirTouch Communications, 1997).

Strategic Intent

Vodafone's focus is on global expansion. They are expanding through partnerships and by purchasing licenses. Notably, Vodafone lacked a significant presence in the United States, the largest mobile phone market in the world. For Vodafone to be considered a truly global company, the firm needed a presence in the Unites States. Vodafone's success in the prepaid phone environment is leading to a further penetration of this type of billing option into other areas in which it competes. Vodafone's strategy is focused on maintaining high growth levels in its markets and increasing profitability; maintaining their current customer base; accelerating innovation; and increasing their global presence through acquisitions, partnerships, or purchases of new licenses. Vodafone's current strategy calls for it to merge with a company with substantial market share in the United States and Asia, which would fill several holes in Vodafone's current geographic coverage. Ideally, the target firm should have a low presence in Britain and Europe because Vodafone has this geography covered.

Company Structure

The company is very decentralized. The responsibilities of the corporate headquarters in the United Kingdom lie in developing corporate strategic direction, compiling financial information, reporting and developing relationships with the various stock markets, and evaluating new expansion opportunities. The management of operations is left to the countries' management, assuming business plans and financial measures are being met. They have a relatively flat management structure. All of their employees are shareowners in the company. They have very low levels of employee turnover, and the workforce averages 33 years of age.

AirTouch

Company History

AirTouch Communications launched it first cellular service network in 1984 in Los Angeles during the opening ceremonies at the 1984 Olympics. The original company was run under the name PacTel Cellular, a subsidiary of Pacific Telesis. In 1994, PacTel Cellular spun off from Pacific Telesis and became AirTouch Communications, under the direction of Chair and Chief Executive Officer Sam Ginn.

Ginn believed that the most exciting growth potential in telecommunications is in the wireless and not the landline services segment of the industry. In 1998, AirTouch operated in 13 countries on three continents, serving more than 12 million customers, as a worldwide carrier of cellular services, personal communication services (PCS), and paging services. Currently, AirTouch uses both digital and analog technology to serve their customers. They also hold a 5.7% interest in Globalstar, LP. AirTouch has chosen to compete on a global front through various partnerships and JVs. Recognizing the massive growth potential outside the United States, AirTouch began their global strategy immediately after the spin-off.

Strategic Intent

AirTouch has chosen to differentiate itself in its domestic regions based on the concept of "Superior Service Delivery." The company's focus is on being available to its customers 24 hours a day, 7 days a week and on delivering pricing options that meet the customer's needs. AirTouch allows customers to change pricing plans without penalty. The company also emphasizes call clarity and quality and extensive geographic coverage. The key challenges AirTouch faces on a global front is in reducing churn (i.e., the percentage of customers leaving), implementing improved digital technology, managing pressure on service pricing, and maintaining profit margins by focusing on cost reduction. Other challenges include creating a domestic national presence.

Company Structure

AirTouch is decentralized. Regions have been developed in the U.S. market and are run autonomously with respect to pricing decisions, marketing campaigns, and customer care operations. Each region is run as a profit center. Its European operations also are run independently from each other to be able to respond to the competitive issues unique to the specific countries. All employees are shareowners in the company, and the average age of the workforce is in the low to mid-30s. Both companies are comparable in terms of size and exhibit operating profit margins in the mid-to-high teens. AirTouch has substantially less leverage than Vodafone.

Merger Highlights

Vodafone began exploratory talks with AirTouch as early as 1996 on a variety of options ranging from partnerships to a merger. Merger talks continued informally until late 1998 when they were formally broken off. Bell Atlantic, interested in expanding its own mobile phone business's geographic coverage, immediately jumped into the void by proposing to AirTouch that together they form a new wireless company. In early 1999, Vodafone once again entered the fray, sparking a sharp takeover battle for AirTouch. Vodafone emerged victorious by mid-1999. Table 10-8 summarizes the chronology of key events in this hotly contested merger.

TABLE 10-8   Merger Timeline

Date/Event	Outcome
Exploratory talks begin on partnering opportunities in 1996	Opportunities for joint ventures, controlled roaming purchasing arrangements, and merger were discussed at the conceptual level only
Sept./early Oct. 1998 High-level meetings take place	Chris Gent, CEO of Vodafone, and Sam Ginn, CEO of AirTouch, met to engage in more formal merger discussions
Oct. 21, 1998	Merger talks terminated
Nov. 13, 1998 Bell Atlantic proposes merger	Bell Atlantic proposes formation of a new wireless company. The proposal contemplated that AirTouch would become part of the new company and that both Bell Atlantic and GTE, which recently had entered into a merger agreement with Bell Atlantic, would contribute their wireless assets to the new company in return for a controlling interest. The discussion evolved into merger talks
Dec. 31, 1998 Merger discussions made public	AirTouch and Bell Atlantic issue a joint press release discussing exploratory talks on Jan. 3, 1999
Jan. 2, 1999 Vodafone makes formal merger proposal	Vodafone offers 5 of its shares, equivalent to .5 ADSs[1], and $6 in cash for each share of AirTouch common stock. An exchange of stock and cash was undertaken to make the offer more attractive in light of potential offers from other suitors and to ensure tax-free treatment
Jan. 7 & 10, 1999 Special board meetings held	The AirTouch board holds a special meeting to review strategic options. AirTouch continues to negotiate with both Vodafone and Bell Atlantic
Jan. 14, 1999 Vodafone ups the ante	Vodafone raises its offer to 5 of its common shares plus $9 for each share of AirTouch common stock
Jan. 15, 1999 Board accepts Vodafone's proposal	AirTouch submits terms and conditions of both proposals to its board. The board votes unanimously to accept the Vodafone proposal, and both parties execute the merger agreement
June 27, 1999 Vodafone and AirTouch merger completed	Transaction valued at about $55 billion

[1] ADS is an American Depository Share representing 10 Vodafone ordinary shares. ADSs were created to allow U.S. shareholders to more easily hold and trade Vodafone AirTouch shares in U.S. markets after the merger.

Motivation for the Merger

Shared Vision

The merger would create a more competitive, global wireless telecommunications company than either company could achieve separately. Moreover, both firms shared the same vision of the telecommunications industry. Mobile telecommunications is believed to be the among the fastest-growing segment of the telecommunications industry, and over time mobile voice will replace large amounts of telecommunications traffic carried by fixed-line networks and will serve as a major platform for voice and data communication. Both companies believe that mobile penetration will reach 50% in developed countries by 2003 and 55% and 65% in the United States and developed European countries, respectively, by 2005 (AirTouch Communications, 1999).

Complementary Assets

Scale, operating strength, and complementary assets were given as compelling reasons for the merger. The combination of AirTouch and Vodafone would create the largest mobile telecommunication company at the time, with significant presence in the United Kingdom, United States, continental Europe, and Asian Pacific region. The scale and scope of the operations is expected to make the combined firms the vendor of choice for business travelers and international corporations. Interests in operations in many countries will make Vodafone AirTouch more attractive as a partner for other international fixed and mobile telecommunications providers. The combined scale of the companies also is expected to enhance its ability to develop existing networks and to be in the forefront of providing technologically advanced products and services.

Synergy

Anticipated synergies include after-tax cost savings of $340 million annually by the fiscal year ending March 31, 2002. The estimated net present value of these synergies is $3.6 billion discounted at 9%. The cost savings arise from global purchasing and operating efficiencies, including volume discounts, lower leased line costs, more efficient voice and data networks, savings in development and purchase of third-generation mobile handsets, infrastructure, and software. Revenues should be enhanced through the provision of more international coverage and through the bundling of services for corporate customers that operate as multinational businesses and business travelers.

AirTouch's Board Analyzes Options

Morgan Stanley, AirTouch's investment banker, provided analyses of the current prices of both the Vodafone and Bell Atlantic stocks, their historical trading ranges, and the anticipated trading prices of both companies' stock on completion of the merger and on redistribution of the stock to the general public. Both offers were structured so as to constitute essentially tax-free reorganizations.

TABLE 10-9 Comparison of Form of Payment/Total Consideration

Vodafone	Bell Atlantic
5 shares of Vodafone common plus $9 for each share of AirTouch common	1.54 shares of Bell Atlantic for each share of AirTouch common subject to the transaction being treated as a pooling of interest under U.S. GAAP
	Share exchange ratio adjusted upward 9 months out to reflect the payment of dividends on the Bell Atlantic stock
	A share exchange ratio collar would be used to ensure that AirTouch shareholders would receive shares valued at $80.08. If the average closing price of Bell Atlantic stock were less than $48, the exchange ratio would be increased to 1.6683. If the price exceeded $52, the exchange rate would remain at 1.54[1]

[1] The collar guarantees the price of Bell Atlantic stock for the AirTouch shareholders because $48 × 1.6683 and $52 × 1.54 both equal $80.08.

The Vodafone proposal would qualify as a Type A reorganization under the Internal Revenue Service Code; hence, it would be tax-free, except for the cash portion of the offer, for U.S. holders of AirTouch common and holders of preferred who converted their shares before the merger. The Bell Atlantic offer would qualify as a Type B tax-free reorganization. Table 10-9 highlights the primary characteristics of the form of payment (total consideration) of the two competing offers.

Morgan Stanley's primary conclusions were as follows:

1. Bell Atlantic had a current market value of $83 per share of AirTouch stock based on the $53.81 closing price of Bell Atlantic common stock on January 14, 1999. The collar would maintain the price at $80.08 per share if the price of Bell Atlantic stock during a specified period before closing was between $48 and $52 per share.
2. The Vodafone proposal had a current market value of $97 per share of AirTouch stock based on Vodafone's ordinary shares (i.e., common) on January 17, 1999.
3. Following the merger, the market value of the Vodafone American Depository Shares (ADSs) to be received by AirTouch shareholders under the Vodafone proposal could decrease.
4. Following the merger, the market value of Bell Atlantic's stock also could decrease, particularly in light of the expectation that the proposed transaction would dilute Bell Atlantic's EPS by more than 10% through 2002.

In addition to Vodafone's higher value, the board tended to favor the Vodafone offer because it involved less regulatory uncertainty. As U.S. corporations, a merger between AirTouch and Bell Atlantic was likely to receive substantial scrutiny from the U.S. Justice Department, the Federal Trade Commission, and the FCC. Moreover, although both proposals could be completed tax-free, except for the small cash component of the Vodafone offer, the Vodafone offer was not subject to achieving any specific accounting treatment such as pooling of interests under U.S. generally accepted accounting principles (GAAP).

Recognizing their fiduciary responsibility to review all legitimate offers in a balanced manner, the AirTouch board also considered a number of factors that made the Vodafone proposal less attractive. The failure to do so would no doubt trigger shareholder lawsuits. The major factors that detracted from the Vodafone proposal were that it would not result in a national presence in the United States, the higher volatility of its stock, and the additional debt Vodafone would have to assume to pay the cash portion of the purchase price. Despite these concerns, the higher offer price from Vodafone (i.e., $97 to $83) won the day (Vodafone, April 22, 1999).

ACQUISITION VEHICLE AND
POSTCLOSING ORGANIZATION

In the merger, AirTouch became a wholly owned subsidiary of Vodafone. Vodafone issued common shares valued at $52.4 billion based on the closing Vodafone ADS on April 20, 1999. In addition, Vodafone paid AirTouch shareholders $5.5 billion in cash. On completion of the merger, Vodafone changed its name to Vodafone AirTouch Public Limited Company.

Vodafone created a wholly owned subsidiary, Appollo Merger Incorporated, as the acquisition vehicle. Using a *reverse triangular merger*, Appollo was merged into AirTouch. AirTouch constituted the surviving legal entity. AirTouch shareholders received Vodafone voting stock and cash for their AirTouch shares. Both the AirTouch and Appollo shares were canceled (Figure 10-4). After the merger, AirTouch shareholders owned slightly less than 50% of the equity of the new company, Vodafone AirTouch. By using the reverse merger to convey ownership

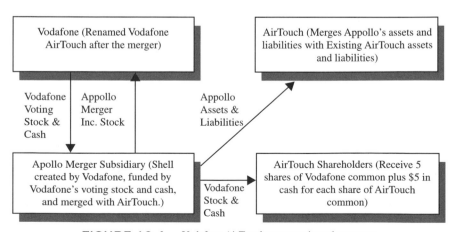

FIGURE 10-4.   Vodafone AirTouch reverse triangular merger.

of the AirTouch shares, Vodafone was able to ensure that all FCC licenses and Air-Touch franchise rights were conveyed legally to Vodafone. However, Vodafone was unable to avoid seeking shareholder approval using this method. Vodafone ADS's traded on the New York Stock Exchange (NYSE). Because the amount of new shares being issued exceeded 20% of Vodafone's outstanding voting stock, the NYSE required that Vodafone solicit its shareholders for approval of the proposed merger.

Following this transaction, the highly aggressive Vodafone went on to consummate the largest merger in history in 2000 by combining with Germany's telecommunications powerhouse, Mannesmann, for $180 billion (see Chapter 1). Including assumed debt, the total purchase price paid by Vodafone AirTouch for Mannesmann soared to $198 billion. Vodafone AirTouch was well on its way to establishing itself as a global cellular phone powerhouse.

Case Study Discussion Questions

1. Did the AirTouch board make the right decision? Why or why not?
2. How valid are the reasons for the proposed merger?
3. What are the potential risk factors related to the merger?
4. Why did the merger happen so quickly?
5. Why was Bell Atlantic interested in a pooling-of-interest accounting treatment? Why was this a concern about Bell Atlantic's purchase price? Would this be an important consideration today? Would this have been an important consideration if the merger had taken place after January 1, 2002?
6. The Vodafone merger will be treated as a purchase of assets under GAAP and will create $3.4 billion in annual goodwill expenses. How has the treatment of goodwill changed for financial reporting purposes after January 1, 2002?
7. Is this merger likely to be tax free, partially tax free, or taxable? Explain your answer.
8. What are some of the challenges the two companies are likely to face while integrating the businesses?
9. How would the collar protect AirTouch shareholders from a decline in Bell Atlantic's stock?

Solutions to these questions appear at the back of this book.

CHAPTER BUSINESS CASE

CASE STUDY 10-2: JDS UNIPHASE–SDL MERGER
RESULTS IN HUGE WRITE-OFF

The Downside of Delay

What started out as the biggest technology merger in history up to that point saw its value plummet in line with the declining stock market, a weakening economy, and concerns about the cash-flow impact of actions the acquirer would have to take to gain regulatory approve. The $41 billion mega-merger, proposed on July 10, 2000, consisted of JDS Uniphase (JDSU) offering 3.8 shares of its stock for each share of SDL's outstanding stock. (SDL Press Release, July 10, 2000). This constituted an approximate 43% premium over the price of SDL's stock on the announcement date. The challenge facing JDSU was to get Department of Justice (DoJ) approval of a merger that some feared would result in a supplier (i.e., JDS Uniphase–SDL) that could exercise enormous pricing power over the entire range of products from raw components to packaged products purchased by equipment manufacturers. The resulting regulatory review lengthened the period between the signing of the merger agreement between the two companies and the actual closing to more than 7 months. The risk to SDL shareholders of the lengthening of the time between the determination of value and the actual receipt of the JDSU shares at closing was that the JDSU shares could decline in price during this period.

The Importance of Collars

Given the size of the premium, JDSU's management was unwilling to protect SDL's shareholders from this possibility by providing a "collar" within which the exchange ratio could fluctuate. With a collar arrangement, predetermined changes in JDSU's share price would have resulted in an upward or downward adjustment in the share exchange ratio to preserve the purchase price paid for each SDL share outstanding. The absence of a collar proved particularly devastating to SDL shareholders, which continued to hold JDSU stock well beyond the closing date. The deal that had been originally valued at $41 billion when first announced more than 7 months earlier had fallen to $13.5 billion on the day of closing, a staggering loss of more than two-thirds of its value.

Billed as the technology deal of the new millennium, the deal was fast becoming the dud of the decade. How did a deal that appeared to make so much sense on paper turn out to be such a disaster in practice?

The Participants: JDS Uniphase and SDL

Through an incredible series of 11 M&As totaling $18 billion since its formation in 1999, JDSU assembled the largest portfolio of optical components in the industry. In fact, JDSU is itself the product of a merger in mid-1999 between JDS FITEL and Uniphase Corporation. JDSU manufactures and distributes fiber-optic components and modules to telecommunication and cable systems providers worldwide. The company is the dominant supplier in its market for fiber-optic components. In 1999, the firm focused on making only certain subsystems needed in fiber-optic networks, but a flurry of acquisitions has enabled the company to offer complementary products. JDSU's strategy is to package entire systems into a single integrated unit, thereby reducing the number of vendors that fiber network firms must deal with when purchasing systems that produce the light that is transmitted over fiber. (Hanks, 2000).

SDL's products, including pump lasers, support the transmission of data, voice, video, and Internet information over fiber-optic networks by expanding their fiber-optic communications networks much more quickly and efficiently than would be possible using conventional electronic and optical technologies. SDL had approximately 1700 employees and reported sales of $72 million for the quarter ending March 31, 2000.

As of July 10, 2000, JDSU had a market value of $74 billion with 958 shares outstanding. Annual 2000 revenues amounted to $1.43 billion. The firm had $800 million in cash and virtually no long-term debt. Including one-time merger-related charges, the firm recorded a loss of $905 million. With its price-to-earnings (excluding merger-related charges) ratio at a meteoric 440, the firm sought to use stock to acquire SDL, a strategy that it had used successfully since 1999.

Motivation for the Merger

The growth of the Internet during much of the 1990s had created an accelerating demand for bandwidth that was driving the construction of significantly more telecommunication network capacity. Telecommunication system providers were developing those network systems based on optical technologies that required state-of–the-art components and modules with increasing levels of integration and complexity. JDSU believed that a merger with SDL would provide two major benefits. First, it would add a line of lasers to the JDSU product offering that strengthened signals beamed across fiber-optic networks. Second, it would bolster JDSU's capacity to package multiple components into a single product line.

Regulatory Concerns

Although few doubted the beneficial effects of the mergers on JDSU–SDL, regulators expressed concern that the combined entities could control the market for a specific type of laser (i.e., 980-nanometer wavelength pump lasers) used in a wide range of optical equipment. SDL is one of the largest suppliers of this type of laser, and JDS is one of the largest suppliers of the chips used to build them. Other manufacturers of pumped lasers, such as Nortel Networks, Lucent Technologies, and Corning, complained to regulators that they would have to buy some of the chips necessary to manufacture pump lasers from a supplier (i.e., JDSU), which in combination with SDL, also would be a competitor. As required by the Hart–Scott–Rodino (HSR) Antitrust Improvements Act of 1976, JDSU had filed with the DoJ seeking regulatory approval. On August 24, the firm received a request for additional information from the DoJ, which extended the HSR waiting period. Such a request was commonplace for mergers of this size involving new rapidly changing and important technologies.

JDS Uniphase Receives Regulatory Approval

On February 6, JDSU agreed as part of a consent decree to sell a Swiss subsidiary, which manufactures pump lasers chips, to Nortel Networks Corporation, a JDSU customer, to satisfy DoJ concerns about the proposed merger.

Canadian-based Nortel paid $2.5 billion in stock for the Swiss operation. Nortel agreed to pay another $500 million in Nortel common stock payable to the extent Nortel's future purchases from JDSU do not meet certain target levels (SDL Press Release, 2001). The divestiture of this operation set up an alternative supplier of such chips, thereby alleviating concerns expressed by other manufacturers of pump lasers that they would have to buy such components from a competitor.

Key Elements of the Deal Structure

On July 9, 2000, the boards of both JDSU and SDL unanimously approved an agreement to merge SDL with a newly formed, wholly owned subsidiary of JDS Uniphase, K2 Acquisition, Inc. K2 Acquisition was created by JDSU as the *acquisition vehicle* to complete the merger. In a *reverse triangular merger*, K2 Acquisition Inc. was merged into SDL, with SDL as the surviving entity. The *postclosing organization* consisted of SDL as a wholly owned subsidiary of JDS Uniphase. The *form of payment* consisted of exchanging JDSU common stock for SDL common shares. The *share exchange ratio* was 3.8 shares of JDSU stock for each SDL common share outstanding. JDSU did not issue *fractional shares* in the merger. Fractional shares arise when a target shareholder is entitled to receive something other than an even number of acquirer shares as a result of a fractionated share exchange ratio (e.g., 3.8 rather 4.0). Instead of a fraction of a share, each SDL stockholder received cash, without interest, equal to dollar value of the fractional share at the average of the closing prices for a share of JDSU common stock for the 5 trading days before the completion of the merger.

Shareholder Approval

Under the rules of the NASDAQ National Market, on which JDSU's shares are traded, JDSU is required to seek stockholder approval for any issuance of common stock to acquire another firm. This requirement is triggered if the amount issued exceeds 20% of its issued and outstanding shares of common stock and of its voting power. (Note that because of such stock exchange rules large transactions still require shareholder approval even if a forward or reverse triangular merger format is used to transfer ownership.)

Fairness Opinions

In connection with the merger, both SDL and JDSU received fairness opinions from advisors employed by the firms. The JDSU board of directors received separate opinions from CIBC World Markets Corporation and Bank of America Securities as to the fairness, from a financial point of view, to JDSU of the exchange ratio provided for in the merger. Similarly, Thomas Weisel Partners, LLC, delivered its written opinion to the board of directors of SDL noting that as of July 9, 2000, the exchange ratio was fair from a financial point of view to SDL shareholders.

Closing Conditions

The merger agreement specified that the merger could be consummated when all of the conditions stipulated in the agreement were either satisfied or waived by the parties to the agreement. Both JDSU and SDL were subject to certain closing conditions. Such conditions were specified in the September 7, 2000 S4 filing with the SEC by JDSU, which is required whenever a firm intends to issue securities to the public. The consummation of the merger was to be subject to approval by the shareholders of both companies, the approval of the regulatory authorities as specified under the HSR, and any other foreign antitrust law that applied. Such foreign authorities included the Canadian Competition Bureau and the German Cartel Office. For both parties, representations and warranties (statements of supposed fact) must have been found to be accurate and both parties must have complied with all of the agreements and covenants (promises) in all material ways. The following are just a few examples of the 18 closing conditions found in the merger agreement.

Tax Status

The merger is structured so that JDSU and SDL's shareholders will not recognize a gain or loss for U.S. federal income tax purposes in the merger, except for taxes payable because of cash received by SDL shareholders for fractional shares. Both JDSU and SDL must receive opinions of tax counsel that the merger will qualify as a tax-free reorganization (***tax structure***). This also is stipulated as a closing condition.

Termination Fee

If the merger agreement is terminated as a result of an acquisition of SDL by another firm within 12 months of the termination, SDL may be required to pay JDSU a termination fee of $1 billion. Such a fee is intended to cover JDSU's expenses incurred as a result of the transaction and to discourage any third parties from making a bid for the target firm.

Financial Reporting

The merger will be accounted for under the purchase method of accounting in accordance with GAAP. Intangible assets, including goodwill from the proposed merger and from past mergers with other firms, of the combined companies totaled $60.5 billion, or about 93% of the combined firms' total assets. Of this figure, goodwill created by the SDL merger totaled $37.4 million (Table 10-10).

The Long-Term Affect of Overpaying

Despite dramatic cost-cutting efforts, the company reported a loss of $7.9 billion for the quarter ending June 31, 2001 and $50.6 billion for the 12 months ending June 31, 2001. This compares to the projected pro forma loss reported in the September 9, 2000, S4 filing of $12.1 billion (JDS Uniphase Press Release, 2000).

TABLE 10-10 Purchase Price Allocation Among Asset Categories

Asset Category	($ Millions)
Tangible Net Assets Acquired	$528,718
Intangible Assets Acquired	
Existing Technology[1]	506,221
Core Technology[2]	175,600
Trademarks and Trade Name[3]	40,840
Assembled Workforce[4]	36,100
Deferred Compensation[5]	1,588,620
Total Nongoodwill – Related Intangible Assets	2,347,381
Goodwill (Excess of purchase price over fair value)	$37,443,561
In-Process Research and Development[6]	$184,600
Purchase Price	$40,504,260

[1] SDL products that are already technologically feasible, including SDL's current product lines.

[2] SDL trade secrets and patents.

[3] SDL trademark and trade name.

[4] 1618 skilled employees across SDL's executive, research and development (R&D), manufacturing, supervisor/manager, and sales and marketing groups.

[5] Estimated intrinsic value of unvested SDL stock options assumed by JDSU. Such options have value to the extent that they encourage SDL employees to remain with the new company at least until such options are fully invested.

[6] New products that qualify as in-process R&D in multiple product areas, typically at the design and testing stage. Value assigned was determined by considering the importance of each project to the overall development plan, estimating costs to develop the purchased in-process R&D into commercially viable products, and estimating the resulting net cash flows from the products when completed.

The actual loss was the largest annual loss ever reported by a U.S. firm. The fiscal year 2000 loss included a reduction in the value of goodwill carried on the balance sheet of $38.7 billion to reflect the declining market value of assets purchased during a series of previous transactions. Most of this reduction was related to goodwill arising from the merger of JDS FITEL and Uniphase and the subsequent acquisitions of SDL, E-TEK, and OCLI. (JDS Uniphase Press Release, 2001).

The stock continued to tumble in line with the declining fortunes of the telecommunications industry such that it was trading as low as $7.5 per share by mid-2001, about 6% of its value the day the merger with SDL was announced. Thus, the JDS Uniphase–SDL merger was marked by two firsts—the largest purchase price paid for a pure technology company and the largest write-off (at that time) in history. Both of these infamous "firsts" occurred within 12 months.

Although these write-offs did not involve an actual reduction in cash flow, they did reflect the cumulative effect of bad management decisions. The lofty JDSU share price in 1999 and early 2000 made it a very attractive acquisition "currency." Management presumed that projected synergies would result in a more than proportional increase in future earnings sufficient to offset the huge increase in shares issued to complete JDSU's string of acquisitions. JDSU issued almost 340 million shares to acquire SDL alone, resulting in the combined firms having more than 1.2 billion shares outstanding in early 2001. The huge amount of shares on the market resulted in a dilution of current shareholder claims on future JDSU earnings.

Case Study Discussion Questions

1. What is goodwill? How is it estimated? Why did JDS Uniphase write down the value of its goodwill in 2001? Why did this reflect a series of poor management decisions with respect to mergers completed between 1999 and early 2001?

2. How might the use of stock, as an acquisition "currency," have contributed to the sustained decline in JDS Uniphase's stock through mid-2001? In your judgment what is the likely impact of the glut of JDS Uniphase shares in the market on the future appreciation of the firm's share price? Explain your answer.

3. What are the primary differences between a forward and a reverse triangular merger? Why might JDS Uniphase have chosen to merge its K2 Acquisition Inc. subsidiary with SDL in a reverse triangular merger? Explain your answer.

4. Discuss various methodologies you might use to value assets acquired from SDL such as existing technologies, "core" technologies, trademarks and trade names, assembled workforce, and deferred compensation?

5. Why do boards of directors of both acquiring and target companies often obtain so-called "fairness opinions" from outside investment advisors or accounting firms? What valuation methodologies might be used in constructing these opinions? Should stockholders have confidence in such opinions? Why or why not?

REFERENCES

AirTouch Communications, *Annual Report*, 1997, www.edgar.com.

AirTouch Communications, *Stockholder Proxy Statement*, April 22, 1999, p. 32, www.edgar.com.

Applied Financial Information, *Mergerstat*, Los Angeles, 2001, p. 15.

Auerbach, Alan J. and James Poterba, "Tax Loss Carry Forwards and Corporate Tax Incentives." In Martin Feldstein, ed., *The Effect of Taxation on Capital Accumulation*, Chicago: University of Chicago Press, 1987.

Auerbach, Alan J. and David Reishus, "Taxes and the Merger Decision," in John C. Coffee Jr., Louis Lowenstein, and Susan Rose Ackerman, eds., *Knights, Raiders, and Targets*, New York: Oxford University Press, 1988, pp. 69–88.

Hanks, Vince, "Gigantic JDS Uniphase," The Motley Fool, Fool.com, November 2, 2000, www.fool.com /dripport /2000/dripport001102.htm.

JDS Uniphase Corporation, S4 Registration Statement, Filed with the Securities and Exchange Commission, September 9, 2000.

JDS Uniphase Press Release, "JDS Uniphase Announces Fourth Quarter Results," July 27, 2001.

Kohers, Ninon and James Ang, "Earnouts in Mergers: Agreeing to Disagree and Agreeing to Stay," *The Journal of Finance*, 73 (3), July 2000, pp. 445–476.

Pahler, Arnold J. and Joseph E. Mori, *Advanced Accounting*, Fort Worth, TX: The Dryden Press, 1997.

Scholes, Myron and Mark A. Wolfson, *Taxes and Business Strategy*, Englewood Cliffs, NJ: Prentice-Hall 1992.

SDL Press Release, "JDS Uniphase and SDL agree to a $41 Billion Merger," July 10, 2000, www.sdli.com /about /release/pr_071000.html.

SDL Press Release, "Sale of Zurich Subsidiary to Nortel Networks Completed," February 14, 2001, www.sdli.com /about /release/pr_021301.html.

Sherman, Andrew J., *Mergers and Acquisitions: From A to Z*, New York: AMACOM Publishing, 1998, pp. 95–122.

Tillinghast, David R. "Tax Aspects of Inbound Merger and Acquisition and Joint Venture Transactions," in David J. BenDaniel and Arthur H. Rosenbloom, eds., *International M&A, Joint Ventures, and Beyond: Doing the Deal*, New York: John Wiley & Sons, Inc., 1998, pp. 151–164.

Vodafone, "Security Registration Statement," *S4 Filing*, U.S. Securities and Exchange Commission, April 22, 1999, p. 387–390.

ALTERNATIVE STRATEGIES AND STRUCTURES

11

LEVERAGED BUYOUT STRUCTURES AND VALUATION

A billion dollars isn't what it used to be.
—Nelson Bunker Hunt

Chuck Brennan, chief executive officer (CEO) of Byzantine International, had completed the transaction after several months of hard negotiating with the firm's board of directors. Along with other senior members of management, he had proposed to take the company private by offering shareholders a substantial premium to the current market price. Although the initial offer was met with significant skepticism from the board, he was able to gain considerable credibility by obtaining financing from Jacob Carter of Carter and Associates, a well-known investor in highly leveraged "middle-market" transactions.

Jacob Carter had been able to finance about 10 similar transactions in related industries during the 1980s and 1990s using relatively little capital. The methodology had been simple. Find target firms with consistent historical earnings growth, solid management, little debt, substantial tangible assets, and mature technologies and production processes in industries with largely stable growth rates. Such firms often displayed predictable cash flows well in excess of their reinvestment requirements. Carter reasoned that the unencumbered assets could be used as collateral for new borrowing, and the excess cash flow could be used to cover the subsequent increase in debt service requirements.

The remaining ingredient for the success of Carter and Associates was to motivate the management of the target firm through generous performance bonuses and stock options. Jacob Carter knew that the prospect of substantial wealth would be likely to cause management to stay focused on improving the operating performance of the highly leveraged firm to meet the quarterly interest and principal repayments. Moreover, earnings resulting from improving performance would be largely tax free, sheltered by the deductibility of interest payments. As the outstanding debt was paid off, the target firm then would be taken public through a reissuance of stock or sold to a strategic buyer. The lenders would be repaid from the proceeds of the sale, and the equity investors would be handsomely compensated for their efforts.

Chuck Brennan was a convert to this line of reasoning and in concert with Jacob Carter was able to convince Byzantine's board that their offer was not only fair for the firm's shareholders but also that it could be readily financed. The celebration following closing was short lived because the enormity of the task that lay before management began to sink in. The methodology used in the takeover was indeed conceptually simple. The challenge would be to make it all happen according to plan.

OVERVIEW

Commonly referred to as leveraged buyouts, highly leveraged transactions often have been romanticized by Hollywood for the daring of those who undertake them or demonized in the popular press for their potentially devastating effects on employees and communities. As is usually the case, the truth lies somewhere in between these extremes.

In a *leveraged buyout* (LBO), borrowed funds are used to pay for all or most of the purchase price. Historically, as much as 90% or more of the purchase price is financed with debt. Typically, the tangible assets of the firm to be acquired are used as collateral for the loans. The most highly liquid assets often are used as collateral for obtaining bank financing. Such assets commonly include receivables and inventory. The firm's fixed assets commonly are used to secure a portion of long-term senior financing. Subordinated debt, either unrated or low-rated debt, is used to raise the balance of the purchase price. This debt often is referred to as *junk bond* financing.

When a public company is subject to an LBO, it is said to be *going private* because the equity of the firm has been purchased by a small group of investors and is no longer publicly traded. Ultimately, the investor group will attempt to realize a return on their investment by once again taking the company public in an initial public offering (IPO) or by selling to a strategic buyer. Buyers of the firm targeted to become a leveraged buyout often consist of managers from the firm that is being acquired. The LBO that is initiated by the target firm's incumbent management is called a *management buyout* (MBO).

Despite the general allure of highly leveraged transactions because of their potential for huge profits, they occur relatively infrequently. The challenges of finding suitable targets, managing a potentially crushing debt load, and implementing highly aggressive cost-cutting measures without fatally damaging the business makes these types of transactions best left to the pros. Perhaps as a testimony to these challenges or in remembrance of the financial debacles of the late 1980s, LBO and MBO transactions comprised a modest 5–6% of all transactions completed during the decade of the 1990s. Moreover, there is little evidence thus far in the new millennium that this is likely to change very much.

This chapter begins with a discussion of the evolution of LBOs (i.e., highly leveraged transactions) in the context of the risks associated with alternative financing options from asset-based or secured lending to pure cash flow–based lending. Subsequent sections discuss typical LBO structures, the risks associated with poorly constructed deals, and how to take a company private. Key shareholder and public policy issues are illustrated in this chapter by a case study of the largest LBO in history, RJR Nabisco. Empirical studies of pre- and postbuyout returns to shareholders also are reviewed. The chapter concludes with a discussion of how to analyze and value LBO transactions.

THE ORIGINS OF LEVERAGED TRANSACTIONS

Interest in highly leveraged transactions remained relatively subdued until the 1980s. Conglomerates that had amassed large portfolios of businesses during the 1960s and early 1970s began to divest many of their holdings. The size of these divested units usually ranged in annual sales from $5 million to more than $250 million. Leveraged buyouts were an increasingly common way to finance these transactions.

THE EMERGENCE OF THE FINANCIAL BUYER

Investors in LBOs frequently are referred to as financial buyers because they are primarily focused on relatively short- to intermediate-term financial returns. Such buyers tend to hold their investments for 5–7 years. Financial buyers tend to concentrate on actions that enhance the target firm's ability to generate cash to satisfy their substantial debt service requirements. The existence of substantial leverage made the potential returns to equity much more attractive than less leveraged transactions (Table 11-1). Financial buyers with a demonstrated ability to identify attractive LBO candidates frequently were able to attract sufficient funding such that they could offer target company shareholders a substantial premium over the target's current public market value.

CHARACTERISTICS OF LBOs IN THE EARLY 1980s

In the 1980s, debt was normally four to five times equity (Lehn and Poulsen, 1988). Debt was likely to be amortized over a 5–7-year period and certainly no more than 10 years. The LBO firm generally was taken public or divested to a corporate buyer whenever the tax benefits provided by the leverage started to diminish. Existing corporate management was encouraged to participate as equity owners. The skill of the financial buyer during this period was largely in constructing a capital structure that would allow for the highest possible leverage while still enabling the firm to meet debt service requirements through

TABLE 11-1   Impact of Leverage on Return to Shareholders[1]

	All-Cash Purchase	50% Cash/ 50% Debt	20% Cash/ 80% Debt
Purchase Price	$100	$100	$100
Equity (Cash Investment)	$100	$50	$20
Borrowings	0	$50	$80
Earnings Before Interest and Taxes	$20	$20	$20
Interest @ 10%	0	$5	$8
Income Before Taxes	$20	$15	$12
Less Income Taxes @ 40%	$8	$6	$4.8
Net Income	$12	$9	$7.2
After-Tax Return on Equity	12%	18%	36%

[1]Unless otherwise noted, all numbers are in millions of dollars.

improvements in operating performance. The transactions normally were characterized by complex capital structures consisting of senior bank debt secured by the target's assets, subordinated unsecured debt, preferred stock, and common equity. Secured debt often comprised about 60% of the total purchase price with unsecured debt or junk financing accounting for about 20–25%. The remainder of the purchase price consisted of preferred and common equity (Roden and Lewellen, 1995).

LBOs IN THE MID-TO-LATE 1980s

LBOs during this period had many of the same characteristics of earlier LBOs, with two notable differences. First, debt was serviced from both operating cash flow and asset sales. Changes in the tax laws reduced the popularity of divesting assets to reduce leverage because asset sales immediately on the closing of the transaction are no longer deemed tax free. Previously, it was possible to buy stock in a company and sell the assets, and any gain on asset sales was offset by a mirrored reduction in the value of the stock. This was made illegal as a result of the Tax Reform Act of 1986. The second half of the 1980s saw the emergence of the nontraditional sources of LBO financing from LBO funds. They provided both secured and unsecured financing. Their sources of funding came from large institutional investors such as life insurance companies and pension funds. These institutional investors also would lend directly to the LBO.

LBOs IN THE 1990s AND BEYOND

From a peak of $66 billion, about one-fifth of total merger and acquisition (M&A) transactions in 1989, the total dollar volume of LBO transactions plummeted to $7 billion in 1991, about 5% of total transactions in that year. During the 5 years ending in 2000, LBOs averaged about 4% of the total dollar volume of M&As. The dollar value of LBOs tends to be small, averaging $40 million to $50 million, with many falling in the $4 million to $5 million range.

Lingering memories of the excesses of LBO financing, the resulting bankrupt cies in the late 1980s, and a serious reduction of suitable candidates for such transactions precluded any significant resurgence of highly leveraged transactions during the decade of the 1990s. LBOs that did take place tended to use a much greater proportion of equity. Reflecting the powerful equity markets of the period, the primary exit strategy during this decade was through stock offerings to the public. Debt-to-equity ratios were typically more conservative than during the 1980s. Equity as a percentage of debt increased to about 20–30%, as compared with 5–10% in the late 1980s. Deals often were structured so that debt repayment was not required until 10 years after the transaction was structured. This tended to reduce pressure on near-term earnings performance. The LBO firm's strategy was to enable the target firm to establish a period of escalating reported earnings to make it more attractive whenever it was ultimately taken public. Moreover, LBO firms often purchased a firm to use as a platform to undertake other leveraged buyouts in the same industry. The acquired firms then would be merged and taken public at a later date.

A common technique used during the 1990s was to wait for favorable periods in the stock market to sell a portion of the LBO's equity to the public. The proceeds of the issue would be used to repay debt, thereby reducing the LBO's financial risk. Once the LBO's shares had traded for a few months, secondary stock offerings often were made as the initial investors liquidated some portion of their equity positions. Whenever the firm had paid off a sufficient portion of its debt, a search was initiated for a strategic buyer willing to pay a premium to the LBO's investors to gain a controlling interest. In addition, LBO investors have become much more actively involved in managing target firms in recent years than they have in the past. Companies such as Clayton, Dubilier & Rice (CD&R) have tended to focus on targeting firms it viewed as having only marginally effective management. CD&R then would bring it new management with considerable previous experi- ence and establish compensation systems that tightly linked management's total compensation to the target's financial performance. This approach is really quite similar to the adoption of a turnaround strategy using a high degree of leverage to finance the transaction.

ALTERNATIVE FINANCING OPTIONS

Once a prospective target has been identified, the buyer has a number of financing options. For the risk-adverse acquirer, the ideal mechanism might be to finance the transaction out of cash held by the target in excess of normal work- ing capital requirements. Such situations are usually very difficult to find. Venture capital investors also may be available to fund the transaction. However, this may represent very expensive financing because the buyer may have to give up as much as 70% of the ownership of the acquired company. Use of the buyer's stock may be an appropriate way to minimize the initial cash outlay, but such an option is rarely available in an MBO or a buyout by privately held companies. The seller may be willing to accept debt issued by the buyer if an upfront cash payment is not important. This may be highly disadvantageous to the buyer if the seller places substantial restrictions on how the business may be managed. The use of a public issue of long-term debt to finance the transaction may minimize the initial cash outlay, but it is also subject to restrictions placed on how the business may be operated by the investors buying the issue. Moreover, public issues are expensive in terms of administrative, marketing, and regulatory reporting costs. For these reasons, asset-based lending has emerged as an attractive alternative to the use of cash, stock, or public debt issues if the target has sufficient tangible assets to serve as collateral.

ASSET-BASED OR SECURED LENDING

Under asset-based lending, the borrower pledges certain assets as collateral. Asset-based lenders look at the borrower's assets as their primary protection against the borrower's failure to repay. Such loans are often short-term (i.e., less than 1 year in maturity) and secured by assets that can be liquidated easily, such as accounts receivable and inventory. Loans maturing in more than 1 year often are referred to as term loans. Acquiring firms generally prefer to borrow funds on an unsecured basis because the added administrative costs involved in pledging assets as security significantly raise the total cost of borrowing. Secured borrowing also can be onerous because the security agreements can severely limit a company's future borrowing. However, in many instances, borrowers may have little choice but to obtain secured lending for at least a portion of the purchase price.

Asset-based lenders generally require personal guarantees from the buyer, in which the buyer is pledging such personal assets as their principal residence. This is especially true in small transactions if the buyer does not have a demonstrated track record in buying and operating businesses. Lenders also have found that the personal guarantee is also an excellent way to motivate the borrower to help the lender recover as much of the collateral as possible in the event the firm is liquidated.

By the early 1970s, many banks had begun to engage in commercial financing as an adjunct to other types of more traditional lending. The adoption of the Uniform Commercial Code in the 1960s greatly simplified and made uniform techniques for obtaining and administering legally enforceable security interests in accounts receivables, inventory, and other types of collateral (Reisman, 1978). During the 1970s and early 1980s, asset-based lenders often were able to charge 5–6 percentage points above bank loan rates. However, increasing competition in the late 1980s and 1990s from commercial banks, which accelerated their move into asset-based lending, narrowed these spreads to 1.5 to 2 percentage points.

Asset-based lenders generally prefer highly liquid assets as collateral. These include collectable accounts receivable and certain types of inventory.

Firms that are likely to have these types of assets are manufacturers, whole-salers, and distributors. Cash and cash equivalents that are needed for working capital purposes (e.g., meeting payroll) are normally not considered as acceptable collateral.

Loan Documentation

The lending process entails the negotiation of a loan agreement, security agree-ment, and promissory note. The *loan agreement* stipulates the terms and conditions under which the lender will loan the firm funds. The *security agreement* specifies which of the borrower's assets will be pledged to secure the loan. The *promissory note* commits the borrower to repay the loan, even if the assets when liquidated do not fully cover the unpaid balance. These agreements contain certain security provisions and protective covenants limiting what the borrower may do as long as the loan is outstanding. These provisions and covenants will be described in more detail in the next section.

The security agreement is filed at a state regulatory office in the state where the collateral is located. Future lenders can check with this office to see which assets a firm has pledged and which are free to be used as future collateral. The filing of this security agreement legally establishes the lender's security interest in the collateral. If the borrower defaults on the loan or otherwise fails to honor the terms of the agreement, the lender can seize and sell the collateral to recover the value of the loan. The process of determining which of a firm's assets are free from liens is made easier today by commercial credit reporting repositories such as Dun & Bradstreet and Experian. These reports also indicate which of the firm's assets currently are pledged as collateral.

Pledging Accounts Receivable

Accounts receivable commonly are used as collateral to obtain secured short-term financing. Accounts receivable represent a highly desirable form of collateral from the lender's viewpoint because they are generally very liquid. However, the lender may encounter problems if the borrower pledges nonexistent accounts, the customer returns the merchandise, or the customer files a claim that the merchan-dise is defective. Receivables for services provided by the borrower often are viewed to be of a lower quality than those based on product sales. Experience shows that customers often argue that the services were not performed up to the level required by the customer's contract. Consequently, they may dispute the actual amount owed. Depending on the extent to which they are collectable, lenders may lend up to 80–90% of the book value of the receivables (Kretlow, McGuigan, and Moyer, 1998, pp. 681–711). Asset-based lenders generally are willing to lend against only those receivables that are due within 90 days. Those that are more than 90 days past due are those that are likely to be difficult to collect. Lenders are not willing to lend up to 100% of the value of the more current receiv-ables because they are aware that some portion of those receivables will not be collectable.

Pledging Inventory

Inventories are also commonly used to provide collateral for LBO transactions. As is true of receivables, inventories are often highly liquid. Inventory consists of raw material, work-in-process, and finished goods. Lenders normally consider only raw material and finished goods inventories as suitable collateral. The amount that a lender will advance against the book value of inventory depends on its characteristics: ease of identification, liquidity, and marketability. In general, lenders will loan between 50% and 80% of the value of inventory. Lenders will tend to loan less if the inventory is viewed as perishable, subject to rapid obsolescence, or as having relatively few potential buyers.

Pledging Equipment and Real Estate to Support Term Loans

A term loan or intermediate-term credit is a loan with a maturity of from 1 to 10 years. Borrowers often prefer term loans because they do not have to be concerned that the loan will have to be renewed. A term loan can be structured in such a way that the term of the loan corresponds with the economic life of the item being financed. Durable equipment and real estate often are used to secure loans. Lenders are frequently are willing to lend up to 80% of the appraised value of equipment and 50% of the value of land. Lenders are unlikely to lend much against special purpose equipment, which is likely to have few potential buyers, and land, which is often difficult to convert to cash rapidly. The cash flows generated by the assets will be used to pay off the loan. Term loans sometimes are used in LBO transactions to reduce the overall cost of borrowing. Because term loans are negotiated privately between the borrower and the lender, they are much less expensive than the costs associated with floating a public debt or stock issue.

Pledging Intangible Assets

Lenders generally loan very little against intangible assets such as trademarks, patents, and copyrights because of the extreme difficulty in determining their liquidation value. However, the borrower may choose to pledge such assets as a "sweetener" to obtain slightly better terms.

SECURITY PROVISIONS AND PROTECTIVE COVENANTS

Security provisions and protective covenants in loan documents are intended to ensure that the interest and principal of outstanding loans will be repaid in a timely fashion. The number and complexity of security provisions depends on the size of the firm. Loans to small firms tend to be secured more often than term loans to large firms.

Security Provisions

Typical security features include the assignment of payments due under a specific contract to the lender, an assignment of a portion of the receivables or inventories, and a pledge of marketable securities held by the borrower. Other features include a mortgage on property, plant, and equipment held by the borrower and the assignment of the cash surrender value of a life insurance policy held by the borrower on key executives.

Affirmative Covenants

An affirmative covenant is a portion of a loan agreement that specifies the actions the borrowing firm agrees to take during the term of the loan. These typically include furnishing periodic financial statements to the lender, carrying sufficient insurance to cover insurable business risks, maintaining a minimum amount of net working capital, and retaining key management personnel acceptable to the lending institution.

Negative Covenants

Negative covenants restrict the actions of the borrower. They include limiting the amount of dividends that can be paid, the level of salaries and bonuses that may be given to the borrower's employees, the total amount of indebtedness that can be assumed by the borrower, and investments in plant and equipment and acquisitions. The borrower also may be required to obtain the lender's approval before certain assets can be sold.

Default Provisions

All loan agreements have default provisions permitting the lender to collect the loan immediately under certain conditions. These conditions might include the borrower failing to pay interest, principal, or both in accordance with the terms of the loan agreement; the borrower materially misrepresenting information on the firm's financial statements; and the borrower failing to observe any of the affirmative or negative covenants. Loan agreements also commonly have ***cross-default provisions*** allowing a lender to collect its loan immediately if the borrower is in default on a loan to another lender.

CASH-FLOW OR UNSECURED LENDERS

Cash-flow lenders view the borrower's future cash-flow generation capability as the primary means of recovering a loan and the borrower's assets as a secondary source of funds in the event of default by the borrower. Cash flow–based lending for LBOs became more commonplace during the mid-to-late 1980s. Aggressive bidding began to force purchase prices to levels well in excess of the value of the target's tangible assets. Borrowers increasingly were seeking funding for amounts well in excess of what traditional asset-based lenders would provide. Consequently, many LBOs' capital structures assumed increasing amounts of unsecured debt. To compensate for additional risk, the unsecured lenders would receive both a higher interest rate and warrants that were convertible into equity at some future date. Unsecured debt often is referred to as ***mezzanine financing***. In liquidation, it lies between the secured or asset-based debt and preferred and common equity. Unsecured financing often consists of several layers of debt, each subordinate in liquidation to the next most senior issue. Those with the lowest level of security normally offer the highest yields to compensate for their higher level of risk in the event of default.

Types of Long-Term Financing

Long-term debt generally is classified according to whether it is secured or not. *Secured debt* issues usually are called mortgage bonds or equipment trust certificates. Issues not secured by specific assets are called *debentures*. Because debentures are unsecured, their quality depends on the general credit worthiness of the issuing company. The attractiveness of long-term debt is its relatively low after-tax cost as a result of the tax deductibility of interest. In addition, leverage can help improve earnings per share and returns on equity. However, too much debt can increase the risk of default on loan repayments and bankruptcy.

Senior and Junior Debt

Long-term debt issues also are classified by whether they are senior or junior in liquidation. Senior debt has a higher priority claim to a firm's earnings and assets than junior debt. Unsecured debt also may be classified according to whether it is subordinated to other types of debt. In general, subordinated debentures are junior to other types of debt, including bank loans, and even may be junior to all of a firm's other debt. The extent to which a debt issue is junior to other debt depends on the restrictions placed on the company by the purchasers of the issue in an agreement called an indenture.

Indentures

An *indenture* is a contract between the firm that issues the long-term debt securities and the lenders. The indenture details the nature of the issue, specifies the way in which the principal must be repaid, and specifies affirmative and negative covenants applicable to the long-term debt issue. Typical negative covenants include maintaining a minimum interest coverage ratio, a minimum level of working capital, a maximum amount of dividends that the firm can pay, and restrictions on equipment leasing and issuing additional debt (Emery and Finnerty, 1992).

Seller Financing

A sometimes overlooked source of financing is to have the seller agree to carry a promissory note for some portion of the purchase price. This may be especially important when the buyer is unable to finance the bulk of the purchase price and is unwilling or unable to put in more equity capital. Seller financing may be used as a means of "closing the gap" on the purchase price. Such financing generally is unsecured. If the business being purchased is part of a larger parent company, the borrower may be able to obtain certain concessions from the parent. For example, the parent may be willing to continue to provide certain products and services to the business at cost to increase the likelihood that the business is successful and that its note will be repaid in a timely fashion.

Bond Ratings

Debt issues are rated by various rating agencies according to their relative degree of risk. These agencies include Moody's Investors Services and Standard and Poor's (S&P) Corporation. Factors considered by these agencies when assessing risk include a firm's earnings stability, interest coverage ratios, the relative amount of debt in the firm's capital structure, the degree of subordination of the issue being rated, and the firm's past performance in meeting its debt service requirements. Each rating agency has a scale for identifying the risk of an issue. For Moody's, the ratings are Aaa, Aa, A, Baa, Ba, B, Caa, Ca, and C, with Aaa the lowest and C the highest risk category. AAA denotes the lowest risk category for S&P. This rating is followed by AA, A, BBB, BB, B, CCC, CC, C, and D.

JUNK BONDS

Junk bonds are high-yield bonds either rated by the credit-rating agencies as below investment grade or not rated at all. Noninvestment grade bonds usually are rated Ba or lower by Moody's or BB or lower by S&P. When originally issued, junk bonds typically yield more than 4 percentage points above the yields on U.S. Treasury debt of comparable maturity. Junk bond financing exploded in the 1980s. Between 1970 and 1977, junk bond issues accounted for about 3–4% of total publicly issued corporate bonds; by 1985, their share of corporate debt issues rose to more than 14%. The sharp growth of junk bonds reflected their growing acceptance by the public debt market to finance the internal growth requirements of high-growth corporations and to finance corporate takeovers, particularly LBOs. Although junk bonds were a popular source of financing for takeovers, about three-fourths of the total proceeds of junk bonds issued between 1980 and 1986 were used to finance the capital requirements of high-growth corporations (Yago, 1991). The remainder was used to finance corporate takeovers. This source of LBO financing dried up as a result of a series of defaults of over-leveraged firms in the late 1980s, coupled with alleged insider trading and fraud at such companies as Drexel Burnham, the primary market maker for junk bonds. The collapse of several large savings and loans, which had been major investors in junk bonds, as well as the onslaught of the 1990–1991 recession compounded, these problems.

Concerns about Quality

The rapid growth of the junk bond market coincided with a growing deterioration in the quality of such issues. Wigmore (1994) found that the quality of the junk bonds issued during the 1980s deteriorated in terms of such measures as interest coverage ratios (i.e., earnings before interest and taxes, or EBIT/interest expense, debt/net tangible book value, and cash flow as a percentage of debt). Cumulative default rates for junk bonds issued in the late 1970s reached as high as 34% by 1986 (Asquith, Mullins, and Wolff, 1989). Despite these high default rates, some portion of the face value of the junk bond issues often was recovered because firms formerly in default emerged from bankruptcy. Altman and Kishore (1996) found that recovery rates for senior secured debt averaged about 58% of the original principal. Taking recovery rates into consideration, they found the actual realized spread between junk bonds and 10-year U.S. Treasury securities was actually about 2 percentage points between 1978 and 1994 rather than more than 4 percentage points when they were issued originally.

Empirical Studies of the Junk Bond Market

Early studies of the junk or high-yield bond market suggested that bonds that were considered below investment grade showed higher returns than those considered investment grade even after the losses resulting from default were deducted from the junk bond yields (Hickman, 1958). Consequently, it made sense for investors to purchase the lower rated bonds as long as their higher yields offset default losses. Although a study by Fraine and Mills (1961) questioned Hickman's conclusions, later studies suggested that default rates on junk bonds were indeed only 2.1% as compared with about zero on investment-grade bonds during the 1970–1984 period (Altman and Namacher, 1985; Fitzpatrick and Severiens, 1984; and Fridson, 1984).

These early studies often did not account for the possibility that the default risk associated with a noninvestment grade bond may increase the longer the elapsed time since its original issue date. Consequently, during periods like the late 1980s, when the issuance of junk bonds reached record levels, the average default rate on junk bonds appeared to be low primarily because newly issued bonds were likely to have relatively low default rates.

Reflecting the cumulative impact of the higher default rates on bonds issued in the early 1980s, it is not surprising that junk bond default rates reached a record level of 10% in the early 1990s. Since then, default rates stabilized at their long-term rate of about 2% during the mid-to-late 1990s. However, the difference on yields between junk bonds and 10-year Treasury securities rose to more than 5 percentage points by the end of the decade as a result of the increasing default rate on high-yield bonds to more than 6% in 1999 (*Business Week*, 1999). Concerns about the rising default rate were exacerbated as a result of worries about the impact of increasing interest rates on slowing the economy.

OTHER SOURCES OF FUNDS

Unlike debt and preferred stock, which are fixed income securities, common stock is a variable income security. Common stockholders participate in the firm's future earnings because they may receive a larger dividend if

earnings increase. Preferred stock has both debt and common equity characteristics. Like common stock, preferred stock is part of shareholders' equity.
Although preferred stockholders receive dividends instead of interest payments,
it is considered a fixed income security. Dividends on preferred stock are
generally constant over time, like interest payments on debt, but the firm is
generally not obligated to pay them at a specific point in time. Unpaid dividends may cumulate for eventual payment by the issuer if the preferred stock
is a special cumulative issue. In liquidation, bondholders are paid first, then preferred stockholders; common stockholders are paid last. Preferred stock often
is issued in LBO transactions because it provides investors a fixed income
security, which has a claim that is senior to common stock in the event of
liquidation. Table 11-2 summarizes the key characteristics of an LBO's capital
structure.

TABLE 11-2   Leveraged Buyout Capital Structure

Type of Security		Debt	
	Backed By	Lenders Loan Up to	Lending Source
Secured Debt (Asset-Based Lending) —Short-Term (<1 Year) Debt	—Liens generally on receivables and inventories	—50–80% depending on quality	—Commercial banks and finance companies
—Intermediate Term (1–10 Years) Debt	—Liens on land and equipment	—Up to 80% of appraised value of equipment and 50% of real estate	—Life insurance companies and LBO funds
Unsecured or Mezzanine Debt (Subordinated and Junior Subordinated Debt, Including Seller Financing) —First Layer —Second Layer —Etc.	Cash generating capabilities of the borrower	Face value of securities	Life insurance companies and LBO funds
Equity			
Preferred Stock	Cash generating capabilities of the borrower		Life insurance companies and LBO funds
Common Stock	Cash generating capabilities of the borrower		Life insurance and venture capital funds

COMMON FORMS OF LEVERAGED
BUYOUT STRUCTURES

As noted previously, LBOs are either asset- or cash-flow based. As a result of the epidemic of bankruptcies of overleveraged cash flow–based LBOs in the late 1980s, the most common form of LBO today is the asset-based LBO. This type of LBO can be accomplished in two ways: (1) the sale of assets by the target to the acquiring company or (2) a merger of the target into the acquiring company (direct merger) or a wholly owned subsidiary of the acquiring company (subsidiary merger).

LENDER COMMITMENT LETTERS

The typical transaction begins with a letter of intent between the seller and buyer, stipulating such basic items as price, terms of sale, assumption of liabilities, and closing deadlines. The acquirer often is asked for a *commitment letter* from a lender, which commits the lender to providing financing for the transaction. Closing is conditioned on the acquirer's ability to obtain financing. The commitment letter allows the lender to have access to the target company's records for credit evaluation and to conduct asset appraisals. It outlines the maximum loan amounts, interest charges, repayment schedule, and ratio of advances to assets pledged. The commitment letter is conditioned on the lender having performed adequate due diligence and the execution of an agreement of purchase and sale between the buyer and seller.

DIRECT MERGER

If the LBO is structured as a direct merger in which the seller receives cash for stock, the lender then will make the loan to the buyer once the appropriate security agreements are in place and the target's stock has been pledged against the loan. The target then is merged into the acquiring company, which is the surviving corporation. Payment of the loan proceeds is made directly to the seller in accordance with a letter of direction drafted by the buyer. For closely held corporations, the lender may make the loan directly to the selling corporation, which then transfers the proceeds as a dividend to its stockholders, or to the buyer, who has responsibility for paying the selling corporation's stockholders. All of these activities, including the closing of the acquisition, the asset-based loan closing, the distribution to the shareholders, and the merger of the target into the acquiring firm, take place simultaneously at the closing.

SUBSIDIARY MERGER

LBOs may be consummated by establishing a new subsidiary that merges with the target. This may be done to avoid any negative impact that the new company might have on existing customer or creditor relationships. If some portion of the parent's assets are to be used as collateral to support the ability of its operating subsidiary to fund the transaction, both the parent and the subsidiary may be viewed as having a security interest in the debt. As such, they may be held jointly and severally liable for the debt. To avoid this situation, the parent may make a capital contribution to the subsidiary rather than provide collateral or a loan guarantee.

LEGAL PITFALLS OF IMPROPERLY STRUCTURED LBOs

Fraudulent conveyance laws take effect whenever a company goes into bankruptcy following a highly leveraged transaction. Under the law, the new company created by the LBO must be strong enough to meet its obligations to current and future creditors. If the new company is found by the court to have been inadequately capitalized to remain viable, the lender could be stripped of its secured position in the assets of the company or its claims on the assets could be made subordinate to those of the general or unsecured creditors. Consequently, lenders, sellers, directors, or their agents, including auditors and investment bankers, may be required to compensate the general creditors. Fraudulent conveyance laws are intended to preclude shareholders, secured creditors, and others from benefiting at the expense of unsecured creditors. The legal basis for these concerns are embodied in the U.S. Bankruptcy Code, the Uniform Fraudulent Conveyance Act, the Uniform Fraudulent Transfer Act, and other state statutes pertaining to fraudulent conveyance.

Avoiding Fraudulent Conveyance

A properly structured LBO should have a balance sheet that indicates solvency at the time of closing. Reasonable cash-flow projections should show the generation of sufficient cash to repay the firm's obligations for at least 1 year after the acquisition. In the case of corporate divestitures, the projected cash flows should include the effect of additional interest and principal repayment and the cost of services previously provided by its parent corporation. Finally, the cash impact of off-balance sheet liabilities, such as pending litigation, also should be quantified and included in the projections.

Lender Due Diligence

The lender can be expected to make a careful evaluation of the quality of the assets to be used as collateral. Receivables will be analyzed to determine the proportion beyond normal collection terms. An assessment of the likelihood that the receivables realistically can be converted to cash also will be made. The receivables also will be evaluated for consignments, bill and hold sales, allowances and discounts, potential bad debts, and unapplied credits or charge backs. A physical inspection of the inventory and inventory records will be made to establish both the quantitative and qualitative values of the inventory. Obsolete and unmarketable goods will be written down in value. Fixed assets will be appraised at their realistic "quick-sale" values by professional appraisers. Values also should be placed on off-balance sheet assets such as patents, trademarks, licenses, franchises, copyrights, and blueprints.

CRITICAL SUCCESS FACTORS

Factors critical to the success of a leveraged buyout include knowing what to buy, not overpaying, and the ability to improve operating performance.

KNOWING WHAT TO BUY

Firms that represent good candidates for an LBO are those that have substantial tangible assets, unused borrowing capacity, predictable positive operating cash flow, and assets that are not critical to the continuing operation of the business (Carow and Roden, 1998). Competent and highly motivated management is always crucial to the eventual success of the LBO.

Unused Borrowing Capacity, Tax Shelter, and Redundant Assets

A number of factors enhance borrowing capacity. These include cash balances on the books of the target company in excess of working capital requirements, a low debt-to-total capital ratio (as compared with the industry average), and a demonstrated ability to generate consistent earnings and cash-flow growth. Firms with undervalued assets may use such assets as collateral for loans from asset-based lenders. Such assets also provide a significant tax shelter because they may be revalued and depreciated or amortized over their allowable tax lives. In addition, operating assets, such as subsidiaries that are not germane to the target's core business and that can be sold quickly for cash, can be divested to accelerate the payoff of either the highest cost debt or the debt with the most restrictive covenants.

Management Competence and Motivation

Although the quality of management is always an important factor in the eventual success of a merger or acquisition, it tends to be critical to LBOs. Although management competence is a necessary condition for success, it does not ensure that the firm's performance will meet investor expectations. Management must be highly motivated by the prospect of abnormally large returns in a relatively short time. Consequently, management of the firm to be taken private is normally given an opportunity to own a significant portion of the equity of the firm.

Attractive Industries

Typical targets are in mature industries such as manufacturing, retailing, textiles, food processing, apparel, and soft drinks. Such industries usually are characterized by large tangible book values; modest growth prospects; relatively stable cash flow; and limited research and development (R&D), new product, or technology requirements. Such industries are generally not dependent on technologies and production processes that are subject to rapid change.

Large Company Operating Divisions

The best candidates for management buyouts are often underperforming divisions of larger companies in which the division is no longer considered critical to the parent firm's overarching strategy. Frequently, such divisions are saddled with excessive administrative overhead, often required by the parent, and expenses are allocated to the division by the parent for services such as legal, auditing, and treasury functions that could be purchased less expensively from sources outside the parent firm. These often represent excellent cost-reduction opportunities once the division becomes independent of the parent. Moreover, lack of attention by the parent often results in missed opportunities for the division because the parent is unlikely to fully fund investment opportunities that it does not consider critical to its overall business strategy.

NOT OVERPAYING

The key to a successful LBO is not to overpay for the acquisition. Although overpaying for any acquisition, highly leveraged or otherwise, almost always impairs the ability of the acquiring firm to achieve expected financial returns, it can be disastrous for LBOs. Forecasted cash flows often are subject to significant error. If the firm's projected operating earnings are even slightly lower than projected, its ability to meet interest and principal payments is jeopardized.

Failure to meet debt service obligations in a timely fashion often requires that the LBO firm renegotiate the terms of the loan agreements with the lenders. In exchange for deferring debt repayments or for reducing interest payments, lenders will demand concessions in the form of increased equity ownership in the LBO firm. The issuance of additional shares to accommodate the lenders' demands for increased ownership dilutes the ownership position of the initial investors. If the parties to the transaction cannot reach a compromise, the firm may be forced to file for bankruptcy. In this circumstance, the value of the initial investors' investment may be wiped out as the firm is forced to reorganize under the protection of the bankruptcy court (see Chapter 13).

Highly leveraged firms often are subject to aggressive tactics from major competitors. Such competitors understand that taking on large amounts of debt will raise the break-even point for the firm. If the amount borrowed is made even more excessive as a result of having paid more than the economic value of the target firm, the competitors may opt to gain market share by cutting product prices. The ability of the LBO firm to match such price cuts is limited because of the need to maintain enough cash flow to meet required interest and principal repayments.

IMPROVING OPERATING PERFORMANCE

Financial buyers succeed through improving operational performance. The discipline imposed by the need to satisfy debt service requirements focuses management's attention on maximizing operating cash flows. Standard tactics include attempting to negotiate employee wage and benefit concessions in exchange for a profit-sharing or stock ownership plan. Outsourcing services once provided by the parent often result in significant savings. Other cost-cutting tactics include moving the corporate headquarters to a less expensive location or to a more functional facility and aggressively pruning marginally profitable customer accounts. It is also commonplace for management to eliminate "loss leader products" (those that supposedly facilitate the sale of more profitable products) and to cancel "frivolous" perks such as corporate aircraft.

Often operating performance can be improved simply by paying more attention to short-term considerations rather than focusing on more involved long-term strategies. This switch in emphasis may result in less money being spent on R&D, new product development, and new technologies. This behavior does not necessarily imply that the LBO firm is mortgaging its future. It may mean that the discipline imposed by debt may compel managers to more clearly prioritize investment opportunities and to concentrate their available resources on those with the shortest payback period. Holthausen and Larker (1996) found that LBOs after being taken public tended to increase capital expenditures and working capital while they were outperforming their industry competitors. Even as the proportion of debt in highly leveraged transactions has tended to drop during the last decade, there is no reason to believe that LBO managers will be any less motivated than in the glory days of the 1980s. As board members, buyout specialists such as LBO funds tend to take a much more active role in monitoring management performance. Empirical studies show that LBOs whose board members actively monitor and motivate management tend to perform better than those whose investors are largely passive (Cotter and Peck, 2001).

IMPACT ON SHAREHOLDER RETURNS OF LEVERAGED BUYOUTS

RETURNS TO TARGET SHAREHOLDERS (PREBUYOUT RETURNS)

The studies cited in Table 11-3 show that the premium paid by LBOs and MBOs to target company shareholders consistently exceed 40%. The distinction made in these studies of highly leveraged transactions between MBOs and LBOs is that in the MBO there is not third-party equity participation in the firm that is being taken private. The management group organizing the MBO provides equity. These empirical studies also include so-called *reverse LBOs*. These are public companies

TABLE 11-3   Returns to Target Shareholders (Prebuyout Returns)

Empirical Study[1]	
Nondivisional Buyouts	Premium Paid to Target Shareholders
DeAngelo, DeAngelo, and Rice (1984) (Sample size = 72 MBOs)	56% (1973–1983)[2] 76% (when there are 3 or more bids)
Lowenstein (1985) (Sample size = 28 MBOs)	48% (1979–1984)
Lehn and Poulsen (1988) (Sample size = 92 LBOs)	41% (1980–1984)
Divisional Buyouts	Return to Parent Corporation Shareholders
Hite and Vetsuypens (1989) (Sample = 151 MBOs)	.55% (1983–1987)
Muscarella and Vetsuypens (1990) (Sample size = 45 MBOs)	1.98% (1983–1988)

[1] MBO, management buyout; LBO, leveraged buyout.
[2] The years in parentheses represent the time period in which the study took place.

that are taken private and later are taken public again. The second effort to take the firm public is called a ***secondary initial public offering***.

As noted previously, ***divisional buyouts*** represent opportunities for improved operating efficiency as the division is removed from the bureaucracy of the parent. Although this may be a source of gain for the acquirer, it does not seem to be true for the shareholders of the parent firm divesting the division. The parent firm's shareholders seem to receive only miniscule returns. The small size of these returns may reflect the division's relatively small share of the parent corporation's total market value. Alternatively, the parent's management may forego the auction process in favor of the division's management. In either case, the parent corporation's share price is unlikely to materially benefit from the divestiture. The fact that parent shareholders experience any gain at all may suggest that the parent's resources are redeployed to higher return investments.

FACTORS DETERMINING PREBUYOUT RETURNS

Table 11-4 summarizes the empirical research, which attempts to identify the factors that explain sizable gains in share price that accrue to prebuyout shareholders.

Anticipated Improvement in Efficiency and Tax Benefits

The most often cited sources of these returns are from tax benefits and from expected post-LBO improvements in efficiency as a result of management incentives and the discipline imposed by the need to repay debt, which motivate

TABLE 11-4   Factors Contributing to Pre-LBO Buyout Returns to Shareholders

Factor	Theory	Evidence[1]
Management Incentives		
Equity Ownership Kaplan (1989–1991) (Sample size = 76 MBOs)	Management will improve performance when their ownership stake increases.	Management ownership increased for MBOs between 1980 and 1986 from 8.3% before the buyout to 29% after the buyout.
Incentive (Profit Sharing) Plans Muscarella & Vetsuypens (1990) (Sample size = 72 reverse LBOs)	Stock option and share appreciation plans motivate management to take cost-cutting actions that might otherwise have been unacceptable.	96% of LBOs had at least one and 75% had two incentive plans in place during the 1983–1988 period. Moreover, the change in shareholder gain is positively correlated with the fraction of shares owned by LBO's officers.
Improved Operating Performance Holthausen & Larker (1996) (Sample size = 90 reverse LBOs)	Equity ownership and incentive plans motivate management to initiate aggressive cost-reduction plans and to change marketing strategies.	For the 1983–1988 period, sales were up by 9.4% in real terms and operating profits were up by 45.4% between the LBO announcement date and the secondary initial public offering. Firm performance also was highly correlated with the amount of ownership by officers and directors.
Kaplan (1989b)		Operating income in LBO firms increased more than in other firms in the same industry during 2 years following the LBO.
Tax Shelter Benefits		
Kaplan (1989a)	An LBO can be tax free for as long as 5–7 years.	Median Value of tax shelter contributed 30% of the premium.
Lehn & Poulsen (1988)		Premium paid to pre-LBO shareholders positively correlated with pre-LBO tax liability/equity.
Wealth Transfer Effects		
Lehn & Poulsen (1988)	Premiums represent a transfer of wealth from bondholders to common stockholders.	Found no evidence that bondholders and preferred stockholders lose value when an LBO is announced.
Travlos & Cornett (1993)		Found small losses associated with the LBO announcement.
Investor Group Has Better Information (Asymmetric Information) on MBO Target		
Kaplan (1988) and Smith (1990)	Investor group believes target worth more than shareholders believe it is.	Found no evidence to support this theory.
Improved Efficiency in Decision Making		
Travlos and Cornett (1993)	Private firms are less bureaucratic and do not incur reporting and servicing costs associated with public shareholders.	Shareholder-related expenses are not an important factor; difficult to substantiate more efficient decision making.

[1] MBO, managed buyout; LBO, leveraged buyout.

aggressive cost cutting. Michael Jensen (1986) argues that managers cannot be trusted to invest free cash flows in a manner that is necessarily in the best interests of the stockholders; debt imposes a discipline that forces them to stay focused on maximizing operating cash flows. Tax benefits are largely predictable and are built into the premium offered for the public shares of the target firm as a result of the negotiation process (Kaplan, 1989b).

Wealth Transfer Effects

The evidence supporting wealth transfer effects is mixed for most LBO transactions. The exception may be for very large LBOs such as RJR Nabisco, where largely anecdotal evidence seems to suggest that a significant transfer of wealth may have taken place between the firm's pre-LBO debt holders and shareholders.

Superior Knowledge

It sometimes is argued that LBO investors have knowledge of a business that is superior to that held by the firm's public shareholders. Therefore, the LBO investors are motivated to pay such high premiums because they understand more effective ways to use the firm's resources. This argument has some intuitive appeal when the firm's management is involved in the proposed buyout. However, there is little empirical evidence to support this proposition.

More Efficient Decision Making

There is also little empirical evidence to support the notion that decision making is more efficient. Nonetheless, the intuitive appeal of the simplified decision-making process of a private company is compelling when contrasted with a public company with multiple constituents directly or indirectly affecting decision making. Examples of such constituents include a board of directors with outside directors, public shareholders, and Wall Street analysts.

FACTORS DETERMINING POSTBUYOUT RETURNS

Table 11-5 summarizes the studies on returns to shareholders following a leveraged buyout. A number of empirical studies suggest that investors in LBOs have earned abnormal profits on their initial investments. The presumption in these studies seems to be that the full effect of increased operating efficiency following a leveraged buyout is not fully reflected in the pre-LBO premium. These studies may be subject to selection bias in that only LBOs that are successful in significantly improving their operating performance are able to undertake a secondary public offering. Mian and Rosenfeld (1993) noted that in many instances the abnormal returns earned by postbuyout shareholders were the result of the LBO being acquired by another firm in the 3 years immediately following the LBO announcement.

TABLE 11-5   Postbuyout Returns to LBO Shareholders[1]

Empirical Study	Impact on Postbuyout Performance
Muscarella and Vetsuypens (1990) (Sample Size = 45 MBOs from 1983–1987)	Of 41 firms going public, median annual return was 36.6% in 3 years following buyout.
Kaplan (1991) (Sample size = 21 MBOs from 1979–1986)	Median annualized return was 26% higher than the gain on the S&P 500 during the 3-year postbuyout period.
Mian and Rosenfeld (1993) (Sample Size = 85 reverse LBOs from 1983–1989)	Of the 33 LBOs that were acquired by another firm during the 3 years following the LBO, cumulative abnormal returns exceeded 21%. Of those not acquired, cumulative abnormal returns were zero.
Holthausen and Larker (1996) (Sample Size = 90 reverse LBOs from 1983–1988)	Firms outperformed their industries over the 4 years following the secondary IPO.

[1] MBO, managed buyout; LBO, leveraged buyout.

ANALYZING LEVERAGED BUYOUTS

An LBO can be evaluated from the perspective of common equity investors only or from the perspective of all investors, including preferred stockholders and debt holders. Because common equity investors often represent less than 10% of the total financing required for the transaction, it normally makes sense to evaluate the transaction from the standpoint of all investors in the LBO.

CAPITAL BUDGETING METHODOLOGY

Conventional capital budgeting procedures may be used to evaluate the LBO. The transaction makes sense from the viewpoint of all investors in the transaction if the present value (PV) of the cash flows to the firm (PV_{FCFF}) or enterprise value, discounted at the weighted average cost of capital, equals or exceeds the total investment consisting of debt, common equity, and preferred equity ($I_{D+E+PFD}$) required to buy the outstanding shares of the target company.

$$PV_{FCFF} - I_{D+E+PFD} \geq 0$$

If this is true, the target firm can earn its cost of capital and return sufficient cash flow to all parties to the transaction, enabling them to achieve their required returns.

If the PV_{FCFE} or equity value, discounted at the cost of equity, equals or exceeds the common equity investment (I_E) in the transaction, common equity investors are able to earn or exceed their required returns.

$$PV_{FCFE} - I_E \geq 0$$

However, it is possible for a leveraged buyout to make sense to common equity investors but not to other investors such as pre-LBO debt holders and preferred stockholders.

The market value of the debt and preferred stock on the books of the target firm before the announcement of the LBO reflects two factors. First, the firm must be able to repay in a timely fashion both principal and interest. Second, the firm must be able to continue to make required dividend payments on preferred equity. The ability to meet these obligations often is measured by comparing such ratios for the target firm as debt-to-equity and interest coverage with those of comparable firms. Once the LBO has been consummated, the firm's perceived ability to meet these obligations often will deteriorate because the firm takes on a substantial amount of new debt. The firm's pre-LBO debt and preferred stock may be revalued in the open market by investors to reflect this higher perceived risk, resulting in a significant reduction in the market value of both debt and preferred equity owned by pre-LBO investors. Although there is little empirical evidence to show that this is typical of LBOs, this revaluation may characterize large LBOs such as RJR Nabisco (see Case Study 11-2 at the end of the chapter).

ANALYZING AND VALUING LBOs: VARIABLE RISK VERSUS ADJUSTED PRESENT VALUE METHOD

Two commonly used methods for valuing leveraged buyouts include the variable risk approach (VRA) and the adjusted present value (APV) method. Although computationally simpler than the VRA technique outlined in this chapter, the APV method rests on highly problematic assumptions. The APV method applied to equity cash flows involves a three-step procedure. First, the target firm is valued without any debt financing and with the projected free cash flows to equity (FCFE) investors discounted at the firm's estimated unlevered cost of equity. Second, the value of the firm's tax savings, which result from financing the transaction with debt, are estimated. Finally, the present value of the target firm without debt and the present value of the tax savings are added together to estimate the present value of the firm's equity including tax benefits. Theoretically, the same equity valuation can be obtained by deducting the market value of debt from the enterprise value of the firm if the analyst is able to estimate the firm's true cost of equity and debt. The key considerations are the choice of discount rate and the assumption that the discount rate is unaffected by changes in the firm's leverage.

The justification for this approach rests on the theoretical notion that the value of a firm should not be affected by the way in which it is financed (Brealey and Meyers, 1996). This notion assumes investors have access to perfect information, the firm is not growing and no new borrowing is required, and there are no taxes and transaction costs. Under these assumptions, the earning power and risk associated with the firm's assets determine the value of the firm. Tax effects can be introduced by adjusting the discount rate used to value the target firm. Although the proposition that the value of the firm should be independent of the way in which it is financed may make sense for a firm whose debt-to-capital ratio is similar to the industry's, it strains credulity when it is applied to highly leveraged transactions. In these situations, the LBO's leverage may be three or four times the industry's average leverage.

Copeland, Koller, and Murrin (2000) argue that the appropriate discount rate applied to both the FCFE investors and to the projected tax savings should be the firm's unlevered cost of equity. However, it is unclear whether this discount rate is the cost of debt or some rate between the cost of debt and the unlevered cost of equity. Assuming a constant debt-to-equity ratio, they argue that future earnings and cash flow will determine the future amount of debt and tax benefits. Under these circumstances, the uncertainty associated with FCFE investors and tax savings should be the same, and the appropriate discount rate also would be the same. In contrast, the cost of debt makes sense if you accept the proposition that uncertainty about the firm's ability to realize the projected tax savings is best measured by using the rate lenders are willing to lend to the firm.

In practice, the debt-to-equity ratio of the highly leveraged firm is not constant; rather, it changes over time as the firm reduces leverage. The driving force behind many LBOs and MBOs is to reduce the firm's debt-to-equity ratio to make the firm more attractive to investors in an IPO or to a strategic investor. Consequently, the levered discount rate changes over time to reflect changes in the perceived risk of the firm. In view of the tenuous nature of the assumptions underlying the APV method and the uncertainty associated with the choice of discount rate, the balance of this chapter focuses on explaining the VRA, which adjusts the discount rate for changes in the leverage of the firm over time.

APPLYING THE VARIABLE RISK APPROACH

What follows is a seven-step procedure to determine if a leveraged buyout opportunity makes sense from the viewpoint of all investors to the transaction. Although the discount rate used in calculating the terminal value may change, conventional discounted cash flow valuation normally assumes that the discount rate remains constant during the cash flow forecast period. Although this may be sensible for many valuation situations, it is inappropriate for valuing highly leveraged transactions. Conventional LBO strategy calls for a rapid reduction of debt and a concomitant buildup of equity. This implies that declining leverage will reduce the cost of equity by lowering the magnitude of the firm's levered beta each period during which the outstanding debt is paid off. If the firm's target debt-to-total capital ratio is used to calculate the weights, the firm's total cost of capital also will decline.

Estimating the Total Cost of the Transaction (Step 1)

The total cost of the transaction normally is viewed as the purchase price of the target firm's outstanding shareholders' equity plus any debt on the target's books that is assumed by the acquirer. For simplicity, we will assume that the LBO target

TABLE 11-6   Estimating the Total Cost of an LBO

Total Cost (Assuming the target firm has no debt)	$ Millions
Buy Back 10 Million Shares @ $50/share	500.00
Transaction Expenses (2% of transaction value)	10.00
Total Purchase Price of Equity	510.00

has no outstanding debt. Thus, the first step involves the estimation of the total cost of buying the stock of the current shareholders of the target firm (Table 11-6).

Determining the Preliminary Mix of Debt and Equity (Step 2)

Step 2 requires the analyst to estimate the borrowing capacity of the firm and to make an assumption about the amount of equity to be invested in the LBO as a percentage of the total purchase price.

Estimating Borrowing Capacity

The amount of total debt the target firm may be able to borrow can be approximated using the average interest coverage ratio (EBIT/interest expense) for other firms in the same industry or by using the interest coverage ratio for recent comparable transactions. If the target firm has a sustainable annual EBIT of $65 million and the industry average interest coverage ratio (EBIT/interest expense) is 1.3, the firm can support up to $50 million in annual interest expense ($65/1.3). If the current prevailing average market rate of interest on transactions of this type is 11%, the firm has a potential capacity to borrow up to $455 million ($50/.11).

Although it is possible that the firm could borrow as much as 89% ($455/$510) of the total purchase price, it is likely to borrow less in practice. Any shortfall between projected and actual cash flows could result in the firm having to borrow additional funds to satisfy working capital requirements. The firm may be able to exceed its potential borrowing capacity only by paying a significantly higher interest rate to compensate lenders for the increase in perceived risk. The increase in interest expense could trigger a downward spiral toward default if the firm is unable to improve operating cash flows.

Estimating the Equity Contribution

For purposes of illustration, the preliminary financing mix is displayed in Table 11-7 using a percentage distribution of debt and equity similar to that used by LBOs during the 1980s. According to a study of 107 LBOs formed between 1981 and 1990 by Roden and Lewellen (1995), debt comprised 85% and equity comprised 15% of the total cost of the average transaction. These transactions accounted for about two-thirds of the total dollar volume of LBOs during that period. Note that in our illustration, borrowing 85% of the purchase price of $510 million gives the LBO investors a small 5% margin of error ($433.50/$455.00).

TABLE 11-7   Approximating the Mix of Debt and Equity

Preliminary Financing Mix	$ Millions
Debt @ 85% of the total cost of the transaction	433.50
Equity @ 15% of total cost	76.50
Total proceeds	510.00

TABLE 11-8   Alternative Cash-Flow Definitions[1]

FCFF Calculation (Enterprise Method)	FCFE Calculation (Equity Method)
EBIT	FCFF
− EBIT (t)	− Interest $(1 - t)$
= EBIT $(1 - t)$	− Principal repayment
+ Depreciation	+ New debt issues
− Gross capital expenditures	− Preferred stock dividends
− Δ Working capital	
= FCFF	= FCFE

[1] FCFF, free cash flows to the firm; FCFE, free cash flows to equity holders; EBIT, earnings before interest and taxes.

Projecting Annual Cash Flows (Step 3)

Step 3 involves projecting free cash flow to the firm (FCFF) and to equity (FCFE). FCFF measures the cash flow available to pay interest and principal repayments, preferred dividends, and common dividends after all other obligations of the firm have been met. FCFE measures the cash flow available for common equity investors after all other financing obligations have been satisfied (Table 11-8). See Chapter 7 for additional detail on these definitions of free cash flow.

These cash flows should be projected annually until the LBO has achieved its target debt-to-equity ratio. Because the LBO wishes to recover its investment and required return by either selling to a strategic buyer or engaging in a secondary public offering, the LBO must make two calculations to determine its target debt-to-equity ratio. The first is to determine at what level of debt relative to equity the firm will have to resume paying taxes. The point at which this occurs depends on the firm's debt repayment schedule and projected pretax income. The second calculation is highly subjective and involves estimating the amount of leverage that may be acceptable to strategic buyers or investors in a secondary public offering at some point in the future. Thus, the target debt-to-equity ratio is that level of outstanding debt relative to equity at which the firm resumes paying taxes and which appears to be acceptable to strategic buyers or investors in a secondary public offering.

Projecting Debt-to-Equity Ratios (Step 4)

The decline in debt-to-equity ratios depends on known debt repayment schedules and the projected growth in shareholders' equity. The change in shareholders' equity is equal to net income (NI) less dividends paid to shareholders. Therefore, year-end shareholders' equity (SE) can be projected in future years assuming no dividends will be paid to equity investors of the LBO as $SE_t = NI_t + SE_{t-1}$.

Calculating Terminal Values (Step 5)

Calculate the terminal value of equity (TVE) and of the firm in year t.

$$\text{Terminal value of equity (TVE)} = FCFE_{t+1}/(k_e - g)$$
$$\text{Terminal value of the firm (TVF)} = TVE + D_t + PS_t$$

The cost of equity, k_e, and g represent the cost of equity and cash flow growth rate during the stable growth period. D_t and PS_t are the amount of debt and preferred stock outstanding at the end of year t. TVF represents the present value of the dollar proceeds available to the firm at time t. These proceeds are generated by selling equity to the public or to a "strategic buyer" and by "rolling-over" the book value of outstanding debt and preferred stock at time t. Alternatively, the terminal value of debt could be calculated by computing the present value of the estimated weighted average coupon rate on total debt outstanding at time t, where the weights represent the percentage each type of debt is of total debt. The terminal value of preferred stock also could be calculated as the present value of preferred stock dividends discounted in perpetuity at the preferred stock's dividend yield.

Adjusting the Discount Rate to Reflect Changing Risk (Step 6)

The high leverage associated with a leveraged buyout increases the risk of the cash flows available for equity investors by increasing debt service requirements. As the LBO's extremely high initial debt level is reduced, the firm's cost of equity needs to be adjusted to reflect the decline in risk, as measured by the firm's levered beta (β_{FL}). This adjustment may be estimated starting with the firm's levered beta in period 1 (β_{FL1}) as follows:

$$\beta_{FL1} = \beta_{IUL1}(1 + (D/E)_{F1}(1 - t_F))$$

where β_{IUL1} is industry unlevered β in period 1; $(D/E)_{F1}$ and t_F are the firm's debt-to-equity ratio and tax rate, respectively; and $\beta_{IUL1} = \beta_{IL1}/(1 + (D/E)_{I1}(1 - t_I))$, where β_{IL1}, $(D/E)_{I1}$, and t_I are the industry's levered β, debt-to-equity ratio, and tax rate, respectively;

$$\beta_{FL2} = [(D/E)_{F2} - (D/E)_{F1}](1 - t_F) + \beta_{FL1}$$
$$\vdots$$
$$\beta_{FLN} = [(D/E)_{FN} - (D/E)_{FN-1}](1 - t_F) + \beta_{FLN-1}$$

Generalizing $\Delta\beta_{FL} = \Delta(D/E)_F \times (1 - t_F)$.

The firm's cost of equity (k_{eF}) may be adjusted as follows:

$$\Delta k_{eF} = \Delta\beta_{FL}(R_M - R_{FR}),$$

where $R_M - R_{FR}$ is a historical average spread between the return on stocks and the risk free rate of return.

This implies a changing cost of equity and weighted average cost of capital over time. The cost of equity declines in line with the reduction in the levered beta. Using the firm's target debt-to-equity ratio to calculate the weights, the weighted average cost of capital also declines as the cost of equity falls. The use of the target debt-to-equity ratio, rather than the projected actual ratio, is appropriate to eliminate gyrations in the cost of capital because of simple fluctuations in the market value of debt and equity. The target debt-to-equity ratio could be set at the industry average debt-to-equity ratio. The beta should continue to be adjusted until the LBO's actual debt-to-equity ratio equals the industry average ratio. At this point, the LBO firm's levered beta should approximate the industry average levered beta.

Because the firm's weighted average cost of capital (WACC) changes over time, the firm's cumulative cost of capital is used to discount projected cash flows. The cumulative cost of capital is represented as follows:

$$PV_1 = FCFF_1/(1 + WACC_1)$$

$$PV_2 = FCFF_2/[(1 + WACC_1)(1 + WACC_2)]$$

$$\vdots$$

$$PV_N = FCFF_N/[(1 + WACC_1)(1 + WACC_2) \cdots (1 + WACC_N)]$$

Making Sense of the Deal (Step 7)

Making sense of the deal requires calculating the PV of FCFF and FCFE including the terminal values estimated in Step 5 and comparing it to the total cost of the transaction. The deal makes sense to common equity investors if the PV of FCFE exceeds the value of the equity investment in the deal and the PV of FCFF exceeds the total cost of the deal, equity plus debt and preferred stock. These conditions suggest that the firm has achieved returns that exceed the minimum returns required by equity investors as well as debt and preferred stock holders. For more information on valuing LBOs, see Damadoran (1997); Kretlow, McGuigan, and Moyer (1998, pp. 796–831); and Westin, Chung, and Siu (1998).

CASE STUDY 11-1: PACIFIC INVESTORS
ACQUIRES CALIFORNIA KOOL IN A
LEVERAGED BUYOUT

Pacific Investors (PI) is a small investment management group with $100 million under management. The objective of their fund is to give investors at least a 30% annual average return on their investment by judiciously investing these funds in highly leveraged transactions. Investors are required to remain in the fund for at least 5 years. PI has been able to realize such returns over the last decade because of their focus on investing in industries that have slow but predictable growth in cash flow, modest capital investment requirements, and relatively low levels of research and development spending. In the past, PI has made several lucrative investments in the contract packaging industry, which provides packaging for beverage companies that produce various types of noncarbonated and carbonated beverages. Because of its commitments to its investors, PI likes to liquidate its investments within 5 years through a secondary public offering or sale to a strategic investor and to use the proceeds of the sale to repay any outstanding debt then return what remains to its investors.

Following its past success in the industry, PI currently is negotiating with California Kool (CK), a privately owned contract beverage packaging company with the technology required to package many different types of noncarbonated drinks. CK's 1999 revenue, EBIT, and net income are $47.8 million, $7.8 million, and $2.1 million, respectively. CK does not have any debt on its balance sheet. With a reputation for effective management, CK is a medium-sized contract packaging company that owns its own plant and equipment and has a history of continually increasing cash flow. The company also has significant unused excess capacity, suggesting that production levels can be increased without substantial new capital spending. Its major customers are the large beverage companies that outsource some or all of their bottling operations to contract packaging companies as well as small start-up specialty beverage companies that devote most of their resources to marketing rather than manufacturing their products. Contract packaging companies give a beverage company a presence in a market where it would be impossible to serve without incurring a substantial capital investment to build a packaging operation on location.

The owners of CK are demanding a purchase price of at least $53.5 million. This price represents a multiple of 7 times EBIT and 26 times net income. These are significantly above multiples for comparable publicly traded companies, which are selling for about 6 times 1999 EBIT and 23 times 1999 net income. PI believes that it can finance the transaction through an equity investment of $13.5 million and a $40 million, 15-year level payment loan from an insurance company. The loan would be secured by the target's fixed assets. The annual interest rate on the loan is 11%. If it proceeds with the transaction, PI would borrow the money at the end of 1999 (Table 11-9).

Revenue for CK is projected to grow at 5% annually through 2004 and then 4% per year thereafter. The deceleration in the growth rate is in line with the overall aging of the population and a slower overall population growth rate. Operating expenses, capital spending, and working capital are expected to grow at the same rate as revenue. The target debt-to-equity ratio for the firm is .5. The cost of equity and capital declines in line with the reduction in the firm's beta as the debt is repaid. The cost of equity during the terminal period is assumed to be 10%. The industry average beta is 1.3 and debt-to-equity ratio is .5. In Tables 11-10, 11-11, and 11-12, PI treats 1999 as the base year or year zero in its calculations. Because the PV of FCFF exceeds the cost of capital, the deal makes sense from the standpoint of both lenders and equity investors. If PI were to sell the business at the end of 2004, equity investors would receive a compound annual average return of 48.3% [($65.33/$13.5)$^{.25}$] over 5 years on their initial investment of $13.5 million. This is well above the 30% return promised by PI to its fund investors. Therefore, PI should do the deal.

Case Study Discussion Questions

1. Why is it important in highly leveraged businesses to adjust for changes in the discount rte as debt is repaid?
2. Assume that Pacific investors valued California Kool using a constant discount rate (i.e., one not adjusted to reflect changes in the debt to equity ratio). Would this change Pacific investors' decision to do the deal? Show your work.

TABLE 11-9   Debt Amortization Table[1]

Year	Annual Payment[2]	Interest[3]	Principal[4]	Ending Balance[5]
1	5.56	4.40	1.16	38.84
2	5.56	4.27	1.29	37.55
3	5.56	4.13	1.43	36.12
4	5.56	3.97	1.59	34.54
5	5.56	3.80	1.76	32.78
6	5.56	3.61	1.95	30.82
7	5.56	3.39	2.17	28.65
8	5.56	3.15	2.41	26.24
9	5.56	2.89	2.67	23.57
10	5.56	2.59	2.97	20.60
11	5.56	2.27	3.29	17.31
12	5.56	1.90	3.66	13.65
13	5.56	1.50	4.06	9.59
14	5.56	1.05	4.51	5.01
15	5.56	0.55	5.01	0.00

[1]Fifteen-year, $40 million loan at an 11% annual rate of interest.
[2]Equal annual payments including principal and interest are calculated by solving the following equation for the annual payment (PMT):

PVA (PV of an annuity) = PMT × PVIAF$_{11,15}$, where PVIFA$_{11,15}$

is the present value interest factor for an annuity for 15 years at 11% interest

[3]Loan balance times annual rate of interest.
[4]Annual payment less interest payment.
[5]Beginning loan balance less principal repayment.

TABLE 11-10   Summary Pro Forma Financial Tables[1]

	1999	2000	2001	2002	2003	2004
Revenue	47.80	50.19	52.70	55.33	58.10	61.01
Less: operating expenses	35.00	36.75	38.59	40.52	42.54	44.67
Less: depreciation	4.90	5.15	5.40	5.67	5.96	6.25
Equal: EBIT	7.90	8.30	8.71	9.15	9.60	10.08
Less: interest	0.00	4.40	4.27	4.13	3.97	3.80
Equals: EBT	7.90	3.90	4.44	5.02	5.63	6.28
Less: taxes @ 40%	3.16	1.56	1.78	2.01	2.25	2.51
Equals: net income	4.74	2.34	2.66	3.01	3.38	3.77
Plus: depreciation	4.90	5.15	5.40	5.67	5.96	6.25
Less: capital expenditures	1.40	1.47	1.54	1.62	1.70	1.79
Less: Δ working capital	0.20	0.21	0.22	0.23	0.24	0.26
Less principal repayment[2]	0.00	1.16	1.29	1.43	1.59	1.76
Equals: FCFE	8.04	4.65	5.01	5.40	5.81	6.21
Plus: interest[2] $(1 - t)$	0.00	2.64	2.56	2.47	2.38	2.28
Plus principal repayment	0.00	1.16	1.29	1.43	1.59	1.76
Equals: FCFF	8.04	8.45	8.86	9.30	9.78	10.25
Equity	13.50	15.84	18.58	21.76	25.41	29.56
Debt	40.00	38.84	37.55	36.12	34.53	32.77
Debt/equity	2.96	2.45	2.02	1.66	1.36	1.11
Beta[3]	2.78	2.47	2.21	1.99	1.81	1.66
Cost of equity[4]	21.30	19.59	18.16	16.95	15.96	15.14
After-tax interest @ 11%[5]	7.00	7.00	7.00	7.00	7.00	7.00
WACC @ D/E = .5[6]	16.58	15.44	14.48	13.67	13.00	12.46

[1] EBIT, earnings before interest and taxes; FCFE, free cash flows to equity holders; FCFF, free cash flows to the firm; WACC, weighted average cost of capital; D/E, debt/equity.

[2] From debt amortization table interest and principal payment columns.

[3] Industry unlevered $\beta_u = \beta_L/(1 + (D/E)(1 - t)) = 1.3/(1 + .5(.6)) = 1.0$
LBO levered $\beta_L = \beta_u(1.0 + (D/E)(1 - t)) = 1.0(1.0 + 2.96(.6)) = 2.78$
$\Delta\beta = \Delta(D/E) \times (1 - t)$

[4] $k_e = 6.0 + 2.78(5.5) = 21.3$
$\Delta k_e = \Delta\beta(5.5)$

[5] Rounded.

[6] LBO's target debt-to-total capital ratio used to calculate weights for the weighted average cost of capital. The weights are calculated as follows:

$$\text{Debt-to-Total Capital (DTC)} = D/(D + E)$$

$$= D/(D + D/.5), \text{ since D/E} = .5 \text{ and E} = D/.5$$

$$= .5D/(.5D + D)$$

$$= .5D/1.5D$$

$$= .33$$

$$\text{Equity-to-Total Capital (ETC)} = 1 - \text{DTC} = .67$$

TABLE 11-11   Leveraged Buyout with Free Cash Flow to the Firm Valuation[1]

Year	FCFF	×	PV Factor	=	Present Value
2000	$8.45		$\dfrac{\$8.45}{(1.1544)}$		$7.32
2001	$8.86		$\dfrac{\$8.86}{(1.1544)(1.1448)}$		$6.71
2002	$9.30		$\dfrac{\$9.30}{(1.1544)(1.1448)(1.1367)}$		$6.19
2003	$9.78		$\dfrac{\$9.78}{(1.1544)(1.1448)(1.1367)(1.1300)}$		$5.76
2004	$10.25		$\dfrac{\$10.25}{(1.1544)(1.1448)(1.1367)(1.1300)(1.1246)}$		$5.37
			Sum of PV of FFCF$_{1-5}$ =		$31.35

Terminal Value of the Firm (TVF):

TVF = TVE (Terminal Value of Equity) + D (Debt)

$$= \frac{\$6.21(1.04)}{.10 - .04} + \$32.77 = \$140.41$$

$PV_{TVF} = \$140.41/(1.1544)(1.1448)(1.1367)(1.1300)(1.1246) = \$73.55$

Total Present Value = $31.35 + $73.55 = $104.90

[1] FCFF, free cash flow to the firm; PV, present value; TVF, terminal value of the firm; TVE, terminal value of equity; D, debt.

TABLE 11-12   Leveraged Buyout with Free Cash Flow to Equity Valuation[1]

Year	FCFE	×	PV Factor	=	Present Value
2000	$4.65		$\dfrac{\$4.65}{(1.1959)}$		$3.89
2001	$5.01		$\dfrac{\$5.01}{(1.1959)(1.1816)}$		$3.55
2002	$5.40		$\dfrac{\$5.40}{(1.1959)(1.1816)(1.1695)}$		$3.27
2003	$5.81		$\dfrac{\$5.81}{(1.1959)(1.1816)(1.1695)(1.1596)}$		$3.03
2004	$6.21		$\dfrac{\$6.21}{(1.1959)(1.1816)(1.1695)(1.1596)(1.1514)}$		$2.81
			Sum of PV of FCFE$_{1-5}$ =		$16.55

Terminal Value of Equity (TVE):

$$TVF = TVE = \frac{\$6.21(1.04)}{.10 - .04} = \$107.64$$

$PV_{TVF} = \$107.64/(1.1872)(1.1669)(1.1510)(1.1389)(1.1296) = \$48.78$

Total Present Value = $16.55 + $48.78 = $65.33

[1] FCFE, free cash flow to equity; PV, present value; TVE, terminal value of equity; TVF, terminal value of the firm.

THINGS TO REMEMBER

The underlying motivation in structuring an LBO is to finance the transaction with as much debt as possible. Much of the debt will be secured with the assets of the target firm. Often, the proceeds from the sale of "redundant" assets are used to pay off debt as quickly as possible. Success in structuring a leveraged buyout is a result of knowing what to buy, not overpaying, and being able to substantially improve operating performance. Firms that represent good LBO candidates are those that have substantial tangible assets, unused borrowing capacity, predictable positive operating cash flow, and assets that are not critical to the continuing operation of the business. Although overpaying for any acquisition, highly leveraged or otherwise, almost always impairs the ability of the acquiring firm to achieve expected financial returns, it can be disastrous for highly leveraged transactions. If the firm's projected operating earnings are even slightly lower than projected, its ability to meet interest and principal payments is jeopardized.

Successful LBOs rely heavily on management incentives to improve operating performance and the discipline imposed by the demands of satisfying interest and principal repayments. The premium paid to target company shareholders by LBO and MBO investors consistently exceeds 40%, substantially above the average 33% paid to the target shareholders in less leveraged transactions. The most often cited sources of these returns are from improvements in efficiency and tax benefits. Tax benefits are largely predictable and are built into the premium offered for the public shares of the target firm as a result of the negotiation process. Post-LBO abnormal returns average between 30% and 40% during the 3 years following the announcement of the LBO. The primary reasons for these gains seem to be improvements in operating efficiency whose value was not captured in the premium paid to pre-LBO stockholders and the potential for the LBO firm to be acquired.

A leveraged buyout can be evaluated from the perspective of common equity investors only or from the perspective of all investors, including preferred stockholders and debt holders. Because common equity investors often represent less than 10% of the total financing required to complete the transaction, it normally makes sense to evaluate the transaction from the standpoint of all investors in the LBO. The high leverage associated with the LBO increases the risk of the cash flows available for equity investors by increasing debt service requirements. As the LBO's extremely high initial debt level is reduced, the firm's cost of equity needs to be adjusted to reflect the decline in risk. This implies a changing cost of equity and weighted average cost of capital over time. Excessive leverage and the resultant higher level of fixed expenses makes LBOs vulnerable to business cycle fluctuations and aggressive competitor actions, which LBOs cannot counteract.

CHAPTER DISCUSSION QUESTIONS

11.1   What potential conflicts arise between management and shareholders in an MBO? How can these conflicts be minimized?

11.2   Describe how and why LBO strategies have changed since the early
       1970s.

11.3   What are the primary ways in which an LBO is financed?

11.4   How do loan and security covenants affect the way in which an LBO is
       managed? Note the differences between positive and negative
       covenants.

11.5   What are the primary factors that explain the magnitude of the premium
       paid to pre-LBO shareholders?

11.6   What are the primary uses of junk bond financing?

11.7   Describe a typical LBO's preferred capital structure in the 1970s and
       early 1980s, and compare it to what you think the structure would look
       like today. Explain any changes between the two periods.

11.8   Describe some of the legal problems that can arise as a result of an
       improperly structured LBO.

11.9   Is it possible for an LBO to make sense to equity investors but not to
       other investors in the deal? If so, why? If not, why not?

11.10 How does the risk of an LBO change over time? How can the impact of
       changing risk be incorporated into the valuation of the LBO?

CHAPTER BUSINESS CASE

CASE STUDY 11-2: EVALUATING
A LEVERAGED BUYOUT OPPORTUNITY

A leveraged buyout firm is considering acquiring Nexus Enterprises. Revenue
in the current year is $3,000,000. Current operating expenses before depreciation
are $2,100,000. Revenue and operating expenses are projected to grow at 15%
per year for the next 5 years and 5% annually thereafter. Capital expenditures and
depreciation in the current year are $250,000 and $200,000, respectively, and they
are expected to grow at the same rate as revenue through the forecast period. The
annual change in working capital is expected to be 5% of revenue based on the
firm's historical performance. Nexus does not intend to pay any dividends during
the forecast period.

Discussions with local lenders suggest that the LBO can be financed with
$1,000,000 in equity capital and $5,500,000 in debt. Thus, if the transaction
were completed at the end of year 0, Nexus's capital structure would consist of
$1,000,000 in equity and $5,500,000 in debt. The interest rate on the debt is 10%
annually. Principal repayments on the debt will be $500,000 annually through the
forecast period. At the end of the fifth year, the remaining debt will be refinanced
at the same rate of interest in perpetuity.

Based on an examination of similar firms, the beta of the firm in the first year of
operation is estimated to be 3.00 and the cost of equity is estimated to be 23.5%.
The spread between the return on stocks and the risk-free rate is 5.5%. The firm's
combined federal, state, and local marginal tax rate is 40%. The risk-free interest

rate is expected to remain at its current level of 7.0% throughout the forecast period. Despite its high leverage, Nexus pays some taxes from the outset. Its tax liability grows rapidly as a result of the firm's rapid payoff of debt. In estimating its WACC, the LBO firm uses its long-term target debt-to-equity ratio of $1 of equity for $1 of debt to calculate the weights associated with debt and equity. This is the ratio that Nexus believes it must achieve to attract a strategic buyer or investors in a secondary public offering.

Nexus provides the following financial information. Based on this information, will the buyout generate sufficient cash to cover interest and principal payments and to provide an appropriate return to LBO firm's equity investors?

1. Calculate free cash flow to equity holders (FCFE) and the firm (FCFF).
2. Calculate WACC using a target debt-to-equity ratio of 1:1.
3. Calculate the terminal values.
4. Calculate present values of FCFE and FCFF.

Year	1	2	3	4	5	Terminal Value
Revenues	$3,000,000	$3,450,000	$3,967,500	$4,562,625	$5,247,019	$5,509.370
Less:						
Operating Expenses	$2,100,000	$2,415,000	$2,777,250	$3,193,834	$3,672,913	$3,856,559
Less:						
Depreciation	$200,000	$230,000	$264,500	$304,175	$349,801	$367,291
= EBIT	$700,000	$805,000	$925,750	$1,064,616	$1,224,305	$1,285,520
Less:						
Interest	$550,000	$500,000	$450,000	$400,000	$350,000	$300,000
Taxable Income	$150,000	$305,000	$475,750	$664,616	$874,305	$985,520
Less:						
Tax	$60,000	$122,000	$190,300	$265,846	$349,722	$394,208
= Net Income	$90,000	$183,000	$285,450	$398,770	$524,583	$591,312

A solution to this case is provided in the back of this book.

CHAPTER BUSINESS CASE

CASE STUDY 11-3: RJR NABISCO GOES PRIVATE—
KEY SHAREHOLDER AND PUBLIC POLICY ISSUES

Although many LBOs involve relatively small companies, a number have involved very large companies. The largest on record occurred in 1988 when the investment firm of Kohlberg Kravis & Roberts (KKR) used a leveraged buyout to purchase RJR Nabisco for $24.6 billion. The transaction caught the attention of the public because of what at the time was its staggering size and because of the antics of many of the key players involved in the transaction. The transaction was made famous in both a best-selling novel and a movie entitled "Barbarians at the Gates." This case study illustrates several important issues associated with MBOs in particular and LBOs in general. These issues deal with the potential conflict of interest facing the management team of a firm that is proposing to take the firm private and the potential redistribution of wealth that some believe takes place among stakeholders of the firm undergoing an LBO.

Background

The largest LBO in history is as well known for its theatrics as it is for its substantial improvement in shareholder value. In October 1988, H. Ross Johnson, then CEO of RJR Nabisco, proposed an MBO of the firm at $75 per share. His failure to inform the RJR board before publicly announcing his plans alienated many of the directors.

The Board's Dilemma

Analysts outside the company placed the breakup value of RJR Nabisco at more than $100 per share—almost twice its then current share price. Johnson's bid immediately was countered by a bid by the well-known LBO firm, Kohlberg, Kravis, and Roberts (KKR), to buy the firm for $90 per share (Wasserstein, 1998). The firm's board immediately was faced with the dilemma of whether to accept the KKR offer or to consider some other form of restructuring of the company. The board appointed a committee of outside directors to assess the bid to minimize the appearance of a potential conflict of interest in having current board members, who were also part of the buyout proposal from management, vote on which bid to select.

An Auction Environment

The bidding war soon escalated with additional bids coming from Forstmann Little and First Boston, although the latter's bid never really was taken very seriously. Forstmann Little later dropped out of the bidding as the purchase price rose. Although the firm's investment bankers valued both the bids by Johnson and KKR at about the same level, the board ultimately accepted the KKR bid. The winning bid was set at almost $25 billion—the largest transaction on record at that time and the largest LBO in history. Banks provided about three-fourths of the $20 billion that was borrowed to complete the transaction. The remaining debt was supplied by junk bond financing. The RJR shareholders were the real winners because the final purchase price constituted a more than 100% return from the $56 per share price that existed just before the initial bid by RJR management (Burrough and Helyar, 1990).

Aggressive pricing actions by such competitors as Phillip Morris threatened to erode RJR Nabisco's ability to service its debt. Complex securities such as "increasing rate notes," whose coupon rates had to be periodically reset to ensure that these notes would trade at face value, ultimately forced the credit rating agencies to downgrade the RJR Nabisco debt. As market interest rates climbed, RJR Nabisco did not appear to have sufficient cash to accommodate the additional interest expense on the increasing return notes. To avoid default, KKR recapitalized the company by investing additional equity capital. In total, RJR sold off more than $5 billion worth of businesses in 1990 to help reduce its crushing debt load. In 1991, RJR went public by issuing more than $1 billion in new common stock, which placed about one-fourth of the firm's common stock in public hands.

When KKR eventually fully liquidated its position in RJR Nabisco in 1995, it did so for a far smaller profit than expected. KKR earned a profit of about $60 million on an equity investment of $3.1 billion. KKR had not done well for the outside investors who had financed more than 90% of the total equity investment in KKR. However, KKR fared much better than investors had in its LBO funds by earning more than $500 million in transaction fees, advisor fees, management fees, and directors' fees. The publicity surrounding the transaction did not cease with the closing of the transaction. Dissident bondholders filed suits alleging that the payment of such a large premium for the company represented a "confiscation" of bondholder wealth by shareholders.

Potential Conflicts of Interest

In any MBO, management is confronted by a potential conflict of interest. Their fiduciary responsibility to the shareholders is to take actions to maximize shareholder value; yet in the RJR Nabisco case, the management bid appeared to be well below what was in the best interests of shareholders. Several proposals have been made to minimize the potential for conflict of interest in the case of an MBO. Borden (1987) proposed that directors, who are part of an MBO effort, not be allowed to participate in voting on bids and that fairness opinions be solicited from independent financial advisors. Lowenstein (1987) proposed that a firm receiving an MBO proposal be required to hold an auction for the firm.

Postbuyout Lawsuits

The most contentious discussion immediately following the closing of the RJR Nabisco buyout centered on the alleged transfer of wealth from bond and preferred stockholders to common stockholders when a premium was paid for the shares held by RJR Nabisco common stockholders. It often is argued that at least some part of the premium is offset by a reduction in the value of the firm's outstanding bonds and preferred stock because of the substantial increase in leverage that takes place in LBOs. However, empirical studies of the change in the value of a firm's outstanding debt at the time of a leveraged buyout announcement provide mixed results. In their studies of numerous LBOs during the 1980s, Lehn and Poulsen (1988) found no evidence that bondholders lose value; however, Travlos and Cornett (1993) found statistically significant losses associated with the announcement of going private. In a lawsuit against RJR Nabisco, it was alleged but never proved that its $5 billion in bonds outstanding at the time of the announcement lost more than 20% of their value (Greenwald, 1988).

Winners and Losers

RJR Nabisco shareholders before the buyout clearly benefited greatly from efforts to take the company private. However, in addition to the potential transfer of wealth from bondholders to stockholders, some critics of LBOs argue that a wealth transfer also takes place in LBO transactions when LBO management is able to negotiate wage and benefit concessions from current employee unions. LBOs are under greater pressure to seek such concessions than other types of buyouts because they need to meet huge debt service requirements. Empirical studies suggest that employment in firms that undergo a leveraged buyout does grow more slowly than for other firms in the same industry (Kaplan, 1989a; Muscarella and Vetsuypens, 1990). However, this appears to result from the more efficient use of labor and the sale of nonstrategic assets following the LBO.

Lowenstein (1985) has argued that the tax benefits associated with LBOs represent a subsidy of the premium paid to the shareholders of the firm subject to the buyout. However, this subsidy is offset by the taxes paid by the shareholders when they sell their stock (Morrow, 1988). If the LBO firm actually is made stronger as a result of the transaction, taxes paid actually may be higher than they would have been if the transaction had not occurred. Furthermore, the eventual sale of the LBO either to a strategic buyer or in a secondary public offering also will generate additional taxes.

Case Study Discussion Questions

1. In your opinion, was the buyout proposal presented by Ross Johnson's management group in the best interests of the shareholders? Why or why not?
2. What were the RJR Nabisco board's fiduciary responsibilities to the shareholders? How well did they satisfy these responsibilities? What could or should they have done differently?
3. Why might the RJR Nabisco board have accepted the KKR bid over the Johnson bid?
4. Explain how bondholders and preferred stockholders may have been hurt in the RJR Nabisco leveraged buyout.
5. Describe the potential benefits and costs of LBOs to shareholders, employers, lenders, customers, and communities in which the firm undergoing the buyout may have operations. Do you believe that on average LBOs provide a net benefit or cost to society? Explain your answer.

REFERENCES

Altman, Edward I. and Scott A. Namacher, *The Default Rate Experience on High Yield Corporate Debt*, New York: Morgan Stanley & Co., 1985.

Altman, Edward I. and Vellore M. Kishore, "Almost Everything You Wanted to Know about Recoveries on Defaulted Bonds," *Financial Analysts Journal*, November/December 1996, pp. 57–64.

Asquith, Paul, David Mullins, and Eric Wolff, "Original Issue High Yield Bonds: Aging Analysis of Defaults, Exchanges and Calls," *Journal of Finance*, 44 (4), September 1989, pp. 923–952.

Borden, Arthur M., *Going Private*, New York: Law Journal Seminar Press, 1987, pp. 1–6.

Brealey, Richard A. and Stewart C. Meyers, *Principles of Corporate Finance* (5th ed.), New York: McGraw-Hill, 1996, pp. 525–541.

Burrough, Bryan and John Helyar, *Barbarians at the Gate: The Fall of RJR Nabisco*, New York: Harper & Row, 1990.

Business Week, "Leveraged Buyout Blues," November 1, 1999, p. 220.

Carow, Kenneth A. and Dianne M. Roden, "Determinants of the Stock Price Reaction to Leveraged Buyouts," *Journal of Economics and Finance*, 22 (1), Spring 1998, pp. 37–47.

Copeland, Tom, Tim Koller, and Jack Murrin, *Valuation: Measuring and Managing the Value of Companies*, 3rd edition, New York: John Wiley & Sons, 2000, pp. 477–483.

Cotter, James F. and Sarah W. Peck, "The Structure of Debt and Active Equity Investors: The Case of the Buyout Specialist," *Journal of Finance*, 59 (1), January 1, 2001.

Damadoran, Aswath, *Corporate Finance: Theory and Practice*, New York: John Wiley & Sons, 1997, pp. 502–537.

DeAngelo, Harry, Linda DeAngelo, and Edward Rice, "Going Private: Minority Freezeouts and Stockholder Wealth," *Journal of Law and Economics*, 27, October 1984, pp. 367–401.

Emery, Douglas R. and John D. Finnerty, "A Review of Recent Research Concerning Corporate Debt Provisions," *Financial Markets, Institutions, and Instruments*, 1 (5), December 1992, pp. 23–39.

Fitzpatrick, J. D. and J. T. Severiens, *Hickman Revisited: The Case for Junk Bonds*, New York: Salomon Brothers, March 1984.

Fraine, Harold G. and Robert H. Mills, "The Effects of Defaults and Credit Deterioration on Yields of Corporate Bonds," *Journal of Finance*, September 1961, pp. 423–434.

Fridson, Martin, *Default Experience of Corporate Bonds*, New York: Salomon Brothers, March 1984.

Greenwald, J., "Where's the Limit?" *Time*, December 5, 1988, pp. 66–70.

Hickman, W. B., *Corporate Bond Quality and Investor Experience*, Princeton, NJ: Princeton University Press, 1958.

Hite, G. L. and M. R. Vetsuypens, "Management Buyouts of Divisions and Shareholder Wealth," *Journal of Finance*, 44, 1989, pp. 953–970.

Holthausen, Robert W. and David F. Larker, "The Financial Performance of Reverse Leveraged Buyouts," *Journal of Financial Economics*, 42, 1996, pp. 293–332.

Jensen, Michael C., "Agency Costs of Free Cash Flow, Corporate Finance, and Takeovers," *American Economic Association Papers and Proceedings*, May 1986, pp. 323–329.

Kaplan, Steven, "The Staying Power of Leveraged Buyouts," *Journal of Financial Economics*, 29, October 1991, pp. 287–314.

Kaplan, Steven, "The Effects of Management Buyouts on Operating Performance and Value," *Journal of Financial Economics*, 24, 1989a, pp. 217–254.

Kaplan, Steven, "Management Buyouts: Efficiency Gains or Value Transfers," *Journal of Finance*, 3, July 1989b, pp. 611–632.

Kaplan, Steven, "Management Buyouts: Efficiency Gains or Value Transfers," *University of Chicago Working Paper*, 244, October 1988.

Kretlow, James R., James R. McGuigan, and R. Charles Moyer, *Contemporary Financial Management* (7th ed.), Georgetown, TX: Southwestern College Publishing, 1998, pp. 681–711, 796–831.

Lehn, Ken and Annette Poulsen, "Leveraged Buyouts: Wealth Created or Wealth Redistributed?" in M. Weidenbaum and K. Chilton, eds., *Public Policy Towards Corporate Takeovers*, New Brunswick, NJ: Transaction Publishers, 1988.

Lowenstein, Louis, *What's Wrong with Wall Street?* Reading, MA: Addison-Wesley, 1987, p. 184.

Lowenstein, Louis, "Management Buyouts," *Columbia Law Review*, 85, 1985, pp. 730–784.

Mian, Shedhzad and James Rosenfeld, "Takeover Activity and the Long-Run Performance of Reverse Leveraged Buyouts," *Financial Management*, 22, Winter 1993, pp. 46–57.

Morrow, D. J., "Why the IRS Might Love Those LBOs," *Fortune*, December 5, 1988, pp. 145–146.

Muscarella, C. J. and M. R. Vetsuypens, "Efficiency and Organizational Structure: A Study of Reverse LBOs," *Journal of Finance*, 45, December 1990, pp. 1389–1413.

Reisman, Albert F., "The Challenge of the Proposed Bankruptcy Act to Accounts Receivable and Inventory Financing of Small-to-Medium-Sized Business, 83," *Commercial Law Journal*, 169, 1978, pp. 177–180.

Roden, Dianne M. and Wilbur G. Lewellen, "Corporate Capital Structure Decisions: Evidence from Leveraged Buyouts," *Financial Management*, 24, Summer 1995, pp. 76–87.

Smith, Abbie, "Corporate Ownership Structure and Performance: The Case of Management Buy-Outs," *Journal of Financial Economics*, 27, September 1990, pp. 143–164.

Travlos, N. G. and M. N. Cornett, "Going Private Buyouts and Determinants of Shareholders' Returns," *Journal of Accounting, Auditing and Finance*, 8, 1993, pp. 1–25.

Wasserstein, Bruce, *Big Deal: The Battle for Control of America's Leading Corporations*, New York: Warner Books, 1998, pp. 113–116.

Westin, J. Fred, Kwang S. Chung, and Juan A. Siu, *Takeovers, Restructuring, and Corporate Governance* (2nd ed.), New York: Prentice-Hall, 1998, pp. 316–343.

Wigmore, Barry, "The Decline in Credit Quality of Junk Bond Issues, 1980–1988," in Patrick A. Gaughan, ed., *Readings in Mergers and Acquisitions*, Cambridge: Basil Blackwell, 1994, pp. 171–184.

Yago, Glenn, *Junk Bonds: How High Yield Securities Restructured Corporate America*, New York: Oxford University Press, 1991.

12

SHARED GROWTH AND SHARED CONTROL STRATEGIES

JOINT VENTURES, PARTNERSHIPS, STRATEGIC ALLIANCES, AND LICENSING

Humility is not thinking less of yourself.
It is thinking less about yourself.

—*Rick Warren*

When it was formed in early 1998, executives at Spanish phone operator Telefonica de Espana and U.S. long-distance giant MCI WorldCom were all smiles as they unveiled a partnership to provide telecommunications services to customers worldwide. They declared in no uncertain terms that the partners would improve substantially the value of their companies. Or would they?

Since then the grand global alliance appears to have stalled. Of the dozen or so initiatives that have been announced by the two partners, none has been implemented. In many markets MCI WorldCom and Telefonica look more like archrivals than allies. For example, MCI WorldCom bought a controlling interest in Brazilian long-distance carrier, Embratel, putting it into direct competition with Telesp, a network operator in Sao Paolo that is owned by Telefonica.

On the surface, the partnership would seem to offer both parties tremendous opportunities. Telefonica is the strongest player in the $50 billion Latin American telecommunications market and could help MCI grow beyond its current position in Brazil and Mexico. In turn, MCI WorldCom is among the strongest players in telecommunications in the United States, the United Kingdom, France, and Germany. The partnership should give Telefonica a much-needed boost in these geographic areas.

Caution by both parties seems to have prevented them from integrating operations or from sharing competitive information. Neither company seems to have been willing to relinquish control over resources. Moreover, MCI WorldCom's largely "go-it-alone" culture does not seem to be compatible for a partnership whose long-term success requires substantial cooperation. What started out as marital bliss ultimately may be doomed by a failure to communicate. How ironic for firms whose primary business is to help others to communicate.

OVERVIEW

For many years, joint ventures (JVs) and alliances have been commonplace in high-technology industries; many segments of manufacturing; the oil exploration, mining, and chemical industries; media and entertainment; financial services; among pharmaceutical and biotechnology firms; and real estate. They have taken the form of licensing, distribution, comarketing, research and development agreements, and equity investments.

High-technology companies engage in literally thousands of alliances with their customers as part of their normal marketing strategies. Oracle claims to have as many as 15,000–16,000 alliances with their business customers. IBM announced $30 billion worth of alliances with companies like Dell Computer and Cisco during 1999. AT&T announced deals with behemoths like British Telecom and Microsoft.

In manufacturing, General Motors and Toyota entered into an unprecedented JV agreement in 1982. For the first time in 60 years, GM accepted something other than a controlling interest in a relationship with another major automotive company. GM believed it could enhance its manufacturing processes and product quality by learning and adopting Toyota's quality manufacturing processes. In turn, Toyota saw an opportunity to gain access to new markets for its products in the United States and in other countries in which GM was well established.

Also in manufacturing, Corning has created numerous JVs in genetic enzymes, fiber optics, and hollow glass building blocks. They also have created JVs through Owens-Corning in fiberglass insulation.

Largely driven by the risks of oil exploration and by the large capital expenses inherent in this activity, the oil and gas industry has been characterized by numerous JVs. Chemical companies, such as Dow, Hercules, and Olin, have used JVs to build new plants throughout the world. When shortages of raw materials threaten future production, these firms commonly form JVs to secure future sources of supply. Shell and Amoco have pooled most of their West Texas oilfields to become the first major oil companies to combine operations across an entire region. Shell and Mobil are doing the same on the West Coast. The use of alliances in the oil and gas industry is expected to expand in the future. Of senior managers from leading U.S. and Canadian oil companies, 84% expect alliances rather than internal operations to be the main source of performance improvements. Alliances often are preferred to acquisitions and divestitures because they bypass or reduce the valuation, tax, and regulatory issues associated with outright changes in control. They also rationalize overlapping oilfield assets and operations while allowing both parents to retain oil reserves as a hedge against oil price increases (Ernst and Steinhubl, 1997).

Concerned about the loss of viewers to cable TV and the Internet, NBC, a unit of General Electric, and Microsoft each invested $500 million in 1995 to create a new news channel available both on cable and the Internet. The JV was intended to provide programming for the expected convergence of TV and the Internet. By early 1999, NBC owned minority positions in Bravo and the American Movie Classics channels; autobytel.com; and Intervu, a video streaming company. In mid-1999, NBC merged several of its key Internet properties with XOOM.com and Snap.com to form the then seventh-largest Internet site and the first publicly traded Internet company partially owned by a major broadcaster (NBC, 1999).

The huge research and development (R&D) requirements, the relatively low success rate, near-term patent expiration of profitable drugs, and the high cost of marketing new drugs have resulted in a dramatic escalation of the use of partnerships in the pharmaceutical industry. Pharmaceutical firms have been encouraged to enter into such relationships to gain access to new skills and to share the risk and cost associated with bringing new drugs to market. In 1998, there were 712 partnerships, up from 415 in 1993.

Although many alliances are created to share risks, others involve partners with complementary skills or operations. Global competition, more sympathetic regulators, and the desire to gain access to technology are also factors contributing to the dizzying pace at which new alliances are being formed. Business alliances also may span several different industries. Despite competing directly with Canon printers, Hewlett Packard has sold more than 20 million laser printers that use a motor made by Canon.

The term *business alliance* will be used throughout this chapter to include JV corporations, partnerships, strategic alliances, equity partnerships, licensing agreements, and franchise alliances. The primary theme of this chapter is that well-constructed business alliances often represent viable alternatives to mergers and acquisitions (M&As) and that they always should be considered as one of the many options for achieving strategic business objectives. The principal differences in the various types of business alliances were discussed in some detail in Chapter 1; as such, they only are summarized in Table 12-1. This chapter discusses the wide variety of motives for business alliances and the factors that are common to most successful alliances. Also addressed are advantages and disadvantages of alternative legal structures, important deal-structuring issues, and empirical studies that purport to measure the contribution of business alliances to creating shareholder wealth.

TABLE 12-1   Key Differences Among Business Alliances

Type	Key Characteristics
Joint Ventures (JV)	• Independent legal entity involving 2 or parties • Ownership, responsibilities, risks, and rewards allocated to parties • Each party retains corporate identity and autonomy
Strategic Alliances (e.g., technology transfer, R&D sharing, cross-marketing)	• Do not involve the formation of separate legal entities • May be precursor to JV, partnership, or acquisition • Generally not passive but involve cross-training, coordinated product development, and long-term contracts based on performance metrics such as product quality rather than price
Equity Partnerships	• Have all the characteristics of an alliance • Involve making minority investment in other party (e.g., 5–10%) • Minority investor may have an option to buy a larger stake in other party
Licensing —Product Licensing —Merchandise and Trademark Licensing	• Patent, trademark, or copyright licensed in exchange for royalty or fee • Generally no sharing of risk or reward • Generally stipulates what is being sold, how and where it can be used, and for how long • Payments usually consist of an initial fee and royalties based on a percentage of future license sales
Franchising Alliances	• Network of alliances in which partners linked by licensing agreements • Often grant exclusive rights to sell or distribute goods or services in specific geographic areas or markets • Licensees may be required to purchase goods and services from other firms in the alliance
Network Alliances	• Interconnecting alliances among companies crossing international and industrial boundaries • May involve companies collaborating in one market while competing in others (e.g., computers, airlines, telecommunications) • Most often formed to access skills from different but converging industries
Exclusive Agreements	• Usually involve rights for manufacturing or marketing specific products or services • Each party benefits from the specific skills or assets the other party brings to the relationship

MOTIVATIONS FOR BUSINESS ALLIANCES

Business alliances are generally not created as a result of one company making a passive investment in another. Money alone rarely provides the basis for a successful long-term business alliance. A partner often can obtain funding from a variety of sources but may be able to obtain access to a set of skills or nonfinancial resources only from a specific source. Obviously, alliances are likely to be lasting only if both parties find the relationship to be a mutually beneficial union. The basis of this union can include risk sharing, gaining access to new markets, accelerating the introduction of new products, technology sharing, globalization, cost reduction, a desire to acquire (or exit) a business, or the favorable regulatory treatment they often receive as compared with M&As.

RISK SHARING

Risk is the potential for losing, or at least not gaining, value. Risk often is perceived to be greater the more money, management time, or other resources a company has committed to an endeavor and the less certain the outcome. To mitigate perceived risk, companies often enter into alliances to gain access to know-how and scarce resources or to reduce the amount of resources they would have to commit if they were to do it on their own.

Sharing Proprietary Knowledge

The driving force behind one-half of all JVs is the desire to acquire proprietary know-how (Berg, Duncan, and Friedman, 1982). Developing new technologies can be extremely expensive. Given the pace at which technology changes, the risk is high that a competitor will be able to develop a superior technology before a firm can bring its own new technology to market. Consequently, high-technology companies with expertise in a specific technology segment often combine their efforts with another company or companies with complementary know-how to reduce the risk of failing to develop the "right" technology. Moreover, by having multiple contacts throughout an industry, it is unlikely that a firm will overlook new innovations or best practices. For example, TiVo, a small manufacturer of set-top boxes that provide interactive TV service, raised $32 million in 1999 through a series of private placements with CBS, NBC, Disney/ABC, Hughes's Direct TV satellite service, and Comcast (a leading cable TV service). By lending to TiVo, these companies would be able to obtain access to the latest technologies that may someday be necessary to remain competitive in their respective markets.

In 1983, Rockwell, Sperry, Boeing, Control Data, Honeywell, Digital Equipment, Kodak, Harris, Lockheed, 3M, Martin Marietta, Motorola, NCR, National Semiconductor, and RCA formed Micro-Electronics Computer Corporation (MCC). MCC was formed to share the cost of developing semiconductor, computer, and software technology that could not otherwise be developed cost effectively by these companies. In 1988, Sematech was founded as a research alliance consisting of IBM, National Semiconductor, Advanced Micro Devices, and other major companies.

The Microsoft and Intel relationship is one of the better known technology partnerships; it is also one of the more confusing. The two cooperate to enhance the "Wintel" world, which combines Windows operating systems with Intel microchips. Although the partnership is viewed as highly successful, there have been disagreements. For example, Intel wants more competition and lower prices on software bundled with personal computers to reduce the pricing pressure on PC components such as microchips as PC prices decline. Microsoft has been very slow to reduce the price of its Windows operating system software, presumably to maintain profit margins.

Sharing Management Skills and Resources

Firms often lack the management skills and resources to solve complex tasks and projects. These deficiencies can be remedied by aligning with other firms, which possess the requisite skills and proprietary knowledge. Building contractors and real estate developers have collaborated for years by pooling their resources to construct, market, and manage large, complex commercial projects. Similarly, the contribution of Dow Chemical personnel to a JV with Cordis, a small pacemaker manufacturer, enabled the JV to keep pace with accelerating production.

GAINING ACCESS TO NEW MARKETS

Gaining access to new customers is often a highly expensive proposition involving substantial initial marketing costs such as advertising, promotion, warehousing, and distribution expenses. The cost may be prohibitive unless alternative distribution channels providing access to the targeted markets can be found.

Using Another Firm's Distribution Channel

To solve this problem, a company may enter into an alliance to sell its products through another firm's direct sales force, telemarketing operation, retail outlets, or Internet site. The alliance may involve the payment of a percentage of revenue generated in this manner to the firm whose distribution channel is being used. Alternatively, firms may enter into a "cross-marketing" relationship in which they agree to sell the other firm's products through their own distribution channels. The profitability of these additional sales can be significant because neither firm has to add substantially to its overhead expense or to its investment in building or expanding its distribution channels.

The Convergence of "Bricks and Clicks"

Although marketing alliances have been commonplace for years, we now are seeing a convergence of conventional brick-and-mortar retail operations and cyberspace distribution channels. Companies are using their recognizable consumer brands and complementary sales and distribution channels to comarket products and services. About 60% of U.S. consumers were online by the end of 2001. Most of these tended to be wealthier consumers. Retailers and Internet companies now are trying to gain access to consumers who are not currently on-line. During late 1999 and early 2000, a slew of partnerships were announced between major retail outlets and Internet players in an attempt to accomplish this objective (Case Study 12-1).

CASE STUDY 12-1: GETTING WIRED— WAL-MART–AMERICA ONLINE AND OTHER INTERNET MARKETING ALLIANCES

During the second half of 1999, the number of marketing alliances between major retailers and Internet companies exploded. Wal-Mart Stores, the world's biggest retailer, and Circuit City, a large consumer electronics retailer, announced partnerships with America Online (AOL). Best Buy, the largest U.S. consumer electronics chain, partnered with Microsoft, which previously had joined with Tandy Corporation's RadioShack stores. Signaling its own strategy of bringing its service to anyone, anywhere, AOL announced in March 2000 partnerships with Sprint PCS and Nokia to help move AOL's service from the desktop to phones, pagers, organizers, and even TVs.

Wal-Mart and AOL

Wal-Mart and AOL have agreed to create a low-cost Web service for consumers who lack access and to promote each other's services. Wal-Mart customers will get software that allows them to set up the service through AOL's CompuServe service. The retailer also will distribute AOL's software with a link to Wal-Mart's Web site, Wal-Mart.com. The Internet access service will be geared to Wal-Mart customers in smaller towns that currently do not have local numbers to dial for online connections. Wal-Mart wants to funnel as many customers as possible to its revamped Web site, which contains a pharmacy, a photo center, and travel services in addition to general merchandise. The alliance gives AOL access to the 90–100 million people who shop at Wal-Mart weekly.

Microsoft, Best Buy, and RadioShack

Through its alliance with Best Buy, Microsoft is selling its products— including Microsoft Network (MSN) Internet access services and hand-held devices such as digital telephones, hand-held organizers, and WebTV that connect to the Web—through kiosks in Best Buy's 354 stores nationwide. In exchange, Microsoft has invested $200 million in Best Buy. Microsoft has a similar arrangement with Tandy Company's RadioShack stores in which it agreed to invest $100 million in Tandy'sonline sales site in exchange for in-store displays promoting Microsoft products and services. Both Best Buy and RadioShack are major advertisers on MSN and share in the monthly revenue from some of the Microsoft Internet access services they sell through their stores. Best Buy has issued 4 million new shares of common stock to Microsoft in exchange for its investment, giving Microsoft approximately a 2% ownership position in Best Buy. Best Buy is using the proceeds from the Microsoft investment to revamp its electronic commerce operation and to fund new store openings. The multiyear pact is nonexclusive.

Circuit City and America Online

AOL and Circuit City entered a strategic alliance to provide in-store promotion of AOL products and services to Circuit City shoppers nationwide, to make AOL Circuit City's preferred Internet online service, and to feature Circuit City as an anchor tenant in AOL's shopping mall. Under the agreement, AOL products and services are displayed prominently in dedicated retail space in Circuit City's 615 stores across the nation. Circuit City will be able to offer consumers everything they need to connect their homes to the Internet. Access to the Internet is available via AOL through dial-up service and developing broadband technologies, including digital subscriber line and satellite, as well as wireless interactive devices. Circuit City is promoting AOL and its in-store offerings in its print and television advertising programs and in other promotional and marketing campaigns. As an anchor tenant on AOL's shopping mall, Circuit City will have access to AOL's more than 32 million subscribers.

Case Study Discussion Questions

1. What are the elements that each alliance has in common? Of these, which do you believe are the most important?
2. In what way do these alliances represent a convergence of "bricks and clicks?"
3. In your judgment, do these alliances deliver real value to the consumer? Explain your answer.

GLOBALIZATION

The dizzying pace of international competition has increased the demand for alliances and JVs to enable companies to enter markets in which they lack production or distribution channels or in which laws prohibit 100% foreign ownership of a business. Moreover, a major foreign competitor might turn out to be an excellent partner in fighting domestic competition. Alternatively, a domestic competitor could become a partner in combating a foreign competitor.

The automotive industry uses alliances to provide additional production capacity, distribution outlets, technology development, and parts supply. Many companies, such as General Motors and Ford, take minority equity positions in other companies within the industry to gain access to foreign markets (Case Study 12-2). Other companies choose to assume a controlling interest (i.e., 51% or more). Exhibit 12-1 illustrates ownership ties between major automotive makers in which one company owns less than 100% of another as of mid-2000.

CASE STUDY 12-2: GENERAL MOTORS BUYS 20% OF SUBARU

In late 1999, General Motors (GM), the world's largest auto manufacturer, agreed to purchase 20% of Japan's Fuji Heavy Industries, Ltd., the manufacturer of Subaru vehicles, for $1.4 billion. GM's objective is to accelerate GM's push into Asia. The investment gives GM an interest in an auto manufacturer known for four-wheel drive vehicles. In combination with its current holdings, GM now has a position in every segment of Japan's auto market, including minivans, small and midsize cars, and trucks. GM already owns 10% of Suzuki Motor Corporation and 49% of Isuzu Motors Ltd. GM now can expand in Asia more quickly and at a lower cost than if it developed products independently.

GM has been collaborating with Fuji on various products since 1995. The move underscores GM's commitment to expanding its current modest position in the Asian market, which is expected to be the fastest growing market during the next decade. GM has sold less than 500,000 in the Asia-Pacific region in 1999, including about 60,000 in Japan (Bloomberg.com, 1999a). In 2002, GM bought the remaining outstanding stock of Subaru.

Case Study Discussion Questions
1. What other motives may General Motors have had in making this investment?
2. Why do you believe that General Motors may have wanted initially to limit its investment to 20%?

COST REDUCTION

Cost reduction through business alliances may come about in a number of ways, such as purchaser–supplier relationships and sharing or combining facilities in joint manufacturing operations.

EXHIBIT 12-1. OTHER AUTOMOTIVE INDUSTRY INVESTMENTS

General Motors: Owns

    49% of Isuzu Motors
    20% of Fiat Auto SPA
    20% of Fuji Heavy Industries Ltd. (see Case Study 12-2)
    9.9% of Suzuki Motors Company

Ford Motor Company: Owns 33.4% of Mazda
Daimler-Chrysler AG: Owns 34% of Mitsubishi Motors Company
Renault SA: Owns 36.8% of Nissan Motor Company
Fiat SPA: Owns

    5% of General Motors
    80% of Fiat Auto, Alfa Romeo, and Lancia

Mitsubishi Motor Company: Owns 13% of Hyundai Motors
Hyundai Motors: Owns 51% of Kia Motor Company
Toyota Motor Company: Owns 51% of Daihatsu Motor Company

Purchaser–Supplier Relationships

During the 1990s, firms became increasingly involved in purchaser–supplier relationships. These also are called logistics alliances. Companies across the spectrum from retailers to computer manufacturing increasingly are forming alliances with providers of "logistics" services. These alliances generally cover both transportation and warehousing services and utilize a single provider for these services.

In January 2001, the U.S. Postal Service (USPS) and Federal Express (FedEx) announced an agreement in which FedEx will haul the USPS's Express Mail and Priority Mail as well as some first class mail. FedEx will provide guaranteed space at a cost of $6.3 billion over 7 years. Moreover, FedEx will pay the USPS at least $126 million to place its collection boxes at post offices. The USPS is expected to save more than $1 billion by phasing out its Indianapolis hub and by allowing a number of leases to expire. In turn, FedEx is guaranteed a specific volume of mail and will have access to a large number of package drop-off points at USPS offices (Schmid, 2001).

In a survey of 50 companies and 20 logistics service providers, Van Laarhoven and Sharman (1994) found that most believed that as a result of logistics alliances, delivery service exceeded their expectations, although cost reductions, which were significant, did not meet expectations. Service improvements resulted from better on-time delivery, and cost reductions came mostly from sharing of resources with other client companies. Of respondents to the survey, 43% indicated that the alliance was clearly successful; 33% said it was moderately so.

The increased use of the Internet for commercial purposes is widely expected to enable businesses to realize the substantial cost savings that to date have been less than expected by more effectively managing their supplier relationships. The global telecommunications network that comprises the Internet is making electronic business-to-business communication increasingly possible for businesses of all sizes. The inherent efficiencies of converting data to electronic form expedite data transmission, storage, retrieval, updating, and analysis. These capabilities now make possible instant communication with a massive number of suppliers. The desire to more efficiently manage the corporate supply chain drove the major auto manufacturers to create what could become the largest online business in terms of revenue (Case Study 12-3). By increasing the efficiency of the purchasing process, both purchasers and suppliers are likely to benefit. Note how the JV concept is used to achieve the desired neutrality and confidentiality demanded by all participants.

CASE STUDY 12-3: AUTOMOTIVE
MANUFACTURERS JOIN FORCES IN
ON-LINE PURCHASING CONSORTIUM:
THE EMERGENCE OF THE BUSINESS
WEB ("B-WEB")

In late February 2000, GM, Ford, and Daimler-Chrysler announced the formation of a JV corporation intended to streamline the process of purchasing materials and services from external vendors. At the outset, the new company, named Covinsint, was expected to manage the purchasing of the bulk of the $600 billion in raw materials, parts, and office supplies used annually by the three auto manufacturers. All ordering will be done via the Internet. So great was the fanfare around this revolutionary idea that an IPO was planned for late 2001. Pundits believed that the IPO could raise as much as $10 billion (*Business Week*, 2001).

By using the Internet, the automakers believe that they, as well as suppliers, can experience substantial cost savings by reducing the time, paperwork, and error rate associated with literally millions of purchases made with more than 30,000 suppliers. By automating much of the purchasing process, the automakers will be able to automatically reorder parts when inventories drop below desired levels, facilitating efforts to minimize inventory investment. Moreover, tracking systems can be put in place to determine the status of orders and to confirm delivery dates. Estimates of the savings that could be realized in the cost of processing a purchase order range as high as 90%. The resulting cost savings to purchasers and suppliers contribute to improvements in profit margins for both parties. Suppliers also could be allowed to do purchasing online through this JV purchasing corporation.

Organizational Considerations

GM, Ford, and Daimler-Chrysler have equal equity stakes in the JV company. However, the JV will be managed as an independent entity. Other investors with smaller stakes include Oracle and Commerce One, which will provide the software required to automate the purchasing process. The JV company will be opened to other auto manufacturers, which may choose to make investments in the company. Eventually, the focus of the company could be expanded to include other industries. Ultimately, equity in the company could be offered to the public. By centralizing purchasing in an independently operated company, the automotive manufacturers were able to overcome previous concerns expressed by various parties. Both suppliers and auto companies had concerns about previous attempts to move purchasing into an online environment because these efforts had involved working with parts exchanges launched by GM and Ford in 1999 using different and potentially incompatible software and systems. Moreover, auto companies were concerned about the confidentiality of the data they would be asked to place on the computer systems of companies managed by their competitors.

The Challenges of Being a Start-Up

Since its inception in early 2000, things have not gone according to plan. Except for the founding partners, other automakers have thus far refrained from participating. Other automakers and suppliers are using alternative portals of their own exchanges to auction and buy parts and materials. Although Covinsint has processed about $1.5 billion in transactions through its auctions and online processing systems, most of that has come from the Ford Motor and General Motors Web sites that were folded into the JV. Covinsint was slow to implement in part because of a 5-month antitrust probe by the Federal Trade Commission. Because of the probe, the three partners were unable to fully staff the venture. Software development suffered. While the antitrust investigation resulted in delay, competitors began to emerge. Volkswagen went out and formed its own exchange. Other exchanges, including the Plastics Exchange, Metal Sources, and E-Steel, expanded to fill the void (Hyde, 2000).

Covinsint Becomes More Competitive

Covinsint has reacted to the emerging competitive threat by launching a number of new products and services. For example, the firm is developing new systems that will help customers handle shipping and import and export activities and manage bids and contracts online. Furthermore, instead of relying exclusively on two software vendors, Oracle and Commerce One, Covinsint is broadening its pool of software vendors. In the future, the firm also hopes to offer software that will facilitate engineering collaboration among carmakers and suppliers. Covinsint also has decided to move away from a fee-per-transaction system to a subscription based-pricing system. The potential for success seems to be there if Covinsint can execute it smoothly. Automotive parts suppliers seem eager for the JV to succeed. In particular, they would welcome software that would enable car and parts suppliers to show each other their production schedules so that they can base their inventories and workload on actual, rather than estimated, demand for cars (*Business Week*, 2001).

Case Study Discussion Questions

1. Why was confidentiality of information such an important issue in forming this alliance? Do you believe this is an issue common to most business alliances? Why or why not?
2. How do you think the initial distribution of ownership in this alliance may have been determined?
3. Do you believe that the start-up problems experienced by Covinsint are common to all business combinations including the integration of mergers and acquisitions? How might such problems be more pronounced in a business alliance in which there are multiple owners?

Joint Manufacturing

Companies also may choose to combine their manufacturing operations in a single facility with the capacity to meet the production requirements of all parties involved. By building a large facility, the firms jointly can benefit from lower production costs resulting from spreading fixed costs over larger volumes of production. This type of arrangement is commonplace within the newspaper industry in major cities in which there are several newspapers engaged in "head-to-head" competition. Similar cost benefits may be realized if one party closes its production facility and satisfies its production requirements by buying at preferred prices from another party with substantial unused capacity.

A PRELUDE TO ACQUISITION OR EXIT

Rather than acquire a company, a firm may choose to make a minority investment in another company. In exchange for the investment, the investing firm may receive board representation, preferred access to specific proprietary technology, and an option to purchase a controlling interest in the company. The investing firm is able to assess the quality of management, cultural compatibility, and the viability of the other firm's technology without having to acquire a controlling interest in the firm.

Alternatively, JVs or strategic alliances may be used as a means of exiting a business. TRW entered into a JV with Elsevier, a large Dutch publishing company in 1990, in which both companies contributed their residential property information companies to form TRW REDI. The property information included data on the physical characteristics of homes and home-selling prices in selected regions throughout the United States. Neither business had been achieving what their parents considered adequate financial returns. Although divestiture was an option open to both TRW and Elsevier, the individual operations had limited value to potential acquirers because of inadequate geographic coverage. However, in combination, the two operations could experience significant cost savings by eliminating overlapping overhead and achieving economies of scale in selling the same data to more customers over a broader geographic area. Moreover, the combined operations could achieve increased purchasing leverage in negotiating with suppliers of unique types of data. TRW REDI's financial performance improved to the point where it could be sold at what the parents considered an acceptable price. First American Title Company eventually acquired the partnership in 1996.

Case Study 12-4 illustrates how a JV may be used to acquire selected assets of another company. In an "acquisition JV," one company purchases a controlling interest in an existing subsidiary of another company. The former wholly owned subsidiary subsequently is managed as a JV corporation.

CASE STUDY 12-4: BRIDGESTONE ACQUIRES FIRESTONE'S TIRE ASSETS

Bridgestone Tire, a Japanese company, lacking a source of retail distribution in the United States, approached its competitor, Firestone, to create a JV whose formation involved two stages. In the first stage, Firestone, which consisted of a tire manufacturing and distribution division and a diversified rubber products division, agreed to transfer its tire manufacturing operations into a subsidiary. This subsidiary was owned and operated by Firestone's worldwide tire business. In the second stage, Firestone sold three-fourths of its equity in the tire subsidiary to Bridgestone, making the subsidiary a JV corporation. Firestone received $1.25 billion in cash, $750 million from Bridgestone, and $500 million from the JV. Firestone also retained 100% ownership in the diversified products division and 25% of the tire JV corporation. For its investment, Bridgestone acquired a 75% ownership interest in a worldwide tire manufacturing and distribution system.

Case Study Discussion Questions
1. What other options for entering the United States could Bridgestone have considered?
2. Why do you believe Bridgestone chose to invest in Firestone rather than pursue another option?

FAVORABLE REGULATORY TREATMENT

As noted in Chapter 2, the Department of Justice (DoJ) has looked on JVs far more favorably than mergers or acquisitions. Mergers result in a reduction in the number of firms. In contrast, JVs increase the number of firms because the parents continue to operate while another firm is created. Project-oriented JVs often are viewed favorably by regulators. Regulatory authorities tend to encourage collaborative research, particularly when the research is shared among all the parties to the JV.

CRITICAL SUCCESS FACTORS FOR BUSINESS ALLIANCES

Robert Lynch (1990) argues that the probable success of a JV or alliance is dependent on a specific set of identifiable factors. A successful business alliance most is often characterized by the following factors: synergy; risk reduction; accountability; clarity of purpose, roles, and responsibilities; a "win–win" situation; compatible time frames for the partners; support from top management; and similar financial expectations.

SYNERGY

To be successful, the partners should have attributes that either complement existing strengths or offset significant weaknesses. Examples include economies of scale and scope, access to new products, distribution channels, and proprietary know-how. As with any merger or acquisition, the perceived synergy should be measurable to the extent possible.

RISK REDUCTION

Product introduction costs can be exorbitant in terms of development and manufacturing costs. By sharing these costs with others, the amount of capital any single partner has at risk is reduced. Risk may be mitigated further by reducing the likelihood of making poor business decisions by allying with those who have access to better information or proprietary knowledge. Risk also can be viewed as the cost of missing an attractive opportunity. This risk may be lessened by having access to a sufficient number of the right resources needed to exploit a perceived opportunity in a timely fashion.

COOPERATION

All parties involved must have the ability to cooperate with one another. A lack of consistent cooperation will result in poor internal communications and reduce the likelihood that the objectives of the JV or alliance will be met. Companies with similar philosophies, goals, rewards, operating practices, and ethics are more likely to be able to cooperate over the long run.

CLARITY OF PURPOSE, ROLES, AND RESPONSIBILITIES

The purpose of any business alliance must be crystal clear. A well-understood purpose drives timetables, division of responsibility, commitments to milestones, and measurable results. Poorly defined roles and responsibilities of the participants inevitably lead to internal conflict and lethargic decision making.

WIN–WIN SITUATION

All parties involved must see the apportionment of risk and awards as equitable. No matter how clear the purpose of the JV or alliance, the ability to achieve objectives will be retarded if middle-level management on down believes that they are being treated unfairly. Internal dissent can result in lower productivity or even outright sabotage. Johnson & Johnson's (J&J) alliance with Merck & Company in the marketing of Pepcid AC is a classic win–win situation. Merck contributed its prescription drug Pepcid to the alliance so that J&J could market it as an over-the-counter drug. With Merck as the developer of the upset stomach remedy and J&J as marketer, the product became the market share leader in this drug category.

COMPATIBLE TIME FRAMES FOR THE PARTNERS

The length of time an alliance agreement remains in force depends on the partners' objectives, the availability of resources needed to achieve these objectives, and the accuracy of the assumptions on which the alliance's business plans are based. Incompatible time frames are a recipe for disaster. The management of a small Internet business may want to "cash out" within the next 12–18 months, whereas a larger firm may wish to gain market share over a number of years. Unfortunately, although time frames initially may be compatible, short-run profit pressures may force the alliance to dissolve because one or more of the partners is no longer able to meet its commitments for the duration of the time period stipulated in the alliance agreement.

SUPPORT FROM THE TOP

It is imperative that top management of the parents of a business alliance involve themselves aggressively and publicly. Tepid support or worse, indifference, will filter down to lower level managers and prove to be highly demotivating. Middle-level managers will tend to focus their time and effort on those activities that tend to maximize their compensation and likelihood of promotions. These activities may divert time and attention from the business alliance.

SIMILAR FINANCIAL EXPECTATIONS

Partners must be in agreement with the goals of the JV or alliance. A goal of gaining market share will have very different financial implications than one focused on quarterly earnings targets. The parties to the venture must agree on what constitutes success. If objectives are quantifiable and milestones are identifiable, success may be defined in terms of how well the venture is doing in meeting these objectives and milestones.

ALTERNATIVE LEGAL FORMS OF BUSINESS ALLIANCES

As is true of M&As, determining the form of a business alliance should follow the creation of a coherent business strategy. The choice of legal structure should be made only when the parties to the business alliance are comfortable with the venture's objectives, potential synergy, and preliminary financial analysis of projected returns and risk. Business alliances may assume a variety of different legal structures. These include the following: corporate, partnership, franchise, equity partnership, or written contract. Technically, a "handshake" agreement is also an option. However, given the inordinate risk associated with the lack of a written agreement, those seeking to create a business alliance are encouraged to avoid this type of arrangement. However, in some cultures, this type of informal agreement may be most appropriate. Efforts to insist on a detailed written agreement or contractual relationship may be viewed as offensive. The five basic legal structures, excluding the handshake agreement, are discussed in detail in the following section. Each has its own implications with respect to taxation, control by the owners, ability to trade ownership positions, limitations on liability, duration, and raising capital. The relative merits of each legal form are summarized in Table 12-2.

CORPORATE STRUCTURES

A corporation is a legal entity created under state law in the United States with an unending life and limited financial liability for its owners. Corporate legal structures include a generalized corporate form (also called C-type corporation), the sub-chapter S (S-type) corporation, and the limited liability corporation (LLC). The S-type corporation contains certain tax advantages intended to facilitate the formation of small businesses, which are perceived to be major contributors to job growth. The LLC is a hybrid structure that contains some of the benefits of both a corporate and a partnership structure.

TABLE 12-2   Alternative Legal Forms Applicable to Business Alliances

Legal Form	Advantages	Disadvantages
Corporate Structures:		
—Generalized	Continuity of ownership Limited liability Provides operational autonomy Facilitates funding	Double taxation High set-up costs including charter and bylaws
—Sub-Chapter S	Avoids double taxation Limited liability	Maximum of 10 shareholders Excludes corporate shareholders Must distribute all earnings Allows only one class of stock

—Limited Liability	Limited liability
	Owners can be managers
	  without losing limited
	  liability
	Avoids double taxation
	Allows an unlimited number of
	  stockholders
	Allows corporate shareholders
	Can own more than 80% of
	  another company
	Allows flexibility in allocating
	  profits and losses
		Lacks continuity of
		  generalized corporate
		  structure
		Owners also must be active
		  participants in the firm

Partnership Structures:		

—General Partnerships	Avoids double taxation
	Allows flexibility in allocating
	  profits and losses
		Partners have unlimited
		  liability
		Lacks continuity of
		  generalized corporate
		  structure
		Partnership interests illiquid

—Limited Partnerships	Limits partner liability (except
	  for general partner)
	Avoids double taxation
		Lacks continuity of
		  generalized corporate
		  structure
		Partnership interests illiquid

Franchise Alliances	Allows repeated application of
	  a successful business model
	Minimizes start-up expenses
	Facilitates communication of
	  common brand and
	  marketing strategy
		Success depends on quality of
		  franchise sponsor support
		Royalty payments (3–7% of
		  revenue)

Equity Partnerships	Facilitates close working relationship Potential prelude to merger May preempt competition	Limited control Lacks close coordination
Written Contracts	Easy start-up Potential prelude to merger	Limited control Lacks close coordination Potential for limited commitment

C-Type Corporations

A JV corporation normally involves a standalone business. The corporation's income will be taxed at the prevailing corporate tax rates. Corporations, other than S-type corporations, are subject to "double" taxation. Taxes are paid by the corporation when profits are earned and again by the shareholders when the corporation distributes dividends. Moreover, setting up a corporate legal structure may be more time consuming and costly than other legal forms because of legal expenses incurred in drafting a corporate charter and bylaws. Although the corporate legal structure does have adverse tax consequences and may be more costly to establish, it does offer a number of important advantages over other legal forms, as discussed next.

Managerial Autonomy

Managerial autonomy most often is used when the JV is large or complex enough to require a separate or centralized professional management organization. The corporate structure works best when the JV requires a certain amount of operational autonomy to be effective. The parent companies would continue to set strategy, but the JV's management would manage the day-to-day operations.

Continuity of Ownership

Continuity refers to the continuation of the corporation's existence over a long period. Unlike other legal forms, the corporate structure does not have to be dissolved as a result of the death of the owners or if one of the owners wishes to liquidate their ownership position. A corporate legal structure may be warranted if the JV's goals are long term and if the parties choose to contribute cash directly to the JV. In return for the cash contribution, the JV partners receive stock in the new company. If the initial strategic reason for the JV change and the JV no longer benefits one of the partners, the stock in the JV can be sold. Alternatively, the partner can withdraw from active participation in the JV, but it can remain a passive shareholder in anticipation of potential future appreciation of the stock. In practice, the transferability of ownership interests is strictly limited by the stipulations of a shareholder agreement created when the corporation is formed.

Ease of Raising Money

A corporate structure also may be justified if the JV is expected to have substantial future financing requirements. A corporate structure provides a broader array of financing options than other legal forms. These include the ability to sell interests in the form of shares and the issuance of corporate debentures and mortgage bonds. The ability to sell new shares enables the corporation to raise funds to expand while still retaining control if less than 51% of the corporation's shares are sold.

Limited Liability

Under the corporate structure, the parent's liability is limited to the extent of its investment in the corporation. Consequently, an individual stockholder cannot be held responsible for the debts of the corporation or of other shareholders. Creditors cannot take the personal assets of the owners.

Chapter S Corporations

A firm having 10 or fewer shareholders may qualify as an S-type corporation and may elect to be taxed as if it were a partnership and thus avoid double taxation. The major disadvantages to an S-type corporation are the exclusion of any corporate shareholders, the requirement to issue only one class of stock, and the necessity of distributing all earnings to the shareholders each year.

Limited Liability Corporations

LLCs were first recognized for tax purposes in 1988. As of the end of 1999, they were permissible in 36 states. The LLC combines features of the corporation and the limited partnership and offers both tax and nontax benefits. Like a corporation, the LLC protects all its owners from liability, whether or not they participate in the management of the company. This feature enables owners to also be managers without running the risk of losing their limited liability protection. Like a limited partnership, the LLC passes through all the profits and losses of the entity to its owners without itself being taxed. Unlike S-type corporations, LLCs can own more than 80% of another corporation and have an unlimited number of shareholders. Also, corporations as well as non-U.S. residents can own LLC shares. The LLC also can sell shares without completing the costly and time-consuming process of registering them with the Securities and Exchange Commission (SEC), which is required for corporations that sell their securities to the public. This arrangement works well for corporate JVs or projects developed through a subsidiary or affiliate. The parent corporation can separate a JV's risk from its other businesses while getting favorable tax treatment and greater flexibility in the allocation of revenues and losses among owners. Finally, LLCs can incorporate before an initial public offering tax free.

The LLC's drawbacks are evident if one owner decides to leave. All other owners must formally agree to continue the firm. Also, all of the LLC's owners must take active roles in managing the firm.

PARTNERSHIP STRUCTURES

Partnership structures frequently are used as an alternative to a corporation. Partnership structures include general partnerships and limited partnerships.

General Partnerships

Under the general partnership legal structure, investment, profits, losses, and operational responsibilities are allocated to the partners. The arrangement has no effect on the autonomy of the partners. Because profits and losses are allocated to the partners, the partnership is not subject to tax. The partnership structure also offers substantial flexibility in how the profits and losses are allocated to the partners.

Typically, a corporate partner will form a special-purpose subsidiary to hold its interest. This not only limits liability but also may facilitate disposition of the JV interest in the future. The partnership structure is preferable to the other options when the business alliance is expected to have a short (3–5-year) duration and if high levels of commitment and management interaction are necessary for short time periods.

The primary disadvantage of the general partnership is that all the partners have unlimited liability and may have to cover the debts of the other, less financially sound partners. Each partner is said to be *jointly and severally liable* for the partnership's debts. For example, if one of the partners negotiates a contract that results in a substantial loss, each partner must pay for a portion of the loss, based on a previously determined agreement on the distribution of profits and losses. Because each partner has unlimited liability for all the debts of the firm, creditors of the partnership may claim assets from one or more of the partners if the remaining partners are unable to cover their share of the loss. The other partners may sue the offending partner if there is any violation of the articles of partnership. Moreover, the entity lacks continuity in that it must be dissolved if a partner dies or withdraws, unless a new partnership agreement can be drafted. Therefore, the partnership structure lacks the continuity of the corporate form. Partnership interests may also be difficult to sell, thus making the partnership difficult to liquidate or transfer partnership. Partnership interests often are sold at a discount that reflects their lack of liquidity, their lack of majority control over the firm, and the need for the new partner to be compatible with the existing partners.

Limited Partnerships

A limited liability partnership is one in which one or more of the partners can be designated as having limited liability as long as at least one partner has unlimited liability. Limited partners usually cannot lose more than their capital contribution. Those who are responsible for the day-to-day operations of the partnership's activities, whose individual acts are binding on the other partners, and who are personally liable for the partnership's total liabilities are called *general partners*. Those who contribute only money and who are not involved in management decisions are called *limited partners*. Usually limited partners receive income, capital gains, and tax benefits, whereas the general partner collects fees and a percentage of the capital gain and income. Typical limited partnerships are in real estate, oil and gas, and equipment leasing, but they also are used to finance movies, R&D, and other projects. Public limited partnerships are sold through brokerage firms, financial planners, and other registered securities representatives. Public partnerships may have an unlimited number of investors and their partnership plans must be filed with the SEC. Private limited partnerships are constructed with fewer than 35 limited partners who each invest more than $20,000. Their plans do not have to be filed with the SEC.

FRANCHISE ALLIANCE

Franchises typically involve a franchisee making an initial investment to purchase a license, plus additional capital investment for real estate, machinery, and working capital. For this initial investment, the franchisor provides training, site-selection assistance, and economies of scale in purchasing. Royalty payments for the license typically run 3–7% of annual franchisee revenue. Franchise success rates exceed 80% over a 5-year period as compared with start-ups, which have success rates of less than 10% after 5 years (Lynch, 1990, p. 253). The franchise alliance is preferred when a given business format can be replicated many times; when there needs to be a common, recognizable identity presented to customers of each of the alliance partners; and when close operational coordination is required. In addition, a franchise alliance may be appropriate when a common marketing program needs to be coordinated and implemented by a single partner. Multistate franchises must be careful to be in full compliance with the franchise laws of the states in which they have franchisees. Such laws often differ considerably from one state to the next.

EQUITY PARTNERSHIP

An equity partnership involves a company's purchase of stock in another company or a two-way exchange of stock by the two companies. It often is referred to as a partnership because of the equity ownership exchanged. However, it is not a partnership in a legal sense. Equity partnerships commonly are used in purchaser–supplier relationships, technology development, marketing alliances, and in situations in which a larger firm makes an investment in a smaller firm to ensure its continued financial viability. In exchange for an equity investment, a firm normally receives a seat on the board of directors and possibly an option to buy a controlling interest in the company. The equity partnership may be preferred when there is a need to have a long-term or close strategic relationship, to preempt a competitor from making an alliance or acquisition, or as a prelude to a possible acquisition or merger.

WRITTEN CONTRACT

The written contract is the simplest form of legal structure. This form is used most often with strategic alliances because it maintains an "arms-length" or independent relationship between the parties to the contract. The contract normally stipulates such things as how the revenue is divided, the responsibilities of each party, the duration of the alliance, and confidentiality requirements. No separate business entity is established for legal or tax purposes. The written contract most often is used when the business alliance is expected to last less than 3 years, when frequent close coordination is not required, when capital investments are made independently by each party to the agreement, and when the parties have had little previous contact. This type of legal structure may evolve into a partnership or corporate structure at a later date once the parties to the agreement feel more comfortable with each other or the original reasons for the written contract change.

STRATEGIC AND OPERATIONAL PLANS

Planning should precede deal-structuring activities. Too often, the parties to a proposed alliance get bogged down early in the process in such details as legal structure, control, ownership, and other deal-structuring issues. They do not spend sufficient energy in determining if the proposal makes good strategic and operational sense in terms of the participants' financial and nonfinancial objectives. Before any deal-structuring issues are addressed, the prospective parties must agree on the basic strategic direction and purpose of the alliance as defined in the alliances' strategic plan, as well as the financial and nonfinancial goals and milestones established in the operations plan.

STRATEGIC PLAN

The strategic plan identifies the primary purpose or mission of the business alliance; communicates specific quantifiable targets such as financial returns or market share and milestones; and analyzes the business alliance's strengths and weaknesses and opportunities and threats relative to the competition. The purpose of a business alliance could take various forms as diverse as R&D, cross-selling the partners' products, or jointly developing an oil field. Chapter 4 describes tools and methods for developing strategic business plans.

OPERATIONS PLAN

The roles and responsibilities of each partner in conducting the day-to day operations of the business alliance are stipulated in an operations plan. Teams representing all parties to the alliance should be involved from the outset of the discussions in developing both a strategic and operations plan for the venture. The operations plan should reflect the specific needs of the proposed business alliance. The operations plan should be written by those responsible for implementing the plan. Strict attention to details before the business alliance is put in place is crucial to its eventual success.

The operations plan is typically a 1-year plan that outlines for managers what is to be accomplished, when it is to be accomplished, and what resources are required. The operations plan also is referred to as the annual operating budget. The short-term objectives of the operations plan must be consistent with the more long-term objectives of the strategic plan. The standard operations plan contains the following elements:

1. An analysis of the current external competitive environment
2. A statement of critical success factors, such as product performance specifications and service and support levels
3. Key objectives and milestones
4. Marketing plan with projected product prices, unit volumes, and net revenue
5. Manufacturing/production/engineering plans
6. A purchasing plan, including the source of needed inputs and their purchase price
7. Implementation schedule with completion dates and the names of individuals responsible for each major activity
8. Contingency plan
9. Financial forecasts for the enterprise, including a monthly budget statement
10. A performance-tracking system to compare actual performance with the budget statement

Note that some deal-structuring decisions, such as the legal form, may affect the financial analysis because of the their tax implications for the cash flow of the business alliance. Nonetheless, the decision to proceed with forming the alliance should never be justified based on tax benefits alone but rather on the overall strategic value of the alliance to the participants.

BUSINESS ALLIANCE DEAL STRUCTURING

Generally speaking, the purpose of deal structuring in a business alliance is to allocate fairly risks, rewards, resource requirements, and responsibilities among participants. The formation of a successful alliance requires that a series of issues be resolved before signing an alliance agreement. Table 12-3 summarizes the key issues and related questions that need to be addressed as part of the business alliance deal-structuring process. This section discusses how these issues most often are resolved. For an excellent discussion of deal structuring in this context, see Ebin (1998), Freeman and Stephens (1994), Fusaro (1995), and Lorange and Roos (1992).

SCOPE

A basic question in setting up a business alliance involves which products specifically are included and excluded from the business alliance. This question deals with defining the scope of the business alliance. Scope outlines how broadly the alliance will be applied in pursuing its purpose. For example, an alliance whose purpose is to commercialize products developed by the partners could be broadly

TABLE 12-3 Business Alliance Deal-Structuring Issues

Issue	Key Questions
Scope	What products are included and what are excluded? Who receives rights to distribute, manufacture, acquire, or license technology or purchase future products or technology?
Duration	How long is the alliance expected to exist?
Legal Form	What is the appropriate legal structure—standalone entity or contractual?
Governance	How are the interests of the parents to be protected? Who is responsible for specific accomplishments?
Control	How are strategic decisions to be addressed? How are day-to-day operational decisions to be handled?
Resource Contributions and Ownership Determination	Who contributes what and in what form? Cash? Assets? Guarantees/loans? Technology including patents, trademarks, copyrights, and proprietary knowledge? How are contributions to be valued? How is ownership determined?
Financing Ongoing Capital Requirements	What happens if additional cash is needed?
Distribution	How are profits and losses allocated? How are dividends determined?
Performance Criteria	How is performance to plan measured and monitored?
Dispute Resolution	How are disagreements resolved?
Revision	How will the agreement be modified?
Termination	What are the guidelines for termination? Who owns the assets on termination? What are the rights of the parties to continue the alliance activities after termination?
Transfer of Interests	How are ownership interests to be transferred? What are the restrictions on the transfer of interests? How will new alliance participants be handled? Will there be rights of first refusal, drag-along, tag-along, or put provisions?
Tax	Who receives tax benefits?
Management/Organization	How is the alliance to be managed?
Confidential Information	How is confidential information handled? How are employees and customers of the parent firms protected?
Regulatory Restrictions and Notifications	What licenses are required? What regulations need to be satisfied? What agencies need to be notified?

or narrowly defined in specifying what products or services are to be offered, to whom, in what geographic areas, and for what time period. Failure to define scope adequately can lead to situations in which the alliance may be competing with the products or services offered by the parent firms. Furthermore, alliances are not static. Products developed for one purpose may prove to have other applications in the future. With respect to both current and future products, the alliance agreement should identify who receives rights to market or distribute products, manufacture products, acquire or license technology, or purchase products from the venture.

In certain types of alliances, intellectual property may play a very important role. It is common for a share in the intangible benefits of the alliance, such as rights to new developments of intellectual property, to be more important to an alliance participant than its share of the alliance's profits. What started out as a symbiotic marketing relationship between two pharmaceutical powerhouses, Johnson & Johnson and Amgen, deteriorated into a highly contentious feud (Case Study 12-5). The failure to properly define which parties would have the rights to sell certain drugs for certain applications and to sell future drugs that may have been developed as a result of the alliance laid the groundwork for a lengthy legal battle between these two corporations.

CASE STUDY 12-5:
JOHNSON & JOHNSON SUES AMGEN

In 1999, Johnson & Johnson (J&J) sued Amgen over their 14-year alliance to sell a blood-enhancing treatment called erythropoietin. The disagreement began when unforeseen competitive changes in the marketplace and mistrust between the partners began to strain the relationship. The relationship had begun in the mid-1980s with J&J helping to commercialize Amgen's blood-enhancing treatment, but the partners ended up squabbling over sales rights and a spin-off drug.

J&J booked most of the sales of its version of the $3.7 billion medicine by selling it for chemotherapy and other broader uses, whereas Amgen was left with the relatively smaller dialysis market. Moreover, the companies could not agree on future products for the JV. Amgen won the right in arbitration to sell a chemically similar medicine that can be taken weekly rather than daily. Arbitrators ruled that the new formulation was different enough to fall outside the licensing pact between Amgen and J&J (Bloomberg.com,1999b).

Case Study Discussion Questions

1. What could these companies have done before forming the alliance to have mitigated the problems that arose after the alliance was formed? Why do you believe they may have avoided addressing these issues at the outset?
2. What types of mechanisms could be used other than litigation to resolve such differences once they arise?

DURATION

The participants need to agree on how long the business alliance is to remain in force. Participant expectations must be compatible. The management of a large corporation may view the alliance as a pivotal part of its long-term strategy; in contrast, the management of a small, start-up operation may be interested in "cashing out" as soon as possible. The expected longevity of the alliance is also an important determinant in the choice of a legal form. For example, the corporate structure more readily provides for a continuous life than a partnership structure because of its greater ease of transferring ownership interests. There is conflicting evidence on how long most business alliances actually last. Mercer Management Consulting in ongoing research concludes that most JVs last only about 3 years (Lajoux: 1998), whereas Booz-Allen and Hamilton (1993) reported an average life span of 7 years.

LEGAL FORM

The corporation and partnership structures are the most common legal forms used in business alliances. As noted previously, partnerships offer tax advantages and greater flexibility in allocating profits and losses than corporate structures. However, a corporate structure may be a more logical choice if the alliance is expected to be large and complex with its own management structure requiring clearly drawn lines of authority, to have an indefinite life span, and to have substantial future capital requirements. If the corporate structure is selected, the participants also need to determine the state of incorporation.

GOVERNANCE

In the context of a business alliance, governance may be defined broadly as an oversight function providing for efficient, informed communication between two or more parent companies. Governance makes those who control the alliance accountable. The primary responsibilities of this oversight function are to protect the interests of the corporate parents, approve changes to strategy and annual operating plans, allocate resources needed to make the alliance succeed, and arbitrate conflicts among lower levels of management.

Traditional Approaches to Governance

Historically, governance of business alliances has followed either a quasi-corporate or quasi-project approach. For example, the oil industry traditionally has managed alliances by establishing a board of directors to provide oversight of managers and to protect the interests of nonoperating owners. In contrast, in the pharmaceutical and automotive industries where nonequity alliances are common, firms treat governance like project management by creating a steering committee that allows all participants to provide input into issues confronting the alliance.

The Need to Modify Traditional Approaches

As companies pursue alliances with different goals, duration, resource contributions, and potentially greater contributions to shareholder value, the traditional governance models will have to be modified. In the past, alliances often have been treated as a sideline by senior management. However, today alliances often are formed to augment a firm's core competencies by drawing on the primary skills of other alliance partners. Consequently, alliances are becoming a key underpinning of a firm's overall business strategy. For highly complex alliances, governance may have to be implemented through multiple boards of directors, steering committees, operating committees, alliance managers, and project committees. For example, the General Electric and Honeywell industrial controls JV recognized that the interaction required to manage the JV was too extensive to be managed by a single board. Consequently, an operating committee and several project committees were established to address issues involving specialized expertise (Kalmbach and Roussel, 1999).

RESOURCE CONTRIBUTIONS AND OWNERSHIP DETERMINATION

As part of the negotiation process, the participants must agree on a fair value for all tangible and intangible assets contributed to the business alliance. The valuation of partner contributions is important in that it often provides the basis for determining ownership shares in the business alliance. The shares of the corporation or the interests in the partnership will be distributed among the owners in accordance with the value contributed by each participant. The partner with the largest risk, the largest contributor of cash, or the person who contributes critical tangible or intangible assets generally is given the greatest equity share of a JV.

Valuing Tangible Contributions

It is easy to value tangible or "hard" contributions such as cash, promissory cash commitments, contingent commitments, stock of existing corporations, and assets and liabilities associated with an ongoing business in terms of actual dollars or their present values. A party contributing "hard" assets, such as a production facility, may want the contribution valued in terms of the value of increased production rather than its replacement cost or lease value. The contribution of a fully operational, modern facility to a venture interested in being first to market with a particular product may provide far greater value than if the venture attempted to build a new facility because of the normal "break-in" period associated with new operations.

Valuing Intangible Contributions

In contrast, intangible or "soft" or "in-kind" contributions such as skills, knowledge, services, patents, licenses, brand names, and technology are often much more difficult to value. Partners providing such services may be compensated by having the business alliance pay a market-based royalty or fee for such services. If the royalties or fees paid by the alliance are below standard market prices for comparable services, the difference between the market price and what the alliance actually is paying may become taxable income to the alliance. Alternatively, contributors of intellectual property may be compensated by receiving rights to future patents or technologies developed by the alliance. Participants in the business alliance contributing brand identities, which facilitate the alliance's entry into a particular market, may require assurances that they can purchase a certain amount of the product or service, at a guaranteed price, for a specific time period.

FINANCING ONGOING CAPITAL REQUIREMENTS

The business alliance may finance future capital requirements that cannot be financed out of operating cash flow by calling on the participants to make a capital contribution, issuing additional equity or partnership interests, or borrowing. If it is decided that the alliance should be able to borrow, the participants must agree on an appropriate financial structure for the enterprise. Financial structure refers to the amount of equity that will be contributed to the business alliance and how much debt it will carry. The financial structure will differ with the type of legal structure selected for the business alliance. Alliances established through a written contract obviate the need for such a financing decision because each party to the contract will finance their own financial commitments to the alliance. Because of their more predictable cash flows, project-based JVs, particularly those that create a separate corporation, sometimes sell equity directly to the public or though a private placement. Banks and insurance companies also may be a source of funding.

OWNER OR PARTNER FINANCING

The equity owners or partners may agree to make contributions of capital in addition to their initial investments in the enterprise. The contributions usually are made in direct proportion to their equity or partnership interests. If one party chooses not to make a capital contribution, the ownership interests of all the parties are adjusted to reflect the changes in their cumulative capital contributions. This adjustment results in an increase in the ownership interests of those making the contribution and a corresponding reduction in the interests of those not making contributions.

EQUITY FINANCING

JVs formed as a corporation may issue different classes of either common or preferred stock. JVs established as partnerships raise capital through the issuance of limited partnership units to investors, with the sponsoring firms becoming general partners. When a larger company aligns with a smaller company, it may make a small equity investment in the smaller firm to ensure it remains solvent or to benefit from potential equity appreciation. Such investments often include an option to purchase the remainder of the shares, or at least a controlling interest, at a predetermined price if the smaller firm or the JV satisfies certain financial targets. In some instances, the general partner may be required, as part of the original agreement, to invest specific amounts of capital in the venture at regular intervals or when certain milestones are reached. These requirements normally are stipulated in the original articles of partnership.

DEBT FINANCING

Non-project-related alliances or alliances without financial track records often will find it very difficult to borrow. Banks and insurance companies generally require loan guarantees from the participating partners. Such guarantees give lenders recourse to the participating partners in the event the alliance fails to repay its debt. The amount that the alliance ultimately can borrow is likely to be based more on the financial viability of the partners than on the venture's cash flows. *Nonrecourse financing* (i.e., loans granted to the venture without partner guarantees) usually is reserved for ventures that already have demonstrated that they are viable businesses.

CONTROL

Control is distinguishable from ownership by the use of shareholder agreements or voting trusts or by issuing different classes of shares. Control issues should be negotiated with an eye to differentiating between day-to-day management and major strategic decisions. The most successful JVs are those in which one party is responsible for most routine management decisions, with the other parties participating in decision making only when the issue is fundamental to the success of the business alliance. The business alliance agreement must define what issues are to be considered fundamental to the business alliance and address how they are to be resolved, either by majority votes or by veto rights given to one or more of the parties. Whichever partner is responsible for the results of the alliance will want operational control. Operational control should be placed with the partner most able to manage the JV. In some cases, the partner with operational control could be a minority owner.

If the partner having the largest equity share does not also have operational control, the partner likely will insist on being involved in the operations of the business alliance by having a seat on the board of directors or steering committee. The partner also may insist on having veto rights over issues it views as fundamental to the success of the alliance. These issues often include changes in the alliance's purpose and scope, overall strategy, capital expenditures over a certain amount of money, key management promotions, salary increases applying to the general employee population, the amount and timing of dividend payments, buyout conditions, and acquisitions or divestitures.

DISTRIBUTION ISSUES

Distribution issues relate to enterprise dividend policies and how profits and losses are allocated among the owners.

Dividend Policies

The dividend policy determines the cash return each partner should receive. How the cash flows of the venture will be divided generally depends on the initial equity contribution of each partner, ongoing equity contributions, and noncash contributions in the form of technical and managerial resources.

Allocation of Profit and Losses

Allocation of profits and losses normally follow directly from the allocation of shares or partnership interests. When the profits flow from intellectual property rights contributed by one of the parties, royalties or payments for know-how may be used to compensate the party contributing the property rights. When profits are to the result of distribution or marketing efforts of a partner, fees and commission can be used to compensate the partners. Similarly, rental payments can be used to allocate profits attributable to specific equipment or facilities contributed by a partner.

PERFORMANCE CRITERIA

The lack of adequate performance measurement criteria can result in significant disputes among the partners and eventually contribute to the termination of the venture. Performance criteria should be both measurable and simple enough to be understood and used by managers at all levels. Performance criteria should be spelled out clearly in the business alliance agreement. Nonfinancial performance measures should be linked to financial return drivers. For example, factors such as market share, consistent product quality, and customer service may be critical to success in the marketplace. Improvements in the venture's performance against these critical success factors ultimately should result in increasing financial returns to the partners.

Balanced Scorecard

The balanced scorecard technique is a widely used performance measurement tool in cross-functional corporate work teams. The concept also can be applied to measuring alliance performance by having the partners agree on a small number (i.e., 5–10) of relevant indicators. The number of indicators should be limited. This enables alliance managers to more easily track performance to plan. The indicators should include financial and nonfinancial, short- and long-term, and internal and customer-focused measures. Examples of performance indicators include return on investment, operating cash flow, profit margins, asset turnover, market share, on-time delivery, and customer satisfaction survey results.

Linking Performance to Individual Incentives

Managers will ignore performance indicators if their compensation is not linked to their actual performance against these measures. The top alliance managers should be evaluated against the full list of balanced scorecard performance measures. The performance of lower level managers should be evaluated only against those measures over which they have some degree of control.

DISPUTE RESOLUTION

No matter how well the participants draft the venture agreement, disputes between parties to the agreement will arise. There are several ways to resolve such disputes. One is a *choice of law provision* in the alliance agreement indicating which state's or country's laws will have jurisdiction in settling disputes. This provision should be drafted with an understanding of the likely outcome of litigation in any of the participants' home countries or states and the attitude of these countries' or states' courts in enforcing choice of law provisions in the JV agreements. Another important clause is the definition of what constitutes a deadlock or impasse when a disagreement arises. This clause should include a clear statement of what events trigger various types of dispute-resolution procedures. Care should be taken not to define the events triggering dispute-resolution procedures so narrowly that minor disagreements are subject to the dispute mechanism. Finally, an *arbitration clause* usually is used to address major disagreements. Such a clause should define the type of dispute subject to arbitration and how the arbitrator will be selected.

REVISION

No matter how well conceived the business alliance was at the time of formation, changing circumstances and partner objectives may prompt a need to revise the objectives of the business alliance. If one of the parties to the agreement wishes to withdraw, the participants should have agreed in advance how the withdrawing party's ownership interest would be divided among the remaining parties. Moreover, a product or technology may be developed that was not foreseen when the alliance first was conceived. The alliance agreement should indicate that the rights to manufacture and distribute the product or technology might be purchased by a specific alliance participant. If revisions cannot be made to meet the needs of the partners, it may be necessary to terminate the enterprise. The events triggering dissolution usually are spelled out in the *deadlock clause*.

TERMINATION

In general, business alliances are not intended to become permanent arrangements. A business alliance may be terminated as a result of the completion of a project, successful operations resulting in merger of the partners, diverging strategic objectives of the partners, and failure of the alliance to achieve stated objectives. Termination provisions in the alliance agreement should include buyout clauses enabling one party to purchase another's ownership interests, prices of the buyout, and how assets and liabilities are to be divided if the venture fails or the partners elect to dissolve the operation. What will happen to key personnel and who owns tangible and intangible property such as trade secrets and patents also should be considered in the termination provisions. In some instances, a JV may convert to a simple licensing arrangement. Consequently, the partner may disengage from the JV without losing all benefits by purchasing rights to the product or technology.

The events leading to termination are usually the same as those stipulated in the deadlock clause. Moreover, the parties normally will be entitled to terminate the venture by mutual consent. Whether it is by mutual consent or through a failure of the dispute resolution mechanism, however, the business alliance agreement should include detailed provisions for terminating the agreement.

TRANSFER OF INTERESTS

JV and alliance agreements often limit how and to whom parties to the agreements can transfer their interests. This is justified by noting that each party entered the agreement with the understanding of who their partners would be. In agreements that permit transfers under certain conditions, the partners or the JV itself may have *rights of first refusal* (i.e., the party wishing to leave the JV first must offer their interests to other participants in the JV). Usually, the agreement will permit the parties to transfer their interests to corporate affiliates without restrictions. Parties to the agreement may have the right to "put" or sell their interests to the venture, and the venture may have a call option or right to purchase such interests. There also may be "tag-along" and "drag-along" provisions, which have the effect of a third-party purchaser acquiring not only the interest of the JV party whose interest it seeks to acquire but also the interests of other parties as well. A *drag-along* provision specifically requires a party not otherwise interested in selling its ownership interest to the third party to do so. A *tag-along* provision allows a participant, who was not originally targeted by the third party, to join the targeted party in conveying its interest to the third party.

TAXES

Each of the different types of business alliance legal structures has different tax implications. Although tax considerations should never drive the transaction, failure to explore their different implications can have painful financial consequences for all parties involved. As is true for a merger, the primary tax concerns of the JV partners will be to avoid the recognition of taxable gains on the formation of the venture and to minimize taxes imposed on the distribution of its earnings.

Corporation

In addition to the double taxation of dividends discussed earlier, the corporate structure may have other adverse tax consequences. Assuming that the partner's interest in the business alliance is less than 80%, its share of the alliance's results cannot be included in its consolidated income tax return. This has two effects. First, when earnings are distributed, they will be subject to an intercorporate dividend tax—7% if the partner's interest in the venture is 20% or more. Second, losses of the business alliance cannot be used to offset other income earned by the participant (Tillinghast, 1998, pp. 163–164). For tax purposes, the preferred alternative to a corporate legal structure is to use a *pass-through* legal structure such as a partnership.

Partnership

Because the profits and losses are allocated directly to the partners, the partnership does not have to pay taxes. Each partner in the JV will report its share of the enterprise's income or loss in its own consolidated return, and no intercorporate dividend tax will be imposed. In addition, the partnership can be structured in such a way that some partners can receive a larger share of the profits, whereas others receive a larger share of the losses. This flexibility in tax planning is an important factor stimulating the use of partnerships and LLCs. These entities can allocate to each JV partner a portion of a particular class of revenue, income, gain, loss, or expense. These *special allocations* can be made in the documents governing the creation of the partnership. Thus, partners need not share the results of the venture on a pro rata basis. However, to be considered legitimate by the Internal Revenue Service (IRS), the special allocations must have an economic impact on the parties receiving the allocation. Therefore, it is not possible to allocate tax losses to a partner that can use them in its consolidated return without requiring that the participant actually bear the loss by experiencing a reduction in the amount it will receive on dissolution of the venture.

Written Contract

The business alliance does not incur any tax because no separate legal entity has been created. Any profits earned or losses incurred by parties to the alliance are taxed at their own effective tax rates.

Noncash Contributions

When one of the partners contributes technology, patent rights, or other property to the JV, the contribution may be structured so that the partner receives equity in exchange for the contribution. Otherwise, it will be viewed by the IRS as an attempt to avoid making cash contributions and will be treated as taxable income to the enterprise.

Start-Up Expenses

If a new corporation has been created, expenses related to the start-up (e.g., advertising, training, and equipment/facility lease payments) are capitalized as deferred expenses and amortized over a 5-year period rather than expensed in the first year. However, once the venture is actively engaged in business, these types of expenses generally can be treated as operating expenses and deducted for tax purposes.

Parent Services Provided to Joint Ventures

Services provided to the JV, such as accounting, auditing, legal, human resource, and treasury services are not viewed by the IRS as being "at risk" if the JV fails. The JV should pay prevailing market fees for such services. Services provided to the JV in return for equity may be seen as taxable to the JV by the IRS if such services are not truly "at risk."

MANAGEMENT AND ORGANIZATIONAL ISSUES

Before a business alliance agreement is signed, the partners must decide what type of organizational structure will provide the most effective management and leadership.

Steering or Joint Management Committee

Control of business alliances most often is accomplished through a steering committee. The steering committee is the ultimate authority for ensuring that the venture stays focused on the strategic objectives agreed to by the partners. To maintain good communication, coordination, and teamwork, the committee should meet at least monthly. The committee should provide operations managers with sufficient autonomy so they can take responsibility for their actions and be rewarded for their initiative.

Methods of Dividing Ownership and Control

Majority–Minority Framework

The first method of control is the majority–minority framework, which relies on identifying a clearly dominant partner. A dominant partner is defined as having at least a 51% ownership stake in the enterprise. In this scenario, the equity, control, and distribution of rewards reflect the majority–minority relationship. This type of structure tends to promote the ability to make rapid mid-course corrections and clearly defines who is in charge. This framework is most appropriate for high-risk ventures where quick decisions often are required. The major disadvantage of this approach is that the minority partner may feel powerless and become passive or alienated.

Equal Division of Power Framework

The second method of control is the equal division of power framework, which usually means that equity is split 50/50. This assumes that the initial contribution, distribution, decision making, and control are split equally. This approach helps keep the partners actively engaged in the management of the venture. This is best suited for partners sharing a strong common vision for the venture and possessing similar corporate cultures. However, this approach can lead to deadlocks and to the eventual dissolution of the alliance, in the absence of mutual respect, good problem-solving skills, and patience by the partners.

"Majority Rules" Framework

Under the "majority rules" arrangement, the equity distribution may involve three partners. Two of the partners have large equal shares, whereas the third partner may have less than 10%. The minority partner is used to break deadlocks. This approach enables the primary partners to remain actively engaged in the enterprise without stalemating the decision-making process. However, it may be difficult to keep the minority partner motivated to remain abreast of all the issues because their share of equity is too small.

Multiple Party Framework

In this framework, no partner has control. Instead, control resides with the management of the venture. Consequently, decision making can be nimble and made by those that best understand the issues. This framework is well suited for international ventures, where a country's laws may prohibit a foreign firm from having a controlling interest in a domestic firm. In this instance, it is commonplace for a domestic company to own the majority of the equity but the operational control of the venture resides with the foreign partner. In addition to a proportional split of the dividends paid, the foreign company may receive additional payments in the form of management fees and bonuses. For an interesting perspective on these types of arrangements, see Armstrong and Hagel (1997).

CONFIDENTIAL INFORMATION

Parties to a business alliance will have access to a substantial amount of confidential information, including proprietary know-how, customers, and employees. The alliance agreement should specify how such information should be treated. Confidential information should never be released without the consent of all parties involved. Moreover, the alliance agreement also should contain clauses preventing the various partners from soliciting the other's employees for purposes of employment or from soliciting the other partner's customers.

REGULATORY RESTRICTIONS AND NOTIFICATIONS

This section provides a brief overview of the regulatory issues confronting business alliances. See Chapter 2 for a more detailed discussion of regulations covering business combinations.

Antitrust Policy

The DoJ has historically looked on business alliances far more favorably than mergers or acquisitions. Nonetheless, JVs may be subject to Hart–Scott–Rodino filing requirements because the parties to the JV are viewed as acquirers and the JV itself is viewed as a target.

For JVs between competitors to be acceptable to regulators, competitors should be able to do something together that they could not do alone. In general, competitors can be relatively confident that a partnership will be acceptable to regulators if in combination they do not control more than 20% of the market. Project-oriented ventures are looked at most favorably. Collaborative research is encouraged, particularly when the research is shared among all the parties to the alliance. However, regulators will move aggressively to investigate any perceived restraint of competition between partners, such as price fixing and market allocation, or any effort to deprive competitors from accessing a much-needed resource.

The regulatory guidelines for joint marketing arrangements are still ambiguous. Such agreements, particularly between competitors, are likely to spark a review by the regulators because they have the potential to result in price fixing and dividing up the market.

Securities and Exchange Commission

If the corporate partners make a public stock offering or a private placement of partnership shares in addition to the infusion of capital, the JV must comply with prevailing federal and state securities laws.

EMPIRICAL FINDINGS

EXCESS RETURNS

There is empirical evidence that JVs create value for their participants. In a study of 136 JVs between 1972 and 1979, McConnell and Nantell (1985) found that excess returns (i.e., the amount of return above what the capital asset pricing model would have predicted) to venture participants averaged 2.15% during the 62 days before the announcement of the JV. In a more recent study, Chan, Kensinger, Keown, and Martin (1997) support these findings. The authors track share price response to the formation of 345 strategic alliances spanning 1983–1992 and conclude that average abnormal stock price response was positive 0.64% for both horizontal alliances involving partner firms in the same industries and nonhorizontal alliances. Notably, at 3.54%, the increase in share price was much greater for horizontal alliances involving the transfer of technical knowledge than for nontechnical alliances. Johnson and Houston (2000) conclude that horizontal JVs create synergy that is shared by all partners, whereas vertical JVs create gains that accrue primarily to suppliers. Finally, partnering firms tend to display better operating performance than their industry peers do over the 5-year period surrounding the year in which an alliance is formed.

IMPACT ON MARKET VALUE

There is also evidence that business alliances may account for a significant amount of the market value of participants. Kalmbach and Roussel (1999) of Andersen Consulting found that alliances account for about 6–15% of the market value of the typical large company in a sample of 870 JVs and 1106 licensing arrangements studied over a 4-year period.

THE GROWING ROLE OF BUSINESS ALLIANCES

The average large company, which may have had no alliances in 1990, now has more than 30 (Kalmbach and Roussel, 1999). During the last decade, the number of reported alliances has been increasing at about 30% per year. Despite rapid growth, there is evidence that most companies have yet to develop the skill to implement alliances successfully. The Kalmbach and Roussel study indicates that 61% of the alliances are viewed as either disappointments or outright failures. This figure substantiates earlier findings by Robert Spekman of the Darden Graduate School of Business Administration that 60% of all ventures fail to meet expectations (Ellis, 1996). These studies do not make allowances for different levels of experience in forming and managing alliances among the firms in their samples. As is true for M&As, cumulative experience is an important factor in increasing the likelihood that an alliance will meet expectations. According to a Booz-Allen survey of 700 alliances (Booz-Allen and Hamilton, 1993), financial returns on investment are directly related to a company's experience in forming and managing business alliances. Companies with one or two alliances in place tended to earn a 10% average return on investment as compared with 15% for those with three to five, 17% for those with six to eight, and 20% for those with nine or more.

THINGS TO REMEMBER

Business alliances may represent attractive alternatives to M&As. The motivations for business alliances can include risk sharing, gaining access to new markets, accelerating the introduction of new products, technology sharing, cost reduction, globalization, a desire to acquire (or exit) a business, and the perception that they are often more acceptable to regulators than are acquisitions or mergers.

Business alliances may assume a variety of different legal structures. These include the following: corporate, partnership, franchise, equity partnership, written contract, or handshake agreements. Handshake agreements generally should be avoided in view of their inherent ambiguity. Corporate legal structures include a generalized C-type, S-type, and LLCs, which contain some of the benefits of both the corporate and partnership structures. Although the corporate structure is subject to double taxation, it does provide for centralized management, continuity of ownership, ease of raising capital, and limited liability. Partnerships frequently are used as an alternative to the corporate structure because of their greater flexibility in allocating gains and losses and their more favorable tax treatment. The written contract is the simplest legal structure and most often is used in strategic alliances.

As is true of M&As, planning always should precede concerns about how the transaction should be structured. All parties must agree on the basic strategic direction and purpose of a proposed alliance as well as the financial and nonfinancial goals and milestones used in establishing the first year's operating plan or budget.

Deal structuring in the context of a business alliance concerns the fair allocation of risks, rewards, resource requirements, and responsibilities among participants. Key issues that must be resolved include the alliance's scope, duration, legal form, governance, and control mechanism. The valuation of resource contributions ultimately determines ownership interests. How profits and losses will be distributed and how performance will be measured also must be determined. Alliance agreements also must be flexible enough to be revised when necessary and contain mechanisms for breaking deadlocks, transferring ownership interests, and dealing with the potential for termination.

Empirical studies suggest that business alliances contribute to shareholder value and that they are likely to become increasingly popular in the future. Nonetheless, their success rate in terms of meeting participants' expectations does not seem to be materially different from that of M&As.

CHAPTER DISCUSSION QUESTIONS

12.1. Under what circumstances does a business alliance represent an attractive alternative to a merger or acquisition?

12-2. Compare and contrast a corporate and partnership legal structure.

12-3. What are the primary motives for creating a business alliance? How do they differ from the motives for a merger or acquisition?

12-4. What factors are critical to the success of a business alliance?

12-5. Why is a handshake agreement a potentially dangerous form of business alliance? Are there any circumstances under which such an agreement may be appropriate?

12-6. What is a limited liability corporation? What are its advantages and disadvantages?

12-7.   Why is defining the scope of a business alliance important?

12-8.   Discuss ways of valuing tangible and intangible contributions to a JV.

12-9.   What are the advantages and disadvantages of the various organizational structures that could be used to manage a business alliance?

12-10. What are the common reasons for the termination of a business alliance?

CHAPTER BUSINESS CASE

CASE STUDY 12-6: BELL ATLANTIC AND VODAFONE FORM WIRELESS OPERATION TO EXPAND GEOGRAPHIC COVERAGE

Background

Bell Atlantic and Vodafone agreed to a business alliance that creates the largest wireless phone company in the United States. This announcement came shortly after AT&T and British Telecom formed a global alliance to link their wireless telephone operations with roaming agreements and other unified services in September 1999. AT&T and British Telecom will provide wireless service to a customer base of 41 million in 17 countries.

Bell Atlantic, the largest local telephone company in the United States, will connect its East Coast network with the West Coast network of VodafoneAirTouch, the world's largest wireless telephone company. Together, their combined 20 million customers will be able to buy less expensive wireless phones and make calls from almost anywhere in the country without having to pay "roaming" charges for out-of-area calls. The driving force behind the creation of the business alliance was to develop a national wireless phone network that will give both companies access to a larger pool of customers. Bell Atlantic gets to reach a national market and Vodafone is able to fill a serious gap in its global coverage. Vodafone's West Coast network is valued at $15 billion. In exchange for this network, Bell Atlantic gave Vodafone a 45% stake in the new company. Bell Atlantic will manage the New York-based JV and control a majority of the seats on the board of directors. The total assets of the JV will exceed $28 billion. The parent companies are expecting to sell a stake in the new company to the public within 2 or 3 years.

Establishing the Partnership

Solely owned by Bell Atlantic and its affiliated companies, Bell Atlantic operated a general partnership, Cellco, whose primary objective was to provide mobile telecommunications services in the United States. Under a new partnership agreement, the Cellco partnership agreement was amended to allow Vodafone AirTouch to contribute certain businesses to the partnership in exchange for a partnership interest. Cellco would retain its current assets, including the mobile and Federal Communications Commission licenses and other government permits, and all current liabilities. Bell Atlantic also agreed to convey certain assets and liabilities, including its interests in GTE's mobile telecommunications assets, to Cellco.

Operation of the Partnership

The partnership will be governed by the partnership agreement, which defines the relationship between the partners in the partnership, including management, the composition of the board, approval requirements for certain matters, restrictions on direct competition between the partners, distributions, transfer of interests, and termination.

The JV agreement provides that Vodafone AirTouch and Bell Atlantic will explore fully the potential for realizing synergies from business initiatives and the relationship between the partnership, Bell Atlantic, and Vodafone AirTouch including the development of new mobile telecommunications technologies, services, and applications. Under the agreement, Bell Atlantic reserves the right to require the partnership to change the name of the partnership to the name designated by Bell Atlantic. In addition, Bell Atlantic has the right to discontinue use of any or all of the partnerships' trademarks and to enter into a nonexclusive royalty-free licensing agreement with any member of the Bell Atlantic group. The agreement may be terminated at any time by mutual consent of both parties or by either party if the other has failed to honor commitments made in the alliance agreement if such failure resulted in a material adverse affect on the partnership. However, if all agreement commitments have been satisfied, either partner can leave the partnership by paying the other $500 million (Vodafone AirTouch, 1999).

The board of representatives, consisting of seven representatives, is responsible for the management of the partnership. The board will decide routine matters by a simple majority vote. Profits and losses will be allocated to the partners in proportion to their respective partnership interests. Transferring partnership interests to entities not currently part of the partnership is prohibited during the first full year of operation. After that, transfers are allowed as long as the other partner is first asked to buy the interest (i.e., each partner has the right of first refusal).

Case Study Discussion Questions

1. What did Bell Atlantic and Vodafone expect to get out of the business alliance?
2. Do you think this alliance will promote or reduce competition in the wireless phone market?
3. Why would Bell Atlantic and Vodafone want to sell a portion of the new alliance to the public?
4. In your judgment, how do you think ownership in the alliance was determined?

5. Why might the partners have selected a general partnership as the appropriate legal structure for this business alliance? Explain your answer.

A solution to this case study is given in the back of the book.

CHAPTER BUSINESS CASE

CASE STUDY 12-7: COCA-COLA AND PROCTER & GAMBLE'S ABORTED EFFORT TO CREATE A GLOBAL JOINT VENTURE COMPANY

Background

Coca-Cola (Coke), arguably the world's best known brand, manufactures and distributes Coca-Cola as well as 230 other products in 200 countries through the world's largest distribution system. Coke sells consumers worldwide more than 1 billion servings of its products daily. Procter & Gamble (P&G) sells 300 brands to nearly 5 billion consumers in 140 countries and holds more food patents than the three largest U.S. food companies combined. Moreover, P&G has a substantial number of new food and beverage products under development. Both firms have been competing in the health and wellness segment of the food market for years. P&G spends about 5% of its annual sales, about $1.9 billion, on R&D and holds more than 27,000 patents. The firm employs about 6000 scientists, including about 1200 people with PhDs.

Both firms have extensive distribution systems. P&G uses a centralized selling and warehouse distribution system for servicing high-volume outlets such as grocery store chains. With a warehouse distribution system, the retailer is responsible for in-store presentations of the brands, including shelving, display, and merchandising. The primary disadvantage of this type of distribution system is that it does not reach many smaller outlets cost effectively, resulting in many lost opportunities. In contrast, Coke uses three distinct systems. Direct store delivery consists of a network of independently operated bottlers, which bottle and deliver the product directly to the outlet. The bottler also is responsible for in-store merchandising. Coke's warehouse distribution is similar to P&G's and is used primarily to distribute Minute Maid products. Coke also sells beverage concentrates to distributors and food service outlets (Coca-Cola Press Release, 2001).

On February 21, 2001, Coca-Cola and Proctor & Gamble announced, amid great fanfare, plans to create a standalone joint venture corporation focused on developing and marketing new juice and juice-based beverages as well as snacks on a global basis (Coca-Cola Press Release, 2001). The new company expected to benefit from Coca-Cola's worldwide distribution, merchandising, and customer marketing skills and P&G's R&D capabilities and a wide range of popular brands. The new company would focus on the health and wellness segment of the food market. Less than 9 months later, Coke and P&G released a one-sentence joint statement on September 21, 2001 that they could achieve better returns for their respective shareholders if they pursued this opportunity independently. Although it is unclear what may have derailed what initially had seemed to the potential partners like such a good idea, it is instructive to examine the initial rationale for the proposed joint effort.

The New Company

Each parent would own 50% of the new company. Because of the businesses each partner was to contribute to the JV, the firm would have annual sales of $4 billion. The new firm would be an LLC, having its own board of directors consisting of two directors each from Coke and P&G. Moreover, the new firm would have its own management and dedicated staff providing administrative and R&D services. Coke was contributing a number of well-known brands including Minute Maid, Hi-C, Five Alive, Cappy, Kapo, Sonfil, and Qoo; P&G contributed Pringles, Sunny Delight, and Punica beverages. The new company would have had 15 manufacturing facilities and about 6000 employees.

Although the new firm was to have access to all distribution systems of the parents, it would have been free to choose the best route to market for each product. Although Minute Maid was to continue to use Coke's distribution channels, it also was to take advantage of existing refrigerated distribution systems built for Sunny Delight. Pringles was to use a variety of distribution systems, including the existing warehouse system. The Pringles brand was expected to take full advantage of Coke's global distribution and merchandising capabilities. Minute Maid was to gain access to new outlets through Coke's fountain and direct store distribution system.

Key Synergies

The new company's sales were expected to grow from $4 billion during the first 12 months of operation to more than $5 billion within 2 years. The combination of increasing revenue and cost savings was expected to contribute about $200 million in pretax earnings annually by 2005. Specifically, Pringles' revenue growth as a result of enhanced distribution was expected to contribute about $120 million of this projected improvement in pretax earnings. The importance of improved distribution is illustrated by noting that Coke has access to 16 million outlets globally. In the United States alone, that represents a 10-fold increase for Pringles, from its current 150,000 points of outlet. Similarly, improved merchandising and distribution of Sunny Delight was expected to contribute an additional $30 million in pretax income. The remaining $50 million in pretax earnings was to come from lower manufacturing, distribution, and administrative expenses and through discounts received on bulk purchases of foodstuffs and ingredients.

P&G and Coke were hoping to stimulate innovation by combining global brands and distribution with talent from both firms in what was hoped would be a highly entrepreneurial corporate culture. The parents also hoped that the standalone firm would be able to achieve focus and economies of scale that could not have been achieved by either firm separately.

Financial Impact on the Partners

The results of the LLC were not to be consolidated with those of the parents but rather shown using the equity method of accounting. Under this method of accounting, each parent's proportionate share of earnings (or losses) are shown on their income statement, and their equity interest in the LLC is displayed on their balance sheets. The new company was expected to be nondilutive of the earnings of the parents during its first full year of operations and contribute to earnings per share in subsequent years. The incremental earnings were expected to improve the market value of the parents by at least $1.5–2.0 billion (Bachman, 2001).

Some observers suggested that P&G would stand to benefit the most from the JV. It would have gained substantially by obtaining access to the growing vending machine market. Historically, P&G's penetration in this market has been miniscule. It may have been this perceived disproportionate benefit accruing to P&G that may have contributed to the eventual demise of the joint venture effort. Coke may have sought additional benefits from the JV that P&G was simply not willing to cede. Once again, we see that no matter how attractive the concept may seem to be on the surface, the devil is indeed in the details when comes to making it happen.

Case Study Discussion Questions

1. In your opinion, what were the motivating factors for the Coke and P&G business alliance?
2. Why do you think the parents selected a limited liability corporate structure for the new company? What are the advantages and disadvantages of this structure over alternative legal structures?
3. The parents estimate that the new company will add at least $1.5–2.0 billion to their market values. How do you think this estimated incremental value was determined?
4. Why do you think the parents opted to form a 50/50 distribution of ownership? What are some of the possible challenges of operating the new company with this type of an ownership arrangement? What can the parents do to overcome these challenges?
5. Do you think it is likely that the new company will become highly entreprenuerial and innovative? Why or why not? What can the parents do to stimulate the development of this type of an environment within the new company?
6. What factors may have contributed to the decision to discontinue efforts to implement the joint venture? Consider control, scope, financial, and resource contribution issues.

REFERENCES

Armstrong, Arthur and John Hagel, *Net Gain: Expanding Markets through Virtual Communities*, Harvard Business School Press, 1997.

Bachman, Justin, "Coke, P&G Try to Juice Snack Sales," *The Associated Press, Orange County Register*, February 22, 2001, Business Section, p. 2.

Berg, Sanford V., Jerome Duncan, and Philip Friedman, *Joint Venture Strategies and Corporate Innovation*, Cambridge, MA: Oelgeschlager, Gunn & Hain, 1982.

Bloomberg.com, "GM Invests in Fuji," December 17, 1999a.

Bloomberg.com, "J&J Sues Amgen," December 11, 1999b.

Booz-Allen & Hamilton, *A Practical Guide to Alliances: Leapfrogging the Learning Curve*, Los Angeles, 1993.

Business Week, "Can Covisint Climb Out of a Ditch," May 21, 2001, p. 128B.

Chan, Su Han, John W. Kensinger, Arthur J. Keown, and John D. Martin, "Do Strategic Alliances Create Value?" *Journal of Financial Economics*, 46 (2), November 1997, pp. 199–221.

Coca-Cola Press Release, "Coca-Cola and Procter & Gamble Announce New Company to Serve Growing Global Demand for Innovative Juices, Beverages, and Snacks," Press Release, February 21, 2001, thecoca-coca-colacompany.com/news/NewsDetail4.asp.

Ebin, Robert F., "Legal Aspects of International Joint Ventures and Strategic Alliances," in David J. BenDaniel and Arthur H. Rosenbloom, eds., *International M&A, Joint Ventures and Beyond: Doing the Deal*, New York: John Wiley & Sons, 1998, pp. 315–360.

Ellis, Caroline, "Briefings from the Editors," *Harvard Business Review*, 74 (1), July/August 1996, p. 8.

Ernst, David and Andrew M. J. Steinhubl, Alliances in Upstream Oil and Gas, *The McKinsey Quarterly*, 2, 1997, pp. 144–155.

Freeman, Louis S. and Thomas M. Stephens, "Advantages, Key Issues, and Tax Strategies in the Use of Partnerships by Corporate Joint Ventures," In *Tax Strategies for Corporate Acquisitions, Dispositions, Spin-Offs, Joint Ventures and Other Strategic Alliances, Financings, Reorganizations, and Restructurings*, New York: Practicing Law Institute, 1994.

Fusaro, Robert F. X., "Issues to Consider in Drafting Joint Venture Agreements," in *Drafting Corporate Agreements*, New York: Practising Law Institute, 1995.

Hyde, Justin, "GM, Ford, DaimlerChrysler Join Online Ordering Forces," CNNfn, February 22, 2000.

Johnson, Shane A. and Mark B. Houston, "A Re-examination of the Motives and Gains in Joint Ventures," *Journal of Financial and Quantitative Analysis*, 35 (1), March 2000.

Kalmbach, Charles Jr. and Charles Roussel, *Dispelling the Myths of Alliances*, Andersen Consulting, 1999, http://www.accenture.com/xd/xd.asp?it=enWeb&xd=ideas/outlook/special99/over_specialed_intro.xml.

Lajoux, Alexandra Reed, *The Art of M&A Integration*, New York: McGraw-Hill, 1998, p. 41, note 7.

Lorange, Peter and Johan Roos, *Strategic Alliances: Formation, Implementation, and Evolution*, Oxford: Blackwell, 1992.

Lynch, Robert Porter, *The Practical Guide to Joint Ventures and Corporate Alliances*, New York: John Wiley & Sons, 1990.

McConnell, John J. and Timothy J. Nantell, "Corporate Combinations and Common Stock Returns: the Case of Joint Ventures," *Journal of Finance*, 40, June 1985, pp. 519–536.

NBC, Press Release May 10, 1999.

Schmid, Randolph E., "Post Office, FedEx Become Partners," *Orange County Register*, January 11, 2001, Business Section, p. 2.

Tillinghast, David R., "Tax Aspects of Inbound Merger and Acquisitions and Joint Venture Transactions," in David J. BenDaniel and Arthur H. Rosenbloom, eds., *International M&A, Joint Ventures and Beyond: Doing the Deal*, New York: John Wiley & Sons, 1998, pp. 151–180.

Van Laarhoven, Peter and Graham Sharman, Logistics Alliances: The European Experience, *The McKinsey Quarterly*, 1, 1994, pp. 39–49.

Vodafone AirTouch, "Listing Particulars Relating to the Issue of Ordinary Shares in Vodafone AirTouch Plc in Connection with the Offer for Mannesmann AG," filing with the Registrar of Companies in England and Wales, October 7, 1999, pp. 363–369.

13

ALTERNATIVE EXIT AND RESTRUCTURING STRATEGIES

DIVESTITURES, SPIN-OFFS, CARVE-OUTS, SPLIT-UPS, BANKRUPTCY, AND LIQUIDATION

Experience is the name everyone gives to their mistakes.
—Oscar Wilde

Stunned by the continued decline in the firm's share price, Joe leaned forward in his chair as he passionately directed his division general managers to improve their units' operating performance. Wall Street had concluded that the conglomerate had become too highly diversified with significant investments in seven different industries. Management had hoped that by diversifying their operations in industries whose fortunes were tied to different stages of the business cycle, the firm would be able to make earnings growth more predictable. In fact, senior management found it increasingly difficult to understand the nuances of the competitive dynamics of so many different industries. This lack of understanding resulted in missed opportunities and poorly performing investments. Consequently, Joe was under considerable pressure to improve consolidated performance, to increase the firm's overall focus, or perhaps even to completely liquidate the business and distribute the cash proceeds to the shareholders.

Last year at this time, Joe's division managers had assured him that plans were in place to materially improve operating performance. Despite a robust economy, the promised improvement did not take place. Joe had lost all patience. His directive to his managers was simple. Improve performance during the coming fiscal year or be divested. Joe was not confrontational by nature, but he felt he had to do something to get his managers' attention. Joe's finance and planning staffs already were using projections submitted by his division managers to value each of the firm's operations as if it were operating independently from the parent. Concurrently, an investment banker had been hired to estimate the after-tax value of each operation as if it had been sold. By comparing the present value of each operation to its sale value, Joe would have some indication of which of his firm's operations should be sold and which should be retained.

The investment banker concluded that one unit would require substantial additional funding if it were to realize the full potential of its technology. Although a cutting-edge unit, few firms seemed to show any real interest in acquiring the largely untested technology. Consequently, the outright sale of the unit did not appear to be an attractive option. However, the stock market was setting new records and many investors seemed to be hungry for "emerging" technology investment opportunities. Consequently, the investment banker recommended that the unit be converted to a wholly owned subsidiary and that a portion of its stock be sold to the public. The resulting proceeds could be used to fund further development of the technology and to establish a market value for the unit. Once established, the balance of the unit's stock could be sold to the public and the proceeds could be used to fund opportunities in the parent firm's remaining operations.

Joe carefully considered his options. Under fire from Wall Street and increasing pressure from his board of directors, he knew he would have to make some very difficult decisions. He knew he was going to face a number of sleepless nights in the coming months.

OVERVIEW

Many corporations, particularly large, highly diversified organizations, constantly are reviewing ways in which they can enhance shareholder value by changing the composition of their assets, liabilities, equity, and operations. These activities generally are referred to as restructuring strategies. Restructuring may embody both growth and exit strategies. Growth strategies have been discussed elsewhere in this book. The focus in this chapter is on those strategic options that allow the firm to maximize shareholder value by redeploying assets through contraction and downsizing of the parent corporation. Divestitures, spin-offs, equity carve-outs, split-ups, split-offs, and bust-ups are commonly used strategies to exit businesses and to redeploy corporate assets by returning cash or noncash assets through a special dividend to shareholders. The intent of this chapter is to discuss why parent corporations may choose to exit certain businesses, how this may be achieved, and how such actions affect shareholder value. This chapter also addresses how firms deal with business failure through voluntary or involuntary reorganization and, in some instances, liquidation.

MOTIVES FOR EXITING BUSINESSES

The motives for exiting businesses are both numerous and diverse. They include changing corporate strategy or focus, a desire to exit underperforming businesses, a lack of fit, regulatory concerns, and tax considerations. Other motives include a need to raise funds, reduce risk, move away from the core business, discard unwanted businesses from prior acquisitions, and avoid conflicts with customers. Although there is empirical evidence to demonstrate that changing corporate strategies or focus are common reasons for firms to exit businesses, the extent to which the other motives are commonplace is less clear.

CHANGING CORPORATE STRATEGY OR FOCUS

Firms may change strategies or focus as a result of a changing competitive or regulatory environment or simply as a result of having learned from past mistakes. Managing highly diverse and complex portfolios of businesses is both time consuming and distracting. This is particularly true when the businesses are in largely unrelated industries. There is a limited understanding by senior management of the nuances of each business and of what constitutes worthwhile opportunities for the parent to fund adequately. A unit may be a small portion of a parent company's sales and may not be receiving sufficient time or attention from management at the corporate level. Often, senior management may not completely understand the opportunities facing such a business, resulting in limited funding of potentially attractive opportunities. A business that is rich in high-growth opportunities may be an excellent candidate for divestiture to a strategic buyer with significant cash resources and limited growth opportunities.

Empirical Evidence

A substantial body of evidence indicates that reducing a firm's complexity (i.e., increasing its focus) can improve substantially financial returns to shareholders. The difficulty in managing diverse portfolios of businesses in many different industries and the difficulty in accurately valuing these portfolios contributed to the "deconglomeration" movement of the 1970s and 1980s. Of the acquisitions made between 1970 and 1982 by companies in industries unrelated to the acquirer's primary industry focus, 60% were divested by 1989 (Petty, Keown, Scott, and Martin, 1993). John and Ofek (1995) found that abnormal returns earned by the shareholders of a firm divesting a business result largely from improved management of the assets that remain after the divestiture is completed. They attributed these returns to increased focus and the ability of management to understand fewer lines of business. As evidence of the challenges of understanding businesses in diverse industries, they also found that 75% of divested units were unrelated to the selling company. Maksimovic and Phillips (2001) find that the probability of divestitures is greatest when divested units are viewed as noncore assets by the parent firm.

Reducing a firm's complexity also has been related to improving shareholder returns in a number of recent studies (Ball, 1997; Burkhart, Gromb, and Panunzi, 1997; Rajan, Servaes, and Zingales, 2000; and Scharfstein and Stein, 2000). Krishnaswami and Subramaniam (1999) also found that gains experienced by spin-offs were greater the more complex the parent was before the spin-off. Presumably, investors were better able to evaluate the spin-off's full potential once it became independent of the parent.

Although asset sales may occur to fund growth investments, the motivations for most of the strategies discussed in this chapter involve a desire to withdraw from underperforming, undervalued, or nonstrategic businesses. Empirical studies show that exit strategies, which return cash to shareholders, tend to have a highly favorable impact on shareholder wealth creation. The share prices of firms that return cash or noncash assets to their shareholders tend to respond much more positively than do the shares of those firms that retain cash generated from the sale of assets for reinvestment in the parent firm (Allen and McConnell, 1998; Lang, Poulsen, and Stulz, 1995). These results suggest that investors often have little confidence in management's ability to invest the funds wisely.

Examples of Achieving Greater Focus

In the late 1980s, TRW divested many of its low-technology businesses to shift into high-technology segments of the information systems and services, space and defense, and automotive parts industries. Although ultimately acquired by Northrop Grumman, TRW presented its shareholders in 2002 with an alternative option to enhance shareholder value in which TRW would spin off its automotive business to shareholders and divest another business, using the proceeds to accelerate the repayment of debt. In 1987, Allegis Corporation reversed its previous strategy of providing a broader range of travel services by selling its hotel and car rental businesses to become UAL Corporation and to concentrate on operating United Airlines. In the late 1990s, General Motors (GM) spun off its Hughes Electronics and Delphi Automotive Parts operations to focus on its passenger car and light truck businesses. In 1999, Allegheny Teledyne spun off its software and engineering systems, communication and electronics, and aircraft engine businesses to focus on its specialty metals businesses.

UNDERPERFORMING BUSINESSES

Parent firms often exit businesses that consistently fail to meet or exceed the parent's hurdle rate requirements. These hurdle rates frequently consist of the parent's cost of capital adjusted for any special risks associated with the business or the industry in which it competes. Baxter International Inc. announced in late 1999 its intention to spin off its underperforming cardiovascular business, creating a new company that will specialize in treatments for heart disease.

Frequently, a parent firm may hang on to operations that have been underperforming for years. The reluctance to sell a poor performer can reflect the parent's emotional attachment resulting from its long history in the business or its unwillingness to admit to mistakes in managing the business. In the instance of an acquisition, management may not want to admit to having paid too much for the business or to having been unable to manage the business effectively (Boot, 1992).

REGULATORY CONCERNS

A firm with substantial market share purchasing a direct competitor may create concerns about violations of antitrust laws. Regulatory agencies still may approve the merger if the acquiring firm is willing to divest certain operations that, in combination with similar units in the acquiring company, are deemed to be anticompetitive.

As a result of an antitrust suit filed by the Department of Justice (DoJ), the government and AT&T reached an agreement effective January 1, 1984, to breakup AT&T's 22 operating companies into seven regional Bell operating companies (RBOCs). The RBOCs became responsible for local telephone service, and AT&T kept responsibility for long-distance service and certain telecommunications equipment manufacturing operations.

LACK OF FIT

Individual businesses may be undervalued because investors believe that there are insufficient benefits from synergy to offset the overhead expenses associated with being part of a holding company. This may have been a factor in AT&T's choice to implement a split-up of its business in the mid-1990s into three separate entities, each with its own stock traded on the public exchanges. In late 1999, a failed attempt to redirect the business into more lucrative telecommunications industry segments such as broadband and wireless caused AT&T to again undertake a strategy to spin off or divest some portions of the firm. See Case Study 13-10 at the end of this chapter.

Companies may divest units after they have had time to learn more about the business. In 1995, Raytheon sold its D.C. Heath textbook publishing company to Houghton Mifflin Company. Although a sizable publishing business on a standalone basis, D.C. Heath did not fit with the other three much larger core businesses of Raytheon, which included defense electronics, engineering, and avionics. Similarly, TRW's decision to sell its commercial and consumer information services businesses in 1997 came after years of trying to find a significant fit with its space and defense businesses.

TAX CONSIDERATIONS

Restructuring actions may provide tax benefits that cannot be realized without undertaking a restructuring of the business. Marriott Corporation contributed its hotel real estate operations to a Real Estate Investment Trust (REIT) in 1989 through a spin-off. Because REITs do not have to pay taxes on income that is distributed to shareholders, Marriott was able to enhance shareholder value by eliminating the double taxation of income, once as rental income to the parent and again when distributed to shareholders.

RAISING FUNDS/WORTH MORE TO OTHERS

Parent firms may choose to fund new initiatives or acquisitions or reduce leverage through the sale or partial sale of units that are no longer considered strategic or are underperforming corporate expectations. Such sales also may result from the need to improve near-term cash flow. Examples include Chrysler's sale of its highly profitable tank division to avoid bankruptcy in the early 1980s. Similarly, Navistar, formerly International Harvester, sold its profitable Solar Turbines operation to Caterpillar Tractor to reduce its indebtedness. Others may view a firm's operating units as much more valuable than the parent and be willing to pay a "premium" price for such businesses.

RISK REDUCTION

A firm may reduce its perceived risk associated with a particular unit by selling a portion of the business to the public. For example, American Express viewed Shearson Lehman as much riskier than its credit card business. Although the firm believed that there were opportunities to sell its credit cards to Shearson Lehman customers, it decided to reduce its exposure to the cyclical securities business by selling a portion of the unit in 1987. Also, major tobacco companies have been under pressure for years to divest or spin off their food businesses because of the litigation risk associated with their tobacco subsidiaries. RJR Nabisco bowed to such pressure in 1998 with the spin-off of Nabisco Foods.

Parent firms may attempt to dump debt or other liabilities by assigning them to a subsidiary and later exiting those businesses. In early 2002, Citigroup sold 21% of its Travelers Property Casualty unit in a $3.9 billion initial public offering (IPO), announcing that the remainder would be sold off at a later date. The parent's motivation for this exit strategy could have been to distance itself from the potential costs of asbestos-related claims by Travelers' policyholders. Similarly, Goodrich passed on its asbestos liabilities to EnPro Industries, its diversified industrial products subsidiary, which it spun off in mid-2002.

MOVING AWAY FROM THE CORE BUSINESS

Management may not believe that investment opportunities in their current core business are attractive. They may believe that their firm's core skills or competencies in manufacturing or distribution can be used to pursue growth opportunities in other industries. Consequently, assets in the current core business may be sold to fund these diversification opportunities. An example would be Dial Corporation's sale of its Greyhound bus operations in 1987. See Case Study 13-1 for a discussion of one of the most dramatic redirections of a corporation's business strategy in U.S. history.

CASE STUDY 13-1: HUGHES CORPORATION MOVES FROM THE DEFENSE INDUSTRY INTO THE ENTERTAINMENT INDUSTRY

Once California's largest manufacturing employer, Hughes Corporation built spacecraft, the world's first working laser, communications satellites, radar systems, and military weapons systems. Today, the one-time defense industry behemoth advertises itself as the world's largest digital entertainment and communications company. To accomplish this transformation, Hughes staged one of the most dramatic shedding of businesses in just a few years in U.S. history. Divestitures included its defense portfolio consisting of communications satellite businesses and even its auto electronics operation. Tens of thousands of its former employees now are working with Boeing, Raytheon, and General Motors. The corporate overhaul created a firm focused on direct-to-home satellite broadcasting with its DirecTV service offering.

From Defense to Direct-to-Home Satellite Communication

DirecTV's introduction to nearly 12 million U.S. homes was a technology made possible by U.S. military spending during the early 1980s. Although military spending had fueled much of Hughes' growth during the decade of the 1980s, it was becoming increasingly clear by 1988 that the lavish spending of the Reagan years was coming to a close with the winding down of the cold war. In line with the move away from military spending, Hughes' CEO, Michael T. Smith, decided not to aggressively pursue a government contract for the F-22, a new jet fighter. This decision proved to be the critical event for Hughes marking its move away from its core defense business.

For the next several years, Hughes attempted to find profitable niches in the rapidly consolidating U.S. defense contracting industry. Hughes acquired General Dynamics' missile business and made about 15 smaller acquisitions. Eventually, Hughes' parent firm, General Motors, lost enthusiasm for additional investment in defense-related businesses. The decision was made that if Hughes could not participate in the shrinking defense industry, then there was no reason to retain any interests in the industry at all. In November 1995 Hughes initiated discussions with Raytheon, and 2 years later it sold its aerospace and defense business to Raytheon for $9.8 billion and merged

Delco with GM's Delphi automotive systems (Shadid, 2001). What remained was the firm's telecommunications division. Hughes had transformed itself from a $16 billion defense contracting behemoth to a more svelte $4 billion telecommunications business.

Since its acquisition in 1987 by General Motors (GM), Hughes has been operating as a wholly owned subsidiary of GM. However, the automaker has allowed investors to buy a tracking stock meant to reflect Hughes' performance. The tracking stock accounts for about 70% of the unit, with GM holding the remaining equity. Under this arrangement, Hughes has its own board responsible for protecting the rights of the holders of the tracking stock. Holders of the tracking stock do not have a claim on Hughes' assets as regular GM shareholders do; they do have rights spelled out in GM's corporate charter. According to the GM charter, if GM sells Hughes or a large part of it, the automaker must convert the tracking stock into GM shares at a 20% premium. By the end of 2000, the value of the tracking stock had a higher market value than GM's automotive operations.

Cultural Impact

Hughes' telecommunications unit was its smallest operation but, with DirecTV, the fastest growing. The transformation was to exact a huge cultural toll on Hughes' employees, most of whom had spent their careers dealing with the U.S. Department of Defense. By moving into commercial communications, Hughes could no longer go back to customers with cost overruns and request price increases. Hughes moved to hire aggressively people from the cable and broadcast businesses. By the late 1990s, former Hughes' employees comprised only 15–20% of DirecTV's total employees.

Restructuring Continues for More Than a Decade

Restructuring continued through the end of the 1990s. In 2000, Hughes sold its satellite manufacturing operations to Boeing for $3.75 billion. This eliminated the last component of the old Hughes and cut its workforce in half. In December 2000, Hughes paid about $180 million for Telocity, a firm that provides digital subscriber line service through phone lines. This acquisition allowed Hughes to provide high-speed Internet connections through its existing satellite service, mainly in more remote rural areas, as well as phone lines targeted at city dwellers. Hughes now can market the same combination of high-speed Internet services and video offered by cable providers, Hughes' primary competitor. It now can offer 225 channels.

General Motors Looks to Sell Hughes

In late 2000, GM put Hughes up for sale, expressing confidence that there would be a flood of lucrative offers. However, the faltering economy and stock market resulted in GM receiving only one serious bid, from media tycoon Rupert Murdoch of News Corporation, in February 2001.

However, internal discord within Hughes and GM over the possible buyer of Hughes Electronics caused GM to backpedal and seek alternative bidders. In late October 2001, GM agreed to sell its Hughes Electronics subsidiary and its DirecTV home satellite network to EchoStar Communications for $25.8 billion (Garsten, 2001).

Case Study Discussion Questions

1. What risks did Hughes face in moving completely away from its core defense business and into a high-technology commercial business? In your judgment, did Hughes move too quickly or too slowly? Explain your answer.
2. Why did Hughes move so aggressively to hire employees from the cable TV and broadcast industry?

DISCARDING UNWANTED BUSINESSES FROM PRIOR ACQUISITIONS

Acquiring companies often find themselves with certain assets and operations of the acquired company that do not fit their primary strategy. These redundant assets may be divested to raise funds to help pay for the acquisition and to enable management to focus on integrating the remaining businesses into the parent without the distraction of having to manage nonstrategic assets. On acquiring Allied Stores in the mid-1980s, Campeau Corporation announced that it would sell 16 Allied operations that were not critical to the firm's overall strategy to help reduce its indebtedness. Campeau undertook a similar strategy after its acquisition of Federated Department Stores in 1989. In 2002, Northrop Grumman Corporation announced that it would acquire TRW. Northrop stated that it would retain TRW's space and defense businesses and divest its automotive operations, which were not germane to Northrop's core defense business.

AVOIDING CONFLICTS WITH CUSTOMERS

For years, many of the RBOCs spun off by AT&T in 1984 have been interested in competing in the long-distance market, which would put them in direct competition with their former parent. Similarly, AT&T sought to penetrate the regional telephone markets by gaining access to millions of households by acquiring cable TV companies. In preparation for the implementation of these plans, AT&T announced in 1995 that it would split up the company into three publicly traded global companies. The three companies included Communications Services (long-distance services), Communications Systems (later renamed Lucent Technologies, a provider of network switches and transmission equipment), and Global Information Solutions (later renamed NCR, a provider of systems integration services). The primary reason for the split up was to avoid possible conflicts between AT&T's former equipment manufacturer and its main customers, the RBOCs.

DIVESTITURES

A divestiture is the sale of a portion of the firm to an outside party generally resulting in a cash infusion to the parent. Divestitures are generally the least complex of the exit-restructuring activities to understand. A firm may choose to sell an undervalued operation that it determined to be nonstrategic or unrelated to the core business and to use the proceeds of the sale to fund investments in potentially higher return opportunities. Alternatively, the firm may choose to divest the undervalued business and return the cash to shareholders either through a liquidating dividend or share repurchase.

HISTORICAL TRENDS

Between 1970 and 2001, divestitures averaged about 40% of total transactions. Divestitures reached a peak of 56% in 1975, the trough of the worst recession since World War II. The surge in divestitures in the early-to-mid 1970s and again in the early 1990s followed the merger boom periods of the late 1960s and the 1980s.

DECIDING WHEN TO SELL

Many corporations review their business portfolio periodically to determine which operations continue to fit their core strategies. As noted earlier in this chapter, changes in the parent's strategy or a desire to achieve a more focused business portfolio can result in certain operations becoming strategically redundant. Such operations become prime candidates for divestiture. Even if a business "fits" within the parent corporation's current strategy, the business may not be earning the financial rates of return required by the parent. Consequently, the parent will conduct a financial analysis to determine if the business is worth more to shareholders if it is sold and the proceeds either returned to the shareholders or reinvested in opportunities offering potentially higher rates of return.

Financial Issues

An analysis undertaken to determine if a business should be sold requires the estimation of four key elements. These elements include the after-tax cash flows generated by the unit, an appropriate discount rate reflecting the risk of the business, the after-tax market value of the business, and the after-tax value of the business to the parent. The decision to sell or to retain the business depends on a comparison of the after-tax value of the business to the parent with the after-tax proceeds from the sale of the business.

Calculating After-Tax Cash Flows

To decide if a business is worth more to the shareholder if sold, the parent must first estimate after-tax cash flows of the business viewed on a standalone basis (i.e., as if it were operated as an independent operating unit). This requires adjusting the cash flows for intercompany sales and the cost of services (e.g., legal, treasury, and audit) provided by the parent.

Intercompany sales refer to operating unit revenue generated by selling products or services to another unit owned by the same parent. For example, in a vertically integrated business, such as a steel manufacturer that obtains both iron ore and coal from its operating subsidiaries, the majority of the revenue generated by the iron ore and coal operations often comes from sales to the parent company's steelmaking operations. The parent may value this revenue for financial reporting purposes using product transfer prices, which may reflect current market prices or some formula such as a predetermined markup over the cost of production. If the transfer prices do not reflect actual market prices, intercompany revenue may be artificially high or low, depending on whether the transfer prices are higher or lower than actual market prices. Intercompany revenues associated with the operating unit should be restated to reflect actual market prices.

Services provided by the parent to the business may be subsidized (i.e., provided at below actual cost) or at a markup over actual cost. To reflect these factors, the cash flows of the business should be adjusted for services provided by the parent at more or less than what the business would have to pay for them if it were operating as an independent organization. Operating profits should be reduced by the amount of any subsidies and increased by any markup over what the business would have to pay if it purchased comparable services from sources outside of the parent firm.

Estimating the Discount Rate

Once the after-tax standalone cash flows have been determined, a discount rate should be estimated that reflects the risk characteristics of the industry in which the business competes. The cost of capital of other firms in the same industry is often a good proxy for the discount rate of the business.

Estimating the After-Tax Market Value of the Business

The discount rate then is used to estimate the present or market value (MV) of the projected after-tax cash flows of the business as if it were a standalone business. The valuation is based on cash flows that have been adjusted for inter-company revenues not on the books at market prices and services provided to the operating unit by the parent firm at something other than actual cost.

Estimating the Value of the Business to the Parent

The after-tax equity value (EV) of the business as part of the parent is estimated by subtracting the market value of the business's liabilities (L) from its MV as a standalone operation. This relationship can be expressed as follows:

$$EV = MV - L$$

EV is a measure of the after-tax market value of shareholder equity of the business, where the shareholder is the parent firm.

Deciding to Sell

The decision to sell or retain the business is made by comparing EV with the after-tax sale value (SV) of the business. Assuming other considerations do not outweigh any after-tax gain on the sale of the business, the decision to sell or retain can be summarized as follows:

If SV > EV, divest.

If SV < EV, retain.

Although the sale value may exceed the equity value of the business, the parent may choose to retain the business for strategic reasons. For example, the parent may believe that the business's products (e.g., ties) may facilitate the sale of other products the firm offers (e.g., custom shirts). The firm may lose money on the sale of ties but make enough money on the sale of custom shirts to earn a profit on the combined sales of the two products. In another instance, one subsidiary of a diversified parent may provide highly complex components critical to the assembly of finished products produced by other subsidiaries of the parent firm. Under these circumstances, the parent may choose to incur a small loss on the production of components to ensure the continued high quality of its highly profitable finished products.

Timing

Timing often has a major influence on the decision to sell a business (Case Study 13-2). Obviously, the best time to sell a business is when the owner does not need to sell to raise new capital or to repay creditors or when the demand for the business to be divested is greatest (Schlingemann, Stulz, and Walkling, 2002). The decision to sell also should reflect the broader financial environment. Selling when business confidence is high, stock prices are rising, and interest rates are low is likely to fetch a higher price for the unit. If the business to be sold is highly cyclical, the sale should be timed to coincide with the firm's peak year earnings. Businesses also can be timed to sell when they are considered most popular. In 1980 the oil exploration business was booming; by 1983 it was in the doldrums. It recovered again by the mid-1990s. What's hot today can be a fizzle tomorrow. A similar story could be told about many of the high-flying Internet-related companies of the late 1990s.

Tax and Accounting Considerations

The divesting firm is required to recognize a gain or loss for financial reporting purposes equal to the difference between the fair value of the consideration received for the divested operation and its book value. However, if the transaction is an exchange of similar assets or an equivalent interest in similar productive assets, the company should not recognize a gain or loss other than any loss resulting from the impairment of value. If the divested division or subsidiary is a discontinued segment, the parent firm must estimate the gain or loss from the divestiture on the date that management approves a formal plan to dispose of the division or subsidiary. For tax purposes, the gain or loss is the difference between the proceeds and the parent's tax (i.e., cost) basis in the stock or assets. Gains are considered capital gains under the tax code, but capital losses on the sale of subsidiary stock is considered an ordinary loss.

CASE STUDY 13-2: GILLETTE ANNOUNCES DIVESTITURE PLANS

With 1998 sales of $10.1 billion, Gillette is the world leader in the production of razor blades, razors, and shaving cream. Gillette also has a leading position in the production of pens and other writing instruments. Gillette's consolidated operating performance during the first 9 months of 1999 continued to be carried by the core razor blade and razor, Duracell battery, and oral care businesses. Excluding certain one-time adjustments, total corporate sales for the first 9 months of 1999 increased by 5% when compared with the same period in 1998; however, operating profits dropped by 5%. In contrast to Gillette's core product areas, sales of Braun products, including electric shavers and oral care products, dropped by 11% and operating profits dropped by 43% during the first 9 months of 1999 over the same period in 1998. Similarly, sales of toiletries and operating profits declined by 5% and 6%, respectively, during the same period. Sales and operating profits of stationery products, which include pens, fell by 11% and 78%, respectively, through the first three-quarters of 1999.

Reflecting disappointment in the performance of certain operating units, Gillette's CEO, Michael Hawley, announced in October 1999 his intention to divest poorly performing businesses unless he could be convinced by early 2000 that they could be turned around (Gillette, 1999). The businesses under consideration at that time comprised about 15% of the company's $10 billion in annual sales. Hawley saw the new focus of the company to be in razor blades, batteries, and oral care. To achieve this new focus, Hawley intends to prune the firm's product portfolio. The most likely targets for divestiture include pens (i.e., PaperMate, Parker, and Waterman). With operating earnings for these businesses down 78% during the first 9 months of 1999, the prospects are for continuing deterioration.

Other units under consideration for divestiture include Braun and toiletries. With respect to these businesses, Hawley apparently intends to be selective. At Braun, where overall operating profits plunged 43% in the first three quarters of 1999, Hawley has announced that Gillette will keep electric shavers and electric toothbrushes. However, the household and personal care appliance units are likely divestiture candidates. The timing of these sales may be poor. A decision to sell Braun at this time would compete against Black & Decker's recently announced decision to sell its appliance business.

Although Gillette would be smaller, the firm believes that its margins will improve and that its earnings growth will be more rapid. Moreover, divesting such problem businesses as pens and appliances would let management focus on the units whose prospects are the brightest. These are businesses that Gillette's previous management was simply not willing to sell because of their perceived high potential (*Business Week*, 1999a).

Case Study Discussion Questions

1. Which of the major restructuring motives discussed in this chapter seem to be a work in this business case? Explain your answer.
2. Describe the process Gillette's management may have gone through to determine which business units to sell and which to keep.

SPIN-OFFS AND SPLIT-UPS

SPIN-OFFS

A spin-off is a transaction in which a parent creates a new legal subsidiary and distributes shares it owns in the subsidiary to its current shareholders as a stock dividend. The shares are distributed in direct proportion to the shareholders current holdings of the parent's stock. Consequently, the proportional ownership of shares in the new legal subsidiary is the same as the stockholders' proportional ownership of shares in the parent firm. The new entity has its own management and is run independently from the parent company. Unlike the divestiture or equity carve-out, the spin-off does not result in an infusion of cash to the parent company. The average size of spin-offs is 20% of the parent's original market value (Schipper & Smith, 1983). Some of the more notable spin-offs include the spin-off of Allstate by Sears; Payless by May Department Stores; Dean Witter/Discover by Sears; CBS by Westinghouse; and Pizza Hut, KFC, and Taco Bell by PepsiCo. See Case Study 13-3.

Accounting and Tax Considerations

If properly structured, spin-offs or split-ups, which consist of multiple spin-offs, are generally not taxable to shareholders. According to the Internal Revenue Service (IRS) Code Section 355, a spin-off must satisfy five conditions for it to be considered tax free to the parent firm's shareholders.

1. *Control:* The parent firm must have a controlling interest in the subsidiary before it is spun off. Control is defined as the parent owning at least 80%

of the voting stock in the subsidiary and 80% of each class of nonvoting stock.

2. *Active Business:* After the spin-off, both the parent and the subsidiary must remain in the same line of business in which each was involved for at least 5 years before the spin-off.

3. *Prohibition Against Tax Avoidance:* The spin-off cannot have been used as a means of avoiding dividend taxation by converting ordinary income into capital gains.

4. *Continuity of Interest:* The parent's shareholders must maintain significant ownership in both the parent and the subsidiary following the transactions.

5. *Business Purpose:* The transaction must have a significant business purpose separate from tax savings.

For financial reporting purposes, the parent firm should account for the spin-off of a subsidiary's stock to its shareholders at book value with no gain or loss recognized, other than any reduction in value due to impairment. The reason for this treatment is that the ownership interests are essentially the same before and after the spin-off.

SPLIT-UPS

A split-up involves creating a new class of stock for each of the parent's operating subsidiaries, paying current shareholders a dividend of each new class of stock, and then dissolving the remaining corporate shell. Stockholders in the new companies may be different because shareholders in the parent company may exchange their stock for stock in one or more of the spin-offs. Some of the most famous split-ups in recent years include ITT, Grace, AT&T, 3M, Baxter, Tenneco, Anheuser Busch, Ralston Purina, General Motors, Corning, Dial, Dun & Bradstreet, and Aetna.

CASE STUDY 13-3: BAXTER TO SPIN OFF HEART CARE UNIT

Baxter International Inc. announced in late 1999 its intention to spin off its underperforming cardiovascular business, creating a new company that will specialize in treatments for heart disease. The new company will have 6000 employees worldwide and annual revenue in excess of $1 billion (*Wall Street Journal*, 1999a). The unit sells biological heart valves harvested from pigs and cows, catheters and other products used to monitor hearts during surgery, and heart-assist devices for patients awaiting surgery.

Baxter conceded that they have been "optimizing" the cardiovascular business by not making the necessary investments to grow the business.

In contrast, the unit's primary competitors, Guidant, Medtronic, and Boston Scientific, are spending more on research and investing more on start-up companies that are developing new technologies than is Baxter.

With the spin-off, the new company will have the currency (i.e., stock and financial resources) that formerly had been siphoned off by the parent to create an environment that will more directly encourage the speed and innovation necessary to compete effectively in this industry. The unit's stock will be used to provide additional incentive for key employees and to serve as a means of making future acquisitions of companies necessary to extend the unit's product offering (*Orange County Register*, 1999).

Case Study Discussion Questions

1. In your judgment, what did Baxter's management mean when they admitted that they had not been "optimizing" the cardiovascular business in recent years? Explain both the strategic and financial implications of this strategy.
2. Discuss some of the reasons why you believe the unit may prosper more as an independent operation than as part of Baxter?

EQUITY CARVE-OUTS AND SPLIT-OFF INITIAL PUBLIC OFFERINGS

Equity carve-outs are often difficult to define. They are most appropriately viewed as hybrid or intermediate transactions. They are hybrid transactions in that they are similar to spin-offs because both result in the subsidiary's stock being traded separately from the parent's stock. They are also like divestitures and IPOs because they result in a cash infusion to the parent. However, unlike the spin-off or divestiture, the parent generally retains control of the subsidiary in a carve-out transaction. They are intermediate transactions in that they are often simply a prelude to another transaction (i.e., the issuance of another portion of or all of the remaining equity in the subsidiary). A potentially significant drawback to the carve-out is the creation of minority shareholders.

There are two basic forms of an equity carve-out: the subsidiary equity carve-out and the split-off IPO. These are discussed in the following section.

SUBSIDIARY EQUITY CARVE-OUT

The subsidiary carve-out is a transaction in which the parent creates a wholly owned independent legal subsidiary, with stock and a management team that is different from the parent's, and issues a portion of the subsidiary's stock to the public. Usually only a minority share of the parent's ownership in the subsidiary is issued to the public (Schipper and Smith, 1986). Although the parent retains control, the shareholder base of the subsidiary may be different than that of the parent as a result of the public sale of equity. The cash raised may be retained in the subsidiary or transferred to the parent as a dividend, as a stock repurchase, or as an intercompany loan. The return of any portion of the proceeds to the shareholder is taxable to the shareholder. An example of a subsidiary carve-out is the sale to the public by Phillip Morris in 2000 of 19% of its wholly owned Nabisco subsidiary.

SPLIT-OFF INITIAL PUBLIC OFFERING

A split-off IPO is a transaction in which a privately held firm "splits off" a portion of the stock of the consolidated entity or parent and offers it to the general public. Such transactions often are referred to as IPOs because they resemble an IPO in which the parent's stock is traded for the first time on a public exchange. The sale of the stock provides an infusion of cash to the parent. As with the subsidiary equity carve-out, this cash may be retained by the parent or returned to shareholders. United Parcel Service's IPO of a small share of its stock in 1999 is an example of a split-off IPO (Case Study 13-4).

CASE STUDY 13-4: UNITED PARCEL SERVICE GOES PUBLIC IN AN EQUITY SPLIT-OFF IPO

On November 10, 1999, United Parcel Service (UPS) raised $5.47 billion by selling 109.4 million shares of Class B common stock at an offering price of $50 per share in the biggest IPO by any U.S. firm in history. The IPO represented 9% of the firm's stock and established the firm's total market value at $81 billion. The share price exploded to $67.38 at the end of the first day of trading. This represented an increase of $17.38 from its initial offering price. With 1998 revenue of $24.8 billion, UPS transports more than 3 billion parcels and documents annually. The company provides services in more than 200 countries.

By splitting off only a portion of the stock for sale to the public, UPS ensured that control would remain in the hands of current management. The proceeds of the stock issue will be used to buy back about 9% of the Class A voting stock held by employees and by heirs to the founding Casey family. The Class B shares have one vote each, whereas the Class A shares have 10 votes. The stock buyback will keep the number of shares outstanding constant at about 1.2 billion shares. The proceeds also will be used to make acquisitions because firms that UPS had attempted to acquire in the past had indicated a strong desire for UPS shares rather than cash.

The beneficiaries of the sale include UPS employees from top management to workers on the loading docks. In a growing trend in U.S. companies to generate greater employee loyalty and productivity, UPS offered all 330,000 employees worldwide an opportunity to buy shares in this highly profitable company at prices as low as $20 per share. Before UPS, the largest IPOs included Conoco in October 1998 at $4.40 billion, Goldman Sachs in May 1999 at $3.66 billion, Charter Communications in November 1999 at $3.23 billion, and Lucent Technologies in April 1996 at $3 billion (*Wall Street Journal*, 1999b).

Case Study Discussion Questions

1. Describe the motivation for UPS to undertake this type of transaction.
2. In what way might a split-off IPO make a company vulnerable to a takeover attempt?

STAGED TRANSACTIONS

Equity may be sold to the public in several stages. A partial sale of equity either in a wholly owned subsidiary (a subsidiary equity carve-out) or in the consolidated business (a split-off IPO) may be designed to raise capital and to establish a market price for the stock. In the United States, many parents initially offer 20% or less of a subsidiary's stock to the public to continue to be able to consolidate the subsidiary's operations. This enables the parent to avoid incurring capital gains taxes that it might have to pay by selling more than that amount, raise some cash, and place a value on the stock. Later, once a market has been established for the stock, the remainder of the subsidiary's stock may be issued to the public. Alternatively, the parent may choose to spin off its remaining shares in the subsidiary to the parent's shareholders as a dividend. Few carve-outs remain under the parent's control in the long-term. After 5 years, parent firms continue to hold more than 50% of the equity of their carve-outs in only about 8% of the 200 carve-outs studied by McKinsey & Company. According to the same study, about 31% of the parents hold less than 25% of the equity and 39% of the carve-outs have been acquired or merged with third parties (Annema, Fallon, and Goedhart, 2002).

Hewlett Packard's (HP) 1999–2000 staged spin-off of its Agilent Technologies subsidiary is an example of a staged transaction. It began with an equity carve-out of a minority position in its wholly owned Agilent subsidiary in late 1999. The spin-off was completed in 2000 when HP issued the remainder of its shares in Agilent to HP shareholders in the form of a tax-free dividend (Case Study 13-5).

CASE STUDY 13-5: HEWLETT PACKARD SPINS OUT ITS AGILENT UNIT IN A STAGED TRANSACTION

Hewlett Packard (HP) announced the spin-off of its Agilent Technologies unit to focus on its main business of computers and printers, where sales have been lagging behind such competitors as Sun Microsystems.

Agilent makes test, measurement, and monitoring instruments; semicon-
ductors; and optical components. It also supplies patient-monitoring and
ultrasound-imaging equipment to the health care industry. Agilent earned
$257 million in net income on sales of about $8 billion for the fiscal year
ending October 31, 1998. For the 9 months ending July 31, 1999, net income
rose 19% to $366 million from $308 million during the same period in 1998.
However, revenue fell by 1.4% to $5.88 billion from $5.97 billion, reflecting
weakness in the Asian markets during the first half of 1999.

HP will retain an 85% stake in the company. The cash raised through the
15% equity carve-out will be paid to HP as a dividend from the subsidiary
to the parent. Hewlett Packard will provide Agilent with $983 million in
start-up funding. HP retained a controlling interest until mid-2000, when
it spun-off the rest of its shares in Agilent to HP shareholders as a tax-free
transaction.

Case Study Discussion Questions
1. Discuss the reasons why HP may have chosen a staged transaction
   rather than an outright divestiture of the business.
2. Discuss the conditions under which this spin-off would constitute a
   tax-free transaction.

TRACKING, TARGETED, AND LETTER STOCKS

Tracking or targeted stocks are separate classes of common stock of the parent
corporation. The parent firm divides its operations into two or more operating
units and assigns a common stock to each operation. Tracking stock is a class of
common stock that links the shareholders' return to the operating performance of
a particular business segment or unit (i.e., the targeted business unit). Tracking
stock represents an ownership interest in the company as a whole, rather than a
direct ownership interest in the targeted business segment or unit. The concept was
introduced in 1984 when General Motors issued a class of stock identified as E
stock, often referred to as letter stock at that time, to buy Electronic Data Systems
(EDS). In 1985, GM issued another class of stock called H stock when it acquired
Hughes Corporation. In 1991, U.S. Steel Company created a USX-Marathon stock
for its oil business and a USX stock for its steel operations. The next year, USX
created a third tracking stock when it sold shares of the USX-Delhi group in an
IPO. For voting purposes, each of the three tracking stocks is considered common
stock of the parent.

TAX AND ACCOUNTING CONSIDERATIONS

For financial reporting purposes, a distribution of tracking stock splits the parent
firm's equity structure into separate classes of stock without a legal split-up of

the firm. Tracking stocks may be issued as dividends to the parent's current share-holders. Unlike the case with spin-offs, the IRS currently does not require the business for which the tracking stock is created to be at least 5 years old and that the parent retains a controlling interest in the business for the stock to be exempt from capital gains taxes. Unlike a spin-off or carve-out, the parent retains complete ownership of the business. Each tracking stock is considered as common stock for the consolidated parent company and not of the subsidiary. In general, a propor-tionate distribution by a company to its shareholders in the company's stock is tax free to shareholders.

THE MOTIVATION FOR TRACKING STOCKS

The purpose in creating tracking stock is to enable the financial markets to value the different operations within a corporation based on their own performance. Tracking or targeted stocks provide the parent company with an alternative means of raising capital for a specific operation by selling a portion of the stock to the pub-lic and an alternative "currency" for making acquisitions. In addition, stock-based incentive programs to attract and retain key managers can be implemented for each operation with its own tracking stock. Although tracking stocks may not be created initially for the purpose of exiting a business, they make such a move easier for the parent at a later date. Following a restructure of its Hughes Electronics subsidiary, GM spun off and subsequently merged its defense electronics unit with Raytheon Corporation in 1997. Dividends paid on the tracking stocks for both USX and GM are based on the performance of each individual operation (Case Study 13-6).

CASE STUDY 13-6: USX BOWS TO SHAREHOLDER PRESSURE TO SPLIT UP THE COMPANY

As one of the first firms to issue tracking stocks in the mid-1980s, USX has relented to ongoing shareholder pressure to divide the firm into two pieces. U.S. Steel had acquired Marathon in 1982 in what was at the time the second largest merger in U.S. history. USX Corp. was formed in 1986 as the holding company for both U.S. Steel and Marathon Oil. In 1991 USX issued its tracking stocks to create "pure plays" in its primary businesses—steel and oil—and to utilize USX's steel losses, which could be used to reduce Marathon's taxable income. Marathon shareholders have long complained that Marathon's stock was selling at a discount to its peers because of its association with USX. The campaign to split Marathon from U.S. Steel began in earnest in early 2000.

On April 25, 2001, USX announced its intention to split U.S. Steel and Marathon Oil into two separately traded companies. The breakup gives holders of Marathon Oil stock an opportunity to participate in the ongoing consolidation within the global oil and gas industry. Holders of USX–U.S. Steel Group common stock (target stock) would become holders of newly formed Pittsburgh-based United States Steel Corporation, a return to the original name of the firm formed in 1901. Under the reorganization plan, U.S. Steel and Marathon would retain the same assets and liabilities already associated with each business. However, Marathon will assume $900 million in debt from U.S. Steel, leaving the steelmaker with $1.3 billion of debt. This assumption of debt by Marathon is an attempt to make U.S. Steel, which continues to lose money, able to stand on its own financially.

The investor community expressed mixed reactions, believing that Marathon would be likely to benefit from a possible takeover attempt, whereas U.S. Steel would not fare as well (Matthews, 2001). U.S. Steel's borrowing costs are likely to rise because its S&P credit rating fell in the wake of the firm's loss of Marathon's dependable cash-flow stream. Nonetheless, U.S. Steel, the eleventh largest steelmaker in the world, could become the takeover target for a foreign steel company.

Case Study Discussion Questions

1. Why do you think USX issued separate tracking stocks for its oil and steel businesses?
2. Why do you believe USX shareholders were not content to continue to hold tracking stocks in Marathon Oil and U.S. Steel?
3. In your judgment, did the breakup of USX into Marathon Oil and United States Steel Corporation make sense? Why or why not?
4. What alternatives could USX have pursued to increase shareholder value?

PROBLEMS WITH TRACKING STOCKS

Tracking stocks may create internal operating conflicts among the parent's business units. Such conflicts arise in determining how the parent's overhead expenses will be allocated to the business units and what price one business unit is paid for selling products to other business units. In addition to creating internal problems, tracking stocks can stimulate shareholder lawsuits. Although the unit for which a tracking stock has been created may be largely autonomous, the potential for conflict of interest is substantial because the parent's board and the target stock's board are the same. The parent's board approves overall operating unit and capital budgets. Decisions made in support of one operating unit may appear to be unfair to those holding a tracking stock in another unit. Thus, tracking stocks can pit classes of shareholders against one another and lead to lawsuits. When GM sold part of its Hughes unit and all of EDS, holders of H shares sued the GM board of directors, complaining that they were underpaid. Although shareholders may be less concerned with potential conflicts of interest when they first receive tracking stocks, the potential for antagonism among different classes of stockholders often grows with time.

Tracking stocks may offer investors the opportunity to invest in a "pure play," but they also may have several unattractive features. Tracking stocks may be penalized if the parent's management continues to operate them conservatively. With a spin-off, the firm has a separate board of directors that can introduce a more aggressive management style than the parent may have been willing to tolerate. Also, tracking stocks may not have voting rights. Finally, the chances of a hostile takeover of a firm with a tracking stock are virtually zero because the firm is controlled by the parent. Hence, there is no takeover premium built into the stock price.

VOLUNTARY LIQUIDATIONS (BUST-UPS)

Involuntary liquidations, normally associated with bankruptcy, are discussed later in this chapter and occur when creditors and the bankruptcy court concur that they will realize more value through liquidation than by reorganizing the firm. Voluntary liquidations reflect the judgment that the sale of individual parts of the firm could realize greater value than the value created by a continuation of the combined corporation. This may occur when management views the firm's growth prospects as limited. This option generally is pursued only after other restructure actions have failed to provide a significant improvement in the firm's overall market value.

Managers may be encouraged to liquidate a company because of the threat that an acquirer will mount a proxy contest for control or launch a tender offer to buy the firm and then liquidate it. Many of the tax advantages to bust-ups compared with nontaxable mergers were removed by the 1986 Tax Reform Act. Before the change in the law, capital gains to the selling firm were not taxable if it adopted a plan of liquidation and all proceeds were paid out to the shareholders within 12 months after the plan was adopted.

In general, a merger has the advantage over the voluntary bust-up of deferring the recognition of a gain by the stockholders of the selling company until they eventually sell the stock. In liquidation, the selling shareholders must recognize the gain immediately. Unused tax credits and losses belonging to either of the merged firms are carried over in a nontaxable merger but are lost in liquidation.

COMPARING ALTERNATIVE EXIT
RESTRUCTURING STRATEGIES

Table 13-1 summarizes the primary characteristics of each of the restructuring strategies discussed in this chapter. Note that divestitures and carve-outs provide cash to the parent, whereas spin-offs, split-ups and bust-ups do not. Equity ownership changes in spin-offs and split-ups only. The parent remains

TABLE 13-1   Key Characteristics of Alternative Exit Restructuring Strategies

	Alternative Restructuring Strategy				
Characteristics	Divestitures	Equity Carve-Outs/ Split-Off IPOs	Spin-Offs	Split-Ups	Voluntary Liquidations (Bust-Ups)
Cash Infusion to Parent	Yes	Yes	No	No	Yes
Change in Equity Ownership	Yes	Yes	No	No	Yes
Parent Ceases to Exist	No	No	No	Yes	Yes
New Legal Entity Created	Sometimes	Yes[1]	Yes	Yes	No
New Shares Issued	Sometimes	Yes	Yes	Yes	No
Parent Remains in Control	No	Generally	No	No	No
Taxable to Shareholders	Yes[2]	Yes[2]	No[3]	No[3]	Yes

[1] Applies to subsidiary carve-outs only.

[2] The proceeds are taxable if returned to shareholders as a dividend or used to repurchase the parent's stock.

[3] The transaction is generally not taxable if properly structured.

in existence in all restructuring strategies except split-ups and bust-ups. A new legal entity generally is created with each restructuring strategy, except for voluntary liquidations. With the exception of the carve-out, the parent generally loses control of the division involved in the restructuring strategy. Only spin-offs and split-ups are generally not taxable to shareholders.

CHOOSING AMONG DIVESTITURE, CARVE-OUT, AND SPIN-OFF RESTRUCTURING STRATEGIES

The reasons for selecting a divestiture, carve-out, or spin-off strategy are inherently different. Parent firms that engage in divestitures are often highly diversified in largely unrelated businesses and have a desire to achieve greater focus or to raise cash. Parent firms that use carve-out strategies usually operate businesses in somewhat related industries exhibiting some degree of synergy and desire to raise cash. Consequently, the parent firm may pursue a carve-out rather than a divestiture or spin-off strategy to retain perceived synergy. Firms engaging in spin-offs are often highly diversified but less so than those prone to pursue divestiture strategies

TABLE 13-2   Characteristics of Divisions That Undergo Divestiture, Carve-Out, or Spin-Off

Exit Restructuring Strategy	Characteristics
Divestitures	• Usually unrelated to other businesses owned by parent • Operating performance generally worse than the parent's consolidated performance • Slightly underperform their peers in year before announcement date • Generally sell at a lower price than carve-outs measured by market value to book assets
Carve-Outs	• Generally more profitable and faster growing than spun-off or divested businesses • Operating performance generally exceeds parent's • Usually operate in industries characterized by high market to book values • Generally outperform peers in year before announcement date
Spin-Offs	• Generally faster growing and more profitable than divested businesses • Most often operate in industries related to other industries in which the parent operates • Operating performance worse than parent's • Slightly underperform peers in year before announcement date

Sources: Cho and Cohen (1997), Hand and Skantz (1997), Kang and Shivdasani (1997), Powers (2001), and Ravenscroft and Scherer (1991).

and have little need to raise cash (John and Ofek, 1995; Kaplan and Weisbach, 1992). Table 13-2 identifies characteristics of divisions that often are subject to certain types of restructuring activities.

The decision to exit a business is essentially a two-stage process. The first stage involves the firm deciding to exit a line of business or product line for one or more of the reasons described earlier in this chapter in the section entitled "Motives for Exiting Businesses." The second stage entails selecting the appropriate exit strategy. Divestitures, carve-outs, and spin-offs are the most commonly used restructuring strategy when a parent corporation is considering partially or entirely exiting a business. The decision as to which of these three strategies to use is often heavily influenced by the parent firm's need for cash, the degree of synergy between the business to be divested or spun-off and the parent's other operating units, and the potential selling price of the division (Powers, 2001). However, these factors are not independent. The higher the potential value or selling price of the business compared with its synergy value, the more likely the parent is to choose a carve-out rather than a divestiture. Table 13-3 approximates this two-stage procedure.

On the surface, it may seem that a divestiture or carve-out generally would be preferable to a spin-off if the after-tax proceeds from the sale of all or a portion of the division exceed their after-tax equity value to the firm. Unlike a spin-off, a divestiture or carve-out generates a cash infusion to the firm, which either can be reinvested or paid to shareholders as a dividend or share buyback. In fact, a spin-off may create greater shareholder wealth for several reasons.

First, a spin-off is tax free to the shareholders if it is properly structured. In contrast, the cash proceeds from an outright sale may be taxable to the parent to the extent a gain is realized. Moreover, management must be able to reinvest the after-tax proceeds in a project that has a reasonable likelihood of returning the firm's cost of capital. If management chooses to return the cash proceeds to shareholders as a dividend or through a stock repurchase, the shareholders also must pay taxes on the dividend at the ordinary tax rate or on any gain realized through the share repurchase at the generally lower capital gains tax rate. Second, a spin-off enables the shareholder to decide when to sell their shares. Third, a spin-off may be less traumatic than a divestiture for an operating unit. The divestiture process can degrade value if it is lengthy. Employees leave, worker productivity generally suffers, and customers may not renew contracts until the new owner is known.

RETURNS TO SHAREHOLDERS

PREANNOUNCEMENT ABNORMAL RETURNS

Empirical studies indicate that the alternative exit restructure strategies discussed in this chapter generally provide positive abnormal returns to the shareholders of the company implementing the strategy. However, the size of the abnormal returns varies widely among the alternative exit strategies (Table 13-4). In general, the magnitude of the abnormal returns are positively related to the size of the division subject to divestiture, spin-out, or carve-out relative to the size of the parent (J.P. Morgan, 1995; Klein, 1986). Moreover, abnormal returns tend to be larger for divestitures and carve-outs if the parent has announced that it will use the proceeds from a divestiture or carve-out to repay debt or pay dividends (Allen and McConnell, 1998; Byers, Lee, and Opler, 1996; Lang, Poulsen, and Stulz, 1995). Finally, abnormal returns tend to be larger if the parent is selling a division unrelated to its core business (Daley, Mehrotra, and Sivakumar, 1997; Desai and Jain, 1999).

TABLE 13-3 Divestitures, Carve-Outs, and Spin-Offs: Selecting the Appropriate Restructuring Strategy

Stage One Considerations (Primary Motive for Restructuring)	Stage Two Considerations		Appropriate	Restructuring Strategy More Likely If Parent
	Need for Cash	Value of Business/Degree of Synergy	Restructuring Strategy	
Change Strategy/Increase Focus	Needs Cash	High Price/High Synergy	Carve-Out	Can retain synergy
		Low Price/High Synergy	Carve-Out	Can retain synergy
		High Price/Low Synergy	Divestiture	Can shield taxable gains
		Low Price/Low Synergy	Divestiture	
	Little Need for Cash	High Price/High Synergy	Carve-Out	Can retain synergy
		Low Price/High Synergy	Carve-Out	Can retain synergy
		High Price/Low Synergy	Spin-Off	Cannot shield potential gains
		Low Price/Low Synergy	Spin-Off	
Underperforming Businesses	Needs Cash		Divestiture	Can shield taxable gains
	Little Need for Cash		Spin-Off	
Regulatory Concerns	Little Need for Cash		Divestiture/Spin-Off	Carve-Out not an option
Lack of Fit	Needs Cash		Divestiture	Can shield taxable gains
Tax Considerations	Little Need for Cash		Spin-Off	Cannot shield potential gains
			Spin-Off	
Raising Funds/Worth More to Others	Needs Cash		Divestiture	Can shield taxable gains
Risk Reduction			Carve-Out	
Moving Away from Core Business			Divestiture/Carve-Out	
Discarding Unwanted Businesses from Prior Acquisitions	Needs Cash		Divestiture	Can shield taxable gains
			Divestiture	
Avoiding Customer Conflicts	Little Need for Cash		Spin-Off	Cannot shield taxable gains

The exceptional abnormal returns for voluntary bust-ups may reflect investors' concurrence with management that continued operation of the firm is likely to erode sharcholder value. Liquidation of the firm results in the firm's assets being redeployed by the firm's shareholders to potentially higher alternative financial returns. Firms that tend to liquidate voluntarily often have low market-to-book ratios, cash

TABLE 13-4 Returns to Shareholders of Firms Undertaking Restructuring Actions

Restructuring Action	Average Preannouncement Abnormal Returns
Divestitures	2.3%
Spin-Offs	3.8%
Tracking Stocks	2.9%
Equity Carve-Outs	3.4%
Voluntary Bust-Ups	17.3%

Study	Preannouncement Abnormal Returns by Study[1]
Divestitures:	
Alexander, Benson, and Kampmeyer (1984):	
53 from 1964–1973	.17
Linn and Rozeff (1984): 77 from 1977–1982	1.45
Jain (1985): 1,107 from 1976–1978	.70
Klein (1986): 202 from 1970–1979	1.12
	When percentage of equity sold is
	<10%: None
	>10<50%: 2.53%
	>50%: 8.09%
Lang, Poulsen, and Stulz (1995): 93 from 1984–1989	2% for firms distributing proceeds to shareholders; (.5)% for those reinvesting proceeds
Mulherin and Boone (2000): 139 from 1990–1998	2.6
Spin-Offs:	
Hite and Owers (1983): 56 from 1963–1979	3.8%
Miles and Rosenfeld (1983): 62 from 1963–1981	2.33
Michaely and Shaw (1995):	
91 master limited partnerships from 1981–1989	4.5%
Loh, Bezjak, and Toms (1995): 59 from 1982–1987	1.5
J.P. Morgan (1995): 77 since beginning of 1995	5%
	6% if spin-off >10% of parent's equity
	4% if spin-off <10% of parent's equity
Vroom and van Frederikslust (1999):	
210 worldwide spin-offs from 1990–1998	2.6%
Mulherin and Boone (2000): 106 from 1990–1998	4.51
Tracking Stocks:	
Logue, Seward, and Walsh (1996): 9 from 1991–1995	2.9%

(Continued)

TABLE 13-4   (*Continued*)

Study	Preannouncement Abnormal Returns by Study[1]
Equity Carve-Outs (Split-Off IPOs)	
Schipper and Smith (1986): 81 for 1965–1983	1.7%
Michaely and Shaw (1995):	
91 limited partnerships from 1981–1989	.4%
Allen and McConnell (1998): 188 from 1978–1993	6.63% when proceeds used to pay off debt; zero otherwise
Vijh (1999): 628 from 1981–1995)	6.2%
Mulherin and Boone (2000): 125 from 1990–1998	2.27%
Voluntary Liquidations	
Skantz and Marchesini (1987): 37 from 1970–1978	21.4%[2]
Hite, Owers, and Rogers (1987): 49 from 1966–1975	13.62%[2]
Kim and Schatzberg (1987): 73 from 1963–1981	14%
Erwin and McConnell (1997): 61 from 1970–1991	20%

[1] Abnormal returns measured from 1–3 days before and including announcement date of restructure action.

[2] Abnormal returns measured during the month of the announced restructure action.

balances well in excess of their operating needs, low debt-to-equity levels, and high equity ownership by senior managers. Such firms often liquidate after takeover attempts (Fleming and Moon, 1995).

POST-SPIN-OFF RETURNS TO SHAREHOLDERS

Empirical studies show that shares in carve-outs and spin-offs tend to significantly outperform the Standard & Poor's (S&P) 500 during the 2 years following the announcement (Table 13-5). In contrast, tracking stocks tend to underperform the gains in the S&P 500.

Carve-outs and spin-offs may tend to outperform the broader stock market indices because their share prices reflect speculation that they will be acquired rather than any improvement in the operating performance of the units once they have been spun off from the parent. One-third of spin-offs are acquired within 3 years after the unit is spun off by the parent. Once those spin-offs that have been acquired have been removed from the sample, the remaining spin-offs do not perform better than their peers (Cusatis, Miles, and Woolridge, 1993). McConnell, Ozbilgin, and Wahal (2001) conclude that many historical studies showing superior post-spin-off returns are indeed heavily biased by the inclusion of one or two firms in the sample whose excess returns are the result of their having been acquired. Spin-offs simply may create value by providing an efficient method of transferring corporate assets to acquiring companies.

In a study of 232 spin-offs and equity carve-outs during the 1990s Booz Allen Hamilton found that only 26% of the units outperformed the broader stock market indices during the 2 years following their separation from the parent (Scherreik, 2002). Smaller spin-offs (i.e., those with a market cap of less than $200 million)

TABLE 13-5   Returns to Postrestructuring Shareholders

Study	Average Annual Returns (2–3 Years Following Announcement)
Spin-Offs	6–11% above the S&P 500[1]
Carve-Outs	3–10% above the S&P 500[2]
Tracking Stocks	2–11% less than the S&P 500[3]

[1] Oppenheimer & Company (1981); Cusatis, Miles, and Woolridge (1993); J.P. Morgan (1999), and McKinsey & Company (1999).
[2] J.P. Morgan (1999) and McKinsey & Company (1999).
[3] McKinsey & Company (1999), Vijh (1999), and Billett (2000).

tend to outperform larger ones (i.e., those with a market cap greater than $200 million) (J.P. Morgan, 1999). This may be a result of a tendency of investors relatively unfamiliar with the business that is spun off by the parent to undervalue the spin-off. McKinsey & Company found that those carve-outs that were largely independent of the parent (i.e., in which the parent tended to own less than 50% of the equity) tended to significantly outperform the S&P 500 (Annema, Fallon, and Goedhart, 2002).

BUSINESS FAILURE

The leading causes of business failure in order of priority include economic factors such as recession, financial factors such as excess operating expenses and excessive leverage, and lack of business or managerial experience (Dun & Bradstreet Corporation, 1997). A study by the U.S. Small Business Administration (1999) traced the experience of 3377 small businesses that had declared bankruptcy between 1994 and 1997. The results are consistent with the study by Dun & Bradstreet (1997). In order of importance, the reasons for filing for bankruptcy include outside business conditions; financing problems; and management-related problems that reflect inexperience, such as selecting a poor location, an inability to manage people, the loss of major clients, and an inability to collect accounts receivable.

During the 2001 recession, the number of public companies declaring bankruptcy reached record proportions, with 255 declaring bankruptcy as compared with 123 in the previous recession in 1991, according to Bankruptcy-Data.com. Moreover, at $256 billion, the amount of assets involved was more than double the previous record of $95 billion in the 1991 recession (Bloomberg News, 2002). With more than $110 billion in book assets, WorldCom became the largest U.S. corporation to declare bankruptcy when it filed with the U.S. Bankruptcy Court on July 22, 2002. Enron Corporation, which sought bankruptcy protection on December 2, 2001, with $63.3 billion in assets, was the second largest on record (Case Study 13-7). Other large or high-profile bankruptcies in 2001 and 2002 included Global Crossing, Polaroid, Bethlehem Steel, and Kmart.

CASE STUDY 13-7: THE ENRON SHUFFLE— A SCANDAL TO REMEMBER

The Best of Times and the Worst of. . .

What started in the mid-1980s as essentially a staid "old economy" business became the poster child in the late 1990s for companies wanting to remake themselves into "new economy" powerhouses. Unfortunately, what may have started with the best of intentions emerged as one of the biggest business scandals in recent memory. The firm that may have had the potential to be a role model for firms in the new millennium instead became a paragon of alleged corruption and fraud.

Enron was created in 1985 as a result of a merger between Houston Natural Gas and Internorth Natural Gas. The resulting firm formed a system with about 37,000 miles of natural gas pipelines. In 1989, Enron started trading natural gas commodities and eventually became the world's largest buyer and seller of natural gas. In the early 1990s, Enron became the nation's premier electricity marketer and pioneered the development of trading in such commodities as weather derivatives, bandwidth, pulp, paper, and plastics. The firm's EnronOnline was the world's first Web-based commodity trading platform. Enron also invested billions in its broadband unit and water and wastewater system management unit and in hard assets overseas. In 2000, Enron reported $101 billion in revenue and a market capitalization of $63 billion (*Business Week*, December 10, 2001). Enron was at the top of its game, but oh what a difference a year can make.

The Virtual Company

Enron was essentially a company whose trading and risk management business strategy was built on assets largely owned by others. The complex financial maneuvering and off-balance sheet partnerships that former CEO Jeffrey K. Skilling and Chief Financial Officer Andrew S. Fastow implemented were intended to remove everything from telecommunications fiber to water companies from the firm's balance sheet. Asset-rich energy companies, such as ExxonMobil, were viewed as essentially dinosaurs in the new millennium by Enron's top management. Skilling's strategy was to create an "asset-light" company by applying Enron's energy trading and risk management skills to power plants and other facilities owned by outsiders. To maintain the firm's credit rating, Enron moved many of its own assets off its balance sheet and into partnerships. Some partnerships required Enron to contribute its stock if its credit rating and stock price fell below a certain point. If this occurred, Enron could be held immediately responsible for more than $4 billion in debt.

Partnerships frequently are used in business to hedge investments (i.e., share risk) or to obtain access to certain expertise or assets. They normally are capitalized by outside investors who bear the risk of the partnership's investments. If any one partner has a controlling interest in the partnership, which is possible with interests of less than 50%, the controlling partner would have to consolidate the affiliates assets and liabilities (debt) on its balance sheet. What distinguished Enron's partnerships were their lack of independence from Enron and the use of Enron's stock as collateral to leverage the partnerships. If Enron's stock fell in value, the firm was obligated to issue more shares to the partnership to restore the value of the collateral underlying the debt or to immediately repay the debt. The resulting issuance of new shares would dilute the ownership interests of the current Enron shareholders. Lenders in effect had direct recourse to Enron stock if at any time the partnerships could not repay their loans in full and in a timely manner. Rather than limiting its risk, Enron was in effect assuming the full measure of risk by guaranteeing the loans with its stock.

Enron also engaged in a number of questionable transactions that inflated its earnings, such as selling time on its broadband system to a partnership at inflated prices at a time when the demand for broadband services was plummeting. Enron then recorded a substantial profit on such transactions. The partnerships agreed to such transactions, because Enron management seems to have exerted disproportionate influence in some instances over partnership decisions although its ownership interests were very small, often less than 3%. Curiously, Enron's outside auditor, Arthur Andersen, may have had a dual role in these partnerships, collecting fees for helping to set them up and for auditing them.

Time to Pay the Piper

At the time the firm filed for bankruptcy on December 2, 2001, it had $13.1 billion in debt on the books of the parent company and another $18.1 billion on the balance sheets of affiliated companies/partnerships (*Business Week*, December 17, 2001). A wave of panic selling began in mid-October when the then-CEO, Kenneth Lay, announced to Wall Street analysts that deals with partnerships would reduce the firm's shareholder equity by $1.2 billion as a result of pending write-offs. Previously, Enron's management had been able to inflate earnings and hide the firm's problems. However, this time the uncertainty surrounding just how the partnerships were being managed and what other time bombs may be lying in wait all but eliminated any chance for Enron to avoid seeking the protection of the federal bankruptcy court.

In addition to the Byzantine partnerships created by Enron, a number of bad investments both in the United States and abroad contributed to the firm's malaise. Enron's 65% investment in the $3 billion Dabhol power plant in India was in dispute with its largest customer who refused to pay for electricity it had used already. Meanwhile, Enron's core energy distribution business was deteriorating, even as it was growing rapidly. Enron was attempting to gain share in a maturing market by paring selling prices. Margins also suffered from poor cost containment. Enron's answer to growing competition in its core business was to enter into highly creative, but risky, new businesses including broadband, metals, and advertising.

November proved to be a pivotal month for the firm. Dynegy Corp. agreed to buy Enron for $10 billion. On November 8, 2001, Enron announced that its net income would have to be restated back to 1997, resulting in a $586 million reduction in profits reported during that period. On November 15, Chair Kenneth Lay admitted that the firm had made billions of dollars in bad investments. Four days later Enron said it would have to repay a $690 million note by mid-December and that it might have to take an additional $700 million pre-tax charge. At the end of the month, Dynegy withdrew its offer and Enron's credit rating was reduced to junk bond status. Enron was responsible for another $3.9 billion owed by its partnerships. Enron had less than $2 billion in cash on hand (*Dallas Morning News*, 2001). The stage was set for Enron to seek protection from its creditors in federal bankruptcy court.

The end came quickly as investors and customers completely lost faith in the energy behemoth as a result of its secrecy and complex financial maneuvers. Enron's stock had reached a high of $90 per share on August 17, 2001; by December 5, 2001, the stock was trading at less than $1. However, even Enron's attempt to declare bankruptcy did not come easy for the firm. Enron's efforts to seek bankruptcy protection were complicated by its difficulty in getting so-called ***debtor in possession financing***. Such financing is intended to allow the bankrupt firm to continue to operate while it attempts to reorganize under the protection of the bankruptcy court. Lenders normally demand collateral in exchange for such financing. However, in this instance, Enron had few unencumbered assets.

The Enron Legacy

In addition to its angry creditors, Enron faced class-action lawsuits by shareholders and employees, whose pensions were invested heavily in Enron stock. Enron also faced intense scrutiny from Congressional committees and the U.S. Department of Justice. By the end of 2001, shareholders had lost more than $63 billion from its previous 52-week high, bondholders lost $2.6 billion in the face value of their debt, and banks appeared to be at risk on at least $15 billion of credit they had extended to Enron. In addition, potential losses on uncollateralized derivative contracts totaled $4 billion. Such contracts involved Enron commitments to buy various types of commodities contracts at some point in the future.

The firm also was saddled with the onerous costs of bankruptcy. A bankruptcy of this size generates huge fees for a variety of consultants who are employed by corporate boards to stave off a "fire sale" of assets in liquidation. The objective is to bring the corporation out of bankruptcy protection as quickly as possible because creditors tend to push more aggressively for liquidation the longer bankruptcy proceedings drag on. By the time the bankruptcy reorganization is over, attorneys' fees could reach $30 million, with a dozen law firms working on the case. High-profile law firms involved with the case included Milbank Tweed; Wachtell, Lipton, Rosen & Katz; Skadden, Arps, Slate, Meagher & Flom; and Cutler & Pickering. Investment bankers, such as the Blackstone Group, charge $350,000 per month and stand to earn $35 million if the firm emerges from bankruptcy. Such advisors are employed to appraise the value of the firm's assets. Estimates of the total fees that could be earned by law firms, investment bankers, and accountants range as high as $300 million.

Questions remain as to why Wall Street analysts, Arthur Andersen, federal or state regulatory authorities, the credit rating agencies, and the firm's board of directors did not sound the alarm sooner. It is surprising that the audit committee of the Enron board seems to have somehow been unaware of the firm's highly questionable financial maneuvers. Inquiries following the bankruptcy declaration seem to suggest that the audit committee followed all of the rules stipulated by federal regulators and stock exchanges regarding director pay, independence, disclosure, and financial expertise. Enron seems to have collapsed in part because such rules did not do what they were supposed to do. For example, paying directors with stock may have aligned their interests with shareholders, but it is also possible to have been a disincentive to aggressively question senior management about their financial dealings. Nonetheless, 99% of the Fortune 200 companies pay their directors with stock.

The Lesson of Enron

Enron may be the best recent example of a complete breakdown in corporate governance, a system intended to protect shareholders. Inside Enron, the board of directors, management, and the audit function failed to do the job. Similarly, the firm's outside auditors, regulators, credit rating agencies, and Wall Street analysts also failed to sound warning bells. What seems to be apparent is that if the auditors fail to identify incompetence or fraud, the system of safeguards is likely to breakdown. The cost of failure to those charged with protecting the shareholders, including outside auditors, analysts, credit rating agencies, and regulators, is simply not high enough to ensure adequate scrutiny.

The problem seems to fall more on inadequate enforcement of existing rules than on outdated generally accepted accounting principles. There were many red flags that seemed to have been ignored. These included insufficient disclosure of related-party transactions and the questionable application of the rules pertaining to recording profits. With respect to profitability, the firm applied very aggressive accounting interpretations.

What may have transpired is that company managers simply undertook aggressive interpretations of accounting principles and then challenged auditors to "show them where they can't" engage in such practices according to GAAP accounting rules (Weil, 2002). This type of practice has been going on since the early 1980s and may account for the proliferation of specific accounting rules applicable only to certain transactions to insulate both the firm engaging in the transaction and the auditor reviewing the transaction from subsequent litigation. The solution may not be more accounting rules because smart managers always will be able circumvent restrictions. Instead, external and internal auditors, as well as board audit committees, need to exercise better judgment in protecting the shareholders' interests.

In one sense, the Enron debacle represents a failure of the free market system and its current shareholder protection mechanisms in that it took so long for the dramatic Enron shell game to be revealed to the public. However, this incident highlights the remarkable resilience of the free market system. The free market system worked quite effectively in its rapid imposition of discipline in bringing down the Enron house of cards, without any noticeable disruption in energy distribution nationwide.

Case Study Discussion Questions

1. In your judgment, what were the major factors contributing to the demise of Enron? Of these factors, which were the most important?
2. In what way was the Enron debacle a break down in corporate governance (oversight)? Explain your answer.
3. How were the Enron partnerships used to hide debt and inflate the firm's earnings? Should partnership structures be limited in the future? If so, how?
4. What should (or can) be done to reduce the likelihood of this type of situation arising in the future? Be specific.

INSOLVENCY VERSUS BANKRUPTCY

When a firm is unable to pay its liabilities as they come due, it is said to be *technically insolvent*. *Legal insolvency* occurs when a firm's liabilities exceed the fair market value of its assets. Creditors' claims cannot be satisfied unless the firm's assets can be liquidated for more than their book value. U.S. courts treat both technical insolvency and legal insolvency as a financial failure of the firm. *Bankruptcy* is a federal legal proceeding designed to protect the technically or legally insolvent firm from lawsuits by its creditors until a decision can be made to shut down or to continue to operate the firm. A firm is not considered to be bankrupt or in bankruptcy until it or its creditors file a petition for reorganization or liquidation with the federal bankruptcy courts.

VOLUNTARY SETTLEMENTS WITH CREDITORS OUTSIDE OF BANKRUPTCY

An insolvent firm may reach an agreement with its creditors to restructure its obligations out of court to avoid the costs of bankruptcy proceedings. The voluntary settlement process usually is initiated by the debtor firm because it generally offers the best chance for the current owners to recover a portion of their investments either by continuing to operate the firm or through a planned liquidation of the firm. This process normally involves the debtor firm requesting a meeting with its creditors. At this meeting, a committee of creditors is selected to analyze the debtor firm's financial position and to recommend an appropriate course of action. The committee either can recommend that the firm continue or that it be liquidated.

VOLUNTARY SETTLEMENT RESULTING IN CONTINUED OPERATION

Creditors may decide to allow the insolvent firm to continue to operate because they believe that they are most likely to recover more of what they are owed than if they force the firm to liquidate its assets. Plans to restructure the debtor firm developed cooperatively with creditors commonly are called *workouts*. Because of the firm's weak financial position, the creditors must be willing to restructure the insolvent firm's debts to enable it to sustain its operations. *Debt restructuring* involves concessions by creditors that will lower an insolvent firm's payments so that it may remain in business. Restructuring normally is accomplished in three ways: an extension, a composition, or a debt-for-equity swap.

An *extension* occurs when creditors agree to lengthen the period during which the debtor firm can repay its debt. Creditors often agree to temporarily suspend both interest and principal repayments. A *composition* is an agreement in which creditors agree to settle for less than the full amount they are owed. A *debt-for-equity swap* occurs when creditors surrender a portion of their claims on the firm in exchange for an ownership position in the firm. If the reduced debt service payments enable the firm to prosper, the value of the stock may in the long run far exceed the amount of debt the creditors were willing to forgive.

Exhibit 13-1 illustrates a debt restructure or composition of a bankrupt company that will enable the firm to continue operation by converting debt to equity. Although the firm, Survivor Incorporated, has positive earnings before interest and taxes, it is not enough to meet its interest payments. When principal payments are considered, cash flow becomes significantly negative. Therefore, it is technically insolvent. As a result of the restructuring of the firm's debt, Survivor Incorporated is able to continue to operate. However, the firm's lenders now have a controlling interest in the firm. Note the same type of restructuring could take place either voluntarily outside the courts or as a result of reorganizing under the protection of the bankruptcy court. The latter scenario will be discussed later in this chapter.

EXHIBIT 13-1. SURVIVOR INC. RESTRUCTURES ITS DEBT

Survivor Inc. currently has 400,000 shares of common equity outstanding at a par value of $10 per share. The current rate of interest on its debt is 8% and the debt is amortized over 20 years. The combined federal, state, and local tax rate is 40%. The firm's cash flow and capital position are shown below.

Income and Cash Flow		Total Capital	
Earnings Before Interest & Taxes	$500,000	Debt	$10,000,000
Interest	800,000	Equity	4,000,000
Earnings Before Taxes	(300,000)	Total	$14,000,000
Taxes	120,000		
Earnings After Taxes	(180,000)	Debt/Total Capital	71.4%
Depreciation	400,000		
Principal Repayment	(500,000)		
Cash Flow	(280,000)		

Assume bondholders are willing to convert $5,000,000 of debt to equity at the current par value of $10 per share. This necessitates that Survivor Inc. issues 500,000 new shares. These actions result in positive cash flow, a substantial reduction in the firm's debt-to-total capital ratio, and a transfer of control to the bondholders. The former stockholders now own only 44.4% (4,000,000/9,000,000) of the company.

Income and Cash Flow		Total Capital	
Earnings Before Interest & Taxes	$500,000	Debt	$5,000,000
Interest	400,000	Equity	9,000,000
Earnings Before Taxes	100,000	Total	$14,000,000
Taxes	40,000		
Earnings After Taxes	60,000	Debt/Total Capital	35.7%
Depreciation	400,000		
Principal Repayment	(250,000)		
Cash Flow	$210,000		

VOLUNTARY SETTLEMENT RESULTING IN LIQUIDATION

If the creditors conclude that the insolvent firm's situation cannot be resolved, liquidation may be the only acceptable course of action. Liquidation can be conducted outside the court in a private liquidation or through the U.S. bankruptcy court. If the insolvent firm is willing to accept liquidation and all creditors agree, legal proceedings are not necessary. Creditors normally prefer private liquidations to avoid lengthy and costly litigation. Through a process called an *assignment*, a committee representing creditors grants the power to liquidate the firm's assets to a third party called an *assignee or trustee*. The responsibility of the assignee is to sell the assets as quickly as possible while obtaining the best possible price. Once the assets have been sold, the assignee distributes the proceeds to the creditors and to the firm's owners if any monies remain.

REORGANIZATION AND LIQUIDATION IN BANKRUPTCY

In the absence of a voluntary settlement out of court, the debtor firm may seek protection from its creditors by initiating bankruptcy or may be forced into bankruptcy by its creditors (Case Study 13-7). When the debtor firm files the petition with the bankruptcy court, the bankruptcy is said to be *voluntary*. When creditors do the filing, the action is said to be *involuntary bankruptcy*. It takes only a group of three creditors who are owed a total of $5000 to place a firm in involuntary bankruptcy. Once either a voluntary or involuntary petition is filed, the debtor firm is protected from any further legal action related to its debts until the bankruptcy proceedings are completed. The filing of a petition allows the debtor firm to stop all principal and interest payments owed to creditors, while preventing secured creditors from taking possession of their collateral.

Bankruptcy may result from unanticipated economic downturns (e.g., Kmart), management incompetence or deceit (e.g., Enron and WorldCom), or misguided government intrusion in the free market system (e.g., PG&E). Ill-conceived efforts by the California state legislature to restructure the state's electricity market pushed the state's largest utility into bankruptcy. The effort to restructure the industry consisted of deregulating the wholesale price of power to be paid to electricity generators by the state's electric utilities while continuing to freeze the price the utilities could charge their customers. The utilities also were required to sell off most of their internal generation capacity and were prohibited from signing long-term contracts with power suppliers. When instituted, the state was in the midst of a significant electricity surplus. Consequently, it was believed that power generators would be encouraged to add capacity, keeping the wholesale price well below the retail price of electricity in the long run. Escalating electricity demands and the unwillingness of state and local officials to license any new capacity since 1987 pushed demand in excess of supply by late 2000. The cost of producing electricity soared in the wake of sharply higher oil and natural gas prices, whereas the cost of hydroelectric power rose in the wake of a prolonged drought in the northwestern United States. Case Study 13-8 illustrates the impact of these events on Pacific, Gas, and Electric, one of the nation's largest utilities.

CASE STUDY 13-8: PG&E SEEKS BANKRUPTCY PROTECTION

Pacific, Gas, and Electric (PG&E), the San Francisco-based utility, filed for bankruptcy on April 7, 2001, citing nearly $9 billion in debt and unreimbursed energy costs. The utility, one of three privately owned utilities in California, serves northern and central California. The intention of the Chapter 11 reorganization was to make the utility solvent again by protecting the firm from lawsuits or any other action by those who are owed money by the utility. The bankruptcy also will allow the utility to deal with all of the firm's debts in a single forum rather than with individual debtors in what had become a highly politicized venue.

The Road to Bankruptcy

September 1996: California's power restructuring efforts were signed into law by then-Governor Pete Wilson.

May 2000: Wholesale power prices begin to rise as demand surges past supply in the buoyant economy. However, the 1996 law prohibits the utilities from passing rising costs on to customers until March 1, 2002.

January 4, 2001: California Public Utility Commission (PUC) disallows PG&E's request to recover the full amount of their cost increases and approves an average 10% increase in retail rates, about two-thirds of what had been requested. The PUC institutes internal audits of the state's private utilities.

January 5, 2000: Credit rating agencies downgrade PG&E and Southern California Edison (SCE) to one notch above junk bonds.

January 10, 2000: PG&E asks then-Governor Grey Davis for help to buy natural gas for customers, saying it does not have enough cash to pay its bills.

January 12, 2000: PG&E lays off 1000 workers.

January 17, 2000: Rolling blackouts are ordered for the first time to avoid overloading the state's power grid. PG&E defaults on $76 million in commercial paper.

January 19, 2000: Then-President Clinton declares a natural gas supply emergency and orders out-of-state suppliers to continue selling gas to PG&E despite concerns about getting paid.

January 23, 2000: The Bush Administration extends emergency orders through February 6.

March 27, 2000: The PUC approves an increase in retail electricity prices by 3 cents per kilowatt hour to bring retail prices more in line with wholesale prices after PG&E states that its debt has grown to more than $9 billion.

April 6, 2000: PG&E files for bankruptcy.

An Alternative to Political Gridlock

Utility industry analysts saw PG&E's move as largely an effort to escape the political paralysis that had befallen the state's regulatory apparatus (*Orange County Register*, April 7, 2001). The bankruptcy filing came one day after Governor Davis dropping his opposition to increasing retail rates. The Governor's reversal, however, came after 5 months of negotiations with the state's privately owned utilities on a rescue plan.

PG&E Shareholders Get Hammered

PG&E's common shares fell 37% on the day the firm filed for reorganization. Fearing a similar fate for San Diego Gas and Electric (SDG&E), the shares of Sempra Energy, SDG&E's parent corporation, also dropped by 35%.

State's Rescue Efforts Burden Future Tax Payers

In an attempt to insulate California ratepayers from escalating wholesale electricity prices, the state entered into a series of 5–10 year contracts with electricity power generators that account for more than two-thirds of the state's projected power needs. The last contracts were signed by the state in June 2001. By September, a slowing economy pushed the wholesale price of electricity well below the level the state was required to pay in the "take or pay" contracts the state had just signed. Estimates suggest that California taxpayers will have to pay between $40 billion and $45 billion in power costs over the next decade depending on what happens to future energy costs (*Orange County Register*, October 2, 2001). PG&E has continued to supply its customers without disruption or blackout while being under the protection of the bankruptcy court.

The State's Second Largest Utility Reaches An Out-of-Court Settlement

Southern California Edison, nearing bankruptcy for reasons similar to those that drove PG&E to seek protection from its creditors, reached agreement with the PUC to pay off $3.3 billion in debt owed to power generators from customer revenues. Previously, the PUC forbade the utility to use monies generated from two previous rate increases for this purpose. The U.S. District Court judge approved the plan on October 5, 2001. Although some creditors complained that the settlement was not reassuring because it did not include a timetable for repayment of outstanding debt, others viewed the agreement as a voluntary reorganization plan without going through the expensive process of filing for bankruptcy with the federal court.

Case Study Discussion Questions

1. In your judgment, did regulators attenuate or exacerbate the situation? Explain your answer.
2. PG&E pursued bankruptcy protection, whereas Southern California Edison did not. What could PG&E have been done differently to avoid bankruptcy?

BANKRUPTCY LAWS AND PROCEDURES

The Bankruptcy Reform Act of 1978 was enacted to make bankruptcy proceedings more flexible than previous laws, which dictated that creditor claims took absolute priority over ownership claims. Moreover, under the 1978 act, the conditions under which companies could file were broadened such that a firm could declare bankruptcy without having to wait until it was virtually insolvent. The intent of making the bankruptcy code less rigid was to increase the likelihood that creditors and owners would reach agreement on plans to reorganize rather than liquidate insolvent firms. Although most companies that file for bankruptcy do so as a result of their deteriorating financial position, there is evidence that some firms are using the bankruptcy code for purposes for which it was not intended.

Companies increasingly are seeking bankruptcy protection to avoid litigation and hostile takeovers. In the mid-1980s, Johns Manville Corporation used bankruptcy to negotiate a reduction in huge liability awards granted in the wake of asbestos-related lawsuits. Similarly, Texaco used the threat of bankruptcy in the early 1990s as a negotiating ploy to reduce the amount of court-ordered payments to Occidental Petroleum resulting from the court's determination that Texaco had improperly intervened in a pending merger transaction. To protect themselves from litigation, Washington Construction Group required Morrison Knudsen Corporation to file for bankruptcy as a closing condition in the agreement of purchase and sale. In doing so, the acquirer believed that it could protect itself from certain liabilities of the target (*Business Week*, March 20, 2000).

Saddled with crushing pension and other retiree benefit obligations, 33 steel companies have sought the protection of the bankruptcy court to either reorganize or liquidate their businesses. In 2001, LTV sold its plants while in bankruptcy to W. L. Ross and Company, which restarted the plants in 2002 in a new company named the International Steel Group (ISI). By simply buying assets, ISI does not have the obligation to pay the pension, health care, or insurance liabilities, which remained with LTV. The Pension Benefit Guaranty Corporation, a quasi-government organization, will pay some portion of the pension obligations. Also in bankruptcy, Bethlehem Steel announced in mid-2002 that it is seeking to lease its operations to Brazilian steelmaker CSN, which would pay Bethlehem a fee to operate several of its plants. Bethlehem then would use the fees to pay its creditors.

The two key chapters in the Bankruptcy Reform Act are Chapters 7 and 11. *Chapter 7* deals with liquidation and provides for a court-appointed interim trustee with broad powers and discretion to operate the debtor firm in such a way to prevent further deterioration in the overall financial position of the firm and the removal of assets by owners before liquidation. ***Chapter 11*** deals with reorganization, which provides for the debtor to remain in possession, unless the court rules otherwise, of the business and in control of its operations. The debtor and creditors are permitted considerable flexibility in working together. This enables them to negotiate debt repayment schedules, the restructuring of debt, and the granting of loans by the creditors to the debtor. If a workable plan cannot be formulated, the firm will be liquidated in accordance with the procedures outlined in Chapter 7.

Filing for Chapter 11 Reorganization

Figure 13-1 summarizes the process for filing for reorganization under Chapter 11. The process begins by filing in a federal bankruptcy court. In the case of an involuntary petition, a hearing must be held to determine whether the firm is insolvent. If the firm is found to be insolvent, the court enters an ***order for relief***, which initiates the bankruptcy proceedings. On the filing of a reorganization petition, the filing firm becomes the ***debtor in possession*** of all the assets. The debtor firm's managers are able to continue to make operating decisions, and they have the exclusive right to propose a reorganization plan during the 120 days after filing for Chapter 11 bankruptcy. The court often grants several extensions if requested by management. Management has 180 days from the filing date to obtain creditor and shareholder approval of a proposed reorganization plan. If management does not propose a plan or if their plan is rejected, creditors can propose their own plan. The creditors may request that the court appoint a trustee instead of the debtor to manage the firm during the reorganization period.

Federal bankruptcy courts evaluate reorganization plans in terms of their fairness and feasibility. Fairness means that the creditor claims are to be satisfied in accordance with the order of priorities listed in the bankruptcy laws. Feasibility refers to whether the assumptions underlying the plan are viewed by the court as being realistic. When the court approves a reorganization plan, creditors and owners are grouped according to the similarity of claims. In the case of creditors, the plan must be approved by holders of at least two-thirds of the dollar value of the claims as well as a simple majority of the creditors in each group. In the case of owners, two-thirds of those in each group (e.g., common and preferred shareholders, secured creditors, and unsecured creditors) must approve the plan. Once approved by all claimant groups, the plan is put into effect. Finally, the debtor

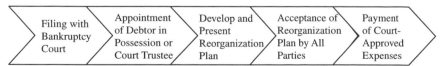

FIGURE 13-1. Procedures for reorganizing in bankruptcy.

is responsible for paying the expenses approved by the court of all parties whose services contributed to the approval or disapproval of the plan.

Chapter 7 Liquidation

If the bankruptcy court determines that reorganization is infeasible, the failing firm may be forced to liquidate. A trustee is appointed by the court to handle the administrative aspects of the liquidation. The trustee convenes a meeting of all creditors to apprise them of the prospects for liquidation. The trustee then is given the responsibility to liquidate the firm's assets, keep records, examine creditors' claims, disburse the proceeds, and submit a final report on the liquidation. The priority in which the claims are paid is stipulated in Chapter 7 of the Bankruptcy Reform Act, which must be followed by the trustee when the firm is liquidated. All secured creditors are paid when the firm's assets that were pledged as collateral are liquidated. If the proceeds of the sale of these assets are inadequate to satisfy all of the secured creditors' claims, they become unsecured or general creditors for the amount that was not recovered. If the proceeds of the sale of pledged assets exceed secured creditors' claims, the excess proceeds are used to pay general creditors.

The order of priority of payment of claims after the pledged assets have been sold is as follows:

1. Past-due property taxes
2. Secured creditors up to the proceeds of the sale of pledged assets; unpaid portions of secured claims become unsecured claims
3. Legal fees and other expenses to administer and operate the bankrupt firm, including legal fees incurred in trying to reorganize
4. Expenses incurred after an involuntary case has begun but before a trustee has been appointed
5. Wages not to exceed $2000 per worker that are owed to those employed by the firm during the 90 days before the initiation of bankruptcy proceedings
6. Unpaid employee benefit plan contributions, up to $2000 per worker, that were to have been paid during the 6 months before the initiation of bankruptcy proceedings
7. Unsecured customer deposits, of $900 or less, resulting from purchasing or leasing a product or service from the firm
8. Income taxes owed to federal, state, or local governments
9. Underfunded pension liabilities up to 30% of the book value of preferred and common equity; unpaid portions become unsecured claims
10. Unsecured creditors, including claims of secured creditors that were not fully satisfied by the sale of pledged assets. All such claimants are paid from available proceeds on a pro rata basis
11. Preferred stockholders, who are paid up to the par value of their stock
12. Common shareholders, who are paid out of the remaining funds on an equal per share basis

Exhibit 13-2 illustrates how a legally bankrupt company could be liquidated with the proceeds distributed in order of priority. The bankruptcy court, owners, and creditors could not agree on an appropriate reorganization plan for DOA Inc. Consequently, the court has ordered that the firm be liquidated in accordance with Chapter 7. Note that this illustration would differ from a private or voluntary out-of-court liquidation in two important respects. First, the expenses associated with conducting the liquidation would be lower because the liquidation would not involve extended legal proceedings. Second, the distribution of proceeds could reflect a prioritization of claims negotiated between the creditors and the owners that differs from that set forth in Chapter 7 of the Bankruptcy Reform Act.

EXHIBIT 13-2. LIQUIDATION OF DOA, INC. UNDER CHAPTER 7

DOA has the following balance sheet. The only liability that is not shown on the balance sheet is the cost of the bankruptcy proceedings, which are treated as expenses and are not capitalized.

Balance Sheet

Assets		Liabilities	
Cash	$35,000	Accounts Payable	$750,000
Accounts Receivable	2,300,000	Bank Notes Payable	3,000,000
Inventories	2,100.000	Accrued Salaries	720,000
Total Current Assets	$4,435,000	Unpaid Benefits	140,000
Land	1,500,000	Unsecured Customer Deposits	300,000
Net Plant & Equipment	2,000,000	Taxes Payable	400,000
Total Fixed Assets	$3,500,000	Total Current Liabilities	$5,310,000
Total Assets	$7,935,000	First Mortgage	2,500,000
		Unsecured Debt	200,000
		Total Long Term Debt	$2,700,000
		Preferred Stock	50,000
		Common Stock	100,000
		Paid in Surplus	500,000
		Retained Earnings	(725,000)
		Total Stockholders' Equity	$(75,000)
		Total Shareholders' Equity & Total Liabilities	$7,935,000

The sale of DOA's assets generates $5.4 million in cash. The distribution of the proceeds results in the following situation. Note that the proceeds are distributed in accordance with the priorities stipulated in the current commercial bankruptcy law and that the cost of administering the bankruptcy totals 18% of the proceeds from liquidation.

Distribution of Liquidation Proceeds

Proceeds from Liquidation	$5,400,000
Expenses of Administering Bankruptcy	972,000
Salaries Owed Employees	720,000
Unpaid Employee Benefits	140,000
Unsecured Customer Deposits	300,000
Taxes	400,000
Funds Available for Creditors	$2,868,000
First Mortgage (From sale of fixed assets)	1,500,000
Funds Available for Unsecured Creditors	$1,368,000

Once all prior claims have been satisfied, the remaining proceeds are distributed to the unsecured creditors. The pro rata settlement percentage of 27.64% is calculated by dividing funds available for unsecured creditors by the amount of unsecured creditor claims (i.e., $1368/$4950). The shareholders receive nothing because not all unsecured creditor claims have been satisfied.

Pro Rata Distribution of Funds Among Unsecured Creditors

Unsecured Creditor Claims	Amount	Settlement at 27.64%
Unpaid Balance from First Mortgage	$1,000,000	$276,400
Accounts Payable	750,000	207,300
Notes Payable	3,000,000	829,200
Unsecured Debt	200,000	55,280
Total	$4,950,000	$1,368,000

STRATEGIC OPTIONS FOR FAILING FIRMS

A failing firm's strategic options are to merge with another firm, reach an out-of-court voluntary settlement with creditors, or file for Chapter 11 bankruptcy. The firm may voluntarily liquidate as part of an out-of-court settlement or be forced to liquidate under Chapter 7 of the bankruptcy code. The implications of each option are summarized in Table 13-6. The choice of which option to pursue is critically dependent on which provides the greatest present value for creditors and shareholders. To evaluate these options, the firm's management needs to estimate the going concern, selling price, and liquidation values of the firm.

Merging with Another Firm

If the failing firm's management estimates that the sale price of the firm is greater than the going concern or liquidation values, management should seek to be acquired by or merge with another firm. If a strategic buyer can be found,

TABLE 13-6 Alternative Strategies for Failing Firms

Assumptions	Options: Failing Firm	Outcome: Failing Firm
Selling Price > Going Concern or Liquidation Value	1. Is acquired by or	1. Continues as subsidiary of acquirer.
	2. Merges with another firm	2. Merged into acquirer and ceases to exist.
Going Concern Value > Sale or Liquidation Value	1. Reaches out-of-court settlement with creditors	1. Continues with debt for equity swap, extension, and composition.
	2. Seeks bankruptcy protection under Chapter 11	2. Continues in reorganization.
Liquidation Value > Sale or Going Concern Value	1. Reaches out-of-court settlement with creditors	1. Ceases to exist. Assignee liquidates assets and distributes proceeds to creditors on a pro rata basis.
	2. Liquidates under Chapter 7	2. Ceases to exist. Trustee supervises liquidation and distributes proceeds according to statutory priorities

management must convince the firm's creditors that they will be more likely to receive what they are owed if the firm is acquired rather than liquidated or allowed to remain independent. Stockholders may be able to recover a significant portion of their cost basis in the stock of the failing company. In a study of 38 takeovers of distressed firms from 1981 to 1988, Clark and Ofek (1994) found that bidders tend to overpay for these types of firms. The failing firm may continue to exist as a subsidiary of the acquiring company or cease to exist as a result of a merger with the acquirer. Although this strategy may benefit the failing firm's shareholders, such takeovers do not seem to benefit the acquirer's shareholders. Clark and Ofek also found that, in most cases, the acquiring firms fail to successfully restructure the acquired firms.

Reaching an Out-of-Court Voluntary Settlement with Creditors

Alternatively, the going concern value of the firm may exceed the sale or liquidation values. Management must be able to demonstrate to creditors that a restructured or downsized firm will be able to repay its debts if creditors are willing to accept less, extend the maturity of the debt, or exchange debt for equity. The resulting improvement in cash flow may demonstrate to the satisfaction of the creditors that the going concern value of the firm is indeed much higher than liquidation or merger strategies. If management cannot reach agreement with the firm's creditors, it may seek protection under Chapter 11.

Holdout Problem

A voluntary settlement may be difficult to achieve because the debtor often needs the approval of all of its creditors. Smaller creditors sometimes have an incentive to attempt to hold up the agreement unless they receive special treatment. The situation may become untenable if there are a large number of small creditors. Consensus may be accomplished by paying all small creditors 100% of what they are owed and the larger creditors an agreed-on percentage. A preference on the part of certain institutions for debt rather than equity and inadequate access by creditors to the necessary information to enable them to value properly the equity they are being offered in a debt-for-equity swap also limit the use of voluntary agreements. Because of these factors, there is some evidence that firms that attempt to restructure outside of Chapter 11 bankruptcy have more difficulty in reducing their leverage than those that negotiate with creditors while under the protection of Chapter 11 (Gilson, 1997).

Prepackaged Bankruptcies

Prepackaged bankruptcies start with the failing firm negotiating with its creditors well in advance of filing for a Chapter 11 bankruptcy. Preferably, the failing company will have unanimous approval of the proposed reorganization plan before any formal filing is made. Because there is general approval of the plan before the filing, the formal Chapter 11 reorganization that follows generally averages only a few months and results in substantially lower legal and administrative expenses (Altman, 1993; Betker, 1995).

Voluntary and Involuntary Liquidations

The failing firm's management, shareholders, and creditors may agree that the firm is worth more in liquidation than in sale or as a continuing operation. All parties involved may believe that continued operation of the firm may cause the value of the firm's assets to deteriorate further. As noted earlier in this chapter, studies show that voluntary liquidations often result in significant returns to the shareholders of the failing firm. If management cannot reach agreement with its creditors on a private liquidation, the firm may seek to liquidate under Chapter 7 of the 1978 Bankruptcy Law. However, the expenses associated with the legal proceedings can result in the creditors receiving much less than with a voluntary liquidation and in the shareholders receiving nothing.

RETURNS TO FIRMS EMERGING FROM BANKRUPTCY

When firms emerge from bankruptcy, they often cancel the old stock and issue new common stock. Empirical studies show that firms emerging from bankruptcy often show very attractive returns to holders of the new stock in the period immediately following the announcement. Focusing on total cash flows generated by the firm, Alderson and Betker (1996) found that between 1983 and 1993, for 89 firms returns on average exceeded the returns on the S&P 500 index. These findings were supported in a study by Eberhart, Altman, and Aggarwal (1999) of 546 firms emerging from bankruptcy at various times between 1980 and 1993. They found that excess returns ranged from 24.6% to 138.8% depending on how they were measured during the 200 days after the firm's emergence from bankruptcy. They also found some evidence that the willingness of informed institutional investors such as banks to accept only equity in the new firm in exchange for debt contributes to the excess returns. The latter conclusion may reflect the willingness of the bankers with access to the necessary information about the firm's financial condition to significantly restructure debt and improve the firm's cash flow.

Despite the short-term favorable results, the long-term performance of these firms often deteriorates in terms of standard accounting measures such as operating profit. For a sample of firms emerging from bankruptcy between 1979 and 1988, Hotchkiss (1995) found that 40% of the firms studied continued to experience operating losses in the 3 years after emergence from Chapter 11. Almost one-third subsequently file for bankruptcy again or have to again restructure their debt.

THINGS TO REMEMBER

Divestitures, spin-offs, equity carve-outs, split-ups, and voluntary bust-ups are commonly used exit strategies to redeploy assets by returning cash or noncash assets through a special dividend to shareholders. Empirical studies show that these restructuring actions can have a highly favorable impact on shareholder returns. Abnormal returns for divestitures average about 1–2%; about 3–3.5% for equity carve-outs, spin-offs, and split-ups; and about 17% for bust-ups.

The motives for firms undertaking these strategies include a changing corporate strategy or a desire to exit underperforming businesses. Tax and regulatory considerations, a desire to reduce risk, abandoning the core business, discarding unwanted businesses from prior acquisitions, and avoiding conflicts with customers are also factors causing firms to restructure.

A divestiture is the sale of a portion of the firm to an outside party generally resulting in a cash infusion to the parent. Studies suggest that the more unrelated a business is to the parent's core business the more likely it is to be divested. Once a business has been determined to be nonstrategic, the decision to sell an operating unit can be reduced to simply comparing the division's after-tax "standalone" value less its operating liabilities with the after-tax proceeds of the sale value of the operation. If the after-tax sale value exceeds the equity value to the parent, the business should be sold.

Equity carve-outs tend to fall into two categories. The first category, the subsidiary equity carve-out, involves a parent selling a portion of the stock in a newly created, wholly owned subsidiary to the public. The second type, the split-off IPO, involves a transaction in which a privately held firm "splits-off" a portion of the stock of the consolidated entity and offers it to the general public. As is true with equity carve-outs, spin-offs entail the creation of a new legal entity. However, there is no cash infusion to the parent as these new shares are distributed, as a stock dividend, to the parent's current shareholders in direct proportion to their current holdings of the parent's stock. In a split-up, the entire company is broken up into a series of spin-offs or newly formed companies, whose shares are distributed to the parent firm's current shareholders as dividends. The parent ceases to exist.

Tracking or target stock transactions, also called letter stocks, are those in which a parent divides its operations into two or more operating units and assigns a common stock to each operation. The tracking stock is owned by the parent and not by the subsidiary. Voluntary liquidations or bust-ups reflect the judgment that the sale of individual parts of the firm could realize greater value than the value created by a continuation of the combined corporation.

A failing firm's strategic options are to merge with another firm, reach an out-of-court voluntary settlement with creditors, or file for Chapter 11 bankruptcy. The firm may liquidate voluntarily as part of an out-of-court settlement or may be forced by its creditors to liquidate. The choice of which option to pursue depends on which provides the greatest present value for creditors and shareholders. A technically insolvent firm is unable to pay its liabilities as they come due; a legally insolvent firm is one in which the firm's liabilities exceed the fair market value of its assets. The firm is not bankrupt or in bankruptcy until a petition for bankruptcy is filed in the federal bankruptcy court. A failing firm or its creditors may file a bankruptcy petition. Once filed, the bankruptcy procedures normally involve a reorganization, debt restructuring, or liquidation. A reorganization in bankruptcy is a business plan, which, if acceptable to the court, creditors, and shareholders, allows the failing firm to continue to operate. Before the firm is able to emerge from bankruptcy, the firm's debt usually is restructured with creditors granting concessions that will lower an insolvent firm's payments so that it may remain in business. Finally, liquidation involves closing the firm, selling its assets, and distributing the proceeds to its creditors and owners. There is usually nothing left for common shareholders.

CHAPTER DISCUSSION QUESTIONS

13-1.   How do tax and regulatory considerations influence the decision to exit a business?

13-2.   How would you decide when to sell a business?

13-3.   What are the major differences between a spin-off and an equity carve-out?

13-4.   Under what conditions is a spin-off tax free to shareholders?

13-5.   Why would a firm decide to voluntarily split up?

13-6.   What are the advantages and disadvantages of tracking or target stocks to investors and to the firm?

13-7.   What factors contribute to the high positive abnormal returns to shareholders before the announcement of a voluntary bust-up?

13-8. What are the primary factors contributing to business failure?

13-9. Why would creditors make concessions to a failing firm?

13-10. What are the primary options available to a failing firm? What criteria might the firm use to select a particular option?

CHAPTER BUSINESS CASE

CASE STUDY 13-9: ALLEGHENY TELEDYNE RESTRUCTURES

Allegheny Teledyne is the creation of the 1996 merger of Allegheny Ludlum Corporation and Teledyne Inc. In 1999, Allegheny Teledyne Inc. reconfigured its operations by creating a new independent company to be spun off to its shareholders. The new company would comprise four former Teledyne units in aerospace and electronics. Combined 1998 revenues of these businesses were approximately $800 million. The intent is to focus the new company on its high-technology competencies and markets in software and engineering systems, communication and electronics, and aircraft engines and components.

Allegheny Teledyne simultaneously is considering a spin-off and public offering of its consumer segment into a standalone public company. Its 1998 revenues were $250 million. Allegheny Teledyne received approval for the proposed tax-free spin-offs of its aerospace and electronics and consumer products business from the IRS. After the spin-offs, Allegheny Teledyne had six operating units. These units included a specialty metals, stainless steel, and flat-rolled producer; a producer of nickel-based super-alloy and titanium alloy products; a producer of zirconium, titanium, niobium, and tantalum; a tungsten mill products and tungsten carbide cutting tools manufacturer; a foundry for large gray and ductile iron castings; and a custom impression die forging company. These businesses, which are Allegheny Teledyne's highest margin operations, had 1998 annual sales of $2.5 billion. Allegheny Teledyne also is exploring selling Ryan Aeronautical, Fluid Systems, and Specialty Equipment, which had combined 1998 revenues of $400 million.

Once all this restructuring has been completed, stockholders would own common stock in each of three distinct companies, each with a clear business focus and the financial ability to pursue individual strategic growth objectives. Although Richard P. Simmons will remain as chair, the Allegheny Teledyne board announced that they would begin looking for his successor as chief executive officer.

Case Study Discussion Questions

1. What are some of the reasons that Allegheny Teledyne considered such an extensive restructuring of its operations?

2. What synergies might there be in the businesses that Allegheny Teledyne is retaining?

3. Why do you think that stockholders might be better off owning stock in each of the three new companies (consumer products, aerospace and

electronics, and metals manufacturing) than just in Allegheny Teledyne Inc.?

4. Why might Allegheny Teledyne be considering spinning off some units and divesting others?

5. Why might it be common for a major restructuring to come at a time when the head of a company is leaving, retiring, or assuming fewer responsibilities?

Solutions to these questions are found in the Appendix at the end of this book.

CHAPTER BUSINESS CASE

CASE STUDY 13-10: AT&T—A POSTER CHILD FOR RESTRUCTURING GONE AWRY

Between 1984 and 2000, AT&T underwent four major restructuring programs. These included the government mandated breakup in 1984, the 1996 effort to eliminate customer conflicts, the 1998 plan to become a broadband powerhouse, and the most recent restructuring program announced in 2000 to correct past mistakes. It is difficult to identify another major corporation that has undergone as much sustained trauma as AT&T.

The 1984 Restructure: Changed the Organization But Not the Culture

The genesis of Ma Bell's problems may have begun with the consent decree signed with the Department of Justice in 1984, which resulted in the spin-off of its local telephone operations to its shareholders. These included Pacific Telesis Group (Pac Tel), Southwestern Bell, Ameritech, Nynex, Bell Atlantic, U.S. West, and Bell South. AT&T retained its long-distance and telecommunications equipment manufacturing operations. Although the breadth of the firm's product offering was changed dramatically, little else seems to have changed. The firm remained highly bureaucratic, risk averse, and inward looking. Decision making remained painfully slow. However, substantial market share in the lucrative long-distance market continued to generate huge cash flow for the company, thereby enabling the company to be slow to react to the changing competitive dynamics of the marketplace.

The 1996 Restructure: Lack of a Coherent Strategy

Cash accumulated from the long-distance business was spent on a variety of ill-conceived strategies such as the firm's foray into the personal computer business. After years of unsuccessfully attempting to redefine the company's strategy, AT&T once again resorted to a major restructure of the firm. In 1996, AT&T spun-off Lucent Technologies (its telecommunications equipment business) and NCR (a computer services business) to shareholders to facilitate Lucent equipment sales to former AT&T operations and eliminate the noncore NCR computer business. However, this had little sustained impact on the AT&T share price.

The 1998 Restructure: Vision Exceeds Ability to Execute

In its third major restructure since 1984, AT&T CEO Michael Armstrong passionately unveiled in June of 1998 a daring strategy to remake AT&T from what was a struggling long-distance telephone company into a broadband Internet access and local phone services company. To accomplish this end, he outlined his intentions to acquire cable companies MediaOne Group and Telecommunications Inc. for $58 billion and $48 billion, respectively. The plan was to use cable-TV networks to deliver the first fully integrated package of broadband Internet access and local phone service via the cable-TV network.

AT&T Could Not Handle Its Early Success

During the next several years, Armstrong seemed to be up to the task, cutting sales, general, and administrative expense's share of revenue from 28% to 20%, giving AT&T a cost structure comparable to its competitors. He attempted to change the largely bureaucratic culture to one able to effectively compete in the deregulated environment of the post-1996 Telecommunications Act by issuing stock options to all employees, tying compensation to performance, and reducing layers of managers. He used AT&T's stock to buy the cable companies before the decline in AT&T's long-distance business pushed the stock into a free fall. He also transformed AT&T Wireless from a collection of local businesses into a national digital business.

Notwithstanding these achievements, AT&T experienced major missteps. Employee turnover became a big problem, especially at the top. Business Services has had four CEOs in the preceding 3 and a half years, and AT&T's other three major businesses each lost at least one CEO between 1998 and 2000. Armstrong also bought Telecommunications and MediaOne when valuations for cable-television assets were near their peak. He paid about $106 billion in 2000, when they were worth about $80 billion. His failure to cut enough deals with other cable operators (e.g., Time Warner) to sell AT&T's local phone service meant that AT&T could market its services only in regional markets rather than on a national basis. In addition, AT&T moved large corporate customers to its Concert joint venture with British Telecom, alienating many AT&T salespeople, who subsequently quit. As a result, customer service deteriorated rapidly and major customers defected. Finally, Armstrong seriously underestimated the pace of erosion in AT&T's long-distance revenue base.

AT&T May Have Become Overwhelmed by the Rate of Change

What happened? Perhaps AT&T fell victim to the same problems many other acquisitive companies have. AT&T is a company capable of great strategic vision but seemingly incapable of great strategic execution. Effective execution involves buying or building assets at a reasonable cost. Its substantial overpayment for its cable acquisitions meant that it would be unable to earn the returns required by investors in what they would consider a reasonable time period.

Moreover, Armstrong's efforts to shift from the firm's historical business by buying into the cable-TV business through acquisition has saddled the firm with a crushing $62 billion in debt.

AT&T tried to do too much too quickly. New initiatives such as high-speed Internet access and local telephone services over cable-television network are still too small to pick up the slack. Much time and energy seems to have gone into planning and acquiring what were viewed as key building blocks to the strategy. However, there appears to have been insufficient focus and realism in terms of the time and resources required to make all the pieces of the strategy fit together. Some parts of the overall strategy were at odds with other parts. For example, AT&T undercut its core long-distance wired telephone business by offers of free long-distance wireless to attract new subscribers. Despite aggressive efforts to change the culture, AT&T continued to suffer from a culture that evolved in the years before 1996 during which the industry was heavily regulated. That atmosphere bred a culture based on consensus building, ponderously slow decision making, and a low tolerance for risk. Consequently, the AT&T culture was unprepared for the fiercely competitive deregulated environment of the late 1990s (Truitt, 2001).

Furthermore, AT&T created individual tracking stocks for AT&T Wireless and for Liberty Media. The intention of the tracking stocks was to link the unit's stock to its individual performance, create a currency for the unit to make acquisitions, and provide a new means of motivating the unit's management by giving them stock in their own operation. Unlike a spin-off, AT&T's board continued to exert direct control over these units. In an IPO in April 2000, AT&T sold 14% of AT&T's Wireless stock to the public to raise funds and to focus investor attention on the true value of the Wireless operations.

Investors Lose Patience

Like many firms that undertake broadbased restructuring efforts, AT&T may have confused frenetic activity with substantive change. Although all of these actions created a sense that grandiose change was imminent, investor patience was wearing thin. Profitability foundered. The market share loss in its long-distance business accelerated. Although cash flow remained strong, it was clear that a cash machine so dependent on the deteriorating long-distance telephone business soon could grind to a halt. Although Armstrong's vision was still a possibility, it was increasingly unclear when it might be realized. Investors' loss of faith was manifested in the precipitous decline in AT&T stock that occurred in 2000.

The 2000 Restructure: Correcting the Mistakes of the Past

Pushed by investor impatience and a growing realization that achieving AT&T's vision would be more time and resource consuming than originally believed, Armstrong announced on October 25, 2000, the breakup of the business for the fourth time. The news rocked Wall Street. The plan involved the creation of four new independent companies including AT&T Wireless, AT&T Consumer, AT&T Broadband, and Liberty Media.

By breaking the company into specific segments, AT&T believed that individual units could operate more efficiently and aggressively. AT&T's consumer long-distance business would be able to enter the digital subscriber line (DSL) market. DSL is a broadband technology based on the telephone wires that connect individual homes with the telephone network. AT&T's cable operations could continue to sell their own fast Internet connections and compete directly against AT&T's long-distance telephone business. Moreover, the four individual businesses would create "pure-play" investor opportunities. Specifically, AT&T proposed the following:

- Spin off in early 2001 AT&T Wireless to shareholders in exchange for Wireless tracking stock.
- Issue tracking stocks[1] to the public in late 2001 for

    —AT&T Consumer operations, including long-distance and Worldnet Internet service and

    —AT&T Broadband (cable) operations. The tracking shares would at a later date be converted to regular AT&T common shares as if issued by AT&T Broadband, making it an independent entity.[2]

- Convert AT&T Liberty Media tracking stock to Liberty Media common and issue to holders of Liberty Media tracking stock, thereby making it an independent entity.
- Retain AT&T Business Services (i.e., AT&T Lab and telecommunications network) with the surviving AT&T entity.

Investor reaction was swift and negative. Investors were not swayed by the proposal because the stock dropped 13% in 1 day—to 23 3/8 the day the restructuring was announced. Moreover, it ended 2000 at 17, down 66% from the beginning of the year. (*Business Week*, February 5, 2000).

The Proposed Restructure Triggers Immediate Hurdles

One of the most immediate challenges that had to be overcome before the restructure could be implemented was how to resolve differences among the four new businesses. The management of AT&T Wireless was upset because AT&T Business Services wanted exclusive rights to use the AT&T brand in marketing to corporations. Wireless wanted to use the brand in selling its high-speed data services to companies. The concern was that customers might become confused

---

[1] Unlike spin-offs, for the issuance of tracking stocks to shareholders to be considered tax free, the IRS does not require the parent and the subsidiary to have been engaged in business for at least 5 years before the spin-off and that the subsidiary is at least 80% owned by the parent. Stock issued by the AT&T cable operations may not have qualified for a tax-free spin-off at the time the restructure was announced because it had been created through a series of acquisitions during the late 1990s.

[2] Unlike spin-offs, tracking stocks are considered common stock issued by the parent on behalf of the subsidiary. To remove such shares from AT&T's books, they must be converted to Liberty Media common by exchanging the new shares for the Liberty Media tracking stock.

if the two units used the same brand to sell to the same market. The issue finally was resolved by allowing Wireless to use the AT&T brand to sell some data services to businesses with 10 or fewer phone lines in no more than three locations.

Immediately following the announcement, the Communications Workers of America (CWA) attacked the proposed breakup expressing concern about the job security and other compensation-related issues. The union contended that the breakup proposal must achieve two-thirds approval from AT&T's shareholders before it could be enacted. In contrast, AT&T's management insisted that it was only one-half. If the unions were proved right in the courts, Armstrong ran the risk of not being able to get approval for his proposal. In early 2001, AT&T announced that it had reached agreement with the CWA to withdraw a lawsuit aimed at impeding the company's plan to break itself into four companies in exchange for certain labor guarantees.

It was also unclear whether Wireless could make the necessary investments as an independent entity to compete effectively in the wireless telecommunications market. A slump in wireless stocks had hampered Wireless's ability to raise funds needed to make its network more competitive. Japanese mobile phone giant NTT DoCoMo Inc. was unwilling to make an investment as long as AT&T Wireless was part of AT&T. DoCoMo wanted to make the investment as a means of entering the U.S. market through minority investments in domestic wireless carriers. With the announcement of the restructuring, DoCoMo agreed to invest $9.8 billion in AT&T Wireless in late November 2000, enabling the business to rebuild its network with new technology, expand overseas, and buy crucial radio spectrum. There was also concern that the postrestructure AT&T would be unable to service the debt remaining on its books, even after a significant amount had been reallocated to the entities that were to be spun off. In early November, reassured asset sales would keep AT&T's debt load manageable, bankers indicated that AT&T could borrow the $15 billion in short-term capital needed to finance the restructuring.

AT&T Wireless Is Spun Off

On July 10, 2001, AT&T Wireless Services became an independent company, in accordance with plans announced during the 2000 restructure program. Wireless is one of six wireless companies with a nationwide network in the United States. AT&T Wireless became a separate company when AT&T converted the tracking shares of the mobile-phone business into common stock and distributed 1.14 billion shares, valued at $19.6 billion. AT&T shareholders were offered a premium of 6.5% to exchange their AT&T shares for shares in AT&T Wireless. Each AT&T shareholder was offered 1.176 shares of AT&T Wireless Group tracking stock for each share of AT&T stock. The exchange ratio represents a 6.5% premium over AT&T's closing price as of April 18, 2000.

AT&T retained 7% of AT&T Wireless, valued at $3 billion. It intends to sell that stake to raise funds to reduce its outstanding debt. AT&T Wireless shares have fallen 44% since AT&T first sold the tracking stock in April 2000 for $29.50 per share, raising 10.6 billion in the then largest-ever U.S. IPO. AT&T Wireless intends to expand through further partnerships with foreign carriers. DoCoMo owns 16% of the company. The DoCoMo investment prevents AT&T Wireless from selling a 17–49% stake to another partner, but it does not preclude a sale of the entire company.

Is It Personal Between Malone and Armstrong?

On August 10, 2001, AT&T spun off Liberty Media Corporation, the television programming unit headed by John C. Malone. As a former AT&T board member, Malone had long been a critic of AT&T CEO Michael C. Armstrong. Malone became an AT&T board member when AT&T acquired Telecommunications Inc. (TCI) for which Malone had been the CEO. As a major TCI shareholder, Malone had received AT&T stock valued at several billion dollars. Malone has never forgiven Armstrong for the loss of more than $1 billion in the value of his shares in AT&T during Armstrong's tenure as AT&T CEO (*Business Week*, August 27, 2001).

AT&T's Future Prospects

In mid-July 2001, Comcast Corp. offered to acquire AT&T's cable operations for $41.3 billion. Armstrong and the AT&T board rejected the offer as inadequate. Other potential suitors such as Disney and AOL Time Warner showed immediate interest. After extended discussions, AT&T agreed on December 21, 2001 to merge its broadband unit with Comcast to create the largest cable television and high-speed Internet service company in the United States. The new company, to be called AT&T Comcast Corp, will have 22 million subscribers and a presence in 17 of the 20 largest U.S. cities. The shareholders of both AT&T and Comcast approved the $27 billion deal in July 2002.

Without the future growth engine offered by Broadband and Wireless, AT&T's remaining long-distance businesses and business services operations appear to have limited growth prospects. After a decade of tumultuous change, AT&T appears to be back where it was at the beginning of the 1990s. In 2002, AT&T entered into discussions with BellSouth for a possible merger of equals. However, with the sale of its broadband unit, it will have a market value of about $30 billion to $40 billion as compared with BellSouth's nearly $80 billion. A deal with BellSouth would reunite AT&T with a piece of the old Bell system, which it had spun off in the 1984 court-ordered breakup. The 1996 Telecom Act bars BellSouth from owning large stakes in cable. This is one reason why AT&T had to get rid of its cable business. The deal makes strategic sense for both parties because neither has the scale to compete with Verizon and SBC. Moreover, the transaction would catapult BellSouth to the forefront of the long-distance business.

Case Study Discussion Questions

1. What were the primary factors contributing to AT&T's numerous restructuring efforts since 1984? How did they differ? How were they similar?

2. Why do you believe that AT&T chose to spin off its wireless operations rather than to divest the unit? What might you have done differently?

3. Was AT&T proactive or reactive in initiating its 2000 restructuring program? Explain your answer.

4. Do you believe that AT&T overpaid for many of its largest acquisitions made during the 1990s? How might this have contributed to its subsequent restructuring efforts?

5. What challenges did AT&T face in trying to split up the company in 2000? What might you have done differently to overcome these obstacles?

REFERENCES

Alderson, Michael J. and Brian L. Betker, "Assessing Post-Bankruptcy Performance: An Analysis of Reorganized Firms' Cash Flows," Working Paper, Saint Louis University, 1996.

Alexander, Gordon J., George Benson, and Joan M. Kampmeyer, "Investigating the Valuation Effects Announcements on Valuing Corporate Sell-Offs," *Journal of Finance*, 39, June 1984, pp. 503–517.

Allen, Jeffrey and John J. McConnell, "Equity Carve Outs and Managerial Discretion," *Journal of Finance*, 53 (1), February 1998, pp. 163–186.

Altman, E. I., *Corporate Financial Distress and Bankruptcy* (2nd ed.), New York: John Wiley & Sons, 1993.

Annema, Andre, William C. Fallon, and Marc H. Goedhart, "When Carve-Outs Make Sense," *The McKinsey Quarterly*, 2, 2002.

Ball, M., "How A Spin-Off Could Lift Your Share Value," *Corporate Finance*, May 1997, pp. 23–29.

Betker, B., "An Empirical Examination of Prepackaged Bankruptcy," *Financial Management*, Spring 1995, pp. 3–18.

Billett, Matthew T., "Long-Term Returns from Tracking Stocks," *Social Science Research Network*, Working Paper Series, June 27, 2000.

Bloomberg News, "A Record Year for Business Bankruptcies," February 4, 2002, www.bloomberg.com.

Boot, Arnoud W. A., "Why Hang on to Losers? Divestitures and Takeovers," *Journal of Finance*, 47 (4), December 1992, pp. 1401–1423.

Burkhart, Mike, Denis Gromb, and Fausto Panunzi, "Larger Shareholders, Monitoring and the Value of the Firm," *Quarterly Journal of Economics*, 1997, pp. 693–728.

Business Week, "Gillette Slims Down," November 8, 1999a, p. 86.

Business Week, "Armstrong's Last Stand," February 5, 2000, pp. 88–92.

Business Week, "Chapter 11 Never Looked So Good," March 20, 2000, p. 44.

Business Week, "A Spin-Off with a Hangover," August 27, 2001, p. 50.

Business Week, "Enron: Running on Empty," December 10, 2001, pp. 80–82.

Business Week, "The Fall of Enron," December 17, 2001, pp. 30–34.

Byers, Steven S., D. Scott Lee, and Tim C. Opler, "Equity Carve-Outs and Management Change," Idaho State University Working Paper, 1996.

Cho, Myeong-Hyeon and Mark A. Cohen, "The Economic Causes and Consequences of Corporate Divestiture," *Managerial and Decision Economics*, 18, August 1997, pp. 367–374.

Clark, Kent and Eli Ofek, "Mergers as a Means of Restructuring Distressed Firms: An Empirical Investigation," *Journal of Financial and Quantitative Analysis*, 29, December 1994, pp. 541–565.

Cusatis, Patrick J., James A. Miles, and J. Randall Woolridge, "Restructuring Through Spin-Offs," *Journal of Financial Economics*, 33, 1993, pp. 293–311.

Dallas Morning News, "Enron Facing Lights Out," November 30, 2001, Business Section, p. 1.

Daley, Lane, Vikas Mehrotra, and Ranjini Sivakumar, "Corporate Focus and Value Creation, Evidence from Spin-Offs," *Journal of Financial Economics*, 45, 1997, pp. 257–281.

Desai, Hermang and Prem Jain, "Firm Performance and Focus: Long-Run Stock Market Performance Following Spin-Offs," *Journal of Financial Economics*, 54, 1999, pp. 75–101.

Dun & Bradstreet Corporation, New York, *Business Failure Record*, 1997.

Eberhart, Allan C., Edward I. Altman, and Reena Aggarwal, "The Equity Performance of Firms Emerging from Bankruptcy," *Journal of Finance*, 54 (5), October 1999.

Erwin, Gayle R. and John J. McConnell, "To Live or Die? An Empirical Analysis of Piecemeal Voluntary Liquidations," *Journal of Corporate Finance*, 3 (4), December 1997, pp. 325–354.

Fleming, Michael J. and John J. Moon, "Preserving Firm Value through Exit: The Case of Voluntary Liquidations," Federal Reserve Bank of New York, *Staff Reports*, 8, December 1995.

Garsten, Ed, "GM to Sell Hughes Subsidiary," *Associated Press, Orange County Register*, Business Section, October 30, 2001, p. 2.

Gillette Corporation, "Restructuring to Improve Performance," Press Release, October 21, 1999.

Gilson, Stuart, "Transactions Costs and Capital Structure Choice: Evidence from Financially Distressed Firms," *Journal of Finance*, 52 (1), March 1997, pp. 161–196.

Hand, John R. and Terrance R. Skantz, "Market Timing Through Equity Carve-Outs," University of North Carolina Working Paper, 1997.

Hite, Gailen and James E. Owers, "Security Price Reactions around Corporate Spin-Off Announcements," *Journal of Financial Economics*, 12, 1983, pp. 409–436.

Hite, Gailen, James Owers, and Ronald Rogers, "The Market for Inter-Firm Asset Sales: Partial Sell-Offs and Total Liquidations," *Journal of Financial Economics*, 18, June 1987, pp. 229–252.

Hotchkiss, Edith S., "The Post-Emergence Performance of Firms Emerging from Chapter 11," *Journal of Finance*, 50, 1995, pp. 3–21.

Jain, Prem C., "The Effects of Voluntary Sell-Off Announcements on Shareholder Wealth," *Journal of Finance*, 40, March 1985, pp. 209–224.

John, Kose and Eli Ofek, "Asset Sales and Increase in Focus," *Journal of Financial Economics*, 37 (1), January 1995, pp. 105–126.

J.P. Morgan, "Monitoring Spin-Off Performance," *Morgan Markets*, New York, June 6, 1995.

J.P. Morgan, "Monitoring Spin-Off Performances," *Morgan Markets*, New York, August 20, 1999.

Kang, Jun-Koo and Anil Shivdasani, "Corporate Restructuring During Performance Declines in Japan," *Journal of Financial Economics*, 46, October 1997, pp. 29–65.

Kaplan, Steven N. and Michael S. Weisbach, "The Success of Acquisitions: Evidence from Divestitures," *Journal of Finance*, 47 (1), March 1992, pp. 107–138.

Kim, E. Han and Hohn Schatzberg, "Voluntary Corporate Liquidations," *Journal of Financial Economics*, 19 (2), December 1987, pp. 311–328.

Klein, A., "The Timing and Substance of Divestiture Announcements: Individual, Simultaneous and Cumulative Effects," *Journal of Finance*, 41, 1986, pp. 685–697.

Krishnaswami, Sudha and Venkat Subramaniam, "Information Asymmetry, Valuation and the Corporate Spin-off Decision," *Journal of Financial Economics*, 53 (1), July 1999, pp. 73–112.

Lang, Larry, Annette Poulsen, and Rene Stulz, "Asset Sales, Firm Performance, and the Agency Costs of Managerial Discretion," *Journal of Financial Economics*, 37 (1), January 1995, pp. 3–37.

Linn, Scott C. and Michael S. Rozeff, "The Corporate Sell-Off," *Midland Corporate Finance Journal*, 2, Summer 1984, pp. 17–26.

Logue, Dennis E., James K. Seward, and James W. Walsh, "Rearranging Residual Claims: A Case for Targeted Stock," *Financial Management*, 25 (1), Spring 1996, pp. 43–61.

Loh, Charmen, Jennifer Russell Bezjak, and Harrison Toms, "Voluntary Corporate Divestitures as an Anti-Takeover Mechanism," *The Financial Review*, 30 (1), February 1995, pp. 21–24.

Maksimovic, Vojislav and Gordon M. Phillips, "The Market for Corporate Assets: Who Engages in Mergers and Assets Sales and Are There Efficiency Gains?," *Journal of Finance*, December 2001, p. 27.

Matthews, Robert Guy, "USX to Spit U.S. Steel and Marathon Oil," *Wall Street Journal*, April 25, 2001, Section C, p. 2.

McConnell, John J., Mehmet Ozbilgin, and Sunil Wahal, "Spin-Offs: Ex Ante," *The Journal of Business*, 74 (2), April 2001, pp. 245–280.

McKinsey & Co., "Spin-Offs May Overshadow Other Investments," *Business Week*, December 13, 1999, pp. 196–197.

Michaely, Roni and Wayne H. Shaw, "The Choice of Going Public: Spin-Offs vs. Carve-Outs," *Financial Management*, 24 (3), Autumn 1995, pp. 15–21.

Miles, James and James Rosenfeld, "An Empirical Analysis of the Effects of Spin-Off Announcements on Shareholder Wealth," *Journal of Finance*, 38 (5), December 1983, pp. 15–28.

Mulherin, J. Haarold and Audra L. Boone, "Comparing Acquisitions and Divestitures," *Social Science Research Network*, Working Paper Series, April 19, 2000, p. 38.

Oppenheimer & Company, "The Sum of the Parts," New York: January 14, 1981.

Orange County Register, "Baxter to Exit Heart Care Unit" July 13, 1999, Business Section, p. 2.

Orange County Register, "PG&E Seeks Bankruptcy," Business Section, April 7, 2001, p. 1.

Orange County Register, "Davis' High-Voltage Recession is Coming," Editorial, October 2, 2001, p. 6.

Petty, J. William, Arthur J. Keown, David F. Scott, Jr., and John D. Martin, *Basic Financial Management* (6th ed.), Englewood Cliffs, NJ: Prentice-Hall, 1993, p. 798.

Powers, Eric A., "Spinoffs, Selloffs, and Equity Carveouts: An Analysis of Divestiture Method Choice," *Social Science Research Network*, Working Paper Series, January 2001, pp. 2–4.

Rajan, Raghuram, Henri Servaes, and Luigi Zingales, "The Cost of Diversity: The Diversification Discount and Inefficient Investment," *Journal of Finance*, 55, 2000, pp. 35–38.

Ravenscroft, D.J. and F. M. Scherer, "Divisional Sell-Off: A Hazard Function Analysis," *Managerial and Decision Economics*, 12, 1991, pp. 429–438.

Scharfstein, David and Jeremy Stein, "The Dark Side of Internal Capital Markets: Divisional Rent-Seeking and Inefficient Investment" *Journal of Finance*, LV (6), 2000, pp. 128–145.

Scherreik, Susan, "Gems Among the Trash," *Business Week*, April 15, 2002, p. 112–113.

Schipper, Katherine and Abbie Smith, "Effects of Re-Contracting on Shareholder Wealth," *Journal of Financial Economics*, 12, 1983, pp. 437–467.

Schipper, Katherine and Abbie Smith, "A Comparison of Equity Carve-Outs and Equity Offerings: Share Price Effects and Corporate Restructuring," *Journal of Financial Economics*, 15, 1986, pp. 153–186.

Schlingemann, Frederik P., Rene M. Stulz, and Ralph A. Walkling, "Divestitures and The Liquidity of the Market for Corporate Assets," *Journal of Financial Economics*, 64 (1), 2002.

Shadid, Anthony, "Hughes Good Offense is No Defense," *Boston Globe*, February 4, 2001, Business Section, p. 2.

Skantz, Terrance and Roberto Marchesini, "The Effect of Voluntary Corporate Liquidation on Shareholder Wealth," *Journal of Financial Research*, 10, Spring 1987, pp. 65–75.

Solomon, Deborah, "AT&T Prepares Its Cable-Access Program," *Wall Street Journal*, June 6, 2001, p. C1.

Truitt, Wesley B., Business Planning: A Comprehensive Framework and Process, Greenwood Publishing, October 30, 2001, p. 183.

U.S. Small Business Administration, " Financial Difficulties of Small Businesses and Reasons for Their Failure," Office of Advocacy, RS 188, March 1999.

Vijh, Anand M., "Long-Term Returns from Equity Carveouts," *Journal of Financial Economics*, 51, 1999, pp. 273–308.

Vroom, Harald Janssens de and Ruud van Frederikslust, "Shareholder Wealth Effects of Corporate Spinoffs: The Worldwide Experience 1990–1998," *SSRN Working Paper Series*, August 9, 1999.

Wall Street Journal, "Baxter Spins Off Heart Care Business," July 13, 1999a.

Wall Street Journal, "UPS Goes Public," November 10, 1999b.

Weil, Roman L., "Fundamental Causes of the Accounting Debacle at Enron: Show Me Where It Says I Can't," Testimony before the U.S. House of Representatives Committee on Energy and Commerce, February 6, 2002.

PART

V

PUTTING IT ALL
TOGETHER

14

THE ACQUISITION PROCESS

THE GEE WHIZ MEDIA CASE

"I am not afraid to die. I just don't want to be there when it happens."

—*Woody Allen*

PART I: PLANNING

THE DREAM

Like most start-up companies, Gee Whiz Media (GWM) was the product of the visionary zeal of its founder Dan Durand. Dan had a longstanding reputation in the local technology community of being a gifted visionary who put a premium on honesty. In the industry, he was known for his integrity in his relationships with employees, customers, and suppliers. This reputation had come from several successful start-ups he had taken public in the 1980s. He found that this was a particularly good way to do business because those with whom he dealt generally were willing to accept his word at face value. This reputation was to serve him well in his next venture.

In the late 1980s, an emerging technology called multimedia caught Dan's imagination. CD-ROMs were one of the few media with the capacity to store such diverse types of information as sound, video, and text. As PCs became commonplace, Dan believed that CD-ROMs would revolutionize in-home entertainment by allowing users to interact easily with the new media. Dan convinced the owner of a local retail computer store to provide space for him to demonstrate the wonders of multimedia. He reasoned that if consumers saw that computers didn't need to be boring, they might buy a complete system including a CD-ROM drive, speakers, and graphics programs. Dan would get a percentage of the sale. Thus, GWM was born.

For several years, Dan evangelized about the virtues of multimedia. However, the pace of acceptance was painfully slow. To energize the growth of multimedia usage, Dan convinced Apple, IBM, Sony, and others to fund his efforts to promote their multimedia technologies. To accommodate additional employees and to gain access to a larger demo area, Gee Whiz Media moved out of the computer retail store and into a small, nearby office park early in 1992. IBM and the others paid Dan from $5000 to $15,000 per month to provide all-day seminars in a small auditorium inside GWM's offices.

With a small staff and increasing revenues, Dan had the perfect niche, promoting multimedia technology applications. They were professional evangelists. They were succeeding. Dan knew that this success was likely to be fleeting, however. As CD-ROMs loaded with multimedia applications were becoming common, the need for GWM as a promotion company would end. Dan knew that just to stay in business he had to change with the industry. His dream that multimedia CD-ROMs would become the mainstay of the interactive home entertainment media and the reference manuals of the future appeared to be coming true. To survive, however, he had to find a new niche.

BUILDING THE BUSINESS PLAN

Dan and his staff of nine met in his home to redefine their place in the multimedia industry. Together, they attempted to summarize the competitive dynamics underlying the multimedia industry. Early pioneers in the industry viewed it as electronic publishing, the conversion of text, video, and music to an electronic medium. Major segments included entertainment (e.g., music videos), games, sports, education, hobbies, "how-to" or training manuals, and career development applications. Game applications proved to be a hit and demonstrated that there was demand for the right content. A game named "Myst" had just been introduced. Players moved through a fantasy-land by clicking a mouse and solving a series of intricate puzzles along the way. "Myst" was doing phenomenally well, and it eventually would sell nearly 1 million copies. Reference CD-ROMs, Dan reasoned, might do even better because they were reusable and beautiful.

More and more small companies were entering the industry. Few resources were required other than the knowledge to develop the requisite software and the creativity to develop exciting content or the rights to use existing content. No one company as of yet dominated the industry, but Dan knew that it was just a matter of time. Although CD-ROMs held great promise, the risk was still great. CD-ROM drives were in less than 30% of personal computers. In the early 1990s, CD-ROM technology was still in its infancy. Video appeared very erratic rather than seamless like the big-screen movie. The format held unlimited promise, however. CD-ROMs could store 600 times more information than a 3-inch square diskette and could be read optically with lasers like a compact disc. Durand saw CD-ROMs as modern encyclopedias, where information could be retrieved by a click of the mouse rather than by flipping pages. Moreover, instead of just text and pictures, a multimedia reference guide could have movies and music.

Several days of brainstorming caused Dan and his staff to agree that they could emulate Myst's success with the right kind of content. They chose to focus on the music entertainment segment because they saw it as large and growing and subject to less intense competition than the game segment. GWM proposed to apply multimedia technology to famous artists in the music industry. Viewers would move through buildings, clicking on objects such as guitars and sheet music that would serve as gateways to a biography of the artist, the lyrics to his songs, and his filmed interviews. None, however, would be labeled. Rather than having a menu or an index, the disk would abandon the traditional, narrative look. Symbols that represent the artist would be used as interactive icons and transitions.

Dan's dream for GWM was to put a well-known artist on a CD-ROM and make it into a nationally recognized brand name. This, he thought, would move GWM from a narrow niche player into a national brand name in the CD-ROM business. It could be an Activision, a Broderbund, or maybe even a Microsoft. After some honest soul searching, Dan and his staff quickly realized that, although they did have an exciting vision and some highly talented technical people and artists on staff, they lacked access to proprietary content, advertising, and a distribution channel to get the CD-ROM to market. Converting the dream to reality was going to take a lot of hard work and money.

Although they had decided on a niche, Dan knew that the challenges would be great. They did have significant brand recognition in this narrow market segment because they were the first to target this market with a unique product on a relatively new medium, CD-ROMs. They also would benefit at least in the short run from the royalty arrangements they had with Apple and others, which would provide some cash-flow stability. Moreover, they were highly motivated by the prospect of dominating a new market and eventually striking it rich by selling to a strategic buyer or by offering stock to the public.

Dan was a realist. He knew that most of these advantages would be temporary. He understood that they had very little leverage in bargaining with customers or suppliers, particularly content owners. Although individuals would be the final consumer of their products, their immediate customers were larger retailers (e.g., Wal-Mart and Bests and software distributors such as CompUSA). GWM was largely at the mercy of retailers who would give those products the greatest exposure on their shelves. The core of GWM's business was an idea that could be copied readily because there were few hurdles preventing others from entering the business, including brassy start-ups as well as the firm's own customers and even suppliers (Figure 14-1).

ANALYZING OPTIONS

Dan decided to address the content issue first. His options were limited by the lack of funds. He could develop the content internally and then pay a license fee

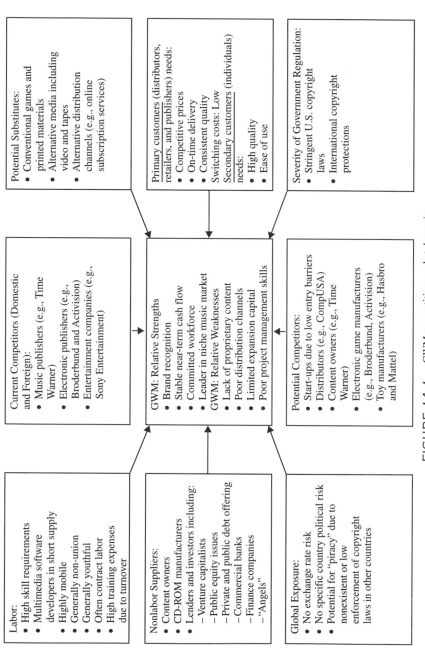

FIGURE 14-1. GWM competitive market dynamics.

to use the artist's name. He realized that this would require substantial time and effort to hire the right talent and negotiate a license arrangement. He thought he could solve this problem and also his concerns about the lack of a cost-effective distribution channel by directly contacting major music publishing companies. Such companies frequently owned the rights to certain music libraries, were in a position to convince the artist to promote the CD-ROM, and had the financial wherewithal to aggressively advertise the product.

GWM was continuing to receive significant fee income from the multiyear contracts it had signed with Apple, IBM, Sony, and others to promote their multimedia products, but this was insufficient to fund GWM's move into the electronic publishing business. Dan, the consummate salesman, was able to get sufficient additional funding through an initial public offering of the company's stock in mid-1993. The timing was right for new technology companies coming to market. Moreover, GWM was one of the few that were profitable as a result of its multi-year fee-based contracts. By late 1993, GWM had introduced several CD-ROMs. The acceptance of the new music CD-ROMs showed great promise. Sales exploded— they more than doubled between 1993 and 1995. Revenue and net income reached $21 million and $450,000, respectively, in 1995.

Emboldened by this success, Dan and his staff worked feverishly to flesh out GWM's business expansion strategy. The essence of GWM's business plan was to grow through the rapid introduction of high-quality multimedia disks targeted at relatively narrow market segments. Dan was ready to shift into high gear by accelerating efforts to introduce new products. Revenue and profit growth would come from increasing GWM's penetration into the music entertainment CD-ROM publishing segment and then expanding into related electronic publishing segments. The central strategic question on Dan's mind was how best to achieve this growth: through internal development, through alliance, or through acquisition?

THE INEVITABLE NEED TO FUND FUTURE GROWTH

To fuel high growth, GWM had to continue to sign more artists, expand staff, increase the size of their facility, and augment their promotion and marketing budget. Although the future continued to hold great promise, the dynamics of the market were changing. By late 1996, industry-wide sales began to slow. GWM's market niche was not immune. Other companies were churning out similar products. The market was getting crowded. Predictions of a multi-billion dollar market by the end of the decade were simply not panning out. Despite the entry of other companies into the marketplace, GWM was able to sustain strong sales and profit growth as a result of its high product quality and excellent brand recognition. However, Dan knew that GWM could not continue to grow faster than the market for very long, especially in the face of increasing competition. Increasing capital outlays and working capital requirements caused free cash flow to deteriorate. Dan was becoming increasingly concerned.

A review of what successful players in the industry were doing convinced Dan that he had to change GWM's formula for success. Go Go Technology (GGT), the fastest-growing industry participant, and Multimedia, Inc., the largest player, were continuing to grow. Unlike others, they were focusing primarily on programming while allowing others to manufacture the disks. Marketing was done largely through alliances with major software companies such as Broderbund, which was well known in the industry. GGT had done an excellent job in entering exclusive marketing relationships with some of the best-known software companies in the nation.

Dan was convinced that the market was moving too fast for him to outsource his development activities and to broaden his product line through purchasing or developing additional content. He felt that he did not even have the time required to enter into strategic marketing arrangements with the major software firms and publishing companies. Such arrangements could take months to negotiate, and the results were highly unpredictable. Dan believed that the multimedia industry was ripe for consolidation. Slower growth at least in certain segments of the market would require consolidation to survive. The cost of developing, buying, or licensing content was becoming too great for the smaller players to survive. Dan carefully considered other options such as the sale of all or a portion of his company to a larger company. But GWM was still his baby. It was his dream, and he wanted to retain control until his dream was realized.

In late 1999, his worst fears were realized when Multimedia, Inc. acquired Fly-By-Nite, Inc. for $15 million. The consolidation phase in the industry that Dan had feared was under way.

GEE WHIZ MEDIA LOOKS TO
GROW THROUGH ACQUISITION

It had become clear to Durand that an acquisition would be the best route to restoring GWM's earlier meteoric growth. Dan enlisted the aid of Kathryn Kim, a senior partner at a respected regional investment banking firm, and proceeded to develop a plan involving an acquisition as the primary means of realizing GWM's business plan. As envisioned by Dan, the acquisition plan really would provide the detail required to implement successfully GWM's business plan through an acquisition strategy. The acquisition plan provided both financial (e.g., minimum return, cash flow) and nonfinancial objectives (e.g., gaining access to distribution channels, content libraries, software development capacity), GWM's resource limitations, further definition of the target industry, and the primary tactics required to complete the acquisition.

As outlined in GWM's business plan, management's primary strategy was to gain market share by extending its existing product line capabilities for converting content focused on niche markets into highly entertaining and interactive multimedia experiences. The means of accomplishing this was through the medium of the CD-ROM. An acquisition was viewed as the best way to implement the business strategy rapidly.

SETTING ACQUISITION PLAN OBJECTIVES

To implement this strategy, GWM sought to identify other related companies with proprietary content or access to proprietary content, effective distribution channels, and excellent design and production capabilities. GWM would look for other CD-ROM companies with widely recognized titles whose growth had matured. Dan believed that it would be easier to rejuvenate old but well-known titles than to build widespread recognition around new ones. By adding new characters or story lines to existing development engines (i.e., the basic software code on which each title is based), it would be much faster and cheaper than starting from scratch each time the company developed a new title. Consequently, GWM could speed development and drastically reduce its costs.

As a normal part of its internal business planning process, GWM would conduct a "peer analysis" to compare its own performance with that of other industry performers. This peer-review process would serve as an important component of the process for searching for acquisition targets. Although it was very difficult to get such data as market share, Dan had ready access to financial information on his primary competitors, which were all publicly traded companies. Dan was aware that financial performance could fluctuate widely because of seasonal factors or accounting reserves. Therefore, he insisted on viewing the trend in key financial indicators by averaging the data over a 3-year period. This had the effect of smoothing out fluctuations in the data (Table 14-1).

Early in the process, Dan and his board of directors decided to stay within the industry they understood. They continued to believe in the long-term promise of multimedia applications. Furthermore, they believed that by staying with what they understood they were more likely to achieve the goals laid out in GWM's acquisition plan. Kim, GWM's investment banker, explained that numerous academic studies confirmed this belief. The company's management was very concerned about the ability to manage the acquired company (i.e., operating risk), earnings-per-share (EPS) dilution (i.e., overpayment risk), and losing the ability to pursue unanticipated opportunities by assuming too much leverage (i.e., financial risk). These concerns drove many of their conclusions and subsequent actions in seeking an acquisition target. Having established acquisition plan objectives, resource capability limitations, and the target industry, GWM set about to define key tactics it would use in making an acquisition.

DEFINING ACQUISITION TACTICS

Based on the following analysis, GWM's management determined that they could not afford to pay more than $100–200 million for an acquisition. In determining the maximum price GWM would be willing to pay for a company,

TABLE 14-1 Comparative Financial Performance Ratios (1998–2000 3-Year Average)[1]

	Gee Whiz Media	Go Go Technology	Fly-By-Nite, Inc.	Hype-O-Tech	Hi Flyer Corp.	Multimedia, Inc.
Profitability Ratios						
EBIT/Sales[2]	.136	.190	.028	.067	.019	.098
Net Income/Sales	.06	.108	.009	.048	.008	.076
EBIT/Total Assets	.186	.279	.041	.121	.031	.187
Net Income/Equity	.294	.248	.068	.169	.052	.220
Net Income CAGR[3]	.354	.359	−.028	−.014	−.044	.196
Activity Ratios						
Sales Growth	.301	.348	−.031	−.021	−.036	.089
Sales/Assets	1.4	1.48	.98	1.11	1.63	1.32
Liquidity Ratios						
Current Assets/Current Liabilities	4.42	4.22	1.61	2.51	1.52	1.86
Working Cap./Sales	.320	.334	.229	.321	.324	.226
Financial Leverage Ratios						
Debt/Total Assets	.586	.215	.816	0.767	0.823	.398
Debt/Total Capitalization	.679	.251	.922	0.883	0.899	.456
Fixed Payment Coverage[4]	1.27	2.90	.886	1.27	1.07	1.49
Market-Based Ratios						
Price/Share ($)	$40.30	$32.50	$3.77	$19.24	$9.60	$66.22
Price/Earnings	16.1	18.1	11	14	10	15.6
Earnings Per Share ($)	2.50	.60	0.19	0.66	0.16	3.01
Price/Revenue	1.04	1.95	0.9	1.3	0.8	1.6
Price/Book	4.74	4.47	.89	2.13	2.88	2.89
Price/Cash Flow[5]	NA	NA	45.6	35.7	NA	19.6
Market Capitalization						
Market Value[6]	$33,000,000	$103,500,000	$12,565,000	$28,462,000	$17,239,000	$368,990,000

[1] Based on normalized financial performance.
[2] Earnings before interest and taxes.
[3] Compound annual average growth rate.
[4] (EBIT + Lease Payments)/(Interest Expense + Lease Payments + Principal Repayments ×(1/(1 − .4)).
[5] NA = not applicable because average free cash flow is negative during this period.
[6] Yearend 2000.

GWM's management laid out the following criteria:

- The minimum acceptable rate of return would be GWM's cost of capital, which Kathryn Kim had estimated to be 15%.
- EPS dilution of the combined organizations would be limited to no more than 2 years following the closing date.
- The combined firm's return on total investment would within 3 years exceed that which GWM could have achieved if it had remained independent.
- Financing the transaction would not violate existing loan covenants or materially increase GWM's borrowing costs.
- Only friendly transactions would be considered.
- Current competitors would be considered as potential targets.
- Ownership would be at least 51% of the acquired firm's outstanding equity.
- The maximum price-to-earnings ratio (P/E) of the acquired company could not exceed 30 times the current year's earnings or 25 times next year's projected earnings.
- The fixed payment (i.e., interest, lease, and principal payments) coverage of the combined companies could not fall below the industry average of 1.0. GWM's management believed the company's attractive fixed payment coverage ratio (almost 2.0 at the end of 2000) would not result in any reduction in their credit rating by the investor community.
- A maximum of one-half of the present value of projected cash flow resulting from synergy would be counted in the purchase price. GWM's management believed that although they would be conservative in their estimate of synergy, history consistently has demonstrated that acquiring companies tend to realize only a portion of anticipated synergy in the desired time frame. Moreover, some portion of the projected synergy should accrue to GWM's shareholders rather than all of it going to the shareholders of the acquired company for the deal to make sense.

PART II: IMPLEMENTATION

INITIATING THE SEARCH FOR ACQUISITION CANDIDATES

The deterioration in GWM's free cash flow from operations, slower than expected market growth, and intensifying competition caused the firm's share price to flounder. GWM's management knew that they would have to strictly adhere to realistic expectations of what the firm could pay for an acquisition. With Kim's assistance, GWM's management team set about determining appropriate criteria for selecting potential acquisition candidates. The primary selection criteria included target industry, size, price range, profitability, and growth rate. Kim cautioned against adding more criteria at this point in the search. "Too many selection criteria," she warned, "would eliminate all potential prospects."

In establishing secondary selection criteria (i.e., those used to reduce the long list developed by applying the primary criteria), Kim advised GWM to focus on targets whose cash flow, asset base, or lack of leverage could be used to finance the acquisition. This was particularly important in view of the deterioration in GWM's own cash flow from operations.

A "short list" of potential acquisition targets was developed following a search of Kim's in-house database of companies, a review of industry literature, and confidential inquiries to GWM's board members as well as law and accounting firms. Current competitors and potential entrants into the market were given particular consideration.

GWM's management decided that control was important; therefore, they would not be interested in acquiring a minority interest in another company. In addition, they had seen how unfriendly takeovers during the 1980s had dramatically inflated acquisition purchase prices as companies were "put into play." Moreover, GWM believed that a friendly takeover would encourage cooperation from the target firm's management to facilitate preclosing integration planning. Control premiums for multimedia companies were believed to be 25–35% of current market value, as suggested by recent transactions.

Because GWM was a publicly traded company, management believed that they had to pay close attention to EPS. Although Durand knew that GWM's true economic value was determined by discounting the firm's future cash flows, he also knew that investors and Wall Street analysts closely monitored fluctuations in EPS as a convenient proxy for economic value. Despite the limitations of this accounting-based performance measure, he knew that over long time periods EPS tended to track other measures of value very well. He knew that if he used GWM's stock to acquire GGT he would have to be sensitive to the potential for near-term EPS dilution.

With this information in hand, Durand was prepared to initiate "first contact" with firms on the "short list." Whenever possible, contact would be made through a trusted intermediary such as a GWM board member, the company's law or accounting firm, or Kathryn Kim. He made it clear to all involved that at this stage in the process, secrecy was of paramount importance. He did not want to create concern among GWM's employees, suppliers, or customers. In addition, he did not want the "marketplace" to get wind of his intentions, which could drive up market values of potential acquisition targets. Professional arbitrageurs frequently made fortunes by buying on rumors and selling shortly before or after a transaction was complete.

FIRST CONTACT

After a somewhat frustrating 2-month search, GWM reduced what had been a lengthy list of 12 candidates to 2. The list was narrowed because the companies did not fit the selection criteria as well as GWM had wanted or because they had rejected GWM's initial overtures through its intermediaries. At Dan's request,

Dana Davies, one of GWM's board members, contacted her former business associate, Barry Chang, the CEO of GGT. Chang said that GGT might be willing to be acquired under "the right conditions." Kathryn Kim recommended further research into GGT's competitive market position and the goals of major shareholders and management before approaching GGT with a formal proposal.

The secret to GGT's success appeared to be its ability to outsource programming activities to service bureaus employing armies of highly skilled software programmers in India and the Philippines. Their hourly rates were a fraction of what domestic software engineers demanded. Moreover, GGT was able to diversify into other types of content to expand its product offering because of significant savings in developing software. GGT demonstrated its clear understanding of market segmentation as it developed titles for such niche hobbyist and educational markets as "Civil War Battlefields Interactive" and a series entitled the "Great Works of Literature Come Alive." Finally, as previously mentioned, GGT had done an excellent job of developing marketing relationships with some of the major software companies.

GGT was following a different business model from other companies in the industry, and Wall Street analysts were taking notice. GGT's approach to this business was to program the disks and have a larger publisher (like Broderbund) distribute them. Other companies such as Fly-By-Nite, Inc., Hype-O-Tech, and Hi Flyer Corp. chose to bear nearly all of the costs for programming and distributing the discs. Rather than contracting out projects (avoiding the price of new equipment, for instance) or developing for others (avoiding the actual manufacture of the disks), these companies wanted to be major players. They also wanted control. Moreover, without a publisher, they didn't need to deal with contracts and the close scrutiny of others. The attractiveness of their business model resulted in GGT's equity market value being more than three times GWM's at the end of 2000. Although the two had grown both earnings and revenue at about the same pace in recent years, investors believed that only GGT would be able to sustain their growth rate through the foreseeable future.

Although GGT was the industry's current "Wall Street darling," a recent speech by Barry Chang at an industry trade association meeting implied that GGT's management was anything but smug about its current market position. By "reading between the lines," Dan believed that Barry was becoming increasingly concerned that Multimedia, Inc., the industry's behemoth, was likely to erode GGT's position by adopting many of the tactics used by GGT. Indeed, Multimedia, Inc. had publicly pronounced in an interview with its chief executive officer (CEO), Carl Widman, that its strategy was to adopt the best practices in the industry and to improve on them. Moreover, it had the financial wherewithal to do this.

After further conversations between Davies and Chang, Dan believed that it was time for a face-to-face meeting with Chang. At that meeting, Dan presented the argument that together their two companies could present an effective counterweight to Multimedia, Inc. Dan wanted to play to Chang's concerns. "Individually," he argued, "their competitive positions were questionable in the long run given the apparent slowdown in industry demand. But together they could benefit from Gee Whiz Media's excellent content library and GGT's lower cost of designing, developing, and marketing CD-ROM products." Chang seemed to be impressed by Durand's compelling logic.

At the end of the meeting, Dan and Barry agreed to sign a confidentiality agreement that would include both parties and to exchange summarized business plans and financial statements for their respective companies. Dan was very interested in seeing in more detail what GGT had done over the last few years and thought it could do over the next few years; Barry was interested in evaluating GWM's ability to finance a transaction. Barry had no desire to waste time with a suitor who could not complete a transaction. Even before GWM began its due diligence review of GGT, Barry initiated a due diligence of his own operations to ascertain exactly what representations he could make if the negotiations reached the stage of a final agreement of purchase and sale. Barry also had his key managers sign affidavits stating that to the "best of their knowledge" what they said about the GGT operations was indeed true.

Dan and Barry also laid out a timeline that would enable GWM to perform a modest preliminary due diligence review. At the end of 30 days, GWM would have to provide a formal letter of intent containing a specific purchase price. Although the letter of intent would be binding, it would contain the standard protections for both parties. GGT would agree not to "shop" for another suitor during the 60-day period the letter of intent was in force, and GWM's offer price would be contingent on performing a more thorough due diligence, gaining a commitment from lenders, and obtaining the requisite board and shareholder approvals.

PRELIMINARY VALUATION

Dan and his CFO, Andy Perez, poured over the 5 years' worth of audited statements that they had received from GGT. Dan expressed some disappointment that the cash-flow numbers tended to jump around from year to year. He was hoping that GGT could demonstrate a stable, predictable cash-flow stream. Predictable cash flows, he reasoned, would enable GWM to convince bankers that GWM could assume significant leverage to purchase GGT for cash and still be able to meet debt service requirements easily. Perez was quick to point out that much of the variation in historical cash flows was the result of nonrecurring or one-time events. For example, he explained that GGT's cash flow was affected negatively in 1997 by a $1.9 million expense associated with an out-of-court settlement of a software copyright infringement lawsuit filed by Fly-By-Nite, Inc. In 2000, free cash flow benefited from the sale of a proprietary software license for $4.5 million to another firm. Perez assured Durand that if the historical numbers were restated to eliminate the one-time occurrences, GGT's cash flow would show a smooth upward trend.

Dan designated Perez as the acquisition project leader with clear authority to draw on others with specialized skills throughout the organization. Perez was quick to establish action teams dedicated to specific aspects of the negotiation process. These teams included financial analysts to refine the initial valuation of GGT and a combined legal and financial team to work on structuring the proposal to GGT's management. Other teams included a multidisciplinary group to conduct due diligence consisting of operations, marketing, and accounting experts and a team consisting of Perez and GWM's treasurer to develop a plan for financing the acquisition. Dan viewed the financing plan as a critical component of the negotiating process because it placed a realistic limit on what he could offer GGT's management and shareholders.

Dan was pleased with the appearance of highly predictable cash flows for GGT between 1996 and 2000. He was, however, quite skeptical of the 32.6% and 28.6% compound growth rate GGT projected for net income and sales, respectively, between 2001 and 2005. Once again, Perez—being the consummate numbers person—cautioned that Dan should reserve judgment until the assumptions underlying the forecast were well understood. Following several days of hectic number crunching by Perez's minions, Perez reported to Durand that the assumptions looked reasonable except for what appeared to be an overly optimistic improvement in the ratio of the cost of goods sold to net revenue built into the forecast period beginning in 2002. This was evident on examination of the common-size income statement, which showed how the projections deviated from GGT's actual historical performance.

Chang was questioned about the realism of this assumption. "This reduction," he explained, "reflected the implementation of a modular software development system that GGT had been working on for several years. This system would enable GGT's developers to more readily reuse existing software code in new product introductions. The resulting reduction in coding time would substantially lower product introduction costs." Dan was familiar with software development projects, and he was well aware that they frequently were implemented well behind schedule and considerably above budget. Furthermore, his experience led him to believe that these types of projects rarely provide the productivity improvements that are expected. Consequently, Dan told Perez to rerun the GGT projections but with more modest growth assumptions and with the cost of goods sold as a percentage of sales in line with the company's historical performance. This, he believed, would provide a more realistic picture that did not depend on what Dan thought were largely heroic assumptions. The preliminary discounted cash-flow standalone value for GGT was $102.7 million, about $6 million more than the market value (including debt) of GWM, despite its significantly smaller size in terms of revenue.

IDENTIFYING SOURCES (AND DESTROYERS) OF VALUE

With the revised forecast, Durand and Perez turned to identifying "hidden" sources of value that GWM could unlock to provide additional cash generated by the combination of GGT and GWM. To identify these sources of value (measured in terms of incremental cash flow), Perez and his associates poured over GGT's financial statements and operations looking for assets not recorded on the books at fair value, underutilized borrowing capacity, and the potential for cost savings (e.g., shared overhead, duplicate facilities). Other potential sources of value included new customer relationships; opportunities for GWM to use new technologies and processes; and intellectual property such as patents, trademarks, and royalty rights. They also looked for factors that would reduce future cash flow such as product quality problems, employee turnover, duplicate customer relationships, and so on. Perez knew from past experience that finding and quantifying potential sources of value frequently would be the difference between a successful acquisition and one that failed to meet expectations.

The present value of total synergy was estimated at $118 million. Very little of the anticipated synergy was expected to be realized during the first full year of GWM's ownership. The full impact was not expected until the third full year of combined operations of the two firms. Perez was aware that he also needed to look for factors that could detract from the future cash flow of the combined entities. A third-party marketing firm was hired to interview a representative sample of GGT customers without divulging that they were hired by GWM. Rather, customers were told, with GGT's blessing, that the marketing firm was conducting a survey for GGT so that the company could better understand its customers' needs. Assumptions made about factors contributing to future cash flows of the combined firms and those detracting from future cash flows were clearly delineated in Perez's presentations to Durand. Moreover, these assumptions would be validated carefully during the more exhaustive on-site due diligence that was to take place before closing.

DETERMINING THE INITIAL OFFER PRICE

Perez's approach to valuation involved a four-step procedure. Initially, GWM and GGT were valued as standalone businesses, with all operating revenues and costs stated at market prices. In the second step, the present value of net synergy was determined by subtracting the sum of the standalone values of GWM and GGT from the present value of consolidated GWM and GGT, including the effects of estimated synergy. The third step entailed the determination of the initial offer price, which was equal to the minimum offer price (i.e., GGT's current share price times total shares outstanding) plus the percentage of estimated net synergy GWM was willing to share with GGT shareholders. Finally, Perez determined if GWM could finance the transaction at the initial offer price determined in the third step.

This initial offer price would be further validated by comparing the discounted cash-flow valuations with purchase prices based on P/E, price-to-revenue, and price-to-book ratios for recent transactions involving comparable companies. These ratios seem to confirm that $150.6 million ($50.20 per share) was a fair price for GGT's outstanding equity. This price represented a 46% premium over GGT's current share price of $34.50 (Table 14-2).

TABLE 14-2 Offer Price Determination[1]

| Financing Metrics | Standalone Value | | Consolidated GWM and GGT | | Value of Synergy |
	GWM (1)	GGT (2)	Without Synergy (3) (1) + (2)	With Synergy (4)	PV Net Synergy (4) − (3)
			$ Millions		
Valuations	72.8	99.6	172.4	290.2	117.9
Minimum Offer Price	103.5	GGT share price ($34.50) at close of business day before offer presented to GGT management × number of GGT shares outstanding			
Maximum Offer Price	221.4	Minimum offer price plus 100% of estimated net synergy			
Initial Offer Price	150.6	Minimum share price + 40% of estimated net synergy, where .4 is portion of synergy GWM initially is willing to share with GGT shareholders			
Initial Offer Price Per Share	50.20	Initial offer price/number of GGT's shares outstanding			
Purchase Price Premium Per Share (%)	.46	Initial offer price/current GGT share price			

[1]For the detailed financial statements underlying this table and others in Chapter 14, see Case Study 8-1 (Chapter 8) entitled "Determining the Initial Offer Price—The Gee Whiz Media and Go Go Technology Saga."

Dan reasoned that a substantial premium over GGT's current share price would preempt other potential bidders from making a "run" for GGT. The last thing Dan wanted at this time was a protracted and contentious bidding war for GGT. Dan knew that GWM did not have the financial resources to outbid companies the size of Multimedia. Nonetheless, even with this lofty premium, the GGT acquisition looked attractive, promising to boost the market value of the combined companies to almost $300 million, including about $118 million in estimated synergy. The expected synergy consisted of a combination of revenue enhancements and cost savings. The additional revenue was expected to come from improved product quality, a broader product offering, and cross-selling to each firm's customers. Production cost-related savings would result from economies of scale (i.e., better utilization of existing facilities) and scope (i.e., the use of existing operations to produce a broader product offering) as well as the elimination of duplicate jobs.

DEAL STRUCTURING

Dan knew that a stock-for-stock purchase was problematic because of the potential dilution in GWM's EPS. Wall Street analysts increasingly viewed GWM's above-average industry growth rate as suspect. With the industry growth slowing, they reasoned that product pricing was likely to get very competitive.

Although GWM had been able to maintain attractive margins in recent years, the lack of new products that had blockbuster potential made the analysts increasingly wary of the firm's ability to sustain both high growth and attractive margins. Continuing delays in introducing new products, the lack of exclusive distribution channels, and the firm's limited proprietary content library heightened this concern.

An acquisition resulting in dilution was not likely to be acceptable to Wall Street. With long-term debt comprising about 60% of total capital, an all-cash transaction did not seem possible. Durand and Perez had to be creative to reduce the initial cash-flow impact of the acquisition on GWM. Consequently, it seemed increasingly obvious that GWM would have to convince GGT that some combination of stock and cash for GGT would be attractive. They would need to know what GGT's management and shareholders would be willing to accept. This required some old-fashioned detective work, such as reading old speeches made by Chang at trade shows and shareholder meetings, reading Wall Street analysts' reports, and looking at the amount of GGT stock accumulated by the company's top management. In addition, because many of the GGT's top managers were quite young, it was possible that they would like to stay with the combined companies or even that they would be willing to hold significant amounts of stock in the new company.

Although Durand wanted to retain several key GGT managers, he believed that in the long term, personality conflicts would arise as a result of his way of doing business and Chang's hard-charging, sometimes "bend-the-rules" approach to things. Moreover, Chang's salary was the highest in the industry; Durand thought it was out of line for what Chang could contribute as a senior manager to the combined firm's ongoing operations. Dan Durand was willing to consider management employment contracts to retain key managers, but he did not want to keep Chang.

Durand, Perez, and their investment banker began to brainstorm different scenarios involving different purchase price compositions. They knew that if an exciting "story line" could be created for the combined companies, it would be possible to convince GGT's shareholders to accept something other than an all-cash or all-stock offer. Indeed, a combination of stock and cash might appeal to a wider range of GGT shareholders. GGT shareholders could continue to hold GWM stock to participate in the potential appreciation, while using the cash portion of the purchase price to diversify their investment portfolios or to satisfy any short-term cash requirements they might have.

To determine the appropriate composition of the initial offer price, GWM's management reviewed 15 alternative scenarios. GWM's own analysis suggested that its standalone equity value could total about $73 million, even without the acquisition of GGT, if their assumptions underlying their current 5-year projections turned out to be correct. Obviously, GWM's management and shareholders would have to be convinced that they could do markedly better to justify the risk associated with acquiring GGT.

Certain financial scenario selection criteria were established to determine the preferred scenario. The most acceptable scenario would be the one that resulted in the highest net present value, the least EPS dilution, substantially exceeded what GWM could have done without GGT in terms of after-tax returns on invested capital, and would most likely be acceptable to shareholders. Moreover, the scenario could not jeopardize the combined companies' ability to satisty loan covenants or maintain fixed payment coverage and debt-to-total capital ratios consistent with the average for other companies in the industry. All-cash and all-stock offers were included in the analysis (although it was felt that neither was a realistic option) as benchmarks or baselines for comparing the other options. The most attractive scenario to GWM consisted of 1.14 shares of its stock plus $12.55 in cash for each share of GGT's stock. However, it was unclear how attractive GGT would find this offer.

NEGOTIATIONS HEAT UP: REFINING THE OFFER PRICE

Although this offer had great appeal from GGT's perspective, the transaction would create a significant tax liability for GGT's shareholders. Dan learned very quickly from Chang that this could be a stumbling block. Although he did not mention it to Chang at this point, Dan was willing to increase the number of GWM shares offered for each GGT share. He also was willing to share up to one-half of the expected synergy if he had to in order to complete the transaction. However, he would only play that card if he were forced to do so. Chang made it clear that although Dan's proposal was "in the ballpark" on a pretax basis, it was wholly inadequate on an after-tax basis. Much of GGT's stock was held by a relatively few shareholders that had a very low tax basis in the stock. Consequently, their tax liabilities from a taxable transaction would be substantial. Chang indicated that Dan either would have to raise the total price on a pretax basis to compensate for any tax liability or increase the equity portion of the offer price, thereby softening the potential tax bite to GGT shareholders. Dan agreed to review his options and get back to Chang. Dan knew that "in the ballpark" meant that Chang was looking for a higher price on both a pre- and after-tax basis. He and Perez would have to be creative to satisfy Chang's demands.

DEVELOPING COUNTER OFFERS

Subsequent analysis indicated that it would be difficult for GWM to increase significantly the share exchange ratio without savaging EPS of the combined firms. Dan and his board of directors did not find these results acceptable. However, GWM was willing to "sweeten" their initial offer by assuming all of GGT's long-term debt, which totaled $3.2 million. Although this change in terms did not address specifically Chang's concern about taxes, it did add to the overall purchase price being offered. Without GWM's assumption of this debt, GGT would have to repay this amount to lenders from the cash portion of the purchase price (Table 14-3).

Although Barry Chang initially expressed disappointment with the offer, he agreed to present it to his board of directors. GGT's board and shareholders found

TABLE 14-3   Determining the Composition of the Offer Price

Cash Per Share ($)	12.55
Share Exchange Ratio[1]	1.14
New Shares Issued by GWM[2]	3.42
Total Shares Outstanding (GWM/GGT)[3]	4.42
Ownership Distribution in Combined Firm	
GGT Shareholders (%)[4]	.77
GWM Shareholders (%)	.23
Offer Price Composition Per Share	1.14 shares of GWM stock + $12.55 for each GGT share outstanding
Offer Price Including Assumed GGT Debt[5] ($ Millions)	153.8

[1] Number of GWM shares to be exchanged for each share of GGT stock.

[2] Share exchange ratio times the number of GGT shares outstanding (i.e., 3 million).

[3] GWM's existing shares plus the new shares issued to acquire GGT.

[4] Number of GWM shares held by GGT shareholders divided by total shares outstanding for the combined firms (i.e., 3.42/4.42).

[5] GGT's outstanding long-term debt at the time of the proposed acquisition totaled $3.2 million.

the improved offer acceptable because it was substantially nontaxable, offered a significant premium over the firm's current share price, and represented an increase (albeit small) of 2.1% (i.e., $153.8/$150.6) in the initial offer price. Durand was happy because he was able to move the deal along without raising the total purchase price to levels that were clearly unjustifiable.

The GWM management team celebrated. They were on the verge of closing the transaction. Dan knew the success of the transaction in the eyes of the GWM shareholder rested on his and his management team's ability to realize the projected synergy. He did not really know if this would be doable, but he was willing to savor the moment and worry about that later. There was much work remaining to be done. Durand and Perez would have to devote more time to conducting due diligence and developing a financing plan. Now that he and Perez had resolved the major business issues, the lawyers could draft the necessary legal documents.

DUE DILIGENCE: LOOKING FOR A NEEDLE IN A HAYSTACK

Durand was a "big picture" guy. He had little interest in details. He understood intuitively the need for a thorough due diligence, but he did not have the temperament to actively participate in such a time-consuming and laborious process. "Andy, you take the lead in due diligence," he barked. "I will attend to the day-to-day operations of GWM that have been neglected during the negotiations." Andy Perez reminded him that due diligence was extremely important to confirm the "sources of value" assumed in the valuation, identify other potential sources of value, and identify any "fatal flaws" that would reduce future cash flows.

Perez urged him to participate at least in the interviews of senior GGT managers. Perez quipped, "What we don't know can hurt us." Dan reluctantly agreed to participate. He understood that, until due diligence had been completed, they would really not know what they didn't know.

Perez organized three teams to conduct due diligence: a financial team, a strategy team, and a legal team. He asked Dan to direct the strategy group; he would handle financial matters, and the attorneys would handle the legal affairs. The strategy and operations teams' responsibilities were to review past business and operating plans to evaluate actual performance to plan (a measure of the competence of management), to evaluate the effectiveness of sales and marketing plans, and to assess customer relationships. In addition, the team was to evaluate the integrity of operations in terms of facility design and layout, software design and development capabilities, and project management skills. Much of this was to be accomplished through a series of personal interviews with midlevel and senior management.

The financial team would concern itself with the integrity of GGT's books (i.e., are they stated in a manner consistent with generally accepted accounting principles, or GAAP) and would conduct an inventory of assets to substantiate their existence and to evaluate their quality. Perez was aware that significant variations from GAAP, as is often the case with the increasingly common use of so-called pro forma statements, could signal that the selling firm was trying to hide something (e.g., true profitability or questionable accounting practices). The legal team would review corporate records, material contracts and obligations of the seller, and current and pending litigation and claims. Each team developed a question checklist to ensure that the due diligence activity was comprehensive.

Following an extensive review of GGT's operations and books, several areas of concern as well as opportunities emerged. Revenue recognition appeared that it might become an issue. This traditionally has been a problem with software companies where products frequently are shipped to distributors on consignment or where service contracts and upgrades can stretch revenue out for years. GWM accountants noted that GGT might have been booking revenue too quickly. When disks were sent to retailers, allowance for the return of unsold disks from the retailers should have been taken into account. Booking revenue too early provides an opportunity to inflate current sales and earnings at the expense of future earnings.

Areas that provided an opportunity for GWM included in-process research and development (R&D) charges. These could be taken by GWM at the time of the acquisition. These charges represent the estimated value of R&D at the target company. Because it is still "in process," the research is not yet commercially viable. Because it may prove worthless, it all can be written off. By separating the expenses from revenues that might be gained in the future from the R&D, however, future earnings can get a big boost. Moreover, some portion of goodwill arising from the purchase could be offset by the increasingly common practice of writing off in-process R&D charges.

As a result of its own internal due diligence activity, GGT felt comfortable with the accuracy of the representations and warranties it was prepared to make in the agreement of purchase and sale. Because GWM was well known to Barry Chang and his management team, their review of GWM's ability to finance the acquisition was limited.

OBTAINING FINANCING: LEND ME THE MONEY, STUPID!

"It's a great deal. Just lend me the money you dunderheads," thought Dan as he and Perez pitched the acquisition proposal to lenders. To raise money, Durand and Perez had to go on the typical road show to make presentations to banks, insurance companies, pension funds, and the like to raise funding. They would need to borrow about $40 million to finance the cash portion of the purchase price. Their challenge was to convince bankers that the cash flow of the combined companies could meet debt service requirements. In the electronic publishing business, few companies had a sufficient amount of tangible assets to serve as collateral. Consequently, lenders focus on the amount and predictability of free cash flow (i.e., cash generated in excess of normal working capital, capital expenditures, and other fixed obligations).

Table 14-4 provides the financial statements for the combined firms including the impact of the additional debt and equity issued to purchase GGT. The combined companies' total debt was expected to reach $70.5 million, including transaction-related debt totaling $40 million. Loan covenants on existing debt require that the new firm's debt-to-total capital be less than one, fixed payment coverage charges be greater than one, and current assets be at least twice current liabilities. At the end of 2001, the new firm's debt-to-total capital was estimated to be .72. Although the fixed payment coverage ratio was .92, slightly less than required, the ratio of current assets to current liabilities was a highly favorable 3.2.

After extended negotiations, a bank agreed to an unsecured loan to GWM of $40 million amortized in equal payments over 15 years at an annual interest rate of 11%. The loan was subject to normal covenants, which restricted the amount GWM could borrow in the future and the types of spending it could undertake without the bank's approval. Furthermore, GWM would have to ensure that certain other financial ratios such as earnings before interest and taxes as a multiple of interest expense did not fall below a contractually determined multiple. Durand felt the covenants would restrict his ability to manage GWM in the future as aggressively as he might want. This provided an incentive for him to use the majority of future free cash flow to accelerate repayment of the loan. He knew that the loss of some control and strategic flexibility was the price he would have to pay to complete the transaction.

INTEGRATING THE ORGANIZATIONS: COMMUNICATE! COMMUNICATE! COMMUNICATE!

Despite the perceived compatibility of the cultures of the two firms, Durand knew from experience that combining the firms would lead to inevitable concerns, particularly among GGT employees, about job security and compensation and

TABLE 14-4 Consolidated Financial Statements Financing Feasibility Analysis

Forecast Assumptions (2001–2005)
New Transaction-Related Borrowing:

Principal ($ Millions)	40
Interest (%)	0.11

Loan Covenants on Existing Debt

Debt/Total Capital	<1.0
Fixed Payment Coverage Ratio	>1.0
Current Assets/Current Liabilities	>2.0

Financial Reporting

Consolidated GWM and GGT Financial Statements Including Synergy & Financing Effects

	Projected Financials					Forecast Comments
	2001	2002	2003	2004	2005	
Income Statement ($ Millions)						
Net Sales	124.9	163.4	199.4	237.6	275.5	See Case Study 8-1 for more detail
Less: Cost of Sales	85.4	111.2	135.1	160.7	186.0	
Gross Profit	39.5	52.2	64.4	76.8	89.4	
Less: Sales, General & Admin. Exp.	17.5	21.2	25.9	30.9	35.8	
Integration Expenses	−5.0	−3.0	0.0	0.0	0.0	
Operating Profits (EBIT)	17.0	27.9	38.4	46.0	53.6	
Plus: Interest Income	0.6	0.7	0.9	1.1	1.3	
Less: Interest Expense	7.6	7.7	7.3	6.8	5.7	Includes interest on current and transaction-related debt
Net Profits Before Taxes	10.0	21.0	32.1	40.3	49.3	
Less: Taxes	4.0	8.4	12.8	16.1	19.7	
Net Profits After Taxes	6.0	12.6	19.2	24.2	29.6	
Earnings per Share ($/Share)	1.6	3.4	5.1	6.4	7.9	Includes 1 million existing + 2.76 million new GWM shares

(*Continued*)

TABLE 14-4 (*Continued*)

Balance Sheet (12/31)

Current Assets						
Cash & Marketable Securities	53.5	55.9	58.1	61.0	64.6	
Other Current Assets	36.9	46.0	55.3	66.8	78.1	
Total Current Assets	90.4	101.9	113.4	127.8	142.7	
Gross Fixed Assets	47.2	58.7	70.3	84.5	98.8	
Less: Accumulated Depreciation	16.1	22.0	29.0	37.5	47.4	
Net Fixed Assets	31.0	36.7	41.3	47.0	51.4	
Total Assets	121.4	138.6	154.7	174.8	194.1	
Current Liabilities	12.3	15.3	18.4	22.3	26.0	
Long-Term Debt	38.8	37.6	36.1	34.5	32.8	
Existing Debt	31.7	33.9	31.5	28.0	18.9	
Transaction-Related debt	38.8	37.5	36.0	34.3	32.5	$40 million, 15-year loan at 11% per annum
Total Long-Term Debt	70.5	71.4	67.5	62.3	51.4	
Common Stock	4.0	4.0	4.0	4.0	4.0	
Retained Earnings	34.6	47.8	64.8	86.3	112.7	
Shareholders' Equity	38.6	51.8	68.8	90.3	116.7	
Total Liabilities + Shareholders' Equity	121.4	138.6	154.7	174.8	194.1	
Addendum:						
Lease Payments	2.0	2.4	2.4	2.6	2.6	
Principal Repayments	5.6	5.6	5.6	5.6	5.6	$40 million, 15-year loan at 11% per annum[1]
Financial Scenario Selection Criteria						
After-Tax Return on Capital-Combined Firms (%)	9.7	13.7	16.7	17.7	20.7	(Net Income + (Interest and Lease Expense) × (1 − .4))/ (Shareholders' Equity + Long-Term Debt + PV of leases)

After-Tax Return on Capital-GWM (%)	12.6	14.4	15.1	15.6	16.2	Same
Key Combined Firm Credit Ratios						
Debt to Total Capital	0.65	0.58	0.50	0.41	0.31	Total Long-term Debt/(Total Long-term Debt + Equity)
Fixed-Payment Coverage Ratio	1.01	1.56	2.15	2.60	3.20	(EBIT + Lease Payments)/ (Interest Expense + Lease Payment + Principal Repayment × (1/(1 − .40)))
Current Assets/Current Liabilities	7.36	6.64	6.15	5.74	5.48	
Key Industry Average Credit Ratios						
Debt to Total Capital	.72					
Fixed-Payment Coverage Ratio	.92					
Current Assets/Current Liabilities	3.15					

[1] Level payment loan

Year	2001	2002	2003	2004	2005	2006	2007	2008	2009	2010	2011	2012	2013	2014	2015
Annual Payment[2]	5.6	5.6	5.6	5.6	5.6	5.6	5.6	5.6	5.6	5.6	5.6	5.6	5.6	5.6	5.6
Interest[3]	4.4	4.3	4.1	4.0	3.8	3.6	3.4	3.1	2.8	2.5	2.5	1.8	1.4	.9	.4
Principal[4]	1.2	1.3	1.5	1.6	1.8	2.0	2.2	2.5	2.8	3.1	3.4	3.8	4.2	4.7	5.2
Ending Balance[5]	38.8	37.5	36.0	34.3	32.5	30.5	28.2	25.7	23.0	19.9	16.5	12.7	8.5	3.8	−1.4

[2] Equal annual payments including principal and interest are calculated by solving PVA = PMT × PVIAF$_{11,15}$ (i.e., future value interest factor for 11% and 15 years) for PMT.

[3] Loan balance times annual interest rate.

[4] Annual payment less interest payment.

[5] Beginning loan balance less principal payment.

about how the new firm would be managed. Although one could expect to lose some key employees to competitors following the acquisition, Durand felt that the situation was manageable if the proper planning was undertaken. He had to start by clearly communicating his own priorities to his subordinates and establishing an appropriate integration team infrastructure.

Before closing, he appointed Amy Pettibone, one of his best operating and project managers, to oversee the operational combination of the two firms once the transaction had been completed. Perez was disappointed that he did not get this assignment, but he understood that spearheading the activities before closing frequently took a different set of skills than those required during the integration of the two companies. Amy had a demonstrated ability to set and communicate priorities, to size up people accurately, to make tough but fair decisions, to establish a timeline, and to stick to even the most ambitious schedule. These were managerial skills crucial to successfully integrating businesses where differences in corporate cultures could be significant. Meshing the software development teams of the two companies would be critical to ensuring that the productivity improvements and acceleration of new product introductions envisioned in GWM's acquisition strategy would be realized. Amy was assigned to head the strategy and operations team during due diligence to familiarize herself with the challenges of integration.

Based on the information collected during due diligence, Amy Pettibone and Andy Perez worked closely to determine what near-term expenditures might be required to ensure that GGT's operations would continue without interruption during the next 12–24 months. This included the identification of key managers that were to be retained, key technologies, and a review of vendors and customers. The pair also reviewed industry-wide operating norms to determine other adjustments that might have to be made in the immediate future. These norms included executive compensation, billing procedures, product delivery times, quality metrics, and employee benefit and compensation packages. Retention bonuses were offered to employees, who were to be terminated within the first full year following the closing, to stay with the firm during that period to ease the integration of the two firms. Such bonuses were equal to as much as 6 months of the employees' salary and benefits, depending on their perceived importance during the integration period.

GWM's management knew that the time to address these issues was before the closing. Issues such as severance expenditures, pension plan buyouts, employment contracts, capital expenditures that should have been made by GGT as part of the "normal course of business," noncompete agreements, and so on, should be addressed as part of the negotiation process. When appropriate, GWM would seek a reduction in the purchase price as at least a possible offset to these types of expenses that were not apparent when the preliminary indication of value for GGT was given in the letter of intent.

Perez was interested in ensuring a smooth transition for all employees immediately following closing. Consequently, he wanted to make sure that all GGT employees would be transferred to current GWM benefit programs and that payroll information was transcribed accurately to the GWM personnel database so that payrolls could continue to be processed without disruption despite the change in ownership. Finally, Perez knew that GGT lock boxes had to be closed and that former GGT banks had to be instructed to forward any checks they might receive from GGT customers to GWM lock boxes.

Key managers at GGT were offered 1-year employment contracts with GWM. Retaining key GGT managers was considered important enough that Durand instructed his attorneys to make the acceptance of employment contracts by designated employees a "condition" of closing. Barry Chang also signed an agreement that he would not work for a competitor or start a business that could compete with the combined firms for a period not to exceed 3 years from the closing date.

Finally, a detailed communications plan was devised for use immediately following closing. The plan included press releases and announcements to employees (addressing questions about job security, compensation, and benefits), customers (providing assurances of an uninterrupted service), and vendors. Durand would speak to GGT employees at their headquarters to answer questions and provide reasonable assurances of continuity of pay and benefits. The lawyers cautioned Dan about not making verbal commitments about job security, which could result in litigation at a later date. In addition, "talk tracks" were written for the salesforce, who were instructed to contact all major customers directly on the day of the announcement of the acquisition of GGT. Nothing was to be left to chance!

THE DREAM COMES TRUE

The stress level rose sharply doing the days just before closing. Heated negotiations were taking place around a number of issues that surfaced during due diligence. Several potential lawsuits involving disgruntled customers and employees had the potential of costing the new company millions of dollars over the next 3–5 years. Although it was not clear if they actually would go to trial, GWM estimated the future value of their potential impact to be $7 million to $10 million. In addition, the new company would have to spend $1 million to $3 million in normal maintenance and repair of GGT operations during the next several years. GGT's management had postponed these expenditures when the prospect of sale came up.

The combination of potential or pending expenses had an estimated present value of $10 million, consisting of $8 million in potential jury awards and $2 million in deferred maintenance. Because they had been identified late in the due diligence process, their impact had not been included in the projected operating cash flows used in GGT's initial valuation. Moreover, Durand was concerned enough about what was uncovered during due diligence that he wanted Chang to agree to put 5% of the purchase in escrow for at least 1 year until all the "surprises" were known.

Despite several days of aggressive negotiating, Durand capitulated and agreed to absorb these additional costs without any reduction in purchase price. Durand believed that the $10 million would be more than offset by certain nonoperating

TABLE 14-5   Adjusted GGT Standalone Valuation ($ Millions)

PV (2001–2005) @ 15%	6.7
PV of Terminal Value @ 10%	96.0
Total PV (Market Value of Firm—Equity + Debt)	102.7
Less Market Value of Debt	3.1
Equity Value	99.6
Plus Nonoperating Assets	
Excess Operating Cash & Short-Term	
Marketable Securities	1.5
PV of Undeveloped Commercial Property	2.5
PV of Unused Process Patents, Software Copyrights,	
and Content Licenses	10.0
Total Nonoperating Assets	14.0
Less Nonoperating Liabilities	
PV of Potential Jury Awards	8.0
PV of Deferred Maintenance	2.0
Total Nonoperating Liabilities	10.0
Adjusted Equity Value	103.6

assets that were identified during the due diligence process. These included GGT's holdings of cash and marketable securities in excess of normal working capital requirements of $1.5 million and a series of process patents, software copyrights, and content licenses that were owned by GGT but were not being used in the operation of the company. Durand believed that by using these assets, the new company could save at least $12 million to $15 million in future expenses that would have been incurred to develop these processes and patents or to gain access to certain types of content. Moreover, GGT owned a piece of undeveloped commercial property that GWM believed could be sold during the next 12–18 months for approximately $3 million. The estimated present value of these nonoperating assets was $14 million (Table 14-5). The equity value for GGT adjusted to include the estimated value of these nonoperating assets and liabilities totaled $103.6 million, $4 million more than the initial estimate made before completing due diligence. Besides, he was tired. He wanted the negotiations to end so that he could get on with the business of growing the combined businesses.

Once the respective companies' boards of directors and shareholder approvals were received, customer and vendor contracts assigned, financing in place, and other closing conditions satisfied, the closing finally took place. For the first time in 6 months both parties could relax. Congratulations were in order for all participants. Whereas Perez's stress level eased, Pettibone's escalated as she faced the challenges of meeting the demanding integration schedule. Durand's role changed from that of the dealmaker to that of the chief executive charged with meeting the expectations of his shareholders and Wall Street analysts. As the CEO of one of the major firms in his industry, Durand was trading one set of challenges for another. But he was happy—he was living his dream.

GEE WHIZ MEDIA CASE STUDY
DISCUSSION QUESTIONS

PART I: PLANNING

Business Plan

1. Describe the industry or market in which GWM competed in terms of the following: customers, suppliers, current competitors, potential entrants, and product substitutes. How should this information be used by GWM management to develop a long-term strategy?*
2. Identify GWM's primary strengths and weaknesses as compared with the competition. How can this information be used to identify threats to and opportunities for GWM?*
3. Give examples of GWM's potential competitors, and describe how they might compete with GWM. What could GWM do to minimize these risks?

Making Strategic Choices

4. Identify the range of reasonable options available to GWM to grow its business. Discuss the key advantages and disadvantages of each option. Of the available options, which would you have selected and why?*
5. Did an acquisition make sense for GWM to realize its business strategy? Why or why not? Describe the motives for the acquisition. (Hint: Consider the traditional motives for acquisitions outlined in Chapter 1.)

Acquisition Plan

6. GWM's acquisition plan identified key objectives, resource capability, the target industry, and appropriate tactics for completing an acquisition. Were all the objectives adequately quantified, and did they have associated completion dates? What other key objectives and tactics might GWM have included? Discuss the importance of these additional objectives and tactics.*
7. Describe GWM's primary business objectives and acquisition plan objectives. How did the acquisition plan objectives support the realization of GGT's business plan objectives?
8. What were the key assumptions made in the GWM business plan used to justify the acquisition of GGT? Consider key assumptions, both explicit and implicit, with respect to the following areas: the market, financial performance, acquisition tactics, valuation, and integration.*

PART II: IMPLEMENTATION

Identification, Search, and Initial Contact

9. Describe various techniques that GWM could have used to identify potential acquisition targets. Describe those that they actually used.

How did they actually make initial contact with GGT management? Why was this approach selected? What are the potential risks involved in contacting a potential acquisition target?

10. What legal documents did GWM and GGT sign before proceeding with due diligence? Why are these documents important and how do they protect the parties involved in the potential transaction? What, if any, risks are involved in signing these documents?

11. GWM would incur significant expenses in conducting due diligence and engaging in what could become protracted negotiations. What protections could GWM have taken to minimize its expenses or to help it recover any costs incurred if the acquisition could not be completed? Why might GGT agree to GWM's demands for such protections?

12. In valuing GGT, Perez used various valuation techniques including discounted cash flow and recent comparable transactions methods. Perez also could have used a variety of other techniques. Indicate other ways in which GGT could have been valued. What are the strengths and weaknesses of the alternative valuation approaches? What might you have done differently to value GGT? Are there any factors that might lead you to believe that Durand paid too much for GGT?*

Determining the Offer Price

13. How was the initial offer price determined? Was it a single purchase price or a range? Why might it have been expressed in terms of a range? How was the purchase price premium determined?

14. Describe how GWM developed its preliminary valuation of GGT. What challenges did GWM encounter, and how were they overcome? How was the preliminary valuation to be used by GWM? What most concerned GWM's management about the financial forecast they had received from GGT? What adjustments did GWM's management make to GGT's projections? Were they appropriate?

15. What were the primary sources and destroyers of value identified by GWM during due diligence? Of these, which do you consider most important and why? How did GWM's management deal with these issues? Do you agree with what they did? Why or why not?

16. What factors did Durand consider in structuring the initial purchase price offer to Chang? What other factors should he have considered?*

17. What additional information would you like to have to make a more informed valuation of GGT?*

Deal Structuring, Financing and Postacquisition Integration

18. Suppose that another CD-ROM media company is sold during the negotiations between GWM and GGT and that the P/E ratio paid for the comparable transaction was higher than what GWM was offering for GGT. How would this information affect negotiations? What would

Chang's likely position be? How could Durand counter Chang's arguments? Assuming Durand still wanted to complete the transaction, how might he have restructured the purchase price to make it acceptable to both firms' shareholders?*

19. Describe the process of offers and counter offers, which resulted in a negotiated agreement. What might you have done differently?

20. What risks was Durand accepting in agreeing to close the deal although several significant liabilities were found during due diligence? Why did he agree to close without reducing the final purchase price? What could he have done to protect GWM from other known or unknown liabilities?*

21. What was the form of payment used by GWM to acquire GGT? (Describe the composition of the purchase price.) Why was this form selected? Was the purchase price taxable or not taxable to GGT shareholders? Explain your answer.

Due Diligence

22. Describe the challenges GWM faced in integrating the two firms. What do you believe were the greatest risks? How did GWM attempt to overcome these risks? What would you have done differently? Be specific.

23. Why is it important to integrate these businesses quickly? Identify both benefits and risks.

24. Why is it important to begin planning for integration before closing?

Financing the Transaction

25. What challenges did GWM face in obtaining financing? What assurances would the lenders want from GWM?

26. In your judgment, how might Durand used GWM's business plan to obtain financing?

27. To what extent do you believe that lenders will tend to focus on the credibility of the assumptions underlying the business plan? Why?

28. Why is it important to include the effects of anticipated synergy in the financing plan?

29. How might lender restrictions affect how GWM could manage the combined firms? Cite examples.

30. Why is financing the transaction sometimes referred to as a reality check?

(Solutions to all asterisked questions are provided in the back of the book.)

Appendix

Solutions to Selected Chapter Business Case Study Discussion Questions

CASE STUDY 1-2: AMERICA ONLINE ACQUIRES TIME WARNER—THE EMERGENCE OF A VERTICALLY INTEGRATED INTERNET AND MEDIA GIANT

1. *What were the primary motives for this transaction? How would you categorize them in terms of the historical motives for mergers and acquisitions discussed in this chapter?*

America Online (AOL) is buying access to branded products, a huge potential subscriber base, and broadband technology. The new company will be able to deliver various branded content to a diverse set of audiences using high-speed transmission channels (e.g., cable).

This transaction reflects many of the traditional motives for combining businesses:

a. *Improved operating efficiency resulting from both economies of scale and scope.* With respect to so-called back office operations, the merging of data, call centers, and other support operations will enable the new company to sustain the same or a larger volume of subscribers with lower overall fixed expenses. Time Warner also will be able to save a considerable amount of expenditures on information technology by sharing AOL's current online information infrastructure and network to support the design, development, and operation of Web sites for its various businesses. Advertising and promotion spending should be more efficient because both AOL and Time Warner can promote their services to the other's subscribers at minimal additional cost.

b. *Diversification.* From AOL's viewpoint, it is integrating down the value chain by acquiring a company that produces original, branded content in the form of magazines, music, and films. By owning this content, AOL will be able to distribute it without having to incur licensing fees.

c. *Changing technology.* At least two profound changes in technology are promoting these types of business combinations. First, the trend toward the use of digital rather than analog technology is causing many media and entertainment firms to look to the Internet as a highly efficient way to market and distribute their products. Time Warner had for several years been trying to develop an online strategy with limited success. AOL represented an unusual opportunity to "leap frog" the competition. Second, the market for online services clearly is shifting away from current dial-up access to high-speed transmission. AOL had been attempting to lobby the government to require that access to the Internet via cable systems be open to the subscribers of any Internet service provider (ISP). As a contingency plan if it could not get "open access" on cable systems, it was developing alliances with local phone companies to use their high-speed digital subscriber line service. By gaining access to Time Warner's cable network, enhanced to carry voice, video, and data, AOL will be able to improve both upload and download speeds for its subscribers. AOL has priced this service at a premium to regular dial-up subscriptions.

d. *Hubris.* AOL was willing to pay a 71% premium over Time Warner's current share price to gain control. This premium is very high by historical standards and assumes that the challenges inherent in making this merger work can be overcome. The overarching implicit assumption is that somehow the infusion of new management into Time Warner can result in the conversion of what is essentially a traditional media company into an Internet powerhouse. Not only did this result in the most expensive merger up to that time but it also created the most unique and the biggest media and entertainment company in the world. Investor confusion following the announcement underscored the difficulty in valuing something that had never been done before.

e. *A favorable regulatory environment.* Growth on the Internet has been fostered by the lack of government regulation. The Federal Communications Commission (FCC) has ruled that ISPs are not subject to local phone company access charges, e-commerce transactions are not subject to tax, and restrictions on the use of personal information have been limited.

2. *Although it is referred to as an acquisition in the case, why is it technically more correct to refer to it as a consolidation? Explain your answer.*

A consolidation refers to two or more businesses combining to form a third company, with no participating firm retaining its original identity. The newly formed company assumes all the assets and liabilities of both companies. Shareholders in both companies exchange their shares for shares in the new company.

3. *Would you classify this business combination as a horizontal, vertical, or conglomerate transaction? Explain your answer.*

If one defines the industry broadly as media and entertainment, this transaction could be described as a vertical transaction in which AOL is backward integrating along the value chain to gain access to Time Warner's proprietary content and broadband technology. However, a case could be made that it also has many of the characteristics of a conglomerate. If industries are defined more narrowly as magazine and book publishing, cable TV, film production, and music recording, the new company could be viewed as a conglomerate.

4. *What are some of the reasons AOL Time Warner may fail to satisfy investor expectations?*

Although AOL has control of the new company in terms of ownership, the extent to which they can exert control in practice may be quite different. AOL could become a captive of the more ponderous Time Warner empire and its 82,000 employees. Time Warner's management style and largely independent culture, as evidenced by their limited success in leveraging the assets of Time and Warner Communications following their 1990 merger, could rob AOL of its customary speed, flexibility, and entrepreneurial spirit. The key to the success of the new companies will be how quickly they will be able to get new Web applications involving Time Warner content up and operating. Decision making may slow to a halt if top management cannot cooperate. Roles and responsibilities at the top were ill defined to make the combination acceptable to senior management at both firms. It will take time for the managers with the dominant skills and personalities to more clearly define their roles in the new company. To their credit, AOL has a good track record in acquiring and integrating companies in a rapidly changing environment. However, it has never before attempted to absorb a company of this size and complexity. If earnings growth slows from historical rates, it is unlikely that investors will assign the excessively high price-to-earnings (P/E) ratios characteristic of Internet firms to the newly formed company.

5. *What would be an appropriate arbitrage strategy for this all-stock transaction?*

Arbitrageurs (arbs) make a profit on the difference between a deal's offer price and the current price of the target's stock. Following a merger announcement, the target's stock price normally rises—but not to the offer price, reflecting the risk that the transaction will not be consummated. The difference between the offer price and the target's current stock price is called a discount or spread. In a cash transaction, the arb can lock in this spread by simply buying the target's stock. In a share-for-share exchange, the arb protects or hedges against the possibility that the acquirer's stock might decline by selling the acquirer's stock short. In the short sale, the arb instructs his or her broker to sell the acquirer's shares at a specific price. The broker loans the arb the shares and obtains the stock from its own inventory or borrows it from a customer's margin account or from another broker. If the acquirer's stock declines in price, the short seller can buy it back at the lower price and make a profit; if the stock increases, the short seller incurs a loss.

CASE STUDY 2-9: EXXON AND MOBIL MERGER—THE MARKET SHARE CONUNDRUM

1. *How does the FTC define market share?*

The market generally is defined by the regulators as a product or group of products offered in a specific geographic area. Market participants are those currently producing and selling these products in this geographic area; potential entrants also are considered market participants. Regulators calculate market shares of all firms identified as market participants based on total sales or capacity currently devoted to the relevant markets. In addition, the market share estimates include capacity that is likely to be diverted to this market in response to a small, but significant and sustainable, increase in price.

2. *Why might it be important to distinguish between a global and a regional oil and gas market?*

The value chain for a fully integrated oil and gas company consists of the following segments: exploration, production, transmission, refining, and distribution. Oil and gas exploration and production is largely a global market subject to substantial competition from numerous competitors. In contrast, the refining and distribution segments of the business can be highly concentrated in the hands of a few oil and gas companies. Such concentration may give the oil and gas company substantial pricing power within a specific region for various types of refined products by owning substantially all of the refining capacity or distribution points, such as gas stations.

3. *Why are the Exxon and Mobil executives emphasizing efficiencies as a justification for this merger?*

Current antitrust guidelines recognize that the efficiencies associated with a business combination may offset the potential anticompetitive effects of increased concentration. The guidelines call for an examination of the net effects of the proposed combination. Proving that the presumed efficiencies justify the merger is difficult because most synergies will not be realized for a number of years. It is therefore difficult to measure their true impact.

4. *Should the size of the combined companies be an important consideration in the regulators' analysis of the proposed merger?*

Size alone should not be a criterion unless it results in anticompetitive practices. Because of the increasing cost of oil and gas exploration and development worldwide, increasing size to realize economies of scale is becoming more important if increasingly scarce world energy resources are to be recovered.

5. *How do the divestitures address perceived anticompetitive problems?*

Requiring one or both of the parties to the merger to sell assets, such as refineries or gas stations, to competing firms can reduce concentration. Such actions will tend to restore competition within a heavily concentrated market.

CASE STUDY 3-3: TYCO RESCUES
AMP FROM ALLIEDSIGNAL

1. *What types of takeover tactics did AlliedSignal use?*

AlliedSignal reinforced its bear hug of AMP with its public announcement of its intent to initiate a tender offer for all of AMP. The move was designed to put pressure on the AMP board and management. Following AMP's rebuff, AlliedSignal initiated a "creeping" tender offer for a portion of AMP's outstanding shares. AlliedSignal also used a consent solicitation to gain effective control of the AMP board through "packing" the board with sympathetic representatives and to neutralize the AMP rights agreement (poison pill) without having to call a special AMP shareholders' meeting. AlliedSignal also used litigation to attempt to thwart AMP's efforts to prevent AlliedSignal from voting its shares.

2. *What steps did AlliedSignal take to satisfy federal securities laws?*

As required by federal securities laws, AlliedSignal informed the AMP board of its intentions to acquire AMP through a hostile tender offer and to file the appropriate schedules with the Securities and Exchange Commission (SEC). AlliedSignal proceeded to file the necessary disclosure documents and consent solicitation materials to be used to obtain consents from AMP shareholders with respect to a series of proposals with the SEC.

3. *What antitakeover defenses were in place at AMP before AlliedSignal's offer?*

The AMP rights agreement, a poison pill, was its primary defense in place before the bid.

4. *How did the AMP board use the AMP rights agreement to encourage AMP shareholders to vote against AlliedSignal's proposals?*

If the AMP board lost majority control following the purchase of more than 20% of AMP's stock by a single individual or entity, the rights could not be redeemed.

5. *What options did AlliedSignal have to neutralize or circumvent AMP's use of the rights agreement?*

AlliedSignal chose to reduce the number of shares it would purchase through its partial tender offer to ensure that it stayed below the 20% ownership threshold. However, AlliedSignal could have increased its offer price to put more pressure on the AMP board to accept its unsolicited bid.

6. *Why did AlliedSignal, after announcing it had purchased 20 million AMP shares at $44.50, indicate that it would reduce the price paid in any further offers it might make?*

AlliedSignal was trying to frighten AMP shareholders into tendering their shares at $44.50. This may have been a prelude to a tender offer for more shares at a later date.

7. *What other takeover defenses did AMP use in its attempt to thwart AlliedSignal?*

Initially, AMP used the "just say no" defense to buy time to add more defenses. The board cleverly used the AMP rights plan to discourage AlliedSignal from immediately moving ahead with its proposed $10 billion tender offer for all of AMP's shares. The board initiated a stock buy-back plan for 30 million shares at $55.00. This was intended to reduce the number of shares available for purchase by AlliedSignal and to communicate to the market what AMP thought its shares were worth. The presumption is that shareholders most likely to sell in a buy-back are the least loyal to the company and are most likely to sell in a tender offer. In addition, AMP set up an employee stock ownership plan (ESOP), enabling it to place some number of AMP shares in "friendly" hands. Finally, AMP used litigation to attempt to block AlliedSignal from voting its shares. Note that as part of the merger agreement with Tyco, these defenses were deactivated. The self-tender and ESOP were terminated and the rights plan was amended so that it would not apply to the merger with Tyco.

8. *How did both AMP and AlliedSignal use litigation in this takeover battle?*

AMP used Pennsylvania antitakeover statutes to try to block AlliedSignal's ability to vote its shares and to prevent AlliedSignal from taking control of the AMP board through its consent solicitation. Both sides used lawsuits to increase the cost of the acquisition and to wear down their opponents.

9. *Should state laws be used to protect companies from hostile takeovers?*

The empirical evidence suggests that target shareholders benefit greatly from a hostile takeover, whereas the acquirer's shareholders may experience modest negative abnormal returns. Some critics of mergers and acquisitions (M&As) argue that the gains to the target shareholders are more than offset by the damage to other constituent groups including employees, communities, customers, and suppliers.

10. *Was AMP's board and management acting to protect their own positions (i.e., the management entrenchment hypothesis) or in the best interests of the shareholders (i.e., the shareholder interests hypothesis)?*

As a result of their resistance, AMP's board was able to secure for its shareholders an additional 15% premium to the original AlliedSignal offer. This is consistent with the shareholder interests hypothesis.

CASE STUDY 4-3: CONSOLIDATION IN THE GLOBAL PHARMACEUTICAL INDUSTRY CONTINUES—THE GLAXO WELLCOME AND SMITHKLINE BEECHAM EXAMPLE

1. *What drove change in the pharmaceutical industry in the late 1990s?*

Profit margin pressures continued to mount on drug companies as a result of the proliferation of managed care, reductions in the number of "me-too" drugs, and new medical breakthroughs in human genome research. The cost of supporting the drug trials necessary to bring new drugs to market based on this research continued to grow. The potential for government intervention further complicated efforts to increase selling prices. Finally, the loss of patent protection for many "blockbuster" drugs and the dearth of such drugs in the pipeline encouraged the remaining independent companies to rethink their strategies of staying independent.

2. *In your judgment, what are the likely strategic business plan objectives of the major pharmaceutical companies and why are they important?*

Major strategic objectives are likely to include the following: (1) gaining access to current patents for drugs that already are generating substantial cash flow or show significant promise of doing so; (2) gaining access to proprietary research pertaining to drugs currently under development; (3) increasing returns on research and development (R&D) spending; (4) obtaining access to new distribution channels for current and new products; and (5) reducing the overall cost of doing business.

3. *What are the alternatives to mergers available to the major pharmaceutical companies? What are the advantages and disadvantages of each alternative?*

Drug companies could enter joint ventures or partnerships or make minority investments in research-oriented biotechnology companies. Although such options are generally less costly, the degree of control is also substantially less. Also, although it may be possible to gain access to new distribution channels through partnering, such arrangements do not address the immediate needs of companies whose backlog of new drugs is limited. Finally, partnering rarely provides the degree of cost savings that can be realized through the consolidation of overlapping portions of merged companies.

4. *How would you classify the typical drug company's strategy in the 1970s and 1980s: cost leadership, differentiation, focus, or hybrid? Explain your answer. How have their strategies changed in recent years?*

Historically, drug companies tended to pursue differentiation strategies that were heavily dependent on the ability of their salesforces to convince physicians, hospitals, and pharmacies to buy their drugs. Although "me-too" drugs were heavily promoted, the salesforce had to be able to convince the customers that there were legitimate reasons to buy them. Today, drug companies seem to be moving toward hybrid strategies involving a combination of differentiation and cost leadership in their targeted markets. Margin pressure continues to force companies to look for ways to reduce operating expenses and improve productivity, often through M&A strategies.

5. *What do you think was the major motivating factor behind the Glaxo SmithKline merger and why was it so important?*

The primary factor seems to be the desire to achieve sufficient scale to support the necessary R&D to commercialize new products based on advances made in gene sequencing. Although cost savings continue to be important, they were likely to have played a secondary consideration. The estimated annual cost savings of $1.7 billion after 3 years represents less than 5% of the combined companies' total cost base.

CASE STUDY 5-7: WHEN COMPANIES OVERPAY—MATTEL ACQUIRES THE LEARNING COMPANY

1. *Why was Mattel interested in diversification?*

With more than one-third of its revenue coming from a mature product like Barbie, Mattel was hoping to take advantage of the children's software market that was growing at 20% per year—about four times the growth rate of the traditional toy market.

2. *What alternatives to acquisition could Mattel have considered? Discuss the pros and cons of each alternative.*

Mattel could have considered building the capability internally by leveraging its small but growing software division. Alternatively, Mattel could have considered creating a joint venture corporation with a leading "edutainment" software company. Both parties would contribute certain assets. Mattel could contribute certain of its most recognized brand name products, and the software company could contribute its technical expertise. Mattel also could have considered licensing certain software products from other companies for distribution under its own brand or taking minority positions in software companies that would develop products for distribution by Mattel. Developing the capability internally may be a high-risk proposition because, given its limited technical resources, Mattel may have missed the opportunity to participate in the accelerating market for interactive children's toys. A joint venture or partnering arrangement may not provide the control Mattel may want to market globally and to produce only products that would not compete directly with Mattel's current products. Licenses and minority investments both suffer from limited control and may be difficult to manage.

3. *How might the Internet affect the toy industry? What potential conflicts with customers might be created?*

As illustrated by eToys success at that time, the Internet poses an interesting new distribution channel for Mattel. However, efforts to exploit this new technology put Mattel in direct competition with its customers, who are already on-line.

4. *What are the primary barriers to entering the toy industry?*

Barriers to entry include the well-established distribution channels of the major manufacturers, based on long-standing relationships with retailers such as Wal-Mart and Toys "R" Us. Companies like Mattel and Hasbro have created substantial brand recognition over the years by spending tens of millions of advertising dollars. Furthermore, brand names are protected by patents and proprietary knowledge. Finally, the top manufacturers have licensing arrangements granting them the exclusive right to market toys based on products provided by the major entertainment companies.

5. *What could Mattel have done to protect itself against risks uncovered during due diligence?*

Mattel could have protected itself by shifting some of the risk to The Learning Company (TLC). This could have been achieved by making part of the purchase price contingent on TLC hitting certain future performance targets defined in terms of profits or revenue. Alternatively, Mattel could have insisted that a portion of the purchase price be put into an escrow account until the full extent of the problems uncovered during due diligence were understood.

CASE STUDY 6-7: DAIMLER ACQUIRES CHRYSLER—ANATOMY OF A CROSS-BORDER TRANSACTION

1. *Identify ways in which the merger combined companies with complementary skills and resources.*

Germany's world-renowned reputation in engineering could be used to raise the overall quality of Chrysler products, whereas Chrysler's project management skills could be used to shorten the new product introduction cycle. In addition, Daimler's distribution network in Europe could provide access to the European market for Chrysler products. Chrysler dealerships could be used to service Daimler cars in the United States. Finally, greater access to capital markets and the combined operating cash flow of the two companies could give DaimlerChrysler the financial strength to build assembly plants and develop distribution networks in Asia.

2. *What are the major cultural differences between Daimler and Chrysler?*

Daimler is largely a conglomerate in which management is decentralized. In contrast, Chrysler's management and decision-making process tended to be highly centralized. Daimler, like many European companies, tended to be very detail-oriented. The reference to lengthy meetings and big reports suggests a very cumbersome and bureaucratic decision-making process. The replacement of key Chrysler managers by Daimler managers may have left many Chrysler managers feeling alienated. The small number of former Chrysler managers reporting directly to the top may have added to a sense of powerlessness. Differences in customs and habits also may have contributed to poor communications. All of these factors tended to reduce loyalty by Chrysler managers to the newly created corporation.

3. *What were the principal risks to the merger?*

The risks to the merger included the loss of key Chrysler operating managers, who were enriched by the merger, and a loss of corporate continuity. Moreover, the lengthy time period required to integrate manufacturing operations and purchasing makes the recovery of the premium paid for Chrysler that much more difficult.

4. *Why might it take so long to integrate manufacturing operations and certain functions such as purchasing?*

Changing manufacturing operations requires changing union work rules, which are set by contract. Such rules could only be renegotiated when current contracts covering the plants expire. Before any significant changes could be made,

DaimlerChrysler would have to inventory/catalog equipment and procedures by plant, benchmark performance, identify best practices, and convince workers at the plant level to change their methods. Purchasing represented both a significant opportunity and major challenge for DaimlerChrysler. Spending on purchased materials for automotive companies represents a major portion of their total cost of production. Therefore, opportunities to buy in bulk offer substantial cost savings. However, integrating purchasing, which often is dispersed across various countries or even plants, could be done only as contracts with existing vendors expire. In addition, much purchasing is done at the plant level, where purchasing agents are accustomed to significant autonomy.

CASE STUDY 7-1: THE HUNT FOR ELUSIVE SYNERGY—@HOME ACQUIRES EXCITE

1. *Did @Home overpay for Excite?*

To answer the question of whether @Home overpaid, it is necessary to estimate the value of synergy, add this estimate to the market value of Excite, and compare the resulting sum to the $6.7 billion purchase price. Note that free cash flow to the firm in the first full year of operation following the merger equals ($500 − $50) × (1 − .4) × 340,000 or $91.8 million.

Using the variable growth model, we can calculate the present value of potential synergy (P_0) as follows:

Year	FCFF ($ Millions)	Present Value Interest Factor	Present Value ($ Millions)
1	91.8	.83	76.2
2	105.6	.69	73.3
3	121.4	.58	70.4
4	139.6	.48	67.0
5	160.6	.40	64.2
6	184.6	.33	61.8
7	212.3	.28	59.4
8	244.2	.23	56.2
9	280.8	.19	53.4
10	322.9	.16	51.7
			$633.6

$$\text{Terminal Value} = \frac{\$322.9 \times (1.05)/(.10 - .05)}{(1.20)^{10}} = \frac{\$6780.90}{6.19}$$

$$= \$1095.5$$

$$P_0 = \$633.6 + \$1095.5 = \$1729.1$$

Maximum purchase price for Excite (including present value of synergy)

$$\$1729.1 + \$3500.0 = \$5229.1 \text{ (versus } \$6700.0)$$

2. *What other assumptions might you consider?*

Other sources of profitable revenue, such as selling additional products and services to the Excite customer base and advertising revenue, could be considered. In addition, some assumption would have to be made about working capital requirements and investment in new server capacity and other support infrastructure.

3. *What are the limitations of the valuation methodology used in this case?*

The valuation is heavily dependent on the choice of assumptions concerning growth rates during the high-growth and stable-growth periods and the discount rates for each period. Almost two-thirds of the total valuation is dependent on the estimation of the residual value or the value of cash flows beyond the tenth year, which is likely to be less accurate than estimates of cash flows during the earlier years of the forecast period.

4. *What alternative valuation techniques could you use?*

The analyst could examine recent transactions of similar companies or consider market valuations of similar companies in the same industry. The latter would have to be adjusted to reflect premiums paid for these types of companies.

CASE STUDY 8-3: TRIBUNE COMPANY ACQUIRES THE TIMES MIRROR CORPORATION IN A TALE OF CORPORATE INTRIGUE

1. *In your judgment, did it make good strategic sense to combine the Tribune and Times Mirror corporations? Why or why not?*

Yes, the combination of the two firms offers substantial cost savings in closing overlapping news bureaus and substantial economies in purchasing major cost items such as news print. The merger also gives both firms larger coverage in the nation's major metropolitan areas in which they can offer consumers both on-line and print access to the content. By expanding their reach in this manner, both firms will be significantly more attractive to advertisers. Moreover, this geographic diversification will help consolidated earnings as slower economic activity in one area is offset by relatively stronger growth in another.

2. *Using the Merger Evaluation table (Table 8-10) given in the case, determine the estimated equity values of Tribune, Times Mirror, and the combined firms. Why is long-term debt deducted from the total present value estimates to obtain the estimated equity values?*

The estimated equity values for the Tribune, Times Mirror, and combined firms are $8.5 billion, $2.4 billion, and $16.4 billion, respectively. The total value of the firm is estimated using free cash flow to the firm, which includes cash flow available to both equity and bondholders. Consequently, deducting the market value of debt from the firm's total market value will give an estimate of the firm's equity value.

3. *Despite the merger having closed in mid-2000, the full effects of synergy may not be realized until 2002. Why? What factors could account for the delay?*

The full effects of synergy are not realized immediately because of bureau leases that must expire or be bought out, severance expenses that offset savings that result from layoffs, management inertia, employee resistance, morale concerns, and the tendency to underestimate the time that is required to implement savings programs. In addition, savings programs often require retraining and relocating workers, which also offset some portion of the savings in the early years.

4. *The estimated equity value for the Times Mirror Corporation on the day the merger was announced was about $2.8 billion. However, as shown in the offer price determination table (Table 8-11), the equity value estimated using discounted cash-flow analysis is given as $2.4 billion. What factors might explain this difference? Why is the minimum offer price shown as $2.8 billion rather than the lower $2.4 billion figure? How is the maximum offer price determined in the offer price determination table? How much of the estimated synergy value generated by combining the two businesses is being transferred to the Times Mirror shareholders? Why?*

The minimum offer price is the market value of the firm because it is unlikely that Times Mirror shareholders would sell their shares at below current market value. The maximum price is the minimum price plus the present value of synergy. Two-thirds of the estimated synergy is being transferred to the Times Mirror shareholders as part of the offer price as a result of the relative bargaining power of the seller versus the buyer.

5. *Does the Times Mirror-Tribune Corporation merger create value? If so, how much? What percentage of this value goes to Times Mirror shareholders and what percentage to Tribune shareholders? Why?*

The merger creates $4.6 billion in value between the premerger and postmerger valuations, of which 37% goes to Times Mirror shareholders, reflecting their equity ownership in the new firm. The remainder goes to Tribune shareholders.

CASE STUDY 9-5: VALUING
A PRIVATELY HELD COMPANY

Note: To estimate the weighted average cost of capital (WACC) for a leveraged private firm, it is necessary to calculate the firm's leveraged β. This requires an estimate of the firm's unleveraged β, which can be obtained by estimating the unleveraged β for similar firms in the same industry. Also, the value of debt and equity in calculating the cost of capital should be expressed as market rather than book values.

Calculating cost of equity (COE) and WACC:

1. Unlevered Beta for publicly traded firms in the same industry $= 2.00/(1 + .6 \times .4) = 1.61$, where 2.00 is the levered beta, .6 is $(1 - \text{tax rate})$, and .4 is the average debt ratio for firms in this industry.

2. Debt/Equity ratio for the private firm $= 5/(2 \times 4) = .625$ where 5, 4, and 2 are the private firm's debt, book value of equity, and the ratio of market value to book value for similar firms.

3. Levered beta for the private firm $= 1.61 \times (1 + .6 \times .625)$
$$= 2.21$$

4. Cost of equity for the private firm $= 6 + 2.21 \times 5.5 = 18.16$

5. After-tax cost of debt $= .10 \times (1 - .4) = 6.0$

6. COC for the private firm $= 18.16 \times \dfrac{2 \times 4}{(2 \times 4 + 5)} + 6.00 \times \dfrac{5}{(2 \times 4 + 5)}$
$$= 18.16 \times .615 + 6.00 \times .385$$
$$= 13.48$$

Valuing the business using the free cash flow to the firm (FCFF) model:

Year	1	2	3	4	5	6
EBIT (EBIT grows at 15% for the first 5 years and 5% thereafter)	$2.30	$2.65	$3.04	$3.50	$4.02	$4.22
EBIT (1 − Tax Rate)	$1.38	$1.59	$1.82	$2.10	$2.41	$2.53
Less (Cap. Expenditures- Depreciation) grows at same 15% annual rate as revenue for 5 years and are offsetting thereafter)	$.115	$.132	$.152	$.175	$.201	$0.00
Equals						
FCFF	$1.26	$1.46	$1.67	$1.93	$2.21	$2.53

Terminal value $= \$2.53/(.1348 - .05) = \$29.83$

$$\text{Present Value of FCFF} = \frac{\$1.26}{1.1348} + \frac{\$1.46}{1.1348^2} + \frac{\$1.67}{1.1348^3} + \frac{\$1.93}{1.1348^4}$$

$$+ \frac{\$2.21}{1.1348^5} + \frac{\$29.83}{1.1348^5}$$

$$= \$1.11 + \$1.13 + \$1.14 + \$1.16 + \$1.17 + \$15.85$$

$$= \$21.56$$

Value of Equity $= \$26.27$ (Market value, or MV, of the firm) $- \$5$ (MV of debt)
$$= \$16.56$$

CASE STUDY 10-1: CONSOLIDATION IN THE GLOBAL WIRELESS COMMUNICATIONS INDUSTRY—VODAFONE ACQUIRES AIRTOUCH

1. *Did the AirTouch board make the right decision? Why or why not?*

Only time will tell which stock, Vodafone or Bell Atlantic's, will outperform. Morgan Stanley concluded that the Vodafone offer was likely to have the higher overall value at the time of the closing. AirTouch shareholders could lock in this higher value if they choose to sell the shares of Vodafone they receive for each share of AirTouch. In addition, the anticipated earnings dilution through 2002 probably would cause the gap between the values of Vodafone's and Bell Atlantic's offers to widen. Intangible arguments for accepting the Vodafone proposal include the probability that Vodafone had the more compatible corporate culture. Both companies shared the same vision and appear to be relatively decentralized in terms of management style. In contrast, Bell Atlantic still is emerging from the highly regulated environment of the landline carriers.

2. *How valid are the reasons for the proposed merger?*

The justification for the merger rests more on faith in the continued expansion of the wireless communication market than on factual evidence. To date, it remains unclear how much business travelers and travel-oriented consumers are willing to pay for wireless communication services. Establishing a global wireless network with global roaming capability is going to be a very expensive proposition. In late 1999, Iridium LLC—a satellite phone venture backed by Motorola, which has an 18% stake in Iridium—went into default on an $800 million syndicated loan. Default on this loan automatically placed Iridium in violation of loan covenants on $700 million in other loans. At the same time, Chase Manhattan Bank demanded that Motorola guarantee at least $300 million of the $800 million syndicated loan. On August 13, 1999, Iridium filed for protection under Chapter 11 of the U.S. Bankruptcy Code because Motorola and Iridium's creditors could not agree on a plan for repaying Iridium's debt. Although this will give Iridium some breathing space, it does not address its key problem—a lack of paying customers. As of August 13, 1999, Iridium had signed 20,000 of the 500,000 it had projected for 1999. In March 2000, Iridium filed for Chapter 7 liquidation. In early 2002, Global Crossing also declared Chapter 11 bankruptcy because of a lack of demand for its state-of-the-art global telecommunications network.

3. *What are the potential risk factors related to the merger?*

Cost savings may not be realized. Even if they are, they represent only about 6% of the total purchase price. Because of the absence of a collar, the AirTouch shareholders could be hurt if Vodafone American Depository Shares decline in value before the closing date. Projected earnings may not be realized as a possible global recession slows the growth of international travel. Achieving global coverage may be more expensive than anticipated. Increased competition from other vendors may cause reductions in the price per minute of usage, which more than offset the projected increase in the number of minutes used.

4. *Why did the merger happen so quickly?*

Once a target announces that it has received an offer from a legitimate potential acquirer, the target has been "put into play." Other potential suitors may make bids for the target, boosting the potential purchase price in an auction-like environment. The key is for the initial bidder to move quickly enough and to make the proposed price attractive enough to preclude others from making a bid.

5. *Why was Bell Atlantic interested in a pooling-of-interest accounting treatment? Why was this a concern about Bell Atlantic's purchase price? Would this be an important consideration today? Would this be an important consideration if the merger had been completed after January 1, 2002?*

The Bell proposal already was dilutive. Purchase accounting would have created substantial annual goodwill charges, which would have exacerbated this situation. AirTouch's board was concerned about this closing condition because its failure to qualify for pooling of interests would have removed Bell from the bidding. The remaining bidder(s) could have found some pretext to lower their offering prices. Note that had this merger been undertaken in 2002, pooling of interest would not have been an option for financial reporting purposes because all such business combinations have to be accounted for using the purchase method of accounting. However, companies no longer have to amortize any goodwill that is created as a result of the business combination.

6. *The Vodafone merger will be treated as a purchase of assets under GAAP accounting and will create $3.4 billion in annual goodwill expenses. Why might the merger have been accounted for financial reporting purposes using the purchase method of accounting? How has the treatment of goodwill changed for financial reporting purposes after January 1, 2002?*

The purchase method improves after-tax cash flow by allowing the acquiring corporation to write-off the excess of the fair market value of acquired assets over their book values. After January 1, 2002, companies no longer have to amortize goodwill, but they may still write-up the book value of acquired assets to their fair market value. However, if goodwill is found to be impaired (i.e., its book value far exceeds its fair market value), the company must reduce its value to reflect more accurately true economic conditions.

7. *Is this merger likely to be tax-free, partially tax free, or taxable? Explain your answer.*

The merger is partially taxable. Cash received will be taxed at the capital gains tax rate because it does not exceed the AirTouch shareholder cost basis in the stock.

8. *What are some of the challenges the two companies are likely to face while integrating the businesses?*

Although the two companies appear to have been managed somewhat similarly in the past and both seem somewhat entrepreneurial, they are likely to suffer the same challenges others experience in international mergers. This includes diminished control over widely dispersed operations, a lack of loyalty or commitment to the parent company, jealousies created by differences in salary and benefit levels, lack of a shared vision in remote operations, and increasingly large percentages of profits whipsawed by currency fluctuations. More specifically, most of the anticipated $3.5 billion in cost savings is expected from economies realized through bulk purchases. This presumes that most of the purchasing can be coordinated sufficiently to realize this objective. This is frequently extraordinarily difficult to implement in highly decentralized operations.

9. *How would the collar protect AirTouch shareholders from a decline in Bell Atlantic's stock?*

The collar guarantees the price of Bell Atlantic stock for the AirTouch shareholders because $48 × 1.6683 and $52 × 1.54 both equal $80.08.

CASE STUDY 11-2: EVALUATING A LEVERAGED BUYOUT OPPORTUNITY

Based on the information given in the case, will the buyout generate sufficient cash to cover interest and principal payments and to provide an appropriate return to the leveraged buyout opportunity (LBO) firm's equity investors?

1. *Calculate free cash flow to equity holders (FCFE) and to the firm (FCFF).*

Year	1	2	3	4	5	Terminal Year
Revenues	$3,000,000	$3,450,000	$3,967,500	$4,562,625	$5,247,019	$5,509,370
− Expenses	$2,100,000	$2,415,000	$2,777,250	$3,193,834	$3,672,913	$3,856,559
− Depreciation	$200,000	$230,000	$264,000	$304,175	$349,801	$367,291
= EBIT	$700,000	$805,000	$925,750	$1,064,616	$1,224,305	$1,285,520
− Interest	$550,000	$500,000	$450,000	$400,000	$350,000	$300,000
= Taxable	$150,000	$305,000	$475,750	$664,616	$874,305	$985,520
Income						
− Tax	$60,000	$122,000	$190,300	$265,846	$349,722	$394,208
= Net Income	$90,000	$183,000	$285,450	$398,770	$524,583	$591,312
+ Depreciation	$200,000	$230,000	$264,500	$304,175	$349,801	$367,291
− Capital Expenditures	$250,000	$287,500	$330,625	$380,219	$437,252	$459,114
− Chg. WC	$150,000	$172,500	$198,375	$228,131	$262,350	$275,468
− Principal Repaid	$500,000	$500,000	$500,000	$500,000	$500,000	$0
= FCFE	$(610,000)	$(547,000)	$(479,050)	$(405,405)	$(325,218)	$224,021
+ Interest × (1 − t)	$330,000	$300,000	$270,000	$240,000	$210,000	$180,000
+ Principal Repaid	$500,000	$500,000	$500,000	$500,000	$500,000	$0
= FCFF	$220,000	$253,000	$290,950	$334,595	$384,782	$404,021

2. *Calculate the weighted average cost of capital (WACC) using a target debt-to-equity ratio of one to one.*

Equity (Y/E)	$1,090,000	$1,273,000	$1,558,450	$1,957,220	$2,481,803	$3,073,115
Debt (Y/E)	$5,000,000	$4,500,000	$4,000,000	$3,500,000	$3,000,000	$2,500,000
D/E Ratio	4.59	3.54	2.57	1.79	1.21	.81
Beta	3.00	2.37	1.79	1.32	.97	.73
Cost of Equity	23.50%	20.04%	16.85%	14.27%	12.35%	10.15%
WACC	14.75%	13.02%	11.43%	10.14%	9.18%	8.08%

1. Equity at the end of year 1 = Net Income + Equity at the end of year 0

$$= \$90,000 + \$1,000,000$$

$$= \$1,090,000.$$

2. β_L in year 2: $\beta_{L2} - \beta_{L1} = (1 - t) \times (D_2/E_2 - D_1/E_1)$ and

$$\beta_{L2} = (1 - t) \times (D_2/E_2 - D_1/E_1) + \beta_{L1}$$

$$= (.6) \times (-1.05) + 3.00 = 2.37$$

3. COE in year 2: $COE_2 - COE_1 = (B_{L2} - B_{L1}) \times 5.5$ and

$$COE_2 = (B_{L2} - B_{L1}) \times 5.5 + COE_1$$

$$= (2.37 - 3.00) \times 5.5 + 23.50$$

$$= 20.04\%$$

4. After-tax interest cost on debt is $10\% \times (1 - t) = 6\%$

3. *Calculating terminal values:*

a. Terminal Value of Equity $= \$224,021/(.1015 - .05) = \$4,349,922$

b. Terminal Value of Firm = Terminal Value of Equity

$$+ \text{Outstanding Debt}$$

$$= \$4,349,922 + \$2,500,000$$

$$= \$6,849,922$$

4. *Calculating present values:*

$$\text{PV to equity investors} = -\frac{\$610,000}{(1.2350)} - \frac{\$547,000}{(1.2350)(1.2004)}$$

$$- \frac{\$479,050}{(1.2350)(1.2004)(1.1685)}$$

$$- \frac{\$405,405}{(1.2350)(1.2004)(1.1685)(1.1427)}$$

$$+ \frac{(\$4,349,922 - \$325,218)}{(1.2350)(1.2004)(1.1685)(1.1427)(1.1235)}$$

$$= -\$493{,}927 - \$368{,}973 - \$276{,}541$$
$$- \$204{,}552 + \$1{,}809{,}702$$
$$= \$465{,}709 < \$1{,}000{,}000$$

(equity investment in the LBO)

$$\text{PV of deal to firm} = \frac{\$220{,}000}{(1.1475)} + \frac{\$253{,}000}{(1.1475)(1.1302)}$$
$$+ \frac{\$290{,}950}{(1.1475)(1.1302)(1.1143)}$$
$$+ \frac{\$334{,}595}{(1.1475)(1.1302)(1.1143)(1.1014)}$$
$$+ \frac{(\$384{,}782 + \$6{,}849{,}922)}{(1.1475)(1.1302)(1.1143)(1.1014)(1.0918)}$$
$$= \$191{,}721 + \$195{,}080 + \$201{,}330$$
$$+ \$210{,}215 + \$4{,}163{,}154$$
$$= \$4{,}961{,}500 < \$6{,}500{,}000 \text{ (total cost of the}$$
LBO including both debt and equity)

Conclusion: The proposed LBO does not make sense because neither equity investors nor lenders can recover their original investment or loans plus their required rates of return.

CASE STUDY 12-6: BELL ATLANTIC AND VODAFONE FORM WIRELESS OPERATION TO EXPAND GEOGRAPHIC COVERAGE

1. *What did Bell Atlantic and Vodafone expect to get out of the business alliance?*

A substantial number of users of wireless devices are business travelers. Securing widespread geographic coverage would give both companies access to more customers. By using existing networks, the two companies could gain access to these new customers far less expensively than if they were to attempt to build their own networks. (It is unclear if the two companies could not simply have cross-licensed access to their respective networks.) In particular, although Vodafone is the world's largest wireless company, it did not have complete geographic coverage in the United States. This significantly reduced the value of the Vodafone franchise given the size of the U.S. market.

2. *Do you think this alliance will promote or reduce competition in the wireless phone market?*

The alliance, or joint venture (JV), is likely to be procompetitive because it will put the partners on a more equal footing with other global competitors such as MCIWorldcom/Sprint as well as AT&T and British Telecom. The JV made it possible for the two partners to achieve national coverage at a price that is far less than if they had tried to build their own networks. Antitrust regulators generally look more favorably on alliances that make it possible for companies to do something that they probably could not have done on their own.

3. *Why would Bell Atlantic and Vodafone want to sell a portion of the new alliance to the public?*

Selling equity to the public will enable the joint venture to finance future capital expenditures, will provide a currency for future acquisitions, and will place a value on the JV that might help to boost the share prices of both companies. The two partners eventually may wish to sell the entire JV to the public.

4. *In your judgment, how do you think ownership in the alliance was determined?*

The distribution of ownership appears to have been based on the valuation of the assets contributed by each party to the joint venture. Each party contributed their network assets, which could be valued either by discounting future cash flows generated by each network or by estimating the cost of building a network in the geographic areas that were not currently covered by Bell Atlantic and Vodafone.

5. *Why might the partners have selected a general partnership as the appropriate legal structure for this business alliance? Explain your answer.*

The partners elected to use the existing Cellco general partnership to preserve the FCC licenses and other government permits needed to conduct business in the U.S. telecommunications market. By simply having Vodafone AirTouch contribute assets directly to an existing legal entity there was no need to transfer ownership of the licenses to a new legal entity and in doing so risk the possibility that ownership would not be wholly transferred. The partners may choose at a later date to change the form of ownership to a corporate legal structure because of their desire to issue equity in the future. The corporate structure often is selected if the proposed alliance is large and complex such that it requires its own organizational structure and internal management. The equity structure of the corporation also will facilitate the sale of the partners' interest in the business if they should choose to exit the business at some point in the future. These benefits are negated by the double taxation of dividends that could have been avoided if a partnership had been the preferred legal structure. Moreover, both companies lose the flexibility associated with the partnership structure, which enables creative ways to distribute profits and losses from the venture in amounts that are disproportionate to their respective ownership shares.

CASE STUDY 13-9: ALLEGHENY
TELEDYNE RESTRUCTURES

1. *What are some of the reasons that Allegheny Teledyne considering such an extensive restructuring of its operations?*

Allegheny Teledyne had a desire to achieve greater focus and to improve its overall profitability and growth potential by exiting underperforming businesses.

2. *What synergies might there be in the businesses that Allegheny Teledyne is retaining?*

All remaining businesses are in some segment of the metals manufacturing or fabrication business, which should facilitate management's understanding of specific business problems and opportunities. In addition, some of the metal alloy products may be used in the production of specialty metals.

3. *Why do you think that stockholders might be better off owning stock in each of the three new companies (consumer products, aerospace and electronics, and metals manufacturing) than just in Allegheny Teledyne Inc.?*

They are pure plays and may be valued more accurately by analysts and investors. Moreover, they will have their own management, who will be focused on operating a single business, and they will not be burdened by Allegheny Teledyne's corporate overhead structure.

4. *Why might Allegheny Teledyne be considering spinning off some units and divesting others?*

The decision to spin off rather than to divest a business may reflect the lack of buyers for the business or a concern that the divestiture process will be too disruptive to the employees, customers, and suppliers of the business.

5. *Why might it be common for a major restructuring to come at a time when the head of a company is leaving, retiring, or assuming fewer responsibilities?*

The chief executive officer (CEO) may be retiring rather than face a firing following the poor performance of the corporation. The CEO also may see this as an appropriate time to retire because a successful restructuring may be viewed as his legacy to the company.

CHAPTER 14. GEE WHIZ MEDIA (GWM)
ACQUIRES GO-GO TECHNOLOGY (GGT)

ANSWERS TO SELECTED QUESTIONS

1. *Describe the industry or market in which GWM competed in terms of the following: customers, suppliers, current competitors, potential entrants, and product substitutes. How should this information be used by GWM's management to develop a long-term strategy?*

    a. Customers: Electronic publishing companies (e.g., Activision and Broderbund) and distributors.

b. Suppliers: Primarily content owners including Prince, famous artists, and record companies. Suppliers had market power and could exact high prices from CD programming companies.

c. Current competitors: GGT and Multimedia Corp were focusing on what they did best (i.e., converting content to electronic media such as CD-ROMs); allowing others to manufacture the disks; and aligning with distribution companies such as Broderbund for marketing, distribution, and advertising.

d. Potential entrants: Few barriers to entry. Many small companies were entering the multimedia industry segment to convert content to CD-ROMs.

e. Product substitutes: Virtually all types of entertainment (e.g., books, tapes, TV, other game CDs, etc).

f. This information could be used by GWM management in developing a long-term strategy by helping to define their customers' needs, suppliers' requirements, relative strengths versus the competition, potential threats and opportunities, and ways in which they can satisfy customer needs better than the competition.

2. *Identify GWM's primary strengths and weaknesses as compared with the competition. How can this information be used to identify threats to and opportunities for GWM?*

a. Strengths

   (1) Market recognition that comes from being first (i.e., "first mover advantage")
   (2) Reputation for honesty
   (3) Multi-year licenses with major software companies (Sony, IBM and Apple) to promote their multimedia products

b. Weaknesses

   (1) Undercapitalized
   (2) Poor project management skills, including few controls and an inability to meet deadlines
   (3) Excessive spending
   (4) Limited access to distribution channels
   (5) No proprietary content

4. *Identify the range of reasonable options available to GWM to grow its business. Discuss the key advantages and disadvantages of each option. Of the available options, which would you have selected and why?*

Rapid industry consolidation suggested that acquisition was the most attractive route for GWM. Time was not on their side. Organic or internal growth through reinvestment of excess cash flow involved significant investment in marketing programs and in developing proprietary content. This also would require substantial time to assemble the right content. An alliance or JV with another competitor or a publisher to obtain content would initiate control issues and require significant amounts of time to negotiate, especially if it involved multiple content suppliers.

6. *GWM's acquisition plan identified key objectives, resource capability, the target industry, and appropriate tactics for completing an acquisition. Were all of the objectives adequately quantified, and did they have associated completion dates? What other key objectives and tactics might GWM have included? Discuss the importance of these additional objectives and tactics?*

a. GWM's stated objectives in its acquisition plan included:

1. Acquiring companies with proprietary content or access to proprietary content, effective distribution channels, and excellent design and production capabilities
2. Acquiring companies with widely recognized CD titles
3. Staying within the multimedia industry that they knew

b. Some of GWM's stated tactics in its acquisition plan included:

1. Achieving a minimum acceptable rate of return equal to its cost of capital of 15%
2. A maximum P/E for the target company of not more than 35 times current year's earnings or 30 times next year's earnings
3. An interest coverage ratio of the combined companies that would not fall below the industry average of 6.2
4. Counting only one-half of the projected cash flow resulting from synergy as part of the purchase price

c. Other tactics could have included a target debt-to-equity ratio.

8. *What were the key assumptions made in the Gee Whiz Media business plan used to justify the acquisition of Go Go Technology? Consider key assumptions, both explicit and implicit, with respect to the following areas: the market, financial performance, acquisition tactics, valuation, and integration.*

a. Market:

1. CD-ROM technology would improve and proliferate.
2. People would use this medium to play games and for reference material.
3. The market would be large and growing.

b. Financial Performance:

1. They could make money without owning content.
2. Initially they felt they could distribute the disks on their own.
3. Growth through acquisition is preferable to organic businesses, JVs, or alliances.
4. It is easier to rejuvenate existing products than to introduce new ones and build a brand image.

5. Although the number of titles produced in the industry in 1996 slowed to 360,000, Durand believed the combined companies could grow faster than the industry.

6. The potential loss of customers and other unanticipated expenses discovered during due diligence could be made up from future cash flows.

c. Acquisition Tactics

1. Acquiring something in their same industry would heighten their chances of success.

2. A friendly acquisition was superior to a hostile one.

3. Wall Street would accept 2 years of earnings dilution.

d. Valuation

1. Present value (PV) of undeveloped commercial property and certain intangible assets equaled $2.5 million and $10 million, respectively.

2. PV of known nonoperating liabilities would not exceed $10 million.

3. PV of net synergy was equal to $117.9 million.

4. Only a few customers would leave.

5. The loan covenants would not prove to be too burdensome.

6. They would generate sufficient cash flow to meet debt service requirements.

7. Discount rate is 15%, and the conventional valuation techniques are adequate to measure value.

8. GGT's software development program would not realize the cost savings embodied in the GGT forecast (Cost of sales reduced from 70% to 65%) by Chang.

9. The combined companies cash flow would grow at the assumed growth rates during the forecast period.

e. Integration

1. The cultures of the two companies are compatible.

2. The software development teams could work together.

3. The two businesses could be integrated quickly.

4. Severance expenses were estimated adequately.

5. Duplicate personnel positions could be eliminated without disruption.

12. *In valuing GGT, Perez used various valuation techniques including discounted cash flow (DCF) and P/E ratios for recent comparable transactions. What might you have done differently to value GGT? Are there factors that might lead you to believe that Durand paid too much for GGT? What are the strengths and weaknesses of the alternative approaches?*

a. P/Es for publicly traded companies are accounting based but represent values the stock market currently places on similar types of companies.

b. Price to book: Accounting based and not useful for companies with few hard assets.

c. Price to revenue: Same as P/Es.

d. Value of recent transactions: Best method if the recent transactions are very similar.

e. Net present value: Assumes accurate projections of the magnitude and timing of future cash flows as well as the discount rate.

What would you have done differently to value GGT?

a. Weighted each valuation technique and computed a weighted average going concern value.

Are there any factors that would lead you to believe that Durand paid too much? Yes.

a. Willingness to retain the $10 million (PV terms) in nonoperating liabilities.

b. Inability to get Chang to put some portion of the purchase price in escrow in view of the anomalies found during due diligence.

16. *What factors did Durand consider in structuring the initial purchase price offer to Chang? What other factors should he have considered?*

a. Impact on GWM shareholders in terms of extent of initial dilution of EPS (his first inclination was to dismiss an all-stock purchase as being too dilutive).

b. Ability to enable the combined companies to outperform what GWM could have done on its own in terms of EPS.

c. Acceptability to GGT management and stockholders.

   1. Durand knew that many GGT managers were young and would be receptive to a deferred purchase price or options.

   2. He also knew that many large shareholders had been shareholders for a long time and probably had a low tax basis in the business.

17. *What additional information would you like to have to make a more informed valuation of GGT?*

a. More comparable, recent transactions.

b. Profitability by customer and product to generate more reliable cash-flow estimates.

c. Listing of informal commitments made to customers and vendors.

d. Listing of potential lawsuits.

18. *Suppose that another CD-ROM media company is sold during the negotiations between GWM and GGT and the P/E paid for the firm exceeded that offered for GGT. How would this information affect the negotiation? What would Chang's likely position be? How would Durand counter Chang's arguments?*

Assuming Durand still wanted to complete the transaction, how might he have restructured the purchase price to make it acceptable to Chang while still making the transaction attractive to GWM's shareholders?
  How would this information affect negotiations?

  a. Chang would want GWM to raise the purchase price for GGT.

How would Durand counter Chang's arguments?

  a. Point out the concessions Durand has made already (e.g., the acceptance of the liabilities for potential lawsuits and willingness to forego escrowing some portion of the purchase price), and argue that the recent transaction is not really comparable.
  b. Together they represented a counterweight to Multimedia, the industry's behemoth.

Assuming Durand still wanted to complete the transaction, how might he have restructured the purchase price to make it acceptable to both firms' shareholders?

  a. Offer to increase the purchase price based on an earn-out formula.
  b. Defer a portion of the purchase price payment to some future period, which would offer a higher future value but a lower present value of the transaction.

  20. *What risks was Durand accepting in agreeing to close the deal although several significant liabilities were found during due diligence? Why did he agree to close without adjusting the final closing price? What could he have done to protect GWM from other known or unknown liabilities?*

  a. What risks was Durand accepting to close the deal even though several significant liabilities were found during due diligence?
    Although deferred maintenance expenses can be reasonably estimated, Durand was accepting a largely unquantifiable potential liability in accepting pending litigation. The open-ended nature of such liabilities makes them particularly risky. Moreover, finding such significant potential liabilities also could be an indication of other potentially significant liabilities that were not uncovered during due diligence. Finally, Durand was assuming that the appraisal of the undeveloped land and the intellectual property were accurate.
  b. Why did he agree to close without adjusting the final closing price?
    It is common in intense, protracted negotiations for a buyer or seller to accept risks "discovered" just before closing because of sheer exhaustion and because of the potential for reopening discussion of issues on which both sides already had reached concurrence. Although such behavior may be understandable, it is seldom a good idea to accept largely unquantifiable risks.
  c. What could he have done to protect GWM from other known or unknown liabilities?

Durand's options were limited. He could have demanded that at least a portion of the purchase price be contingent on the satisfactory resolution of the lawsuits. Because they were acquiring 100% of the stock, other remedies were not available. If GWM simply had purchased the assets or some portion of the assets, Durand could have sought full indemnification from such liabilities from the seller or at least capped the total amount that GWM would have to pay. However, these options assume that the seller will have sufficient future assets with which to cover potential future liabilities.

INDEX

A

Accountants, 16
Accounting abuses, 393–398, 465–467
Accounting discrepancy red flags, 396
Accounting objectives, 186
Accounts payable (days), 458
Accounts receivable, 563
Acid-test ratio, 457
Acquirer, 6
Acquiring company, 6
Acquisition, 5
Acquisition plan, 199–205
 defined, 169, 199
 example, 204–205
 management objectives, 199–200
 market analysis, 200
 objectives, 199–200, 206
 resource availability, 201–202
 schedule, 203
 tactics, 202–203
Acquisition process, 167–264
 business plan, 172–199. *See also* Business plan
 closing, 245–250
 deal structuring, 232–233
 due diligence, 234–238. *See also* Due diligence
 example, 703–731. *See also* Gee Whiz Media case
 financing plan, 238–242
 first contact with target company, 224–227
 integration plan, 243–245
 merger/acquisition implementation plan, 199–205.
  See also Acquisition plan
 negotiation phase, 227–242
 overview, 168–169, 218
 phases, listed, 170–172
 planning, 169–170
 postclosing evaluation, 252–253
 postclosing integration, 250–252
 preliminary legal documents, 225–227
 screening process, 222–223
 search process, 219–222
Acquisition process flow diagram, 171
Acquisition-related customer attrition, 293
Acquisition subsidiary, 501
Acquisition tactics, 202–203
Acquisition vehicle, 501, 505–507
Activity-based systems, 196
Activity ratios, 457–458
Adjusted present value (APV) method, 579–580
Adler, Fred, 331
Advance notice provisions, 141
Advance ruling, 525
Adverse competitive effects, 84
Affirmative covenant, 565
Agency problems, 28
Agreement of purchase and sale, 246–248
Airline industry, 101
Albertson's acquisition of American Stores, 303–304
Alcoa takeover of Reynolds Aluminum, 118–119
Allegheny Teledyne, 691–692, 752
Allegis Corporation, 646
Alliances. *See* Business alliances
Allianz-Pimco merger, 310–311
AlliedSignal-AMP attempted takeover, 153–157
AlliedSignal-Honeywell merger, 79–80
Almanac of Business and Industrial Financial Ratios,
 401
Alternative business alliance structures, 12–13. *See also*
 Business alliances
Alternative exit/restructuring strategies, 643–671
 comparing/choosing strategies, 664–667
 divestitures, 652–656, 666
 equity carve-outs, 658–661, 666

Alternative exit/restructuring strategies (*continued*)
  motives for exiting business, 645–652
  returns to shareholders, 667–671
  spin-offs, 656–657, 666
  split-off IPO, 659
  split-ups, 657–658
  tracking stock, 661–664
  voluntary liquidations (bust-ups), 664
Alternative minimum tax, 529
Amazon.com, 181, 190, 395
America Online (AOL), 44–45, 190, 191
American Airlines-TWA merger, 313–316
American Express, 648
American Society of Appraisers (ASA), 474
Americans with Disabilities Act, 101
Ameritech-SBC Communications merger, 99–100
AMT, 529
Analysis paralysis, 176
Annual report, 69
Annual reporting requirements, 69
Annual Statement Studies, 401
Annuities, 344–345
Antigreenmail provisions, 142
Antitrust laws, 72–96
  adverse competitive effects, 84
  AlliedSignal-Honeywell merger, 79–80
  alternative to imminent failure, 87
  BP Amoco-Arco merger, 77–78
  business alliances, 633
  Clayton Act, 74
  collaborative arrangements, 90–92
  consent decree, 79
  define the market, 81–82
  efficiencies, 86–87
  entry analysis, 85
  FTC/DoJ decision-making process, 81–87
  Hart-Scott-Rodino Act, 74–78
  HHI, 83
  JDS Uniphase-SDL merger, 87–90
  market concentration, 83
  MCI WorldCom-Sprint merger, 92–94
  merger guidelines, 80–87
  Microsoft acquisition of Intuit, 85–86
  Microsoft antitrust case, 94–96
  procedural rules, 78–79
  Sherman Act, 73
  Staples-Office Depot merger, 82
  state laws, 97
AOL, 44–45, 190–191
AOL-Time Warner merger, 44–51, 733–735
Apple Computer, 185
Appraisal rights, 129
Appraisers, 474
APV method, 579–580
Arbitrageurs ("arbs"), 17
Arbitration clause, 628
Articles of incorporation, 138
ASA, 474
Asset-based lending, 242, 562–564
Asset-oriented methods of valuation, 347, 349, 365–367
Asset purchase, 515–517, 521–522

Asset purchase agreement, 246–248
Asset swaps, 194
Asset turnover, 458
Assignee, 679
Assignment, 679
Assumptions, 410–411
  @Home-Excite merger, 387–388, 742–743
AT&T, 92, 194, 364, 651
AT&T restructuring, 692–698
Attorneys, 15
Audit, 464
Average collection period, 458

B

Back-end merger, 128
Back-end plans, 137
Backward integration, 8
Balance sheet assumptions, 410
Balanced scorecard, 627
Bank loans, 238–239
Bank Merger Act, 98
Bank of America, 375
Banking industry, 98
Bankruptcy, 676, 679–686, 688
Bankruptcy Reform Act, 682
"Barbarians at the Gates," 591
Barriers to entry, 85
Baxter International, 657–658
BCG, 188
Bear hug, 117–118
Bell Atlantic-Vodafone alliance, 636–638, 750–751
Benchmarking, 304
Bergen Brunswick, 365
Berkshire Hathaway, 24–25
Best practices, 251
Beta (β), 335–337
β_1, 336
β_{FL}, 583
β_{FL1}, 583
β_u, 336
Bethlehem Steel, 682
Black-Scholes option pricing model, 374
Blank check preferred stock, 137
Board of Governors of the Federal Reserve System, 98
Boeing, 190
Bond ratings, 567
Bonsignore, Michael, 110
Bonus, 300, 301
Book value, 365
Boot, 522
Bossidy, Larry, 110
Boston Consulting Group (BCG), 188
Bougie, Jacques, 102
BP Amoco-Arco merger, 77–78
Breakup fees, 47, 129
Breakup value, 349, 367–368
Bridge financing, 238
Bridgestone-Firestone alliance, 610
British Telecom, 598
Broadcom Corporation, 395

Brokers, 221–222
Buckhorn Inc. v. Ropak Corp., 144
Buffet, Warren, 25
Build strategy, 193
Buildup method, 480–482
Bush, George H.W., 72
Bush, George W., 73
Business alliances, 12–13, 597–641
   antitrust policy, 633
   confidential information, 632
   control, 626
   critical success factors, 611–613
   deal structuring, 620–633
   debt financing, 626
   defined, 599
   dispute resolution, 628
   distribution issues, 627
   duration, 623–624
   empirical findings, 633–634
   equity financing, 625–626
   financing ongoing capital requirements, 625
   governance, 623–624
   legal form, 613–619, 623
   management/organizational issues, 631–632
   motivations for, 601–611
   operations plan, 619–620
   overview, 599–601
   owner/partner financing, 625
   performance criteria, 627
   regulatory restrictions/notifications, 633
   resource contributions/ownership determination,
     624–625
   revision, 628
   scope, 620–622
   SEC, 633
   strategic plan, 619
   taxes, 629–631
   termination, 628–629
   transfer of interests, 629
   types, 12–13, 600
Business attractiveness matrix, 183–184
Business cases. *See* Case studies
Business combination provisions, 97
Business Cycle Development, 215
Business failures, 671
   bankruptcy, 679–686, 688
   emerging from bankruptcy, 688–689
   insolvency, 676
   strategic options, 686–688
   voluntary settlements, 677–679
Business judgment rule, 144
Business-level strategies, 187–192
Business-market attractiveness matrix, 191–192
Business objectives, 186–187
Business plan, 172–199
   business attractiveness matrix, 183–184
   business-level strategies, 187–192
   business-market attractiveness matrix, 191–192
   communication document, as, 197
   core competencies, 183–185
   corporate-level strategy, 187

   defined, 169
   example, 197–199
   external analysis, 173–182
   framework for development, 174
   functional strategies, 192–195
   how to compete, 178–182
   implementation strategy, 192–195
   industry/market attractiveness matrix, 177
   internal analysis, 182–185
   key activities, 172
   market segmentation, 175–178
   mission statement, 186
   objectives, 186–187, 206
   share growth matrix, 189–190
   strategic controls, 196
   where to compete, 175–178
Business risk premium, 481
Business strategy, 169, 187–192
Business Week, 215
Bust-ups, 664
Buyer due diligence, 234
Buying undervalued assets (q-ratio), 27–28
Buyouts, 6

C
C-type corporations, 615–616
Cable industry, 194
California's Proposition, 65, 101
Call option, 374
Campeau Corporation, 651
Capellas, Michael, 121
Capital asset pricing model (CAPM), 333, 479
Capital budgeting, 348
Capital budgeting process, 348
Capital budgeting theory, 238
Capital gains taxes, 529
Capital lease, 357–358
Capitalization rate, 346, 474, 478–482
CAPM, 333, 479
Carve-outs, 658–661, 666
Case, Steve, 48
Case Corporation acquisition of New Holland, 291–293
Case studies
   Albertson's acquisition of American Stores, 303–304
   Alcoa takeover of Reynolds Aluminum, 118–119
   Allegheny Teledyne, 691–692, 752
   Allianz-Pimco merger, 310–311
   AlliedSignal-AMP attempted takeover, 153–157
   AlliedSignal-Honeywell merger, 79–80
   American Airlines-TWA merger, 313–316
   Ameritech-SBC Communications merger, 99–100
   AOL-Time Warner merger, 44–51, 733–735
   AT&T restructuring, 692–698
   Baxter International, 657–658
   Bell Atlantic-Vodafone alliance, 636–638, 750–751
   Berkshire Hathaway, 24–25
   BP Amoco-Arco merger, 77–78
   Bridgestone-Firestone alliance, 610

Case studies (*continued*)
  Case Corporation acquisition of New Holland, 291–293
  Circuit City-AOL alliance, 604
  Cisco Systems, 287–289
  closing, 249–250
  Coca-Cola-P&G attempted alliance, 638–640
  corporate shell game, 486–487
  Covinsint, 607–609
  Daimler-Chrysler merger, 320–322, 741–742
  Dell Computer, 180–181
  discussion questions, solutions, 733–758
  earnouts, 244
  Enron, 672–676
  Exxon-Mobil merger, 105, 303, 736
  First Union-Wachovia merger, 262–264
  Ford-Volvo merger, 451–456
  GE-Honeywell merger, 106–111
  Gee Whiz Media. *See* Gee Whiz Media case
  GHS, Inc., 484–485
  Gillette, 655
  Glaxo Wellcome-SmithKline Beecham merger, 207–210, 738–739
  GM-Subaru alliance, 605
  Hewlett Packard spin-off of Agilent, 660–661
  Hewlett-Packard takeover of Compaq, 119–123
  @Home-Excite merger, 387–388, 742–743
  Hughes Corporation, 649–651
  JDS Uniphase-SDL merger, 87–90, 547–553
  Johnson & Johnson sues Amgen, 622
  leveraged buyout (LBO), 584–588, 590–591, 748–750
  loss of key employee, 468–469
  Mattel acquisition of The Learning Company, 255–261, 740
  MCI WorldCom-Sprint merger, 92–94
  McKesson HBOC, 234–235
  Microsoft acquisition of Intuit, 85–86
  Microsoft antitrust case, 94–96
  Microsoft-Best Buy alliance, 603–604
  Microsoft-Radio Shack alliance, 604
  misstated revenue, 466
  Northrup Grumman-TRW merger, 439–441
  Pacific, Gas, and Electric (PG&E), 680–682
  Pacific Wardrobe-SurferDude merger, 492–496
  PepsiCo acquisition of Quaker Oats, 210–213
  Pfizer hostile takeover of Warner-Lambert, 157–162
  reps and warranties, 237
  RJR Nabisco LBO, 591–594
  solutions to selected questions, 733–758
  Staples-Office Depot merger, 82
  sustainable competitive advantage, 185
  Travelers-Citicorp merger, 323–325
  Tribune-Times Mirror merger, 444–451, 743–744
  Tyco-AMP acquisition, 153–157, 737–738
  UPS, 659–660
  USX Corp., 662–663
  valuing privately held company, 492, 744–745
  Vodafone AirTouch-Mannesmann merger, 51–58, 239–240, 540–547, 746–748
  Wal-Mart/AOL alliance, 603

Cash and marketable securities, 369–370
Cash cows, 190
Cash-flow based lending, 242
Cash-flow concepts, 337–341
Cash-flow lending, 565–567
Casual pass, 134–135
Celler-Kefauver Act, 67
Cendant, 394
Centralized vs. decentralized structure, 296–297
CERCLA, 101
Certificate of incorporation, 138
Chapter 7 liquidation, 684–686
Chapter 11 reorganization, 683
Chapter business cases. *See* Case studies
Chapter S corporations, 616
Choice of law provision, 628
Chrysler, 648
Circuit City-AOL alliance, 604
Cisco Systems, 191, 287–289, 598
Citigroup, 21, 648
Classified board elections, 139
Clayton, Dubilier & Rice (CD&R), 561
Clayton Act, 74
Clean Water Act, 101
Closely held companies. *See* Privately held companies
Closing, 245–250
Closing conditions, 226
Closing documents, 246–248
CNH Global, 291–293
Co-insurance, 22
Coca-Cola, 191
Coca-Cola acquisition of Cadbury Schweppes, 102
Coca-Cola-P&G attempted alliance, 638–640
Collar/collar agreement, 47, 439
Combined firms' ability to finance transaction, 408–410
Commercial/industrial real estate industry, 194
Commitment letter, 570
Common-size financial statements, 398
Common stock, 568
Communication plans, 250–251
Communications industry, 98
Comparable companies method, 349, 361–362
Comparable firm approach to valuation of trademarks, 375
Comparable transactions method, 349, 362
Compensating balances, 239
Compensation plans, 300–301
Competitive advantage, 185
Composition, 677
Comprehensive Environmental Response, Compensation, and Liability Act (CERCLA), 101
Comptroller of the currency, 98
Concentration ratios, 81, 83
Conexant, 395
Confidentiality agreement, 225
Conglomerate discount, 24
Conglomerate era (1965–69), 30–31
Conglomerate mergers, 7
Consensus decision making, 317
Consent decree, 79
Consent solicitation, 141

Consolidation, 6
Constant-growth valuation model, 351–353
Consultative selling, 306
Contingency plans, 169
Contingent events, 398
Contino, Maria, 496
Continuing growth value, 353
Continuity of interests requirement, 523, 525
Control premium, 8, 345
Control share provisions, 97
Controlling interest, 345
Core competencies, 183–185
Corning, 598
Corporate capital gains taxes, 529
Corporate charters, 96, 138
Corporate culture, 252, 309–316
Corporate focus, 24
Corporate-level strategy, 187
Corporate mission statement, 186
Corporate restructuring, 5, 145, 148
Corporate shell game, 484–487
Corporate structures, 613–616, 630
Corporation's bylaws, 138
Cost-avoidance approach to valuation of trademarks, 374–375
Cost-cutting tactics, 574
Cost leadership, 188
Cost of capital, 334–335
Cost of debt, 333–334
Cost of equity, 332–333
Cost of preferred stock, 334
Cost savings-related synergies, 407
Costa, Domenic, 496
Covenants, 238–239
Covinsint, 607–609
Cox Communications, 194
Cramdown, 115
Cross-border transactions, 102–103
Cross-default provisions, 565
Cross-sectional comparisons, 398
Crown jewels lockup, 130
Crutchfield, Edward, 263
Cultural profiling, 312
Culture, 309
Cumulative voting rights, 139
Current ratio, 457
Customer lists, 534
Customer service drivers, 363–364
Customer surveys, 375–376

D
D. F. King & Company, 16
Daimler-Chrysler merger, 320–322, 741–742
Data room, 237
Davis Polk & Wardwell, 15
Days in inventory, 458
D.C. Heath, 647
DCF methods, 345–346, 348–357
de Vink, Lodeijk, 158–160
Dead hand, 138

Deadlock clause, 628
Deal breakers, 227
Deal structuring, 232–233
Deal-structuring process. *See* Structuring the deal
Debentures, 566
Debt, value of firm's, 357–358
Debt-for-equity swap, 677
Debt restructuring, 677
Debt-to-equity ratio, 458, 580
Debtor in possession, 683
Debtor in possession financing, 674
Decentralized vs. centralized structure, 296–297
Default provisions, 565
Defense industry, 100
Defensive acquisition, 148
Deferred revenue, 396
Defined benefit pension plans, 376
Defining the market, 81–82
Definitive agreement of purchase and sale, 246–248
Dell, Michael, 180
Dell Computer, 180–181, 190, 598
Deregulation, 26
Destroyers of value, 403–404
Deutsche Telekom, 364
Deyhimy, Lauri, 496
Dial Corporation, 649
Differentiation, 190
Digital subscriber line (DSL) services, 92
Direct issuance costs, 485
Direct merger, 570
Directory of National Trade Associations, 216
Discount rate, 346, 474. *See also* Capitalization rate
Discounted cash flow (DCF) methods, 345–346, 348–357
Discretionary assets, 230–231
Discussion questions, solutions, 733–758
Distribution channels, 186
Diversifiable risk, 335
Diversification, 20, 22–25
Divestiture, 5
Divisional buyouts, 575
Divisional organization, 296
Dogs, 190
DoJ, 71
Double taxation, 615
Drag-along provision, 629
Drexel Burnham, 567
DSL services, 92
Due diligence, 234–238
    buyer, 234
    lender, 571–572
    limiting length/scope, 236–237
    preliminary information request, 265–276. *See also*
        Information request—due diligence
    revalidation, 302
    seller, 237–238
    team approach, 236
Dun & Bradstreet, 221
Dunlap, Al "Chain-Saw," 397
Dun's Review, 401

E

Earnings management, 393
Earnings per share (EPS), 457
Earnings smoothing, 397–398
Earnouts, 243–244, 510–513
Ease of entry, 85
EBITDA, 346
eCompanies, 375
Economic Indicators, 215
Economic information, sources, 215
Economic Report of the President to the Congress, 215
Economies of scale, 20–21
Economies of scope, 21
Effective control, 9
Efficiencies, 86–87
Ego-driven decision making, 27
Eight-factor test, 127
Electronic commerce marketplace, 91
Elsevier, 609–610
Emergency Planning and Community Right to Know Act (EPCRA), 101
Employee availability, 299
Employee benefit plans, 102
Employee retention, 251
Employee retirement and pensions, 102
Employee Retirement Income and Security Act, 102
Employee stock ownership plan. *See* ESOP
Employee turnover, 279–280
Encyclopedia of Associations, 216
Enron, 394, 672–676, 679
Enron bankruptcy, 359
Enterprise cash flow, 337–339
Enterprise DCF method, 348–350
Enterprise value, 228, 378
Entry analysis, 85
Entry barriers, 85
Environmental laws, 101
EPCRA, 101
EPS, 457
Equal division of power framework, 632
Equity carve-outs, 658–661
Equity cash flow, 339–341
Equity DCF method, 349–350
Equity partnership, 600, 614, 618
Equity per share method, 349, 365
Equity value, 378
Equity value of firm, 359–360
Era of mega-mergers (1992–2000), 32
Error, sources of, 393–398
Escape clause, 138
ESOP, 10–12
    acquisition vehicle, as, 507
    alternative to divestiture, as, 11
    establishing a plan, 11
    leveraged plan, 11, 507
    management buyouts, and, 11–12
    private companies, 488–489
    takeover defense, as, 145, 147
Esser, Klaus, 51–58
Estate of James C. Hall v. Commissioner, 477
Example. *See* Case studies, Gee Whiz Media case

Exchange offer, 126
Exclusive agreements, 600
Exit strategies. *See* Alternative exit/restructuring strategies
Expense investment, 194
Experian, 221
Experience curve, 188
Experienced acquirers, 37
Extension, 677
External analysis, 173–182
Exxon-Mobil merger, 105, 303, 736

F

Faber, Joachim, 311
Failing firms. *See* Business failures
Fair market value, 473
Fair-price provisions, 96, 142
Fair value, 473
Fairness opinion, 14
Fairness opinion letter, 14
False invoices, 397
Family Medical Leave Act, 101
Family-owned businesses. *See* Privately held companies
Fastow, Andrew S., 672
FCC, 98
FCFE, 339–341
FCFE method, 349–350
FCFF, 337–339
FCFF approach, 348–350
Federal antitrust laws. *See* Antitrust laws
Federal Communications Commission (FCC), 98
Federal Deposit Insurance Corporation, 98
Federal securities laws, 68–71
Federal Trade Commission. *See* FTC
FedEx, 606
FIFO, 471
Finance concepts. *See* Rudimentary finance concepts
Financial economies of scale, 22
Financial modeling, 391–459
    collar argument, 439–441
    complex vs. simple models, 420, 438
    defined, 392
    example (case study), 418–438
    key formulas, 416
    model-building process, 398–411
    postmerger share price, 411–415
    primary objective, 392
    SER, 411, 438–439
    step 1 (value acquirer/target as standalone businesses), 398–402
    step 2 (value consolidated firm), 403–404
    step 3 (initial offer price for target firm), 405–408
    step 4 (combined firms' ability to finance transaction), 408–410
    synergy, 403–408
    underlying assumptions, 410–411
Financial objectives, 199–200
Financial ratio analysis, 401, 457–458

Financial restructuring, 5
Financial risk, 201–202
Financial Services Modernization Act, 26
Financial synergy, 22
Financing contingencies, 242
Financing plan, 238–242
Finders, 221–222
Fiorina, Carly, 120
First contact with target company, 224–227
First-generation poison pills, 137
First-in, first-out (FIFO), 471
First Union-Wachovia merger, 262–264
Five Forces framework, 178–179
Fixed charge coverage ratio, 458
Fixed SER, 438
Flip-in rights plans, 137
Flip-over pill, 137
Float, 117
Floating SER, 439
Florida Steel, 181
Focus groups, 375
Focus strategy, 190
Focused firms, 24
For cause provisions, 141
Forbes, 215
Ford-Volvo merger, 451–456
Form 8K, 69, 220
Form 10K, 69, 220
Form 10Q, 69, 220
Form S-1, 220
Form S-2, 220
Form of acquisition, 513–521
Form of acquisition vehicle, 505–507
Form of payment, 509–514
Fortune, 216
Forward integration, 8
Forward triangular merger, 526–527
Fractional shares, 550
Franchise, 13
Franchise alliance, 600, 614, 618
Fraudulent conveyance, 571
Free cash flow, 337
Free cash flow to equity investors (FCFE), 339–341
Free cash flow to the firm (FCFF), 337–339
Freeze-in, 115
Friendly takeover, 8, 114–116
FTC
    antitrust complaints, 78–79
    creation, 72
    website, 73
Functional integration, 302–309
Functional organization, 296
Functional strategies, 195–196
Funk and Scott's Index of Corporations and Industries, 216
Future value (FV), 342–343
Future value compounding, 343
Future value of annuity (FVA), 344–345
FV, 342–343
FVA, 344, 345

G
GAAP, 394
Gates, Bill, 85
GE-Honeywell merger, 106 111
Gee Whiz Media case, 703–731. *See also* Case studies
    acquisition plan objectives, 709
    acquisition tactics, 709–711
    analyzing options, 705–707
    business plan, 704–705
    communication, 722–727
    counter offers, 719–720
    deal structuring, 717–719
    due diligence, 720–722
    financing, 722
    first contact, 712–714
    implementation, 711–729
    initial offer price, 716–717
    integration, 722–727
    planning, 703–711
    preliminary valuation, 714–715
    refining the offer price, 719
    searching process, 711–712
    solutions to discussion questions, 752–758
    sources (destroyers) of value, 715–716
General Motors (GM), 598, 646
General partners, 617
General partnership, 616–617
Generally accepted accounting principles (GAAP), 394
Gent, Chris, 51, 55–57
Geometric mean, 333n
Georgeson & Company, 16
GHS, Inc., 484–485
Glaxo-Wellcome-SmithKline Beecham merger, 207–210, 738–739
Global exposure, 182
GM, 598, 646
GM-Subaru alliance, 605
Going concern value, 347, 365–366
Going private, 558
Going public, 484–485
Golden parachutes, 143–144
Goodrich, 648
Goodwill, 532, 534–535
Gordon model, 351, 353–354
Governance, 232
Greenmail, 144–146, 530
Gross, Bill, 311
Gross profit margin, 457
Growth rates, 356–357

H
Hamel, Gary, 183
Handshake agreement, 613
Hart-Scott-Rodino Act (HSR), 74–78
Hawley, Michael, 655–656
Herfindahl-Hirschman Index (HHI), 83
Hewlett, Walter, 121
Hewlett-Packard, 184
Hewlett Packard spin-off of Agilent, 660–661

Hewlett-Packard takeover of Compaq, 119–123
HHI, 83
High-growth period, 356
High-speed cable access to the home, 92
High-yield (junk) bonds, 568
Highly leveraged transactions, 5. *See also* Leveraged
    buyout (LBO)
Hill & Knowlton, 17
Historical M&A waves, 29–32
    conglomerate era (1965–1969), 30–31
    era of mega-mergers (1992–2000), 32
    horizontal concentration (1897–1904), 30
    increasing concentration (1916–1929), 30
    retrenchment era (1981–1989), 31–32
Holding company, 8–9
Holdout problem, 688
@Home-Excite merger, 387–388, 742–743
Honda, 21, 183
Horizontal merger, 7
Hostile takeover, 8, 114, 116–117
How to compete, 178–182
HSR, 74–78
Hu, Jenny, 496
Hubris, 20, 27
Hudson, William J., 154
Hughes Corporation, 649–651
Human resources, 308–309
Hunt, Nelson Bunker, 557
Hybrid strategies, 191

I

IBM, 341–342, 598
ICC, 100
Illiquidity discount, 482–484
Implementation strategy, 192–195
Inc, 216
Incentive pay, 300
Incentive systems, 196
Income approach to valuation, 345–346, 348–357
Income statement assumptions, 410
Indemnification, 516
Indenture, 566
Industrial/commercial real estate industry, 194
Industry, 175
Industry information, sources, 215–216
Industry/market attractiveness matrix, 177
Industry Norms and Key Business Ratios, 401
Industry specific regulations, 97–101
Industry Survey, 216
Information request—due diligence, 265–276
    assets, real/personal property matters, 269
    conduct of business matters, 269–271
    corporate matters, 266
    financing/accounting matters, 267–268
    information system matters, 274–275
    intellectual property matters, 271
    legal compliance matters, 273
    litigation, disputes, claims matters, 273
    management, labor, personnel matters, 271–273
    risk-management matters, 268–269

    securities matters, 266–267
    tax matters, 267
Information sources. *See* Sources of information
Information technology (IT), 305
Ingram Micro, 365
Initial offer price for target firm, 405–408
Initial public offering (IPO), 15, 483
Insider trading, 71
Insider trading laws, 71–72
Insider Trading Sanctions Act, 72
Insolvency, 676
Institutional investors, 17
Insurance industry, 100
Intangible assets, 370, 534–535
Integration manager, 244
Integration plan, 238–242
Integration planning, 282–289
Integration process, 277–327
    board of directors, 297–298
    business alliances, 316–318
    communicating to stakeholders, 289–295
    community, 294–295
    compensation, 300–301
    corporate culture, 309–316
    customer commitments, 291–294
    decentralized vs. centralized structure, 296–297
    difficulty of, 280
    due diligence data revalidation, 302
    employee turnover, 279–280
    finance, 306
    functional integration, 302–309
    human resources, 308–309
    importance, 278–279
    international considerations, 310–311
    investors, 294
    IT, 305
    manufacturing and operations, 304–305
    marketing, 307
    middle management, 298
    organizational structure, 296
    overview, 278
    performance benchmarking, 304
    planning, 282–289
    purchasing, 307–308
    R&D, 308
    sales, 306–307
    senior management, 298
    staffing issues, 298–301
    success factors, 280–281
    suppliers, 294
    team approach, 285–287
Integration success factors, 281
Integration work teams, 286–287
Intel, 180
Intellectual property, 372–376
Interim financing, 238–239
Intermediate-term credit, 564
Internal analysis, 182–185
International Steel Group (ISI), 682
Internet Explorer, 185
Internet focused industries, 178

Internet service providers (ISPs), 92
Interstate Commerce Commission (ICC), 100
Intrinsic value, 346
Inventory turnover, 457
Investment bankers, 14–15
Investment boutiques, 15
Investments in other firms, 370–371
Investor's required ownership percentage (IOR), 487
Involuntary bankruptcy, 679
IOR, 487
IPO, 15, 483
ISPs, 92
IT, 305

J

James, Barrie G., 161
JDS Uniphase-SDL merger, 87–90, 547–553
Johns Manville Corporation, 404, 682
Johnson, H. Ross, 592
Johnson, Lyndon, 72
Johnson & Johnson sues Amgen, 622
Joint manufacturing, 609
Joint venture, 193, 600. *See also* Business alliances
Jointly and severally liable, 617
Junior debt, 566
Junk bonds, 567–568
"Just say no" defense, 145, 149
JVs, 600. *See also* Business alliances

K

Kekst & Company, 17
Keller, Helen, 277
Kennard, William, 48
Kennecott Cooper Corp. v. Curtiss Wright Corp., 127
Kennedy, Robert, 72
KKR-RJR Nabisco LBO, 591–594
Kmart, 679
Kohlberg Kravis & Roberts (KKR), 591–594
Kozlowski, L. Dennis, 155
Kroll Associates, 16

L

Labor and benefit laws, 101
Large investment banks, 15
Last-in, first-out (LIFO), 471
Lawrence Bossidy, 153–155
Laws. *See* Regulatory considerations
Lawyers, 15
Lay, Kenneth, 673–674
LBO, 5. *See also* Leveraged buyout (LBO)
Leadership, 316
Leases, 357–358
Legal documents, 225–227
Legal form of selling entity, 508–509
Legal insolvency, 676
Legislation. *See* Regulatory considerations
Lender commitment letters, 570
Lender due diligence, 571–572

Letter of intent (LOI), 129, 225–227
Letter stocks, 483, 661
Leverage ratios, 458
Leverageable ESOP, 488
Leveraged buyout (LBO), 5, 557–596
    analyzing, 578–584
    APV method, 579–580
    asset-based lending, 562–564
    capital budgeting analysis, 578–579
    cash-flow lending, 565–567
    commitment letter, 570
    common stock/preferred stock, 568–569
    critical success factors, 572–574
    direct merger, 570
    historical overview, 559–561
    improving operating performance, 574
    junk bonds, 567–568
    legal pitfalls, 571–572
    overpaying, 573
    postbuyout returns, 577–578
    prebuyout returns, 574–577
    security provisions/protective covenants, 564–565
    subsidiary merger, 570–571
    VRA method, 580–584
Leveraged employee stock ownership plan, 11
Leveraged ESOP, 488–489, 507
Levered β, 336–337
Levin, Gerald, 48–49
License agreement, 13
Licensing, 600
LIFO, 471
Like-kind exchanges, 509
Limited liability corporations (LLCs), 616
Limited partners, 617
Limited partnership, 617
Lipton, Marty, 137
Liquidation, 688
    bankruptcy, 684–686
    voluntary, 664
Liquidation value, 349, 365–367
Liquidity, 481
Liquidity discount, 482–484
Liquidity ratios, 457
LLCs, 616
Loan agreement, 563
Lock-up, 146
Lockheed-Martin, 190
Lockup options, 129–130
LOI, 129, 225–227
Long-term contracts, 397
Long-term debt, 566
Long-term debt to total capital, 458
Long-Term Economic Growth, 215
Loss corporations, 528
LTV, 682
Lynch, Robert Porter, 316

M

M&A activity, 4
M&A failures, 38–40

M&A process
  merger failures, 38–40
  merger waves, 29–32
  motivations, 19–29. *See also* Motivations for
    M&As
  participants, 13–19
  phases, 167–264. *See also* Acquisition process
  shareholder benefits, 32–38
  societal benefits, 40–41
  terminology, 5–13
  valuation. *See* Valuation
M&A valuation. *See* Valuation
M&A waves. *See* Historical M&A waves
Macro value drivers, 364
Madigan, John, 444
Maier's law, 461
Majority-minority framework, 631
Majority rules framework, 632
Manage earnings, 393
Management buyout, 5
Management buyout (MBO), 558. *See also* Leveraged
  buyout (LBO)
Management compensation, 29
Management entrenchment theory, 115
Management integration team (MIT), 286
Management objectives, 199–200
Managerial pride (hubris), 27
Managerialism, 29
Managers, 317
Manipulation of reported income, 465–467
Mannesmann, 53–54, 364
Manufacturing and operations, 304–305
Market analysis, 178–182, 200
Market assumptions, 410
Market-based methods of valuation, 346, 349, 360–364
Market concentration, 83
Market power, 81
Market power theory, 29
Market profiling, 178–179
Market risk premium, 481
Market segmentation, 175–178
Market structure, 80
Market value of firms' debt, 357–358
Marketability discount, 482–484
Marketable securities, 369–370
Marketing, 307
Marketing intangibles, 534
Markets, 175
Markewich, Sam, 391
Marriott Corporation, 648
Materials ordering, 304
Mattel acquisition of the Learning Company, 255–261,
  740
McCall, Charles W., 234
McDonald's, 191
MCI WorldCom-Sprint merger, 92–94
McKesson HBOC, 234–235
Merger
  back-end, 128
  conglomerate, 7
  defined, 6

direct, 570
  economic perspective, 7–8
  forward triangular, 526–527
  horizontal, 7
  legal/structural perspective, 6–7
  reverse, 484–487
  reverse triangular, 527
  short form, 6, 513
  statutory, 6, 519
  subsidiary, 6, 570–571
  vertical, 7
Merger/acquisition implementation plan, 199–205.
  See also Acquisition plan
Merger agreements, 248
Merger and acquisition (M&A) activity, 4
Merger and acquisition waves. *See* Historical M&A
  waves
Merger arbitrage, 17–18
Merger failures, 38–40
Merger guidelines
  horizontal mergers, 80–87
  vertical mergers, 87
Merger of equals, 6–7
Mezzanine financing, 240, 565
Micro value drivers, 363
Microsoft, 180, 191, 598–599
Microsoft acquisition of Intuit, 85–86
Microsoft antitrust case, 94–96
Microsoft-Best Buy alliance, 603–604
Microsoft-Radio Shack alliance, 604
MindSpring, 92
Minority interest, 345
Minority investments, 12
Mismanagement (agency problems), 28
Mission statement, 186
Misstated revenue, 465–466
MIT, 286
Model-building process, 398–411. *See also* Financial
  modeling
Modified Porter competitive framework, 179
Monferino, Paolo, 292
Monitoring systems, 196
Monthly Bulletin of Statistics, 215
Monthly Labor Review, 215
Monti, Mario, 103, 107
Moody's Investors Services, 567
Morrison, Robert, 211
Motivations for M&As, 19–29
  buying undervalued assets (q-ratio), 27–28
  diversification, 22–25
  managerialism, 29
  market power, 29
  mismanagement (agency problems), 28
  overview, 20
  strategic realignment, 25–27
  synergy, 19–22
  tax considerations, 28
Multi-period comparison, 398
Multi-tiered offers, 128–129
Multimarket approach, 191
Multiple party framework, 632

Murdoch, Rupert, 650
Muris, Timothy, 73

N
Navistar, 648
NBC, 599
Negative covenants, 565
Negotiation phase, 227–242
Net operating losses (NOLs), 528, 530–531
Net present value (NPV), 238, 348
Net profit margin, 457
Net purchase price, 228
Net synergy (NS), 403–404
Netscape browser software, 185
Network alliances, 600
New organization. *See* Integration process
New York State v. Visa USA, Inc., 91
Niche focus approach, 191
Niche strategies, 190
"No comment" statement, 135
No-shop agreement, 129
No-shop provision, 226
NOLs, 528, 530–531
Noncompete agreement, 226, 300
Nondiversifiable risk, 335
Nonfinancial objectives, 200
Nonleveraged ESOP, 488, 507
Nonoperating assets, 369, 376. *See also* Valuation of
   nonoperating assets
Nonoperating liabilities, 376
Nonrecourse financing, 626
Nonrecurring expenses, 395
Normalization of data, 231–232, 400
Normalized cash flows, 401
Northern Trust Company v. Commissioner, 477
Northrop Grumman, 651
Northrop Grumman-TRW merger, 439–441
NPV, 238, 348
Nucor Steel, 181

O
Objectives
   business, 186–187
   business/acquisition plan, compared, 206
   financial, 199–200
   management, 199–200
   nonfinancial, 200
Off-balance sheet liabilities, 376
One-tier offer, 128
Open-access issues, 91–92
Open-market purchases, 125
Operating bureaus, 98
Operating cash-flow requirements, 251
Operating lease, 357–358
Operating risk, 201
Operating synergy, 19–21
Operational intangibles, 534–535
Operational restructuring, 5
Operational value drivers, 364

Opportunity cost, 332
Option pricing theory, 374
Options, 374
Oracle, 191, 598
Order entry, 305
Order for relief, 683
Organizational structure, 296
Other assumed liabilities, 229
Overfunded pension plans, 376
Overpaying, 40
Overpayment risk, 202

P
P/E ratio, 480
Pac-man defense, 145–146
Pacific, Gas, and Electric (PG&E), 680–682
Pacific Wardrobe-SurferDude merger, 492–496
Packard, David, 121
Parsons, Richard, 48–49
Partnership structures, 617–618, 630
Passive minority investments, 12
Patent license agreements, 373
Patents, 372–373
Payment-in-kind, 228
Pension Benefit Guaranty Corporation, 682
Pension plans, 376
PepsiCo acquisition of Quaker Oats, 210–213
Performance benchmarking, 304
Periodic reporting requirements, 69
Periodic reports, 69
Permanent financing, 240
Personnel information systems, 301
Pfizer hostile takeover of Warner-Lambert, 157–162
Pickens, T. Boone, 28
Pitofsky, Robert, 77
Pittman, Robert, 48–49
Plant consolidation, 305
Pledging
   accounts receivable, 563
   equipment/real estate, 564
   intangible assets, 564
   inventory, 564
Poison pills, 135–138
Poison puts, 137–138
Pooling of interests, 158n, 532
Porter, Michael, 178
Portfolio balance theory, 189
Portfolio power, 108
Post-LBO buyout returns, 577–578
Postbid (active) defenses, 133, 144–149
Postclosing evaluation, 252–253
Postclosing integration, 250–252. *See also* Integration
   process
Postclosing organization, 501, 507–508
Postmerger EPS, 412
Postmerger integration organization, 285–287
Postmerger returns to shareholders, 35–38
Postpurchase decision activities, 171
Prahalad, C. K., 183
Pre-LBO buyout returns, 574–575

Pre-merger returns to shareholders, 33–35
Pre-tender offer tactics, 124–125
Prebid (preventive) defenses, 133, 135–144
Preferred stock, 334, 569
Preferred stock plans, 133, 137
Preliminary legal documents, 225–227
Premerger integration planning, 282–285
Prepackaged bankruptcies, 688
Prepurchase decision activities, 171
Present value (PV), 344
Present value of annuity (PVA), 344–345
Pretax cost of debt, 333–334
Preventive defenses, 133, 135–144
Price leadership, 188
Price-to-Earnings (P/E) ratio, 480
Private investigators, 16
Private limited partnerships, 617
Private placement, 15
Privately held companies, 461–497
    accounting abuses, 465–467
    areas commonly understated/overlooked, 471–473
    auto expenses/personal life insurance, 469–470
    benefits, 469
    capitalization rate, 478–482
    defined, 462
    depreciation expense, 470
    difficulties in valuation, 463
    ESOPs, 488–489
    family members, 470
    inventory, 471
    manipulation of reported income, 465–467
    marketability/liquidity discount, 482–484
    owner/officer's salaries, 467–468
    professional service fees, 470
    rent/lease expenses, 470
    reserves, 470–471
    Revenue Ruling, 59–60, 477
    reverse mergers, 484–487
    shareholder returns, 489
    shell corporations, 484–487
    travel and entertainment, 469
    valuation methodologies, 474–478
    valuation professionals, 474
    venture capital method (ownership share), 487–488
Pro forma financial statements, 394
Problems, solutions, 733–758
Process effectiveness, 304
Proctor and Gamble, 21
Product differentiation, 190
Product life cycle, 188–189
Product-market matrix, 23
Product or service organization, 296
Production planning, 304
Production/product intangibles, 534
Profiling targeted markets, 178–179
Profitability ratios, 457
Promissory note, 563
Protective covenants, 564–565
Proxy battles, 16
Proxy contests, 119–124
Proxy solicitations, 69

Proxy solicitors, 16
Proxy statement, 123–124
P_{TPP}, 238
Public limited partnerships, 617
Public offering, 15
Public relations, 16–17
Public utilities, 101
Purchase accounting, 532–538
Purchase of assets, 515–517, 521–522
Purchase of stock, 515, 517–518, 522
Purchase price, 227–231
Purchaser-supplier relationships, 606–607
Purchasing, 307–308
Purchasing value drivers, 364
Put option, 374
Putting it all together. *See* Gee Whiz Media case
PV, 344
PV_1, 238
PV_{AD}, 228
PV_{DA}, 228
PV_{ND}, 228
PV_{NPP}, 228
PV_{OAL}, 228
PVs, 228
PV_{SYN}, 238
PV_{TC}, 228
PV_{TPP}, 228
PVA, 344–345

Q

Q-ratio, 27
Qualitative data, 81
Quality control, 305
Question marks, 190
Quick (acid-test) ratio, 457

R

Railroad industry, 100
Range effect, 108
Ratio analysis, 401, 457–458
Raytheon, 647
R&D, 308
Reagan, Ronald, 72
Real options, 374
Real property exchanges, 509
Recapitalization, 145, 147
Refining valuation, 231–232
Regulated industries, 97–101
Regulation 10b-5, 72
Regulation 14e-3, 72
Regulatory considerations, 65–112
    airlines, 101
    antitrust laws, 72–96. *See also* Antitrust laws
    banking, 98
    benefit plan liabilities, 102
    communications, 98
    cross-border transactions, 102–103
    defense, 100
    environmental laws, 101

insider trading laws, 71–72
insurance, 100–101
labor and benefit laws, 101
overview, 66–67
public utilities, 101
railroads, 100
Securities Act of 1933, 68
Securities Exchange Act of 1934, 68–69
state antitakeover laws, 96–97
state antitrust laws, 97
Williams Act, 69–71
Reincorporation, 143
Relative value methods, 346, 360–364
Replacement cost method, 347, 349
Reps and warranties, 236–237, 284–285
Required rate of return, 332
Research and development (R&D), 308
Reserves, 397–398
Resource availability, 201–202
Resource Conservation and Recovery Act, 101
Restricted stock, 483
Restricted tender offers, 126
Restructuring, 145, 148
Restructuring strategies, 644. *See also* Alternative
    exit/restructuring strategies
Retention bonuses, 196
Retrenchment era (1981–89), 31–32
Return on equity (ROE), 457, 480
Return on investment (ROI), 457, 480
Revenue overstatement, 465–466
Revenue recognition, 397
Revenue-related synergy, 406
Revenue Ruling, 59–60, 477
Revenue rulings, 477
Reverse LBOs, 574
Reverse mergers, 484–487
Reverse triangular merger, 527
Right of first refusal, 629
Right-to-know laws, 101
Ripp, Robert, 154–155
Risk
    defined, 335
    diversifiable, 335
    financial, 201–202
    nondiversifiable, 335
    operating, 201
    overpayment, 202
Risk premium, 333
Risk sharing, 501
RJR Nabisco, 648
RJR Nabisco LBO, 31–32, 591–594
Road show, 241
Robbins, Anthony, 485
Robinson Lerer & Montgomery, 17
ROE, 457, 480
ROI, 457, 480
Rosso, Jean-Pierre, 291–292
Rudimentary finance concepts, 332–345
    beta, 335–337
    cost of capital, 334–335
    cost of equity, 332–333

cost of preferred stock, 334
FCFE, 339–341
FCFF, 337–339
pretax cost of debt, 333 334
risk, 335
time value of money, 341–345
Rule of law, 518

S
S corporations, 616
Sales, 306–307
Same or comparable industry method, 349, 363
Scale economies, 20–21
Schedule 13D, 70, 75
Schedule 14A, 220
Schedule 14D-1, 71, 75
Schedule 14D-9, 71
Schrempp, Jurgen, 321–322
Schroeder, Gerhard, 56
Scope economies, 21
Screening process, 222–223
Search process, 219–222
Second-generation poison pill, 137
Secondary initial public offering, 575
Section 338 election, 522
Secured debt, 566
Secured lending, 562–564
Securities Act of 1933, 68
Securities and Exchange Commission (SEC)
    eight-factor test, 127
    filings, 220
    insider trading, 72
    proxy contests, 123
    tender offer, 127
    website, 67
Securities Exchange Act of 1934, 68–69
Security agreement, 563
Security provisions, 564–565
Self-tenders, 148
Seller due diligence, 237–238
Seller financing, 241, 566
Seller representations/warranties, 236–237, 284–285
Senior debt, 566
Sequent Technology, 21
SER, 411, 438–439
Service mark, 374–376
Share buyback plans, 145, 147–148
Share control provisions, 97
Share-exchange ratio (SER), 411, 438–439
Share-growth matrix, 189–190
Share repurchase plan, 147–148
Shared goals, 312
Shared services, 313
Shared space, 313
Shared standards, 312–313
Shareholder benefits, 32–38
Shareholder interests theory, 115
Shark repellants, 138–143
Shell corporations, 11, 484–487
Sherman Act, 73

Short form merger, 6, 513
Short sale, 19
Short-term marketable securities, 369
Silver parachutes, 143–144
Simpson Thatcher & Bartlett, 15
Skadden Arps Slate Meagher & Flom, 15
Skilling, Jeffrey K., 672
Small businesses. *See* Privately held companies
Smith, Michael T., 649
Societal benefits, 40–41
Solutions to selected questions, 733–758
Sources of information
  cost of debt, 334
  economic information, 215
  financial information, 220–221
  individual companies, 220–221
  industry information, 215–216, 401
  websites, 220
Sources of value, 403
Special allocations, 630
Special meetings, 141
Special purpose entity, 359
Split-off IPO, 659
Stable growth rates, 357
Staffing issues, 298–301
Staffing strategy sequencing, 298
Staged transactions, 515, 520–521, 660–661
Staggered board elections, 139
Stakeholders, 169
Standalone business, 398
Standard and Poor's (S&P) Corporation, 567
Standstill agreement, 115, 145
Staples-Office Depot merger, 82
Stars, 189
Start-up companies, 309
State antitakeover laws, 96–97
State antitrust laws, 97
Statistical Abstract of the United States, 215
Statistical Yearbook, 215
Statutory consolidation, 6
Statutory merger, 6, 519
STB, 100
Steere, William C., 158–160
Steering committee, 631
Stock float, 117
Stock-for-assets purchase, 515, 520
Stock-for-stock purchase, 515, 519–520
Stock lockup, 129–130
Stock purchase, 515, 517–518, 522
Stock watch programs, 133–134
Strategic alliances, 600. *See also Business alliances*
Strategic controls, 196
Strategic realignment, 20, 25–27
Street name, 134
Street sweep, 124–125
Strengthening board's defenses, 139–141
Stromfeld v. Great Atlantic & Pacific Tea Company, 127
Structuring the deal, 499–554
  business alliances, 620–633
  form of acquisition, 513–521
  form of acquisition vehicle, 505–507

  form of payment, 509–514
  forward triangular merger, 526–527
  legal form of selling entity, 508–509
  linkages/interactions, 504–505
  overview, 500–504
  postclosing organization, 507–508
  purchase accounting, 532–538
  purchase of assets, 516–517
  purchase of stock, 517–518
  reverse triangular merger, 527
  staged transactions, 520–521
  statutory merger, 519
  stock-for-assets purchase, 519
  stock-for-stock purchase, 519
  tax-free reorganizations, 522–528
  taxable transactions, 521–522
  taxes, 521–532. *See also* Taxes
  type A reorganization, 524–525, 528–529
  type B reorganization, 525, 528–529
  type C reorganization, 525–526, 528–529
Subordinated debentures, 566
Subsidiaries, 9
Subsidiary equity carve-out, 658–659
Subsidiary merger, 6, 570–571
Success factors, 183
Successful deals, characteristics, 233
Sullivan & Cromwell, 15
Sunbeam, 394
Super-fund, 101
Super-majority rules, 142
Super-voting stock, 142–143
Surface Transportation Board (STB), 100
Survey of Current Business, 215
Surveys, 375–376
Sustainable competitive advantage, 185
Sustainable growth rate, 353
SWOT analysis, 172
Syndicate, 15
Synergy, 19–22, 403–408
Synergy assumptions, 410
Synthetic-lease arrangements, 359

T
Tag-along provision, 629
Takeover, 6
Takeover decision tree, 130–132
Takeover defenses, 132–151
Takeover litigation, 145, 148–149
Takeover tactics, 115–132
Takeover tactics/defenses, 113–163
  advance notice provisions, 141
  antigreenmail provisions, 142
  bear hug, 117–118
  casual pass, 134–135
  consent solicitations, 141
  cumulative voting rights, 139
  decision tree, 130–132
  empirical studies, 132–134, 149–151
  ESOP, 147
  fair price provisions, 142

"for cause" provisions, 141
friendly/hostile takeover, 115–117
golden parachutes, 143–144
greenmail, 144–146
"just say no" defense, 149
limiting shareholder actions, 140–142
litigation, 148–149
LOI, 129
open-market purchases, 125
pac-man defense, 146
planning, 133–134
poison pills, 135–138
predicting likelihood of being acquired, 132–134
proxy contests, 119–124
recapitalization, 147
reincorporation, 143
restructuring, 148
share repurchase/buyback plans, 147–148
shark repellants, 138–143
silence, 135
silver parachutes, 143–144
special meetings, 141
staggered/classified board elections, 139
stock watch programs, 133–134
street sweep, 124–125
strengthening board's defenses, 139–141
super-majority rules, 142
super-voting stock, 142–143
tender offer, 125–129
theory, 115
tin parachutes, 143–144
white knights/squires, 146
Tangible book value, 365
Tangible book value method, 349, 365
Target, 6
Target company, 6
Targeted stocks, 661
Tax accountants, 16
Tax-free reorganizations, 522–528
Tax Reform Act of 1986, 528–530
Taxable transactions, 521–522
Taxes, 521–531
    advance rulings, 525
    AMT, 529
    business alliances, 629–631
    capital gains tax, 529
    continuity of interests requirement, 523, 525
    divestitures, 654–655
    greenmail, 530
    loss corporations, 528
    NOLs, 528, 530–531
    restructuring strategies, 648
    revenue rulings, 477
    section 338 election, 522
    spin-offs, 656–657
    tax-free reorganizations, 522–528
    taxable transactions, 521–522
    tracking stock, 661–662
Technically insolvent, 676
Technological change, 26–27
Telecommunications Act, 98

Telecommunications Reform Act, 26
Tender offer, 8, 125–129
Tender offer solicitation/recommendation statement, 71
Tender offer statement, 71
Term loan, 564
Terminal value, 353–354
Termination fee, 129
Texaco, 682
Third-generation poison pills, 137
Thomas' Register of American Manufacturers, 216
Thompson, G. Kennedy, 263
Time value of money, 341–345
Time Warner, 44
Times interest earned, 458
Tin parachute, 143–144
Toehold strategy, 129
Total consideration, 228
Total purchase price, 228
Toxic Substances Control Act (TSCA), 101
Toyota, 598
Tracking stock, 661–664
Trademark, 374–376
Travelers-Citicorp merger, 323–325
Tribune-Times Mirror merger, 444–451, 743–744
Trigger points, 170
Truman, Harry S., 499
Trustee, 679
TRW, 646
TRW REDI, 610
TSCA, 101
Turner, Ted, 48
Two-tiered offer, 128
Tyco, 394
Tyco-AMP acquisition, 153–157, 737–738
Type A reorganization, 524–525, 528–529
Type B reorganization, 525, 528–529
Type C reorganization, 525–526, 528–529
Type D reorganization, 523
Type E reorganization, 523
Type F reorganization, 523

U

UAL Corporation, 646
Underground economy, 465
Undervaluation of assets theory, 42
Underwriter spread, 485
Unfriendly takeover, 8
United Parcel Service (UPS), 659–660
United States v. Primestar, 91
Unlevered β, 336
Unocal v. Mesa, 149
Unrelated diversification, 23–24
Unsecured financing, 565–567
Unutilized/undervalued assets, 370–376
UPS, 659–660
U.S. Census Bureau publications, 215
U.S. Industrial Outlook, 215
U.S. Postal Service (USPS), 606
U.S. Steel Company, 661
USX Corp., 662–663

V

Valuation, 331–389
  adjusting firm value, 376–377
  asset-oriented methods, 365–367
  breakup value, 367–368
  comparable companies, 361–362
  comparable transactions, 362
  constant-growth model, 351–353
  DCF methods, 348–357
  enterprise method, 348–350
  equity method, 350
  error, sources of, 393–398
  finance concepts, 332–345. *See also* Rudimentary
    finance concepts
  growth rates, 356–357
  liquidation value, 365–367
  market-based methods, 360–364
  modeling, 391–459. *See also* Financial modeling
  nonoperating assets, 369–376. *See also* Valuation of
    nonoperating assets
  privately held companies, 461–497. *See also*
    Privately held companies
  replacement cost method, 347
  same or comparable industry method, 363
  tangible book value, 365
  value driver-based, 363–364
  variable-growth model, 353–355
  weighted average method, 367–368
  zero-growth model, 350–351
Valuation assumptions, 410
Valuation objectives, 186
Valuation of nonoperating assets, 369–376
  cash and marketable securities, 369–370
  intellectual property, 373–374
  investments in other firms, 370–371
  overfunded pension plans, 376
  patents, 372–373
  real options, 374
  service marks, 374–376
  trademarks, 374–376
  unutilized/undervalued assets, 370–376
Valuation professionals, 474
Value driver-based valuation, 363–364
Value drivers, 398
*Value Line Investment Survey for Company and
  Industry Ratios*, 401
Variable growth valuation model, 353–355
Variable risk approach (VRA), 580–584
VC, 240–241, 487
Vendor financing, 397
Venture capital method (ownership share), 487–488
Venture capitalist (VC), 240–241, 487

Vertical mergers, 7
Vodafone AirTouch, 51–53
Vodafone AirTouch-Mannesmann merger, 51–58,
  239–240, 540–547, 746–748
Voluntary bankruptcy, 679
Voluntary liquidations, 664
Voluntary settlements with creditors, 677–679
VRA, 580–584

W

WACC, 334–335
Wachtell Lipton Rosen & Katz, 15
Wal-Mart, 191
Wal-Mart/AOL alliance, 603
Wall Street Journal Index, 216
WARN, 101
Warren, Rick, 597
Waste Management, 394
Watts, J. C., 65
WD-40, 191
Wealth transfer effects, 576–577
Weighted average cost of capital (WACC),
  334–335
Weighted average method of valuation, 367–368
Welch, Jack, 103, 106–107
Where to compete, 175–178
White knight, 8, 145–146
White squires, 145–146
Wilde, Oscar, 643
Willes, Mark, 444
Williams Act, 69–71, 75, 126
Williams Act 14(d) reporting requirements, 128
Williams Companies, 191
Winding-up. *See* Alternative exit/restructuring
  strategies
Winner's curse, 27
Wood, Scott, 76
Worker Adjustment and Retraining Notification Act
  (WARN), 101
Workouts, 677
World Trade Annual, 215
WorldCom, 394, 679
Written contract, 614, 618–619

Y

Yahoo!, 190, 395

Z

Zero-growth valuation model, 350–351